CW01301501

Fred

The Collected Letters and Speeches of Colonel Frederick Gustavus Burnaby

Volume 1: 1842-1878

Edited and Introduced by Dr John W. Hawkins

THIRD CARLIST WAR, 1873/74
To sum up, Colonel Burnaby is a thoroughly good fellow and will oblige me and the world much if he gives to the light his maiden volume, that on his experiences with the Carlists, which is wasting in manuscript and stowed away somewhere.
John Augustus O'Shea, *Tinsley's Magazine*, August 1883

RUSSO-TURKISH WAR, 1877/78
There are many, though, who will be glad to know that Captain Burnaby was taking copious notes of all that passed and it is, I believe, his intention to write a book on the winter campaign in the Balkans.
Francis Francis, *The Times*, 15 February 1878

Fred

*The Collected Letters and Speeches of
Colonel Frederick Gustavus Burnaby*

Volume 1: 1842-1878

Edited and Introduced by Dr John W. Hawkins

Helion & Company Limited

Helion & Company Limited
26 Willow Road
Solihull
West Midlands B91 1UE
England
Tel. 0121 705 3393
Fax 0121 711 4075
Email: info@helion.co.uk
Website: www.helion.co.uk
Twitter: @helionbooks
Visit our blog http://blog.helion.co.uk/

Published by Helion & Company 2013

Designed and typeset by Farr out Publications, Wokingham, Berkshire
Cover designed by Farr out Publications, Wokingham, Berkshire
Printed by TJ International, Padstow, Cornwall

Original material © Dr John W. Hawkins. Primary documents and quotes as individually attributed.
Images © as individually noted
Maps © Helion & Company Limited 2013. Maps designed by Steve Waites

ISBN 978 1 909384 51 4

British Library Cataloguing-in-Publication Data.
A catalogue record for this book is available from the British Library.
All rights reserved. No part of this publication may be reproduced, stored in a retrieval system, or transmitted, in any form, or by any means, electronic, mechanical, photocopying, recording or otherwise, without the express written consent of Helion & Company Limited.

Front cover: Painting of Burnaby by Ethel Mortlock, hanging in the Officers' Mess of the Royal Horse Guards Mounted Regiment, Knightsbridge, London © Household Cavalry Regimental Collection Trust. Spine: Caricature of Burnaby from the *Hornet*, 24 October 1877. Inside rear dustjacket flap: Caricature of author by Dick Leech. Rear cover: Caricature of Burnaby from the *Penny Illustrated*, 31 January 1885.

For details of other military history titles published by Helion & Company Limited contact the above address, or visit our website: http://www.helion.co.uk.

We always welcome receiving book proposals from prospective authors.

Contents

List of illustrations	viii
List of maps	ix
Foreword by Lieutenant General Sir Barney White-Spunner KCB, CBE	x
Preface	xii
Acknowledgements	xiv
Introduction	xvi

Part 1: A Life in Brief (1842-1878) — 25
1. Family background, education and early years, 1842-64 — 25
2. *Vanity Fair*, early travels in Spain, 1868-70 — 33
3. Travels in Russia, Turkey and France, 1870-71 — 39
4. First Khiva attempt; the Carlist War, 1872-73 — 44
5. First Sudan trip; Gordon at Sobat, 1874-75 — 53
6. Ride to Khiva, 1875-76 — 61
7. Ride through Asia Minor, 1876-77 — 70
8. Russo-Turkish War; Battle of Tashkessan, 1877-78 — 82

Part 2: Letters (1856-1878) — 95

Part 3: Speeches (1878) — 337

Part 4: Other Writings by Fred Burnaby (1875-1878) — 343
1. *Annual Report of Proceedings of the Aeronautical Society of Great Britain*, 1875, pp. 28-30. — 344
2. 'The Practical Instruction of Staff Officers in Foreign Armies' in *Journal of the Royal United Services Institute* vol. 16, no. 68 (January 1872), pp. 633- 44. Reprinted with the same title as a pamphlet (London: W. Mitchell & Co., 1876). — 346
3. 'In Memoriam' *On horseback through Asia Minor* (London: Sampson Low, 7th edition, 1878), pp. xxxii-xl. — 359

Part 5: Sketches, Obituaries and Extracts from Selected Memoirs — 367

1	'Portraits in Oil. XCII. The Latest Lion' in *The World*, 26 April 1876.	372
2	'Men of the Day – No. CXLIII: Captain Frederick G. Burnaby' in *Vanity Fair*, 2 December 1876.	374
3	'Men and Women of the Day. No. LXXXVIII: Capt. Frederick Gustavus Burnaby' in *The Hornet*, 24 October 1877.	376
4	"Radford in Asia Minor" in *The World*, 20 November 1877.	378
5	'Pictures in Little, – N° 12. "His name the Synonym of Daring"' in *The Owl*, 20 May 1882.	383
6	'Colonel Fred Burnaby at Home' in *The World*, July 1882.	384
7	'Explorers I have met' by John Augustus O'Shea in *Tinsley's Magazine*, vol. 33 (August 1883); and extracts from *Roundabout Recollections* (London: Ward and Downey, 1892).	388
8	Eugene Schuyler 'Colonel Fred Burnaby: recollections of his career' in *New York Daily Tribune*, 22 January 1885.	395
9	Anonymous 'Colonel Burnaby as a journalist' in *Northern Echo*, 27 January 1885.	399
10	Henry Tracey Coxwell 'Colonel Burnaby's ballooning' in *Pall Mall Gazette*, 27 January 1885.	400
11	Edward Marston 'Colonel Fred Burnaby: a publisher's reminiscence' in *Publishers' Circular*, 1 February 1885. Reprinted in *After work: fragments from the workshop of an old publisher* (London: W. Heinemann, 1904), pp. 168-72.	403
12	Thomas Gibson Bowles 'Colonel Frederick Gustavus Burnaby' in *Vanity Fair*, February 1885.	405
13	Martin Farquhar Tupper 'Colonel Fred. Burnaby' in *The Brooklyn Magazine*, vols. 2-3 (1885), pp. 89-90. Reprinted in *My life as an Author* (London: Sampson Low, Marston, Searle & Rivington, 1886), pp. 328-30.	406
14	Henry William Lucy 'Fred Burnaby' in *Faces and Places* (London: Henry and Co., 1892), pp. 1-22.	408
15	Evelyn Burnaby *A Ride from Land's End to John O' Groat's* (London: Sampson Low, Marston & Co., 1893), pp. ix-xxii [Introduction]	420
16	Archibald Forbes *Czar and Sultan: the adventures of a British lad in the Russo-Turkish war of 1877-78* (Bristol: J.W. Arrowsmith, 1894), pp. 316-8.	427
17	Henry William Lucy, extract from 'Ups and Downs in My Life' *Strand Magazine*, vol. 31 (January 1906), pp. 33-40.	429

18 Julian Hawthorne 'Fred Burnaby, the hero that was' in *New York Tribune*, 26 April 1908. 437
19 Amy Charlotte Stuart Menzies (née Bewicke), *Memories Discreet and Indiscreet by a Woman of No Importance* (London: Herbert Jenkins, 1917), pp. 52-60. 440

Part 6: Poems and Songs (1879-1885) 447

List of illustrations

Somerby Hall, Leicestershire (*The Graphic*, 31 January 1885)	26
Don Alfonso in Catalonia (*Illustrated London News*, 5 April 1873)	36
Burnaby and the Carlists (*The Graphic*, 31 May 1875)	45
Don Carlos in Navarre (*Illustrated London News*, 8 September 1873)	46
Major-General Charles George 'Chinese' Gordon (*Vanity Fair*, 19 February 1881)	54
The hunting parties. Back row – Russell, Burnaby, Vivian, Gordon-Cumming. Front row – Levick, Ranfurly, Coke, Arkwright, Dr. Meyer (*The Graphic*, 6 March 1875)	57
HRH the Duke of Cambridge (*Vanity Fair*, 23 April 1870)	65
Cockles Pills advertisement (Author's collection)	66
Burnaby and Radford in Asia Minor (*The Graphic*, 19 May 1877)	76
Burnaby on his return from Asia Minor (*Mayfair*, 1 May 1877)	77
Burnaby and Radford in Bulgaria (*Illustrated London News*, 31 January 1885)	79
Captain Fred Burnaby (*Mayfair*, 2 October 1877)	80
Baker and Burnaby at Kamarli (Fife-Cookson)	86
Baker and Burnaby at Tashkessan (Fife-Cookson)	86
Burnaby at Birmingham (*The Owl*, 20 May 1882)	383
On the ground, Crystal Palace, 14 September 1874 (*Mayfair*, 3 July 1877)	430
In the air, Crystal Palace, 14 September 1874 (*Mayfair*, 3 July 1877)	431
(*Strand Magazine*, January 1906)	432
(*Strand Magazine*, January 1906)	433
(*Strand Magazine*, January 1906)	434
Burnaby at Abu Klea (*New York Daily Tribune*, 26 April 1908)	439

List of maps

Burnaby's travels with the Carlist forces, 1873 (Steve Waites)	48
Egypt and the Sudan, 1874/5 (Steve Waites)	58
Burnaby's ride to Khiva, 1875/6 (Steve Waites)	64
Burnaby's travels in Asia Minor, 1876/77 (Steve Waites)	71
Burnaby's route in the the Russo-Turkish War, 1877/8 (Steve Waites)	84
The region around Lake Van, 1876/7	313
Russia's fortresses, 1872	353

Foreword

Lieutenant General Sir Barney White-Spunner KCB, CBE

There are few Victorians as interesting or as controversial as Fred Burnaby. Soldier, politician, adventurer, publisher, balloonist, giant, strong man, socialite, author and raconteur, he aroused a great variety of emotions and he had, in his own words, what "my old nurse used to call a very contradictorious spirit". The Duke of Cambridge, the Army's Commander in Chief, could not abide him; his brother officers disliked his showmanship, and the fact that he wrote about their affairs in *Vanity Fair*; the public thought of him as a national hero who had that quality of "pluck" which our great grand-parents so admired, and his soldiers adored him. This was because Burnaby, or Colonel Fred as he was universally known, was an operational soldier who sought out wars wherever he could find them at a time when his regiment, and mine, The Royal Horse Guards – The Blues, were largely restricted to rather dull public ceremonial. Colonel Fred was not necessarily a soldier by conviction; he served more because he enjoyed the excitement of fighting, and the more dangerous the conflict the better. He recorded the number of enemy he killed in Sudan in his game book, which may have offended the more sensitive of his contemporaries but was considered very good form by others and certainly helped his image as a warrior. He was killed in 1885 in the skirmish at Abu Klea, in the desert north-west of Khartoum, when he was serving with the camel column sent ahead to try to save Gordon. He had no official position there and was officially on leave, but he just thought it was too good an opportunity to miss. He was struck down whilst trying to close a gap in the square, despite desperate efforts by Corporal Mackintosh of The Blues to save him, which cost Mackintosh his own life. After the battle a young soldier was found trying to revive him saying "Here lies the bravest man in England and with no one to help him". "Many of the men" wrote a brother officer, "just sat by his body and cried".

The Blues went into mourning when news of his death reached England and all regimental social events were cancelled, although The Duke of Cambridge was pilloried in the press for still attending the theatre. Queen Victoria wrote in her diary that it was "a sad end to his brave and strange life". Private Cameron of The Blues wrote a poem, which, although probably not in line for a literary award, captured the soldiers' mood, ending:

> The soldiers' friend, the best of men,
> Beloved of all his corps,
> So mourn you Royal Horse Guards Blue
> Brave Burnaby no more.

It was not so much the loss of the man, controversial as he was, but rather that an icon of the Victorian age had been struck down and one who had been an inspiration to a generation of Household Cavalrymen. His legacy is as varied as was his life and takes many different guises. In the great Tissot portrait of the languid explorer; in his huge jack boots in the Household Cavalry museum; in his books, many of which have now been re-published; and in the dinner held every year in his honour by the officers of my regiment where what is celebrated is his spirit of adventure and his desire above all to be an operational soldier.

I am therefore delighted to have been asked by Dr Hawkins to introduce this collection of his letters and speeches. They offer an invaluable insight to one of the great and most colourful Victorians, and great British military characters, and are as important as history as they are entertaining to read.

London
3 April 2013

Preface

On looking through a South Wales newspaper, *The Cambrian*, of 26 January 1872 (for another purpose entirely), it was hard not to have one's interest piqued on encountering this description of an unidentified British officer *en route* to St. Petersburg.

> Just as we started from Berlin we made another acquaintance … an officer of the Blues, height 6ft. 4in. in his stocking feet, wrapped up in a splendid Astracan 'Shuba', and to whom I had previously called Chambers's attention, as to his being a magnificent Russian. Our guardsman is a perfect marvel, he speaks nine living languages – Russian included – and has travelled over pretty nearly the whole of this world, occupying his 'leave' in so doing: and if he could only get 'leave' in the next, there is no knowing where he would not go.

What was his name and why, unlike the rest of the party, was it not given by the author of the letter? Why was he going to St. Petersburg? What had made him learn nine languages? Exactly where had he travelled? What was his fate?

Some of these questions were answered quite easily. His name was Fred Burnaby and he had probably asked the letter writer not to mention his name since his jaunts abroad were frowned upon by the powers that be in Horse Guards. In his youth he had been a notable gymnast, pugilist and swordsman. He had been to Russia at least once previously, probably because he was an extreme Russophobe and wanted to know his potential enemy better. He became fascinated with modern languages after failing to appreciate the classics while at school (where he was described as a 'duffer'). By 1872 he had travelled very extensively in Europe and North Africa and had most likely visited Central and South America. More travels were to come. In 1875 he made a journey across the Egyptian and Sudanese deserts by camel to visit Gordon at Khartoum. In 1876 and 1877 he would undertake rides to Khiva and through Asia Minor that made him a household name when his stories of these journeys were published. In 1878 he was present at the battle of Tashkessan and retreated with Baker Pasha's force across the Rhodope Mountains during the Russo-Turkish War. 1880 saw him contesting Birmingham unsuccessfully on behalf of the Tory party. He was an experienced aeronaut and the first person, in 1882, to make a solo crossing of the British Channel in a balloon. Less than a decade after his first visit to the Sudan he was wounded at the second Battle of El Teb and he would die in hand-to-hand fighting at the Battle of Abu Klea the following year. In this original collection of his letters, articles and speeches, which complements his two volumes of travel writing (*A Ride to Khiva* and *A Ride through Asia Minor*), his own voice can once again be heard.

Acknowledgements

Fred Burnaby first impinged himself on my consciousness while writing my PhD thesis on Henry Gardner's Trust for the Blind at Kingston University in 2010. He turned up as the travelling companion of Colonel and Mrs. Robert Richardson-Gardner (Henry Gardner's son-in-law and daughter) on their trip to Moscow and St. Petersburg during the winter of 1870/71. Fred was a sufficiently intriguing character that I took a few weeks off to undertake some preliminary research on him, resulting in the publication of 'Burnaby the spy?' in the December 2011 issue of *Soldiers of the Queen*. Andy Smith, editor of *SOTQ*, was delightfully easy to work with. A copy of this article came into the hands of Nicholas Davidson, tutor in Modern History at my old college, St. Edmund Hall, Oxford, with whom I had been discussing a quite different research proposal. He first suggested that an up to date biography of Burnaby might find a market and encouraged me to give it serious consideration. When I did so I reached the conclusion that what might be required was not simply a rewrite of previous biographies, but a collected edition of his letters and speeches, perhaps with an introduction presenting some new material that has turned up on Burnaby's life over the last sixty or so years.

The number of publishers likely to be interested in a work of this type was extremely limited and I was fortunate enough to come across Helion within only a few weeks of commencing my search. From the outset Duncan Rogers proved not only enormously supportive in a general sense, but was an active collaborator in the additional research that proved necessary.

Burnaby's handwriting was notoriously poor and even when he made an effort at legibility it can still be extremely difficult to read. Rebecca Shorter, the archivist at St. Edmund Hall, happens also to be an expert palaeographer and made clear to me much that had previously been obscure.

Among the many specialist areas where my own knowledge is sadly lacking is that of late Victorian actresses and courtesans. Fortunately Ron Shee was able to identify 'Mrs. Phoenix', with whom Fred travelled to Paris in 1876, as her *alter ego* Fanny Lear and to provide a copy of a *carte de visité* photograph of Burnaby in ethnic dress that I had never seen before. The Conservative Party historian Lord Lexden pointed out to me Burnaby's involvement with the Primrose League and kindly facilitated access to the archives of the Carlton

Club.

In volume two will be found a complete list of the archives and libraries holding Burnaby primary material, including several in the United States. In all cases the staff could not have been more helpful, either in locating and preparing documents in advance of personal visits, or of making and sending copies from the more remote locations.

Unfortunately there are no living descendants of Fred and Lizzie Burnaby. It was possible to trace a small number of living collateral relations, but regrettably none of these had inherited the family papers made available to previous Burnaby biographers. I am, in any event, thankful to them for taking the time to respond to my enquiries.

Lizzie Burnaby was a quite extraordinary woman in her own right and richly deserves a biography. Fortunately one is currently being written, by Rosemary Raughter. Rosemary is an established historian with a number of important books to her credit. She has been extraordinarily helpful in drawing to my attention matters concerning Fred and Lizzie that I would otherwise never have come across and making available copies of the surviving fragments of the Burnaby family archive.

In any prolonged writing assignment the encouragement of family and friends is critical; my thanks, therefore, go out to all of mine who have helped with the reading and researching. They know who they are!

Introduction

'Fred Burnaby, though picturesque and colourful, was a minor figure who missed by a hair's breadth getting into the main channels of history.'
Louis Blake Duff, *Burnaby*, 1926

Duff's assessment of Burnaby as a minor figure is unfair. Scarcely forty years before he made this comment, Fred Burnaby had been second only to General Gordon among the Soldiers of the Queen in the affection of the British public and, by the time of his death in hand-to-hand combat at the battle of Abu Klea in 1885, he was nothing short of a national hero. His accounts of his travels in Central Asia and Asia Minor ran to numerous editions and as a 'special correspondent' he was a frequent contributor to several newspapers. His wife's estates in Ireland came to be known as 'The Burnaby', despite the fact that he never lived there, and, according to Duff, his name was chosen for a town in British Columbia he had never visited.[1] Following Abu Klea, songs and poems were written describing his death and mourning his loss, while the popular papers devoted not columns but pages to his obituaries.

This is not to say he was universally popular. By 1885 he was no longer on friendly terms with the Prince of Wales and was an embarrassment at Horse Guards, particularly to the Duke of Cambridge. By at least one account he was not on speaking terms with the other officers of his regiment, the Blues, and he was estranged from his wife, who had moved to Switzerland ostensibly for health reasons. He once described his own spirit as 'contradictorious' and there were certainly contradictions in his behaviour, with a frequent failure to conform to what were considered social norms.

Yet Burnaby was far more than a soldier, traveller and controversialist. Speaking seven foreign languages more or less fluently he was a renowned linguist and, in an age when ballooning was still in its infancy, he was an acknowledged pioneer and made the first solo crossing of the English Channel in 1882. He wrote an important article on the subject of ballooning and developed aeronautical navigation aids, while fully recognising that the future

---

1 Louis Blake Duff, *Burnaby* (Welland County Historical Society, Canada: Tribune-Telegraph Press, 1926).

of aviation lay in heavier-than-air flight. His interest in the training of staff officers resulted in the presentation of a paper on this subject at the prestigious Royal United Services Institute, based on personal observations made in Prussia and Russia.

He mixed easily in society and, for a time, became part of the circle of the Prince of Wales, travelling with him as ADC to Vienna for the Exhibition in 1872, but his bluffness could also lead him into trouble. Among his close friends was Thomas Gibson Bowles, with whom he founded, in 1868, the first British version of *Vanity Fair*, a satirical magazine that became famous for its colour lithograph caricatures. This did not go down well with his military superiors and he was ordered to give up his involvement, although he continued to act as a correspondent for *The Times* and other newspapers. One of the illustrators of *Vanity Fair* was J.J. Tissot, who painted an iconic portrait of Burnaby now hanging in the National Portrait Gallery in London. Sir Algernon Borthwick, later Lord Glenesk, the owner of the *Morning Post* was also counted amongst Fred's friends and he developed close relationships with T.H.S. Escott, editor of the *Fortnightly Review*, Edmund Yates, editor of *The World* and Henry Lucy, the respected political journalist and sometime editor of *Mayfair*. Burnaby published three books in his lifetime: *A ride to Khiva*; *On horseback through Asia Minor*, and *A Ride across the Channel and other adventures in the air*; the first two of these can still easily be found, for example as modern Oxford University Press editions with introductions by Peter Hopkirk. Among his literary correspondents were Lord Houghton and Frank Harris. His speeches, mainly of a political nature given between 1878 and 1884, were also widely and extensively published in the contemporary press. A political novel, *Our Radicals*, was edited, completed and published by Burnaby's personal secretary shortly after his death. Probably the least said about this the better.

He was well-connected politically, particularly with Sir Drummond Wolff and Lord Randolph Churchill, whom he had helped to found the Primrose League in 1883, and with the latter of whom he intended to stand as a Conservative candidate for the UK parliamentary seat of Birmingham in 1885. It was then not at all uncommon for a serving soldier to sit as an MP and, given that he had made a notable impression on his party in the 1880 General Election, when he had stood unsuccessfully against Joseph Chamberlain and John Bright in Birmingham, a parliamentary future was almost assured had he lived. He also found time to play his part in the Great Game.

Six biographies of Burnaby have been written, but to a greater or lesser extent all of these have contained errors and lacunae. The first, by R.K. Mann, appeared in 1882. It would be tempting to assume that Mann was a pseudonym – no other works by this author have been traced – but for a letter written by Burnaby on 13 August 1884 to T.H.S. Escott, which specifically refers to Mann as having been introduced to him by Mr. Leprière.[2] Burnaby continues in this letter to say that his only involvement with the project was the provision (by his personal secretary, James Percival Hughes) of copies of some speeches he had delivered and that he had no pecuniary interest in the project. In fact the work largely consists of extracts from Burnaby's already published letters, which, presumably, his secretary had also provided. In the bibliography to his own later work Thomas Wright suggests that Mann's book was revised by Burnaby prior to publication, but this seems not to have been the case. In any event it contains several errors as to dates. As an example, Mann places Burnaby with the Carlists 'under fire at the battles of Allo, Dicastillo, Viana and Mañeru' in 1874, but these actions all took place in the summer and autumn of 1873, so Burnaby must have joined Don Carlos immediately after recuperating from typhoid in Naples earlier that year and this is borne out by the dates of his despatches to *The Times*.[3] This and many other mistakes have been perpetuated in practically all subsequent books and articles on Burnaby.

An expanded edition of this book was published by Mann in collaboration with the better known James Redding Ware shortly after Burnaby's death in 1885.[4] The Mann & Ware book was announced within days of Burnaby's death, the implication being that it had been planned beforehand and that Fred had been involved in its supervision, but it again contained errors.[5] Referring to the period after Burnaby's return from his 1870/71 trip to Russia, the authors state: 'The remainder of 1871, and nearly all of 1872, he passed in England, doing regimental duty and enjoying life. His tentative work as a newspaper correspondent had not been continued between 1868 and 1872.'[6] As will be seen this is incorrect on two counts. In a review of Ware & Mann's biography,[7] the reviewer made a justifiable criticism of the work: 'The chief objection to it is that it has been compiled largely from Burnaby's own published writings, and from the contributions of special correspondents to the public newspapers. One seems to feel the want of more personal and private testimony as to his career, such as might be gathered from his more intimate friends and relations.' Despite the authors' attempt to debunk some of the myths that had grown up around him by the time of Fred's death and their description of some of the

---

2 The letter is in the British Library Escott Papers (Add. 58776 f.60). 'Mr. Leprière' was presumably Lieutenant George Philip Leprière (1855-1949), a well-known balloonist.
3 Thomas Wright, *The life of Colonel Fred Burnaby* (London: Everett & Co., 1908), p. 70.
4 Ware (1843-1909), was a jobbing writer who also wrote under the pseudonym Andrew Forrester. He makes at least one reference in this book to 'the short memoir by Mann', implying that Mann may not actually have contributed in any meaningful way to the revised edition (p. 339).
5 *Freeman's Journal*, 7 February 1885.
6 James Redding Ware and R.K. Mann, *The Life and Times of Colonel Fred Burnaby* (London: Leadenhall Press, 1885), p. 82.
7 *Morning Post*, 22 September 1885. This review may have been written by Sir Algernon Borthwick, the paper's proprietor and editor, who had known Burnaby well.

less savoury incidents with which he was involved, the book still comes across as closer to a hagiography than a critical biography.

'Life, Speeches and Adventures of Colonel Burnaby', an anonymous pamphlet, was also published in 1885.[8] It contained no original material and Mann would have had grounds for charges of plagiarism had he not himself borrowed so extensively already from Burnaby's own letters and speeches.

Much of the same ground was covered in 1906, albeit in a little more detail, by Thomas Wright.[9] To be fair to Wright he was the first of Burnaby's biographers to mention his involvement with the foundation of the Primrose League, but he also made several basic errors (including the dates of Burnaby's first balloon flight with Henry Lucy and his almost fatal flight with M. de la Marne). Wright was also given access to certain family papers by Burnaby's widow, by then Mrs. Aubrey Le Blond, and by his son, Harry, but Burnaby still seems a distant figure.

In 1926 there was a short work by Louis Blake Duff, *Burnaby*, again with almost no original primary material, and then a gap of three decades until the most recent biography by Michael Alexander in 1957, *True Blue*. Superficially there was a great deal of information available to Alexander: anecdote, contemporary reportage, Burnaby's own published writing and his many obituaries. Although Alexander also had access to a few of his private letters that his family chose to make available, the opportunity to interview those who had known Fred well had been lost – by then all of his friends and enemies were long dead and much of his voluminous correspondence had disappeared.[10] The result was probably the most readable and enjoyable of the early biographies, but Alexander still failed to dig far below the surface of the secondary sources or question much of what was by then accepted Burnaby lore.

Meanwhile, memoirs were being written by a number of people who had known Burnaby well, the most important of which was by his widow. Lizzie's memoirs published in 1928, *Day In, Day Out*, contained five chapters about Fred (and none on her two other husbands).[11] With the exception of one or two personal letters that had not appeared in previous biographies of Burnaby, Lizzie's book added almost nothing to an understanding of him as a man. Fred's brother, Evelyn, produced a short volume describing a journey he made

---

8   *Life, speeches and adventures of Colonel Fred Burnaby* (London: Diprose & Bateman, 1885).
9   This was not Thomas Wright the balloonist, whom Burnaby had known well, but a kinsman and namesake who wrote a number of popular biographies.
10 Michael Alexander, *The True Blue: the Life and Adventures of Colonel Fred Burnaby, 1842–85* (London: Rupert Hart-Davies, 1957).
11 The other relevant works are: (1) R.K. Mann, *The Life, Adventures and Political Opinions of Frederick Gustavus Burnaby* (London: F.V. White & Co., 1882); (2) Henry William Lucy, 'Fred Burnaby' in *Faces and Places* (London: Henry and Co., February 1892), pp. 1-22; and (3) Mrs. Aubrey Le Blond (formerly Burnaby), *Day in, Day out* (London: Bodley Head, 1928).

on horseback from Land's End to John O'Groats in 1893.[12] The introduction to this contained many reminiscences of his brother, but again with almost nothing original. In 1892 Henry Lucy devoted a chapter of his memoir, *Faces and Places*, to Burnaby.[13] Lucy had known Burnaby well from 1874, when they had shared a balloon ascent from Crystal Palace, but even much of his material had appeared previously in magazine articles. One of Burnaby's contemporaries was a Guards officer, Captain Stuart Menzies, whose wife wrote a series of reminiscences popular in the early years of the twentieth century. These included sketches of both Fred and his brother and at least provide a little additional colour. He is also mentioned in many other works by contemporary authors, including Frank Harris.[14]

The third major category of secondary material on Burnaby comprises descriptions by participants of the military campaigns in which he was involved. Many British volunteers served with the Turkish army in the Russo-Turkish War of 1877/8 and several of these produced memoirs, not least Valentine Baker Pasha, Burnaby's close friend.[15] Although in theory present as a civilian, Fred's considerable assistance to Baker is recognised in all of those memoirs in which he is mentioned, as it was by the special correspondents of *The Times* and other newspapers.

Numerous histories of the Egyptian campaigns of 1884 and 1885 contain descriptions of the two battles of El Teb and that of Abu Klea, in all three of which Burnaby was engaged. In the second volume of her memoirs Mrs. Stuart Menzies wrote: 'There have been various conflicting accounts of how Colonel Burnaby met his death at Abu Klea, and it is curious that out of the accounts given to me by friends present at the battle, no two are alike.'[16] Burnaby is also referred to in the campaign diaries and letters of General Lord Wolseley.[17]

There are three modern sketches of Burnaby. The first is that by Roger Stearn in the *Oxford Dictionary of National Biography*.[18] This does a good job of

12 Evelyn Burnaby, *A Ride from Land's End to John O' Groat's* (London: Sampson Low, Marston & Company, 1893).
13 Henry William Lucy, 'Fred Burnaby' in *Faces and Places* (London: Henry and Co., 1892), pp. 1-22.
14 Frank Harris (ed. by John F. Gallagher), *My Life and Loves* (Paris: privately printed, 1922-27). [Avalon Travel Publishing, 1991, pp. 389-92.]
15 Valentine Baker, *War in Bulgaria: a narrative of personal experiences* 2 vols. (London: Sampson Low & Co., 1879).
16 Mrs. Stuart Menzies (née Amy Charlotte Bewicke), *Memories Discreet and Indiscreet by a Woman of No Importance* (London: Herbert Jenkins, 1917), pp. 52-60.
17 Lord Wolseley, ed. Adrian Preston, *In relief of Gordon: Lord Wolseley's campaign journal of the Khartoum relief expedition, 1884–1885* (London: Hutchinson, 1967); and Lord and Lady Wolseley, ed. Sir Arthur George *The letters of Lord and Lady Wolseley, 1870–1911* (London: W. Heinemann, 1922).
18 Roger T. Stearn 'Burnaby, Frederick Gustavus (1842–1885)' in *Oxford Dictionary of National Biography* (Oxford: Oxford University Press, 2004). The DNB entry of Burnaby's wife is also worth reading: Peter H. Hansen 'Le Blond [née Hawkins-Whitshed], Elizabeth Alice Frances (1860–1934)'.

summarising the key elements of Burnaby's life and places him well in a late Victorian context, while citing some useful secondary sources. The second is a chapter in the autobiography by Alan Tritton, who is best known as a banker, but who is also a great grand-nephew of Burnaby.[19] The third is a chapter in Max Hastings's *Warriors*.[20]

So what is the purpose of this addition to the Burnaby canon? It is certainly not merely to repeat the stories told in the existing books about Burnaby. Most of these publications can be found quite easily and despite their shortcomings they still make a good read. However, since the last full biography was written, in 1957, some new material on Burnaby has surfaced, mainly comprising unpublished private correspondence and letters to newspapers not previously attributed to him. What has been attempted here is therefore the following:

- To provide in a single work all of Burnaby's known letters, speeches and journal articles, many of which have not previously appeared in their entirety in any of the biographies. (Parts Two, Three and Four)
- To introduce and annotate this material in such a way as to provide context for Burnaby's actions and opinions and to provide continuity between the phases of his life in which they were written. This section takes the opportunity to correct some of the errors and omissions of previous works. (Part One)
- To reproduce a selection of character sketches and obituaries of Burnaby, mostly written by people he knew well, providing an overview of how he was regarded by his contemporaries. (Part Five)
- To collect a representative sample of the songs and poems written about Burnaby, both during his life and after his death. (Part Six)
- Recognising the disparity in various eye witness accounts of the battle of Abu Klea and Burnaby's death, to reproduce a representative sample of these. (Part Seven)
- Given that Burnaby was a popular figure in the illustrated journals as well as the daily press, to provide examples of the cartoons and caricatures in which he appeared. (Part Eight and other text)
- To provide a comprehensive bibliography of Burnaby literature, including manuscript sources.

The number of letters and speeches has dictated that the collection be split into two volumes. In order to balance the quantity of material in each and to choose a sensible chronological break point for the bulk of the material, the following plan has been adopted.

---

19 Alan George Tritton, *The Half Closed Door* (Brighton: Book Guild, 2008).
20 Max Hastings, *Warriors* (London: HarperCollins, 2005).

	Vol. 1	Vol. 2
Part One: a life in brief	1842-1878	1878-1885
Part Two: letters	1856-1878	1878-1885
Part Three: speeches	1878	1878-1885
Part Four: other writings	1875-1878	1878-1885
Part Five: sketches, obituaries, etc.	1876-1885	
Part Six: poems and songs	1879-1885	
Part Seven: Abu Klea		1885
Part Eight: images		1870-1885
Appendix: guide to letters and speeches		1842-1885
Bibliography		1842-1885
Index		1842-1885

Volume 1 therefore covers the period of Burnaby's life during which he acted as a special correspondent during the Third Carlist War, visited Gordon in the Sudan, made his famous rides to Khiva and through Asia Minor and rode alongside Baker Pasha in the Russo-Turkish War. Volume 2 deals with his entry into politics (including fighting the General Election of 1880), marriage, voyage by balloon across the English Channel and participation in the two battles of El Teb and the battle of Abu Klea.

Parts Five and Six would have fitted more comfortably into Volume 2 from a chronological point of view, but it is not as though Burnaby's ultimate fate is not well known. A comprehensive index to both volumes is contained in Volume 2, as is an appendix listing all of the letters and speeches, etc. included in both volumes.

This work does have at least one obvious shortcoming. Despite having traced and contacted several descendants of Fred's siblings and his daughter-in-law, it has not been possible to locate Burnaby's papers to which at least three of his previous biographers/memoirists had access (Wright, Alexander and Le Blond). These comprised not only various letters that he had written and received, but his commonplace books, of which there were several, and his collection of press-cuttings (he actually subscribed to an agency for this purpose). At some time after the death of Fred's son, Harry, his American widow went to live in Ireland in an old farmhouse on the Burnaby estate. On her death in 1979, by which time the dwelling was apparently in a very sorry state, it was bought by a local golf club which carried out a complete renovation. Anecdotally much of the contents were destroyed at the time, although some fragments of letters survived and came into the hands of a local school. These, which include parts of letters from Lord Beaconsfield, Don Carlos and Private Woods (who was with Burnaby when he died) are probably all that remain of Burnaby's personal archive.

There is no evidence that these papers included anything important ignored by the previous authors, but it is just possible they contained some information on his life during periods on which he was otherwise silent, for example between 1859 and 1867. In fact, despite a determined effort it has proved remarkably difficult to locate more than a modest amount of new primary material on Burnaby, particularly in connection with his earlier travels. The question arises as to why Burnaby failed to record these travels, given that he took pleasure from his writing and clearly enjoyed describing his later adventures. One also wonders why he never collected together and published as a single volume his letters from Spain during the Carlist War (he did get as far as writing a preface), or why he did not write of his experiences during the Russo-Turkish War (during which he was observed assiduously taking notes). Burnaby was certainly an enigma.

In April 2013, shortly before the manuscript for the first volume of *Fred* had to be delivered to Helion & Company, Julian Barnes published *Levels of Life*. The middle part of his book, which I enjoyed in its entirety, describes an *affair* between Fred Burnaby and Sarah Bernhardt. Barnes dates this as having taken place in the 'mid-1870s' over a period of several months, during which period Fred remained in Paris. In one of the conversations between the lovers Fred refers to the ascent he had made from Crystal Palace the previous year with Henry Lucy; this actually took place on 14 September 1874, placing the conversation in 1875. Unfortunately it never took place. Fred could have stayed in Paris for a prolonged period only during one of his long leaves and his presence during these is well accounted for during the winters of 1874/5 (Egypt and the Sudan), 1875/6 (Khiva), 1876/7 (Asia Minor), 1877/8 (the Russo-Turkish War) and 1878/9 (by which time he was engaged to Elizabeth Hawkins-Whitshed). I wish the *affair* had taken place (Fred deserved at least one passionate relationship *à la* Harry Flashman), but it did not.

Part 1

A Life in Brief (1842-1878)

1 Family background, education and early years, 1842-64

The Burnabys

Frederick Gustavus Burnaby was born just outside the town of Bedford in the old rectory at St. Peter's Green on 3 March 1842. His immediate family circumstances were comfortable, but unremarkable. His paternal grandfather, Edwyn Andrew Burnaby (1771-1825), whose manorial home was Baggrave Hall in Leicestershire, had come into the possession of Somerby Hall, also in Leicestershire, on the death of his father-in-law in 1812. On his own death Baggrave Hall was left to his oldest son, Edwyn Burnaby, and Somerby Hall to a younger son, Fred's father, the Rev. Gustavus Andrew Burnaby.[1] Along with the Somerby estate came the advowsons to the parishes of Somerby and the neighbouring Burrough-on-the-Hill.

Gustavus was a member of what has inelegantly been called the 'squirearchy'; hunting and keeping a good table were at least as important to him as his ecclesiastical duties. He married Harriet Villebois, one of three surviving daughters of Henry Villebois of Marham Hall, Norfolk, in 1833. From 1835 until 1866 he was rector of St. Peter de Merton, Bedford. The first opportunity for a presentation at Somerby did not occur until 1855 on the death of Thomas Hanbury, who had held the living for over forty years. Hanbury's long-serving curate, Septimus Rolleston, was then initially granted the living, but Gustavus arranged an exchange with him in 1866 and then remained at Somerby as vicar until his death in 1872. By all accounts he found life in Bedford more

---

1 Baggrave Hall was famously purchased in the 1980s by Asil Nadir, the disgraced former head of Polly Peck.

Somerby Hall, Leicestershire
(*The Graphic*, 31 January 1885)

conducive than Somerby.

Fred had two older sisters, Mary and Anna, with whom he maintained a correspondence during his youth and both of whom married in due course. Throughout his life he remained close to his younger brother, Evelyn Henry Villebois Burnaby (1848-1924), who, after initially studying law, followed their father into the church, Fred having shown no inclination to do so. The story is told that Fred was always upset by funerals, but that he had a good memory for biblical verses. Evelyn was rector and patron of Burrough from 1873 to 1883.

Fred's formal schooling began, as was then common, at the age of nine at the old building of Bedford Grammar School under its headmaster, Dr. Brereton. In May 1852 he was removed to a private school at Tinwell, Rutland, run by the Rev. Charles Arnold and remained there for two and a half years. In January 1855 he started at Harrow where he boarded with Mr. Oxenham at a house now known as Moretons.[2] The fagging system was rife at Harrow and had been decried in an article in *Punch* a few years before, probably written by Douglas William Jerrold. By this time Fred's size, strength and appetite were already giving rise to stories that would later be related by his early biographers and his combative character would have made him temperamentally unsuited to a fagging role, so it is no surprise that his days there were numbered. The trigger is supposed to have been a letter against the fagging system that he himself wrote to *Punch* ('The Toad under the Harrow'), but no trace has ever been found. A contemporary at Harrow, Lord Claud Hamilton, M.P. (1843-1925), described him as a 'hopeless duffer' who was obliged to leave school and join the army.[3] In any event during 1857 he moved schools again, this time to Oswestry under the Rev. Stephen Donne, where he lived with Donne's

---

2 This information was provided by Harrow. Wright, p. 20, states that it was "'Middlemist's House", afterwards known as "Cruickshank's"'.
3 *York Herald*, 20 August 1879.

family as a 'parlour boarder', rather than in one of the school houses. He never excelled in the classics at Harrow or Oswestry, but developed a keen interest in modern languages. The likelihood is that even by then it had been determined that his career would be in the army and a year in Oswestry would have been an interim step towards this.

Had he wished to do so, Fred would have had no difficulty tracing his Burnaby forebears as far back as at least the fifteenth century. In fact he claimed direct descent from King Edward I, a conceit that eventually led to a cooling of his friendship with the Prince of Wales. Solidly positioned as members of the landed gentry, the Burnaby family had produced successful men of commerce, literature and law, with a speciality in the church and the army. Fred's great grandfather, the Ven. Dr. Andrew Burnaby, had been archdeacon of Leicester and his father was a canon of Middleham in Yorkshire. His second cousin once removed, Richard Beaumont Burnaby, had risen to lieutenant-general in the Royal Artillery and had served with Wellington at Waterloo. His uncle, Edwyn Burnaby, had been a captain in the Prince of Wales's Dragoon Guards and later High Sheriff of Leicestershire, while his great uncle, John Dick Burnaby, had been a colonel in the Grenadiers. His first cousin, Edwyn Sherard Burnaby, was also commissioned in the Grenadier Guards and rose to major-general, having distinguishing himself at a young age in the battle of Inkerman; in 1880 he became the Member of Parliament for Leicestershire North. By the time of Fred's return from Turkey in 1877, eight Burnabys, all related, held regular army commissions, many of them serving with great distinction.[4] Fred would even have had a precedent for a naval career. A distant cousin, Vice-Admiral Sir William Burnaby (1710-1777), had served as Commander-in-Chief, Jamaica immediately before Admiral Lord Rodney and another of his cousins was a serving naval captain.

The Blues

During the years of Fred's schooling the progress of the Crimean War dominated international news. Given his size and strength it was entirely natural that Fred should have gravitated towards a career in the army and his father would have had no reason to demur once it was plain that he did not have a calling to the church. With the army established as his preferred career, considerable thought would have had to have been given as to the division of the army to which he should aspire. His social position, physical stature

---

[4] These were: Lieutenant-General C.H. Burnaby, RA; Colonel E.S. Burnaby, Grenadiers; Colonel R. Burnaby, RE; Captain A.D. Burnaby, RA; Captain F.G. Burnaby, Royal Horse Guards; Major E.B. Burnaby, 10th (North Lincolnshire) Regiment; Major E.B. Burnaby, 51st (2nd Yorkshire West Riding) Regiment; and Lieutenant R.B. Burnaby, 70th (Surrey) Regiment. Another distant cousin, H.B. Burnaby, was then a captain in the Royal Navy.

and a private income eminently qualified him for the Guards and given his father's interest in hunting (his godfathers were both Masters of Foxhounds), it is hardly surprising that he was pointed in the direction of the heavy cavalry. The next question was which regiment.

The Royal Horse Guards (Blue), sometimes referred to as the Oxford Blues or simply the Blues, had a long and honourable history. Their origins could be traced to Colonel Unton Croke's Regiment of Horse, which was formally raised as the Royal Regiment of Horse Guards by King Charles II in 1661. They had subsequently fought with Marlborough at Blenheim and with Wellington in the Peninsular War and at Waterloo. When not fighting, which was increasingly the case from 1815 onwards, they had important ceremonial duties and acted as domestic peace-keepers, leading one critic to describe them as the finest mounted police in the world. In precedence they ranked immediately after the First and Second Life Guards, with whom they jointly comprised the Household Cavalry, although in some respects by the middle of the nineteenth century the Blues were considered even more prestigious.

There was a strong family connection with this regiment. Fred's elder sister, Anna Glentworth Burnaby, had married in 1862 Duncan James Baillie, who was the Colonel commanding the Blues from 1866 to 1875. Not only this, but Duncan succeeded his elder brother, Hugh Smith Baillie, in that role, who had married Fred's widowed aunt, Lady Glentworth (formerly Eva Maria Villebois). Finally, if it had been needed, Gustavus Burnaby could have put in a good word for his son with the Commander-in-Chief of the Army, the Duke of Cambridge, for whom he had acted as Chaplain.

Joining a regiment such as the Blues was not to be considered lightly. Apart from the matter of the initial and subsequent purchases of commissions,[5] the pay would be insufficient to cover the on-going costs of uniform, horses, grooms and social necessities, probably amounting to £1,000 a year. Many of those who took up such commissions never expected to see actual fighting and membership was more like that of a club or exclusive society. The duties of heavy cavalry regiments like the Blues were largely ceremonial and confined to the 'season' from Spring until the end of the Summer and officers were often free to take extended periods of leave during the winter months. Those who eschewed the actual field of battle were disparagingly referred to as 'carpet knights', but of this Burnaby could never legitimately be accused.

To prepare him for his army entrance examinations, Fred's father sent him for a year to Dresden, Saxony, to study privately under Professor Hughes at 4 Marian Strasse. This was not an unusual move and among other famous soldiers

---

5 The official initial cost of a cornet's commission in the Blues at this time was £1,250, with further sums being payable on promotion to lieutenant, captain, major and lieutenant-colonel. However, the purchase of commissions was abolished in 1871 as part of the Cardwell army reforms.

to have studied in Dresden was Sir Gerald Graham, under whom Burnaby fought at the second battle of El Teb and who, like him, was of massive stature. By all accounts Fred enjoyed his time there, honing his language skills, learning to play the cornet to a good standard and bathing in the Elbe. Fred referred to this as his 'top dressing'. He did well in the army examinations of 1859 (as the youngest entrant coming seventh of the 150 or so sitting the exam that year) and entered the Blues as a cornet (second lieutenant) in September 1859. By this time he stood six feet four inches in his bare feet, measured forty six inches around the chest and weighed fifteen stone when in good condition, although he was inclined to put on weight easily. His complexion was often described as sallow, which combined with a dark moustache (which he seldom bothered waxing) gave him a Latin appearance. His first promotion, to lieutenant, came in September 1861.

Primary sources dealing with his life immediately on entering the army are hard to find. His early biographers agree that he devoted almost all of his time to developing his prodigious strength, engaging in boxing, fencing, gymnastics and weightlifting. Alexander states that one of the pugilists with whom he sparred was 'the famous Jimmy Paddock', but even if such a match did take place this is probably an error for Tom Paddock, the 'Redditch Needlepointer', who indeed had an impressive ring career, but retired in 1860 and died in 1863 at the age of 41.[6] Whether Burnaby ever fought or sparred with the more famous John C. Heenan, 'the Benicia Boy' (1834-1873), is not known, but he certainly attracted the soubriquet 'Heenan' in his regiment and later in the national press. Burnaby continued to act as a judge of amateur boxing competitions after his own retirement from the ring.[7]

One of the few athletic exploits of Burnaby reported in the contemporary press occurred at Boveney Lock near Windsor on 1 April 1864, when for a wager he undertook to walk, run, hop, ride and row the distance of a quarter of a mile in under a quarter of an hour, which he duly accomplished with four minutes and forty seconds to spare.[8]

The National Army Museum still displays a pair of massive Indian clubs with which Burnaby used to exercise. For many years a barbell that he used was to be seen at the London Fencing Club in Cleveland Row and was even displayed at the Naval, Shipping and Fisheries Exhibition held at London in 1905 – it reportedly weighed a hundredweight and a half. Burnaby retained his membership of the London Fencing Club long after he fenced competitively and was still on its committee at the time of his death. Numerous anecdotes

---

6 Alexander, p. 20.
7 *Morning Post*, 17 July 1867.
8 *Birmingham Daily Post*, 7 April 1864. News of the wager even reached France, where a report appeared in *Le Petit Journal* of 26 April 1864.

attesting to his prowess were related, some of which have survived until today in various versions. It is hard to escape the conclusion that he was considered something of a freak and, to the extent that he was fêted by the higher ranks of society, including the Prince of Wales, it was because he was different and not because he fitted the usual stereotypes.

Fred also indulged in traditional country pursuits when at Somerby, fishing and hunting with the Oakley Hunt on a succession of large horses with names such as Ahasuerus, Beelzebub and Belial. He also took up ballooning in 1864, of which more later, and found time for pigeon shooting at Hurlingham Gardens.[9]

Quite when Fred's health first suffered a serious deterioration is not known. Several of his obituarists refer to him having suffered a breakdown brought on by over-exertion and that, following this, he was advised to give up athletic activities and undertake a period of travel. It is supposedly at this time that he visited Central and South America, with Henry Lucy, among others, stating that he had gone there big game hunting. It was out of character for Burnaby never to refer to this trip and no personal or public letters from Central or South America have survived. The date of such a trip is also uncertain. His early biographers imply that it took place in the early 1860s, but there is no primary evidence to support this and some to the contrary (for example, his exploit at Boveney Lock in 1864). Another explanation is that the trip was indeed made, but later, possibly in early 1865.

Hooker vs Burnaby

In December 1864 Burnaby appeared in court on a charge of assault in the action *Hooker vs Burnaby*. In the company of two fellow junior officers from his regiment, Adderley and Westcar, Burnaby had been invited to shoot on an estate in Kent and had come to blows with its owner, compounding the assault by kicking his host. Among other things the owner had accused him of being a 'swindler', to which Westcar had responded on his behalf that he was confusing him with another officer of the same name in the Guards. If the similarity in name had simply been a coincidence Burnaby might have allowed the matter to pass, but the person referred to was his cousin, Colonel Edwyn Sherard Burnaby of the Grenadiers. One way or another both personal and family honour were at stake.

The 'swindle' referred to by Hooker involved a horse race at Newmarket in October 1862 between *Tarragona*, owned by Colonel Burnaby, and *Michel Grove*, owned by Mr. Wyon. It was alleged by a punter at the meeting that Burnaby had laid a bet with the Hon. Captain Arthur Annesley, also of the

9   *Morning Post*, 29 June 1868.

Grenadier Guards, designed to 'ramp' the odds and had then caused his jockey to 'pull' his horse. Burnaby and Annesley were called before the committee of the Jockey Club under its Chairman Admiral Rous, who to the astonishment of many observers failed to provide an immediate acquittal. The Jockey Club committee met again in November at which Rous withdrew as conflicted and they subsequently issued a half-hearted statement to the effect that the committee had found no evidence against Burnaby and Annesley, leaving their reputations somewhat tainted.

Both Burnaby and Hooker retained eminent counsel. Burnaby chose John Walter Huddlestone, QC (1815-1890), who had a strong reputation at the criminal bar and later became a Member of Parliament successively for Canterbury and Norwich and a High Court Judge. Hooker's brief was Serjeant William Ballantine (1812-1887), later famous for his part in the Mordaunt divorce case, involving the Prince of Wales, and the case of the Tichborne claimant.

The Hooker assault case was described in detail by the court reporter of *The Times* and subsequently gave rise to a series of letters published in *The Times* and elsewhere. This is the first occasion on which Burnaby's judgment can be seriously questioned, not only by involving himself in the affair in the first place, but in making matters worse by not reaching an out-of-court settlement. Even if his original behaviour could have been justified as a 'matter of honour', his decision to fight the suit in court and then not to appear as a witness in his own defence must be considered bizarre. Neither Burnaby nor the plaintiff came off well, although Burnaby lost on a majority verdict and was ordered to pay damages of £150, compared to the £500 claimed by Hooker. Perhaps more importantly the judge, Baron Martin, implied that Burnaby was unfit to hold the Queen's commission: 'If there is a word of truth in the plaintiff's case and the defendant is still in the army he won't be long in it.' Horse Guards considered the matter and eventually reached the conclusion that one punishment was sufficient, probably because Burnaby retained the support of his fellow officers. He would certainly have been severely reprimanded and it is possible he may have been strongly encouraged to leave London for a spell and to keep quiet while he was away, but if he did travel at this time he was back in London by August 1865 making further balloon ascents from Crystal Palace. All things considered he was lucky to retain his commission, notwithstanding which he was promoted to captain, by purchase, in July 1866. For the remainder of his life he kept himself out of court, but he came close again on at least two occasions and this was certainly not the last time on which his judgment can be called into question.

Fred had gained a good knowledge of German, French and Italian while living in Dresden, but in 1867 he decided to learn Russian while recuperating from another bout of illness, 'gastric catarrh', in Nice with his brother Evelyn (they had travelled there after taking the waters at Schwalbach near Wiesbaden). Hiring a personal instructor, Mr. Hoffman, with whom he spoke nothing but Russian on long walks, he had mastered the basics of the language by the time he returned to England. The next language he was to learn was Spanish.

In 1868 Fred, along with Valentine and Samuel Baker and numerous others, became founder members of the Marlborough Club, with rooms in the heart of club-land at 52 Pall Mall. The Club's patron, and most important member, was the Prince of Wales, who, from 1863 until his accession to the throne in 1901, occupied Marlborough House, on the opposite side of Pall Mall. Fred later also became a member of the Bachelors' Club and, when his interest in politics began to develop, the Junior Carlton and later the Carlton.[10] Almost all of Fred's surviving correspondence from this period is on notepaper from one of the several barracks at which his regiment would be based, including the Knightsbridge Barracks at Hyde Park, the Albany Street Barracks at Regent's Park and, when the Royal Family was in residence, the Spital Barracks at Windsor.

So passed for Fred the first years of the 1860s. The Crimean was now a distant memory and nothing on the horizon suggested the Blues or any other cavalry regiments would be called into action in the immediate future. Domestic military duty during the summer months was not particularly onerous and winter leave could be spent travelling, but other interests were required.

---

10 The Bachelors Club was founded at the end of 1880, when Fred would not have been eligible to become a member, having married Lizzie only the year before. His letter to T.H.S. Escott written on the Club's notepaper in 1883 suggests that by then at least he did feel he was qualified to become a member.

2   *Vanity Fair*, early travels in Spain, 1868-70

Spain and the Carlist Wars

Fred Burnaby must have visited Spain for the first time during the 1860s and continued to do so regularly and for prolonged periods until shortly before his final trip to Egypt in 1884. According to Thomas Gibson Bowles he spoke Spanish like a Castilian and by his own account could go for a week without speaking English during his visits. Yet Spain was in constitutional and political foment for the whole of the period during which he made his visits, the reason for which had its roots in a controversial law passed well before he had been born, in 1830.

Under strict Salic Law, elements of which still applied to much of Europe during the eighteenth and early nineteenth centuries, one of the key tenets was agnatic succession, whereby females were absolutely excluded from inheriting a throne. On acceding to the throne of Spain in 1700, Philip V brought with him from France a variant known as semi-Salic law, under which females of a direct line from previous sovereigns could inherit, but only if there were no males with a valid claim to do so (including younger brothers of a former sovereign). In 1789 Charles IV of Spain issued a Decree, never formally promulgated, abolishing the semi-Salic system and reintroducing the mixed succession system that had pre-dated the accession to the throne of the Bourbon Philip V. Under this system a daughter of the sovereign could succeed to the throne if there was no son, even if there was a surviving younger brother of the sovereign. This is the form of succession still operating in Great Britain today, although soon to be changed.

In 1829 Ferdinand VII of Spain was married for the fourth time, on this occasion to his niece, Maria Christina of the Two Sicilies, who almost immediately fell pregnant. His three previous marriages (one of which was to another niece and another to a first cousin) had only produced daughters, none of whom had survived, and he must have feared that even if his new wife did bear him children who would survive they might well be female. Ferdinand, who had never been on particularly good terms with his younger brother, the Infante Carlos Maria, Count of Molina, was persuaded early in 1830 to ratify the largely forgotten Decree of his father, Charles IV, which he did by inducing the Cortes to issue a legal instrument commonly known as the Pragmatic Sanction of 1830. Carlos was therefore removed from being next in line of succession as long as Ferdinand's new wife produced children and this she did. The Infanta Maria Isabella Luisa was born in 1830 and the Infanta Luisa Fernanda in 1832, the effect of the Sanction being that the former would be declared Queen on his death. This happened quite quickly. Ferdinand died in 1833 and his older daughter succeeded him as Isabella II of Spain, with her mother acting as Regent.

Sovereigns and Pretenders of Spain (Houses of Bourbon and Savoy): 1748-1931

Sovereign	Lived	Reigned	Pretender	Lived	Claimed
Charles (Carlos) IV	1748-1819	1788-1808			
Ferdinand VII	1784-1833	1813-1833	Infante Carlos Maria (Carlos V)	1788-1855	1830-1845
Isabella II	1830-1904	1833-1870	Infante Carlos Luis (Carlos VI)	1818-1861	1845-1861
Amadeo I	1845-1890	1870-1873	Don Juan Carlos (Juan III)	1822-1887	1861-1868
Alfonso XII	1857-1885	1874-1885	Don Carlos (Carlos VII)	1848-1909	1868-1909
Alfonso XIII	1886-1941	1886-1931	Don Jaime (Jaime III)	1870-1931	1909-1931

Notes: 1. On the abdication of Charles IV in 1808, Ferdinand VII reigned very briefly before being deposed in favour of Joseph Bonaparte.
2. Isabella II left Spain in 1868, but did not abdicate until 1870.
3. The Spanish Cortes declared a Republic in 1873/4 following the abdication of Amadeo I.

Isabella's long reign was highly troubled from the outset, not least because of the First Carlist War of 1833 to 1839, during which her uncle, the Infante Carlos Maria (who adopted the title King Carlos V), sought the throne he felt that he had been unfairly denied. He had some grounds for this, for example arguing that the Sanction should not apply to the claims of those born before it had been introduced. Carlos was ultimately unsuccessful and was exiled following his final defeat in 1839. In 1845 he renounced his rights to the Spanish throne in favour of his eldest son, the Infante Carlos Luis, Count of Montelin (Carlos VI). Although Carlos VI married in 1850, there were to be no children of the union and when he died unexpectedly of typhus in 1861 his place as Pretender was taken by his surviving younger brother, Don Juan Carlos, Count of Montizón (Juan III). Juan Carlos had two sons, Don Carlos, Duke of Madrid (1848-1909) and Don Alfonso, Duke of San Jaime (1849-1936). Don Juan Carlos had taken no part in the brief Carlist uprising of 1860 led by his brother and even after his death did not seek to promote his cause. In 1868 he formally abdicated his rights to the Spanish throne in favour of his elder son, Don Carlos (Carlos VII). Unlike his father, frequently criticised for his liberal tendencies, Don Carlos was a strong traditionalist and took his responsibilities seriously with respect to his claim on the Spanish throne, especially after the abdication of Isabella in 1870. Also unlike his father he had a strong physical presence and natural leadership skills, although he had no military training.

In 1843 the Regency terminated and Isabella acceded to the throne in her own right reigning until 1868, but only with the support of the army. Burnaby is known to have been in Spain at least briefly early in 1868 and then for longer periods in the winter and spring of 1868/69 and 1869/70, doubtless tempted by the possibility of civil war. In 1868 Isabella was forced to leave Spain, the coup becoming known as 'the Glorious Revolution'. One of those to support the insurgents under General Juan Prim was Antoine d'Orléans, Duke of Montpensier (1824-1890), Isabella's brother-in-law. She abdicated formally in 1870 and the Cortes, which believed it was better to have the throne filled rather than vacant, looked round for a likely candidate to elect. Various names were considered, including King Louis I of Portugal (sometimes referred to as Don Fernando), Amadeo, Duke of Aosta (also known as the Prince of Carignano), the second son of King Vittorio Emanuel II of Italy, and Montpensier himself. The election was held in November 1870; Amadeo received 191 votes and Montpensier 27, possibly influenced by the fact that earlier in the year Montpensier had killed in a duel the Infante Enrique, Duke of Seville, and served a month in prison. Enrique had been the brother of Francis, Duke of Cadiz, Isabella II's consort. Lacking popular support, Amadeo I reigned for only two years and abdicated in 1873, when the Cortes declared the First Spanish Republic. This lasted less than a year and in 1874 Isabella's oldest son was installed as Alfonso XII of Spain. Whether his father was Isabella's consort is a matter of dispute, but uncertainty on this point was frequently used for propaganda purposes by the Carlists. Montpensier's consolation prize was that his daughter, Mercedes, briefly became Queen Consort to King Alfonso XII.

Meanwhile, the Third (and last) Carlist War had commenced in April 1872.[1] Forces sympathetic to the Carlist cause had begun to gather in the Basque Provinces even before Don Carlos crossed the border from France for the first time in May 1872, but there was insufficient time to organise them and within

---

1 The Second Carlist War was a localised and fairly low key affair that took place between 1846 and 1849.

Don Alfonso in Catalonia
(*Illustrated London News*, 5 April 1873)

days they were overcome by a small government army under General Moriones at Oroquieta. It was November 1872 before the Carlist forces managed to regroup in the Basque Provinces and Navarre under General Dorregaray, while Don Carlos' younger brother, Don Alfonso, took nominal control in Catalonia.

In May 1873 Dorregaray won an important victory at Eraul in Navarre, defeating a government army led by General Navarrese. Three months later Don Carlos re-entered the Basque Provinces and an escalation of the uprising became inevitable. The temptation for Burnaby to make another visit to Spain was now too great to resist, doing so briefly during the summer after he left Naples and then again from August to October. The Carlist forces met with several further successes, not least because Don Carlos adopted a policy of reintroducing limited autonomy to regions such as Catalonia, Valencia, Aragon and the Basque Provinces. Several important towns were occupied during the campaign, including Estella, but sieges to Bilbao and San Sebastian were eventually raised and the Carlist forces had to withdraw from Catalonia in 1875. Eventually, in February 1876, government forces re-took Estella, effectively Don Carlos's capital, and the Pretender and his staff went into exile in France. Thus the Third Carlist War came to an end and Don Carlos never returned to Spain.

An idler in Spain

Fred's first long visit to Spain of which we have any record commenced in November 1868, following another of his periodic bouts of illness (perhaps even his first serious one), although he had also been in Madrid during May of that year.[2] Some evidence of a slight feeling of guilt on his presence in Spain is shown by his signing of his letters to *Vanity Fair* 'Convalescent' and those to the *Morning Post* 'An idler in Spain'. He travelled overland via Paris and Pau, on the northern edge of the Pyrenees, then on to Bayonne, San Sebastian, Madrid and Seville. He remained there, with side trips to Cadiz, Gibraltar and Tangiers, until May 1869, sometime after his leave would normally have expired had he not been officially convalescent. By December 1869 he was back in Spain, dividing his time between Madrid and Seville, and remained there until April 1870. With the length of his time in the country and his dedication to languages it is easy to understand why his Spanish became so fluent, but it was also during this period that he recommenced lessons to perfect his Russian.

One of Fred's closest friends in London was Thomas Gibson Bowles (1841-1922), the illegitimate son of a British politician, Thomas Milner Gibson (1806-1884), and Sally Bowles. Tommy Bowles' father educated his son in France and arranged for him a post as a civil servant at Somerset House, but his real talent was writing and by 1866 he was a regular contributor to the *Morning Post* of Algernon Borthwick, later Lord Glenesk. By 1868 he was confident enough to start his own weekly newspaper, but he could not do this on his own. Most versions of the story of the foundation of *Vanity Fair* relate that Burnaby lent Bowles half of the £200 capital required, although other candidates have occasionally been proposed.[3] Burnaby's letter to his brother from Madrid in February 1869 in which he states: 'I begin to think my share looks promising in that speculation' seems to confirm not only that he provided at least some of the finance, but that it was an equity investment and not a loan. He is also generally acknowledged to have been the person who suggested the journal's title, taken from John Bunyan's *Pilgrim's Progress*, which would have

---

2 Lucy states that Burnaby's first visit to Spain was before he visited South America, which if it happened at all must have been some time before 1868. However, he also states that his second visit to Spain, by implication before 1871, 'provided him with the rare gratification of being shut up in Barcelona during the siege, and sharing all the privations and dangers of the garrison'. Although Burnaby almost certainly visited Barcelona he left no record thereof and the city was not besieged at any time when Burnaby was likely to have been in Spain. Lucy may have confused Barcelona with Bilbao or San Sebastian, but Burnaby was not present at these sieges either, both of which occurred during the Third Carlist War after he had returned to England. Finally, Lucy states that Burnaby was in Seville when he learned of his father's illness in 1871, which was definitely not the case (he was returning from his trip to Russia and Turkey).
3 Leonard E. Naylor in his biography of Bowles, *The irrepressible Victorian* (London: Macdonald, 1965), p. 19, suggests that the co-financier may have been another friend, Charles Waring.

been compulsory reading for the son of a Bedfordshire clergyman. Through his membership of the Marlborough Club and a growing circle of influential friends, Fred would have been in a good position to provide Bowles with gossip and leads for stories. Discretion was not one of Fred's strengths.

Bowles obviously thought that Burnaby could write entertainingly and published twenty one of his letters from Spain in *Vanity Fair* between December 1868 and April 1870. Burnaby was also on good terms with Borthwick and six additional letters from Fred were published in the *Morning Post* during this same period. Together with a few family letters quoted by early biographers, they fill in some of the gaps that would otherwise exist in the *Vanity Fair* letters. The cessation of Burnaby's writing for *Vanity Fair* in April 1870 was quite abrupt and it would seem that his financial interest in the journal also ended at around this time. No documents have been discovered to substantiate the story that pressure was brought on him from Horse Guards to terminate his involvement, but a strong hint may have been sufficient as he still had ambitions for promotion in his regiment. The matter was referred to in a letter Tommy Bowles wrote to the Prince of Wales in 1877:

> It is impossible I can avoid seeing that this is not an isolated case, but one of many beginning four years ago, by which your Royal Highness has shown a feeling of personal animosity towards me for which I am at a loss to account. And I cannot refrain from recalling here the conversations which in previous years your Royal Highness has had with Captain Burnaby in which you have intimated to him your opinion that he would do well to cease to be what for many years he has been, my intimate friend.[4]

Burnaby undoubtedly had a number of irritating habits. One of these was using what he considered to be phonetic representations of direct speech of foreigners who spoke English with a poor accent. Several examples of this can be found in his letters from Spain, where Americans, French and Germans are treated equally impolitely. Tempting as it would have been to omit or edit these, they have been left to stand in the transcripts provided in Part Two.

---

4 Quoted in Naylor, pp. 50-1.

3 Travels in Russia, Turkey and France, 1870-71

Bored with Spain?

These two long visits to Spain must have been enough to satisfy Fred's taste for Spanish food and culture for the time being. When his winter leave began at the end of 1870 he needed somewhere else to go.

Although Burnaby ceased to write for *Vanity Fair* in April 1870, he continued to act as a correspondent for the *Morning Post*, notably on a trip to Russia and Turkey during the winter of 1870/71. It is quite probable that a journey to Russia was not his first choice that winter; his friend Tommy Bowles was sending back despatches from within besieged Paris where, with James Tissot, he was a member of *Les Éclaireurs de la Seine*, and his original intention may well have been to see something of the Franco-Prussian War. However, this was not to be.[1] It is also possible that he had to remain in England longer than he had wished. His father's health had declined during the year and only began to improve again towards its end.

On his arrival in Moscow in December 1870 he wrote to his sister Annie asking her to 'please cut out and send me here any letters which may appear in the *Morning Post*'. Attempting to identify these despatches is slightly complicated by the fact that most of that newspaper's pieces on Russia and Turkey around this time were usually headed 'From our Correspondent'. Four, however, stand out as being very likely to have been written by Burnaby.

The first, headed 'From our Special Correspondent, St. Petersburg', appeared on 8 December 1870 and comprised two letters of the 1 and 3 of December. The writer apparently spoke some Russian and was concerned with his digestion, so it was almost certainly Burnaby. The second, datelined 'Russia, from our special correspondent, St. Petersburg, Dec. 10' appeared on 16 December 1870. The first part of the letter deals with the influx of Parisians to the Russian capital, escaping the siege of their own city, and relates a story concerning Russian marital infidelity. The second part returns to the subject of army estimates also

---

1 Although the war did not formally come to an end until May 1871, the siege of Paris was over by January and Burnaby did pass through the city, by then in the hands of the Paris Commune, on his way home.

mentioned in the first and provides a lengthy quotation from a local newspaper, the *Birjevouai Vedomosti*, on Russia's increasingly militaristic posture.[2] The third, datelined 'St. Petersburg and Moscow, from a Correspondent', appeared on 8 February 1871; apart from the fact that the writer had recently visited both cities, there is a reference to the writer's love of Seville and to goose livers (Burnaby's own liver was always a source of concern to him). It contains little of real importance, dealing with the diversions offered by Moscow (which he much preferred to St. Petersburg) and local religious and other customs. The fourth, datelined 'Notes from Turkey, from an Occasional Correspondent, Constantinople, Feb. 17' appeared on 6 March 1871. The writer mentions having passed through Kiev and Odessa (then in the grip of a cholera epidemic), which Burnaby is known to have done. All four represent typical examples of Burnaby's style. In her memoirs, Burnaby's widow states that: 'In 1870 the *Morning Post* published various letters from his pen in Russia', so there may still be more to be identified.[3]

While visiting Russia may have been his less preferred alternative in 1870/71, Fred probably felt that a resumption of an armed conflict with Russia was almost inevitable and in this he was correct. In 1871 the Treaty of Paris, which had brought the Crimean War to a conclusion, was effectively ended and thereafter it was a question of when, not if, Russia would find a pretext for further encroachment on the decaying Ottoman Empire. Travelling from Moscow to Constantinople would give him the opportunity of seeing at first hand some of the territory over which such a conflict would be fought.

In the summer of 1871 Burnaby presented a paper to the prestigious Royal United Services Institute, which was reprinted in its journal early in 1872.[4] The paper provided a description of staff officer training methods in the Russian army, with which he was clearly impressed. He had probably witnessed the manoeuvres described therein during his visit of the previous winter.

Although the trip has not been commented on by previous biographers, Burnaby was back in Russia during the winter of 1871/72. Oddly, he does not seem to have written any letters to the *Morning Post* or *The Times* while on this trip. In 1868 Colonel Robert Richardson-Gardner, DL, FSA (1827-1898) had unsuccessfully contested the seat of Windsor and Eton for the Conservative Party.[5] For the next few years he waited patiently to re-contest the seat, which

---

2 *Birjevouai Vedomosti* ('Exchange Statements') was published by Karl V. Trubnikov.
3 Le Blond, p. 48.
4 Frederick Gustavus Burnaby, 'The Practical Instruction of Staff Officers in Foreign Armies' in *Journal of the Royal United Services Institute* vol. 16, no. 68 (January 1872), pp. 633-44. Reprinted as a pamphlet (London: W. Mitchell & Co. 1876). Valentine Baker's paper 'Organisation and employment of cavalry' was published in vol. 17 of the *Journal*.
5 There were some superficial parallels between Richardson-Gardner and Burnaby. In both cases the first time their names appeared in the press related to public brawls – Richardson-Gardner's occurred in the billiard room of Swansea Assembly Rooms in 1849 and he was also fined as a

he indeed won in 1874 and held until his resignation in 1890. In the winter of 1871/72 Robert and his wife, Maria Louisa, daughter of Henry Gardner, a wealthy brewer, made the railway journey of over 1,500 miles from London to St. Petersburg and Moscow. The trip was described by Robert in a series of letters written to his brother, John Crow Richardson of Swansea, and published in both the *Cambrian* and the *Windsor and Eton Herald* (which Robert co-owned). These letters were subsequently collected and republished with minor amendments and corrections as a short book. Robert names most of his travelling companions, including Lt.-Col. Money of the North-East London Rifles (of which unit Robert himself had been until recently Honorary Colonel), Captain Chambers of the Canadian army and 'a respected Russian officer', Lt.-Col. Isenbeck. However, one of his travelling companions was described only as a 'Captain in the Blues'. Of this officer Robert wrote:[6]

> Just as we started from Berlin we made another acquaintance ... an officer of the Blues, height 6ft. 4in. in his stocking feet, wrapped up in a splendid Astracan 'Shuba', and to whom I had previously called Chambers's attention, as to his being a magnificent Russian. It seemed he had previously travelled with Isenbeck, and so he added materially to the pleasure of the salon party as far as Wilna. Our guardsman is a perfect marvel, he speaks nine living language – Russian included – and has travelled over pretty nearly the whole of this world, occupying his 'leave' in so doing: and if he could only get 'leave' in the next, there is no knowing where he would not go.

At this time Burnaby's travels were not well known to the public, but his ballooning exploits were and it may be considered odd that Robert, a social climber, did not recognise him on introduction, at least by reputation or through his connections with *Vanity Fair*; the nine languages may also have been a small exaggeration at this stage of Burnaby's life.

That it was definitely Burnaby and that he soon continued on to St. Petersburg from Wilna is apparent from an article written in French and re-published in the *Windsor and Eton Herald* on 17 January 1872, having originally been published in the *Journal de St. Petersburg* of 3 January 1872 (OS). Referring to a diplomatic reception at the Winter Palace on the first day of the year, there is included a report of presentations: 'During the reception, the following persons had the honour of being presented to their Majesties

---

result. Both were well above average height, although Richardson-Gardner was two inches shorter than Burnaby, both were letter writers to newspapers, and both married heiresses. Both were staunch Conservatives and, like Burnaby, Richardson-Gardner's caricature appeared in *Vanity Fair*. Richardson-Gardner's colonelcy related to the North East London Rifles, a militia unit, rather than the regular army.

6   Robert Richardson-Gardner, *A trip to St. Petersburg* (London: T. Brettell and Co., 1872).

[the Czar and Czarina], namely: ... Mr. Burnaby, major of the Horse Guards; Mr. Richardson-Gardner, a retired colonel of the regiment of volunteers; ...'. So not only was Richardson-Gardner presented to the Czar (and his wife to the Czarina), but also 'Major' Burnaby of the Horse Guards; the fact that Burnaby is described by Wright as an 'extreme Russophobe' obviously did not preclude him from making as many Russian contacts as he could.

The railway journey from Berlin to St. Petersburg took the small party two days and two nights, their route passing through Dantsig, Marienburg, Königsberg, Eydtkuhnen, Wiersbolow, Kovno and Wilna (now Vilnius in Lithuania), where Burnaby left them. A little beyond Wilna the route would also have taken them through Dunaburg (now Daugavpils in Latvia) and it may well be that Burnaby had a particular reason for visiting this area. At some time after his return to England he made an investment in the Dunaburg & Witepsk Railway Company, which was quoted on the London Stock Exchange and which shares he still held in 1878.[7] Where else he visited on this trip is not known, but Isenbeck, whom Richardson-Gardner thought Burnaby had met previously, travelled on by rail from St. Petersburg to Nijni-Novgorod, several hundred miles to the east of Moscow, and it may have been that Burnaby followed him there.

Various anecdotes have been related concerning Burnaby and Russians, for example that as a wager he allowed a Russian artillery officer to bind him hand and foot with a rope, undoing it in less than half the time it took the Russian to tie it.[8] In a conversation with a journalist, Archibald Forbes, during the Russo-Turkish War, Count Paul Schuvalov, who described him as an old friend, remarked of Burnaby that: '... he was my guest at the mess of the *Garde du Corps* when he was last in St. Petersburg, and our crack giant, old Protassoff-Bakmetieff, was not in it with Burnaby either in stature or in strength.'[9] Following the publication of *On horseback through Asia Minor* Burnaby was *persona non grata* in Russia, so the occasion of his entertainment must have been on his way either to or from Khiva the previous year.

Not only had Burnaby's fluency in Russian grown during his two visits, but so had his distrust of the Russian government. He was certainly not the only person to predict that when a suitable opportunity arose, engineered or otherwise, Russia would move south through the Balkans and towards Constantinople, most probably accompanied by a parallel move south around the eastern end of the Black Sea into Anatolia. Likewise he was one of a

---

7 Shakespeare Birthplace Trust, Stratford. Autograph Collection: Maslin collection, 1840-1907 (formerly M4a). No.8 (1/2).
8 Ware, p. 119.
9 Forbes, p. 318. General Count Protassoff-Bakmetieff was commander of the bodyguard of the Hussar regiment and Imperial adjutant-general. The *Garde du Corps* was the personal bodyguard of the Imperial Russian Monarchy.

number of those greatly concerned by Russia's inexorable advance southwards into Central Asia ever closer to India, still regarded as the jewel in the crown of the Empire. Burnaby felt strongly that Britain should be proactive in reversing this encroachment and realised that first hand observation might be a good way of raising public awareness. The obvious place to visit would be Khiva, then an independent khanate to the south of the Russian border, known to be next on the list of territories that the Russian government wished to annex.

4 First Khiva attempt; the Carlist War, 1872-73

The lure of Khiva

In May 1872 Burnaby found himself with some light military duties, accompanying the Prince of Wales as ADC to Vienna for the international exhibition. His father's health declined again that year and he died in July, following which his mother moved their London residence from 32 Upper Berkeley Street to 36 Beaufort Gardens. By then he had been in the Blues for over twelve years; he had seen no military action and could have no short term expectation of achieving his majority. Always restless, some form of adventure strongly beckoned.

His first attempt to visit Khiva was made in the winter of 1872/73, in the hope that he would arrive in time for an expected attack on the khanate by the Russian General Constantin von Kaufmann (1818-1882). The only European to have visited the city within the last decade was the Hungarian, Arminius Vambéry, who had done so in disguise in 1863. Despite the protestations of the Czar of Russia that his country had reached its natural southern frontier, his generals in Central Asia continued to press south and seldom lacked opportunities for picking fights with the warlike tribes of the region, who were not averse to taking Russians as slaves. In fact Kaufmann commenced his assault on Khiva in the spring of 1873 and the Khan had capitulated by the summer of that year.

Burnaby was accompanied on his attempt by his servant George Radford, a trooper in the Blues, who was of his own height, although not so large. The intended route was to travel eastwards overland from Asia Minor. They set out for Brindisi, but only reached as far as Naples. There he succumbed to typhoid and became seriously ill; by March there was a press report stating that he had been ill for over a month and that he had 'passed through the delirious and other stages, but had not yet shaken off some of the acute symptoms'.[1] His mother, who had been widowed the previous year, came out to nurse him and when he was sufficiently recovered they moved on to Seville for a further period of convalescence. In June 1873 Fred's sister-in-law died in childbirth

---

1 *Morning Post*, 12 March 1873.

First Khiva attempt; the Carlist War, 1872-73   45

Burnaby and the Carlists
(*The Graphic*, 31 May 1875)

and his mother felt it was her duty to return to England.[2] Soon after this Fred must have made a decision also to make his way back, but determined to do so via Vitoria and San Sebastian, in other words through the heartland of the Carlist forces, a part of Spain with which he was not familiar. The journey from Seville to Vitoria was made by train, but from that point on the railway line was unsafe and he had to proceed by diligence (public stagecoach). The route to San Sebastian took him through Alsasua and Beasain. Between the last two of these towns his coach was stopped by a party of Carlists, but he was allowed to proceed after a polite interrogation and reached San Sebastian safely. From there it was but a short journey the following day to Irun and the border crossing at Henduza, whence he undertook the final leg of his journey to England through France.

2   Evelyn Burnaby had married Winifred Crake on 4 May 1871 at Hastings; she died in childbirth in May 1873 (GRO ref. Melton Mowbray 7a 158), which confirms the date when Fred was recovering in Seville. The dates of publication of the forty or so letters in *The Times* that he wrote while with the Carlist forces are between 15 August and 5 November 1873, so that it is quite clear he only spent a few weeks back in London.

Don Carlos in Navarre.
(*Illustrated London News*, 8 September 1873)

Back to Spain

Without exception his early biographers suggest that he spent a year or so resting in England before returning to Spain, but this is not the case. It was in August 1873, not 1874, that he made his way back to the northern provinces of Spain. Temperamentally Burnaby would have found himself more in sympathy with the Carlist cause than that of the government, although the general feeling in Britain was not entirely pro-Carlist, due to alleged atrocities by Carlist irregulars. Before leaving he was appointed, or appointed himself, 'Special correspondent with the Carlist Forces' to *The Times*. He was far from the only such special correspondent, although at that time the majority of foreign correspondents based themselves in Madrid, or just across the French border at Hendaye. The Carlist military authorities in general and Don Carlos in particular were very happy to have their side of the conflict reported fairly in the international press and so Fred and the other correspondents were made welcome. Among those with whom he came into contact were John Augustus O'Shea of the *Standard*, an unidentified journalist and artist of the *Illustrated London News*, Baron von Wedell of the *Cologne Gazette* and Baron von Walterskirchen of the Viennese *Vaterland*. The following year the *ILN* sent out another of its artists, Irving Montagu; Archibald Forbes of the *Daily News* returned after a visit to India during the winter of 1873/4 and the *New York Herald* sent out Januarius Aloysius MacGahan.

Burnaby and Don Carlos, who, like Fred, had a striking physique, soon developed a strong mutual respect and he was given wide access to the military operations carried out by Don Carlos's generals. Over the course of the next three months, around forty of his despatches were published by *The Times* (one or two may also have been lost in transit). It is almost certain that Fred originally intended to collect these letters and publish them in book form on his return, but he never did so. However, he did go so far as to draft a preface that was found written in one of his commonplace books among his papers on his death. Towards the end of an item in the *World* in 1876 that mentions Burnaby in passing, the author poses the question, 'What about a manuscript teaching adventures on a campaign with the Carlists, including the wonderful performance of a wizard at St. Esteban, written by a certain officer, but withheld from publication in deference to a hint from higher powers? Surely it might see the light now without any serious danger to international friendship.'[3] Whether or not a completed manuscript actually existed is debatable, but the suggestion that Burnaby was discouraged from collecting and publishing the letters may well be correct.

Burnaby left London with his servant, George Radford, and his friend, Charles Needham, a captain in the First Life Guards, on 8 August 1873, travelling by train to Bayonne in France and thence by horse to Biarritz. It took a few days for them to have their papers put in order and they then continued on horseback to St. Jean de Luz and across the border to Bera[4] in Almeira, arriving on 11 August. They probably passed through Irun, since Burnaby would have been familiar with this route as a result of his trip in the opposite direction only a few months previously. Almost immediately they continued south-east to Elizondo, also in Navarre. Having established contact with the Carlist forces, the remainder of August was spent in a south-westerly movement through Arraiz, Estella, Dicastillo, Allo, Los Arcos and Viana, from all of which Burnaby returned despatches to *The Times*. Still within Navarre he then turned north to Aras and Alsasua, before entering Guipuzcoa Province and passing through Bergara on the way to the coastal town of Lequeito, via Azpeitia. Pausing only briefly, he then headed south-west back to Bergara followed by an east-west-east traverse to Zumarraga, Tolosa, Zumarraga again, Durango and Villa Real (now Urretxu), before turning south-east to Avarzuza

---

3   *The World*, 31 May 1876. Burnaby passed through St. Esteban in August 1873 and again on his way home, when John Augustus O'Shea performed some magic tricks with a coin.
4   Burnaby was equally inclined to refer to this town as Bera or Vera.

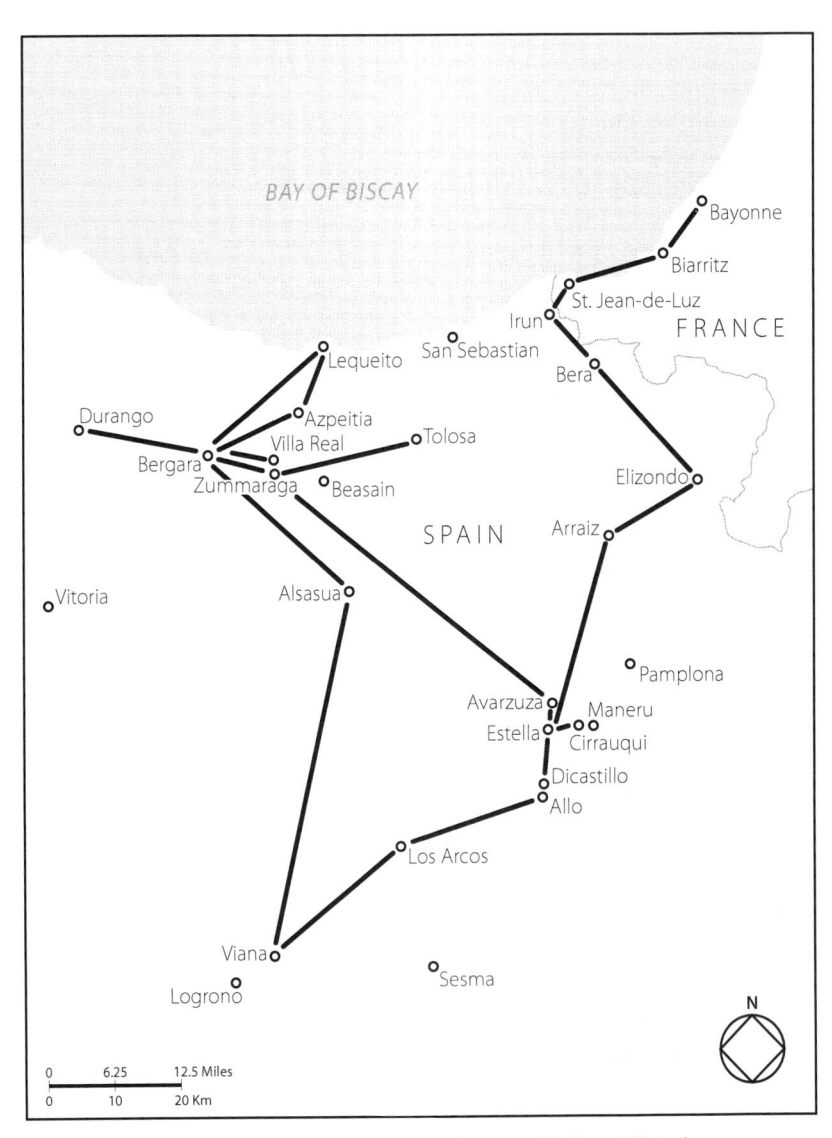

Burnaby's travels with the Carlist forces, 1873 (Steve Waites)

and back to Estella. There was then one final short journey east to Cirauqui and Mañeru, before he returned to the Royalist Headquarters at Estella at the beginning of October. He remained there until the end of the month, when he bade farewell to Don Carlos and made his way home to London. It was on this return journey that Radford had the accident Burnaby related in the 'In memoriam' to Radford he added to the seventh addition of his *On horseback through Asia Minor*.

The military actions with which he was involved during this journey on horseback of over 1,000 miles were the battles of Allo (22 August), Dicastillo (24 August), Viana (4 September) and Mañeru (6 October), as well as the siege of Tolosa and the capture of Estella (26 August). None of these would have been described as a major engagement, but they were not without their casualties. Despite his lengthy despatches, Burnaby never once mentioned any situations of danger or difficulty in which he found himself. The following anecdote only appeared after his death in a brief unattributed additional obituary in *The Times* sent from Paris.[5]

> Great regret is felt here at the death of Colonel Burnaby, who has left many friends in Paris, for he was popular in France, as indeed wherever he went, and it is felt that a braver man never lived. A friend has just given me an instance of his total disregard of danger.
>
> During the civil war in the Basque Provinces, the Carlists were attacked by a column of Liberals at the church of Dicastillo. Colonel Burnaby, whose stature exceeded six feet, was standing in front of the soldiers of Don Carlos, calmly watching the fighting, when a body of the enemy suddenly appeared within a hundred yards, and delivered a murderous volley, which brought down several men behind him. The commanding officer gave the order to kneel and fire under cover of the parapet wall. This was obeyed promptly enough, but Burnaby remained standing on the same spot, until the attack was repulsed. One man was shot dead, and an officer had his ear cut off by a bullet, within a few feet of him. Wherever fighting was going on there the Colonel loved to be.

Irving Montagu, the war artist who was another of the special correspondents in Spain, mentions in his memoirs of the war the propensity of Burnaby and Don Carlos to make inspections together.

> By the way, talking of San Marcial brings me to Don Carlos, who, more than once, visited that stronghold during the war, accompanied by his friend Colonel Burnaby, and which led to a supposition on the part of the Republicans that whenever, through field-glasses, they saw officers of broader proportions than

5 *The Times*, 23 January 1885 (Paris, 22 January 1885).

usual on the ramparts, His Majesty and his friend were *en évidence*.[6]

Montagu also mentioned Burnaby in other articles he wrote some years after the war. These have been quoted by his early biographers and are reproduced here.

> The Carlist campaigns were, in a general way, more dangerous to civilians than soldiers on either side, for both sides gave each other a wide berth. As an instance of that mode in which the so-called war was carried on, I may mention that, when at Irun – which was held by the Alfonsists and shelled by the Carlists from Fort San Marcial, which is situated on the Trois Couronnes, Basses Pyrenées – when the Carlists were within ordinary range at Fort San Marcial, it was quite safe to walk on the ramparts, for neither party by any chance reached the other. Frequently, by the aid of a decent telescope, I have seen two exceptionally tall men walking on the ramparts of Fort San Marcial, in singular contrast with the men about them. O'Donovan and myself quite agreed that these two figures could only be those of Burnaby and Don Carlos, for they were the only two men amongst the Carlists who were inches above six feet. Again both figures would be seen smoking. Burnaby and Don Carlos were inveterate smokers.
>
> I must often have watched Burnaby as I looked along the line of fire between Fort San Marcial and Irun. It was proverbial that the shot on each side fell equally short, but, nevertheless, it takes some amount of pluck to watch a shell coming towards you. We were informed at the time – and I believed then, as I do now, that the news was not false – that, when the Carlists quite made up their minds to give the assault, it would be led by Burnaby and another officer of the guards, who had volunteered upon seeing that the Carlists themselves funked it. The order given was that a breach was to be made in the walls near the church, and the assault to be wholly concentrated at this point. Mind, it was only a report, and plenty of false news came into Irun, but it created a large amount of anxiety. Ultimately we were given to understand that it was due to Don Carlos himself that his plan was never carried out. It was said among us specials and others, that the Don held that if the assault were led by an Englishman or two, in the result it might lead to some international squabble. But a statement was circulated amongst the town folk to the effect that his Highness Don Carlos had refused to accept the proffered services of the English soldiers, as the honour of Spain, of the royal race, and of victory itself, required that the struggle must be in the hands of the Spaniards. Therefore the offer had been clearly and distinctly refused. I think I saw outward signs of inward joy upon the faces of many Alfonsists as this news spread through the besieged town – if, indeed, it could be said to be in a state of siege. No, I was never with Burnaby at any moment during the Carlist

---

6   Irving Montagu, *Wanderings of a war-artist* (London: W.H. Allen & Co. Ltd., 1889), p. 239.

First Khiva attempt; the Carlist War, 1872-73   51

movement, but at almost any instant I might have shaken hands with him.[7]

The main problems with these is that Burnaby never mentions the siege of Irun or the Fort San Marcial in any of his despatches and the majority of military activity in this area took place in 1874, not 1873 (which, to be fair, is when most people by then thought Burnaby had been in Spain). There is also evidence that Montagu did not arrive in Spain until 1874. In the second of the four chapters of his memoirs dealing with his time in Spain, Montagu refers to the death of Marshal Concha as having occurred sometime previously. In fact Concha had been killed in June 1874, so it is probable that Montagu was writing of a time almost a year after Burnaby had returned to England. One is left to speculate as to the identity of the second tall figure, if he was not simply a figment of Montagu's imagination.

The likelihood is that Burnaby adhered strictly to a non-combatant role during his time with the Carlist forces, fully recognising that it would not be in the best interests of the Carlist cause if he or other non-Spaniards involved themselves in the actual fighting. This is supported by the despatch he wrote in which he mentioned the 'absurd' story that had appeared in *Español* suggesting that it was his intention to raise an international legion for the support of Don Carlos.

It has been speculated by his early biographers that Burnaby returned home before the expiration of his leave, having eventually become disillusioned with the somewhat amateurish manner in which the war was being prosecuted and the reluctance of either side to take decisive action. A more convincing explanation is provided by one of his fellow correspondents, John Augustus O'Shea, who believed that Burnaby was recalled prematurely from Spain by the War Office, a complaint having been made by the Government in Madrid that the Carlists were boasting that one of Queen Victoria's 'Blue Guards' was giving military counsel to Don Carlos.[8] Notwithstanding this he remained on good terms with Don Carlos for the rest of his life and also, in due course, came to be on terms of familiarity with King Alfonso XII, whom he had first met in London during Alfonso's time at Sandhurst.

On his return to England Burnaby did not entirely lose interest in the Carlist cause and other soldier-adventurers took up the mantle of 'special correspondent'. One such was Lord Melgund, formerly an officer in the Scots Guards and later to become 4th Earl of Minto. He spent much of 1874 with the Carlists and wrote a letter to Burnaby in September of that year, which he

7 Ware & Mann give no source for the first quotation and that for the second quotation as *The Welcome*, 1883, but the relevant article has not been identified. Irving Montagu certainly did write for *The Welcome*, notably contributing a piece 'At the front' on special correspondents for the issue that also contained Burnaby's obituary by M. MacMaster, in February 1885 (no. 178).
8 John Augustus O'Shea, 'Explorers I have met' in *Tinsley's Magazine*, vol. 33 (August 1883), p. 99.

forwarded to Delane, still editor of *The Times*.

Perhaps because he had been absent from his Regiment for almost all of the time between December 1872 and November 1873, Burnaby seems not to have been granted a period of leave over the winter of 1873/74. During the summer of 1874 his thoughts must have turned to his plans for the following winter and given the determination that was such an obvious part of his character it is surprising that he did not immediately make another attempt at Khiva. In fact in the winter of 1874/5 Burnaby visited Egypt and the Sudan, apparently for the first time, traveling overland to Khartoum. On this trip he was once again engaged as a special correspondent of *The Times* and it is likely that he was retained specifically by its editor, John Delane, to meet and report on Colonel Charles Gordon.

5 First Sudan trip; Gordon at Sobat, 1874-75

Egypt and Sudan

Placing Gordon's presence in Khartoum and the British expeditions to Egypt and the Sudan of 1882 to 1885 in context requires a brief review of the secession of Egypt from the Ottoman Empire. In 1798 Napoleon had invaded Egypt, then an Ottoman province, and the French forces were only expelled in 1801 by a combination of British and Ottoman forces. The Ottoman troops were largely Mamluks, from the ruling military caste, and were sent from Rumelia, one of the Balkan provinces of the Ottoman Empire, under the command of Muhammed Ali Pasha. With the British and French gone, Muhammed Ali realised that his position in Egypt was extraordinarily powerful as the Porte had no other forces with which to oppose him and he seized power, declaring himself ruler of Egypt. After some unsuccessful attempts to regain control, the Porte eventually reached the conclusion that there was nothing they could do and in 1805 granted him the titles Pasha and Governor, but not content with this he adopted the additional title of Khedive (roughly Viceroy), which was also held by his successors, although only recognised by the Porte in 1867.

The strategic importance of Egypt increased dramatically during the 1850s and 1860s with the construction of the Suez Canal, which was financed mainly by a combination of French and local capital. Although invited to participate in its financing and construction, the British Government opposed the project from its inception to its completion. Notwithstanding some operating difficulties following its opening in 1869, it became clear very quickly that the new canal would have a major impact on the level and patterns of world maritime trade. By the time Burnaby arrived in Egypt in late 1874, it was also clear that the Egyptian government had over-reached themselves financially in supporting the construction of the canal. Before the end of 1875 the British government had bought Egypt's shares from the Khedive, Ismail Pasha, who was widely and increasingly considered to be an unreliable ruler. Thereafter the British and the French, who remained the majority shareholders, would be forced to protect their interests.[1]

---

1 Although England and France initially acted jointly, when armed intervention became necessary in

Major-General Charles George 'Chinese' Gordon
(*Vanity Fair*, 19 February 1881)

Meanwhile, Charles George Gordon had entered the service of the Khedive of Egypt in 1874. Gordon had joined the Royal Engineers in 1852, fought in the Crimea and enjoyed a conventional military career until 1860, when he volunteered for service in China. After some initial duties in and around Beijing, he was appointed as an engineer officer in support of the militia raised to combat a rebel force from Taiping advancing on Shanghai, but by 1862 he was appointed commander of a Chinese element of this force that came to be known as 'the Ever-Victorious Army'. His unit enjoyed considerable success against the rebels, well-reported in the British press, before being disbanded in 1864. Gordon was promoted to Lieutenant-Colonel and thereafter became known to the British public as 'Chinese Gordon'. A variety of less active posts followed and in 1872 he was sent to inspect the British military cemeteries in the Crimea. While passing through Constantinople he was introduced to a representative of the Khedive of Egypt, who opened negotiations for Gordon to serve as a regional governor. In 1873 Gordon received a definite offer and proceeded to Egypt early in 1874. He was been given the rank of Colonel in the Egyptian army and appointed by the Khedive to govern a large area of

1882, Britain was forced to act alone.

the Sudan with the object of suppressing the Nilotic slave trade, then largely centred on the southern Sudan.

Gordon's appointment had the full approval of the British government, not least because it was unsure of what to do with him. It also felt its public popularity would be enhanced in being associated with a high profile attempt to reduce the slave trade. The Nilotic slave trade had existed since at least mediaeval times, with Egypt being one of the main takers of slaves from the Sudan and further south for most of this period. Until the 1850s Egypt itself had continued to encourage the trade, but in 1854 under increasing European influence Muhammad Sa'īd Pasha, the Khedive, bowed to pressure for its abolition in Egypt, although it could do little to influence the trade in the Sudan where its power was still limited. Despite the fragmentation of the Ottoman Empire the Egyptian government had been trying to extend its influence south along the Nile from the 1820s. In 1871 Sir Samuel Baker, the elder brother of Valentine, was sent on an expensive expedition along the White Nile by Ismail Pasha, by then Khedive, and succeeded in establishing bases at Khartoum and Gondokoro, but little else. Gordon made some progress during the three years following his appointment, establishing further outposts as far south as the border with Uganda and doing much to discourage the slave trade, although in 1876 he clashed with the Egyptian Governor of Khartoum and abruptly left for England.

The route taken by Gordon to Khartoum in February 1874 was essentially that to be followed by Burnaby a year later. From the southern end of the Suez Canal he travelled by steamer with his small team and a military escort as far as Suakin, a port on the west coast of the Red Sea. From there the overland route to Berber by camel passed through Tamai and the oasis of Aryah, where the party stopped briefly, still managing to achieve what would normally be a twelve day journey in nine days. Gordon's team comprised a mixture of amateurs and professionals. Among the latter were Colonel Charles Chaillé-Long (1842-1917) and Major William Campbell, both Americans who had fought in the US Civil War and later accepted commissions with the Egyptian Army. He took as his secretary and interpreter Auguste Linant de Bellefonds, the younger son of Louis Linant de Bellefonds (1799-1883), better known as Linant Pasha, a noted and highly respected French Egyptologist. The younger Linant was fluent in Arabic and had a good knowledge of several of the languages spoken in Central Africa. Also in the party was Frederick Russell, the son of William Howard Russell, the Irish special correspondent of *The Times*, who had travelled up the Nile with the Prince and Princess of Wales five years before. He was not Gordon's choice, but the Khedive wanted someone with the Expedition who could act as a correspondent. The party was completed by de Witt, a German naturalist supposedly from Hamburg,[2] and Gordon's nephew, William Anson, who had previously worked for the Post Office in England. Already at Khartoum were a civilian marine engineer, Mr. J. Kemp, and an Italian soldier, Romolo Gessi (1831-1881), whom Gordon later described as a 'brilliant mercenary' and who had fought alongside Garibaldi in Italy and with the British army in the Crimea, where he and Gordon had first met. Later in the year his party was augmented by Lieutenants William Harold Chippindall and Charles Moore Watson, both on secondment from the Royal Engineers.

There is a tendency to think of Burnaby's trip to the Sudan as an extended Cook's tour, but this is far from accurate, as can be seen from the fate of Gordon's party. Anson did not even live to see Gondokoro, succumbing to blackwater fever *en route*. Linant and de Witt reached Gondokoro, but died there and were buried alongside Edwin Higginbotham, Samuel Baker's engineer who had heroically transported his steamers across the desert to Korosko. They were followed shortly after by Campbell, who died of typhus at Khartoum. Long travelled further south with the Austrian explorer Ernst Marno (1844-1883), who had been sent out by the Geographical Society of Vienna to join the Expedition, and by September 1874 Gordon had heard nothing of them for six months, although they did eventually return. Russell became seriously ill almost immediately and was invalided to Cairo once he regained sufficient strength, where he fell in with Burnaby's party for the return trip. The health of Kemp, Chippindall and Watson failed next. Chippindall was sent to Cairo and Watson travelled north with Burnaby when he left Khartoum on his way back to England. Kemp was also sent back to England. Meanwhile Linant Pasha's elder son, Ernest, had travelled to Khartoum with the two Royal Engineers officers and attached himself to Gordon's retinue. Within a few months he was killed by natives. Gessi managed to survive for six years, but also died of fever contracted on the Nile and was followed two years later by Marno. Long, unusually, survived Africa and went on to a successful life as a diplomat and author. Two more Europeans subsequently took up service with Gordon: the Italian Carlo Piaggia (1827-1882), who survived only a few years, and the German Isaak Eduard Schnitzer (1840-1892), later better known as Mehemet Emin Pasha. Burnaby, who had almost died of typhus only two years before, must have realised the risks he was taking.

Burnaby's journey to the Sudan via Alexandria and Cairo would have been straightforward until he reached the southern end of the Suez Canal. From there, so far as Suakin on the west coast of the Red Sea, he travelled on a self-catering steamer, the Dessouk, where he found that he was also called on to

---

2 It has been speculated that de Witt was, in fact, a barrister from Bremen called George Spretzer, who fled home to avoid a criminal investigation. See Alice Moore-Harell, *Egypt's African Empire: Samuel Baker, Charles Gordon & the Creation of Equatoria* (Eastbourne: Sussex Academic Press, 2010), p. 215.

First Sudan trip; Gordon at Sobat, 1874-75   57

The hunting parties. Back row – Russell, Burnaby, Vivian, Gordon-Cumming.
Front row – Levick, Ranfurly, Coke, Arkwright, Dr. Meyer
(*The Graphic*, 6 March 1875)

assist with the navigation. The journey of some 750 miles took five days and involved a close brush with a coral reef. Among his fellow passengers were three shooting parties. The largest, also to disembark at Suakin and then travel on by land to Kassala in Abyssinia, comprised four officers of the Foot Guards: Captain Vivian, Viscount Coke (heir to the Earl of Leicester) and the notorious womaniser Sir William Gordon-Cumming (alongside whom Burnaby was to fight at Abu Klea and who was to later to be the central figure in the 'Royal Baccarat Scandal' at Tranby Croft). Also in this party was a surgeon in the Coldstream Guards, Arthur Myers, who later wrote a memoir of the expedition and recalled: 'Burnaby is the most industrious of our party, and may frequently be seen holding a conversation with one of the crew with the assistance of an Arabic vocabulary (Sacroug),[3] and he is making rapid progress in their language.'[4] This party was to have been joined by Lord Charles Ker of the Scots Guards,[5] but on his arrival at Cairo he was immediately recalled to England.

There were also two smaller shooting parties on board. One comprised the 4th Earl of Ranfurly and Mr. Charles Arkwright, of whom the latter had prior experience of the region. The other comprised the 7th Earl of Mayo, a lieutenant in the Grenadier Guards, and a Mr. Flower. Both of these parties were heading for Massowah (now usually Massawah), almost four hundred miles and two

3 Gabriel Sacroug, *The Egyptian travelling interpreter, or, Arabic without a teacher* (Cairo, 1874).
4 Arthur Bowen Richards Myers, *Life with the Hamran Arabs* (London: Smith, Elder & Co., 1876).
5 Lord Charles John Innes-Ker (1842-1919), younger son of the 6th Duke of Roxburghe, later Lieutenant-Colonel.

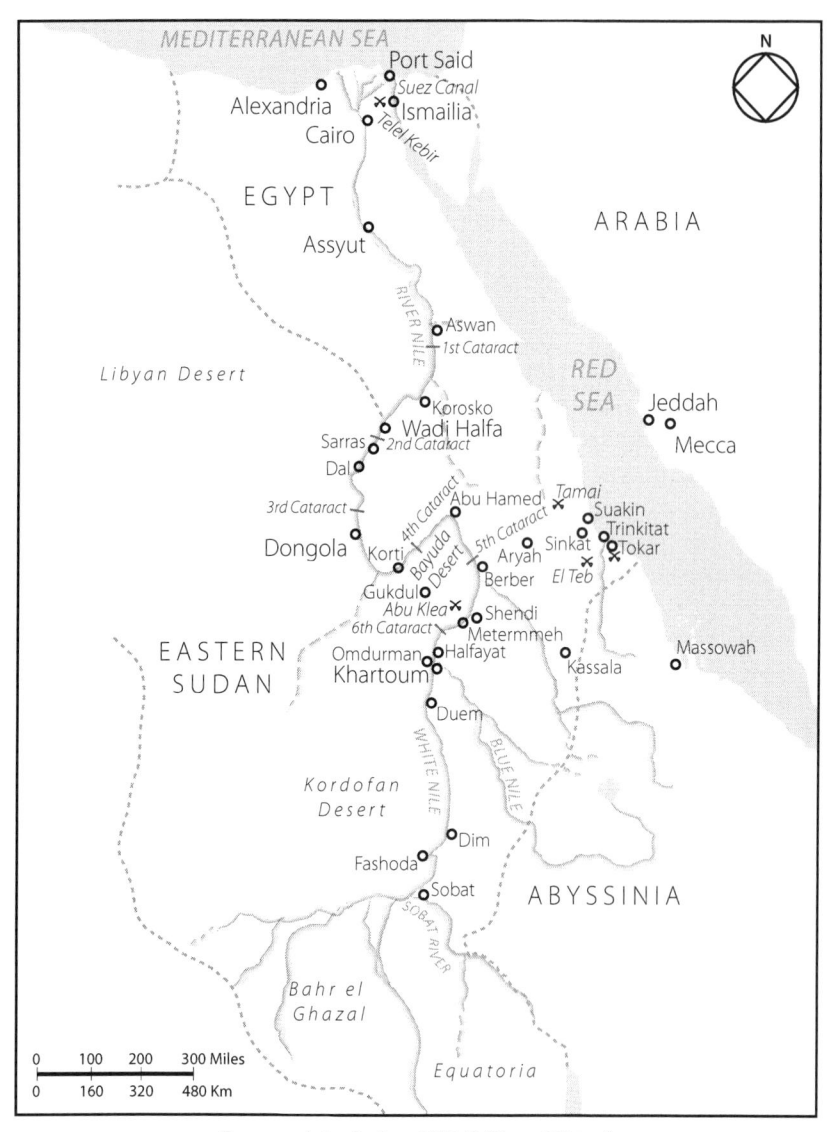

Egypt and the Sudan, 1974/5 (Steve Waites)

days steaming further south than Suakin. While on his expedition, Ranfurly contracted dysentery in the Bogos country to the west of Massawah (now in Eritrea). Despite regaining contact with the larger Guards expedition and benefitting from the care of Myers, he died at Suakin in May. Mayo also went down with fever while travelling in the Mareb and had to return to the coast, but survived.[6]

The group was completed by Frederick Russell, one of Gordon's assistants, who was returning from sick leave in Cairo, and Mr. Marcopoli, both of whom were to travel across the desert with Burnaby to Khartoum. Marcopoli, who had worked for Sir Samuel Baker before losing his confidence, was a Greek who spoke and read Arabic fluently and had an excellent knowledge of the region. He was travelling to Khartoum to take up a position with Gordon as an interpreter and administrator, but he eventually lost his trust as well. As the steamer was leaving Suez Mr. C.M. Kenny-Levick of the Her Britannic Majesty's Packet Agency, who acted as post-master, arranged for a photograph to be taken of some of his passengers, which was subsequently the basis for an illustration in the *Graphic*.

While the game-shooters travelled south either towards Kassala by camel, or onwards by steamer to Massowah, Fred took the overland caravan route from Suakin to Khartoum via Berber, which was the same as that taken by Gordon. Burnaby had elected not to bring Radford with him and hired a Nubian as his servant. The leisurely journey from Sinkat to Berber took fifteen days, rather than the nine taken by Gordon, and like them they stopped at Aryah. The inherent boredom of the desert journey was relieved only by an encounter with a slaving caravan. At Berber they boarded one of the Nile steamers and passed by Metammeh and Halfayah on the way to Khartoum, continuing immediately onwards to Sobat, where they found Gordon. The total journey took a further twenty five days, including some enforced halts.

Gordon and Burnaby had little in common. The former was no lover of journalists and resented Fred's intrusion (he rejected the presence of Henry Morton Stanley on the grounds that 'I object to being daily logged'). Fred did not form a wholly positive impression of Gordon, although he was happy later to plead his cause for political reasons. Gordon gave Burnaby permission to travel even further south, but he placed restrictions on what subjects he was allowed to write about in his dispatches. Probably because of this, when Gordon left Sobat for Lardo, another of his stations, Fred returned to Khartoum and, after a short stay, to England. Burnaby's four letters to *The Times* were colourful, but due to the constraints under which he apparently wrote constituted little more than a travelogue. Notwithstanding this he managed to annoy Gordon

6   Dermot Robert Wyndham Bourke (7th Earl of Mayo), *Sport in Abyssinia; or, the Mareb and Tackazee* (London: John Murray, 1876).

with their contents, who wrote to one of his staff officers: 'If you see or hear from Burnaby, tell him that it is on the understood ground that he ceases this sort of correspondence and limits it to descriptions of country and *dead objects*, etc.'[7] Burnaby's final letter describes the locations of four of Gordon's stations, at Ratichambé, Bor, Lardo and Gondokoro, of which the last was almost another 450 miles upriver from Sobat. From the style of the letters it would be easy to imagine that he had actually made this trip himself, but he did not do so. Burnaby occasionally referred to this trip elsewhere, including anecdotes concerning the discomforts associated with riding both a cow and a lovesick camel, in *A ride to Khiva*.

On his return journey Burnaby travelled in the company of the young officer of the Royal Engineers to whom Gordon had addressed his letter of complaint about Burnaby, Lieutenant Charles Watson. Like most of Gordon's other European officers, Watson's health had deteriorated badly in the Sudan and he had been sent back to England. The journey by steamer from Lardo to Khartoum brought about a swift recovery in Watson's health and in order to avoid simply retracing their outward journeys they decided to travel the 600 miles from Khartoum to Korosko by camel via Shendi and Abu-Hamed, which they achieved in 22 days. Burnaby and Watson thus became probably the only two serving officers in the British army who had travelled to or from Khartoum by both of the main overland routes. On reaching Korosko, to the south of Aswan, they found a little time to play the part of a typical Cook's tourist, visiting the temple at Philae and shooting the rapids of the First Cataract with Lord Francis Cecil and his wife, who were on their honeymoon. They continued by steamer to the railhead at Asyut, visiting Thebes and Carnac *en route*. The last part of their journey to Cairo was by train, which they reached on 2 April and were received by the Khedive on the following day.

While in Khartoum on his way back to England, Burnaby noticed a newspaper report stating that the Russians had forbidden entry to their territories in Central Asia to all Europeans. Since his last attempt to visit Central Asia in 1873 the Russians had annexed Samarkand and were within sight of both Khiva and Bokhara, further to the east. On his return to London he began planning in earnest for a second attempt at Khiva, this time starting from Russia itself and heading south east, rather than eastwards from Asia Minor.

Several parts of his journey through Egypt and the Sudan were not described in detail in the letters published in *The Times* and one is left to wonder yet again why Fred did not take the opportunity of relating these incidents, or of publishing a memoir of his travels.

---

7   Stanley Lane-Poole, *Watson Pasha: a record of the life-work of Sir Charles Moore Watson, Colonel in the Royal Engineers* (London: John Murray, 1919), p. 74.

6   Ride to Khiva, 1875-76

The Great Game

When Burnaby began his parliamentary assault on Birmingham in 1880, one of the subjects on which he expressed the strongest opinions was the 'Eastern Question' and he was undoubtedly well qualified to do so. In its purest form the Eastern Question was simply that of who should be allowed to assume control of the European territories previously held by the Ottoman Empire, which had been in decay since the end of the seventeenth century. During the eighteenth century Russia pushed steadily south engaging in several conflicts with Turkey, its ultimate objective being Constantinople. The Crimean War of 1853 to 1856, in which the Ottoman Empire was supported by Great Britain and France, brought a temporary halt to Russia's ambitions and placed Turkey under international protection. This bought it some time, but it had famously been described by then as 'the sick man of Europe' and the ultimate disintegration of the Ottoman Empire was inevitable.

    Meanwhile, Russia was equally ambitious further to the east. In the early nineteenth century there had been a vast area of Central Asia south of Russia and north of India that retained a fierce independence. By 1863, the southern Russian frontier had been pushed south to a wavering line running east from the northern end of the Caspian Sea. By 1876, despite assurances by the Russian Emperor that it had no further territorial ambitions in Central Asia, it had advanced another four hundred miles south and was already beginning to exert its influence in the independent khanates even further south, among them Khiva, Bokhara and Samarkand. Despite its vast size and remoteness, the area attracted a variety of travellers from the seventeenth century onwards, many of them officers of the armies of Britain and Russia. Their efforts to influence the politics of these regions were famously described by Kipling as 'the Great Game'.[1]

---

1   Peter Hopkirk's *The Great Game* (London: John Murray, 1990) is indispensable on this subject. George MacDonald Fraser's *Flashman and the Great Game* is also a good read, featuring, as it does, Burnaby's contemporary Sir Harry Paget Flashman, VC, KCB, KCIE (1822-1915). The periods of absence from their regular duties taken by these officers were often euphemistically described as shooting leave, in connection with which see also John Ure's *Shooting Leave* (London: Constable

Reports of a probable advance by the Russians on the warlike tribes around Khiva had led Burnaby to make his first attempt, probably not particularly well planned, in the winter of 1872/73. Details of his proposed route are not known, but he may well have hoped to travel more or less due east from the Mediterranean through Baghdad, Teheran and Merve, thereafter turning north towards Khiva and the Aral Sea. Had he been successful, he would have been the first Englishman to visit since Captain James Abbott and Lieutenant Richmond Shakespear in 1840 and the first European since Vambéry in 1863. As it was he was beaten by the American journalist and war correspondent Januarius MacGahan, who took a route similar to that which Burnaby would eventually follow and reached Khiva just after the fall of the city to the Russian army in the summer of 1873. MacGahan had hoped to proceed from Khiva to the oasis of Merve, but was prevented from doing so. Although MacGahan, like Burnaby, was a special correspondent during the Carlist War, their paths did not cross until shortly before Burnaby left London in November 1875.

Burnaby's decision to attempt the journey to Khiva was made early in 1875 at Khartoum, as he returned from his rather unsatisfactory meeting with Gordon. Being Burnaby, a newspaper report that the Russians had, unusually, closed the area to foreigners made him even more determined to succeed where he had failed a little over two years previously. There had been changes during this short period relevant to his planned trip. In 1871 Russia had succeeded in repudiating the clause of the 1856 Treaty of Paris preventing them from operating a fleet in the Black Sea, somewhat earlier than implied by Burnaby (who referred to it as 'The Black Sea Treaty'), but it took Russia a few years to increase its naval presence. In Central Asia, Samarkand had been annexed to the imperial dominions and Russian troops were quartered in Khivan territory. Burnaby was convinced that the Russians had a reason for keeping foreigners out of their Central Asia conquests, most likely because their ultimate aim was British India. General von Kaufmann, in command of Russian forces in Central Asia, was also notoriously shy of journalists.

The Ride

Burnaby left London quietly, initially for St. Petersburg, on 30 November 1975 with several letters of introduction provided by Count Peter Schuvalov, the Russian Ambassador to the Court of St. James's. Burnaby had developed a cordial relationship with Schuvalov (1827-1889), who had been sent to England in 1873 to negotiate the marriage between Queen Victoria's second son, then the Duke of Edinburgh, and the Grand Duchess Maria Alexandrovna, daughter of Czar Alexander II. He also benefited from advice provided by Januarius

and Robinson, 2009).

MacGahan and several Russians living in London. The general consensus was that he would be made most welcome in St. Petersburg, but the closer he came to Khiva the more difficult would he find it to obtain permission from local administrators to proceed further. As with his trip to Egypt the previous year, Burnaby decided not to take with him his servant, Radford, although he noted that 'he had been with me in several parts of the world'.

In St. Petersburg Burnaby met Eugene Schuyler, the United States' Secretary of Legation, apparently for the first time. Schuyler had travelled in the Central Asia region and also spoke Russian, so he was a useful source of information. It is not clear whether he met the British Ambassador to St. Petersburg, Lord Augustus Loftus, but in a private letter written a few years later Burnaby described him as a 'wretched imbecile', so it is possible he did not make the effort. He also failed in his attempts to meet Count Paul Schuvalov (1830-1908), brother of the British Ambassador, whom he was to encounter across the battlefield in the Russo-Turkish War a few years later. Despite a letter of introduction he also failed to meet General Milutin, the Minister of War, who nevertheless, no doubt reluctantly, confirmed his permission to travel through Russia proper, but stated that he could not answer for his safety if he ventured 'beyond Russian territory'. Behind the scenes it was likely that Milutin was already putting pressure on the British Foreign Office to recall Burnaby, but it took some weeks for this pressure to take effect. In any event this permission was sufficient for Burnaby to begin his journey as originally conceived, although by then he had devised a fall-back plan, which was to go straight to Persia and then head east via Merve and Bokhara to India, staying south of the presumed southern border of Russia (almost the same route that he had proposed on his attempt of 1872/3). Burnaby wrote to thank Milutin for his permission and advised him that after reaching Khiva he hoped to continue south to Merve, Meshat, Herat and then through the Bolan Pass to Shikapoor on the River Indus. He would return to European Russia via Cabul, Bokhara and Kasala, or a more easterly route through Cachemire (Kashmir), Kashgar and Tashkent. This must have incensed the Russians even more, since the area to the north of India was one that they very much considered their own. Either route home would have been extraordinarily ambitious, involving a round trip from Kasala of some 4,000 miles, and it is hard to believe that Burnaby really thought he could achieve this in the limited time available before the period of his leave expired. However, that Khiva was not his preferred ultimate destination should come as no surprise and it would have been out of character for Burnaby to attempt something that had been done before. Not only had Khiva been reached previously by Vámbéry, Abbott and MacGahan, but they had each written popular works describing their own undoubted adventures (respectively *Travels in Central Asia, From Herat to Khiva* and *Campaigning on the Oxus*), to each of which Burnaby refers in his the book he wrote about his journey.

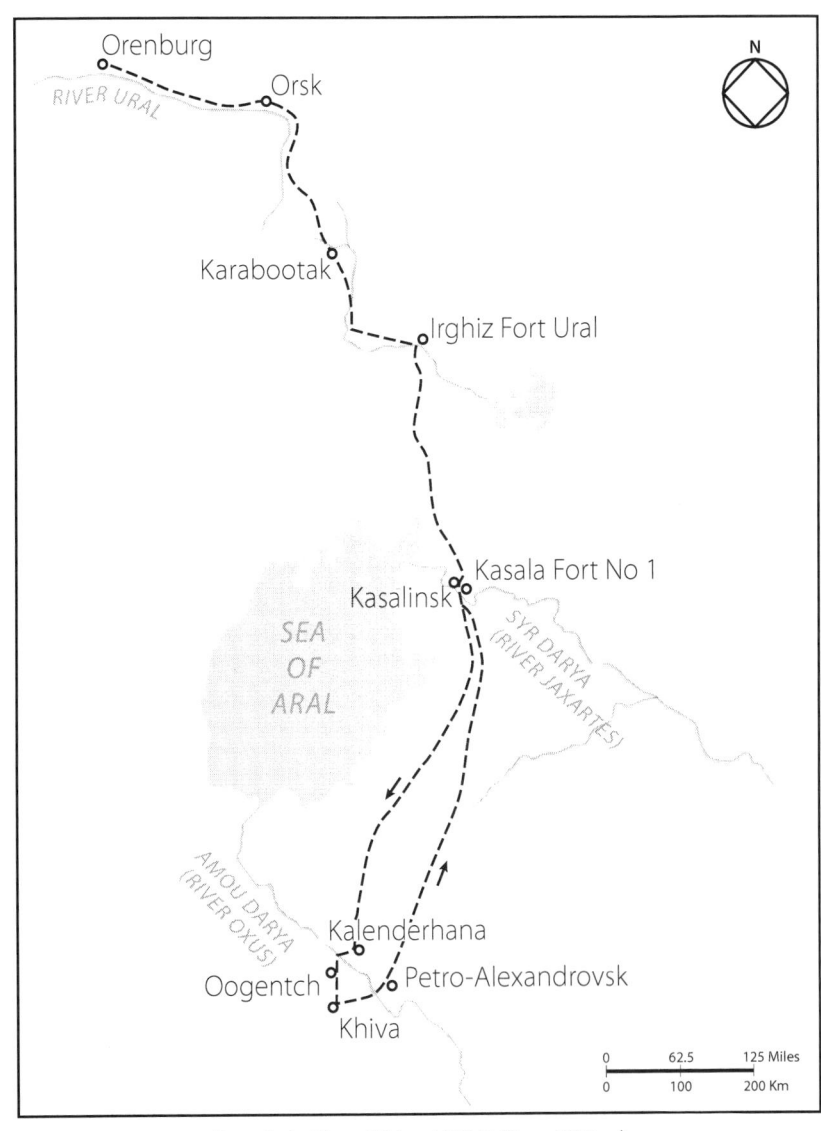

Burnaby's ride to Khiva, 1875/6 (Steve Waites)

HRH the Duke of Cambridge
(*Vanity Fair*, 23 April 1870)

Despite numerous obstacles, Burnaby did succeed in reaching Khiva. He travelled as far as Sizeran by train, on to Samara and Orenburg by troika and thence on horseback for the final 370 miles to Khiva, which leg he covered in thirteen days, initially in conditions of extreme cold. The journey he made is more than adequately described in the book he wrote immediately on his return, *A Ride to Khiva*, which remains in print today. It is an adventure classic and deserves to be read in its entirety.

Notwithstanding his ambitious plans, Burnaby delayed in Khiva for several days after having met the Khan and then decided to set off for Bokhara rather than Merve, perhaps realising the impracticability of his original thinking. As it was, Burnaby's ambition to travel further was to be thwarted and, while making his preparations for departure, he was summoned by the local commandant to Petro-Alexandrovsk, around which he had detoured on his outward journey. There he was presented with a telegram, widely reported at the time to come from the Duke of Cambridge, officially recalling him to England. The genesis of the telegram was unclear, but its existence became known to the British public by no later than 19 January 1876, although it had apparently still not

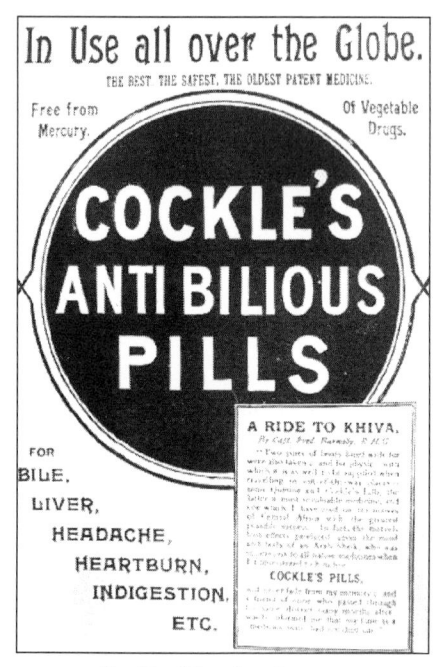

Cockles Pills advertisement
(Author's collection)

caught up with him even by early March.[2] He eventually arrived back in London at the end of that month to accusations from St. Petersburg that he had been expelled by the Khan of Khiva, which he swiftly denied in letters to the *Standard* and the *Morning Post*, placing the blame squarely upon Milutin.

Regardless of whether the Duke of Cambridge had sent the telegram, within days of Burnaby's return he had a meeting with him, as a result of which he wrote an enthusiastic letter to Gathorne Hardy, the Secretary of State for War, recommending that he should also interview him. There is no reference in this letter to the telegram requesting his return from Khiva, which is itself surprising, and there is also the clear implication that Burnaby was not previously well known to the Commander-in-Chief. It is also obvious that he found Burnaby personally convincing and placed credence in his warning of the Russian advance southwards towards India.

Burnaby the author

Despite Burnaby's failure to reach Merve, which would only be achieved by

---

2   *Hampshire Telegraph*, 19 January 1876 and *Times of India*, 16 March 1876.

Edmond O'Donovan in 1879, he had obtained quite enough material to write the book he had seemingly already planned. It was published within a few months of his return and included twenty appendices dealing with the Russian advance eastwards and other subjects (although some later reprints included only the first of these).

Burnaby was paid only £750 by his publisher, Cassel, for the publication rights of *A ride to Khiva*, who marketed the book astutely to a public keen for information on Russia. Neither party can have imagined that it would run to eleven editions within a year of its first publication and that his reputation as an adventurer and a writer would be indelibly established. Although Cassell eventually sent him a cheque for another £250 (which he gave to charity), Fred felt strongly that he had been taken advantage of and never used Cassell again. Cockle's Pills, long a staple of Burnaby's supplies when travelling and of which he was known to be a strong supporter, took full advantage of his fame and used his name prominently on their advertisements, for which they paid him a gratuity of £100. Noting that the proprietors of Cockle's Pills mainly advertised in Liberal newspapers, Burnaby decided that they were probably pro-Russian and therefore donated the money to the Stafford House Committee, a Turkish relief charity.

Writing only a year after Burnaby's death, Charles Thomas Marvin (1854-1890), a prolific writer on Russia with an extensive knowledge of the country and its people, devoted a chapter of his book on travels in Central Asia to Burnaby's ride.[3] He was a great admirer of Burnaby and those like him, 'typical of a class of officer ready at a moment's notice to secretly ride off and reconnoitre the position of England's enemy, no matter in what part of the world that enemy may be'. Nevertheless he thought the actual journey considerably overpraised, noting in particular that it was not uncommon for the wives of Russian officers to make the winter journey from Orenburg to Kasala by sleigh and that the ride from Kasala to Khiva, itself no longer a dangerous city, was regularly undertaken by merchants and Cossacks. He also felt that *A ride to Khiva* was far less exciting and graphic than Vámbéry's *Travels in Central Asia* or MacGahan's *Campaigning on the Oxus*.

Another of those who reviewed *A Ride to Khiva* was his near contemporary, Henry James (1843-1916), who was more impressed with Burnaby's strength of body than strength of intellect: "[*A Ride to Khiva*] offers a very entertaining image of a thoroughly English type of man – the robust, conservative, aristocratic soldier, opaque in intellect but indomitable in muscle ... who takes his stand, with a sort of physical tenacity, upon the faith that, by the eternal

---

3   Charles Thomas Marvin, 'Captain Burnaby's Ride to Khiva' in *Reconnoitring Central Asia, pioneering adventures in the region lying between Russia and India* (London: S. Sonnenschein, Le Bas & Lowrey, 1886), pp. 177-210.

fitness of things, England must be the longest-armed power in the world."[4]

In March 1877, almost a year after Burnaby's return and the publication of *A ride to Khiva*, the manner of his recall gave rise to questions being raised in the House of Commons, principally by Mountstuart Elphinstone Grant Duff (1829-1906), the Conservative member for Elgin Burghs.[5] It is likely that this was prompted by an article in *Vanity Fair*, written by Tommy Bowles, stating that the Duke of Cambridge had not acted of his own volition in recalling Burnaby, but under pressure from the Foreign Office, which had itself received representations from the Russian Government. Grant Duff's concern was that Burnaby had apparently been ordered to return from a private journey in the country of one of Britain's allies, where he was perfectly entitled to travel as he wished. Moreover, it seemed that the British government had bowed to unjustified pressure from an ally in sending the telegram of recall, which had been carried by the Russians 900 miles beyond the end of the telegraph line to reach him in Khiva. George Goschen (1831-1907), then a member of the Liberal Opposition, added that the Russian administration was remarkably obliging in carrying the telegram such an extraordinary distance if they did not have a vested interest in its delivery. Gathorne Hardy denied the charge of bowing to Russian pressure and would only say that the Government had its reasons for requesting Burnaby's return, although it was far from clear what these might have been. The affair rumbled on for another week or so with the Lords Elcho and Dorchester also becoming involved, arguing that the Foreign Office should have been defending the rights and dignity of a British officer travelling abroad, rather than putting pressure on the War Department. The Earl of Derby, Secretary of State for Foreign Affairs, was forced to make a statement to the effect that although Burnaby's journey was private, his position as a holder of the Queen's Commission on leave meant that he was subject to recall on political considerations and that this could not be construed as a violation of his personal liberty. He also referred to Burnaby's high character and efficiency and popularity as an officer. The matter did not entirely end there, but the government stonewalled and offered no further information on their reasons for the recall. However, what the questions had done was raise the awareness of Burnaby in both houses of Parliament and thereafter his name was often mentioned as an expert on the Orient and as a skilled linguist.

Meanwhile, copies of the book had become available in Russia, where the anti-Russian sentiments expressed therein caused great annoyance. No doubt the half-hearted attempts to keep him out of Khiva were now thoroughly regretted, but it was too late. While the Parliamentary questions were being asked *The World* quoted from an anonymous article about Burnaby that had

---

4 *Nation*, vol. 24 no. 1, 29 March 1877.
5 See *Hansard* for 5, 8 and 12 March 1877.

appeared in Moscow's *Vetchernaia Gazeta* (*Evening Gazette*):[6]

> You know Captain Burnaby of the Guards. I wrote you a letter last November about his book, the Ride to Khiva, which made such a noise. He obtained leave when the Russians established themselves in Khiva, rode there on horseback, and was recalled from Central Asia by a telegram from the English Commander-in-Chief, forwarded to him by the Russian authorities. The book of this *chaveniste*[7], as I have already told you, is full of details of Russian chauvinism. Not long ago in the House the Government was asked if Burnaby had not been recalled at the request of the Russian Government. The answer of the Ministry was no. We ourselves recalled him. Many Russian papers consider him as an English Military spy. That Burnaby was really a spy I do not credit, but that he was a spy *con amore*[8] I will grant.

During his journey one of the things that had impressed Burnaby was the size and quality of the fruit grown near Khiva, particularly the melons, and he brought back with him some of seeds. One of the firms to whom he provided samples was Thomas Methven & Sons of Edinburgh, who cultivated the fruit and in 1879 sent examples to, among others, the Scottish Horticultural Association, the Royal Caledonian Horticultural Society (RCHS) and John Webster (1814-1890), the long-serving head gardener at Castle Gordon, Moray. The *Gardener's Chronicle*, in which the seeds had been advertised by Methven at 2s 6d per packet, later descibed one of the fruits grown by Webster:

> The fruit, which weighed 9lb., was cut on November 1, having changed little or nothing in appearance for the previous three months. It was of oblong form, 14 inches long, with a white firm fibrous flesh, 2 inches deep, remarkably full of juice, and when cut on December 8 was quite sound, and pleasantly but not richly flavoured. The colour was dark green and the surface rough. We hear that it has been grown this season up to 20lb. weight. Such a succulent mass must be a blessing in the deserts of Khiva, but here it must be regarded rather as a curiosity than an acquisition.[9]

Despite this faint praise, it was awarded a first class certificate from the RCHS and Prince Edward of Saxe-Weimar, who was then staying at Castle Gordon (he had married a daughter of the Duke of Richmond, whose ancestral home it was), wrote to Burnaby congratulating him on the manner in which the fruit had been received.

---

6 *The World*, 9 May 1877.
7 Chauvinist: in this sense a militant or fanatical devotion to and glorification of one's country.
8 Literally 'with love', but in this context motivated out of love, or zeal.
9 *Gardener's Chronicle*, 3 January 1880, p. 3 and 11 December 1880, p. 760.

7 Ride through Asia Minor, 1876-77

The Eastern Question

In the summer of 1876 Burnaby added another new and dangerous sport to his repertoire – cycling. He took lessons at Crystal Palace and practised in the lanes near Somerby on a 'Coventry Spider'.[1] His enthusiasm for the activity was noted by Tommy Bowles, who included a spoof article in *Vanity Fair*: 'On a bicycle down the Euphrates, being a random extract from the next work of the distinguished author of the *Ride to Khiva*, written after the "Convention" has got into working order.'[2] Meanwhile, having identified what he obviously must have hoped was a recipe for success, Fred began to plan another journey for the winter of 1876/77, although he almost found himself on an official mission instead.

Within three months of Burnaby's return from Khiva the situation in the Balkans deteriorated with the declaration of war by Montenegro and Serbia on Turkey on 18 June 1876. The declaration had been precipitated by an uprising of ethnic Serbs in Herzegovina the previous year, which spread into Bosnia and rapidly became one of the most significant rebellions against Ottoman rule in her European dominions.

The Serbian and Montenegrin armies, despite unofficial assistance from Russia, were poorly prepared and inadequately resourced, failing to make any significant headway against the Turkish divisions. On 26 August Serbia asked the Great Powers of Europe to intercede with the Ottoman Empire on their behalf, as a result of which, in early September, Turkey granted a one month truce. Although the negotiation of a permanent peace treaty commenced immediately, it soon became clear that the terms proposed by Turkey were unacceptable to Serbia and Montenegro and, more importantly, were considered too harsh by the European Powers.

The truce expired in early October and the Turkish army resumed its offensive. There was little the Serbian and Montenegrin forces could do to

---

1 *St. Louis Globe-Democrat*, 28 May 1876.
2 *Vanity Fair*, vol. 20 (17 August 1878), pp. 85-6. The 'Convention' was the supposedly secret Cyprus Convention of June 1878.

Ride through Asia Minor, 1876-77 71

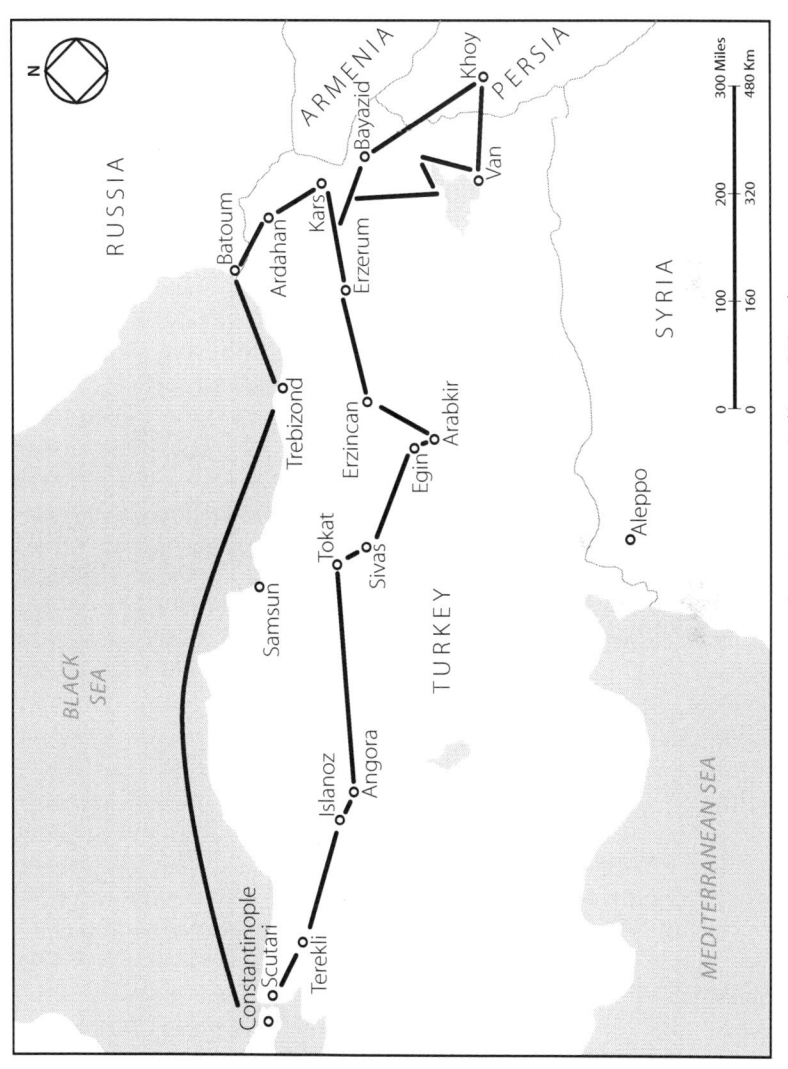

Burnaby's travels in Asia Minor, 1876/7 (Steve Waites)

resist them and finally, on 31 October, Russia, with the tacit support of the other Powers, stepped in and gave an ultimatum to Turkey to enter into a new truce within 48 hours. By this time Russia had begun a partial mobilisation of its armed forces and was well-placed to strike south into the Balkans should its ultimatum be ignored. Turkey complied and arrangements by the Powers for policing the truce commenced in earnest, although in London a contingency plan had already been prepared.

The agreement between Russia and Turkey provided that the line of demarcation between the two armies would be determined by Military Delegates, acting jointly, sent by each of the Powers to the headquarters of the Turkish, Serbian and Montenegrin armies. The three delegates initially selected by Britain were, respectively, Major-General (later General) Sir Arnold Burrowes Kemball (1820-1908), Major (later Colonel) Thomas Gonne (*c*.1838-1886) of the 17th Lancers, Military Attaché at Vienna, and Burnaby. Kemball had already had a long and distinguished military and diplomatic career, largely in India, but by 1876 he was president of the international commission to determine the position of the Russian-Persian border. Gonne was later to become Military Attaché at St. Petersburg and Assistant Adjutant to the Dublin Army District. Whereas the names of Kemball and Gonne had been suggested by Lord Tenterden, Permanent Under-Secretary at the Foreign Office, that of Burnaby was suggested by Gathorne Hardy, to whose attention he had been drawn by the Duke of Cambridge after his return from Khiva. This decision had been made as early as 24 October, but within a week the original arrangements had been scrapped. It transpired that the other Powers intended to send only two delegates (to the Serbian and Montenegrin frontiers) and that they intended to use for this purpose their Military Attachés at the respective embassies, rather than sending out additional personnel. Britain was anxious not to be seen to be acting heavy-handedly and decided to adopt the same approach, so that Colonel (later Lieutenant-General Sir) Wilbraham Oates Lennox, RE, VC (1830-1897), already attached to the Diplomatic Service and newly appointed as Military Attaché at Constantinople, was given the job of going to Montenegro instead of Burnaby.[3] This did not prevent *The Times* from speculating that the reason for Burnaby's replacement was a belated recognition that his appointment might have been seen as antagonistic by the Russians, whose territorial ambitions he had criticised freely in his recently published book.[4] Fred's disappointment at not being given the assignment is evident from a letter he wrote to Lord Beaconsfield at the time.[5] He must

---

3   National Archives. Foreign Office Records: Affairs in Turkey, Further Correspondence 424/44 (Part VI) and 424/45 (Part VII).
4   *The Times*, 6 November 1876.
5   Bodleian Library special collections. Hughenden papers, BXXI/142-1/1404 ff.137-138.

have been even more disappointed when it became clear that the appointment of Lennox was less than inspired. Sir Henry Layard, the British Ambassador at Constantinople, wrote to Gathorne Hardy in October 1877 expressing his poor view of Lennox's performance and shortly afterwards Hardy met with Lennox, commenting in his diary that he 'did not impress me favourably with his judgement nor foresight'.

In retrospect this was a pivotal moment for Burnaby. Despite the War Office having been involved in his recall from Khiva earlier in the year, it retained sufficient confidence in his abilities to propose him for a sensitive assignment, notwithstanding his lack of diplomatic experience. Had he actually gone to Montenegro and made a success of his task his future career might have followed a very different path.

There is some evidence that Burnaby actually considered a return to Africa during his next period of leave. On two occasions the *World* speculated that he might combine a visit to Central Africa with an attempt to find Henry Morton Stanley. Stanley had famously located David Livingstone in 1871, but by 1876 Stanley himself was in a remote part of Africa tracing the course of the Congo River and firm news of his eventual success did not reach Britain until August 1877.

The long journey that Burnaby eventually decided to undertake instead was perhaps less dangerous than his ride to Khiva, but no less arduous. His ostensible reason for visiting Anatolia (Turkey in Asia) was to understand whether there was any truth in the stories of Ottoman brutality towards the nominally Christian inhabitants of Armenia. Burnaby, who it must be remembered was an ardent Russophobe and therefore pro-Ottoman almost by definition, felt that the Ottoman Empire's reputation for the poor treatment of indigenous people in its territories might be exaggerated. A more natural destination would have been Bulgaria, where atrocities had been reported in August 1876, but these could scarcely be denied and had already been covered in depth by Januarius MacGahan, so he had to look elsewhere. The other advantage of Anatolia was that the farther east he travelled the more he would approach Russian territory and the more he would be able to judge that country's war preparations. It is clear that Fred considered a visit to Turkey inevitable at some stage and, according to the *World*, had 'devoted all his spare time since his return from Khiva to learning Turkish'.[6]

Shortly before he left for Turkey he wrote to the man who would ultimately bear a large part of the responsibility for his death at Abu Klea. In November 1876 Sir Garnet Wolseley returned from his governorship of Natal to take up a seat on the Council of India. His had become a household name since the successful Ashanti Campaign of 1873/4 and he was the rising star of the

6 *The World*, 31 May and 27 November 1876.

army with a distinguished career in the Crimea, India and Canada. Whether Burnaby had met Wolseley previously is not clear, but he made the assumption that if Britain did become embroiled in what he considered would be the inevitable war between Russia and Turkey, Wolseley would be involved, or at least in a position to influence the officers that would be selected for the campaign. Burnaby made a plea to be selected for a position on his staff, not least because of his fluency in Russian and the progress he was making in Turkish. Wolseley's reply has not survived, but from this time on he developed a great respect for Burnaby's bravery and intelligence.

On horseback

Burnaby was said to be on excellent terms with three of London's leading society hostesses: Lady Molesworth, Countess Waldegrave and the Marchioness of Ely. The reasons for Fred's popularity with this stratum of society can readily be understood from his letter to Lady Molesworth from Constantinople – risqué and humorous, with a touch of adventure.

Burnaby left London in late November on the boat train from Charing Cross with his servant, Radford. One of his travelling companions on the first part of his trip, as far as Paris, would definitely not have been approved of by his servant. 'Mrs. Phoenix' also known by a variety of other names, including Fanny Lear, was a beautiful and talented American courtesan who had gained notoriety through an affair with the Grand Duke Nicolas Constantinovich (1850-1918), a grandson of Czar Nicolas I and nephew of Czar Alexander II. Born Harriet Clarissima Ely in Philadelphia in 1848, she was the daughter of a prominent Minister, the Rev. Ezra Ely, and was briefly married to a railway clerk named Beale Blackford. On her husband's sudden and unexplained death she embarked on a professional career in Philadelphia and New York that eventually forced her to flee America. After staying for a short time in London, where she attracted the attention of the Prince of Wales, she took up residence in Paris. When Fred Burnaby wrote one of his letters to the *Morning Post* from St. Petersburg in 1871 he noted that the city was full of courtesans who had fled from Paris in the wake of the Franco-Prussian War and one of these was Fanny Lear. Among the Americans in St. Petersburg with whom she became friendly was Eugene Schuyler, secretary of the American legation. Aiming high professionally, she commenced a three year relationship with the Grand Duke Nicolas, which the Royal family initially tried to cool by sending him to participate in the Khiva campaign in the spring of 1873, where his demeanour impressed the American journalist, Januarius MacGahan. The trip Nicolas made from St. Petersburg to 'Fort No. 1' via Nijni-Novgorod and Orenburg was almost exactly the same as that followed by Burnaby less than two years later. The affair recommenced when Nicolas returned from the front and Fanny was eventually thrown out of Russia when it transpired that Nicolas had given her a Romanov necklace stolen by him from his mother. Nicolas, who also had some radical political ideas, was officially declared insane and banished from St. Petersburg, first to Orenburg and later to Turkestan. Count Peter Schuvalov, the head of the 'Third Section' (secret police) in St. Petersburg, did not come out of the affair very well and was sent to London to negotiate the marriage of the Grand Duchess Maria Alexandrovna to the Duke of Edinburgh. By the time Fred and Fanny met he was on close terms with Schuyler, MacGahan and Schuvalov. Fanny's memoirs, published in Brussels in 1875, were considered scandalous, and she eventually died in obscurity in Nice in 1886.[7]

Between Paris and Marseille Fred fell in with William Ballantine, the fashionable barrister who had represented Hooker in the assault case in which he had been involved a decade earlier, although he forbore from mentioning this connection in his letter to Lady Molesworth.

At Marseille he boarded a Messageries Maritimes steamer for Constantinople via Smyrna, arriving at his destination in early December, taking a room at the Hotel du Luxembourg. He was once again in a good position to gain up to date knowledge of the political situation through meeting Eugene Schuyler, by now Secretary of the United States' Legation in Constantinople, Antonio Gallenga (1810-1895), veteran correspondent of *The Times*, George Sala (1828-1895) of the *Daily Telegraph*, who had recently visited Januarius MacGahan in Philippopolis, Bulgaria and William Arthur White (1824-1891), Britain's Consul-General to Serbia in Belgrade. He did not take the opportunity of calling on another acquaintance, General Ignatieff, the Russian Ambassador to the Porte. There is some evidence that his original intention was first to reconnoitre the passes in the Balkan Mountains through which the Russians would have to advance if they marched on Constantinople, but this would have eaten into a significant part of his leave and the idea was not pursued.[8] He did, however, inspect part of the long defensive line to the west of Constantinople between the Sea of Marmara and the Black Sea (the Chekmagee Lines), which he believed would be manned by British troops in the event that Britain came into the war that he viewed as inevitable as an ally of Turkey.

Before leaving he met with Sir Henry George Elliot (1817-1907), Britain's Ambassador to Constantinople, their conversation subsequently being reported by him to the Earl of Derby:

Captain Burnaby of the Royal Horse Guards, who is about to proceed to visit

---

7 Fanny Lear [Harriet Clarissima Blackford, née Ely], *Le Roman d'une Americaine en Russie* [*The Romance of an American in Russia*] (Brussels: A. Lacroix et Cie, 1875). A translation into English is included in: Eva and Daniel McDonald, *Fanny Lear, love and scandal in Czarist Russia* (Bloomington, IL: iUniverse, 2011).
8 *The World*, 27 November 1876.

Burnaby and Radford in Asia Minor
(*The Graphic*, 19 May 1877)

Kars, Erzeroum, and the neighbouring districts, tells me that he has had some conversation with the Armenian Patriarch upon the disposition of the populations. The Patriarch had told him, as stated by Mr. Zohrab, that the Kurds were not to be relied upon. The Armenians, on the other hand, were, he said, well affected by the Turkish Government; but the Patriarch added, with emphasis, that if the Slav Provinces were to be rewarded by exceptional privileges for having risen in insurrection against the Porte, the Armenians would probably think that their interest prescribed a similar course upon themselves.[9]

Within a few days of his arrival Burnaby had completed his reconnaissance, purchased horses, hired a local servant (Osman), crossed by ferry to Scutari and commenced his ride. Travelling east and, initially, a little south, his path ran roughly parallel to the southern coast of the Black Sea through Angora and Arabkir as far as Erzeroum, which he referred to in a letter to his mother as the traditional location of the Garden of Eden. By this stage he had suffered

9 National Archives. Foreign Office Records: Affairs in Turkey, Further Correspondence 424/46 (Part VIII).

Burnaby on his return from Asia Minor
(*Mayfair*, 1 May 1877)

various misfortunes with his horses, dismissed Osman for pilfering and hired a more reliable replacement, Mohammed, who got on much better with Radford. A surprise awaited him in Erzeroum. The Russian Consul there had recently received a telegram from the Russian authorities in the Caucasus that apparently read as follows:

> Two months ago, an Englishman, a certain Captain Burnaby, left Constantinople with the object of travelling in Asia Minor. He is a desperate enemy of Russia. We have lost all traces of him since his departure from Stamboul. We believe that the real object of his journey is to pass the frontier, and enter Russia. Do your best, sir, to discover the whereabouts of this aforesaid Captain. Find means to inform him that in the event of his entering our territory, he will be immediately expelled.

Somehow or other the Russians had procured a photograph of Fred and distributed copies to their frontier stations in case he attempted to enter Russian territory. Clearly the Russians were still smarting over Fred's visit to Khiva the previous year, doubtless exacerbated by the strong anti-Russian stance he had adopted in the best-selling book describing his ride. In any event he had no intention of crossing the border and his party then turned south to Van, east again to Khoi (in Persia) and then north past Mount Ararat and through Kars to Ardahan, where the horses were sold. The last part of this journey was delayed by Burnaby suffering first from a bout of dysentery and then rheumatic fever. Radford had also been ill earlier in the journey, with Burnaby complaining jocularly that he had had to look after his own servant. Fresh mounts were hired for the relatively short ride to Livana, from which his party took a river boat to the port of Batoum, now in Georgia, on the east coast of the Black Sea. Including detours the total distance travelled on horseback through a harsh winter in a period of something over four months was over 2,000 miles. The return journey to Constantinople was made in only five days by steamer from Batoum via Trebizond and within another eight days, by early April, Fred and Radford had retraced their outward route and were back in London. Mohammed had declined to go with them as far as Constantinople, being fearful of travel by water and overdue to join the regiment into which he had been conscripted shortly before taking service with Burnaby.

Other private letters from this journey have survived in part in a short-lived journal titled *Mayfair*, which first appeared with a Christmas edition in 1876 and folded in February 1880. Henry Lucy was editor of the journal, with which Burnaby was said to be 'intimately connected', and one of its main contributors.[10] From the first issue Burnaby's name was prominent. To whom the letters were written is uncertain (it may well have been Lucy himself), but extracts from them were printed with his permission in editions of *Mayfair* published in February, March and April 1877, while he was still in Asia Minor. Extracts from another were forwarded to *The Times* by their Special Correspondent in Pera, also appearing in February. Since it was Burnaby's clear intention to publish a book describing this journey, it is somewhat surprising that he permitted this, but he always found it difficult to avoid publicity and these letters may well have been intended to whet the public appetite.

Although arduous, the journey did not contain many moments of genuine excitement or events of special interest and Burnaby must have been concerned how he would fill a couple of volumes of narrative, which is what he had agreed to provide his new publisher, Sampson Low, as the justification for his much increased advance of £2,500. He had become friends with Montagu Corry while at school and by 1877 Corry (later Lord Rowton) was private secretary to the Prime Minister, Lord Beaconsfield. In May he wrote to Corry seeking official reports as 'padding' for what would he thought might otherwise be a rather slim publication – a technique he had also adopted with his previous book. In early July he made a balloon ascent and he then left England for Bad Homburg where he planned to spend a month writing the story of his

10 *Birmingham Daily Gazette*, 4 June 1878.

Burnaby and Radford in Bulgaria
(*Illustrated London News*, 31 January 1885)

journey.[11] Homburg, which Burnaby had visited many times previously, was a popular place for the British to take the waters and among those there at the same time were the Duke of Cambridge and John Thadeus Delane, editor of *The Times*, with whom he could be found walking round the Kursaal (the public hall at the spa).[12] The concentration of British Army officers in Homburg led the *Pall Mall Gazette* to comment that war with Russia could not possibly be imminent. In an article on the history of Homburg written on 12 August, its author, who clearly knew Burnaby, noted his presence in the town and observed: 'He will probably, unless engaged with the troops in the East, spend his leave during the coming winter in a quiet trip to Timbuctoo.'[13] Later in August, before returning home, he visited Berlin, where *The World* speculated that he was 'half-inclined to offer his services to the Turks'.[14] Knowing that his friend Valentine Baker was in Turkey must have tempted him to consider this

11 *Western Daily Press*, 19 July 1877.
12 *Royal Cornwall Gazette*, 24 August 1877.
13 *St. Louis Globe-Democrat*, 2 September 1877 (reprinted from the *Philadelphia Times*).
14 *The World*, 8 August 1877.

Captain Fred Burnaby
(*Mayfair*, 2 October 1877)

option, but there can never have been any serious question of him throwing up his Queen's commission.

On horseback through Asia Minor, published in October 1877, was another success; as with *A ride to Khiva* it remains in print today and is still an amusing read. Although not quite in the same league of popularity as his first book, it soon ran to seven editions. By the time of its publication Russia had declared war on the Ottoman Empire, as Burnaby had predicted. One critic noted that much of the book's humour depended on the antics of Burnaby's servant, Radford, whom he had taken with him on this trip. On his return *Mayfair* commissioned a 'character portrait' of Burnaby from Wallis Mackay, one of its regular illustrators, for which Burnaby posed in 'a rough blue jacket, with astrakhan collar, and a cap of the same material … [and] huge boots [that] came well above the knee'.[15]

Any publicity …

On 17 and 27 October 1877, soon after the publication of *On horseback through Asia Minor*, *The Times* ran two lengthy reviews that essentially provided a

---

15 A reminiscence of Mackay was included in Ware & Mann, pp. 348-8, although he incorrectly recalls the commission as having been carried out the previous year after Burnaby's return from Khiva.

précis of both volumes. Within a few days of the appearance of the second review, Douglas William Freshfield wrote to the editor suggesting that certain of Burnaby's descriptions of Russian "atrocities" inflicted on Turks should be taken with a pinch of salt. Freshfield, apart from being a prominent lawyer, was a mountaineer and author, who edited the *Alpine Journal* from 1872 to 1880 and was an active member of the Royal Geographical Society and the Alpine Club, serving as President of both organizations. Despite this he was not a linguist or an expert on the Eastern Question and his stated motivation was that he simply felt Burnaby was being unfair to the Russians, who might have been responsible for atrocities from time to time, but probably no more so than the Ottomans.

Burnaby, predictably, replied that he stood by what he had described and dealt with a few specific points raised by Freshfield, and he was not the only one to enter into correspondence on the subject. He also pointed out that, unlike himself, Freshfields could speak neither Russian nor Turkish. The editor also published letters from Edmond Beales, a barrister and champion of the Reform Movement, and Stewart Erskine Rolland, a journalist and supporter, some years previously, of the Circassia independence movement. Beales took the position that despite his knowledge of the region, he could not confirm some of the more frightful Russian atrocities described by Burnaby. Rolland, on the other hand, stated that Freshfield was wrong to suggest that he supported his view and that he felt the accusations of the worst Russian atrocities should be taken seriously and if possible investigated.

Both Burnaby and Freshfield felt obliged to write further letters defending their respective positions, but it is hard to escape the conclusion that Burnaby must have thought that the exchange would do nothing to harm sales of his latest book.[16]

Burnaby had for some time been a well-known figure in the higher levels of British society, but his two travel books now made him an immediately recognisable figure on a much wider stage. This included not only the British public at large, but also the reading public of many European countries and America. His fluency in several languages no doubt helped in this. Although the most famous visit of Giuseppe Garibaldi to England was in 1864, he visited again a few years before his death in 1882. Mrs. Stuart Menzies, the wife of one of Burnaby's fellow officers, asked him to arrange an audience with Garibaldi, whom he had apparently known for some time. This meeting she described in one of the volumes of her memoirs, noting how easily Burnaby could switch from Italian to French and English as the conversation required.[17]

16 For the full exchange of letters, see correspondence columns of *The Times*, 1 to 7 November 1877, inclusive.
17 Stuart Menzies, pp. 52-60.

8   Russo-Turkish War; Battle of Tashkessan, 1877-78

The next leave

The late summer and early autumn of 1877 passed quietly for Burnaby, but by November he was on his way back to Constantinople. A so far unidentified copy of *Mayfair* from the autumn of 1877 noted that: "Captain Burnaby's next tour will be in Central Africa, his intention being to visit Timbuctoo and the king of Dahomey."[1] Within a few weeks, however, *Mayfair* was also the source for the comment that he "stands fast to his intention of not visiting either Timbuctoo, or any other outlying region, for the space of two years".[2] This article also reported that he was off to Bulgaria at the end of the month, with the intention of travelling to the seat of the Russo-Turkish War and visiting Plevna, then under siege. Henry Lucy, the editor of *Mayfair*, was close to Fred and presumably had all of this information directly from him. It is of particular interest in so far as no previous comment had been made of his refraining from distant travel, or of not writing any more books for a prolonged period; it is also only the second time that Timbuctoo had been mentioned as a possible destination for a future journey, although it would do so frequently again. French explorers had rediscovered the ancient trading city in 1815 and despite the fact that by then its days of glory were long gone it retained an aura of wealth and mystery that continued to attract adventurers like Burnaby.

War in Bulgaria

The proximate cause of the Russo-Turkish war of 1877/78 was the "Bulgarian Atrocities", perpetrated by irregular, mainly Muslim, forces of the Ottoman Empire (Bashi-Bazouks), who brutally suppressed the Bulgarian uprising of April/May 1876. News of the atrocities was transmitted to the west by two men who knew Burnaby well, Januarius MacGahan and Eugene Schuyler, of whom

---

1   *Edinburgh Evening News*, 16 October 1877.
2   *Western Mail*, 7 November 1877. Either the same or a later *Mayfair* article (*Pall Mall Gazette*, 13 November 1877) announced that he did not intend to write a book concerning his journey to Bulgaria and that nor would he "take up his pen again till after an interval of two years".

the latter was to write one of Burnaby's most balanced and considered eulogies. Their reports galvanized public opinion in Britain against the Ottoman Empire and led to strong doubts over whether the western powers would ever again support Turkey in a conflict with Russia, which legitimately felt that it had a duty of care for the Orthodox inhabitants of its southern neighbour.

On 24 April 1877 Russia declared war on Turkey and persuaded Romania to allow its troops to pass through that country and an attack was launched, the ultimate target being Constantinople. A simultaneous attach was launched in the Caucasus region south towards Kars and Erzeroum, where Burnaby had travelled only a few months before. Numerous actions took place during the following months, with the Russians and their supporters moving steadily towards Constantinople and Erzeroum. Whether Britain should intervene remained a political hot potato, but by then certain elements in Britain were already taking positive action to help Turkey.

On 12 December 1876 the Duke of Sutherland, no friend of either Gladstone or his Liberal government, had chaired a meeting at Stafford House, his London home, "to consider what steps could be taken to alleviate the great sufferings which prevailed amongst the Turkish soldiers". At this meeting it was decided to form a committee, of which the Duke would be chairman, for the purpose of inviting subscriptions from the public with a view to supplying sick and wounded Turkish soldiers with warm clothing and medicines. This became known as the Stafford House Committee and Burnaby was one of the first to endorse the subscriptions for which it advertised. It also provided Fred with a passport to visit Turkey in November 1877, when he was appointed in a civilian capacity to visit and report on the work of the Stafford House Committee doctors in the field.[3] It was 6 November by the time Fred left London with Radford. Arriving in Constantinople on 18 November, he proceeded north-west, first to Adrianople (now Erdine, Turkey) and then on to Phillippopolis (now Plovdiv, Bulgaria), but his aim was to then turn north to Plevna (now Pleven, Bulgaria), which was under Russian siege and defended by Osman Pasha.

By 28 November he was in Adrianople, where he met one of his oldest and closest friends, Valentine Baker. Baker (1827-1887) was somewhat older than Burnaby and like him a cavalry officer, having previously commanded the elite

---

3   Archibald Forbes in his memoir of the Russo-Turkish War (*Czar and sultan: the adventures of a British lad in the Russo-Turkish war of 1877-78* (Bristol: J.W. Arrowsmith, 1894), p. 60, states that: "Colonel Burnaby of *The Times* accompanied Gourko's raid, which lasted more than a month. During all that time he never found an opportunity for forwarding a single letter, and he brought back to Bucharest a pile of correspondence which by that time was out of date and of which I believe he had finally to make a book." This famous raid took place during July and August 1877 when Fred Burnaby, still a Captain, was almost without doubt in England and Germany, so either this was one of his Burnaby cousins, or Forbes made a mistake in the name.

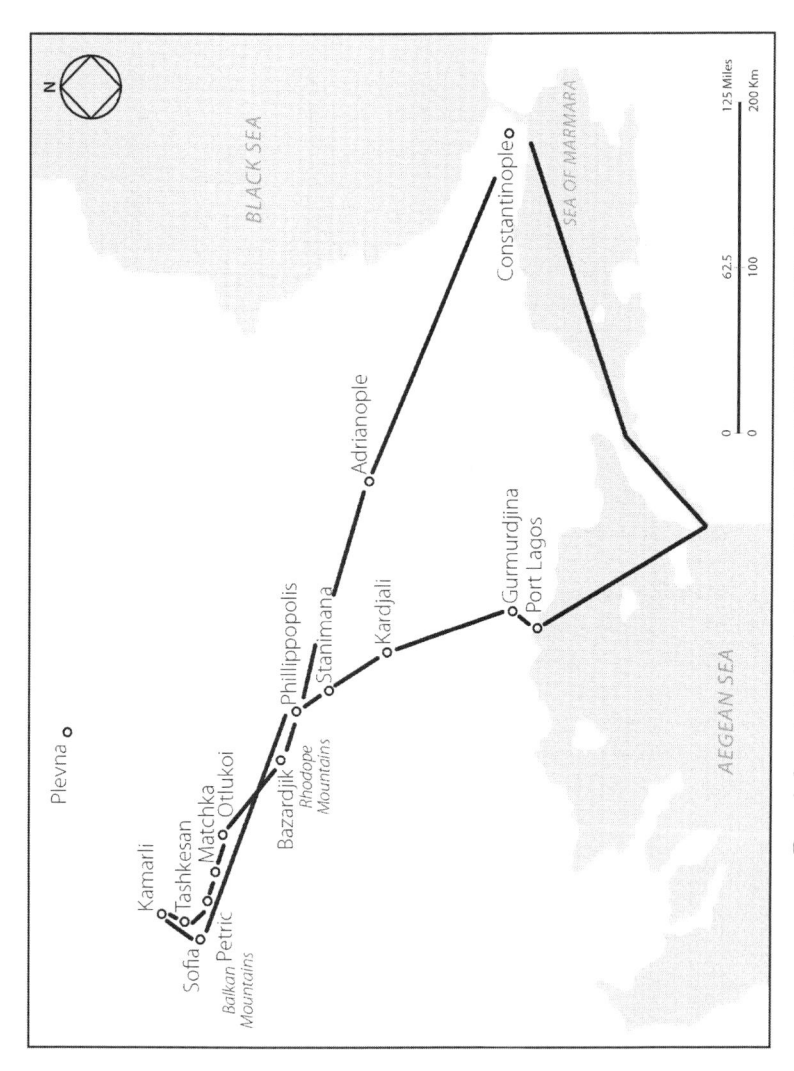

Burnaby's route in the the Russo-Turkish War, 1877/8 (Steve Waites)

10th Hussars. On reaching the age at which he had to give up this role, he was appointed Quartermaster-General at Aldershot in 1873, having the previous year made an unsuccessful attempt himself to reach Khiva through Khorasan, in the company of Captain William Gill, RE.[4] In 1875 his British Army career came to an untimely end. He was accused of indecently assaulting a young lady, Miss Dickinson, in a railway carriage between Woking and Esher and although he denied the charge he offered no defence. The case gave rise to great excitement with extensive press coverage and large crowds gathering outside the Croydon court room where he was tried. Found guilty, he was sentenced by the judge to a year in prison and a fine of £500. In his closing address the judge said: "I mean to spare you those physical indignities [hard labour] which to you would be so dreadful, hoping that you may at some distant day be allowed to resume the brilliant service to the country of which you are undoubtedly capable". Whatever the rights or wrongs of the matter, his family and almost all of his friends stood by him, as did many of his fellow officers who felt that the worst of which he might have been guilty were standard "light cavalry tactics". Clearly he would have to leave the army and, in a letter to Gathorne Hardy, the Duke of Cambridge offered three alternatives of increasing severity: (a) resignation with the sale of his Commission (valued at around £4,500); (b) unconditional resignation with no sale of his Commission; (c) dismissal without compensation. The recommendation of the Duke of Cambridge was the first, on the same basis that had been applied when Burnaby had come before the court on his assault charge, in other words that the court had already levied a financial penalty and it would be wrong for the army to levy a second. He was strongly against the third alternative since he felt it would jeopardise the chances of Baker entering military service overseas.

Although Gathorne Hardy's own opinion was that dismissal was the most appropriate course of action, he allowed himself to be persuaded by the other members of the Cabinet that the most lenient course would be sufficient punishment, particularly as Baker had been devoted to the army for twenty seven years with a previously exemplary service record.[5] The problem was that Queen Victoria had taken a personal interest in the case and had reputedly sent Miss Dickinson an autograph letter and requested that she be sent a photograph of her. When she heard the decision of the Cabinet she wrote to Lord Salisbury requesting them to reconsider the matter, insisting that in her view dismissal was the only appropriate outcome. At the following Cabinet meeting they acceded to her request, which on learning news of the decision

4   The book he wrote about this trip was *Clouds in the east: travels and adventures on the Perso-Turkoman frontier* (London: Chatto & Windus, 1876).
5   In fact the *Derby Mercury* of 18 August 1875 reported that many years previously, while serving as a junior lieutenant in Ceylon, Baker had been involved in a case involving a lady's maid in which he had been lucky to escape serious censure.

Baker and Burnaby at Kamarli (Fife-Cookson)

Baker and Burnaby at Tashkessan (Fife-Cookson)

the Duke of Cambridge described as deplorable.[6]
Widely regarded as one of the finest cavalry officers in the British Army, strenuous efforts were made for his reinstatement, but these failed and in 1877, after his release from prison, he entered the service of the Ottoman Army, initially in a high position with the gendarmerie holding the rank of major-general. Baker was only one of a number of British officers that had taken service under the Sultan. Others that served with distinction on his staff during the Russo-Turkish War included Colonel Noel Charles Allix, formerly of the Grenadier Guards (1846-1925), Colonel Charles George Baker, VC, formerly of the Bengal Police Battalion (1830-1906), later taken prisoner by the Russians, Captain James of the Scots Greys and Captain Thackeray.[7]

It was on his way to take up his command with Mehemet Ali Pasha that Baker and Burnaby met at Adrianople. Baker felt that for Burnaby to try to enter Plevna would be suicidal and dissuaded him from the attempt. This was just as well since, after a prolonged siege, the city fell to the Russians on 10 December 1877 and, according to *The World*, "the Muscovite sentries on the road to Plevna had orders at once to shoot any suspicious looking stranger above six feet in height."[8] However, Burnaby immediately accepted Baker's offer to remain with his force as a non-combatant and they continued north-west to Sofia.

The Battle of Tashkessan

Shortly before the arrival of Baker and Burnaby in Sofia, both the Turkish Minister of War (Redif Pasha) and the Commander-in-Chief of the Ottoman forces on the Danube front (Abdul Kerim) had been replaced due to their failure to prevent the Russian advance as far as the Balkans, despite the superior numbers of the Turkish forces. The new Commander-in-Chief was Mehemet Ali Pasha (1827-1878), who had been born in Germany, but travelled to Turkey when young, embraced Islam and gained the favour of Mehemet Emin Ali Pasha (1815-1871), who later became High Vizier. He was commissioned in the Ottoman army in 1853 and appointed brigadier-general in 1865, subsequently gaining further promotions.

Mehemet Ali was more open minded when it came to external help than had been Abdul Kerim and immediately accepted assistance from Valentine Baker, who had been languishing for the previous three months in Constantinople with a severe attack of typhoid. Mehemet's instructions were to gather his

---

[6] The relevant correspondence is contained in the Earl of Cranbrook Family Archive held at Ipswich Record Office: Correspondence Concerning Colonel Baker (HA43/T501/87).
[7] Baker, VC later joined Baker Pasha in Egypt and succeeded him as head of the Egyptian gendarmerie. Allix was declared bankrupt in 1900.
[8] *The World*, 19 December 1877.

forces in Sofia and then raise the siege of Plevna, but he soon realised that with the calibre of troops at his disposal this would be impossible. Moreover, his defensive position was weak and he feared he would soon be outflanked by the Russian forces when they made their way through the Balkan passes. On realising this, his new priority became the defence of the Orkhranie Pass, through which the main road between Plevna and Sofia crossed the Balkans. The period of his command was, however, very brief. His honesty in reporting these facts to Constantinople resulted in his own dismissal and replacement by Shakir Pasha, who now took over the defensive positions at Orkhranie.

Osman Pasha's gallant defence of Plevna finally gave out on 10 December and General Gourko's besieging force was released and left free to advance south towards Sofia. Shakir Pasha's main force of around 14,000 men, reduced by more than a quarter from its original numbers as a result of cold, disease and desertion, was concentrated on the Plevna-Sofia road about five miles north of the village of Kamarli. It was in an unsustainable position and it was clear that the force would have to retreat before the Russian army. The question was when and how. About ten miles south-west of Shakir Pasha's headquarters on the road to Sofia lay the village of Tashkessan (now Sarantsi, Bulgaria), where a slight ridge crossed the valley floor of the pass. A little to the east of Tashkessan the Plevna-Sofia road divided, with the other branch leading further east through the village of Kamarli and then south through the Rhodope Mountains. Valentine Baker was provided with a small brigade of fewer than 3,000 men and instructed by Shakir Pasha to hold the defensive line across the road at Tashkessan, permitting his main force to retreat south across open country and join the eastern route at Kamarli. If all went according to plan, when the main force had made its safe escape, Baker's much smaller force would follow.

Baker chose his position carefully. His forward line was on the lower part of the ridge that lay across the valley, but he knew this would not hold indefinitely and a stronger line was formed higher up the ridge, to which he knew he would be able to retire at the appropriate time. The Russian attack came on the morning of 28 December and, as described by Burnaby in his speech at the Savage Club and in Radford's In Memoriam, lasted all day. By the time the sun set Baker had lost nearly a third of his force, but the bulk of Shakir Pasha's main army was now able to retreat under cover of darkness to Kamarli, where they were joined by Baker's remnants. For the successful outcome of this action against overwhelming odds Baker was widely applauded by his Ottoman employers and later promoted to lieutenant-general. In England this textbook example of a rearguard action was, at the time, hardly mentioned.

The retreat of the whole of Chakir Pasha's army south across the Rhodope Mountains was under conditions of great hardship and a further action was fought at Meska on 6 January 1878. Losses were heavy in the freezing conditions, but a considerable force succeeded in reaching the coast near Gumurd-jina (now Komotini, Greece), having made a fighting retreat over a period of three weeks through Philippopolis, Stanimana, and Kardjali. Burnaby, still wearing his bowler hat, pea-jacket and trousers, encouraged Baker's troops to follow his non-combatant "suggestions" with the use of a large stick. Whether he really did leave notes in villages through which they passed, written in Russian to provoke their pursuers, is not known, but it is something of which he would have been quite capable and scarcely designed to ensure his survival should he have been captured. Of course, his handwriting was so poor that it is doubtful whether they could have been deciphered.

The hackles of the British public were raised when an attempt to poison Baker Pasha and Burnaby at Gumurd-jina was widely reported in *The Times* and elsewhere, although Burnaby never mentioned the incident in his own writings. It was also described shortly afterwards by one of the Stafford House doctors who participated in the retreat, Herbert D. Crook of Bristol. Of his first meeting with Burnaby, at Sofia around 8 December 1877, Crook wrote: "I did not go with General Baker, as he started too early, but I went with Captain Burnaby, of Khiva renown. He is an immense man and marvellously strong, and is most agreeable company."[9] Another of the doctors with Baker's force was John Gill. After crossing the Rhodope Mountains Baker Pasha and his party were briefly entertained by the Archbishop of Gumerd-jina, following which several of the party became seriously ill. Gill, who treated them, was convinced that deliberate poisoning was involved, although this view was not shared at the time by Crook. Later in the year an unidentified correspondent for the *Daily News* also expressed doubt, causing Gill to write irritably to the paper in response, but not entirely accurately; "I may add that several surgeons of the Stafford House Committee, and in the Turkish service, were also present, and were entirely agreed as to the symptoms being due to irritant poisoning, and I do not think it possible that a skilled observer could have held any other opinion."[10] John Gill impressed both Burnaby and Valentine Baker very favourably, Baker effectively using him as a staff officer on at least one occasion. After the conflict had ended Burnaby wrote a private letter to Lord Wolseley recommending Gill for a position in Cyprus, the administration of which Britain had taken over following the cessation of hostilities and the Congress of Berlin. In a speech at Birmingham in 1880 Burnaby mentioned that he had visited Cyprus, which he believed was of strategic value to Britain as a stepping stone to the Suez Canal, but it is unlikely that he did so on this trip.

Burnaby, Baker and many of the wounded troops embarked from Porto Lagos, located near Gumurd-jina on a bar separating Lake Vistonida from

9   *Western Mail*, 27 December 1877.
10 *Daily News*, 13 and 15 August 1878.

the Aegean Sea, for Gallipoli on 27 January and reached Constantinople on 2 February. Under pressure from the British government, which had sent (and then withdrawn) a battle-fleet to the Dardanelles, Russia had accepted a truce offered by the Ottoman Empire on 31 January, but its troops continued to move towards Constantinople. Burnaby was still apparently in Constantinople on 17 February,[11] perhaps hoping to see further action, but he must have departed for England overland via Vienna very soon thereafter. His faithful and long suffering servant, George Radford, contracted typhoid *en route* and died at the Military Hospital, Hougham near Dover on 22 February, where he was buried a few days later with military honours; Fred was the chief mourner and led a detachment of the Blues.[12] Burnaby caused to have carved on his gravestone: "He was a brave soldier, a faithful servant, and as true as steel." According to Wright, Radford was initially replaced by a polyglot Swiss, but this arrangement evidently proved unsatisfactory and before long another trooper of the Blues had been recruited, Henry Storey.

Fred's popularity was undiminished. *Mayfair* reported that he intended to go down to Torquay, where he proposed to spend a few weeks quietly "before the war breaks out".[13] If so he was soon back in London and on 27 February he was a guest at a dinner given by Gathorn Hardy, still Secretary of State for War, in honour of Prince and Princess Christian. Soon after this he made a speech at the Savage Club, at a meeting chaired by George Sala, in which he described in some detail Baker's generalship during the battle of Tashkessan and the subsequent fighting retreat. This was widely reported, including in *Mayfair*, and was generally credited with Baker's subsequent re-election to the Army & Navy and Marlborough Clubs, from which he had been forced to resign after being cashiered.

Baker also returned to London after the retreat across the Rhodope Mountains, where he and Burnaby entertained Eugene Schuyler to dinner at the Marlborough Club, of which meeting Schuyler wrote in his diary: "Baker and Burnaby have got back, having accompanied Suleiman Pasha in his retreat to Enos and Gallipoli. Baker is sad and quiet. Burnaby is full of spirits."[14]

---

11 This is according to the date of a letter to his mother quoted by Wright, p. 141. In fact there is circumstantial evidence that he left Constantinople a day or two before this and was in Vienna by 16 February.
12 The *Morning Post* of 23 February 1877 stated that Radford had been transferred to a military hospital in London, but his death certificate states that he died of typhus fever and pneumonia at the Military Hospital, Western Heights, Hougham, so this seems unlikely. The certificate also states that he had contracted the typhus six days previously, so if this was at Vienna Burnaby must have left Constantinople before 16 February.
13 *Hampshire Telegraph*, 9 March 1878.
14 Eugene Schuyler and Evelyn Schuyler Schaeffer, *Eugene Schuyler, Selected Essays, with a memoir by Evelyn Schuyler Schaeffer* (New York: Charles Scribner's Sons, 1901), p.112. Schuyler gives the date as 1 February, but it more likely to have been 31 March.

On 3 March, within two weeks of Burnaby's return to England, Russia and Turkey entered into a settlement under the Treaty of San Stefano, by which the Ottoman Empire would recognize the independence of Romania, Serbia and Montenegro, and the autonomy of Bulgaria. The Russians pulled back from their most advanced positions, but retained considerable territorial gains in the Caucasus including Batoum, Ardahan and Kars, although they withdrew from Erzeroum.

In *The Times* of 15 February 1878, their correspondent, almost certainly Francis Francis, wrote: "There are many ... who will be glad to know that Captain Burnaby was taking copious notes of all that passed and it is, I believe, his intention to write a book on the winter campaign in the Balkans." This report proved ill founded and Burnaby stood by his undertaking of temporarily abandoning writing, although there is no doubt he would have had adequate material. He had almost certainly been the author of several short telegrams sent to the *Morning Post* in November/December, there was a letter to the Stafford House Committee and some private letters were again published with his permission in *Mayfair* in March and April, one of which also described the battle of Tashkessan.[15] These letters formed the basis for one section of the In Memoriam for George Radford he added to the seventh edition of *On horseback through Asia Minor*, which appeared shortly after his return to England. Although Radford had not accompanied Burnaby to either Khartoum or Khiva, the In Memoriam dealt with their longstanding relationship and the hardships they had shared during the Third Carlist War, their ride through Asia Minor and the Russo-Turkish War.

The omission to publish anything longer may have been because Burnaby wished to leave the field clear to Valentine Baker, who, in 1879, published his two-volume *War in Bulgaria*, being a personal account of the actions in which he had been engaged, rather than a full history of the Russo-Turkish conflict.[16] In this Baker was generous in his praise of Burnaby's contribution, particularly during the retreat of the 5th Division, which he commanded, over the Rhodope Mountains.[17] As a civilian Burnaby could not be credited explicitly with having made a military contribution, but Baker left his readers in no doubt that Burnaby played a critical role. He also made it clear that Burnaby did more than this. "During all this long and trying retreat we had suffered much. I had been so constantly occupied that I had no time to think of personal requirements. But my good friend, Captain F. Burnaby, used to watch me like a child, and was always ready with some sustenance that might prevent

---

15 The British Library holds copies of *Mayfair, a Tuesday journal of politics, literature and science* for 1876/77, 1879 and 1880, but not 1878. It has not been possible to locate copies for 1878 elsewhere, so reprints of the *Mayfair* articles in other journal have had to be relied upon.
16 Baker, vol. 2, pp. 293-4.
17 Baker, vol. 1, pp. 278-9.

my strength from failing."

Another memoir of the same campaign was written by John Fife-Cookson, who had been appointed an additional Military Attaché at the British Embassy in Constantinople at the outbreak of the conflict and spent some time in the field with Baker.[18]

> On the 25th, Christmas Day, Captain Burnaby entertained a number of Englishman at dinner, including Baker Pasha and his staff, some of the medical men and correspondents, and myself. A goose was one of the luxuries set before us; and I believe that one of Captain Burnaby's servants had already been into Sofia twice before he succeeded in obtaining a good one; in fact he had then ridden altogether about 120 miles. Even then the result of the expedition did not quite satisfy Radford, Captain Burnaby's servant, who cooked the dinner.

The goose obviously failed to impress Valentine Baker, whose own memoir recalled the main course as having been turkey. This was not Fred's only contribution to culinary services while in Bulgaria. At a farewell dinner for departing surgeons held a few weeks previously one of the courses, all of which were named for volunteer officers, was *ananas à la Burnaby*.[19]

Another person who enjoyed Fred's Christmas hospitality was the author of two letters to *Vanity Fair* in January and February 1878 under the title "From the front" and signed "*Quand-Même*" (literally, "Even when"). From a reference to the delivery of despatches, it is most likely that this was Fife-Cookson, who made two other references to Burnaby.[20]

> It was night before our tent was pitched, and had it not been for the kindly help of Captain F. Burnaby and Captain James of the Scots Greys ... we should have passed another stormy, freezing night with unprepared stomachs.
>
> Burnaby had a narrow escape; he was standing with Allix, when the latter called up a trumpeter, who was instantly shot dead between the two.

Those who depicted Burnaby as a mindless butcher were far from the mark, but his indifference to danger is very well attested.

Burnaby the spy?

The question arises as to whether Burnaby ever provided semi-official reports

---

18 John Cookson Fife-Cookson, *With the armies of the Balkans and at Gallipoli in 1877-1878* (London: Cassel, 1879), p. 136.
19 *The World*, 19 December 1877.
20 *Vanity Fair*, vol. 19, 5 January and 9 February 1878.

of his journeys to the British government and there is some evidence that he did. Following his return from Anatolia in early 1877 he certainly met with the Duke of Cambridge and, most likely, the Secretary of State for War, Gathorne Hardy.[21] Reports are also referred to on a number of occasions in the literature on Burnaby, for example by Tommy Bowles in his obituary in *Vanity Fair*: "After his Ride to Khiva, and again after his journey through Asia Minor, he made most full and valuable reports to the Horse Guards; they were received and used ... After the Russo-Turkish war, when he accompanied and assisted Baker Pasha in his masterly retreat across the Rhodope Mountains, and in the various hard-fought battles incidental thereto, he again made the most valuable reports to the Horse Guards ..."[22]

The reports were also mentioned by his wife in a letter from John Delane in 1882 quoted in her memoirs: "It may surprise and probably please you as it certainly did me, considering the somewhat ungracious reception you met with at the Horse Guards, to hear that H.R.H. [the Duke of Cambridge] at a dinner on Wednesday at the Austrian Embassy praised your enterprise and intelligence in very warm terms and spoke of the information you had collected as to the progress of Russia in Central Asia and the routes by which she could advance on India as of the utmost value and importance."[23]

References to "Confidential Reports" also occur in Burnaby's private correspondence, for example in a letter from him to Lieutenant-General Sir Frederick Fitzwygram in 1883.[24] If any of these reports have survived, they have yet to be located.[25]

The existence of such reports would be the hardest evidence to support the accusation that Burnaby engaged in espionage, to which Andrew Roberts came close in his biography of the Marquess of Salisbury, describing Burnaby as "an adventurer and spy", although the thought of the six feet four inch tall and forty six inch chest Burnaby acting clandestinely would be absurd and there

---

21 Quoted in Alexander, p. 81.
22 Burnaby's obituary by his close friend, Thomas Gibson Bowles, in *Vanity Fair*, February 1885.
23 Letter to Burnaby from John Thadeus Delane, editor of *The Times*, quoted by Mrs. Aubrey Le Blond (formerly Burnaby) in her memoirs, *Day In, Day Out*, p. 56. The date of the letter quoted by Le Blond (6 May 1882) is almost certainly incorrect.
24 Leicestershire, Leicester and Rutland Record Office: DE1274/2/266.
25 A series of confidential reports under the general title "Russian advances in Asia" were produced by the Intelligence Department for the years 1870 to 1887. These included summaries of expeditions to the area, but none of these makes reference to Burnaby even in passing, including during the period in which he made his journey to Khiva. Likewise a series of reports entitled "The Theatre of War in Asiatic Turkey" made no mention of Burnaby's ride in 1876/77 and a separate memorandum by Colonel Home, Assistant Quartermaster General, dated 12 August 1878 specifically stated: "The information we have on the topography of Asia Minor is exceedingly meagre. When it was requisite recently to put together in a tangible form information on this subject it became apparent that the few travellers who had visited the country had not reported on the subjects it was desirable to know about." All of these reports are in the National Archives, Series WO33.

is certainly nothing in the Hatfield House archives of the Salisbury family to support this.[26] Sinan Akilli, a Turkish historian, has also analysed Burnaby's contribution to the politics of the Great Game, but falls short of describing him as an agent of the British government, secret or otherwise.[27]

Spies were, of course, employed, but these were usually local people who were paid for their work; Burnaby himself refers in a letter from El Teb to "the reports of my spies" and they also feature in *Our Radicals*.[28] His discretion on intelligence and other matters also left something to be desired as in his letter to Lady Molesworth, which could easily have been intercepted, wherein he was quite open about the likely point of weakness in the defensive line that would be occupied by the British army if called upon to defend Constantinople.[29] Another confusion may have arisen from the fact that officers on leave who volunteered to participate in overseas engagements (an officially frowned-upon, but accepted practice) were often employed in support posts, such as transport or "intelligence", and this was indeed the case with Burnaby when he arrived in Egypt in 1884 and was appointed initially to the Intelligence Department by General Lord Wolseley, although he subsequently took on a more active logistics role.[30]

26 Andrew Roberts, *Salisbury: Victorian Titan* (London: Weidenfield and Nicholson, 1999), p. 217.
27 Sinan Akilli, "Propaganda through Travel Writing: Frederick Burnaby's Contribution to Great Game British Politics" in *Edebiyat Fakültesi Dergisi/Journal of Faculty of Letters* vol. 26 no.1 (June 2009), pp. 1-12.
28 Quoted in Le Blond, p. 80.
29 Somerset Archive and Record Service: DD\SH/59/274 N.D. WW56/1-16.
30 Quoted in Le Blond, p. 82.

Part 2

Letters (1856-1878)

Introduction

The documents reproduced in this section fall into the following categories:
- Letters written to and received by Burnaby, including those written to newspapers and journals (by date of writing).
- Selected contemporary newspaper articles relating to Burnaby's life or career (by date of publication).
- Selected letters and diary entries written by third parties relating to Burnaby's life or career (by date of letter or diary entry).

A full list of all documents contained in this section together with an explanatory key is provided in the Appendix in Volume 2.

By far the largest single group of letters is that written from Spain, which can be divided into two sub-groups. The first, comprising letters written between 19 December 1868 and 9 April 1870, were addressed by Burnaby to *Vanity Fair*, the *Morning Post* and his family. The second, comprising letters written between 12 August and 16 October 1873, were all addressed to *The Times*. This sub-group has been preceded by the brief preface Burnaby intended to use for an abortive collection of these letters.

A smaller group of various dates comprises letters Burnaby wrote to the *Morning Post* and *The Times* during other trips, such as those to Russia, Turkey, Sudan and later trips to Spain. With these may be included a small number of 'political' letters Burnaby wrote to newspapers, mainly *The Times* and the *Birmingham Daily Gazette*.

For reasons explained elsewhere, very few of Burnaby's personal letters have survived, other than those already published, or in a far-flung variety of archives. All those that have been found have been included here, even if the only source for them is previous biographies, or even if they are fragments, or trivial in nature.

Newspaper reports of events in Burnaby's life have only been included to the extent that they seem to add significantly to our knowledge of his activities.

In this category, for example, comes the court report of *The Times* describing the case of Hooker vs. Burnaby and the associated correspondence.

Very limited use has been made of diary entries, but those of General Lord Wolseley are too important to omit, even though most have been quoted by previous biographers.

FGB001
Harrow School; Undated [c. 1856]
Burnaby to his father
My dear Papa, I hope you are quite well. You will be very glad to hear I have got my remove, and got it quite easily, as seven fellows below me got it.[1] Give my love to dear mamma. I think my eyes are better. Finch gave me a dinner yesterday at Fuller's. At least it was a kind of early tea on a pheasant and some other things. There were three of us there, and between us we finished him well. He was rather a large pheasant. Give my love to May and Annie. And now with best love, I remain, Your ever affectionate son, Frederick G. Burnaby.

FGB002
Oswestry School; 12 October 1857
Burnaby to his father
My dear Father, Many thanks for the post office order, which I received on Saturday. I expect I shall be able to go up in December, for the other day I met a captain in the army at dinner, and he said they want officers so bad now that they wink at the age, and that a cousin of his got in a little while ago at 16. I had a letter from Colonel Yorke the other day, saying he would let me know when the next examination is to be. He is the Secretary to the Council of Education. Give my love to dear Mother and Annie, and hoping that Evelyn is not quite annihilated at the idea of going to school. Believe me, your very affectionate son, F. Burnaby.

FGB003
4, Marian Strasse, Dresden; Undated [c. 1858]
Burnaby to his father
My dear Governor, Many thanks for your kind letter, which I received quite safe. I called on Paget today. He was very kind, but said he had received no letter from my uncle, so I suppose it was lost. I have, however, written to my uncle to ask him for another. I like Dresden very much. The old professor is a capital fellow. I am getting on very well with the cornet, and German is becoming easier every day. Write and tell me how much Benham makes. It is awfully hot, but we live almost the whole day in the Elbe, so it is very comfortable. They have got capital bathing places there – large rafts with houses on them and capital places to spring from so and so feet from the water. The scenery is lovely. Give my best love to Mamma and Annie, and with best love to all friends,

---

1   The 'remove' was an intermediate class at some British public schools, usually for pupils of about 14 years of age, designed to introduce them to the responsibility of a more senior position. The implication here is that he had done sufficiently well in his examinations to achieve promotion to this class.

Believe me ever your very affectionate son, F. Burnaby.

Anon01
Hooker v. Burnaby
The Times, 15 December 1864
The declaration in this case alleged that the defendant had assaulted and beaten the plaintiff. The defendant pleaded "Not guilty".

Mr. Serjeant Ballantine and Mr. Prentice appeared for the plaintiff and Mr. Huddlestone and Mr. Henry James for the defendant.

The learned Counsel, in opening the case, said that the assault complained of was most gratuitous and most brutal. The plaintiff in this action was a gentleman of good family and position residing near Tunbridge-wells, and held extensive shooting rights over his own and adjoining lands. Through the default of his wife's trustees he had been compelled to enter into a composition with his creditors, and had in consequence of his impoverished circumstances thought fit to divide the rights and expenses of his shooting with a Mr. Westcar. In the middle of last September Mr. Westcar, accompanied by the defendant Lieutenant Burnaby, an officer in the Royal Horse Guards Blue, came down to the plaintiff's property to enjoy the shooting. The defendant was a person whose extraordinary muscular powers far surpassed his intellectual powers, for he could box like a trained prize-fighter, and among his brother officers passed under the *sobriquet* of "Heenan". On the day that Mr. Westcar and the defendant arrived they dined with the plaintiff, and the following morning they all went out shooting. During the course of the day the defendant thought fit to make a most insulting remark to the plaintiff, which the latter responded to, and a rather fierce dispute took place. About two hours after the defendant, seeing that the plaintiff had laid down his gun, walked up to him and on the plaintiff refusing to apologise for the language he had used, struck him several violent blows in the face, and kicked him again and again in a most brutal manner, inflicting upon an inoffensive man the most severe injuries. These were not the customs of the present day, and doubtless the jury would mark their sense of the defendant's misconduct by awarding ample damages to the plaintiff.

His Lordship inquired whether there was no method of settling the matter.

Mr. Serjeant Ballantine said he was afraid not.

Mr. John Hooker, the plaintiff, was then called, and said, – I live at Brenchley, in Kent, near Tunbridge-wells, upon an estate my family have held for many years. I possess the right of shooting over a considerable extent of country. I entered into an arrangement with a gentleman named Westcar, an officer in the Royal Blues, to permit him to shoot with me. That arrangement was entered into before the last season commenced. Mr. Westcar came down, accompanied by the defendant, on the 7th of September last. They shot the day they came down in the afternoon. We all dined together. Another officer named Adderley was also present at dinner. No misunderstanding took place on that day, and we separated at 12 o'clock. We went out shooting again on the following day. Mr. Westcar had appointed to meet me at 9 o'clock, but as he did not come I went on by myself with the gamekeeper. I came up with them in a turnip-field. A Mr. Walmsley was with me then. Mr. Adderley and Mr. Burnaby were with Mr. Westcar. Mr. Burnaby continually complained of the scarcity of birds, and when we came to the end of the turnips he said, looking towards me, "If I were Westcar I would give this d____d shooting up; it will never be of any use to him." I said, "The sooner the better if he brings such sportsmen as you down here, who only grumble and make him discontented." I had heard that they had been shooting sparrows and robin red-breasts on their way. "Sportsmen", said he to me, "do you call yourself a sportsman? You know more of the Bankruptcy Court and of poaching than of sporting." I must explain that I had made an assignment of my property for the benefit of my creditors, in consequence of the trustee of my wife's property having absconded. All my neighbours had treated me very kindly in the matter. Hearing what he said I naturally got out of temper, and I hardly know what I did say. I have no doubt that I told him that my debts would be paid as soon as his, and that I believed he only kept up his position by feats of strength – such as walking matches and boxing. After we had exchanged a few such remarks he fired off his gun in the air, and challenged me to fight him on the spot. I had heard a description of his power from his own lips the night before. He had shown his arm to me, and asked me to feel its substance, and I had seen him throw weights; therefore I told him that I had never had on the boxing gloves in my life, and that it was not likely I was going to fight with a trained pugilist. He then squared up in my face, and I told him to stand off or I would blow his brains out if he hit me. I said that to deter him from hitting me, but I had no intent of carrying my threat into effect. Mr. Westcar made some observation, and we walked down the field, and the quarrel appeared in some degree to be settled. We went lo the carriage, which was standing at the bottom of the field, and had some refreshment, and we then continued our shooting. I walked with the party the whole time. About two hours after the disturbance we came to a piece of hops which I said contained birds. They refused to go through it, and I gave my gun to a person named Mainwearing, who had then joined us, and requested him to go through the hops with the keeper while I acted as guide to the rest of the party. I had reached the field at other side of the hops when the defendant, giving his gun to Mr. Westcar, who had in the meanwhile asked me to apologize, walked up to me and said, "Do you mean to apologize?" I said "Certainly not." But before the words were out of my mouth he struck me with one hand under the eye, and with the other on the temple, and almost stunned me. He then kicked me with all his force on the hip and followed up the blows. He struck me in the face two, or three times without stopping. I endeavoured to parry the blows as well as I could, but I did not attempt to strike the defendant. He then stopped to take breath, and again proceeded to strike and kick me. He kicked me on the groin inside the thigh; he hit me on the side of the head and several other parts of the body. He again stopped and asked me if I had had enough, and would I apologize. I said certainly I should not apologize, but that he should hear of the matter again. He then commenced hitting me again and struck me a violent blow in the mouth. He seemed to watch his opportunity, and when I was unprepared to hit me in the mouth. He then, kicked me again on the top of the knee, and as he did it I caught his foot and tried to throw him back and throw him. I could not do so, however; he hopped about on one leg and kept hitting me with all his force on both ears. At this time Mr. Mainwearing came up with my gun, and I took it and threw it over my shoulder, telling the defendant he dared not have acted in the manner he had done if I had had my gun with me. We then walked to the carriage, and as we were getting in he said to me, "Let me give you a little bit of advice; put a poultice on your mouth." I was then suffering very much from the effect of the blows; my nose and mouth were bleeding. I saw a medical man the following day. I suffered greatly; for three or four days afterwards my ears discharged blood and matter, and I was deaf, to come extent. I believe I have now entirely recovered from the effects of the injuries

Mr. Baron Martin – Cannot this matter be settled?

Mr. Huddlestone – Of course, I cannot Justify Mr. Burnaby's conduct altogether, but if your Lordships were aware of the expression used by the plaintiff you would not be surprised at our going on with the case.

Mr. Baron Martin – If there is a word of truth in the plaintiff's case and the defendant is still in the army he won't be long in it. Don't you think it could be settled?

Some consultation then took place between the learned counsel, but without any result.

Cross-examined. – I was so angry at the time that I don't exactly know what I did say. They had not had good sport, but it was entirely their own fault, because they refused to go where the birds were. They said it was as bad as walking a measured mile to follow up the birds. I said to the defendant, after he had alluded to my bankruptcy, "You make your money by swindling your brother officers, and doing feats of strength for wagers. I thus explained what I meant by swindling, but I certainly used that word. Some other very strong expressions were used between us. Some were very low and coarse; what he said to me I tried to reply to in the same terms and I think I succeeded pretty well. I said as much as I possibly could say – there is no doubt about that. I don't know that I was in an unusually bad temper that morning. I am usually in a good one. I did not threaten to shoot my friend, Mr. Walmsley's, dog. I heard Mr. Westcar on the previous day say he would shoot the keeper's dog, when I said, "Come, a joke is a joke." My own friend, Mr. Walmsley, told me Mr. Westcar said he thought I ought to apologize. Mr. Walmsley told me Mr. Westcar said I was in the wrong, and if I was he thought I ought to apologize. Mr. Walmsley had not heard the whole of the dispute. I considered that the apology ought to come from the defendant. Mr. Westcar said to me, on one occasion, "I would advise you to apologize; because Burnaby is a queer fellow to have any dealings with." Mr. Westcar said to me, in reference to my calling Burnaby a swindler, "You have no right to make use of that expression. The person to whom you refer was in the Guards and not in the Blues." Mr. Westcar expressed his sorrow to hear the dispute, but not more as against one person than the other. I never said that I should like to give Burnaby a thrashing were it not that I know he would take a mean advantage of me by going to law.

Re-examined – I used the word "swindler" after the allusion to my being bankrupt before strangers. I never was a bankrupt, but made an arrangement with my creditors. Of coarse an allusion to the matter under such circumstances gave me very great pain.

Mr. Shaftesbury Edmund Walmsley said he was a land agent in London. He was one of the shooting party on 8th of September. He had not been present at the commencement of the dispute, but he came up to them while it was going on. He heard some abusive language passing between the parties. The defendant fired off his gun, and invited the plaintiff to do the same, for the purpose of their fighting. The plaintiff refused, and two hours afterwards the attack upon the plaintiff by the defendant was made. The witness described the blows and the kicks in nearly the same terms as the plaintiff. He said that he saw the defendant kick the plaintiff three times.

Mr. Baron Martin – You saw him kick the plaintiff?

Witness. – Yes, my Lord, distinctly.

Mr. Baron Martin – Are you sure of it?

Witness. – I will swear it my Lord.

Examination continued. – The plaintiff was much injured and the blood was streaming from his mouth. The plaintiff had never threatened to shoot his dog that morning.

Cross-examined. – Witness's dog had run wild that morning, and he himself had shot at it. He did not hear the plaintiff threaten to give the defendant a thrashing. Mr. Westcar said they ought to try and make the matter up.

Mr. Thomas Mainwearing corroborated the evidence of the two previous witnesses.

Mr. Buckstone Skilletoe, a medical man, described the injuries received by the plaintiff. There were severe injuries to the left side of the mouth, the left eye, and the left ear, with a severe bruise on the outside of the thigh and the top of one of his knees. There was a mark of a blow or a kick on the inside of the thigh, but no definite bruise. There were also many other bruises.

That being the plaintiff's case, Mr. Huddlestone intimated that he should not call any witnesses on behalf of the defendant.

Mr. Serjeant Ballantine summed up the case on behalf of the Plaintiff in very strong language against the defendant.

Mr. Huddlestone replied, on behalf of the defendant, who, he said, had undoubtedly, under great provocation acted in a manner that was very unjustifiable. The jury must, however, recollect that the defendant, a British officer, had been stigmatized in the presence of his brother officers as a swindler; and, as the days of duelling were past, all he could do was to inflict a summary chastisement upon the offender. In the heat of the moment he had, perhaps, gone farther than he ought to have done, but he had now been ready to offer an ample apology for the assault, and had offered to pay a handsome compensation to the plaintiff. The latter, however, had declined any satisfaction but a large pecuniary one, and had employed a hired advocate to trumpet forth his wrongs and to flap every abusive epithet in the English dictionary upon the defendant.

Mr. Baron Martin interrupted the learned counsel, who had used the word "hired" three or four times in reference to Mr. Serjeant Ballantine, and said that such remarks were not proper.

Mr. Serjeant Ballantine – We are both "retained". That is the term generally made use of among the profession.

Mr. Huddlestone asked pardon for using the expression, and concluded by praying the jury in estimating the amount of damages to take into consideration the amount of provocation the defendant had received.

Mr. Baron Martin, in summing up, said the only question for the jury was the amount of damages the plaintiff was entitled to. That was entirely a question for the jury, and one with which the judge had nothing to do; but he must tell them that they were bound to regard not only the absolute bodily pain suffered by the plaintiff, but also the indignity to which he had been put by the acts of the defendant. It would not in most cases of this kind be unreasonable to suppose that the plaintiff had rather exaggerated his case, but here the defendant, although he had three witnesses, had not thought fit to endeavour to contradict the plaintiff in the slightest degree, and therefore the account of the latter must be assumed to be substantially correct. The counsel for the defendant had said that the days of duelling were passed, and it was to be hoped that they never would be restored, but he was afraid that if people were to be compelled to submit to such an outrage as the plaintiff's case detailed without adequate compensation, the custom would be revived in some way or another. This was the first ease he had tried wherein two gentlemen of position were concerned where one had conducted himself as the defendant had done. The learned judge then proceeded to read over the evidence to the jury, remarking that the observation of the defendant to the plaintiff to put a poultice to his mouth was a gross insult, and must be considered as an aggravation to his previous conduct. The question of damages was, however, one entirely for the jury, and they must now consider to what amount they considered the plaintiff entitled.

The jury retired, after some consultation, during which they sad four were for giving a large amount and eight for a more moderate sum.

His Lordship, after about half an hour, sent for the jury, and asked them whether they were likely to agree.

The jury said they were not likely to agree. There were then two for giving a large sum, and ten for a smaller amount.

His Lordship remarked that by the amount claimed in the record they could not give more than 500*l*. Would the learned counsel on both sides accept the verdict of the ten?

One of the jurymen said he was quite ready to wait until 5 o'clock in the morning.

The foreman said there was not the slightest chance of their coming to an agreement.

His Lordship said, under those circumstances, he should discharge the jury if the learned counsel- refused to accept the verdict of the ten.

The counsel on both sides having then agreed to accept the verdict of the ten, a verdict was given for the plaintiff for 150*l*.

FGB004
Regent's Park Barracks; 16 December 1864
Burnaby to Editor – The Times, 17 December 1864
Sir, – May I be permitted, as the defendant in this case to say a word or two in my own defence, not having had the opportunity afforded to me (contrary to my own expressed wishes) at the trial of this case on Wednesday last? I deny in the first instance most positively that I ever kicked the plaintiff while upon the ground, and trust that I may, through your columns, give my version of this very unpleasant affair. Mr. Hooker, as admitted by his own evidence, commenced the dispute by objecting in a most offensive manner to my venturing to express an opinion as to the shooting; and he continues his evidence by further admitting that he hardly "knows what he did say". Had myself and witnesses been called they would have stated upon oath that Mr. Hooker indulged in a tirade of coarse and vulgar abuse that few men would or could have submitted to. The terms "swindler of my brother officers" and other words of a like character were freely applied to me, and he himself proposed fighting, or, to use is own words, "give me a sound thrashing", and when I fired off my gun and expressed myself as willing to accede to his request, was at once met by his threat "to blow my brains out if I touched him."

It was not for some two hours after this, and after consulting with my two friends and brother officers, Mr. Adderley and Mr. Westcar, and through them expressing my willingness to withdraw any expression of my own calculated to hurt the plaintiff's feelings and accept an apology, and allow the plaintiff to withdraw the term "swindler", and the other offensive epithets he had applied to me, and upon his refusal so to do, that I personally addressed him. I then asked him for an apology, to which he replied he would make no apology "to a bully like myself", and upon his saying this I kicked him twice behind. He then caught at my leg, and endeavoured to throw me, and to prevent this and in the scuffle I struck him several times. I again deny that I ever kicked the plaintiff while upon the ground, and I deny that he was ever on the ground all, and I pledge my word of honour that his statement as to my kicking him in any way, save as already mentioned, is utterly false, and that Mr. Adderley, and Mr. Westcar, who were both in court as well as myself were prepared to have fully substantiated the truth of this statement, had we been called. I may also state that the plaintiff himself proposed to accept 50*l.* damages prior to the hearing of the case, which I declined acceding to, feeling then, as I do now, that, however much I may regret my loss of temper on the occasion, I did only that which the same amount of provocation any gentleman in my position would have done, feeling as I do that I could not have again met my brother officers, and that I should have been unworthy to retain Her Majesty's commission, had I allowed so gross, and, as I venture to assert, so unprovoked an insult to have passed without notice.

I again repeat that it was against my wish that myself and witnesses were not called. I did as others would have done – submitted to the advice of the eminent counsel to whom my defence was intrusted, and although I do not for one moment complain of the conduct of my case, I must, however, again express my deep regret that I had not the opportunity afforded me of laying this, my present statement, before the jury and the public.

In conclusion I may observe that while admitting my proficiency in manly exercises, it is only fair to call attention to the fact of my adversary being a young man, standing 6ft. 2in., and my superior in weight.

I have the honour to remain, Sir, your obedient servant, Fred. Burnaby.

Royal Horse Guards, Regent's-park Barracks, Dec, 16.

JMH01
Brenchley, Kent; 19 December 1864
Hooker to Editor – *The Times*, **20 December 1864**
Sir, – my attention having been directed to a letter from Mr. Burnaby contained in *The Times* of Saturday last, I trust you will give me the opportunity of replying thereto. I could have wished that he had not made it necessary for me to do so, but, as his account of the affair is so totally opposed to the sworn testimony

given on the trial, a substantially correct report of which appears in *The Times* of the 15th inst., I have no alternative.

Mr. Burnaby appears to imagine that, by starting with the denial of that which was never stated to have occurred, either by me or my witnesses, his task would be somewhat easier in endeavouring to convey to the public an impression that the expression of feeling exhibited by both judge and jury was called forth by a misrepresentation of the facts.

Another impression Mr. Burnaby would in like manner attempt to convey in his statement that he had no opportunity afforded to him on the trial of saying "a word or two" in "his own defence". Why, Sir, whose fault was that? Surely he had, in instructing his own solicitors and counsel, given to them his "own version of this unpleasant affair", and can it be conceived that they would not have called upon him and his alleged witnesses to enlighten the jury with that "version" if they had not felt assured that the evidence they were prepared to give would not in the least degree refute the testimony given by me and corroborated by several independent witnesses?

So much, then for Mr. Burnaby's alleged reason for desiring still to continue before the public, who must attach such weight to it as it deserves.

It would be a very unpleasant occupation to again go through the evidence given by me on the trial, but I must with your permission refer to some portions contradictory to Mr. Burnaby's assertions. He states that I commenced the dispute "as admitted by" my "own evidence". In no portion of that evidence will there be found any such admission. On the contrary, Mr. Burnaby commenced the affair by an offensive remark and gesture respecting the shooting, accompanied by a coarse and vulgar expression. My reply contained no such expression, and could only have been offensive to him by the truth of the desire it expressed, – viz., that the sooner his friend did give up the shooting, as he recommended, the better I should like it if he brought down such sportsmen as him. This was followed by an insulting and offensive rejoinder by Mr. Burnaby; "the war of words then waxed wrath". I deny most positively that I ever invited him to fight, and this denial was corroborated on the trial by the evidence of Mr. Walmsley. The fact was Mr. Burnaby was himself the challenger; he fired off his gun and commenced to square up to me, and it was only from my threat to use my gun that he did not then strike me. A reference to your report of the evidence will confirm this statement. What Mr. Burnaby means by his allegation that I offered to "give him a sound thrashing", and that when he expressed his willingness to accede thereto, I threatened to blow his brains out, I do not know.

I also deny most emphatically, Sir, that the defendant, through "his two friends and brother officers", in anyway expressed his "willingness to withdraw any expression of his calculated to hurt my feelings", upon my doing the same. As I stated in my evidence, and as was the fact, an apology was demanded of me, and as an inducement for giving it I was told that Mr. Burnaby was "a queer fellow to deal with." Feeling, Sir, that the apology ought to have come from him, I declined to make one.

This, however, is merely begging the question. My complaint was, and is, that we afterwards proceeded with our shooting, and after the lapse of two hours, the dispute having apparently ended, Mr. Burnaby, taking advantage of my having parted with my gun, came up to me, and what then took place I will give from your own report of my evidence, which is strictly correct. Mr. Burnaby then walked up to me and said, "Do you mean to apologize?" I said "Certainly not." But before the words were out of my mouth he struck me with one hand under the eye, and with the other on the temple, and almost stunned me. He then kicked me with all his force on the hip and followed up the blows. He struck me in the face two, or three times without stopping. I endeavoured to parry the blows as well as I could, but I did not attempt to strike the defendant. He then stopped to take breath, and again proceeded to strike and kick me. He kicked me on the groin inside the thigh; he hit me on the side of the head and several other parts of the body. He again stopped and asked me if I had had enough, and would I apologize. I said certainly I should not apologize, but that he should hear of the matter again. He then commenced hitting me again and struck me a violent blow in the mouth. He seemed to watch his opportunity, and when I was unprepared to hit me in the mouth. He then kicked me again on the top of the knee, and as he did it I caught his foot and tried to throw him back and throw him. I could not do so, however; he hopped about on one leg and kept hitting me with all his force on both ears.

The above, Sir, is an account of the attack made upon me by the defendant, whose demur that he ever kicked me while upon the ground, and that I never was on the ground at all, was entirely gratuitous, because I never asserted anything of the kind, either on the trial or elsewhere. As much reliance may also be placed upon his statement as to kicking me twice behind. My back was never towards him. All the wounds and bruises about my person as deposed to by the surgeon on the trial were in front.

With reference to the assertion that I "proposed to accept 50*l*. damages prior to the hearing of the case", I beg to give this my most emphatic and unqualified denial. Neither I, my solicitors, nor counsel at any time ever solicited any arrangement, nor were any overtures ever made on behalf of the defendant until after the jury had retired to consider their verdict, when, as my solicitor informed me, an offer had been made to him by the defendant's counsel to give me a verdict for 50*l*. and an ample apology, but I declined acceding thereto, considering that the offer had come too late.

Mr. Burnaby very ingenuously acknowledges and appears to be proud of his proficiency in manly exercises. I would ask him, Sir, in what do these consist. If in striking, kicking, and otherwise brutally ill-treating one who offers no defence I leave you and your readers to judge whether it is a proficiency to be proud of or for which he will find many admirers.

In conclusion, I beg to state that the defendant's last assertion as to my height, size and age is as equally erroneous as the other statements contained in his letter.

I have the honour to remain, Sir, your obedient servant.

John M. Hooker, Brenchley, Kent, Dec. 19.

HEW01
Regent's Park Barracks; 20 December 1864
Westcar to Editor – *The Times*, 21 December 1864
Sir, – It was far from my desire to bring my name before the public in connexion with this painful matter, which no one can more regret than myself, but Mr. Hooker's letter in your columns of to-day leaves me no alternative, in common justice to Mr. Burnaby, but to reply thereto, and give my statement of this unfortunate affair.

I have for some time past had a shooting arrangement with the plaintiff, Mr. Hooker, he finding the land and I paying all the other expenses, including gamekeeper. I very seldom avail myself of this shooting, and when I do generally stop at a farm in the neighbourhood belonging to my father. In September last I had invited Mr. Burnaby and Lieutenant Adderley (another brother officer), and upon their coming down I asked Mr. Hooker to meet them. We dined together, and in the course of conversation after dinner Mr. Burnaby and Mr. Hooker, who are both gentlemen of athletic proportions, discussed various subjects in connexion with throwing weights, and each boasted of his strength; some trials took place between them, and Mr. Hooker to some extent lost his temper, but at the close of the evening all parted on friendly terms, arranging to meet on the following day and shoot together. We did not meet in the early part of the day, as arranged, but eventually came together, and upon Mr. Hooker proposing to shoot over some ground that we had been trying prior to our meeting, Mr. Burnaby objected, saying we should find no birds, to which Mr. Hooker replied "that he did not understand shooting there, although, perhaps, he might in his own country", adding some taunting expressions as to Mr. Burnaby's shooting. We had very little sport, and Mr. Burnaby about 2 o'clock in the day made an observation to the effect he should advise me to give up the shooting. This seemed greatly to annoy Mr. Hooker, who asked Mr. Burnaby what he meant by interfering between him and myself, and also if Mr. Burnaby imagined that he (Mr. Hooker) had been over the ground before, to which the latter replied that he thought it probable he had. This remark appeared further to annoy Mr. Hooker, who lost his temper, asked Mr. Burnaby if he intended to call him a poacher, saying, "that although he might be an architect he got his living honestly, and did not, as Mr. Burnaby did, make money by swindling his brother officers, attending prize fights, and going into training for all sorts of blackguard affairs", that he, Mr. Burnaby, "wished to get up a quarrel", and then taunted him with being afraid to hit him for fear of getting a licking, adding, "if I did lick you you'd take the law me." Upon this being said Mr. Burnaby fired off his gun and offered to fight the quarrel out, when Mr. Hooker said, "If you hit me, I'll blow your brains out."

From this moment the dispute was carried through on both aides in a spirit of bitterness which, although most lamentable, it was futile to attempt to moderate. To me the quarrel was from the first a source of regret, knowing as I did both parties, having been acquainted for some years with Mr. Hooker and Mr. Burnaby being my brother officer and guest. I did my best to make peace, and, having spoken to Mr. Burnaby, who professed himself willing to adopt any course myself and Mr. Adderley would suggest, I repeatedly spoke to Mr. Hooker, and urged upon him to apologize for the gross insult he had offered to my friend in applying the term "swindler" to him; and this term I insisted he should withdraw. Mr. Hooker, however, positively refused to give any apology or to withdraw the word; and, after again conferring with Mr. Adderley, we both felt we must leave matters to take their course, and that we had no alternative but to intimate to Mr. Burnaby that he was, in our opinion, bound to resent the affront, and some two hours after the commencement of the quarrel, during which time both Mr. Adderley and myself had anxiously attempted to amicably arrange matters, Mr. Burnaby went up to Mr. Hooker and demanded an apology, to which Mr. Hooker replied, "That he would not apologize to a bully like himself." What afterwards took place has been described by Mr. Burnaby in his letter, which has already appeared in *The Times*, and I am prepared to pledge my word of honour to its strict accuracy. I state most positively that Mr. Hooker was never upon the ground at all; that Mr. Burnaby kicked him twice only; those kicks were administered behind and Mr. Burnaby did not strike Mr. Hooker until the latter had seized his leg, and was endeavouring to throw him over. I wish to add that the statement I have now made I furnished to Mr. Burnaby's solicitors; that Mr. Adderley and myself attended the trial of the case, and both were prepared to give evidence to the effect of my present statement. I cannot, of my own knowledge, state whether the offer to settle upon payment of 50*l*. was made, except that Mr. Burnaby so informed me when in the court, and stated he had refused to compromise the matter.

I must express my regret at addressing you at this length, but I feel that I have only one course to pursue, and that is to place the correct facts before the public. I should have readily done so had Mr. Burnaby been in the wrong, and I only regret finding myself called upon to give the most explicit denial of the accuracy of Mr. Hooker's statement, as it again appeared in of his letter of to-day; and, in addition, I avail myself of this opportunity of publicly contradicting the allegation advanced by Mr. Hooker to the effect that I introduced the name of, or hinted at, Mr. Burnaby's having been mistaken for another gentleman.

In making these remarks, I feel that a very faithful statement of a scuffle of this description can seldom be expected from the immediate parties.

In conclusion, I wish to add that Mr. Adderley is acquainted with the purport of this letter, and that I have his authority for saying that the statement I now beg the favour of your affording a place in your columns is, in his opinion, strictly correct.

I have the honour to remain, Sir, your most obedient servant, H.E. Westcar.
Royal Horse Guards, Regent's-park Barracks, Dec. 20.

MBBA01
Regent's Park Barracks; 20 December 1864
Adderley to Editor – *The Times*, 21 December 1864
Sir, – Mr. Westcar, of my regiment, has written you a letter in connexion with this affair, for the strict accuracy of which I vouch; and feeling, as myself and brother officers do, that if the report of this trial were true in substance, and if Mr. Burnaby had committed the brutal assault laid to his charge, he would be unfit to remain our associate, I look to that spirit of fair play which is always accorded by the press to all classes to ask the favour of your permitting me through your columns to state most positively that Mr. Hooker and his witness most grossly exaggerate the real facts of this case. I speak as an independent eye witness of the entire affair from beginning to end, and pledge my word that Mr. Burnaby never kicked Mr. Hooker in any part of his person, save in the first instance giving him one or two kicks behind. The scuffle did not occupy two minutes; no blow was struck by Mr. Burnaby until his leg had been laid hold of by his opponent, and immediately he was released he ceased striking. In fact, however much the matter is to be regretted, it was one of those fracas of the moment between two hot-blooded men equally matched as to size and strength, and the plaintiff and his witnesses have enlarged this into an assault of a most violent and disgraceful character.

I have the honour to remain, Sir, your most obedient servant, M.B.B. Adderley.
Royal Horse Guards, Regent's Park Barracks, Dec. 20.

H&M01
7 St. Martin's Place; 20 December 1864
Horn & Murray to Editor – *The Times*, 21 December 1864
Sir, – A very few words will dispose of the only material points in Mr. Hooker's letter which appears in *The Times* of to-day.

Mr. Burnaby's counsel called no witnesses, because in law no amount of provocation justifies a blow, and as it was admitted that Mr. Hooker had, without justification, called Mr. Burnaby a swindler and had decline to apologize when asked, it would have been wasting time to call witnesses in corroboration, even though the witnesses could and would have shown that the whole course of Mr. Hooker's conduct was grossly insulting, and calculated to provoke a breach of the peace.

Before the trial commenced we were the bearers of a message to Mr. Burnaby from his counsel to the effect that Mr. Hooker's counsel would take a verdict for 50*l*. Mr. Burnaby declined to agree to this, feeling that he was justified in the course he had taken.

The fact is that the whole of the plaintiff's account of his grievances is one-sided and exaggerated. We do not propose entering further into this, but we must observe that Mr. Hooker was well enough to go to London the morning after the assault, and to call on his solicitors in the city, and instruct them to write to Mr. Burnaby threatening an action for damages, which they did on the very same day. We would add, in conclusion, that when the jurymen told the Judge they could not agree on the verdict, the foreman said so his Lordship, "Eight of us think this is not a case for excessive damages; there was great provocation."

We are, Sir, Your obedient servants, Horn and Murray, Defendant's Attorneys.

7, St. Martin's-place, Trafalgar-square, Dec. 20.

[*.* It seems unfortunate that Mr. Burnaby and his friends were not called at the trial to give in the witness box their explanation of the circumstances in which the cause of action arose. Their obvious remedy is to apply for a new trial; but we cannot permit the case to be re-tried in our columns, and can insert no further letters on the subject.]

Anon02
Hooker v. Burnaby
The Times, 3 January 1865

We understand that the field-marshal commanding-in-chief does not consider himself called upon to take any steps with regard to the case of the Lieutenant of the Blues. On the whole we think the decision is wise, and not inconsistent with injustice. Lieutenant Burnaby has to pay 150*l*. damages, and probably as much more in costs – no light penalty for his misconduct; and it is in the spirit, if not in deed, in accord with the letter of the Mutiny Act, that punishment by a civil tribunal should bar further proceedings before a military court. While we quite admit the absence of a necessity for further stirring up this matter, we by no means wish to stand in the light of apologists for Lieutenant Burnaby. Although the imputations of cowardly brutality made against him by some of our contemporaries are quite unwarranted, his conduct on the occasion appears to have been far from that which we should like to see imitated by the gentlemen of the army. He and Mr. Hooker appear to have abused each other like fishwives, and Mr. Burnaby to have ended the discussion after a fashion natural enough among navvies, but not quite in harmony with the feelings of gentlemen. But if his brother officers are satisfied, no one else is likely to suffer by his being retained in the army, and we can find no fault with the Duke of Cambridge for not acting upon the extra-judicial remark of Baron Martin. At the same time this kind of appeal to fisticuffs is not very creditable to the army, and is not likely to add to the reputation of the regiment to which Lieutenant Burnaby belongs. Upon this subject we find some apposite passages in the last published volume of the "Duke of Wellington's Despatches". In reviewing the proceedings of courts-martial during the military occupation of France, the Duke lays it down to be "a military offence for an officer to take the law into his own hands, and beat a man with his fists". In the same case he says:– "I wished to mark my disapprobation of the mode, but too common among the officers of the army lately, of making use of their fists upon every occasion in which their anger might be excited". Again he says, "It is also important for the discipline and for the reputation of the army that the mode recently too common of each officer revenging his own cause by knocking down and beating him who may have offended him should be checked and discontinued, and this can be done effectually only by the sentences of general courts-martial". In another and much stronger case – where an officer received the first blow in an affray in a theatre at Boulogne, and in which the court passed a most lenient sentence in consequence – the Duke asks the court if it is "proper for a general court-martial to sanction in so many terms by its sentence the principle that a British officer, when struck, no matter on the part of whom is the provocation, nor where the scene occurs, shall return the blow with his fists? Is there no authority to whom complaint can be made, and is there nothing to be done, according to the common received notions of officers and gentlemen, excepting to use violence and fighting in a public theatre?" It must be recollected that this was uttered in the days of duelling and by one who "went out" himself. – *Army and Navy Gazette.*

FGB005
Pau; 16 December 1868
Burnaby to Editor – *Vanity Fair*, **19 December 1868**
My journey from Paris was made in the company of one of the most free, easy, and enlightened citizens of Yankeydom it has ever been my fate to travel with. On my taking my seat at Paris, he accosted me with, "Wall, I rather think you are a Britisher?" On my replying "Yes", "I reckoned as much", he continued, "when I seed you a-making tracks for this here division, where there are seven of us already." Why did not you locate yourself in another car? I marked you as a Britisher, too, 'cos you did not say *Pardonnez moa*, and rise your cover (*Anglicè*,

take off your hat) to everybody, but squatted down just as free and as content with yourself as I should have been myself." I replied that I was compelled to enter that compartment, as all the others were full. "Wall", he said, "could you not chaw (*Anglicè*, tip) the guard and get him to put on another carriage, as I don't care if I don't lay my blessed limbs up 'twixt here and Bordeaux." I said this was quite out of the question in France, and asked him how long he had been in Europe. "Not very long", he said, "I fust tuk up in your diggings fur a month or so as I wanted to see a 'lection, but you can't chalk water with us; why you han't no rows; you all went and voted jist for all the wurld as if you were going to meeting. I had hoped to have seen a few hats broken jist in a friendly sort of way you know, but you was all as soothin' as sheep." I suggested that if he had been in Ireland he might probably have had his wishes gratified. "Ah, yes", he replied "rot them Irishmen, they ain't got nothin', only stomachs, so they kum to us to fill 'em, and they won't wark, but want all to be masters, – masters indeed – idle loafers!" A Frenchman who understood a little English here began with "Mais messieurs, you are one leetle bit cruel to poor leetle Ireland. Why you go stop 'Habas Korpoos Act for? You nevair do that in your own country."[2] I answered that it was impossible to keep Ireland in order without its temporary suspension. "Ah", he said, "you call England one free land, but I do read in the *Figaro* that a man in London was prisonéd for two weeks for playing cards in a cabaret one Sunday. Do you call that liberal?" I replied I knew nothing of that case, but it was generally supposed we had much more liberty in England than in France. "Ah", he said, "what you liberale? Look you, after 1789 every one of all the religions could hold any public office in La France, but with you only one ten or twelve years back you permit the Jews to be in your Senate." I next remarked that we had liberty of the press; this rather dumbfoundered my friend, for an instant, but with the ready aptness of a Mossoo[3] who is never to be convinced, he said, "Yes, sare, you can abuse your own government, and also the one the other; and some leetle day more and you have revolution." I shook my head at this. He went on: "We know it; what did you not pull down railings for? What did you not let Murphy make preach for? We have our leetle chronic (chronicle?) in Paris." My two talkative companion got out at Bordeaux, and after a monotonous and uninteresting view of the Bas Pyrenees covered with snow out of the right-hand window, I arrived at Pau shivering with the cold. I have been here four days, and my experience of its variable climate is not such to induce me to make a protracted stay. Imagine to yourself a dull heavy sky laden with moisture, and a warm

---

2   A Bill to suspend 'Habeas Corpus' in Ireland was enacted on 16 February 1866 'to empower the Lord Lieutenant … to apprehend and detain until the first day of March 1867 such Persons as He or They Shall Suspect of Conspiring against Her Majesty's Person and Government'.
3   Nineteenth century slang for a Frenchman.

damp soil steaming with disagreeable exhalations! The aborigines tell me this state of things will not last, but it will probably terminate in fine weather, or else a frost; and a friend informs me last year there was skating. With such a changeable climate, I strongly counsel all weak-chested people to beware, and in preference wend their way towards Algiers or Nice, where they will at least see the sun. One could almost believe one were in an English or American town, as that language – pure or drawled through the nose – meets one at every corner. There are very few Spaniards, most of them having joined their Queen at Paris; and the Russian families, *habitués*, of the place, were so frightened by the inclemency of last winter that they have not returned. Ices are not to be obtained anywhere; I tried to get one to-day at several *confisseur*s, and they all replied, "*Monsieur, à present il fait trap froid pour le glaces!*" The English society is made up of much the sort of people you would expect to meet at Walton-on-the-Naze, or any second-rate Brighton; there is, however, a pack of fox-hounds which three times a week pursues wretched bagmen.[4] and on Saturday there is to be *une grande chasse*. I am told it is the correct thing to turn out in scarlet, but as I am not really travelling for *la chasse*, and should not like to degrade my tops, if I had them with me, by pursuing madly a fox well saturated with aniseed. I shall attend in the modest butcher boot of the period.[5] Last evening some American young ladies, who are stopping in the same hotel as I am, asked me to join them in a game of threading the ring, to be followed by hunt the slipper. I readily assented, as one was very pretty. Oh, Vanity, you would have laughed at the agile way your correspondent got rid of the ring when the ugly girls were hunting for it, and how he was caught at last with it by the pretty one, who looked up in his eyes and said, "I guess I have fixed you this time." American young ladies are free-and-easy, as well as their mammas; they do not wait for an introduction, but begin talking to you as if they had been on intimate acquaintance for years. On my passing one some biscuits to one at dessert, this evening, she said, "Oh please not; I feel so swollen, I guess I'll burst if I stuff any more."

Truly, a wonderful people!

FGB006
San Sebastian; 30 December 1868
Burnaby to Editor – *Vanity Fair*, 2 January 1869

The monotony at Pau during three or four days' incessant rain was diversified a few days since by a fire. I was awoke about twelve o'clock at night by a great

---

4   In this sense one who trails a bag depositing scent for the hounds to chase in the absence of live prey.
5   'Butcher boot' was then a description of informal hunting dress, sometimes also known as 'ratcatcher'.

noise in the street below my window. Dressing as quickly as possible, I hurried downstairs to see what was the matter, when I was told that a house close by us was in flames; so having a little of the amateur fireman in my composition, I hastened to the seat of action to see how our friends on this side of the Channel would bestir themselves on the occasion. The street, where the house was burning, was blocked up at both ends by soldiers; but, to my surprise, they made way directly, saying "*Monsieur, va faire la chaine*"; and before I knew where I was I was seized by a gendarme, who said, "*Il faut travailler, Monsieur*", and I found myself making one of three long rows of men busily engaged in passing buckets. I should have worked with much more energy if I had not been in evening dress; but when a man is travelling with only one pair of black trousers, and finds himself next to a drunken Frenchman who persists in spilling at least half of each bucket over those said nether garments, he speedily finds his philanthropy cool; so waiting till the gendarme's back was turned, I bolted towards the fire. There were two small hand engines at work, but their power was barely sufficient to throw water half way up the side of the house; so, foreseeing that it would probably burn some time, I determined to return to my hotel, but on arriving at the end of the street I found myself as if in a mousetrap, which it is easy to enter but impossible to escape from, for the soldiers placing their bayonets in uncomfortable proximity to my digestive organs, said, "*On ne passé, Monsieur.*" How long this disagreeable state of things would have lasted I really cannot say, but luckily, after a few minutes, a bugle sounded for the soldiers to barricade another street; so, seizing my opportunity, I made my escape.

I went a few days ago with a Spanish gentleman who is residing at Pau to see the government establishment of stallions, situated about three miles from the town. I do not remember to have ever seen cleaner or better ventilated stables; the principal one is more than 100 yards long, by about 30 in width, and some 35 feet high, and contains fifty horses, most of them thoroughbreds bought in England, and some few of Arab and Syrian extraction. The Government keeps these stallions solely for the sake of improving the breed of horses, as they are let out to the farmers at the most ridiculously low rates, the farmers in return generally selling the young horses to the Government for the army, at prices ranging from 600 francs for the light to 800 for the heavy cavalry. In consequence the breed of horses is improving every day; and their cavalry, from having been the worst, are now as well mounted as any in Europe. The stud groom who showed us over the stables informed me that the Arab horses do not eat half as much hay or corn as the English or French ones. My Spanish friend was very much astonished at hearing of hay being given to the horses as in Spain they do not think it good for them, so on my interpreting this to the groom, he said, "*Mais, monsieur les Espagnols sont si bêtes.*" The little Spaniard was furious when I told him this, and said, "They think us *bêtes* do they? and at the same time give a Spanish firm the contract for 200,000 Chassepots.[6] *Bêtes*, indeed, tell him!" When I told the groom what the Spaniard had said, he replied "Yes, but they probably will be so badly made that they won't go off, and so the contract will be broken." I dared not give the Spaniard this answer, as he was so excited I am sure he would have struck the Frenchman; so I told him that the Spaniards were considered a very industrious and clever nation by the French; which eventually appeased the little man.

I arrived at Bayonne on Christmas Eve, and hearing there was to be a midnight Mass in the Cathedral determined to attend. The service and tones of the magnificent organ, one of the finest in France, were most impressive; but what particularly struck my attention was the very small number of men present – there must have been nine women to every man. I have observed this before – that the congregations abroad are principally made up of the fairer sex. Why is this? Are they more easily impressed and really more religious than we are, or do they attend only for the sake of being admired and criticising their neighbours' bonnets? On Christmas Day I went over the fortifications, which are in a dilapidated state, and would soon crumble away under the fire of the heavy artillery which could be brought against them in the present day. There are two infantry regiments and two squadrons of hussars at Bayonne, the latter particularly smart-looking men in everything but their stocks, where you often see an inch or two of dirty shirt protruding. They are very well mounted, and much taller than the average of Frenchmen one sees. The infantry are very young soldiers and look quite boys, but are capable of making long marches. An officer told me, when at Bayonne, that twice a week regularly they march out 25 kilometres for practice; very good work, considering the weight each man carries.

All Frenchmen are full of the letter which appeared in the *Times* on our giving up Gibraltar; they are delighted with the idea, for "should you give it up to the Spaniards", a French officer remarked to me, "we shall very soon be their bankers, and take care of it for them." They do not, however, like the idea of our establishing ourselves at Ceuta,[7] for they think we may encroach on their territory in Northern Africa, as if England had not already more land than she knows what to do with; but alas! Frenchmen will always judge us by their own grasping standard.

During my stay at Bayonne, I drove over to visit Biarritz, and was well repaid for my journey by a view of the most magnificent sea I have ever witnessed. There was a gale blowing at the time, and the large masses of rocks, which

---

6   The 'Chassepot', officially known as 'Fusil modèle 1866', was a bolt-action, breech-loading rifle used extensively during the Franco-Prussian War.
7   Ceuta was, and remains, an autonomous city of Spain, an exclave on the North African coast surrounded by Morocco.

generally stand some sixty feet out of the water, were swept over by mountains of waves such as I have never seen before. I had a splendid view from the emperor's garden, which faces the ocean, his château standing on the very brink of the cliffs. As the season is over in Biarritz most of the shops are shut up, but there are a few English families who remain here for economy during the winter, for in the winter the hotels reduce their charges by almost half. I arrived at San Sebastian last Sunday, and am much pleased with the town; it is surrounded on three sides by magnificent mountains, and on the fourth its shores are lashed by the Atlantic. The citadel thoroughly commands the town and port, and is fortified with a few batteries of guns; but judging by the dates of 1785 and 1803, which are impressed on most of them, they would be more dangerous to their friends than their enemies should they ever have to be used in earnest, and this, as the Alcalde[8] observed to me, is a possible contingency in these troubled times; poor artillerymen, I pity them! San Sebastian certainly strikes one as a warmer town than Pau, notwithstanding its proximity to the sea, but still it is many degrees colder than Seville. It has a very fair company performing at the theatre.

The elections for civic appointments, which have resulted in the defeat of the Republican party, except in some few of the principal towns, have passed off very quietly, and without more disturbances and riots than took place in England last month, and those few riots we hear of were more owing to the wine freely distributed by the agents of each candidate than to any deep political feeling: but, notwithstanding this apparent apathy, the general opinion of all Spaniards, Monarchists as well as Republicans, is, that Spain is, as it were, undermined, and full of gunpowder, which only requires the spark to devastate the whole population, and that spark, they say, will be struck by the quantity of foreign money which is now being freely circulated by the emissaries of the different aspirants to the throne, and will be fanned into flame owing to the delay which will elapse before the Cortes[9] assemble. Montpensier's[10] principal organ – the *Correspondencia* – advocates him, and ridicules the idea of the Duke of Aosta or the Prince of Carignano. *Las Novedades* repudiates Espartero[11] on account of

8   An 'Alcalde' was a traditional Spanish municipal magistrate.
9   Strictly speaking the *Cortes Generales*, the national legislative assembly of Spain.
10 Antoine Marie Philippe Louis d'Orléans, Duke of Montpensier (1824-1890) was the youngest son of King Louis Philippe of France. In 1846 he married the Infanta Luisa Fernanda of Spain, the daughter of King Ferdinand VII. During the Spanish revolution of 1868 he supported the insurgents under General Juan Prim against Queen Isabella II of Spain, his sister-in-law. When, in 1870, the Cortes voted for the next King and chose Amadeo I of Spain with 191 votes, Montpensier received only 27 and left Spain, only returning in 1874. His daughter, Mercedes, became Queen Consort of Spain after her marriage to Alfonso XII, son of Isabella II.
11 Don Joaquín Baldomero Fernández-Espartero y Álvarez de Toro (1793-1879) was a Spanish general and political figure, associated with the progressive wing of Spanish liberalism. He took the credit for the victory over the Carlists in 1839 and was created Duke of La Victoria by Isabella II as a result. He later served as Prime Minister and, effectively, dictator. The title Prince of Bergara

his great age – seventy-five; as on his death Spain would be again plunged into the same embarrassing circumstances she stands in at the present time, and his short reign would enable the banished Queen's agents to intrigue and plot for her return. It hints at Montpensier as being a likely candidate. The *Esperanza* openly advocates Don Carlos, who, it says, has been brought up in misfortune, and knows the real necessities of the country. It finishes its article with "*Viva la Unidad Catolica! Viva las libertades patrias!! Viva el Rey Don Carlos VII. !!!*" The *Siglo* ridicules Montpensier, in common with some other of the ultra papers; but, notwithstanding the Duke of Montpensier is very much ridiculed and laughed at by certain factions, there exists an enormous party for him, at the head of which, the whisper is, stands General Prim.[12] Some say, however, that Prim is ambitious on his own account. My own opinion, formed from carefully-weighed-over conversations with partisans of all sides, is that before six months are over, Europe will see either Prim or Montpensier at the head of affairs in Spain.

FGB007
Madrid; 1 January 1869
Burnaby to Editor – *Morning Post*, 6 January 1869

Happily hotel-keepers are generally bad prophets, and their predictions are seldom accomplished, or else, instead of penning you this letter in a cheery room looking out on the Puerta del Sol, with a bright sun blazing at he window, my cold corse [sic] would be affording a most luxurious repast to the crows inhabiting some lonely pass or dell in the wilds of the bleak mountains between San Sebastian and Burgos. The hotel-keeper at San Sebastian, with the view probably of keeping a customer, told me that the road was infested with *banditti*, who would upset the train, and then carry off the passengers with the design of exhorting a heavy ransom for their captives, when my relations at home would be agreeably surprised by receiving as a new Year's gift a piece of nose or ear in an envelope, with a quiet intimation that the present would be repeated by return of post should the demanded money not be forthcoming. Luckily, however, all these little details of the dangers of the road turned out so many myths, as far as I was concerned, and I reached Madrid having experienced no greater misfortune than that of the cork of a bottle of varnish having got

---

was granted to him by Amadeo I in 1870.
12 Don Juan Prim (1814-1870) was a Spanish general and statesman. He rose to the rank of lieutenant-colonel in the First Carlist War, but subsequently fell out with Espartero and was exiled from Spain for some years. On his return he held several important appointments, but left Spain again as Isabella II became more tyrannical. In 1868 he returned with General Franciso Serrano (1810-1885), who became regent the following year, while Prim became president of the council. Prim was largely responsible for the election of Amadeo I as King of Spain by the Cortes in 1870 and was assassinated shortly thereafter.

loose, and the contents making beautiful for ever the fronts of my dress shirts. Our train was two hours behind time, but that, I am told, is a thing of daily occurrence now, as the company, since the revolution are no longer fined for any delay in the delivery of the mails. I took a walk in the afternoon, and with the exception that the guard in front of the different public buildings, instead of being dressed as soldiers, are attired in every conceivable costume, from the worn-out old shooting jacket and wide-awake,[13] to the Andalusian jacket with its broad red *faja* or belt containing the most formidable-looking dagger, and presenting a revolutionary and cut-throat appearance, and that the names of the streets are in some instances altered, as, for example, La Calle de la Reina to that of La Calle de Prim, I really should not have observed any difference in Madrid since my visit here last May. Beggars still pester you at the corner of every street; and walking down the Paseo del Prado, the Rotten-row of Madrid – a broad road, perhaps a mile in length – I was accosted by no less than thirty-seven. This state of things would not be so objectionable if they did not persist in displaying the diseases and other ailments from which they are suffering openly to the public, in order more thoroughly to arouse the charity of the passers-by. But though externally the state of things appears very much as before, there is a sort of dark cloud hanging over the faces of the Spaniards one meets with; and they all, Republicans as well as Monarchists, are agreed that this tranquillity cannot last, and that sooner or later the revolution, which has been inaugurated under such good auspices, will germinate either into a military despotism or else a fearful civil war; for unfortunately, at the present moment, Madrid is inundated with mischievous place-hunters, all seeking preferment, and as the different candidates for the vacant throne freely promise their partisans all sorts of future rewards should they succeed in attaining the desired prize, these agents are in many instances, it is feared, determined not to wait for the assembling of the Cortes, but to seize the first favourable opportunity for creating a disturbance, in the hope of furthering their particular patron's claim. It is also much to be regretted that the press have so mixed themselves up with the different aspirants to the throne. Each candidate has his own particular organ, which, not content with legitimately and fairly advocating his claims, writes down and scurrilously abuses the character of every other claimant; and with respect to the Republican newspapers, they openly urge and invite their party to rise, and not give time to the priests, who advocate Montpensier's claim to a man, to cajole and frighten their superstitious hearers into voting for the monarchy, and upholding their Church intact as before. The Government have lately been trying to get back the arms which were freely distributed to the populace when the rising took place. This has been met by the most determined opposition from the republican press, who exhort the citizens to

---

13 A soft, low-crowned felt hat.

stand to their arms, and use them, if needs be, in defence of their rights and privileges.

I went to see "The Grande Duchesse" last evening;[14] it is being performed at the Buffo Theatre[15] with great success. I procured a stall near the orchestra, and was much amused by a conversation I had during the *entr'acte* with a violin player, on the subject of the revolution. He told me that he had been given a chassepot, and that all the orchestras were armed, but that the big drum had taken no less than three. I asked him what they were going to do with them; he informed me that he had taken his to a neighbour, a blacksmith, who was going to convert it into a muzzle-loader, and that it would then make a capital *escopeta*[16] to shoot the small birds in the neighbourhood of Madrid. Poor man! I pity him; the first time he discharges his blacksmith's converted muzzle-loader, his fiddling days will be numbered.

FGB008
Madrid; 5 January 1869
Burnaby to Editor – *Vanity Fair*, 9 January 1869
We are living in very stormy times in this small capital, which barely numbers half a million of inhabitants; for every day, and I may say almost every hour, one hears of fresh outbreaks, plots, and counter-plots – defeats of the Republicans in some towns by that indefatigable General Caballero de Rodas,[17] only to be succeeded by risings in other districts. These disturbances at present are for the most part limited to the southern and eastern provinces of Spain, viz., Andalusia and Catalonia. Those in Andalusia are fomented by the money of the Montpensier faction and the agency of the suppressed priests; and the ill-feeling in Catalonia has been raised to boiling point by the agents of Don Carlos, who are leaving no stone unturned to ensure his chance as Spain's future leader. The Republican party, though extremely numerous, and which, if properly organised and subject to wise leaders would have a great prospect in its favour, is so broken up and divided, owing to the mutual dislikes and jealousies of its chiefs, as to strikingly resemble the parable of the house divided against itself. The Monarchical party, on the other hand, headed by Topete[18], Sagasto, and Serrano, all of whom stand pledged to Montpensier, is not animated by the same antagonistical feelings; and if these chiefs can only gain over Prim to

---

14 *La Grande-Duchesse de Gérolstein* was an *opéra bouffe* by Jacques Offenbach (1791-1880). The plot is a satirical critique of militarism.
15 A theatre specialising in the performance of comic opera and operetta.
16 Shotgun.
17 General Antonio Caballeros de Rodas (1816-1876), Spanish soldier and politician, Captain-General of Cuba (1869/70).
18 Juan Bautista Topete y Carballo (1821-1885), Spanish Admiral and politician. He was elected a member of the Cortes in 1869 and served as Minister of Marine.

their views, the country may be saved the misery of a civil war, into which – as is acknowledged by all sides – it is rapidly drifting. But Prim – like the newly elected President of the United States[19] – is a singularly taciturn leader. He says nothing, but probably thinks a great deal; and when it happens to him to state clearly his own views on the subject of a future Government, should they coincide with those of the other three chiefs, each Spaniard may bless him as a saviour of the nation; but if, tempted by wishes of personal aggrandisement, he should incline himself to the Republican division and express his readiness to accept its Dictatorship, a flame will be kindled which will not only consume the little wealth there is left in the country, but which will probably prove fatal to the ambitious man who has kindled the bonfire. If the Republican party, instead of creating risings at intervals, were to plot a general insurrection all through the southern districts, General Caballero de Rodas would find more employment for his troops than they would be capable of performing, especially as the army in the South has lately been reduced by 8000 men, who have been sent to re-establish order in Spain's reactionary colonies. But isolated outbreaks such as those of Cadiz and Malaga, though plainly denoting the amount of ill-feeling against the acting Government, are easily crushed, and each successive failure is one more trump card in the hands of the powers that be. This morning there is a rumour that a rising has taken place in Granada, and that General Caballero de Rodas has marched there from Malaga; and there is also an *on dit* that Barcelona has declared for Don Carlos, but I only give you this information on casual hearsay information, so do not give more credence to it than it deserves. There is, however, very little doubt that the clemency which the Government showed towards the rioters of Cadiz was very ill-timed, as it is attributed by the ignorant inhabitants of each town in the South to timidity and wavering; and this opinion is fostered and encouraged by the Republican newspapers, which openly advocate resistance, and the non-surrender of the arms put into the people's hands the day of the national rising. The most disaffected town next to Malaga is Alicante, and I shall not be at all surprised if in my next letter I may have to give you an account of an outbreak in that quarter. The state of things in Andalusia, according to *El Pensamiento*, is as bad as it can be: the olive proprietors are plundered, herds of cattle are openly driven away, and the robbers, not satisfied with plundering the rich, rob even the poor peasants, whose sole support, perhaps, is one cow. Salt and tobacco, formerly the principal monopolies of the Government, are openly sold in the streets, and meetings are held advocating the re-distribution of property.

The public amusements and theatres of Madrid go on just the same as ever, with the exception that most of the pieces have political jokes and innuendos, which are immensely relished by the audience.

---

19   General Ulysses S. Grant (1822-1885).

Disgusting pictures of the late Queen are sold and placarded in some of the streets, but I am glad to hear that the Government have issued an order prohibiting their sale. *La Epoca*, which, up to the present time, has not expressed an opinion, begins to show a slight bias towards the Queen's son, and is, in consequence, being well abused by the other papers.

The cancan, as danced in the Mabille[20] and certain places of that description in Paris, is becoming immensely popular, and is performed at almost every theatre during the *entr'actes*, I went to Las Novedades, a well-known theatre, a few nights ago, and perhaps my views may be slightly more for conserving or keeping the vestments of the ladies in the ballet to a decorous degree of length than those which are held in these days of revolution; as here the ballet dancers can please themselves, and let the spectators study anatomy; for the principal *danseuse* had on very little more attire than our first mother in the garden of Eden. *Bailes de Mascaras*, or masked balls, are also held almost every evening; but, as in Paris, are only attended by the non-respectable class of the female population.

Bull fights still go on, though they are very poor affairs, as in the cold weather the bulls are not fierce, and will not fight. I attended one last Friday; the first four bulls were *embolados*, that is to say, had balls on their horn so as not to be able to do any injury; these were in turn tortured and killed. The last two, however, were *toros de puntas*, and between them killed seven horses before their own sufferings were put an end to. Cock fights are also publicly held every Sunday morning. If a society for the prevention of cruelty to animals existed at Madrid it would have more than enough to do.

Nearly all the portraits in the picture gallery of the royal family have been removed to private rooms and are not shown except to strangers passing through Madrid, of whom, as you may imagine, there are at present very few. Our Minister, Sir John Crampton,[21] is a regular attendant at the Gallery and spends a great deal of his time in copying pictures. He is now engaged in painting the Three Graces of Rubens.

Here is the speech of the leader of the late insurrectionists at Malaga, which I have translated literally for your readers:

> National Guards, – to live without honour is a life of insult. To die with glory is the death of heroes. Have we armed a town which has always been the first in action when its liberties have been assailed, only to cowardly retreat, without, in the slightest degree, showing that valour exists in our breasts? Where is the

---

20 The Bal Mabille, a dance hall in Avenue Montaigne noted for assignations, founded by Charles Mabille and his sons. It closed in 1875.
21 Sir John Fiennes Twisleton Crampton, Bt. (1805-1886), was a British diplomat. He was Ambassador to the United States from 1852 to 1856, Minister Plenipotentiary to Russia from 1858 to 1860 and Minister to Madrid from 1860 to 1869.

greatness of your souls? If cowardly and timorous chiefs abandon the sacred cause of the people; if they never have conscientiously held the tenets which they possessed, and only called themselves Republicans to turn the country to their own profit, it remains for us to declare to the whole of Spain that we fight for our honour, for our liberty, and for justice. National Guards, you have decided yesterday to die at your posts sooner than dishonoured to quit them. To arms! to die to-day is to live for ever, like the martyrs of Cadiz. Avenge the insult that the defenders of the modern Saguntum[22] are suffering in their prisons and in exile. To your posts! To arms! *Viva la Republica!*

Enrique Romero.

Malaga, 31 de Diciembre, 1868."

I am afraid this renewed clemency will have the contrary effect to what the Government imagine. A tremendous row was expected here last night, owing to Prim's unpopularity with the National Guard, on the subject of disarmament. The troops were all prepared, but the people were afraid and dared not rise.

FGB009
Madrid; 11 January 1869
Burnaby to Editor – *Vanity Fair***, 16 January 1869**
Andalusia, if one may judge by Seville, is much more tranquil than the accounts which I read in the Madrid newspapers had caused me to suppose. The only outward difference in the appearance of the town is that the large and handsome gates through which the Queen passed on her last visit to Seville, and which she ordered should be always preserved in memory of her, were pulled down by the mob and destroyed on the day of the general rising; and that the box at the opera which the Duke of Montpensier and the Infanta used to occupy has had the royal arms removed from it. The theatrical company has had a very bad season, as the higher class of Sevillanos have been afraid to appear in public; and so all the boxes have been untenanted. Though the Republicans carried the day at Seville in the municipal elections, it was only owing to the timidity of the "upper ten" in the monarchical clique, who declined to mix themselves up in the matter, and did not vote at all. The more energetic of their set are, however, now using every endeavour to induce these backward gentlemen to come forward and give their votes on either the 15th, 16th, or 17th inst., which are the days appointed for the election of deputies; the 14th being the inaugurating day. It is to be hoped these recreant monarchists will not fear this time, but will manfully come forward; or else the Seville Republicans will again carry all

---

22 A large and commercially prosperous town in Eastern Spain, which sided with the local Greek colonists and Rome against Carthage. Its inhabitants were defeated, with many killed, by Hannibal in 218 BC after a lengthy siege.

before them. The Government at Madrid appear to be pretty confident of the result; but, from what I can gather from well-informed men of both sides, I think it will be a very near contest, for, though Madrid is monarchical, Madrid does not represent Spain; in fact, there is great jealousy between the capitals of the different provinces, such as Seville and Barcelona and their big brother; for the inhabitants of these districts say, and with some reason, that Madrid ought never to have been made the capital, placed as it is in such a blank, sterile, unproductive district, and containing but half a million of inhabitants, all of whose supplies are drawn from the provinces. Formerly, it was the fashion in Spain for the landed proprietors to live a great deal in the large provincial towns, and thus, by spending their money in the neighbourhood of their own estates, their tenantry to some extent benefitted by the outlay of the capital. But of late years the correct thing has been for all to go to Madrid who can afford it; and this has naturally caused some little ill-feeling among the dependants and provincial tradesmen who used to gain by their presence.

I stayed a day at Cordova *en route* here, and went over the battlefield of Alcolea.[23] All the officers on both sides who fought have since received a grade in rank; but the victors grumble a great deal, and do not see that the men who fought against the revolution should participate in its advantages. This has caused a good deal of jealousy in the military departments.

The inhabitants of Malaga have had a severe lesson, and will not recover it for some time, as an immense deal of property has been destroyed in their town. Up to yesterday afternoon eighty-eight civilians and six women had been buried. The assailants lost one commandant or major, two captains, one lieutenant, one *alferez* or ensign, and thirty-five rank and file killed. They had 173 wounded severely and thirty-six slightly so. There is very little doubt that if the Cadiz and Malaga outbreaks had occurred simultaneously, it would have required a much stronger force to compete with them. I was talking this morning with an Englishman who was at Malaga, and saw the fight from the top of an adjacent house. He told me that the people fought with the greatest bravery, men who had been carried away wounded as soon as their injuries had been attended to returning to their posts and firing away harder than ever. And all for what? If you ask them, they say for a Republic, and if you ask how a Republic will better them, they tell you they do not know, but they have been told so. There is very little doubt that the two risings have originated through the agents of the different candidates to the throne, who freely lavish money, and induce the ignorant peasants to rise and erect barricades; telling them, among other things, that should Don Carlos or the ex-Queen come back, all the land now belonging to the rich will be divided amongst them; and these

---

23 General Serrano's revolutionary army decisively defeated a loyalist force under Manuel Pavía, Marquis de Novaliches at the bridge of Alcolea on 27 September 1868.

tales the uneducated masses, urged on by the priests, freely believe.

There is a great feeling at the present moment against the French Emperor, against whom all the papers – monarchist as well as republican – are bitterly inveighing, on account, as they allege, of the large purchases of arms which are being made in France by the agents of Don Carlos and the ex-Queen for the purpose of promoting civil war in Spain. It is also declared that men are being openly enlisted to fight for Don Carlos, and the report concludes by stating that Prim when in exile had not the same long sufferance shown to him and urge that a force should be despatched at once to the north to guard the frontier, and that more care than ever should be displayed by the Government officials in examining luggage coming from France into Spain, with the view of preventing any arms making their way here.

This morning the news has arrived here of several officers having been arrested in Catalonia who are deeply implicated in the Carlist plot. The officers in the regiment here tell me that should this be proved against them they will undoubtedly be shot, as the Provisional Government has issued a notice to the troops that no indulgence will be shown to any officer discovered in treasonable intercourse with the emissaries of any claimant to the throne, but that in all cases the capital punishment will be dealt out. This remains to be proved, however, and it will be singular if a Provisional Government which lately pardoned 600 rioters in Malaga, after much blood had been shed, will venture to inflict the capital penalty, especially as there is such a strong feeling in the country in favour of its abolition.

There is a great outcry against the lavish expenditure which has been lately taking place amongst the Government officials. The Provisional Government, during the three months of their office, have been spending at the rate of one million and a half pounds sterling annually – half as much again as was ever wasted in the most lavish times of Gonzales Bravo;[24] and the critics say that if half a million is enough for the whole of the expense of the Swiss Government, surely £800,000 ought to be enough for Spain and ask if this is the time to be wasting money on public buildings in Madrid, and keeping up a standing army of 800,000 men, to be employed against each other; the taxes, they say, should not be wasted on destructive weapons, or drivelling priests, but should be directed to national schools and universities.

Affairs look very black in Cuba, and a fresh force of 8,000 men are under orders. The idea of selling the island to the United States is very unpopular, though really the Spaniards, like ourselves, lose more than they gain by their colonies, who draw away all the life-blood from the country and send but little back. What the army has got to fear in this instance is not the insurgents, but

---

24　Luis Gonzales Bravo (1811-1871), Spanish journalist and politician, Chairman of the Council of Ministers 1843/44.

the climate, yellow-fever, and cholera, which decimate fresh regiments, and render all newcomers more or less unable to do hard work till they have been acclimatised to its pernicious influences. The army of General Caballero de Rodas is also to be dissolved, and he is to return to his office as Director-General of Artillery, at Madrid. This looks as if the Government thinks there is no danger of any fresh risings in Andalusia; or is it because it at any heart wishes for some more disturbances and a little unchecked mob law, in order to disgust the Republicans with the license of their own party? The next few days will settle this question. I have just heard it announced that the Government intend to send a force to the north to be on the watch for Don Carlos, but should affairs in the colonies go on as at present, there will soon be no soldiers left to send.

FGB010
Seville; 14 January 1869
Burnaby to Editor – *Morning Post*, **19 January 1869**
I travelled from Madrid in the same compartment with a young lieutenant who had been wounded in the riots at Cadiz, and a French physician and his wife. The latter, who spoke a little broken Spanish, asked the officer how he met with his wound. He described it in the following manner:– "The insurgents were at the barricades, and my colonel gave the order to charge. We charged, they ran, we were very valiant and pursued. I ran after the leader, a very fat man; he, out of breath, fired through my shoulder; but I, with undiminished ardour, presented my pistol, cocked it" (here in his excitement, suiting the action to the word, the lieutenant drew his pistol, cocked it, and pointed it at the French lady). You can imagine the scene that ensued in the carriage. The lady, on finding that the pistol was a loaded one, nearly fainted, and, after having been energetically slapped on the back for some minutes by her husband in order to bring her round, she recovered sufficiently to be able to change her carriage at the next station, amidst the suppressed *sacrés* of her husband, who bitterly inveighed against a land where revolvers are carried about loaded. What annoyed him most was not the pointing [of] the pistol at his wife, who was very ugly, but having to act porter in changing the numerous little feminine parcels the carriage was filled with.

The anecdote was never finished, but I expect that the fat insurgent fared worse than the lady. In the hotel in which I am staying there are, besides the French family, an American stockbroker and his wife and daughter. The American, with the familiarity of his nation, instantly struck up an acquaintance, and the evening of our arrival told us that disturbances were every night expected at Seville, thereby nearly sending the poor little French lady into another fit of hysteria, and with ideas thoroughly impressed with republicanism, revolver, Bowie knives and barricades, we retired to rest. About five in the morning

I was awoke by a noise as if something very heavy was rolling about in the street below, so I got up and put my head out of the window to see what was the matter. To my great amusement I saw that from every other window heads were protruding, and the next one to mine was occupied by a large red ball in a nightcap, which I soon recognised as the cranium of my loquacious friend of the night before. "What is the noise?" I asked. "Hush!" he said, they are making barricades. I guess they will be coming here soon, to make use of our portmantyrs to block up the streets with." "Jonas", a shrill voice screamed from the inside of the room, "Jonas, come away, come to bed or you will be shot"; and I saw my friend drawn away by the strings of his nightcap, a skinny arm looming in the distance. I determined at last, as the noise increased, to go and see what was the cause of it, when to my amusement I found that it was occasioned by two obstreperous mules harnessed to a cart laden with stone slabs for repairing pavement; they had managed to upset the contents, and the row was caused by the Spanish carters trying to replace by the means of levers the slabs in the wagon. When Jonas came down to breakfast I told him this, and asked him how he could bring his wife and family to Spain during such troublesome times. "Wall", he said, "my wife likes pictures, so we fust toured to Rome and then to Dresden, and I reckon we have 'spected all except Mrillers and Vlaskeys – *Anglicé*, Murillos and Velasquez – and when we have jotted them down in our m'randum legers it will be time for me to get back to 'Change'." The climate here is perfectly charming, though it is perhaps what some people would call a little too hot during the day, as in the sun the thermometer goes up to 95; but there is a great difference as soon as the evening comes on, as then it will register barely 52. These changes render invalids very liable to colds; but still, notwithstanding this drawback, which most of the Southern wintering-places share, there is a brightness and freshness in the atmosphere which must be experienced to be appreciated, and all bilious people will here find more relief under this blue sky than even from Du Barry's most delicious Revalenta Arabica food,[25] whose advertisement has reached even beautiful Seville, and which is in great request among the religious community, on account of the miraculous cure of the Holy Papa, which is announced on the advertising placard. There is a very strong Republican party here, as was proved by the result of the municipal elections, but it is not nearly so certain that this time they will conquer their opponents, the Monarchists, by the same overwhelming majority as before, since the garrison of Seville has been lately increased by several regiments, and each soldier of the age of 25 has the right to suffrage; and as their minds have been fully impressed by their officers that

---

25 Du Barry's *Revalenta Arabica* was a proprietary preparation of lentils with supposed restorative properties sold in the eighteenth and nineteenth centuries as a diet for invalids. It was reputed to have been used successfully by Pope Pius XII.

the first thing the Republican party talk of doing, if they gain their point, is to retrench the expenditure and cut down the standing army, thereby taking the bread and cheese out of the soldiers' mouths, it is naturally to be expected that these men will vote for the Monarchists; but still it is to be apprehended that the Republican party will have a majority, for the upper classes, who were too apathetic or timid to vote during the municipal elections, are still in the same vacillating frame of mind, and are all divided by different part feeling, some for Don Carlos, others for the Duke of Aosta, who has a few supporters among the non-influential middle classes, and, lastly, the Duke of Monpensier, who, though personally disliked on account of his closeness in money matters, is yet looked upon by the heads of the party as by far the best of all the many candidates whose claims up to this time been advanced. The fair sex are stirred up by the priests, who influence their religious feelings by telling them that *la libertad de cultos*,[26] which the Republican party advocate, is the next thing to atheism; and, as Spanish women take everything for granted that is told them by their spiritual advisers, there are, as you can easily imagine, a good many little domestic quarrels in the families of the Republican irreligious *pater-familiases*[27] and their priest-incited helpmates. I was dining last evening with an arrant Republican leader, and of course the prevailing topic was *la libertad de cultos*. The hostess turned to me after a fierce discussion with her lord and master, and said – "Señor, you are heretics in your country, as you do not know any better; but still you believe in God, do you not?" I of course said "Yes". "Ah", she went on, "if my husband has his way we shall very soon be worshipping the sun and moon, and have the Turkish priests trying to convert our children; we shall have plurality of worship." I could not help here mischievously insinuating "And perhaps plurality of wives." This added fuel to the flame; the other ladies present took up the cudgels, and for the rest of the evening I was eyed with the most savage glances by the hen-pecked Republicans. Tomorrow is the first day of the elections, but it is expected that they will go off quietly, on account of the large force quartered here in the case of a disturbance, the rioters knowing they will meet with no mercy from the troops, who are still very angry at the losses suffered through riots at Cadiz and Malaga.

Placards are being surreptitiously left about by the agents of Don Carlos, containing the most violent abuse of the other candidate, and openly advocating rebellion against the Provisional Government. If these emissaries are caught they will have a short shrift and a long cord, as one of the principal magistrates informed me that the orders from Madrid are to be very alert, and strict to the last degree against anyone caught conspiring against the present Administration. The desire that is in the heart of every true well-wisher of Spain

---

26 Religious freedom.
27 The heads of family households. The correct plural is actually *patres familias*.

is that the country may be saved a civil war; but it is impossible to conjecture what will be the result of these machinations if the Government *pro tem* does not use the most decisive measures against these agitating Carlists.

FGB011
Seville; 26 January 1869
Burnaby to Editor – *Morning Post*, 2 February 1869
The elections passed off much more quietly than one would have expected, considering the extreme antagonism which exists between the Republicans and their Monarchical rivals, the former, as was anticipated, winning by a large majority. Only one disturbance took place during the three days' voting, and that was occasioned by an altercation between a lieutenant in an infantry regiment and a civilian. The latter publicly accused the officer of unduly influencing his soldiers with a view of obtaining their votes for the Government candidates. The lieutenant irritated at his charge, drew his sword and cut his declaimer across the shoulders; upon which the wounded man produced a revolver and shot the other's sword arm; the spectators then interfered and they were both removed to the hospital. The case is being investigated by the civil power with the usual slowness that characterises Spanish officials, and in about six months hence we shall hear the rights of the case. Universal suffrage does not have an effect of lessening bribery, judging by the open way it is carried on. There is an old adage which says that every man has his price if you only bid high enough, but here the free and independent electors are to be bought at the most moderate rate, an enterprising Republican shopkeeper obtaining 50 votes for 50 packets of cigarettes, the value of each packet being 2 *reals*, or 5*d*. Assassinations are, I regret to say, of frequent occurrence, and a most cold-blooded one was perpetrated a few days ago on the servant of a French gentleman who resides a short distance from Seville. The latter, hearing the report of a gun, sent his gardener to the spot, where, encountering a party of men shooting, he informed them that they were on private property and that they must leave the field. Upon this, one of their number answered that since the revolution the land belonged to the people, and at the same time presenting his gun, shot the poor fellow, who, I have since been told, is not expected to recover.

The announcement that the Pope will not receive their Ambassador has been met with the most violent outcry by all sides, and it is daily expected that the Government will proclaim *libertad de cultos*. This morning the municipal officers have been making an inventory of all the jewels belonging to the cathedral and different churches, and which are used for decorating the images carried about the streets during *La Semana Santa*.[28] The irreligious Republicans

28   Holy Week.

are delighted at this movement on the part of the powers at Madrid, and privately wish for the conversion of these precious gems into specie to liquidate some of the expenses entailed upon the country through the fanaticism which has prevailed from time immemorial in Spain. There is a capital club at Seville,[29] and a foreigner meets with the greatest kindness and attention from the members who vie with each other in showing hospitality to strangers. Their civility, however, is carried to a superfluous extent, for if one is in a hurry, and leaving with a friend, a pantomime has to be gone through at the porch, which consists in your companion shrugging his soldiers and pointing at the door for you to pass first. Etiquette requires that you with a corresponding gesture should do the same, and at last after many mutual bows Spanish ceremony allows one to make a move. There is also much tact shown by the lower orders, very different from the same class in England who laugh at foreigners' mistakes, and frequently openly ridicule them; but here the poor Spaniards do everything in their power to comprehend the stuttering traveller, and not content with pointing out the way to the hotel, will often accompany him till he is safely lodged, and reject the little return in the shape of money which is offered, their national pride being roused at the idea that they could do an act of civility merely for the sake of reward. It is to be hoped that Bradshaw,[30] in his continental directions to travellers this year, has left out that absurd notice which informs Englishmen that it is considered an incivility not to accept a cigarette when offered to you. This paragraph has caused many non-smoking Britons the most intense discomfort. An old gentleman informed me that he had puffed away seven paper cigars between Madrid and Cordova, and had been ill in consequence, all through his fear of offending the susceptibility of his neighbour, who every time he lit one himself offered his case to the other passengers. It is needless to say that this statement in Bradshaw, however true it might have been 100 years ago, is now entirely without foundation, as there are many Spaniards who do not indulge in tobacco.

The news has just reached us by telegraph that four generals have been promoted to the rank of marshals. This has caused an outburst of anger on the part of the economical retrenchment-wishing partisans of Republicanism, who say that it is a new method of increasing the pay of the military chiefs, without getting any additional service from them in return, and thereby still more impoverishing the country, whose national deficit has been largely augmented by the grade in rank given to officers in the army up to the rank of colonel. One of the generals who has just been promoted was 10 years ago a sergeant, and is

---

29 Probably 'Circulo de Labradores y Propietarios de Sevilla' (Seville Farmers' and Businessmen's Club).
30 George Bradshaw (1801-1853), English cartographer, printer and publisher, especially of railway guides and timetables. Burnaby seems not to have realised that his business was now carried on by others.

now Under Secretary for War. It may be thought that great services rendered in the field have caused this sudden promotion; but such is not the case. Each successful *pronunciamiento*[31] brings its advantages in the shape of military rank, and a discontented officer who has the luck not to be found out and shot will soon rise to the top of the tree. This naturally explains the latter part of the despatch, which informs us that several officers are absent from their regiments without leave. Echo murmurs, where? Don Carlos probably could solve the problem.

FGB012
Seville; 5 February 1869
Burnaby to Editor – *Morning Post*, **11 February 1869**
Two Englishmen, whose faces are well known in the "Row" during the season, and who are now making a flying tour through Spain, arrived here last week. Their first impressions at the frontier were not of the pleasantest order, as they were taken by the customs-house officials for Carlists, owing to one of them having in his portmanteau a Scotch cap with a coronet in silver on it, and also a portable camp bed. The former was thought to be a Carlist cap with badge denoting high military rank on the part of the wearer, and the latter a proof that its owner was ready at once to commence the campaign. Finally, however, discovering the travellers were English, their suspicions were lulled, and my two countrymen were permitted to continue their journey. But they had not ended their troubles, for at Burgos one of them was arrested by the police, who thought he was a French criminal they had received a telegram from Paris to be on the watch for, and who was supposed to have escaped to Spain. After about an hour's detention an officer arrived who spoke French, and on disclosing his nationality the prisoner was at once released, with many bows and excuses for the mistake. The two friends procured a courier at Madrid, and I trust the latter part of their tour may be more propitious than its commencement.

A report lately in circulation has gained considerable credence among certain classes, with reference to the manner in which the *employé* whose duty it was to take an inventory of the jewels and works of art in the cathedral executed his office. It is to the effect that, not satisfied with examining the ornaments of the shrines, he insisted upon inspecting the *caja*s, or caskets, which contain the consecrated bread used in administering the sacrament to the dying. The priest who accompanied the official remonstrated, saying that even he himself could not touch the holy caskets without being attired in the vestments prescribed by the rubric as proper when engaged in that duty; but the man persisted, saying there was a strict order from the Provisional Government that every article

---

31 Literally a declaration, it was a form of military rebellion or *coup d'état* peculiar to Spain in the nineteenth century.

in the cathedral composed of either silver or gold should be registered in the inventory. The poor *cura*, hesitating before offending earth or heaven, chose the latter, and has in consequence ever since been undergoing the penances imposed on him by his bishop as a punishment for his sin. The consecrated bread is held in the greatest veneration by all true Catholics; and it is the custom, when the priests carrying the *caja* containing it to the house of some sick person encounters on his road a carriage, for the occupant to get out, kneel in the dust, and relinquish his seat to the holy father. The ex-Queen, who with all her faults was very charitable, invariably complied with this usage – followed herself in the procession to the dying man's house, and if the family were in distressed circumstances left a considerable sum towards alleviating their poverty.

I went over the barracks a few days ago with the colonel of a regiment quartered here. The Spanish soldier is a very economical animal, and does not put his Government to much expense, as all he receives is 5*d.* daily, or 17 *cuartos*.[32] With this sum the private has to find himself in food, exclusive of bread, and all his under-clothing, including boots, stockings, brushes, &c. The colonel assured me that some men were so careful that at the end of their service they returned to their homes with two or three pounds in their pockets. They are enlisted for four years in the actual army and four years in the reserve. When in the reserve they are allowed to resume their former trades and employments, receive no pay from the Government, but are liable to be called out should the country require them. The officers either enter the army after having been trained in military colleges, or are at the age of 15 attached to regiments as cadets for three years. In this case they live at home with their parents, and go to the regiment every day for instruction from regimental schoolmasters kept for that purpose. Should the regiment be removed they are transferred to the one relieving it, and are examined every six months as to their progress, &c.; but failing in two examinations running, they are disqualified from further attempts. At the end of three years they have to pass a final examination, and then enter the army acquainted with French, history, and drawing, and thoroughly *au fait* to all military duty. In this manner the State acquires trained officers, instead of having to teach them their drill after joining. When cadets are supported by their parents, who also pay 2*s.* a day to the regiment towards the cost of their education, &c.

One of the minor annoyances travellers are subjected to in this country is the habit the natives have of smoking the instant they have breakfasted, without any regard to those who are commencing. A Yankee staying at Seville was very indignant at this, and said, "I reckon I'll chaw them tomorrow"; and in fact came he down very early and finished his breakfast before anyone else had

---

32 At this time 8 *cuartos* = 1 *real*.

began, and then, arming himself with a gigantic pipe loaded with Cavendish,[33] created such an atmosphere that the dons, accustomed to a mild cigarette, could not sit in the room, and finally sent a waiter to ask him to desist. "Tell them señor", he said, "if they will come to an understanding not to light them paper macaronis in future till I have done eating I will do the same with my clay, as paper nastinesses take away my stomach for breakfast just as much as 'backy' does theirs." I am glad to say this compromise was accepted, and now we can breakfast free from smoke and its attendant expectoration.

Gigantic preparations are being made for the Carnival, which begins on Sunday next. It is to have a political character, as in one of the processions men are to be dressed as priests, and are to go through a play turning everything connected with former abuses into ridicule. Spain, from having been one of the most religious nations, has made a leap in the other direction. How strange it is that the first consequence of every revolution should be a greater tendency to irreligion! This is no more than the French drama of the last century, though enacted under less bloody auspices.

The Montpensier star is, I hear, very much in the ascendant in Madrid; and it is rumoured that, should he not be elected at the meeting of the Cortes, an instant appeal will be made to arms, as the army is said to have been bought by his agents, and it is well known that he is the most popular candidate with the Government, including all the officers of both army and navy. But *canards* are now of such frequent occurrence that not much attention can be paid to them, though this one, from the quarter when it comes, is more trustworthy than most.

FGB013
Seville; 7 February 1869
Burnaby to Editor – *Vanity Fair*, 13 February 1869

The provisional Government is at present busily engaged in introducing changes, and in altering the different laws relating to murder, assassination, &c., and not before it was required. In Spain a criminal who stabs or wounds his victim even in the presence of spectators, has every chance of evading justice, as the first thing which happens is that all the bystanders instead of assisting the wounded man, run off in different directions; for, should the authorities arrive, they arrest every one found with the body, and take them indiscriminately to gaol, where they are kept for three or four days without being examined, the result of which is that sooner than come forward and say what he knows of the circumstances, each eye-witness, dreading incarceration, prefers to see the murderer escape scathless.

---

33 'Cavendish' was a process of curing and cutting tobacco, usually for pipes, bringing out the naturally sweet taste.

The pickpockets here are not behind their brothers in England and France in the adroit manner in which they accomplish their felonious purposes. A short time since, an old gentleman took his place in a train coming from Cordova to Seville and was followed by a lad of about sixteen. The old gentleman, who had a very showy gold chain suspended from an elaborate white waistcoat, shut his eyes and speedily began to slumber; the boy, who had placed himself in the opposite seat turning to the other passengers, said "My old uncle has gone to sleep, what fun it will be to play him a trick. I will pretend to steal his watch, and when he wakes he will be so frightened as he will think some robber has got it." They all concurred, thinking it would be a good joke, and the boy with the greatest deliberation relieved the old gentleman of his watch and chain. "It will be perhaps as well to take his purse, too", continued the nephew; "poor old uncle how alarmed he will be": then turning to the other travellers, "Don't tell him", said he, "for a minute or two if he wakes when the train stops, but let him find it out himself." On arriving at the next halting-place the lad got out for a minute or so, and was accidentally left behind. A station or two farther on the old gentleman awoke, and discovering he was minus watch, chain, and purse, turned to the passengers and said, "Some scoundrel has robbed me." They all roared with laughter, at which he got furious, when one of them taking pity on him, said: "Oh, never mind, it is only your nephew who has taken it for a lark to alarm you." "What nephew?" said the old man, "I have no nephew"; and to their disgust they found that they had been innocently abetting in a most cunning robbery.

The medical art does not seem to have advanced here since the past century, judging from the fact that bleeding is still looked upon as the universal and only remedy for every ill the flesh is subject to. There is at the present moment residing in Seville an English physician who has long since retired from practice, and who now, influenced by charitable motives, has been attending the poor sick people without taking any fee. He tells me that the great difficulty he experiences is getting the chemists to make up his prescriptions properly. There are always a great many sufferers from ophthalmia, as is common with most towns in the Peninsula. The houses are whitewashed; and this, combined with the glare of the sun, produces most disastrous effects to the eyesight of the inhabitants. The Spanish doctors use the most violent remedies, in the shape of caustic, &c., and those who are not blinded through the primary cause speedily become so under the hands of the faculty. A few days ago a man suffering from ophthalmia called upon my friend, and he prescribed an ointment, which he told the patient to have made up, at the same time observing that it should be a red colour. The latter, finding that the ointment was of a dirty brown, instead of using it, brought the pot to the doctor, who, on examination found that it did not contain the proper ingredients; and on inquiring the reason at the chemist's, the man said – "Why, señor, I have not got all the drugs to make up your prescription, so I have put some others instead, in order that you should not lose your money's worth; and they must be of use, as our own medical men prescribe them for bad eyes." Pleasant for the patient; especially when the doctor told him that, had he used the ointment, he could not have answered for the consequences.

There was an immense meeting held last Friday in front of the *Ayuntamiento*, or town-hall, in commemoration of the anniversary of the execution of twenty-five men, who were shot twelve years ago for an attempt to rebel against the Government then in power. At least, that was the pretended grounds upon which these revolutionists based their rising; but the real object, as discovered by documents found in their possession, was in the confusion to plunder the houses of the bankers and principal inhabitants of the town. Luckily for Seville, its then governor was a man of few words and prompt action; and communicating at once with the Government at Madrid, and getting the necessary authority, he dealt out to the twenty-five ringleaders the same fate that the bankers and other families registered in the discovered document would have met with at the hands of the mob, and had them shot in front of the *Ayuntamiento*. On counting the number of bodies, it was found there were twenty-seven; and it turned out that two inquisitive ruffians, wishing to see the execution, had climbed up a tree overhanging the firing party. This so incensed the soldiers who had to carry out the sentence, that they purposely shot high, and the two unfortunate lookers-on paid with their lives for their curiosity.

My prediction in my letter to you dated a month back will, I think, be speedily realised, and we shall see, in spite of all the efforts to the contrary of Napoleon and the Republican party, Montpensier King of Spain. If the Cortes should be unfavourable to him, which is not likely, as the Government have pretty well made their soundings clear, he will be proclaimed by the generals and colonels at the head of their regiments simultaneously in all the provinces; but this throne purchased by treason to his sister-in-law, will not prove a bed of roses. It will require the greatest tact on his part to keep above water, and already there are many significant allusions to be heard, to the fact that strange princes have met with rough usage at the hands of the Mexicans ere now and in this southern climate the native blood ferments as rapidly, and is quite as pitiless, as on the other side of the ocean. Montpensier's uniform has been ordered to be sent to Madrid to-day, as it will probably be wanted for his triumphal entry. This looks like business. In any case, nothing can save the country from a civil war, for Don Carlos' party are making great strides, especially at Malaga, where the hatred to the Government, owing to the late disasters, has been artfully employed by agents in furtherance of his ends.

The first day's carnival has just finished; there has been very little animation owing to the fear which still exists among the aristocracy, of the Republicans.

A strange drama is announced to be performed in the principal theatre on the 12th, being no less than the "Passion and Death of our Lord". I enclose you the bill announcing it as otherwise I could not expect you to believe that such a performance would be permitted, even in revolutionary Spain.

FGB014
Seville; 16 February 1869
Burnaby to his father (extract)
I have just been calling on the daughter of the Marquis Sancha Scha, and they have been arranging theatricals in which I am to play the part of an enraptured lover. They have given me a book of thirty pages to learn by heart, bad enough in one's own language, but the devil in a strange one. What do you think of the last two letters in *Vanity Fair*? They give more idea of Spanish life and customs than you will see in any books published on Spain, which in fact are written by travellers who know nothing of the country, its habits or language. We had a curious performance last Sunday at the theatre – "The Passion of Our Lord". There was an immense applause when it finished, and the actor who represented our Saviour, having been unfastened from the Cross, came to the footlights and bowed to the audience. There was a good deal of crying among the women in the gallery while our Saviour was being scourged, as it was done in such a natural manner they took it in earnest. ... Judas very successfully hanged himself, the applause was so deafening that he had to reappear and hang himself over again.
... You have no idea of this climate; it is too lovely. Nice is no more to be compared to it than London is to Bedford.

FGB015
Seville; 18 February 1869
Burnaby to his brother (extract)
My dear Evelyn, – Thanks for your letter just received. I have not much news to tell you as the conversation in Seville has ever but one end, and that is the question of government, and the probabilities of civil war. I am going to act the lover to a bright-eyed Spanish girl this evening in some private theatricals; you would laugh if you could see my get-up – an enormous cloak and broad brim crowned hat. One of the necessary things in the role is to sing an amorous ditty below the window, but as I have no more voice than an old crow, it has been settled that I am to go through the pantomime with a guitar, and another Lothario's to pipe a strain to the fair lady, being carefully concealed in the background of the stage. What a pity it is I was not born a 'Mario'; it is humiliating, to say the least, making love under false pretences, even though one does have the post of honour in the play.
Vanity Fair has a capital caricature of Bright this week; I begin to think my

share looks promising in that speculation.[34]

We have had an anomaly actually, two days' rain, and I am writing with a thermometer as low as seventy degrees. My cold is all right, but my old liver will not leave me in peace, I think Prometheus' vulture must be at work upon it. Tell the Governor sherry is as dear as it is in England, the price averaging from 4*s*. to 5*s*. a bottle. The reason is that all the supply goes to England, where it is in great request, and here, in consequence of the heat, it is quite unsuited as a dinner wine. The consumption here is principally of a red wine, between a Burgundy and a claret, and a light Manzanilla which can be bought at about eighteen pence a bottle. That is the real wine of the country, and great quantities of it go to Xeres, where it is bought by the merchants, who load it with alcohol, and it is then sent to England, where it is sold as sherry.

I was much amused yesterday by seeing an American tooth-drawer go through the same performance we saw at Nice, but with this exception, that he failed at the first pull, and the sufferer was so incensed by the pain that he drew his knife, and would have struck the charlatan dentist, if it had not been for the bystanders.

Love to all, and wishing that Madame Rachel could renovate your gullet and my liver as easily as she makes antiquities beautiful for ever.[35]

FGB016
Seville; 21 February 1869
Burnaby to Editor – *Vanity Fair*, **27 February 1869**
Seville brightened up for the carnival, and there have been a few balls and drums. The only difference one remarks between a Seville and a London ball-room is that in the former, the rigodon, or quadrille, is not the same in two of the figures as in England, and that after each dance the happy male walks into a corridor, where a servant is standing who presents a cigarette, on finishing which he returns to his partner. The señoras and señoritas show much appreciation for *dulces*, or sweetmeats, generally carrying a small bag of these delicacies to the theatre, and, during the *entr'actes*, distribute them to their friends. At a ball last Thursday, one divine Andalusian relieved me of at least ten enormous *dulces* made of cream, sugar and fruit, and if the gentleman to whom she was engaged for the next dance had not appeared she would have accepted as many more. There is, however, this to be said, that the ladies eat little else, as their breakfast and dinner consist of chocolate, bread, fish, and vegetables; for they seldom taste meat, and rarely take exercise, except for an

---

34 This caricature appeared in *Vanity Fair* on 13 February 1869, so the letter to his brother must have been dated 15 February 1869, not 1868 as stated in his brother's memoir (p. xxiii).
35 Sarah Rachel Russell, otherwise Madame Rachel (?-1880), was a 'con artist' who operated a beauty salon from which she guaranteed her clientele everlasting youth.

hour or so during the afternoon in a close carriage drawn by magnificent mules, some as much as sixteen hands high. The result is that they are very pale and age rapidly, at thirty being old women. It is a great pity, for if they were only half as much out of doors as our country women they would get a little colour; and this, with the beautifully-shaped feet and hands, small waists, luxuriant black hair, and large piercing eyes they possess, would render them irresistible, at least to the susceptible heart of your correspondent. There remains, however, one great thing to be said in their behalf, and that is, that no Madam Rachel has ever set up business in Seville, and so you have the satisfaction of knowing that the alabaster Venus with whom you are dancing is all real, and no deceptive piece of goods made up for sale to the highest bidder in the matrimonial auction-mart. Spanish wives do not receive any dower from their fathers, and the bridegroom takes his lady for better for worse with nought but her trousseau, having to wait till the death of the parents for her fortune. The consequence is that marriages are made up through love alone, and mammon enters little into the suitor's calculation. They generally marry very young. The lover, having first of all ascertained the state of the young lady's feelings towards him, appeals to her parents, when, if approved by them, he is considered the señorita's *novio*;[36] but the interesting couple have not half the liberty of an English engaged pair, as they are never allowed to be alone for a minute, the mamma keeping a lynx-like eye over them till the marriage ceremony is concluded. The only way they have of talking to each other without the presence of a third party, is at night, when the señorita comes to the iron-barred window, through which she holds a loving conversation with her long-cloaked, closely muffled-up lover; this is called to *pelar la pava*, literally to pluck the turkey, but owing its derivation to the fact of its having been established in order to take in the watchful mamma. This clandestine wooing is very popular, and is to be seen every evening at Seville. The grated window, tenanted on the one side by a sylph-like form and on the other by an amorous *majo*, is very suggestive of the ancient days of chivalry; as are also the narrow streets, scarcely 10 feet in width, and massive-built structures, through which I nightly wend my way on leaving the theatre.

The performance in the theatre of the passion and death of our Lord, which I announced to you in my letter as fixed for the 11th came off on that evening, and has been repeated several times, every episode being put on the stage from the last supper to the crucifixion itself, when the actor representing our Saviour was fastened up on a cross, and went through the form of tasting the vinegar, and finally pretended to die amidst the sounds of thunder. The audience were so pleased at his acting that they encored, and, as soon as the man could be unloosed from the springs which attached him to the cross, he came forward and bowed to the enthusiastic spectators, after which he was fastened up again

---

36 Literally 'groom'.

for the final act of the lowering and burial. When Judas hanged himself on a tree the earth opened and swallowed up his body, at the same time vomiting out fire and smoke. This so delighted the gallery that they cried out *otra vez* (encore); and Judas had to hang himself over again and be re-swallowed, amidst the applause of the spectators, I must give the ladies in Seville the credit of saying that hardly any attended, and several of them have since told me that a theatre is not the proper place for such exhibitions, though all very well in a cathedral. This performance was given at Madrid some years back, but the authorities put a stop to it after the first evening; it has been brought out again now, as in these days of revolution there is no sort of restriction on the managers of theatres, and they can exhibit to the public whatever they think will draw the best house, entirely regardless of decency, or the effect on the morals of their audience.

The state of affairs in Cuba has at last wakened up the Government, and they are making redoubled efforts to furnish cannon and breech-loaders to the 6000 regulars and 4000 volunteers who shortly embark for that destination. The cannons are all on Krupp's, the Prussian, principle, which is the one most in favour with Spanish artillery officers. Their breech-loaders are being rapidly converted from the old muzzle-loading system, at an expense of 40 *reals* per gun. In mechanism they much resemble the Snider-converted weapon.[37]

The firm of Portilla, White, and Co., who have an enormous iron manufactory in Seville, are very busy supplying stores to the Government.[38] Some idea of the business that this firm do can be gained from the fact that, besides the native coal which they make use of, they import annually 15,000 tons from England at an expense of 30*s*. per ton. They are now engaged making experiments with gun carriages, which they can manufacture at a much less expense than if bought from the different Continental companies.

Don Fernando's[39] chance of the crown has been discussed lately with some animation; but it is a very unpopular idea, as, should the kingdoms of Spain and Portugal ever merge into one, the Portuguese would wish Lisbon to be the residence of the Court, and the Spaniards Madrid. The latter say that there are enough ballet-girls in Spain already without more being imported from the adjacent country (alluding to Don Fernando's supposed partiality to that genus of biped), and that the finances are bad enough now; but to what state would they arrive if Madrid were turned into a stage, and its inhabitants into ballet-girls, ruled over by a dancing master. The telegraph has just flashed the news that this candidate has publicly renounced all thoughts of the throne. Poor

---

37 The Snider system was one of those used to convert muzzle-loaders into breech-loaders.
38 Also known locally as Hermanos Portilla y White, a company that started life as grain merchants.
39 'Dom Fernando' is a reference to King Luís I of Portugal (1838-1889), who had a long string of mistresses.

Spain! She is like an old maid of forty, who has been made love to by several beaux, and been jilted by all, and at last, in despair, accepts the only one who will propose himself. Unpalatable as the lover may be, still he is better than nobody, and so we may soon expect to see the ardent Montpensier hand his blushing bride to the altar.

FGB017
Seville; 1 March 1869
Burnaby to Editor – *Vanity Fair*, 6 March 1869

I was invited last week to a *tentadero* by a famous bullfighter, a fellow who, though immensely rich, still works on his own estate like a common peasant, and whose boast consists in having bred the bull which killed the celebrated Matador Pepe. We agreed to start at 7 a.m., and having with difficulty climbed into the high-peaked Andalusian saddle with which my steed was furnished, rode to the place of rendezvous where I found some twenty horsemen; they carried spears, about eighteen feet in length, armed with a sharp spike, bound round with string to within an inch of the end in order to prevent the point penetrating beyond that distance. If I had not been placed under the especial care of one of the principal *toreros*, I should have been a little uneasy at the malicious expression worn by my companions, who seemed to derive no little amusement from my English dress and manner of riding; and the more so as last year, when some Englishmen, who had been invited to a *tentadero*, were lunching in a farm-yard, the Spaniards quietly slipped away and let in a ferocious bull as a mild practical joke, and stimulant to their guests' digestion. At length we made a start, and rode for 10 miles through a grassy country until we came to a large prairie where some eighty bulls were feeding. Now began the task of testing the courage of the herd; two or three horsemen rode at them, and drove out one of the young bulls; they then pursued, one on each side, till getting within distance, the man on the left struck him just above the tail at the moment his hind legs were in the air. If this is well done, the bull rolls completely over; the rider then reins in his horse and waits till he rises, when the same thing is repeated until the poor beast, tired of this sport, turns at bay and charges one of the horses. The Andalusian then shows his good riding, for, wheeling short round, he dashes up to the very horns of the bull, strikes him with his spear, and gallops off at full speed before the enraged animal can turn. The picador now comes up, his right leg cased in iron and his horse blindfolded, to receive the charge on his spear. If the bull repeats his onset, and especially if he gores the horse, he is complimented by being called *muy guapo!* a term applied indiscriminately to a savage bull or a pretty girl, and is marked as fit to figure in the ring. If, on the contrary, he philosophically lies down and refuses to face the spear, he is put aside to spend his life peacefully in agricultural pursuits, a disgrace which any right-minded bull, according to Spanish notions, ought to shrink from as worse than death. Some of the horsemen were very *distinguée* looking, and I found that many of my companions, whom I thought professionals, were noblemen who had come out for a little amateur bull-tilting, and they showed to much more advantage in their smart Andalusian jackets than they ever do on the Prado. At one o'clock a repast of cold meat and sausages was spread out on a *poncho,* and, as there were no forks, they pulled out their knives (ugly instruments, with blades ten inches long, equally useful for cutting one's own dinner or other people's throats), and taking a piece of meat on the point of these weapon, crammed it into their mouths, the blade disappearing in the most alarming manner down their throats. Drinking now commenced. We were placed in a circle, and a man carried round a goat-skin of wine with a wooden tap to it, which he put into one's mouth and tilted up the skin until symptoms of suffocation setting in, he carried it to the next person. The sport soon began again, and these centaurs, who ride like Arabs, looked very graceful as they galloped over the plain managing their heavy *garrochas,* or spears, with the greatest dexterity; no easy task either, for if the point once strikes the ground, the rider is scooped out of his saddle without any chance of recovering himself. The sport concluded at five with a grand carousal, but I could not wait till the drinking bout was finished and so rode hack to Seville, inwardly anasthematising the clumsy native saddle, which will not permit the least rise in the stirrup, and causes much loss of leather to the rider accustomed to the English pig-skin.

FGB018
Seville; 7 March 1869
Burnaby to his brother (extract)
We are to have the Veil of the Temple Scene tomorrow at the Cathedral, that is a large white veil is hung over the altar; and during the mass, fireworks are let off, and the veil is split from top to bottom in order to represent the rending of the Veil of the Temple, but you will see it all described in *Morning Post* and *Vanity Fair.*

FGB019
Seville; March 1869
Burnaby to his brother (?) (extract)
I get up at 8.30, to have a Spanish lesson from 9.15 to 10.45, breakfast at 11.00, and then to the barber's, walk about till 12.30, when I return and study Russian till 1.30, when I have another Spanish master, who comes till 2.30. After which I pay visits till 4, write letters at the club or read papers from 4 till 5, and then go out for a stroll. I dine at 6. At 7.30 I return to the club and talk and chat till 9.30, when I go to some reunion or other till 12. We have an immense procession today in favour of freedom of worship and abolition of the

army. These Radicals would abolish everything if they could. I am busy learning another language, not a verbal one, but a more expressive one. You have heard, of course, that the Spanish señoritas are celebrated for the way they manage their fans. A very pretty little Andalusian is teaching me the language of the fan, and as there are some 200 signs with it, it is not so easy as one would think.

FGB020
Seville; 9 March 1869
Burnaby to Editor – *Vanity Fair*, **13 March 1869**
There is a very general idea among English people that the hapless traveller in Spain, in addition to the discomforts of slow railway travelling in some parts, and seven-miles-an-hour diligences in others, is subjected to bad inns, cooking poisoned with garlic, and beds tenanted by myriads of unmentionables. These three latter delights I can unequivocally state to exist only in the imaginations of those tourists who, having made a hasty journey through the country, and wishing to acquire an idea of importance among their country-people, on account of the supposed hardships they have so gallantly encountered, on their return home embellish their adventures with dirty beds, extortion, and garlic; which, though, perhaps, true 30 years ago, are now as exceptional in a Spanish provincial inn as a tolerable bottle of claret or anything else, for dinner, than "Chops, 'am and heggs, hand poultry, sir", in an English one. The cooking instead of being bad, or indifferent, in the *fondas*, or hotels is as a rule, quite equal to any in France; and the *tables d'hôte* are conducted on precisely the same principles, the only difference being, that the *olla*, a sort of national dish, consisting of every sort of vegetable stewed for some time with small pieces of bacon, is handed round after the soup. The beds are invariably clean and the traveller has the satisfaction of knowing exactly what his bill will be; for the custom is, when you arrive at an hotel, for the landlord to ask you on what floor you require your room, the prices in Andalusia ranging from five to eight shillings a day, and this comprises breakfast and dinner, with white and red wine of the country, attendance included. Sherry is as dear as in England, averaging about twenty-two *reals* a bottle (4*s*. 5*d*. of our money), the reason being that England is the great market for all wine of this class, as, on account of its strength and the climate, it cannot be drunk here with impunity. The hotel proprietors keep but a small supply in their cellars, and that is only called for by American and English travellers, who are made to pay for their alcoholic propensities. The abstemious native seldom tastes anything stronger than the wine of the country, which he dilutes with water till it attains the palest possible amber hue, and he views the stalwart Saxon, who consumes a bottle of Jerez or sherry, with the same gaze of wonder as the Lilliputians did Gulliver's to them insatiable appetite and unquenchable thirst.

Intense politeness reigns in the language used by the highest as well us the extreme dregs of society. On taking leave of a Spanish friend, after making a call, if on a gentleman, you say, "I kiss your hand", if a lady, "*a los pies de usted, señora*" ("at your feet, Madam") the host or hostess at the same time telling you to consider their house, property and all that they possess yours and at your entire disposal. If a mendicant begs of you in the street, he says, "*Señorito, la limosnita*" ("Little Sir, a little alms") in the name of the most holy "Virgin". You decline, asking him to pardon you for the sake of God, but should you give him a *cuarto* he showers blessings on your head, and tells you to "go with God, who will pay you back some day".

FGB021
Cadiz; 15 March 1869
Burnaby to Editor – *Vanity Fair*, **20 March 1869**
A few days ago I was asked to join a shooting party which was to take place on the land of a gentleman residing in the neighbourhood. On arriving at the rendezvous, I was rather surprised to see that the keepers carried cages with them, which, on examination, turned out to contain partridges; and, on asking the meaning of this, one of them said "Señor, it will be very hot about eleven, and the señores will want to rest and have their breakfast, and then the tame partridges will come in useful." I was quite dumbfounded at this, as, although there are some gentlemen in England who buy pheasants to be turned out the night before for their friends to shoot, I was not aware that this custom had as yet been imported into Spain; and so, not wishing to display my ignorance, I waited for the mystery to be cleared up. At last we arrived at a spot where our breakfast was spread out in a shady hollow; and the keeper, with the greatest caution, surrounded us with some bushes, which he stuck in the ground, and then placed the cages containing the birds about twenty yards off. I asked the man on my right if they were to be turned out. He laughed and said, "Oh, no! you do not understand; at this time of year the male partridges are very brave and amorous; so we catch some hens and train them to call, and we shall soon see some of their *novios* strutting up very valiantly." As he was speaking, in fact, two gallant cocks flew up, and settled for a moment near their cages. This was the signal at once for a general family shot, which left the poor victims fluttering on the ground. "Why did you not shoot?" asked my friend. I replied that I thought five guns were enough for two birds, particularly as they were sitting. "Ah, yes", said the owner, "we always shoot sitting if we can, as it is more certain. Some shoot them when they run up to the cages; but that, to say the least, is rash, as one might miss; but flying, of course, it would be still more in favour of the partridges escaping; and we don't come out for that, but to kill what we can." Our bag at the end of the day was not great, as the game was very scarce; it consisted of nine partridges, a snake, and a fox; and I must say that I felt rather ashamed of myself on returning home with these spoils hung behind

the break drawn by four mules which conveyed our party.

This town still shows traces of the late rising, as the houses which look on the sea are, for the most part, covered with shot-holes, which have been plugged up with cement to prevent damp entering. In one of the narrow streets I came across, yesterday, an old announcement with these words printed on it in large black letters – "*Pena de muerte al ladron*" ("Death penalty for thieves") – very significant of the late outbreak. Almost all the inhabitants possessing any means have left, and the greatest terror still exists amongst the few that remain, as they say immense quantities of arms have been brought into Cadiz, concealed under the long cloaks of persons ill-disposed to the Government, during the last two months. So much paralysis of trade has taken place lately, in consequence of the belief that there is shortly to be another rising, that the *gobanador-general* has issued a manifesto entreating the people not to be alarmed by groundless apprehensions, as the state of feeling in the town is not at all such as to justify any alarm. This is the third governor there has been here since the disturbances; and, as he has only been in power a few days, the timid inhabitants are asking what he can possibly know about the feeling towards the Government.

There is to be a demonstration tomorrow in favour of the abolition of *quintas* (or conscriptions); but as there are at the moment 4,000 soldiers in the barracks who are waiting till transports can be obtained to convey them to Cuba, I think the republicans will have too much regard to personal consequences to attempt any more barricade nonsense at present.[40] When these men sail, however, the garrison will be reduced to four regiments; and in these inaccessible streets soldiers fight at a great disadvantage, as every window is a loophole, and, as soon as they have charged and taken one barricade, the insurgents escape along the roofs of the houses and form another in the rear of their opponents, thus exposing them to a fire from both ends of the street, as well as a galling shower of missiles from the roofs. Under these circumstances, and if the ill-feeling in the town is as great as it is represented to be, the Government, to ensure order, should have at least a force of six regiments in the garrison, as, should a rising take place, it would be futile to withdraw men from Malaga as a reinforcement, since that would be the signal for more disturbances in the latter place; and, the army having been much reduced by the incessant drafts to Havana, a simultaneous outbreak in the two towns would be a very bitter pill for the Government to swallow, and might turn out to be a very indigestible one.

---

40 Numerous rebellions against Spanish rule occurred in Cuba during the nineteenth century, occasionally necessitating the strengthening of the garrisons. Spain finally withdrew from Cuba in 1898.

FGB022
Cadiz; 15 March 1869
Burnaby to his father (extract)
I came here last Saturday, and I am going the day after tomorrow over to Africa for a few days. It is pleasant here, but not more than 110 degrees of heat, which is not half hot enough for me. Most of the houses are riddled with shot holes, the effects of the late riots. There will probably be another riot before long, as the Government are aware that the people have enormous quantities of arms stored away ready to use on the first favourable opportunity. I have been rather idle in writing to the papers lately, as what with keeping up my Russian and moving from place to place, one has little time for that sort of correspondence.

FGB023
Tangiers; 17 March 1869
Burnaby to his sister, Annie (extract)
I came here last Tuesday. It is a wild and uncivilised place with inhabitants almost naked, and savage to the last degree. But you will read in *Vanity Fair* an account of the goings on. I find I can make myself understood among the Arabs by a sort of mixture of French, English, Spanish, and Russian, and it is rather amusing inventing a language to speak to them in. I have bought you some Spanish slippers, which I hope you will like. I had some good fun the other day at Gibraltar in the hotel. A Belgian officer wished to make love to the wife of a Spaniard, who was quite deaf, and he asked me to interpret his compliments for him, and so he began in French to me. I translated it into Spanish to the Spaniard's little daughter, and the child bawled the compliments into her mother's ear. The lady smiled very contentedly to the Belgian, who was scowled at by the Spanish husband, while the other people staying in the hotel were greatly amused.

FGB024
Tangiers; 17 March 1869
Burnaby to Editor – *Vanity Fair*, 3 April 1869
I arrived at Gibraltar last Thursday, after a tedious week spent at Cadiz, which has little to recommend it to the traveller in the way of works of art, but which is worthy of a visit from the epicure, simply for the sake of tasting the *pescadilloas fritas par las friaderas*, which are small pieces of whiting and other fish cut up and fried, in a manner worthy of the table of Lucullus,[41] and drinking pure Manzanilla, which is to be met with in a perfection utterly unknown on our side of the Channel, on account of the brandy which is compelled to be added in order to enable it to make the sea voyage without turning. It is a

---

41   Lucius Licinius Lucullus (*c*.117 BC-57 BC), Roman politician and gastronome.

singular thing that more English families who are compelled to reside abroad on account of the treacherous climate at home, do not think of Gibraltar as a winter residence, for with respect to its temperature and salubrity it does not find a rival in Spain; it is by far the prettiest and most romantic spot in the Peninsular, and, notwithstanding its stony nature, has been converted in many places, by means of the extraneous soil, into luxurious gardens and shrubberies, which afford cool and sequestered retreats during the summer months from the burning rays of an almost tropical sun. It also possesses, owing to its garrison, another attraction, for two or three times a week a capital military band plays on the Alameda, and until the Cuaresma, or forty days' rest to the digestive organs, commences, a very fair Italian company gives nightly performances in the theatre. In addition to these advantages there are a pack of fox hounds, which, under the management of their gallant master, Colonel Hankey,[42] of the 83rd, show very fair sport twice a week, in a very rough country, the steep rocks and loose stones of which are, however, compensated for by the magnificent panoramas occasionally seen of the neighbouring mountains, the blue sea, with the bleak coast of Africa sternly standing out in the distance, and ruined remnants of former pirate castles jotted here and there along the shore, recalling to one's mind the day when fair Andalusia was still in the ruthless hand of the Moor, and when old Gib itself was tenanted by a tribe of freebooters who swept the seas in place of the tame and domestic scorpions who are now principal residents on the rock. But to counterbalance all these charms the traveller has to put up with bad hotels, bad cooking, and prices exorbitant in comparison with those of the Spanish provincial towns. It would answer well to any enterprising innkeeper to set up business on the rock, and build a decent hotel, as, by reducing the charges a fourth, he would be able to make a very fair profit, and would easily, by providing eatable food, draw the whole of the custom from the hands of the extortionate and ignorant harpies who own the few places of accommodation for the voyager that Gibraltar possesses. I suspect that this drawback is the reason why so few English families are to be met with, and why many tourists, when travelling, visit every other town in Spain, but pass by Gib on the other side, preferring the *fondas* of Malaga and Valencia, with their varied *table d'hôtes* to the raw and tough beef-steak seldom met with out of the British Isles.

But enough with Gibraltar, and let us pass on to Tangiers, with its wild Moorish population in picturesque Arab dress and closely muffled up women, who are forbidden under the heaviest penalties of the Koran from showing their faces to the unbeliever. I was fortunate enough on my arrival to fall in with a Parisian acquaintance, who at once introduced me to the French Minister, who, with the inherent politeness of his nation, instantly placed his house and

42 Augustus Barnard Hankey (1824-1903).

horses at my disposal during my stay, and at the same time told me that his nephew, who is a thorough master of Arabic, would show me everything that was to be seen in the place. This was invaluable; for I had long wished to see the Moorish dancing-girls go through their performance which is a thing that many English people think they have seen, but that few travellers have really witnessed, as their couriers get up a performance in which Jewish girls are dressed up in the Moorish dress and go through a Hebrew jig as different from the real native dance as the valse from the habanera. Thanks to the exertions of the French Minister's nephew, who frequently disguising himself as an Arab, penetrated into places inaccessible to other Europeans, I eventually found myself, after a capital dinner at the legation, in a low room with four dancing-girls, who had been smuggled to the spot in different disguises. To describe the dance would require the pen of Alexandre Dumas, with the figurative poesy of Victor Hugo; the graceful poses in which they threw themselves, while two other dark-eyed damsels were tum-tumming on a species of harp, had reached their culminating point, when tap-tap thundered at the door, and the owner of the house rushed in to say that the Pasha had in some manner discovered that Moorish dancing girls were performing before some infidels with uncovered faces, and that he had sent some soldiers to search the house, and if there were any Mooresses there to take them off to prison. You can scarcely imagine the scene of confusion: the dancing-girls ran up to the top of the house to hide themselves and we sallied forth to meet the foe, the Frenchmen armed with sword-canes, and I with an old bed-post, snatched up for the fray; but directly the soldiers who had been sent to search found that they would meet a firm opposition, they, though armed to the teeth, beat a retreat, invoking all the curses they could think of – not any on us, but on our fathers and grandfathers, at least ten generations back. Some Jews happened to be passing at the time, and they instantly took our side, quite delighted to see the Moorish Soldiers who freely tyrannize over them, afraid of three Europeans, and retorted in Arabic chaff to the imprecations showered on our heads by our discomfited opponents, to the effect that those "whose hearts were as soft as butter would be beaten by the Pasha when they returned for not having captured the unbelievers". In the meantime the Mooresses had made good their retreat, and I returned much amused with the customs and manners of this wild and uncivilised people.

FGB025
Seville; 27 March 1869
Burnaby to Editor – *Vanity Fair*, **3 April 1869**
The holy week commenced last Sunday, with a procession of priests, carrying palm branches round the cathedral to commemorate Christ's triumphal entry into Jerusalem, after which Grand Mass was performed. On Monday and Tuesday there were no processions, but on Wednesday afternoon two *pasos*, or

large platforms, covered with velvet embroidered with gold, and supporting wooden images of life-size, representing our Lord praying in the garden, with his crucifixion, and carried on the shoulders of twenty or thirty men, who are hid from view by trappings, were paraded about the town headed by priests burning incense and bands of music playing sacred marches purposely out of tune, in order to add to the dolefulness of the ceremony. In the evening the final performance of the passion, concluding with an act called the "Resurrection", written expressly for the occasion by the company's second comic actor, who takes the part of St. Peter, was given in the theatre. In this representation the curtain draws up and you see four Roman soldiers with a centurion keeping guard over Christ's sepulchre, and grumbling at their duty of having to watch over a corpse. All of a sudden the rumbling sound of thunder, imitated by a large sheet of tin shaken at the back of the stage, is heard; the soldiers become frightened, and throwing themselves on their knees invoke Jupiter; but the din increases, the tomb opens, and a framework of canvas appears, connected by wires to the ceiling of the stage. This canvas is painted and arranged like a cloud, and on it stands the actor who takes the *rôle* of our Saviour, holding a crucifix which be brandishes enthusiastically as he is drawn up during his ascension, which was the final exhibition of the piece; and, to please the audience, pigeons were loosed from the side scenes with photographs of the principal actors and actresses fastened to their wings. Of course this produced a free scramble among the deities in the *paraiso*, or gods in the gallery; and whilst the poor pigeons were being torn to pieces in the realms above, an encore was insisted upon by the spectators in the *lutacas* or stalls below. The curtain rose again, more birds were let go, and the artist a second time ascended from the sepulchre waving his crucifix, amidst the yells of the excited beholders. Thus ended this disgraceful spectacle; and I regret to say, pecuniarily speaking, it has been a success and brought grist to the mill of the administration who exhibited it to the Sevillian public; for, though the boxes were invariably empty, and no ladies ever attended, still crowds of farmers and rustics from the neighbouring villages, attracted by the novelty of the piece, and the remote chance of a pigeon for supper, have flocked to the theatre. The company have cleared, after paying all expenses, 6000 dollars, or about £1200; and the author of the "Resurrection" received 2000 dollars for the composition, as a very rigid Catholic lady confided to me this afternoon, a small reward for risking his salvation, though more than the hundred piece of silver which Judas received for his villainy; which caused me to observe that the value of money had deteriorated considerably since those days, and that there is not the same difference now between 3000 *duros* and a hundred pieces of silver as existed during the time of the Roman Governor, Pontius Pilate, and an irreligious *libertad-de-cultos* wishing actor who plays the part of the Pope's great predecessor. On Thursday at mid-day the Archbishop of Seville gave new clothes to thirteen beggars, and washed their feet. This sanitary office being concluded, they sat down to a sumptuous repast spread in the hall of his eminence's palace, and were waited upon by that dignitary and other high officials of the Church. The Duke and Duchess of Montpensier, when in Seville, go through the same operation; so one of the infinitesimally small results of the revolution is that thirteen beggars lose a good dinner, and the chance of an ablution, till the Holy Week next year. I must say I do not envy their Highnesses the Infantas the feet-washing ceremony of 1870, for an Andalusian vagabond with twelve months' abstinence from soap and water is not the sweetest of animals, but what will he become in twenty-four?

FGB026
Seville; 10 April 1869
Burnaby to Editor – *Vanity Fair*, 17 April 1869
A reprieve was granted a few days since under the following singular circumstances to a soldier sentenced to be shot for assassinating the serjeant of his company. A member arose in the Cortes and stated that at 5 o'clock a soldier was to be executed at Granada, and he begged the War Department to reprieve the criminal. Everybody looked at the large clock in the hall. It was a quarter to 3, and the poor wretch had only two hours and a quarter more to live. General Prim, the First Minister for War, answered that the soldier could not be pardoned by the War Department, that his crime was horrible, and that he had murdered his serjeant in the most cold-blooded and premeditated manner; but that, notwithstanding this, the House, in use of its privilege, could remit the sentence should it think fit. These words had scarcely died away on the general's lips, when all the members started to their feet and remained motionless, and without utterance. This mute, but eloquent appeal forcibly touched the public who occupied part of the hall, and they gave vent to their feelings with a cheer. The unanimous assent of the House was given to the proposition, with the exception of one obtuse member, who, though he was for reprieving the condemned, proposed that the question should be first of all well discussed. This observation was received with an ironical laugh, and the remark that there was not much time to waste; in fact, it would have been rather ludicrous that whilst some of the members were eloquently advocating a remission of the sentence, the precious moments should be wasted, and the reprieve arrive too late. General Prim now read out a despatch which he had written to the Captain-General of Granada, communicating the order for a reprieve. But it was half-past 3, and the slightest delay or accident in transmitting the telegram along the wires would prove fatal. The anxiety in the House was very great till an hour afterwards, when the General read out a return message from the Captain-General, at Granada, acknowledging the receipt of the order, which was the signal for another cheer, in which both the members and public heartily joined. This clemency on the part of the Cortes has caused

great indignation amongst the officers all through the army, and certainly with reason; for, if discipline is to be maintained amongst hot-blooded young men, it can be only secured by the knowledge that the punishment will inevitably follow its infraction; and some of the old generals gravely shake their heads and say, that when a soldier receives a pardon for shooting a non-commissioned officer, his comrades will expect to get the order of merit for shooting a general. This opinion is concurred in by all other officers of the service, who are bitterly cursing the republican and levelling principles which are showing themselves among the deputies in the Cortes.

A duel took place last Wednesday between a Frenchman and a Spaniard. The question arose at the *table d'hôte* of the Hôtel de Paris, in Madrid, in the following manner:– Two Frenchmen, discussing General Prim's shooting party at Toledo, one of them stated as his opinion that the shooting was all a pretence, and that the General had only gone there to obtain his share of the jewels lately stolen from the Cathedral. A Spaniard, overhearing this, asked the Frenchman if he meant what he said, and, on the latter repeating his words, he was reproved by a stinging box on the ear from the irate Castilian. The duel took place next day not far from the Delicias,[43] with swords. The Frenchman, who was a good fencer, slightly wounded his opponent in the arm, but the latter, without regarding the rules of fencing, as applied to parrying and lunging, at the same instant ran his opponent through the body, and at the present moment the poor Gaul lies in a very precarious state, and it is not expected he can recover.

FGB027
Seville; 25 April 1869
Burnaby to Editor – *Vanity Fair***, 1 May 1869**
Russians tell us that foreigners visiting their country during the summer, come away without having been able to form any idea of the habits and customs of the inhabitants, who are only to be seen in their true character when the ruthless frost has chained up the Neva, and the double windows, with which every house is provided, have been sealed up for six long months; and this same statement, as relating to the customs of a nation, is equally applicable to the little province of Andalusia, for the natives do not get into the full swing of their amusements, which consist in dancing, singing, and bull-fighting, till the glorious spring has transformed Seville and the adjacent country into one large flower-garden, making the meadows sparkle with tints of every hue, and perfuming the air to such an extent with the scent of orange blossom, that one involuntarily chimes in with the old Spanish bard who softly sang, "*El que no ha visto Sevilla, no ha visto maravilla*".[44]

---

43 The Paseo de Delicias is a park in Seville.
44 He who has not seen Seville has not seen a marvel.

The three days' fair, for which Seville is so justly famed, began last Sunday. It is held on a piece of waste ground about a square mile in extent, on the outskirts of the town, and is looked upon by Andalusians much in the same way as Christmas is by English people, that is to say, as an excuse for uniting all the branches of the family under the same roof, and for unlimited feasting and gaiety. In addition to the booths erected in every available spot in the fair for the sale of horses, sheep, and kine, which form the chief objects of barter, each Sevillian who can afford the luxury has his own *tienda*, or tent, where he spends the day surrounded by his friends, the elders of the party playing *tresillo*[45] and chess, while the more merrily disposed pass the time with dancing, guitar-playing, and charades.

The *Circulo de Propietarios*, or club composed of gentlemen owning property in the neighbourhood, puts up an enormous *tienda*, which, from noon till midnight, is crowded with their señoras and graceful daughters, and in which giddy valses, alternating with quadrilles and lancers, are sustained with the greatest animation. This *tienda* is one of the prettiest sights I have ever witnessed, as at night it is brilliantly lit up with a thousand lights, flashing on the flowers placed in every corner, and reflected back by the bright eyes of the Sevillianas, who come attired in *maja*, or the national Andalusian dress, which consists of a small *balañés* hat coquettishly perched on the side of the head, a short black velvet jacket open in front and displaying an embroidered shirt, with studs and turn-down collar, and round their taper waists a white *faja*, or broad sash-like belt, which supports a red skirt reaching to the ankles, the *tout ensemble* culminating in the tiniest little feet cased in shoes with red bows and silver clasps. Married ladies hardly ever dance, and are much surprised when they hear that some English husbands do not object to their wives dancing. "Pacific dances, such as quadrilles", a little señora, who has only been married three months, remarked to me, "I can understand, but valses never." I retaliated by saying that to the pure all things are pure, even the valse; on which she playfully rejoined that I was a naughty, wicked, unbelieving, *libertad de cultos*-wishing heretic, who ought to know better.

The races came off last Wednesday and Thursday with great *éclat*. The course is a circular one, about three-quarters of a mile in extent, and a good view of every part of it can be had from the stand. This is the second year that races have been held here, and they are so popular that the gentlemen of Seville are thinking of establishing a Jockey Club, and having a meeting every spring. Five races out of six on the first day were carried off by horses belonging to officers at Gibraltar, and the same thing was repeated on the morrow; the fact is, the Spaniards have no idea how to train a horse, and their own animals have done no work till a fortnight previous to the races, when they were dosed with physic,

---

45 Otherwise 'ombre', a trick-taking card game.

and in this state galloped off their legs, so the consequence was they came to the post looking more dead than alive. It is a great pity that the Andalusian noblemen do not pay more attention to the matter, as the Spanish horse, with a cross of the Arab, is a very fast beast, with great endurance, and if properly trained would carry off a good many races, even in England, amongst our own second-rate platers. I was much amused during the last race by a young Spaniard, who, on observing an English jockey finishing, asked his friend (who was looked upon as a great authority in sporting matters) why the rider moved his hands about so much. The juvenile Nimrod, who did not like to show his ignorance, replied, "Ah, yes, you know! A horse gets his mouth very parched at the end of a race, and the jockey jerks about the bit to promote the saliva and quench his thirst!" A fact!!

FGB028
Seville; 7 May 1869
Burnaby to Editor – *Vanity Fair*, **15 May 1869**
Since my last letter there has been considerable alarm in Seville, owing to a conspiracy having been discovered which originated with the officers of an infantry regiment, who, discontented with the commissions and promotions given away by Prim to his partisans, tried to induce the men under their command to make a *pronunciamiento* in favour of the Prince of Asturias.[46] This plot, luckily for the Government, was disclosed by a sergeant, and the ringleaders are now safely imprisoned in Ceuta. I say luckily for the Government, as I firmly believe that, should one regiment in this garrison pronounce, the example would be followed by all the rest, so strong a reactionary feeling is setting in throughout the army. A few days since I accompanied an officer over the barracks. He introduced me to his colonel, and on my asking if the lieutenant-colonel was also doing duty, he rather seemed to shirk the question; but, later on, when alone with my friend, he said "The fact is, nobody associates much with our lieutenant-colonel. Two years ago he was the sergeant in my squadron, and General Prim has now made him second in command of the regiment. I suppose because he thinks he is more to be trusted than we are." This was followed up by an energetically rolled out *"Caramba!"* which did not bode much goodwill to the First Minister for War.

Last Sunday's bull-fight was attended with more than the ordinary number of casualties. In addition to two bull-fighters badly wounded, one picador was fearfully bruised, and another killed outright. This last fatal accident happened in the following manner, and probably owing to a system of knavery which exists amongst the picadors, almost equivalent to that which has disgraced and

---

46 Prince of the Asturias is the title granted to the heir to the Kingdom of Spain; it was then Alfonso, eventually to reign as Alfonso XII.

brought the prize-ring into such contempt in England; with this difference – that instead of selling the fight, the picadors sell their horses' lives to the owner of the *ganaderia*, or proprietor of the bulls; that is to say, they agree for a certain remuneration that, when charged by the bull, they will let their lances slip through their hands, so that the point should not cow him, and allow their horses to be gored by the animal. The principal merit in a *toro muy bravo*, to Spanish eyes, consists in his never flinching when receiving the lance of the picador, but following up and goring the horse. The man who was killed last Sunday allowed a very fierce seven-year-old bull to charge him, and the beast, not feeling the point, and getting his horns well under the horse, threw both steed and rider some six feet in the air, the horse falling with all his weight upon the unfortunate picador, who paid with a broken neck for his double dealing. The bullfight was not stopped, but went on the same as before, my neighbour observing to me that the man had been confessed and received absolution before entering the ring, so really it did not matter, and that the fellow merited his fate for deceiving the public.

All good Catholics are up in arms about the atheistical speech made a few days ago by a Señor Suñer in the Cortes on the *libertad de cultos* question. In his speech he said, "There exist two ideas of religion, one of which is the old one falling into decay, which is Faith, Heaven, and God, but the new idea is Science, Earth, and Man. I am delighted from this Republican bench to proclaim this, for during the last twenty-five years I have sought the opportunity to state my opinions. Buddhism saw the light seven hundred years before Christianity, and in its moral doctrines was much in advance of those preached by Jesus, eldest son of Mary." He was concluding his blasphemous speech by indecent allusions to the Virgin, when the President called him to Order, and said that he was diverging from the question, and must confine himself to the subject. This gave rise to considerable indignation amongst the Republicans, who, instead of routing the orator, and backing up the authority of the President, rose in a body and left the hall; thus making it evident that their ideas on religious subjects were about on a par with their atheistical brother, Señor Suñer. What a pity Mr. Bradlaugh is not a Spaniard! his little superstitions would make him an ornament to the Republican bench.

Seville looks like a gigantic tent, and presents quite a new aspect, as all the streets are covered over with *toldos* or awnings, spread from the flat roofs of each house to its *vis-à-vis* across the way. The heat is intense – the thermometer in my room registering from 97° to 105° at nine o'clock in the morning; and without these *toldos* as a protection against the sun it would be impossible to pass along the streets. The Sevillanos live in the patios or courts of their houses, which are also covered with awnings kept well sprinkled with water; and with these precautions one does not find the heat at all excessive. At seven in the evening the whole population turn out on the Paseo, or Row of Seville, a long and broad drive planted with orange trees by the side of the Guadalquivir,[47] and where a band plays. At ten they return home, and the night winds up with balls in the patios and music and singing. English ladies have a mistaken idea about their Spanish sisters, as it is commonly believed in England that the señoras smoke; such, however, is not the case; I never saw a Spanish lady yet who smoked, although I could not say as much for some of the young married ladies of the period in our own island. But to counterbalance this false impression I have discovered that the idea which prevails here of my fair countrywomen is that they are addicted to intoxicating fluids, have large feet and hands, and waddle when they walk. What strange and erroneous notions the fair sex of both the countries have of each other!

FGB029
Madrid; [December] 1869[48]
Burnaby to his sister, Annie (extract)

… All the embassy people are very civil, and got me directly into the principal club. They play *rouge et noire* here, and also *monte*, in fact these fellows are always gambling. The picture gallery is very interesting. It is by way of being the first in the world. … I have great fun, now I can thoroughly speak the language, talking to the Spaniards about bull-fighting. "Ah", they say, "a bull-fight is the finest sight in the world." So I say to them, "Oh, but you should see a man-fight, which we have in England that is something like a fight"; and then they always say, "How cruel and barbarous you English are!" If you see any more letters in the *Morning Post* signed 'An Idler in Spain', you will know who is the author. There may be one some day this week. I am quite a regular Spaniard, as from one week's end to another, I never speak English. There is sure to be a civil war in Spain, which will probably break out the end of March, and which will cost an immense amount of bloodshed, as the parties are very evenly divided.

FGB030
Madrid; 21 December 1869
Burnaby to Editor – *Vanity Fair*, 1 January 1870

By the time this letter is in print Christmas will have arrived, bringing a holiday – to everything except the stomachs – to Spaniards as well as Englishmen. For here, as in our own country, it is the time-honoured custom to make merry at *Pascua*,[49] and, if possible, to assemble all the members of the family under the

---

47 The river that passes through Madrid.
48 Wright (p. 57) implies that this letter was written by Fred soon after his letter to Annie from Tangiers in March 1869, but it is more likely to have been written when he returned to Spain at the end of 1869.
49 Passover.

ancestral roof, Senators, as well as ordinary beings, have a respite from work, the Cortes are suspended, Prim and Serrano are resting their King-hunting brains by a shooting expedition in, the mountains of Toledo, and Castelar,[50] the great republican orator, is starring in the provinces, and making little social speeches to his constituents.

On account of the disturbed state of affairs there has been little going on in the fashionable world. The Regent has given a few dinners and receptions. The best families in Madrid, however, would not attend them, and the society was made up of the *Corps Diplomatique* and the originators of the revolution. However, Mrs. Prim – or, to give her that title which her husband so little merits, the Marquesa of Castillejos – is a host in herself. She is immensely ambitious, and many people say that the revolution in September would never have happened if it had not been for the pressure she put upon her husband, and the curtain lectures she read him. A petticoat is generally at the bottom of all mischief; but it would be indeed singular if history should have to record in its annals that a Queen was driven from the throne of her ancestors through the devices of the wife of the son of a pettifogging Catalonian lawyer. The General himself looks worn and ill, and does not appear to enjoy the same robust health as his brother conspirator, the Regent Serrano. The latter is not at all unlike Lord Granville in face, and he has a frank and open expression, very different from that of his colleague, whom, judging by his looks, I certainly should not like to meet on a dark night, that is to say, if he knew I had any money about me. The only person who gives dances and drums is the Countess of Montijo, the mother of the Empress of the French. Her salons are thronged by the best society of Madrid on Thursdays and Sundays for balls, and on the other evenings for *tertulias* or receptions. Notwithstanding her advanced age, the Countess still preserves all the freshness and vivacity of youth, and possesses in the greatest degree that charm which the late Lady Palmerston had of thoroughly identifying herself with each of her guests. She is, in consequence, beloved by all, and if there is one person in the world who has no enemies it is the mother of the Empress Eugénie. She speaks French and English with the same facility as her native tongue, and is as thoroughly *au fait* of all the politics of the day as was the noble lady whose name I have mentioned above. It would require the descriptive pen of the *Daily Telegraph* to paint in words the lovely *Madrileñas* who crowd her ball-rooms. Spanish ladies are proverbially beautiful, but such clusters of choice exotics as are to be seen at the Condessa's quite take by surprise and dazzle the traveller, who, as a rule, leaves Spain with but a scanty knowledge of the wealth of beauty concealed within its boundaries. The balls generally begin at half-past ten and end at half-past one; the dances

---

50 Emilio Castelar y Ripoll (1832-1899), Spanish republican politician, was briefly a president of the First Spanish Republic in 1873.

are confined to the rigodones or quadrilles, and valses; lancers and galops are unknown, and valsing is not so general as in England. The cotillon, however, is to be seen to perfection; and the late terpsichorean leader of those dances in Belgravia who was as indispensable to a ball as Gunter and Coote[51] would find many figures unknown to him.

Poor Farlop has quite lost his heart; and if it were not for the greater attraction of fox-hunting and a stud of hunters awaiting him in England would never be able to tear himself away. As it is, however, he has sent a telegram to the M.F.H.[52] in his county, saying that it is very cold here, and asking if there is a frost in England, I am sure he is hoping inwardly that the answer will be in the affirmative, in order that he may have an excuse for staying, and also of doing what is so dear to all who hunt, whether they like it or not – viz., having a good grumble about the confounded horses eating their heads off and doing nothing.

Madrid – to use the style of the Paris correspondent of the *Wire* – has been kept alive this week by a jolly number of murders and robberies. A member of the Cortes was attacked yesterday at the door of his house by two men who, placing their knives against his heart, asked him politely for his watch and purse. He judiciously assented to their courteous request; they then said, "Good bye", telling him to remain with God. The police are making strenuous endeavours to discover the perpetrators of such a brazen-faced act, and it is to be hoped that this outrage on an influential person may be indirectly the means of benefitting the community at large. The papers are full of satirical remarks about the Duke of Genoa – Little Thomas as he is called;[53] in one of the second-rate theatres they have a play about him. It would be too ridiculous if Prim, against the will of the entire nation, were to attempt to establish that candidature. What surprises me most is that, inhabiting a country where murder is so common, Prim has not long ere this been assassinated. His worst enemies must allow he is a brave man, as, though he is perfectly aware of the hatred he is held in by all classes, he walks and drives in the streets alone and unaccompanied.

The Minister Figuerola,[54] who has been making such unwarrantable attacks on the Queen-Mother Cristina, with reference to the Crown jewels, has received a letter from the secretary of the latter, asking him in common fairness to say in the press what he has said when beneath the shelter of the Cortes, so that the lady may have a chance of obtaining justice, and the case investigated before the tribunals of law by bringing an action against the Minister for libel;

---

51   Gunter and Coote were providers of musical entertainments in London.
52   Master of Fox Hounds.
53   Prince Thomas of Savoy, Duke of Genoa (1854-1931).
54   Laureano Figuerola, Minister of Finance.

for so long as he confines himself to statements in his ministerial capacity no legal redress can be obtained. If Figuerola is a gentleman, he will accede to such a moderate request, and give the Queen-mother the opportunity of showing her innocence to the world. I say innocence, as it is the universal opinion that the charge is one trumped up for political purposes, and to irritate the nation against the Bourbons. As it is, however, its grossness and unsubstantiability have aroused the chivalrous feeling of all Spaniards, and done more good than harm to the cause of the Prince Alfonso.

FGB031
Madrid; 25 December 1869
Burnaby to Editor – *Morning Post*, 3 January 1870

A bright and frosty morning, with the sun sparkling in at the window, has inaugurated our Christmas. The sounds of revellers keeping the streets alive till early dawn, with bands of music and singing, reminded me of the time-honoured custom of ushering in the 25th December to the same strains in Old England, and the cosmopolitan system of Christmas boxes was palpably displayed by the congratulations I received on the advent of the *Pascua* from all the club and hotel waiters, shopkeepers and barbers of the metropolis of the Peninsula. In England the good old folks pass the day by going to church in the morning, feeding the poor children on their estates in the afternoon, and acquiring indigestion and nightmare by an unlimited supply of roast turkey, plum pudding and snapdragon[55] in the evening. In the country of the Cid the inhabitant amuses himself in a very different manner, viz., with cock-fighting, followed by a *corrida* of bulls, and then a light dinner and the present of a box at the opera to his wife and children as dessert. Thus Christmas-day passed at Madrid to the great gratification of all except the cocks and bulls, innocent accessories to the amusement of the pleasure-finding in blood-shedding *Madrileños*. But I dare say your readers will by this time have had enough of the bull rings with its concomitant horrors, and may like to know a little of what is going on here in the political world.

Who is to be King? That is the question which is not only puzzling all the heads on the other side of the Pyrenees, but which has caused many a brain to throb and ache from San Sebastian to Cadiz, and from that representative of the monarchs, the Regent Serrano, to his antagonistic rival the Republican Castelar. Prim is still bent on his own solution to the enigma, viz., that of placing a puppet on the throne, and pulling the strings of government himself, and the young Duke of Genoa is the battle-cry of him and his party. They represent, however, but to an infinitesimal extent the feeling of the country

---

55 Snapdragon was burnt brandy. The name was also given to a game played at Christmas when raisins were taken from a bowl of burning brandy and eaten while still alight. (OED)

at large, and Tomasito, or Little Thomas, as the young duke is depreciatingly called, would be foolish in incurring the risk of possible murder and certain exile, which would stare him in the face if he accepted the unenviable task of making himself the nominal head of a Government ruled by Prim's brains and ambition. The Prince Alfonso has a great many allies amongst the old Conservative families, who, although opposed to the weak and vicious reign of Queen Isabella, would gladly hail a restoration in the person of the rightful heir. Prim and his sycophants, however, question this. They acknowledge that he is the eldest son of his mother, but hint that it is a wise child who knows his own father, thus seeking to throw the stain of illegitimacy on the poor boy. Montpensier is undoubtedly the only person capable of cutting the Gordian knot of Spain's pecuniary embarrassments; but Prim is averse to his candidature, as the duke is too well aware of the misappropriation of the public revenue which has been going on since the outbreak of the Revolution, in September, 1868. The *parvenu* general is absolutely detested by all classes, and a desire for the return of Caballero de Rodas, the officer commanding in Cuba, is openly expressed. He is a Montpensierist, and a friend of the resigned Minister of Marine, Admiral Topete, and has a large number of friends in the army, who would side with him, especially if he declared himself against Prim and for the duke. Thus matters stand at present. The Cortes is prorogued till the first week in January, and the gallant general at the head of affairs is giving a grand shooting party to 28 of his friends at Toledo. His salary as Minister is £1,200 annually. He certainly, as the Republicans observe, makes it go a great way, as he keeps open house all the year round, and entertains a regal state about him. All this time the poor and destitute in the unions are starving from the want of funds to supply them with the absolute necessities of life. The press is very free-spoken on the matter. I send you an extract from the *Gorda*, a satirical paper which has a large circulation, and which numbers amongst its collaborators men in the best society of Madrid. Here is what it says:– "We are ignorant what widow, what orphan, priest, sick person in the hospital, or pauper in the union will dare to die of hunger now that Prim has furnished his palace so regally. And this is as clear as the light of day. The empty purse of widows, orphans, priests, sick people, and paupers is what really has decorated the splendid palace of the general. Let us search the treasury; there we have not a centime. In the establishments of charity not a farthing. In the town halls not a halfpenny. The provincial deputations have not a *real*. Our commerce has not enough to pay what it owes. Industry has only its mother, which is necessity. Taxpayers have not enough to meet the dues, and yet in the department of the Minister of War there is sufficient for a magnificent hunting excursion to the mountains of Toledo. The public misery has challenged the Revolution of September. Prim has picked up the gauntlet. That everybody may see that he is a coward he insults wretchedness with his ostentation." I need not continue, as this will be quite sufficient to let your readers know what is spoken and printed. The *Epoca*, one of the principal papers, and which has been publishing the most interesting letters from its correspondent at Suez, this morning astonished the world by announcing in an amusing article that its correspondent has written all his letters which were simply derived from the fertility of his imagination and what he has read on the subject, without having left Madrid. Truly the Spaniards, like the Hebrew race, are a peculiar people.

FGB032
Madrid; 4 January 1870
Burnaby to Editor – *Vanity Fair*, 8 January 1870
Weeping, wailing, and gnashing of teeth are to be heard in all the barbers' shops in Madrid; and Rachel, the wife of the little Jewish hairdresser in the Puerta del Sol, is not to be comforted, for the great Prim has issued an edict that all officers, soldiers, and bandsmen who choose, like Absalom and Sampson of biblical tradition, to allow their hirsute honours, in the shape of whiskers and beard, to develop themselves, can do so with impunity. In consequence of this permission, faces like scrubbing-brushes, with bristles of every length and colour, are to be met with in the Spanish army; and a dirty and slovenly look has taken the place of the smart, clean-looking faces I used to see in the ranks last year. Those officers and men who have taken advantage of this order are distinguished by the name of Primistas; and the *Madrileños* say that the General's adherents and partisans can be easily distinguished from the numerous other factions into which public opinion is split up by their uncleanly, scrubby, and unsoldierlike appearance.

The President's message on the Cuban question has not been received with much satisfaction. It begins by saying that the United States is the first nation in the world, and that for the present its Government will not interfere in Cuba; but it leaves an *arrière pensée* that public opinion may be too strong for the Ministry, and that ultimately they may be forced to recognise the insurgents. The proud Spaniards do not like the idea of the Americans swaggering about being the first nation in the world, and an old deputy in the Cortes ironically remarked to me, that it is a pity Troppmann[56] did not succeed in escaping to America, as a lad of his principles would have had a seat in Congress side by side with Morrissy, the prize-fighter,[57] in five years, and would have been President in ten. Affairs in Cuba do not appear to be progressing favourably. The rebels are committing great devastations, by burning down the plantations

---

56 Jean-Baptiste Troppmann (1848-1870) was a French serial killer, guillotined outside Paris's La Roquette prison.
57 John Morrissey (1831-1878), also known as Old Smoke, was an Irish bare-knuckle boxer and a gang member in New York in the 1850s, who later became a Democratic State Senator and US Congressman.

of the landowners friendly to the Government, and the yellow fever is making fearful havoc with the soldiery. Spain has already sent 35,000 of the flower of her young men to find a grave on those pestilential shores, and I hear that Caballero de Rodas is asking for more reinforcements. He will get them, as on this point the Spaniards are piqued in their self-pride; and with the loss of Cuba they would not like to hear the taunt of the world, "*Sic transit gloria Hispania*"[58].

But let me leave the tobacco-growing island, and, like the lame devil, Asmodeus, lift off the roofs of some of the houses in Madrid, and then fly with your readers to the pinnacle of the highest steeple in the capital, and from that elevated position peer into what is passing in society. Whither shall we look first? Ah, there is the palace, three years ago inhabited by a gay and festive Court; now, alas, triste and sombre. In one part of the building a faint attempt at illumination appears, like a spark of its past glory faintly attempting to struggle into flame. It comes from the apartments formerly allotted to the Duke of Montpensier, and now tenanted by the Regent and his wife, the Duchess de la Torre; and as it is Thursday, on which night they hold receptions, the sounds of music and dancing reach our ears. Innumerable male forms fill the salons; but what a dearth of the fair sex! In all, there are not more than fifteen or twenty, and these, if not the wives of ambassadors and ministers, are the dames and daughters of the revolutionists of the period, and of recently-appointed generals. Little beauty decorates the ball-room, save in one person, viz., that of the fair hostess, who is certainly the most distinguished looking woman in the Peninsula. If loveliness and unaffected kindness made a Queen, the Duchess de la Torre would have long ago held that position; and if it were not for the crafty old Minister of War, she might be so now, instead of the wife of a Regent; but as people say here, at the same time shrugging their shoulders, *quien sabe* what may occur? More impossible things have happened. It is now one o'clock, and everybody is leaving the Regencia, after a light supper of ices, bonbons, sweetmeats, sandwiches, and hot punch. So let me raise the roof of the Casino in the Carrera de San Geronimo, and we shall there see the men who have just left the palace hard at work over the mysteries of *trente et quarante*. Roulette has been stopped, because the Ministers say that it is a nasty, low, gambling game; but its elder brother, *rouge et noir*, is allowed to be carried on with impunity, and to any extent. There are social distinctions and laws about losing one's money in Spain as well as in England; for although a ringman can make a book at Tattersall's and in the betting-ring, woe to him if he establishes a pot-house[59] and keeps a list. But we are too far off to hear the conversation; let us fly a little nearer. "Well", observes a deputy in the club

---

58 Thus passes the glory of Spain.
59 A small tavern.

to his friend, "so the people at Barcelona pelted Ruiz Zorilla, the Minister of Grace and Justice, and threw a bottle of vitriol at him. Prim has telegraphed for his return to Madrid. We shall have a change in the Ministry." "Serves him quite right", says the other; "what business has he to try and introduce the civil marriage law. Society is coming to a pretty pass; we shall soon be like the dogs in the streets. I never used to attend mass before the *Libertad de Cultos* Act was passed; but now I make a point of going, to show people that I am not an Atheist, like the late Republican member, Señor Suñer de Capdevila." "Yes", continues his companion, "the man who wrote the pamphlet to prove that there is no God, and that the Holy Virgin and her Son never existed. We shall not be settled till the Frenchman comes to the throne; but Prim is so obstinate about the matter, and the Duke has made himself so many enemies by his pride and reserve. Well, we shall see!"

But, my dear Vanity, as it is now four in the morning, I shall get off to bed, and can only conclude this letter by telling you that a ministerial crisis is imminent, owing to the entire failure of the candidature of the Duke of Genoa, thus making one more stepping-stone for the owner of the palace at San Telmo, the thrifty Duke of Montpensier.

FGB033
Madrid; 10 January 1870
Burnaby to Editor – *Vanity Fair*, 15 January 1870

The crisis is at an end, and Prim has succeeded in forming a Ministry. The changes, however, from the former members are but few, and the *Progressist* faction still remains the predominant element in the Cabinet. The principal alterations are, first, Topete's accepting the part of Minister of the Marine, which your readers will remember he abandoned when his colleagues announced their determination to support the candidature of the Duke of Genoa, he being morally compromised to the Montpensier interest; and, secondly, Ruiz Zorilla's[60] giving place to Montero Rio, a man of much the same calibre and opinions as himself: so, on the whole, little has been done, and the poor old Spanish state coach will be tooled along the road to ruin by, to all intents and purposes, the same bad whips as before. Serrano is thoroughly impressed with the difficulties of the situation, and in a conversation with Prim last Wednesday, he said, "This state of things cannot last, but if it does I shall abandon the Regencia at the end of the month." Upon which the General observed, "Duke, if you resign your post, I give you my word of honour, as a *caballero de España*, that I, too, will give up the Ministry of War, as we have been together now far too long to be separated." That Prim said this I have no doubt, as my authority

---

60 Manuel Ruiz Zorrilla (1833-1895) was a Spanish politician, serving as prime minister of Spain for a little over ten weeks in the summer of 1871 and again for eight months in 1872/73.

is one that can be relied on; but that he would stand by his words if it came to the point is a very different question, and one which I should be sorry to answer in the affirmative. Six weeks ago the General solemnly assured Admiral Topete that if he quitted the control of the Marine, he, Prim, would also resign the appointment of Minister of War. It is one thing, however, to promise and another to perform, and the gallant officer is a beautiful example of the veracity of the proverb. In the meantime, new candidates for the throne are on the *tapis*: first, the Conde de Paris,[61] and, secondly, Prince Napoleon.[62] They are, however, both of them equally impossible, and have been suggested by the partisans of the Government, merely as a means of prolonging the present state of things, and to keep a little longer the purse of the nation under control. Poor king, I pity him, whoever he may be, who finally accepts the onerous task of ruling the Peninsula, for his predecessors will have eaten up all the lean and fat of the country, and will have only abandoned the Government to him through an inability to swallow the bone – well gnawed, however, they will assuredly leave it.

The theatres have been crowded during the *Pascua*, and one of the minor administrations has netted a considerable sum by placing on the stage the birth of our Saviour, the visit of the Kings from the East with their presents, and finally, as a sensation act, an exciting fight between one of the shepherds and the Old Gentleman. The latter vanquishes the pastor and carries him down to the land of gridirons, upon which the happy thought strikes the victim of mentioning the Virgin's name, when he is instantly released, and transported back to his companions, who, watching their flocks by night, have just heard of the promised Messiah.

The late Republican member, Señor Suñer de Capdevila, has brought out a work called "God". It is an absolute denial of every attribute which in all Christian nations is conceded to the divinity, and such is the state of religious feeling in Spain that, badly written and argued as the pamphlet is, 70,000 copies have already been sold. The priests have published several treatises in answer, all of which only serve to advertise Suñer's work which thus gains additional publicity. To give your readers an idea of its contents, I need only quote the last few sentences: "Man cannot be uppermost in the scale if God is not at the lower end of the balance. Man cannot be man if God exists as God. Man is science – God is ignorance. Man is truth – God is error."

---

61 Louis Philippe Albert d'Orléans (1838-1894) was the grandson of Louis Philippe I, King of France. He was a claimant to the French throne from 1848 until his death.
62 Napoléon, Prince Imperial (1856-1879), was the only child of Emperor Napoleon III of France. To the embarrassment of the Government, he was killed while serving with the British Army in the Zulu campaign.

FGB034
Madrid; 17 January 1870
Burnaby to Editor – *Vanity Fair*, **22 January 1870**

I have shown your readers a little of the high life above stairs, and now I purpose for the nonce to lift the curtain and for a short time to go behind the scenes; so let me accompany them to a rehearsal in the theatre. These generally take place in the morning, from ten to eleven. The stage, as in England, is in semi-darkness, and I have to feel the way in order not to break my nose against an artificial tree, or black an eye, and fracture a bone by falling into the infernal regions represented by an open trap-door. Two candle-ends enable the prompter to read the play, but make the darkness (to use a paradox) still more transparent to the spectators. Around the fire – or, as I ought to describe it, the charcoal brazier – stand a knot of actors and actresses, some enveloped in Russian furs, others clad and wrapped up to their mouths in the national cloak. All are shivering with the cold, and are anxiously awaiting the moment to commence the performance. They are making bets about the success of the piece – some prophesy a glorious triumph for what is to be a fearful failure; and others a general collapse, with the harmonious accompaniment of the hissing of the gods in the gallery, for a great success. Such is theatrical life, and nothing is so deceptive as the calculation of an actor, with the exception of the prognostications of an impresario.

Those actors and actresses who arrive in time grow impatient, and the poor stage-manager, frantic from agitation of mind and perspiration of body, has to leap about and tranquillise them, at the same time appeasing their ire by fining the absentees. These latter, if they are of the fair sex, generally pay for their delinquencies in bonbons, which are eaten with greediness by the sterner portion of humanity. Finally, amidst the yawns of some, the jests of others, and the general weariness of the whole troupe, the rehearsal begins. If it is the first time, the prompter does not sit in his accustomed place, but is honoured by a seat on the stage, with a table in front of him. The actors, with their hats on, read their parts aloud, generally contriving to beat the prompter by a good half-length at the end of each sentence. The actresses do the same, but amuse themselves as well by talking in the midst of the performance with their numerous male friends, who throng the side scenes. In fact, everything goes to the bad, and, to use a Spanish expression, marches to Mephistopheles; while the poor author, especially if he is new to his profession, tears his hair in dismay. Jealousy is not a stranger to the stage, and malice, hatred, and all uncharitableness are frequently engendered, owing to a performer thinking that the part which in his or her opinion ought to have been the allotted one has been improperly bestowed. Fernando and Lola, rabid with rage, declare that Alonso and Carmen, who have to play the principal characters, will damn the piece; they will destroy the whole effect. "We shall be hissed; all the papers will say that the acting has been detestable." "Yes, and we shall lose our reputation as performers; and God knows if we shall then be able to find managers who will engage us next season in Madrid. Let us go to the Director." "But who will go?" "Why, you, of course; you know he thinks you very pretty, and admires you." "On the contrary, I have always heard he was your particular friend." "Well, perhaps, it will be better to send Maria; he never says no to her." "What a capital idea; just the thing. Ah! there she is; let us ask her." By this slight outline your readers will see that there is not much difference behind the scenes between a Spanish and an English theatre. The same egotistic ideas and the same predominant passions prevail in the one as in the other; and to be the friend of the manager is to be an idol to whom all the company bear incense and fall down and worship.

But, enough of the stage, which is but the imitation of real life, as it is time to think of the sterner realities of existence. After a storm comes a calm, but between the two generally exists an interregnum, which is being filled up at the present moment by an animated debate in the Cortes on the estimates for the current year. Señor Riul Comez, a Deputy, informed the Cortes that the gross amount of the country's annual income amounts to 10,000 millions of *reals*, and that the expenditure amounts to 2,700 millions, which makes the disbursements represent 27 per cent. of our entire assets. In France they are about 17 per cent., in Belgium 8½ per cent., and in England from 7 to 8 per cent. If next I make the calculation how much of this national income belongs on an average to each Spaniard, I find that the 10,000 millions of *reals* divided amongst the number of our population, as known by the census, leaves to each individual 600 and odd *reals* of income a year, or deducting taxes, 456; finally leaving a *real* and 17 *maravedis* daily (a little more than threepence of our money), for the subsistence of each person in the kingdom; and with this sum they have to clothe and feed themselves. With these facts, openly stated in the Spanish House of Parliament, there can be little wonder at the number of beggars that meet one's eye at every corner of the street all over the Peninsula.

FGB035
Madrid; 6 February 1870
Burnaby to Editor – *Vanity Fair*, **19 February 1870**
"Murder will out" is a saying we have in England though that it is not a truism the amount of undiscovered assassins clearly shows. In Spain, the proportion of undetected perpetrators of crimes of this nature is enormous; in fact, hardly seven per cent., according to statistical dates [sic], ever being brought to justice. Lately, however, we have been – to use a Yankee expression – fetched right up at Seville by the discovery of a notorious murderer under very singular circumstances. Some three years ago, a horrible crime was committed at Pamplona. A father, mother, and their three children were attacked at night by

some *banditti*, and all killed, with the exception of the eldest son, a boy of fifteen, who, badly wounded and stunned, was believed by the robbers to be dead. The lad, however, when he came to himself, had every feature of the horrible scene just witnessed impressed on his memory, and particularly the appearance of the chief of the band, who was marked on the cheek by a large scar, the result of a former encounter. In Spain, the police are of little use; in fact, it would be strange if they were, as, badly paid, and their wretched stipends constantly for weeks in arrear, they are many of them in league with the criminals, who bribe their connivance at a higher rate than the Government recompenses their services; and the latter are bad payers, whilst with the former it is money down. It is not to be wondered, then, that, at the end of a year, the assassins were still at large; and the poor boy, seeing that all attempts to bring them to justice through the aid of the police were unavailing, determined – true to the southern blood that thirsted in his veins for vengeance – to go himself on their track, and, in his own person, proclaim the vendetta against the murderers of his mother. The first intelligence he received was that the captain of the band had gone to the United States, and for one year he silently tracked his prey through all the cities of the Union. The next thing he heard was that the ruffian had sailed to Belgium; but six months' search in that kingdom proved equally fruitless; and having lost all traces of the murderer, he thought it possible he might have returned to Spain; so, obtaining an order from the Government to visit all the prisons in the Peninsula, he made up his mind to search each one in succession, in the faint hope of meeting with some fresh clue to the assassin. A few days ago he arrived here, and on entering the gaol the first person he recognised was the murderer. The scene that ensued, I am told, passes all description; for the young man threw himself on the wretch, who in vain endeavoured to hide himself behind the other prisoners, and crying out, "My three years have not been wasted", nearly succeeded in strangling him. The warders, however, interfered when the fellow was at the last gasp, and by their united endeavours the avenger was removed from his victim. But, as everybody asks, when will the culprit be tried? In this country justice, as the Spaniards say, marches very slowly; and a prisoner who has got money can generally get off. Years may elapse till the scoundrel is condemned; and when his sentence is carried into effect, so much time will have passed since the crime that people will be found to pity the murderer and petition the Government for a reprieve. But if their efforts are fruitless, and the law takes its course, what happens? The condemned man is made a martyr of. The last two days before his execution, he is put in the *Capilla* (chapel) and is allowed to have what he likes. The Brothers of *La Caridad* (charity) – a religious society, recruited from amongst young men of the best families – stand in the streets and go from house to house collecting money for him. Finally the awful moment arrives. The brothers all bring the donations to the *Capilla*; some is reserved for masses for his soul, and the criminal makes his will and leaves the rest – often a very considerable amount – to his family or friends. Finally, escorted by all the Brothers of *La Caridad*, the procession sets out to the principal square in the town, filled with a yelling throng of the same nature that used to disgrace our own streets when public executions took place. For there are two sights which always draw large audiences – the one the bull ring and the other the *garotte*. Mothers take their children and watch the condemned man as he is placed by the executioner in a low chair at the back of which stands a post with an iron collar, which by means of a rapidly revolving screw, can be made to contract from the size of the circumference of a man's neck to barely an inch in diameter. This is adjusted to the criminal, the priest reads a prayer, and when he comes to the words "*El Unico Hijo*" – the Only Son – the executioner turns the handle, the neck is at once broken, and instantaneous death ensues. Formerly, when the fatal words were uttered, it was the custom of the Andalusian mothers to soundly box their children's ears, with the view of impressing the scene on their memory, and, with an infantine yell of pain and the prolonged hum of a great multitude, the criminal was ushered into eternity.

In politics I have not got much to tell you. Montpensier is still as unpopular as ever amongst the *Sevillaños*; in fact, it is rather strange, that in the place where he is best known he should be least liked. Last Sunday the Infanta, his wife, and daughters walked in the Paseo, and not a hat was taken off when they passed by. Barcelona is the Duke's stronghold, and the industrious Catalonians will hail with delight the day he comes to the throne, but Andalusia is different; and the Duke has made himself very unpopular by still addressing people in the second person singular. The Republicans are furious at this, and say, "As if he is a bit better than we are", and, "after all, he is nothing but a French *gallo*", or cock (a depreciatory term used when talking of Frenchmen, on account of their pronunciation, which rather resembles the crowing of that bird). You will have seen long ere this that at Oviedo the Duke lost the election. It was the best thing that could happen to him. Most of the Unionists were very annoyed at his standing, for in the event of his success, and his taking a seat in the Cortes as deputy, he could have been but a listener to the debate, as his strong French accent would have exposed him to the ridicule of the Republicans, and he would have been made a subject for derision if he had attempted to open his mouth. The only thing the Duke has to do is to bide his time, and when the lovers of order and economy are on the threshold of ruin, he will be elected, as the only means of saving society from universal bankruptcy.

The Cortes has been converted into a bear-garden this week. First, by a Señor Figueras openly accusing a Colonel Luque of having been the assassin of a Republican deputy, who headed the insurrection in Cadiz. General Prim, amidst a great hubbub, asked the speaker to retract his words, saying that the colonel was one of the bravest and best officers in the army. Figueras refused, whereupon the general ordered the expression referring to Luque to be written down; upon which the deputy informed him that, according to an article in the Constitution, no words of a member can be taken in writing inside the House against his consent, but that he was ready to answer for what he had said both inside and outside the Cortes. Colonel Luque has gone to Madrid, so probably there will be a duel to-morrow – a most satisfactory way of settling the knotty point of whether the deputy was murdered or not. And when this feat of arms is over the belligerents will shake hands, and say they are satisfied. Such is life!

The *prempuestos*, or estimates for the Church, have been the subject of a most interesting debate. The clergy are at the present moment receiving a revenue of £1,700,000, and the Republicans are up in arms for suppressing it altogether. Señor Barcia electrified the Catholic portion of the house by saying the defenders of this gross abuse defend it as a just substitute for tithes and first fruits, but they do not reflect that these were Levitical offerings, and that the Hebrew is not the Christian law. "If in the entity of Christ had entered that of Moses, if in the old religion had entered hope what would have become of Christ, and what would have become of the redemption? This, señores, could not be; the testament of another cannot enter mine, since from their union nought but a monstrosity would result. On this account Moses did not enter into Jesus. Moses, who was the old man remained behind, and Jesus, who was the new, marched in front. A great noise was heard over the whole earth, and this signified that the old world had ceded its post to the new, and that slavery was giving place to liberty." Castelar followed him up by a magnificent speech, which would occupy at least five columns of the *Times*, and which was a thunderbolt of eloquence. He was cheered repeatedly from all sides of the house, and his discourse has done more to relieve Spain from this unjust tax than, if possible, the abuses to which it gave rise.

FGB036
Seville; 27 February 1870
Burnaby to Editor – *Vanity Fair*, **5 March 1870**
The revolution seems not to have confined itself to the annihilation of social order, but to have communicated its decomposing influences to the clerk of the weather works, as never in the memory of the oldest Sevillians has this Eden of Andalusia known such a continuous downfall of the elements. Seville does nothing but shed tears for her Government, for her poor dying of starvation, and for fear of her streets being left in total darkness during the night, for that is what we are threatened with by our kind and paternal lawgivers at Madrid. To explain this I should tell your readers that, previous to the expulsion of Queen Isabella in 1868, octroi duties[63] or taxes on edibles and

---

63   Local taxes collected on various articles brought into a district for consumption.

other substances existed in all the towns of the Peninsula. A certain proportion of this sum was deducted by the provincial authorities for the necessities of the towns, and the surplus was remitted to Madrid to add its quota towards the national revenues. But when the gallant savers of their country from the despotism of a woman and from the misappropriation of its finances made their triumphant entry into the capital, by way of offering incense to the gods in the gallery, the impresarios – Prim, Serrano, Figuerola, and Co. – took off the price of admission to that part of their theatre, and told the clamorous multitude that they should buy their bread and butter without having any octroi to pay. Upon this there was great cheering and clapping of hands by all the populations. The extravagant Government of poor Isabella was vituperated, and the economical *régime* of friend Prim and Co. lauded to the skies. At the same time all the taxes collected were ordered to be sent to Madrid, and the provincial towns were desired to cease making any deduction for their own expenses. But as it was necessary to introduce some measure to counterbalance the loss sustained by the abolition of the above-mentioned duty to the revenues a bill was passed to establish a sort of poll tax on all individuals who, not being absolute beggars, possessed the felicity of being able to call themselves Spaniards; and each of the corporations were ordered forthwith to execute this mandate, to forward the amount so levied to the capital, when they should receive the sum necessary for the requisites of their different towns and villages. But this measure proved so unpopular that in the centre of Government, in Madrid itself, it was found impossible to carry it into effect; the *Madrileños* refused to pay, and the authorities felt that they lacked the prestige, power, and *savoir faire* sufficient to put it in force. The same thing resulted in all the large towns; and, from their not having received any remittances from the exchequer towards their expenses, universal bankruptcy stared them in the face. *Mais revenons a nos moutons*, or rather to the gas, for that is the question which most vividly affects the peaceable part of this community. 125 people were admitted into the hospitals in Seville in the month of November last from stabs and wounds received at night, and 600 thieves were released from the prisons last year through the inability of the Government to pay for their keep – what then will be the proportion of assassinations if we are left in utter darkness? This is a problem which requires a Babbage's[64] calculating machine to solve, and I shall leave it to the profoundly learned diviners of your Machiavelically-arranged acrostics to fathom. The reason why we are to have our gas supply cut off is as follows: The corporation owes the company 35,000 dollars, and the latter refuses to furnish any more gas until they are paid, giving the authorities the term of ten days to make up their mind. The Alcaldes tore their hair in

---

64 Charles Babbage, FRS (1791-1871), an English mathematician, philosopher, inventor and mechanical engineer who originated the concept of a programmable computer.

dismay, and telegraphed to Madrid. The Government replied that if they would forward the amount of the poll tax they should at once receive the money. The poor Alcaldes asked if papa in the capital, with all his soldiers, can't make his children pay and keep them in order, how he can expect his delegates in the provinces to be more successfully than himself. But things at last have become so serious that the Government have been compelled to have recourse to the old system of duty on some articles of consumption. This is to be fixed by the towns themselves, and at the present moment all the big-wigs in Seville are busily engaged in endeavouring to discover what will be the least unpopular articles to tax to enable them to meet their liabilities and the expenses for the future. The present state of things is becoming more unbearable every day, and the landowners of Andalusia, who were among the first to abet the revolution, are now bitterly cursing its consequences and their own folly. "What would not we give to have Isabella back once more", said an old marquis to me in the club last night, and one who had been first to join the movement in September. "She was only *purgatorio*, but we are now in *el inferno*." It was a true remark; and as yet Spain is not at the bottom of her misery, for, as the Italian bard sang, "Hell is divided into seven stratas", and that last and most terrible of all is the absolute decadence of all hope, and this is fast seizing the minds of most of the well-to-do landowners, who are selling their properties at any sacrifice in order to place their persons and what is left to them in security across the border.

The management of the opera-house here, not satisfied with the representation of the "Passion", which I informed your readers of last year, has announced a new performance for the *Cuaresma* (Lent), which is entitled, "The Man God". I send you an extract from a prospectus which was handed me in the theatre last evening: – "Principal scenes: The House in Bethany. The Virgin Mary's House. The Abode of the Departed Spirits. Purgatory. The Padre Eterno. The Olive Grove. Ascension of Jesus, and the Descent of the Angel. A View of Cedron, and the Apparition of the Great Serpent. Mount Calvary. Earthquake, and the Awakening of the Dead. The Resurrection and the Trinity. Music performed: Chorus of Angels. Chorus of Patriarchs in the place of Departed Spirits. Chorus of Demons taking Judas to the Flames awaiting him in Hell. Chorus of Lamentations during the Scourging. The management hope that the well-educated and discriminating public in Seville will appreciate the immense sacrifice it has made to put this performance worthily on the stage and that the theatre will be filled during the *Cuaresma*; for by this means the spectators will give a proof of their love to the Christian religion, and a solemn denial to the infamous detractors of our dear and highly-civilised country."

FGB037
Seville; 14 March 1870
Burnaby to Editor – *Vanity Fair*, 26 March 1870

Spain's religious and social observances have reaped the fruits of the revolution equally with her finances, for never has there been a country where so many Biblical representations have seen the light, not only in the lower scale of the social ladder, but even in the best society of Madrid. The *Epoca* informs me in its fashionable intelligence that the Señora Carvajal has given "St. Peter in his Prison", amongst other *tableaux vivants*, to a crowded and fashionable audience, and that her daughter represented the angel with perfect propriety; that Señor Baena was St. Peter, and two other gentlemen the soldiers. When a taste for religion on the stage pervades the crust of the pie, it is not to be wondered if the fruit partakes of the savour, and that we are now having the extraordinary drama of "The Man-God" in the principal theatre of Seville. I will endeavour to give your readers an account of this theological performance.

The curtain draws up to the grand music of the "Stabat Mater",[65] and discloses a lake with mountains in the distance; a chorus of Jewish girls come on, and the twelve disciples, two-and-two, including Judas ornamented by a large red beard, and St. Peter in the rear. Jesus follows them surrounded by little children, whom he blesses. Mary Magdalene then appears in a *demi-monde* costume, and asks for forgiveness, which is accorded her. Judas is very angry at this, and there is a dispute between him and Peter; after which the penitent makes a speech, bidding farewell to her past life. The scene then changes to a bridge near Jerusalem, with an avenue of olive-trees, on whose branches several little Jewish boys are balancing themselves; some children strew palm branches on the stage; after which Peter and John lead in a donkey with Jesus on its back. We are now introduced to two Jewish priests, who complain of the moneylenders being turned out of the temple, and agree that Christ must be killed; the Virgin Mary then appears with a halo of light thrown on her face, kneels down and thanks God that the son of her entrails is to save the world. A transformation scene, however, displays to her three angels, one carrying a cross, and the other two nails and a hammer; they say that her son must first be crucified; she prays to God for pity, and Mary Magdalene tries to console her, but to no effect. Jesus then shows her a vision of purgatory, in which the departed spirits and the great serpent are seen wriggling about in the flames, and tells her that these souls through him will be saved from their torments. Judas looks very frightened when he sees the fire, shakes his head pensively, and leaves the stage. The ceremony of washing the disciples' feet is next gone through, and Jesus kisses all the disciples with the exception of Judas, who

---

65 *Stabat Mater Dolorosa* (The sorrowful mother stood), the first line from a thirteenth century catholic hymn to the Virgin Mary.

turns away, to the astonishment of the eleven. They then have supper, a chorus of angels is heard in the distance, and incense is burnt in the background; a curtain is drawn up and shows the *Padre Eternel* with one foot on a globe, representing the earth. Judas now goes to two priests, and offers to sell his master; they give him thirty pieces of silver, each of which he bites, and rings on the ground, to see if it is genuine, as he says there is a great deal of bad money about. One of the priests remarks that Jesus may really be the Son of God, as he has saved some people from the dead, but the other answers that, man or God, he must die, or there will be a revolution. Christ is then taken prisoner in the olive grove, and Judas tears his hair, and runs to the High Priest, throws the money in his face, and says that the beasts of the field and birds of the air shun his presence and avoid him. He then proceeds to a field, where he hangs himself on a tree; but the earth opens and swallows him up, thunder is heard, flames issue from the opening in the floor, and numerous demons dance a war-dance of triumph on the stage. There is great applause from all parts of the house, at the hanging and swallowing up, which are invariably encored.

Pilate's Hall is the next scene, with three Roman lictors and a mounted guard before the door. Pilate reads a letter from his wife, saying that she has had a dream to the effect that the Jews are going to bring before him a prisoner who is really the Son of God. He is very perplexed what to do; but the Jews howl and yell, so he orders the scourging to be inflicted. Jesus is instantly stripped of all save a flesh-coloured tight-fitting jersey, the executioners belabour him with their rods, and the blood runs down on the stage. He faints, and the Virgin Mary offers up a prayer. A procession is then formed of a Roman band playing a funeral march, some guards two lictors, and a crier, who reads out the sentence, followed by the executioner carrying a ladder, and two others with nails and hammers, which they jingle on the stage, the two thieves and Jesus staggering under the cross. The acting is really good; and as the actor stumbles and gives way beneath his burden all the female part of the audience cry and sob, and the man next me observes, "*Caramba*, it is very sensational, and nearly as good as 'the bulls'". The lights are now subdued, and we come to a large hall with the two thieves fastened up on crosses, and Jesus in the background being nailed to the wood. He is raised up and placed between them. Presently he asks for water, and one of the executioners tells him to drink blood, or wait for water till he arrives in heaven. The thieves make horrible faces and contortions. Jesus dies, and a blind man being led in with a lance in his hand, is told to thrust, and wounds him in the side. Blood pours down, but another miracle is performed, and the blind man receives his sight. He kneels down, and says that they have killed the Son of God. A tremendous noise is heard, part of the Temple in the distance falls down, and men dressed as corpses and skeletons run about the stage. A halo of light appears on Jesus and the pardoned thief's face, and the audience clap enthusiastically.

The next scene is the lowering and burial, with the guard of Roman soldiers around the tomb. The trumpets in the citadel sound the *reveille*, and one of the soldiers observes that it is the morning of the third day, and their watch is at an end. A tremendous thundering, however, is heard, the earth shakes, the soldiers pray to Jove, the tomb opens, and the actor is drawn up by the means of wires, brandishing a flag in one hand, and a cross in the other. The women in the theatre put up their pocket-handkerchiefs, and begin to console themselves with bonbons, and the men read the *Correspondencia* during the *entr'acte* which ensues. We then see the Roman soldiers with the priests trying to tempt them to say that Christ has been stolen; they refuse, however, saying that "Romans are not to be bought by Jews." The next act is the garden where Jesus makes himself known to some of the apostles, and afterwards to Thomas, who insists in placing his fingers in the print of the nails. And the performance is finally brought to an end by a scene, representing Heaven, with the Trinity, Abraham, Moses (with the Ten Commandments in his hand) and all the angels. Blue lights are burnt, the orchestra play a grand triumphal march, and the intelligent Sevillian public leaves the theatre, criticising the death-scene, betting about the weight of the cross, and saying Judas's part ought to have been played by Peter, because the actor who represents that *rôle* squints, and has, according to popular opinion, a more Judas-like expression than his companion.

FGB038
Seville; 3 April 1870
Burnaby to Editor – *Morning Post***, 11 April 1870**
The official gazette has published General Prim's plan for supplying the army with recruits, and which, accepted by the Cortes, has become law to the nation. As at the present moment the military systems of foreign countries are somewhat occupying the public attention in England, it may interest your readers to know the changes that have taken place in the organisation of the Spanish army. Up to the present date each province, with the exception of Navarre and the Vasongadas, which, by an ancient law, are exempt from the blood tax, has had to furnish a *quinta*, or proportion, of young men to meet the requirements of the service. This quota was fixed according to the number of inhabitants, and on an appointed day all the youths of 18 years had to draw lots for who was to win the undesirable prize of serving their country. Those who were fortunate enough to obtain a number higher than the total demanded for the *quinta* were freed from the conscription; their less-favoured-by-fortune companions could only redeem themselves by paying £80 to the government, or by procuring a substitute. The length of service was eight years, of which four were passed in the regular army and four in the reserve; that is to say, at the expiration of the first period a man could return to his family. He received no pay, but had to be prepared at any moment to join his regiment if required.

The *quinta* signifies a fifth part, but it has been rarely found necessary to enrol so many recruits. The name, however, has been retained, and if there is a word which is more odious to a Spanish Republican than Montpensier, it is that of *quinta*. Spain found herself, after the revolution of 1868, split up into as many factions as provinces, and the cry of the Republicans was, "*Abajo los Borbones; Abajo las Quintas.*" ("Down with the Bourbons. Down with the *quintas*.") At the outset the provisional Government, to tranquilise them, intimated through Rivero that there would be liberty for all, and he concluded his speech to the mob, after throwing the Queen's picture from the window of the town hall, with "*Viva la igualdad.*" ("Long live equality") It can be imagined, then, the fury of this party on discovering that Prim, instead of abolishing forced military service, as they had hoped, has taken the term *igualdad* in its widest sense, as henceforth every able-bodied Spaniard of 20 years, with the exception of the natives of the privileged provinces, must serve his country either actively or in the reserve. There are naturally some limits to this law, and ecclesiastics, and sons who support their aged parents, are not included; but, with slight modifications, it strikes home to everyone. For the future the Cortes will annually vote the contingent necessary for the active army. Rich and poor will draw lots, and those on whom the fate falls, if unable to pay the fine, must serve for four years, at the end of which time they may return to their homes and be for two years in the first reserve; at the expiration of this period they are entirely free. The second reserve is composed of the remainder of the young men. These can marry, and are, to most intents and purposes, civilians; but, should the nation require their services, they can instantly be transferred to the first reserve, and from thence fill up the vacancies in the army. The Carlists are profiting by this Republican excitement; their emissaries are busily engaged fomenting the ill feeling, and it is the general opinion that the slightest attempt on the part of any town to resist the application of the new military law will be the signal of a fresh Carlist rising. This apprehension paralyses industry; all those who can afford it leave the country, and thus the money which should stimulate trade is spent in foreign lands. The landed proprietors complain bitterly of the way in which they are taxed, having to contribute 25 per cent. of their rents, and, as the latter principally depend upon the produce of the olive groves, which some years return a large interest, and others are a dead loss, the owners, notwithstanding having to pay the Government collectors to the day, bankruptcy is the rock on which, sooner or later, all must founder. On this account any movement against the authorities, no matter under what banner, will call forth many new adherents, for, as they say themselves, civil war is dreadful; but delay is absolute ruin, and each day seeing their properties swallowed up to be invested in foreign securities for the benefit of the triumvirate in Madrid, is not calculated to calm the political passions which are at fever heat in all parts of the Peninsula. In spite, however, of these apprehensions of disturbances, Seville is becoming more and more crowded by people, who arrive from all parts to witness the processions in the Holy Week. Excursion trains are running at ridiculously low rates, to enable the country people to satisfy their cravings for images, shrines, virgins, and bull-fights. Amongst the few English visitors are the Marquis and Marchioness of Blandford and the Marquis and Marchioness of Ely, who, attracted by the loveliness of the weather and the many attractions which induced Byron to call the fair capital of Andalusia the garden of Spain, are residing in the *Fonda de Londres*, the only really good hotel in the place. Our Minister, Mr. Layard,[66] is winning golden opinions in Madrid, and he is immensely popular with all classes. I send you an extract from the columns of the *Epocha*, which will enable your readers to see how much his appointment has been appreciated by the *Madrileños*. It says that "Mr. and Mrs. Layard, in spite of their short residence amongst us, have acquired the sympathies of all by their frankness, tact, and amiability. Mr. Layard is an artist and a scholar, he knows our literature as well as that of his own country, and he is a great admirer of our ancient and contemporary poets. It seems that it is destined for him to be like Lord Howden, who familiarised himself to such an extent with our society and customs that at the end of a few years he thought himself, and was believed by all, to be a Spaniard."

FGB039
Seville; 9 April 1870
Burnaby to Editor – *Vanity Fair*, **16 April 1870**
All the world and his wife have arrived at Seville. Apartments are not to be had for love or money; prices have quadrupled, and the landlords have lost their bilious, woe-begotten look, caused by the scarcity of foreigners this winter who, fearing garlic, mosquitoes, insects which can be described in four letters, and Republicans, have taken their wives and their purses to see the sun in other climes. It is needless to tell you, and the 5000 intelligent readers who have visited the South of Spain, my dear Vanity, that the first three plagues only exist in the imagination of Alexandre Dumas; but the remaining million who weekly partake of the fruit of the knowledge of good and evil in your columns are in ignorance of the comforts which can be met with in the hotels of this capital, which are as exempt from the torture to one's nose and the little torments of one's body, as any in our own country. The fourth-mentioned plague, however, the political bugbear, is in full force, and that he can make himself very disagreeable if he likes was palpably displayed to us last evening. I must first inform you that the Government has lately passed a law making every able-bodied Spaniard of twenty years of age a soldier. Strange to say, the

---

66 Sir Austen Henry Layard (1817-1894) was a British traveller, archaeologist, politician and diplomat. He served as envoy extraordinary to Madrid from 1869 to 1877.

martial sons of the Peninsula do not bound into the air with delight at the sight of a red coat, or, rather, I should say a blue one, and the idea of 5½d. a day pay to find their rations, underclothing, tobacco, and washing does not enrapture them with military ardour. The Republicans are least of all impressed with the charms of this forced enlistment, as it is principally employed in driving them from the barricades, which from time to time they playfully construct, and their faces are perfectly rabid with rage at that patriotic and disinterested General, Don Juan Prim. An announcement was placarded upon the walls a few days ago that the lots for those who must serve in the active army would be drawn this morning. Infuriated groups of food-for-powder[67] collected themselves in the streets and squares. *Abajo las Quintas!* Down with the *Quintas* – or conscription – could be heard at every moment, and those accustomed to read the signs of the times on men's faces foretold a row. The telegraph then brought us the news of a rising at Barcelona on the same account, and that General Baldrich[68] had left Madrid to quell it. The excitement in Seville was increased to fever pitch by the wires' next communication, of desperate fighting in Gracia, in the immediate neighbourhood of the capital of Catalonia, and the Sevillian would-be apers of the United States swore a great oath to imitate their Barcelona brethren. Spaniards, like ourselves, have a proverb, which says, "Dogs that bark don't bite", and it has been beautifully exemplified on this occasion. Not, however, that affairs have passed off entirely peaceably, but after the talk and bragging that has been going on in the Republican clubs, we have been dreaming of nothing else but the entire extinction of the garrison, and the instant re-division of everybody's goods and chattels amongst the lovers of equality.

Last evening was the time appointed for the rising; but when, at eight o'clock, I strolled into the Plaza Nueva, the principal square, at one end of which is the Town Hall, where the lots for the *Quintas* are drawn, no signs of disturbance could be seen, save a few knots of men and boys talking rather more noisily than usual. "Only jabber", said my friend and companion, B___. "Come along, old man; they won't kick up a row tonight. Let us go back to the hotel." We had not been there, however, for more than half an hour when his courier informed us that the people were shouting in the square, and that the troops were firing at the mob. My dear Vanity, have you ever had a martial friend? If you have, and are, like myself, a highly nervous, sensitive individual, you can conjecture my feelings when B___, lighting a cigar as long as himself, said, "Come along, old fellow, it will be capital fun." "Capital fun, indeed", I thought, "making oneself an animated target!" but he dragged me away with him, and in a few minutes we found ourselves in the midst of a mob of some 500 ragamuffins, who were

67 Cannon fodder.
68 General Gabriel Baldrich, sometime Governor of Puerto Rico.

busily engaged in abusing and pelting six of the *Guardia Civil*, or gendarmes, who were in front of the Town Hall. Finally, however, these guardians of the peace lost their patience, and fired over the heads of their vituperators, who ignominiously ran away, leaving B___ and your correspondent alone in the Plaza. Luckily, however, the six sportsmen took pity on us, and we walked away, admonished by the buzzing of a few bullets rather nearer my hat than was pleasant that our room was more desirable than our company. It would have been fortunate if all had come off as scathless as ourselves, but the fates decreed otherwise; for a few minutes later, in the Calle de Sierpes, an adjacent street, where a company of infantry had been stationed, there were more stones thrown, a little boy shouted *"Muera Prim!"* and the captain commanding ordered his men to fire, which they instantly did. One person was killed and sixteen wounded, and tranquillity, as the Spanish newspapers tell us, from that moment has reigned in Seville. If the rioters had been shot, it would not have mattered; but, unfortunately, three of the victims were, like B___ and myself, only lookers-on, attracted by that weakness of the female sex, which I am sorry to say is not entirely confined to the ladies – curiosity. A few minutes after the soldiers had fired, a battery of artillery was posted in the square, and mounted soldiers patrolled the streets, which were quickly abandoned by all passengers.

Lady Charlotte Schreiber,[69] with her husband, has been staying here, and also the Earl of Strathmore, but they had left – alarmed by the rising in Barcelona – just before this little *émeute*[70] occurred. Amongst the other visitors are the Marquis and Marchioness of Blandford and the Marquis and Marchioness of Ely, who have the intention of remaining for the fair and races, which take place the week after next.[71]

FGB040
St. Petersburg; 1 December 1870
Burnaby to Editor – *Morning Post*, **8 December 1870**
The 1st of December has ushered in the ruthless winter with all its northern accompaniments of sleighing, skating, and other Russian diversions. The *izvozstichik*, or cabman, has awoke from the state of lethargy in which he has been immersed during the last six months, and, having unscrewed the wheels of his vehicle, which very much resembles a coffin without the lid, and placed it on runners, out-Herods Herod[72] in his endeavours to attract a passenger

---

69 Charlotte Schreiber (1812-1893) was the eldest child of the 9th Earl of Lindsay. On the death of her wealthy first husband she married Charles Schreiber, her son's tutor, and spent fifteen years travelling Europe and amassing an unparalleled collection of eighteenth century ceramics.
70 Disturbance, or rebellion.
71 The Marchioness of Ely (1821-1890), with whom Burnaby was on good terms, was a close friend of Queen Victoria.
72 *Hamlet*, act 3, scene 2.

by extolling the swiftness of his horse, the softness of the cushions, and the lowness of his fare, for in the capital of the Czar there is no regular fixed tariff, and the drivers, if an arrangement is not made with them beforehand, often astound the indignant foreigner by the exorbitance of their demands, which he is finally, after much wrangling, obliged to satisfy. But there is so much competition amongst these modern Jehus[73] that anyone knowing a little of the language is able to drive from street to square, and from one friend's house to another – for the distances are frequently very wide, as the city covers a vast expanse of ground – at a much less rate than in London or any other European capital. "How much to the Nevsky Prospect (or what may be called Les Boulevards Italiens[74] of St. Petersburg)?" I ask, when I leave my hotel. "Sixty kopecks", cries one eager *izvozstchik*. "Fifty", yells another. "I will take the *baryen* for 40", vociferates a third"; and the matter is finally ended by a howling applicant, who offers to gallop the whole distance for 25, the entire transaction taking much less time to enact than to describe on paper. But if 12 deg. below freezing point increase the amusement of some, they throw a gloom over the lovers of "*la chasse au renard*"; for although men will hunt here when the ground is as hard as a brick, once melting appears to injure the hardy little horses' hoofs, it is useless to think of Mr. Jorrock's sport of kings now, as the depth of snow puts the chase entirely out of the realms of possibility. I dare say I shall astonish some of my readers by writing of hunting at St. Petersburg; but the fact remains that there is pack of hounds hunted by a former whip in the county of Norfolk, which pursues alternately, or rather as Providence wills it, hares, foxes, and wolves, for all is fish that comes to the net. The country is a large, flat, boggy tract of ground; but there are no obstacles, and this absence of danger is not unpleasing to the Russians. These last, however, do not greatly patronise *le sport*, which is principally confined to the natives of our own isles. But if the loss of this, our national diversion, is a deprivation during the few hours of daylight, there is plenty to reanimate us at night; for the bewitching little Patti[75] – who, by the way, looks prettier than ever – is the idol before whom every worshipper of the muse falls down and does obeisance; and on the evenings when she sings it is next to impossible to obtain a stall. If *les Russes* inhabit an icy region this has not frozen their admiration of the diva, and the enthusiastic reception she invariably meets with must be seen to be imagined, for the most powerful in the art of word-painting would be utterly inadequate to the task of depicting it to his readers. The Marquis de Caux appears to be

---

73 2 Kings 9-10, a bloodthirsty king of Israel.
74 Le boulevard des Italiens is one of the four 'grands boulevards' running east to west in Paris, being named for the théâtre des Italiens, later the Opéra-Comique.
75 Adela Juana Maria Patti (1843-1919), wealthy Sicilian Italian soprano who married the Marquis de Caux, Equerry to Napoleon III, but left him in 1878 to live with the tenor, Ernesto Nicolini, whom she married in 1886 after obtaining a divorce.

a paragon of husbands, for I see him again here, as I have witnessed him in almost every capital in Europe, occupying a stall in the front row, and filled with conjugal adoration for his spouse, taking in her every movement through his extra powerful glasses. On the evenings when there is no opera we are enlivened by a performance of the lower extremities of humanity, or ballet, which, could they only witness it, would delight the eyes of the managers of the Alhambra, and would fill the sanctified elect of Exeter Hall[76] with sorrow. For 200 pairs of legs pirouetting in a thousand fantastic ways would be to some anything but an edifying spectacle, and, although we are told King David danced before the altar[77], we must presume that he did so in a decorous manner, and not with all the appetising little gesticulations of the ladies of the ballet. But everything goes down in Russia, and next in their own estimation to their noble selves and *la* Patti, I think I should have to place *la première danseuse*, a pretty little blonde, who performs some most astounding evolutions, and displays great ingenuity in placing her foot where certainly nature never intended it to go.

The Czar is still in his country palace, but he is expected shortly to gladden his loving subjects by his presence in the capital, for when he arrives the season will be duly opened by a court ball which inaugurates a succession of gaiety till Lent, and then all good Christians will have to fast for 40 days to make up for their previous sins, finally brought to a climax by over-eating and drinking during the Carnival. I must say that an occasional abstention from the fleshpots of Egypt seems to have its advantages, for foreigners do not appeal to the doctor half as often as English people, and an obligatory rest to the digestive organs appears to answer quite as well as the physician's prescriptions. But to leave Patti, the ballet, and indigestion, and let me turn to graver subjects. There is, for the nonce, quite a lull in our political excitement; connected with the Eastern question, and the only people who, apparently, are not satisfied with the idea of a conference are the followers of Mahomet. For the better educated Turks in St. Petersburg are not at all pleased by the turn that affairs have taken, and more especially so far as England is concerned. "Heaven defend us from our friends" is their cry, and the true believers shake their heads in a meaning way. For they say we are sure to come the worst off, we always have done so hitherto, and not owing to the devices of our foes so much as to the agency of our allies. "Ah! it is all very well for England to call herself our friend; we have received more abuse during the last week from the English press than from the most Sultan-detesting Russian newspaper." It is universally declared here that Gortschakoff has virtually carried his point, and that John Bull, after

---

76 Exeter Hall, on the north side of the Strand, was used for holding religious and philanthropic meetings, including those of the Protestant Reformation Society and the Protestant Association; it was demolished in 1907.
77 2 Samuel 6-14.

his usual roaring, will have to eat, metaphorically speaking, humble pie. This conference, they urge, is only a form, and it is stated that the Czar signed the order for the contractors to commence building the Black Sea fleet the very day following the surrender at Sedan, and not after Metz, as was given out by some of the London journals. Public report announces that eight ironclads are fast being constructed at Nicolaev, and numerous gun boats at Kertch. But at the same time I know· for a fact that the Emperor of Russia has quite recently professed the most amicable sentiments to the Turkish Ambassador in respect to the Porte, and that he gave him his word of honour that he had not the slightest desire or even inclination that the friendly relations between the two countries should ever be interrupted. Indeed, if he had any such intentions, Russia still requires considerable time to complete her military disposition. It is true that the reserves are fast being mustered, but these troops are not yet supplied with breech-loaders, and have not been taught how to handle them. Abuse is freely lavished on Austria by the various periodicals, and she is much more disliked than England. Most of the Russians that I have conversed with greatly sympathise with the French, and the psalm-singing King of Prussia does not occupy the same place in their affections as he does in the Czar's, his nephew. The heir to the throne is very anti-Prussian, and does not take the pains to conceal his antipathy to the German nation. So, though a war with Prussia is now next to impossible, when a fresh Emperor dons the purple it would be not only probable but almost a matter of certainty. When it does take place the Russians must be better prepared than they are at present, for in these days of railways a campaign commenced by the Prussians in April would, with the opposition that is now at the disposal of the Czar, not unlikely terminate by October, and leave the invading force time to return to their country after having destroyed both St. Petersburg and Moscow.

I must conclude this letter by telling you that Todleben, the celebrated engineer general, has given it as his opinion that it will be useless for the Prussians to attempt reducing Paris by a bombardment until they can open fire with at least 500 guns of superior calibre to those mounted by the besieged garrison, and those abundantly supplied with ammunition.

FGB041
St. Petersburg; 3 December 1870
Burnaby to Editor – *Morning Post*, **8 December 1870**
At the present moment 209,259 soldiers in the Russian forces are supplied with Carl breechloaders, the rest of the troops being armed with muzzle-loaders. But by the 1st of January, 1871, 497,695 of the old-fashioned weapons will have been converted into breech-loaders on the Krenk system, and 100,000 new rifles will be also in readiness; thus bringing the number up to 647,695;

which with the quantity already issued will amount in all to 856,954.[78] Forty thousand new and 62,000 converted rifles are to be prepared during the year 1871 on Krenk's system, and orders have been given for 30,000 revolvers, with 14,000 carbines, from foreign sources. The military authorities, however, are in favour of the Berdan[79] small-bore as the arm for the future, but they intend temporarily to arm all their soldiers in European Russia with the Krenk, and the forces in Turkestan, Siberia, and the Caucasus district with the Carl breech-loader. The excessive rapidity with which these rifles are being made will enable the above dispositions to be almost entirely carried into effect by the end of the present year. The war estimates for the year 1871 amount to 24,885,792 roubles and 35 copecks; they are in excess of the preceding year's by 4,471,924 roubles and 95 copecks. This difference is accounted for by the fortifications which are being strengthened and constructed in the various provinces; by large augmentation to the parks of artillery, by a contract that has been taken in the United States for 100 mitrailleuses[80] and a million metallic cartridges, by an order that has been given to Nobel for 100 mitrailleuses, by the various pieces of machinery which are to be manufactured in the Government arsenals for 320 weapons similar to Nobel's by the equipment of 15 mounted batteries of artillery, by the construction of 100 mountain carriages for 3lb. cannon, by the large addition that is to be made to the cavalry and artillery remounts, and by the small-arm re-armament and an enormous quantity of cartridges which are to be supplied. After these data, which can be relied on, who can wonder if Prince Gortschakoff's first official letter to the Governments implicated in the celebrated Treaty, and which had certainly no right on its side in 1870, may have something more powerful to enforce its demands by the end of 1871?

FGB042
St. Petersburg; 10 December 1870
Burnaby to Editor – *Morning Post***, 16 December 1870**
If the war has been a means of preventing *la jeunesse* of St. Petersburg from sunning itself at Nice and swelling the profits of the bank at Monaco, this deprivation has been somewhat atoned for (to the juvenile mind) by the vast inroad of fair and frail Parisians who, launched from their beleaguered city, are seeking a happy-go-lucky existence in the capital of the Czar. For there is nothing so *chic* to the young idea in Russia as to be the proprietor of a French Aspetia.[81] However old and ugly she may be, that does not so much signify;

78 The Carl and Krenk systems were alternative methods of converting muzzle-loaders into breechloaders.
79 Named for Hiram Berdan of New York, who invented a new form of cartridge primer, which he patented in 1866.
80 Volley guns with multiple barrels of rifle calibre.
81 Aspetia was a Milesian woman who was famous for her involvement with the Athenian statesman

it is the correct thing to possess one, and so he pays for the luxury. I need hardly say that the more pretty and celebrated of that nameless profession who figure in the photograph shops by the side of kings and bishops had formerly no necessity to leave their native land, and the victims of ruthless time and bankruptcy were the only sisters who paraded themselves within this frost-bound Empire. "*Mais la Guerra a change tout cela*", for almost all the naughty ladies who lately owned the best-turned-out equipages in the *Bois* have arrived, and the hotels are becoming inundated by this deluge of depravity. Indeed, as an old Scotch parson drawled out the other evening at the *table d'hôte*, "Sir, I canna bring my daughter Kate to feast here, for maybe some young officer will be making eyes, and mistaking her for one of these flaunting Jezebels." Poor old gentleman! He need not have been afraid of an equivocation, as Kate's personal attractions, entirely innocent of paint, and the nature of her gloves and shoes, were not such as to cause the most excitable of ardent Russians to imagine her a Frenchwoman. With the exception of the above-mentioned individuals, there are a few foreigners in St. Petersburg. But I had almost forgotten to mention to you that we have a distinguished author and M.P., who is collecting materials for a book on Russia and the Russians, and who purposes to visit all the winter fairs in the country by way of collecting information for his volumes. The natives are very much amused at the attempts that have so often been made to describe them by various British writers; and as an old Russian who knows England very well observed in a sarcastic tone, and with a good deal of truth – "What should you think in London of a Frenchman who cannot even speak or read your language and who after a few months sojourn in England writes a book on your manners and customs? Would you not feel inclined to laugh both at him and his production?" But we shall see, and as our political scribe has the pen of a ready writer, let me hope that his essay will be a success.

The interest which has so lately engrossed everyone in connection with the Eastern question and the siege of Paris has been entirely eclipsed by a never flagging source of conversation, namely universal conscription or military service for all alike, irrespective of rank or Mammon, for most of the merchants and all of the mammas in St. Petersburg are highly indignant and up in arms at the late proclamation of the Czar that every Russian on attaining his majority must serve his country. Formerly all the nobility, as well as those of the commercial class who paid taxes up to a certain amount, were excepted from forced enlistment, but by the present arrangement every little masculine darling who if of the *grand monde* was probably intended for diplomacy, or if of the middle class for the office, will have to face the national enemy. The poor old colonels and generals, and in fact all the military authorities, are being constantly harassed and worried to death by anxious parents who eagerly

Pericles.

enquire whether interest or money will not buy off the little hopefuls. But it is useless appealing, for the one man in Russia has issued his edict, and there can be but little doubt that it will be sooner or later carried into effect. The lower orders, and consequently the great majority of the people who were always liable to serve, are in ecstasies at the idea of their masters having to enter the ranks and shoulder the rifle with themselves, for they say "the cleverest of us will be made officers, and social rank will then give way to relative merit." Poor people! they labour under a sad delusion; for their autocrat, who is only aping the system of his Prussian uncle, is not likely to copy the ordinances for promotion which have but so lately proved so very prejudicial to the French army.

Russian peasants have a somewhat unceremonious way of chastising conjugal infidelity, judging by what lately happened in the village of Shihanag; for an inhabitant of this little hamlet, on having discovered his spouse and a centurion alone together in an old pensioner's house, under rather peculiar circumstances, avenged himself in the following manner:– First of all he whipped his naughty dame most severely, and the dragged her before the *starost*, or head man of the village. This worthy, assisted by a council of elderly individuals, endowed with about as much sense as their president, decided that the accuser should be allowed to punish the culprit. This he did, and in the following manner – first of all he denuded his wife in the centre of the village and in front of the *starost's* house, and the having obtained two men to sit on her head and feet to prevent any struggles, he flogged the poor creature till he was compelled to desist from exhaustion, and till, to use the words of the narrator, the ground was saturated with blood. The castigation part of the punishment being concluded, the judges thought that it would be but proper to punish the other delinquents, and this they did by sentencing the pensioner in whose house the rendezvous had taken place to pay a fine of three roubles, which sum was instantly spent on brandy for the benefit of the assembled company. It was then settled that the centurion, the principal offender, should provide a further supply of spirits, and satisfy the injured husband's honour by giving him five loads of wood. This was instantly done, and the inhabitants, spectators, and participators in the scene returned to their huts, highly pleased with the satisfactory manner by which the infringement of one of the commandments had been punished. In England the Divorce Court soothes the indignant husband with money, in Russia the peasant was assuaged with *vodka*; but the difference matters little, as in both cases the same result is arrive at. However, wife-beating is not included in the British code, so delinquent wives have some little advantage; but I dare say the female sex would consent to even personal flagellation if the sauce for the goose were equally sauce for the gander. Perhaps the great Mill[82] will

---

82 John Stuart Mill (1806-1873), British philosopher, political economist and civil servant.

introduce this change some day; the Russian ladies say he will and they eagerly devour his works and translate them to their consorts.

The *Moscow Gazette* states that the entire military estimates throughout all the districts of Russia for the year 1871 amount to 148,511,177 roubles, being in all 3,821,426 roubles more than those of 1869, and that telegraphs to various military stations are fast being constructed by order of the Ministry of war.

The *Birjevouia Vedomosti* of St. Petersburg of the 9th inst. has the following articles on the two different sides of opinion in Russia. It says:–

> The Pessimists declare that everything will remain as before. It is useless to say that Gortschakoff's first circular in general and in its details, by its tone and by its meaning, has thoroughly corresponded to the importance of the object, and to the dignity presented by Russia herself. We will not contend that the moment chosen was excessively opportune, for France could not oppose us, even if she wished it, and Prussia would have to co-operate, although she might be unwilling. The measure taken was perfectly correct, but what has since happened calls forth a serious doubt. England and Austria have only picked a quarrel on the matter of form, but they have done so in a highly threatening and serious manner. The national feeling has manifested itself most energetically in these countries against Russia. There is no doubt that our diplomats have understood the real dimensions of the prepared resistance even better than the public. On this account they have allowed Count Beust[83] to say so many biting things to us. But this is a small matter. He straight out accuses Russia as if her way of acting excites the Eastern nations to rise, owing to the example of a Power whose prestige, according to Beust's expression, is so great in their eyes. It will be pleasant to Lord Granville to employ against us the phrase of one despatch, that the matter is one of a principle as yet not fulfilled. 'Principles!' exclaim the Pessimists; but the real principles must be realised. Little by little an opinion has been formed, first in England and then in Austria, on account of the manifests of Russia, which remain for us without fruit, and for the other Powers not a source for fear – that the first Russian vessel of war which appears in the Black sea must be pitilessly destroyed. Lord Granville in his last despatch, as the telegraph informed us, has almost given a formal expression of this threat, insisting that Russia, until a general resolution has been come to, has no right to carry out her intention with respect to the Black Sea fleet. The English and Austrian papers speak still plainer, and declare without any ceremony that Gortschakoff's first circular, in consequence of its character, must be considered as not existing, or as if recalled. Therefore, on this account, the whole strength of the Black Sea question consists in the coming Conference. But what is this Conference? First of all, a means of prolonging the

---

83 Count Friedrich Ferdinand von Beust (1809-1886) was a German statesman who also served as Foreign Minister of Austria between 1866 and 1871.

affair, and tying Russia's hands for a time. In the meanwhile many things may happen and act against us. It was not for nothing that Prussia initiated the idea of a Conference, as she, by doing so, made herself the mistress of the position, and can henceforth barter with both sides and close with the one who will give her most. What is there improbable that by this means she will not succeed in disposing England to the views of a special German policy, and finally abet her at the Conference? It is not for nothing that we have heard rumours of a treaty between Napoleon and Prussia on the subject of his re-establishment on the French throne. Let us allow that he may occupy the throne of France, and, as the principal culprit in the Treaty of Paris, that he may have a voice in the Conference. What will happen afterwards? Why, this ambitious man will acquire prestige with his people, and where can he obtain it better than in Russia? This master of intrigue can easily direct the boiling passions of the French. There is already one party in France not satisfied with the actions of Russia, and it is easy to make it the *point d'appui*. France would have at the outset a sufficient fleet to obtain in the Black Sea those distinctions which have not fallen to its lot in the German ocean; and the Pessimists conclude with a deep regret that it is evident that Russia will be bound as before, and God knows whether the sword will not have to be used to cut the Gordian knot.

The Optimists will say, and not without reason, that it is the will of our lord the Emperor to have a fleet in the Black Sea; and they affirm that in consequence, there can be no question whether the other Powers like it or not. Gortschakoff in his answers strives, with all tact and mildness of expression, to place the fact of Russia's resolution as unchangeable in any event. He also says, quite straightforwardly, that peace may be disturbed if the appeal of Russia to the other Powers should meet with an unfavourable reception, or if a positive variance of opinion should exist between them and us; but at the same time he does not disallow the possibility of their consent. In non-diplomatic language this signifies that Russia is ready for every event, and if from any accident peace should be disturbed, that no responsibility can be attached to us. The Optimists then say that measures are already being taken to carry out the resolutions contained in the circular of 7th of November, and that of this fact they have no doubt. The official paper has declared that there is no necessity for private subscriptions, and that the national Exchequer will pay for the Black Sea fleet, which will be carried on in the estimates. So after all, whatever may be the results of the Conference, that can have no effect on Russia. She enters on it without any obligation, and only out of delicacy to the Powers protecting Turkey, and at the same time ready with an inflexible programme which is known to all. Let us suppose the worst, and that the Conference only veils different expedients which are hostile to Russia. Peace and war, it is true, are not always at our disposal; but in this case war would result against our wish and will. Against the coalition Russia would also have a coalition, though Prussia in all probability would remain neutral awaiting events.

But against the feeble strength of those representatives of Turkey, England, and Austria would arise a new and young strength, and to whom the future belongs. On Russia's side would stand the sympathies of all Slavonians, and on the other an active ally – that noble American nation which has an account to settle with England. The American papers become day by day warmer in their amicable feelings towards Russia, and the President's message to Congress clearly counsels awakening the Alabama question. Russia is free for action in conformity to her dignity as a Power, and her benefit as a nation.

The *Birjevouia Vedomosti* then concludes by saying:

We have noted both these forms of opinion, which are diametrically at variance. But they agree in one respect in the general wish, taking in some the form of a doubt, and in others that of a belief, that Russia must not in any case recede from the step taken by her. Up to this time the question turns on the feeling of the Powers; but if manhood and arms should have to support the strength of the pen and reason, then all are unanimous to resolve their doubts and manifest their belief alike. The whole question rests on this: Are we, for the sake of the self-interests of some Powers, to take up the sword to cut the Gordian knot of our time?

FGB043
St. Petersburg and Moscow; [December 1870]
Burnaby to Editor – *Morning Post*, 8 February 1871

What a glorious change the traveller experiences on arriving at Moscow after the damp and fetid atmosphere of the capital, which oppresses his spirits to such an extent that some 15 *petit verres*[84] *per diem* are absolutely essential to prevent him from committing suicide through indigestion. For in St. Petersburg everything is gloomy and *triste*, but here all is bright and gay. I am not, of coarse, writing of the indoor life of the two cities, but of the climate which surrounds them, and the variation is almost as striking as would be a flight of the imagination from Dante's "Inferno" to Milton's "Paradise" before the Fall; for the Russian capital is, if possible, more sombre even than our own smoke-enveloped London, and appears to be as fatal to humanity as the doctors, for the deaths exceed the births in the population. But once in sight of the Kremlin and one breathes a new existence, for when my servant draws the curtains I am awakened by such a flood of light that, were it not for the icy framework which encases the double crystals, I could well imagine myself in the south of France, or at fair and lovely Seville.[85] And inside the house the fancy might still feast

---

84 A liqueur said to aid digestion.
85 This reference to Seville, a favourite city of Burnaby, is one of the clues to his authorship of this

itself on the chimera of its first awakened delusion, for all is warm and sunny, and 20 degrees below zero only make themselves appreciable when the hardy pedestrian, who resembles a polar bear by the thickness of his furs, musters up courage sufficient to leave the hospitable threshold and boldly cross the Rubicon; for then his moustache is instantaneously turned into an icicle, and, although endowed by nature with luxuriant black whiskers and beard, he might be mistaken for the patriarch David by the hoary grizzliness which his hirsute honours assume. But the air he breathes is like the gaseous bubbles of *eau de seltz*[86] in comparison to the pea-soup resembling exhalations of St. Petersburg, and the buoyancy of the atmosphere imparts itself to the spirits, for the foot steps the pavement with a firmer tread, and blue devils[87] and *revalenta arabica* are equally unknown to the ruddy-faced inhabitants of Moscow. The very *coup d'oeil*[88] which meets the eye at every turn is both novel and picturesque, and how shall I attempt to depict it to the reader? Let me suppose him gifted with the wings of Icarus, or like the lame devil, Asmodeus, seated on the pinnacle of a spire, and taking a bird's-eye view of all around. The *entourage* would perhaps recall to his mind the Christmas holidays of childhood, when his infantine entity delighted itself by gazing in at the confectionery shop windows, for the Twelfth-day cakes, representing towers, churches, cathedrals, and domes, might well form a miniature panorama of the edifices in the Holy City. For Moscow appears to be as rich in saints and relics as the Vatican, and the subjects of the King of the Cannibal Islands would not more thoroughly believe in the virtue of their fetishes than these poor *mujiks*[89] in their miracle-working images. Spaniards have long been thought to be the most religiously superstitious nation in existence, but they are very Voltaires or even Bradlaughs[90] in their tenets of negation compared to the emancipated Russian serfs. In every hut or hovel one sees an effigy illuminated by a lamp which is never suffered to burn out, and the amount of bowing and scraping which is gone through by the peasant on entering must be seen to be believed. Occasionally in the course of my peregrinations through the streets I meet an enormous vehicle drawn by six horses, and driven by a bareheaded coachman. Every one bows to the ground as the gigantic conveyance meanders past. "Who is inside?" I ask of a bystander, "a grand duke, the governor, or has the Czar arrived?" "Oh no, *barzen*," he replies, "the mother of God is the passenger, and she is going to visit and cure some sick person." The fact is that there is an old image called the

article.
86 Carbonated water, often used in making cocktails.
87 Blue devils and red monkeys are said to be the characteristic apparitions that haunt drunkards.
88 A 'stroke of the eye' and thus a glimpse, or a glance.
89 A Russian peasant.
90 Charles Bradlaugh (1833-1891), atheist politician and founder of the National Secular Society.

Iberian virgin[91], which the priests, on receiving large sums of money, send out to the houses of their almost moribund parishioners. This figure is supposed to possess miraculous properties, and invalids have much faith in its healing virtues when their doctor's remedies fail. But a visit from their physician only costs them five roubles, and the saint's is a matter of several hundred, so they prefer to begin with their leech and leave spiritual intercession as a final resort. It is a funny sight when travelling on the Volga steamers to witness three labourers breakfasting on deck; for at almost every mouthful one of the party bounds into the air and manipulates himself; and, if any church comes in sight, a sort of St. Vitus's dance of mummery, crossing, and scraping is performed by the Russian sailors on board for the period of several minutes. The educated classes with whom I have conversed say it is absolutely necessary to foster these religious observances among the lower orders, for the rustics are so ignorant that were they not to see some object to bow down to perpetually staring them in the face, they would entirely forget the existence of a deity, and would relapse into mere eating, drinking, and sleeping, which, when they are not crossing themselves, appear to be their principal occupations, for the *mujik* is scarcely capable of learning a servant's duties, or at all events, if competent, to perform them, the Russian aristocracy, as well as the hotel-keepers, prefer being served by Russians from their German-speaking provinces, or by Tartars. These last form a most important element in the waiting community; they are Mahometans, very honest, and of never-failing sobriety. When engaged as *garçons* they allow their hair to grow like Europeans, but once every year they return to their villages to solace the faithful wife, who has been in the meanwhile tilling the ground, with the marital presence, and for the space of a month or so renew their nomad habits and pursuits. The Russians in the capital are quite astonished at the sobriety of these hard-working worshippers of the Prophet, for the temperance society has but few adherents on the banks of the Neva. But if the amount of brandy daily swallowed at St. Petersburg causes its inhabitants to die like Strasburg geese, without even the cursory satisfaction of tempting the gourmand world by their decease, the same cannot be said of the Celestial Bohea[92] – the *ne plus ultra* of Muscovite beverages. For the teapot is even more indispensable to the Moscow sleigh driver than Truman and Hanbury's peculiar to the London cabby. I suppose the reason is that the Chinese decoction contains some hidden element which makes it an unfailing specific against King Frost, for I often see a peasant enter a *traktir* or restaurant and drink 10 or even 15 tumblers of the gossip and

---

91 An icon of the Virgin Mary, often depicted with a wound on her face, of which several copies existed; one of the earliest was said to protect the Iberian (or Iveron) Monastery on Mount Athos from its enemies.
92 A species of black tea.

scandal stimulating decoction to the sweet sounds of an enormous mechanical organ, which constitutes a necessary part of almost every Russian tea drinking establishment, and finally he will go out and sleep in the open, where the temperature is so fatal that were it not for what he had previously imbibed his rest would know no awakening.

FGB044
Moscow; [27] December 1870
Burnaby to his sister, Annie (extract)
I left St. Petersburg yesterday at 12 mid-day, and arrived here at 10 this morning. The weather was something awful – 22 degrees below zero, with a cutting wind, and I got my ear frost-bitten going to the station; but once inside the railway train everything was all right, as the carriages are admirably warmed with double windows to prevent the cold from getting in, and a stove in every compartment. Do write me a line to say how the dear old governor is, and please cut out and send me here any letters which may appear in the *Morning Post*.

FGB045
Moscow; 29 December 1870
Burnaby to his father (extract)
Dear old Governor, I hope this letter finds you better and yourself again. I like Moscow much better than St. Petersburg, but notwithstanding the brightness of the climate, it does not agree with me, and I shall not stay here long, as my liver is like a Strasburg goose's in size, but in the course of three weeks I shall leave for Kiev and Odessa, and then work round by steamer to Constantinople and Spain; I do not know if my letters reached the *Morning Post*, but I flatter myself that the last two or three have been very good works of composition. The friends of the Berosdines called on me yesterday, and I went in the evening to their house. Madame de Berosdine comes to Moscow herself next week, and then I will write to you all about them. What a bore my liver is! I put some mustard and cayenne mixed together next my skin last night, and I am raw today in consequence. However, I am getting very near twenty-seven, so I suppose it is time to expect some ailments or other, particularly after twelve years racketing about in London. At all events I must congratulate myself that I am as well as I am, as poor Adderley, Baring and Westcar my contemporaries are already gone to their account. Ask Evelyn to write to me and tell me all the news. By the way you have had your Xmas day, and ours had not arrived yet. The Russian calendar is twelve days later than the one England and all civilised countries go by. Some years ago there was an attempt made by the late Czar to change to the modern system of computation, but the people were so ignorant that they would not have it on any account, as they declared that putting on

the calendar twelve days would shorten their life by that amount of time, and make them twelve days older. Good-by, dear old Governor, love to all. Your affectionate son, Fred.

FGB046
Constantinople; 17 February 1871
Burnaby to Editor – *Morning Post***, 6 March 1871**
I remained a few days at Kiev and Odessa on my way here. The operations of fortifying the former of these two towns have been temporarily discontinued, owing to the frozen state of the ground and the continual fall of snow. Todleben's[93] plans, however, are to be fully carried out as soon as the spring arrives. They consist of a series of forts, which are to be constructed on various natural elevations and eminences at a distance of from three to four miles from Kiev, and which are to be connected with each other by strong earthworks. The celebrated engineer general is keenly alive to the error in the former system of fortifications, which allowed cities to be bombarded as well as their defences, and he is determined to render this in the present instance almost an impossible contingency. Great animation is visible in the harbour at Odessa. Thirty-six of Krupp's heaviest steel siege-guns have lately passed through *en route* for Nicolaev and Kertch. The latter place is said to have been made quite a second Cronstadt,[94] and at Nicolaev a strict order has lately been issued prohibiting any one not immediately connected with the military departments from visiting the arsenals. Movements of troops are incessantly going on, and the movements in the military districts could not be much greater even had hostilities already commenced. The Russian press continue to lash Austria with the most violent invectives, and Prussia, or rather Germany, by no means escapes scot free. It is a singular thing that in Russia the sympathies of the nation at large should be almost entirely French; and that in Turkey, for whose defence so many gallant Gauls bit the dust in the Crimea, the Pashas talk of the ruin of their late allies and defenders in the most matter-of-fact and indifferent manner. Gratitude to the *Giaour*[95] is evidently not a tenet in the Koran. But, notwithstanding this coldness and apathy about the misfortunes of France, the true believers are leaving no steps untaken to secure their own safety; 10 magnificent iron-clads lie in the Bosphorus ready for immediate use, and hundreds of native workmen, under the direction of 80 English engineers, are engaged in the arsenals and dockyards. Torpedoes are being constructed in very large numbers, and many

---

93   General Eduard Todleben (1818-1884), German military engineer involved in a number of important Russian military campaigns, including the siege of Plevna.
94   Traditionally the seat of the Russian Admiralty, noted for its fortifications having been built very quickly.
95   An offensive ethnic slur used by Turkish people to describe all who are non-Muslim, particularly Christians.

of the troops are already supplied with breech-loaders. The physique of the men themselves leaves nothing to be desired, but they are drilled in a very careless sort of way; and the slouching manner in which they loaf about the streets, and even march on parade, shows a striking contrast to their well-drilled neighbours; for the Russian soldier is now a very different sort of individual from that which fought in the Crimea. He was then a serf, he is now a free man; and the knout is numbered with the past, as corporal punishment is abolished throughout the service. He is also well fed, clothed, and housed, and in fact is very much better off as a soldier in the point of bodily comforts than he would be in his wooden hut and in his native village. In addition to these advantages he is taught to read and write, and in many cases he learns a trade; so when he returns home it is not as a penniless vagrant, but as a man who is able to earn his own living, and capable of benefiting the community at large.

The ravages and damage which the late conflagration occasioned in Pera[96] are still but too palpably apparent, and great misery is the result, as hundreds of poor people are utterly penniless, and entirely dependent on the charity of others. The subscriptions which were made by the British public both at home and abroad have done much to alleviate the distress, but more money is still required. The £10,000 which the Sultan put his name down for still exists but on paper, and numerous are the evasive answers returned to those whose duty it is to collect and expend the sums which have been subscribed on behalf of the sufferers. However, the Commander of the Faithful[97] is able to find resources for the various palaces which are being constructed for him on the Bosphorus, so perhaps later on, and when these are finished, the houseless Christians in Constantinople may reap the benefit of his liberality.

The Turks are certainly getting much more Europeanised in their tastes, as at a ball given last Wednesday by General Ignatieff[98], the Russian Ambassador, many of them appeared thoroughly to enjoy themselves, and, taking off their red fez caps, valsed away quite as hard as their Christian partners. The Turkish ladies, too, are beginning to show a symptom of insubordination at the state of thraldom in which they are kept, and quite a scene took place the other day at the public garden. Turkish women are not allowed admittance to this place of resort, but one of them insisted, and, producing the entrance fee, desired to be let in; however, the gatekeeper was inexorable, and the poor dame was baffled in her attempt. In some of the harems the inmates are allowed much more liberty than before, and the daughter of Mustapha Pasha frequently takes rides into the country, accompanied only by her English governess and a groom. An

---

96 Now Beyoğlu, a westernised district on the European side of Constantinople that suffered a great fire in 1870.
97 Another title of the Caliph or Sultan, then Abdülaziz I (1830-1876).
98 Count Nikolay Pavlovich Ignatieff (1832-1908), Ambassador to Constantinople from 1864 to 1877.

American lady who is residing here occasionally visits the wives of some of the high functionaries, and lends them books. I have been trying to persuade her to take in a few copies of Stuart Mill on "The Rights of Women"; but she will not do so, as she says it would not be fair to the husbands. Report says that the Duke of Sutherland[99] is shortly expected to arrive at Constantinople, and that one of the Sultan's palaces is being got ready for his reception.

FGB047
Proposed preface to collected letters on the Carlist campaign
The season was over, the last valse had been danced, and very nearly the last man had left town, when the idea suddenly occurred to me that if I remained much longer I should probably be that unenviable individual myself. What was to be done? Homburg? – No, I had been there at least a dozen times. Baden and Wiesbaden? – the same thing. Switzerland would be inundated, and by the people I wanted to avoid, viz. my own countrymen, who are very charming in their country, but rather a bore out of it.

One afternoon while meditating on this knotty point whither to betake myself, I was awoke to a sense of the outer world by a newspaper boy, who shouted in an ear, "*Hecho*, sir, only a halfpenny; huge slaughter, thousands killed, and only a halfpenny, sir."

The thought struck me to go to the Peninsula. It was true I had often been there before, but principally in the Southern Provinces, Andalusia and Valencia, and the war then going on was in the north, and, as the Basques are of a different type, character and habits to the inhabitants of the south, it would be something new; and besides that, my excursion might be turned to military advantage, studying the guerrilla tactics for which the Spanish chiefs are so famed.

A few afternoons later, I mentioned my intentions to my friend Needham, in the 1st Life Guards, who offered to accompany me, at all events to the end of the month, when he would be obliged to return to his regiment. The next ten days were employed in buying saddles, maps, and the thousand and one little arrangements which are always necessary before entering upon a campaign; I had great difficulty, however, in obtaining a good chart, as almost all the maps of the Northern Provinces had previously been bought up by the Republican and Loyalist officers. However, at last everything was arranged, and on the 8th August we found ourselves at Charing Cross.

How difficult it is to induce English servants to travel as lightly equipped as their masters. Needham and myself had carefully instilled into the minds of our faithful attendants the necessity of leaving behind everything that was not

---

99 George Granville William Sutherland Leveson-Gower, 3rd Duke of Sutherland (1828-1892), politician.

absolutely essential; but, in spite of this, his man arrived at the station with a portmanteau of brushes. Very dear in the eyes of the servant was this treasured leather case, and my man glanced encouragingly at him and reproachingly on his master at not having been allowed to bring his own cleaning apparatus. But the thing was done, and the luggage had been registered, so there was no help for it; and making a mental oath that the confounded brushes should be either lost or left behind in France I found my place in a carriage, the guard whistled, and we were off.

There was no dawdling *en route*, and we made tracks, as the Americans say, straight through to Bayonne, which we reached the following afternoon; and here we were fated to leave the railroad and travel by a very different means of locomotion for a long time to come. However, it was necessary to remain a couple of days in France. Horses had to be bought, and Carlist passports to be procured, without which any attempt to reach Don Carlos's headquarters would have been in vain.

I had been provided with numerous letters of introduction to Royalists, and especially to the Marques de Sapaza, whose father is a devoted adherent to the Carlist cause.

In a few hours after our arrival we hired a carriage and drove over to Biarritz, to call upon some of the Carlist companies who had made that pretty little watering-place their headquarters. Here the news that I had received about Don Carlos and his cause was most conflicting. According to one man, the king had twenty thousand soldiers in arms, while another equally well-informed person apprised me there were fifty thousand Carlists in the field.

Many grumbled at the apparent inaction of the Royalist Commander-in-chief, Elio,[100] and said he was much too old for his work. But some said they approved of the great caution this leader exhibited, and praised his military qualities. Biarritz was filled with Spaniards of every variety of opinion in politics. There were Alfonsists and Isabellists, Montpensierists and Carlists, Republicans and Socialists, all living in the same hotels, dining at the same *tables d'hôte* and discoursing together with the greatest apparent courtesy and affability.

At the latter establishment, that all-important and first question to all Castellans, "*Que hay de Nuevo?*" – "Is there any news?", to which the almost invariable answer, accompanied by a melancholy shrug of the shoulders, was made – "Nothing". Our arrival created a slight sensation in this colony of exiles, and for the nonce gave them something to talk about. "Do not be a fool and go", said one. "I should like to accompany you", remarked his friend. "You will die of starvation and be eaten up by fleas", said a third. "Oh, do tell his Majesty

---

100 Joaquin Elio y Ezpeleta (1808-1873) was a Carlist general. He had been condemned to death for his participation in the conspiracy of San Carlos de la Rápita, but was pardoned by Isabella.

how much we all love him and his cause!", added another, and by far the most attractive of the group, a dark-eyed raven-locked señorita of about eighteen, whose passionate utterances and gesticulation betrayed her Andalusian birth, even if her graceful form and her accent had not already betrayed her Sevillian origin. "But why go there?"

The following morning a little surprise was prepared for us – a magnificent dish of trout, served up at breakfast by the Alcalde's wife, our hostess. She was a comical old lady in her way, and observed, after seeing we had done good justice to her viands, "Your lordships must know those fish are rarities, exquisite in their way, and delicate to the taste. Generals, colonels, bishops, *cura* frequently come to me. They say, 'Little lady, for the love of God, his Holy Son, and the Little Virgin, just two pounds of fish, only two pounds quick; for our stomachs are fasting, and crave for the dainty.' But I answer, 'Little sirs and your lordships, the sweet little dears are not to be caught; they will not catch themselves; they are in the water underneath the little stones.' Little beauties! So tender and nice are they, I preserve them for your excellencies, for the king, his Majesty Carlos Septimo, and for great Señores like your lordships who arrive with a suite and train. Perhaps their excellencies may see his Majesty tonight, and then they may greet him with, 'Most illustrious, we have some little fish in a tin box. The dainties came from a little river near ____. The Alcalde's wife, dear little lady, who loves your Majesty, sends these exquisite little morsels to lay at your majesty's feet.' But if your lordships do not see the king, why, then the fish will feel highly honoured by your lordships eating them."

A Carlist officer happened to come in as we were finishing our breakfast, and he informed me that an attempt was very likely to be made on Estella, so we determined to push on.

FGB048
Vera; 12 August 1873
Burnaby to Editor – *The Times*, **15 August 1873**
I was detained a few days at Biarritz, owing to the necessity of obtaining Carlist passports, buying horses, &c., and making the thousand and one arrangements which are always essential previous to entering upon a campaign. The time, however, was not thrown away, as I had the opportunity of conversing with several of the Carlist Junta who are now residing in the neighbourhood. The French authorities do not allow these persons to show themselves in the towns, but make no objection to their remaining in the Province. One afternoon, while calling upon an old General, or rather Admiral, though he is known by the last-named title, and who is the chief promoter of the Carlist movement on the frontier, I observed that many of the principal adherents to the cause appeared despondent of success, and could not understand Don Carlos's tardiness in advancing upon Madrid, the more particularly as the Republican troops were

almost to a man engaged in the South. "Yes", replied the General, "it is quite true, we are losing an opportunity which may not occur again; but we have no money, and our forces are not half armed. We have some 18,000 men drilled and organized, but what is that? We could put 50,000 into the field to-morrow, but money is wanting. The King has sacrificed all his personal property, but we have such difficulty in negotiating loans. I cannot understand why England does not help us. Her interests are identical with ours respecting Cuba, and, with regard to France, it would suit MacMahon[101] far better to have a strong Conservative ally at Madrid, in the event of another war with Germany, than the present vacillating and Socialistic Cabinet, which is no Government at all. They tell me England is afraid, in the event of our success, we should repudiate the debt. Why, it is all nonsense. We should be cutting our own throats if we were to do so. We shall pay for everything incurred up to the date of Amadeo's abdication and for ourselves, but not one *cuarto* for the Republicans. It is also given out that we shall return all the Church property which has been sold and passed into other hands to the clergy. This is too absurd. The Neo-Catolica press, which is the King's worst enemy, on account of its extreme and uncompromising tone, would like us to do so, but it is what His Majesty would never dream of."

Another Carlist nobleman, a personal friend of Don Carlos, with whom he is in constant correspondence, related to me how Cabrera's[102] name had been mixed up in the present rising: "When", began my informant, "the officers of one of the most distinguished corps in Spain had resigned on account of the line of conduct pursued by General Cordova,[103] and, a little later, Amadeo had abandoned Madrid, the garrison became excessively discontented, and everybody was conspiring on his own account; but at last it was determined that three officers should be chosen who should select a course which should be followed by all their comrades. This was done, and it was resolved that Queen Isabella should be asked whether her party had sufficient elements in itself to insure a chance of success. The Commission visited Her Majesty, and she told its members that she herself had abdicated all her rights in favour of the Prince of Asturias, and that his party were not prepared at present for any movement; that all she wished for was the welfare of the country, and that the Commission had her sanction to take whatever steps they might think best for Spain. The delegates returned to Madrid, and Don Carlos was then thought of. His election was, as a rule, disliked by the officers. He was supposed to be a *tonto* (fool), and it was not until I, happening to meet one of the Commission

---

101 Marie Edmé Patrice Maurice de Mac-Mahon, 1st Duke of Magenta (1808-1893) was a French general and politician. He served as Chief of State of France from 1873 to 1875 and as the first president of the Third Republic from 1875 to 1879.
102 Ramon Cabrera y Griñó, El Conde de Moralla (1806-1877), a Carlist general.
103 Don Fernando Fernández de Córdova y Valcárcel (1809-1883), a Spanish general and politician.

at Biarritz, proposed that I should present him to the King, and then he could judge for himself what sort of a person Don Carlos really was, that the idea was first entertained. Well, I presented my friend to His Majesty, and they conversed together for more than three hours. Finally the official was so satisfied that he wrote an account of his interview to Madrid, stating at the end of the letter – "Don Carlos is not a Napoleon I as a general or a politician, but he is a Napoleon I in comparison with either Don Francisco de Asis[104] or Amadeo." The result was the Commission determined, if possible, to create a fusion between the Alfonsist and the Carlist branches, and to invite Cabrera to enter Spain. The plan for the fusion was as follows: – Don Carlos was to name a Commissioner, and the Prince of the Asturias was to do the same. These two were to elect a third. The united forces of both parties were then to march upon the capital, and on their arrival the three were to form a Government composed half of Alfonsists and half of Carlists. A plebiscite was then to be appealed to, and the nation asked which of the two candidates it preferred for the Throne. The one elected was to assume the Crown, and the other receive the highest social position in the nation next to that of the Sovereign; in fact, hold a much higher rank than that which was formerly enjoyed by the Infantas of Spain, Don Carlos, though he did not actually say he would accept this plan, wrote word that he "would transact with the idea as a line of conduct" – I use His Majesty's own words – and, with respect to Cabrera, the King said he would receive not only him, but every Spaniard who had fought for the cause of the Royal Family, with open arms. Cabrera was then staying at the Hotel de Rose, in Wiesbaden. The Commission went to see him. He would not give any decided answer, but said he would send a person to Biarritz in six days to represent him. The Commissioner returned, but no one arrived from Cabrera. Some days elapsed, and the General was again written to, when at last, after considerable time had elapsed, a relative of his arrived, not from Wiesbaden, but from Madrid. He had received no instructions whatever from the General, except a telegraphic message desiring him to go to Biarritz and see the Junta. The plan for the fusion of the two Royal Branches was then communicated to him and by him to the General, who approved the idea, but did not say he would personally aid in its execution; and Don Carlos, tired with this delay, finally entered Spain without him. El Conde de Moralla is now advanced in years, and his family ties are so strong that they overcome his inclinations. But now the thought of any fusion has died away, Don Carlos is making war on his own account; and, if the Republican army does not vastly improve in discipline and respect to its officers, we shall succeed; but if we had a million sterling, resupply our men with arms, we should be at Madrid in six weeks." I thanked the Marquis for his information, and soon afterwards my pass arrived, with a

---

104 Marie Francis Ferdinand of Bourbon (1822-1902), King Consort of Spain.

special order permitting me to attach myself to the King's Headquarters; so last Monday I left Biarritz and rode to St. Jean de Luz, a pretty little town near the frontier, and the following day started for Bera.[105] It was a very hot afternoon, and a very trying road for the horses; the heat of it reminded me somewhat of Chobham ridges,[106] and the worst of the steps by the Duke of York's Column,[107] but lovely and picturesque scenery well repaid the journey. At last, after a ride of some five hours, we arrived at Bera yesterday the quarters of 3,500 Carlists, but to-day a deserted village, as the troops left this morning for a destination which, for obvious reasons, I must not mention. To-morrow we shall join them, and I take the opportunity of a few hours rest to write this letter, which has to be carried by hand over the mountains.

FGB049
The Palace of Carola, Elizondo; 15 August 1873
Burnaby to Editor – *The Times*, 19 August 1873

There is an old saying that necessity makes a man acquainted with strange bedfellows, and certainly the vicissitudes of a march through a country when in a state of war render the changes from one quarter to another equally peculiar. At Bera we were billeted in a sort of hovel over a blacksmith's forge, and the beds were so infested with vermin that I was glad to select a soft plank on the floor; while here we are lodged in a very comfortable country house, known by the name of *El Palacio de Carola*. Just before we left Bera two Carlist officers paid us a visit; they were smart-looking fellows, and had formerly been in the Civil Guard, that Corps which the Government at Madrid relied upon so thoroughly. I was told that many of the *Guardia Civil* have come over to the Royalists; that men are leaving the Republican Army in great numbers on account of the time of their service having expired; and, according to my informants, it would not be easy to induce volunteers worth having to enlist for the cause of the "*Republica Federal*".

The Deputation of Navarre, now resident at Bera, provided us with a guide in the form of a Carlist soldier, armed to the teeth and decorated with the insignia of Don Carlos – a heart worked in red worsted, worn on the left side. A military sort of blue cloak, thrown back over a stained shirt, and some patched overalls were his attire, which culminated in a red cap with a tassel, the distinguishing badge of the Royalists. He wore no socks, but white canvas

---

105 Burnaby must have made some mistake concerning the day of the week on which he left Biarritz. He departed from London on Friday 8 August, arriving in Bayonne the next day (Saturday 9) and riding immediately to Biarritz. He left Biarritz for St. Jean de Luz on Sunday 10 and St. Jean de Luz for Bera on Monday 11, writing his first letter from there on Tuesday 12.
106 The army's training ground in Surrey.
107 The Duke of York Column is a monument to Prince Frederick, Duke of York. It is sited near Waterloo Place and the steps down to the Mall are known as the Duke of York Steps.

shoes protected his feet against the rugged nature of the roads. I tried very hard to induce him to leave his rifle behind, and proposed that the cloak should be strapped on to a saddle, and his cap turned inside out, which would give it a dirty brown and not a Carlist colour, as there was a possibility of meeting a column of the enemy on the march, and our guide's garb would have been very compromising; but nothing on earth would induce him to relinquish his breechloader, an extraordinary sort of weapon, which looked much more dangerous for its possessor than the foe. He had shot an officer of the Carabineers only three weeks before with it, we were informed, and according to his own account it was the perfection of a weapon. However, at last I induced him to reverse his cap, abandon the cloak, and also his luggage contained in a pocket handkerchief – in which, by the way, he said there was enough to last him for six months – and fasten all these *impedimenta* on one of our spare horses. We were fortunate in getting something to eat previous to our start. Our hostess, the blacksmith's wife, a very religious Catholic, wished to make the creed an economy to her pocket, as she told me it was a fast day, so we could not have any meat. I retorted by saying all soldiers have a special dispensation from His Holiness the Pope, and that we must have some meat directly, or the Alcalde should be informed. The dreaded name of this potentate, so feared by the Spanish peasantry, had the desired effect, and a very savoury stew was the result. Our route lay for some 15 miles along the shores of the Bidassoa, a river abounding with salmon and trout, and famous for the many sanguinary struggles on its banks, during the early part of the century, when the Iron Duke drove the French out of the Peninsula. A low range of mountains on either side of our path, and covered with vegetation, ran due south from Bera. Presently we came to a fine old bridge, with two of its arches utterly destroyed. "This was the handiwork of the cursed Republicans", said the guide. "They do this to annoy the country people; it does not affect us in the least, as we know the fords. The soldiers wish to ruin our farmers by preventing them selling the produce of their fields. In Catalonia, not content with destroying the means of communication, the troops have even burnt the crops. They think by this means to frighten us into surrender, but they mistake their men. Here it was I shot the Carabineer when in the act of blowing up the bridge. We fired upon them from the top of a height, there on the left", at the same time pointing to a thicket which darkened a neighbouring crag. "We were only seven, and they were more than 100, but nine of them bit the dust, and will not be able to swagger to their comrades of how they helped to starve the country people". Our guide was recognized by many of the passers-by, and being with a Carlist soldier was quite sufficient to insure a cordial welcome. "*Vayan Ustedes con Dios*" – "Go with God", said the old peasant women, bending beneath the weight of their pitchers, as they saw us. "*Viva Carlos setimo, Viva el Rey*" – "Long live Carlos VII, long live the king", shouted our companion in return. One aged woman however, to a certain degree, belied the general state of enthusiasm which prevailed. When we passed, seeing us with the soldier, she screeched *"Viva Don Carlos"*, but a little later, when our servants rode by, thinking it was well to be quite safe, as she thought they looked too well dressed to be Carlists, she changed her tone, and cried *"Viva la Republica"*. After some four hours' march we left San Esteban to our right, a small town sometimes garrisoned by Carlists, sometimes by Republicans; now held by two companies of Royalists, which form part of the 5th Battalion of Navarre. The men of this regiment present a soldier-like appearance. They are fine, broad-shouldered, deep-chested fellows, and all armed with breech-loaders. However, the officers complain bitterly that the rifles are of so many different systems that great confusion is the consequence. "It would not signify so much", they said "if each company had rifles of the same pattern, as they could arrange for the ammunition being of one kind; but when it comes to having the right of a squad requiring different cartridges from those of the men in the centre and left, it gives us great difficulty in furnishing them with a fresh supply when their pouches are empty and they themselves are under fire". Two hours more and Elizondo came in sight – a long, clean little town, with a very homely English appearance, most of the cottages with small gardens, well stocked and in good order. I rode up to the guard-house and told the officer on duty we wished to see the Colonel. "He is instructing the battalion" was the reply, "but I will direct an orderly to take you to him". In a few minutes we arrived at the drill ground, where eight companies of 100 strong were being put through the various battalion formations by their commanding officer. The men performed the different evolutions with very fair steadiness, and were all paying great attention to their instruction. It was easy to see that their heart was in the trade, and that they were working with a will. When the battalion dispersed I walked up to the Colonel, showed my Carlist pass, and asked quarters for ourselves and our five horses. He at once sent off his adjutant to the Alcalde, with an order to provide us with the best accommodation that could be procured, and also with forage, and told me to apply to him for everything I required. I am still many miles from the Carlist head-quarters, and great uncertainty apparently prevails among the officers of this battalion as to where the King is at present. However, I shall receive information at a town a little further on. I am told no action of any importance has occurred lately, and the Carlists are evidently not in a hurry to begin, as they require time to thoroughly organize their regiments, and money and arms to equip them. This letter will have to be carried by hand 40 miles before it can be posted, which will cause considerable delay in its arrival.

FGB050
Arraiz, Navarre, 17 August 1873
Burnaby to Editor – *The Times*, 21 August 1873

I found the officers at Elizondo very gentlemanly and obliging. The Carlists are grossly misrepresented in this respect by the Republican press, which declares that the Royalist army is commanded by the dregs of the nation. There is no truth whatever in the statement, and as a rule the captains and subalterns of the King's forces are socially, as well as intellectually, superior to the mass of the Government officers, who were often only corporals and sergeants in the time of Amadeo and Isabella. Another element exists in the lower ranks of the Carlists, which is absolutely deficient in the opposing forces, and the powerful lever which I am about to mention has, before this, made men taken from the plough fight with greater determination than trained soldiers. I allude to the deeply religious character which the present war is assuming. It is not so much a question of party among the simple mountaineers who are now voluntarily sacrificing their lives to the cause, as a belief that they are fighting for *Dios*, who has been insulted by the Republicans; and this insult, in their opinion, can only be wiped out by the sword. "God, Country, and King", is the Carlist watchword. I had an opportunity one afternoon of seeing the 5th Battalion of Navarre paraded for the purpose of attending Mass. It was a striking spectacle, these men dressed is quaint and varied garb, for as yet the regiment has not been supplied with uniforms, and both officers and soldiers dress after their own individual fancy. Sashes of different colours and hues; caps of every shape and form, with long tassels, sometimes reaching half-way to the waist; daggers and pistols of old-fashioned workmanship, even before the date of percussion locks; some men with shoes, others with *alpargatas* or sandals; and here and there an officer in jackboots and an attire which reminded me of one of Poole's smoking suits[108] – such was the scene which presented itself to my view. But the manifest devotion with which these swarthy mountaineers followed every word which fell from their priest's lips and repeated like one man the guttural, deep-toned responses was well worthy of notice. Old men and women with young children were there too; wives and fiancées kneeling beside the pillars, each one praying for the safety of him she loved; the mother gazing on her son, who was receiving the priest's benediction and hearing the exhortation to serve well and faithfully his God, Country, and King. But at last the service was over. No laughter could be heard as the men left the church. There was a stern, grim look on their countenances, such as would well have become one of Cromwell's Ironsides in the days when to kill a Cavalier was reckoned a saintly deed in the eyes of the Almighty.

---

108 Founded in 1806, Henry Poole & Co. is a gentleman's bespoke tailor, still trading and located at 15 Savile Row, London.

I could not gather much information of Carlist doings at Elizondo, but a report was goings about that the King had marched from Puente la Reina to attack Estella, and that two companies of Republicans were in the neighbourhood of Bera. So, taking the advice of the Commander of the Garrison, I determined to ride to Almanda, and inquire of the Carlist officers in that village what direction I must take to arrive at head-quarters. I had ordered my servant to call me at 4 the next morning in order to make an early start, but on being awoke I was told that our pack-horse was dead lame. I soon found out to my cost that the poor brute could not put his foot to the ground, and so I determined to buy a mule, but, not being able to obtain one at any price, I resolved to speak to the Adjutant of the Garrison. He settled the difficulty in a moment. "What, they won't sell" he said "why, then, we must requisition" and he instantly sent an order to the Alcalde to provide two mules, in case of any accident happening to one of them on the road. "What you must do in future when you want anything", said my friend, "is to go to the officer commanding, and he will supply all that you require". The whole way up the road, which lost itself in the distance amid the clouds above us, so precipitous and steep was the ascent, we kept meeting Carlist detachments and carts conveying supplies to the forces in front. Every building at each convenient turn was garrisoned and fortified. At last we arrived at this little village, and on showing the Alcalde my pass he at once ordered us billets and forage for the horses. "Our accommodation is not very grand", said the good-natured official, "but we will give you the best we can". I remarked that General Dorregaray[109] had slept in the same house only a week ago. "Yes, that he did", said the host, "and such a nice gentleman he was too – not a bit stuck up. Why, he conversed quite affably. Only think, a real General with the like of me." "I cannot give you fish, señores", he continued, turning to us, "but you shall have the best my house contains." "Here, Maria", shouting to his daughter, make an omelet directly; prepare the *puchero* and kill two chickens. That was what we gave the General, and he said he never enjoyed anything more." After dinner the officer commanding the detachment here came in to see us. He told me we must not go south to Pampeluna, as it was strongly garrisoned by Republicans, but that the best route would be a mountain path which skirts the above-mentioned town on the east. "It would not do for you to be captured with a Carlist pass", he added, "as the Republicans are no respecters of nationality, and your back against a wall, a short shrift, and six bullets might be the result." It is needless to say I mean to act upon his advice, and hope that the next letter I write will be from the head-quarters of Don Carlos.

---

109 Antonio Dorregaray y Dominguera (1823-1882), a Carlist general.

FGB051
Carlist Headquarters, Estella; 18 August 1873
Burnaby to Editor – *The Times*, **21 August 1873**

The last letter which I wrote was from Arraiz and very probably it may have been lost in transit as the means of communication are excessively difficult. However, in the above-named town I heard that an attempt to capture Estella would probably be made by the Carlists, so we determined to push on, not to spare the horses, but to arrive there as soon as possible. After riding, however, 24 miles down the most perpendicular passes and out-of-the-way cross-country roads which can well be imagined, we found ourselves at a village called Anor, a few miles north of Pampeluna with our horses quite knocked up, and still leagues distant from Estella. A halt was therefore absolutely necessary. The Alcalde's house was placed at our disposal, and on the morrow, after an early breakfast, I was informed that an officer had arrived from head-quarters *en route* for Bera. "What is the news?" was the first question. "News! Why, have you not heard the King is besieging Estella?" The words were hardly out of his mouth before we commenced preparations for a start. In three-quarters of an hour we were *en route* for Estella, our guide taking great care to avoid Pampeluna, on account of the Republican forces stationed in that fortress. Steeper and steeper became the path, and each moment more exciting was the news brought by the people we met. "The King has left his quarters." "He is on the march." "His Majesty is at the head of the Division." "*Viva Carlos Setimo!*" "Down with the Republicans! Estella is taken!" "No, it is not taken, it is being besieged." "It will be taken." "Viva!" And at last, on arriving within 10 miles of the town, I was told by a priest – the holy man in his enthusiasm doffing his saintly hat and waving it in the air – that Estella had fallen, the Carlists had entered the town, and the Republicans had retired into the citadel. We were assured Don Carlos was in Estella that His Majesty had personally directed a battery, and the bombardment had been incessant. "*Viva! Viva!*" With all these reports becoming each moment more frequent, notwithstanding the exaggeration so common to the Spanish character, I began to think there really must be some good foundation for them. "Faster, faster!" was the cry; but we were obliged from time to time to dismount and lead our poor beasts down the almost impracticable passes which barred our passage. The sun began to disappear beneath the horizon, and "*dos horas mas*" ("two hours more") was the answer of our guide to the repeated interrogatories as to when we should arrive. Spanish leagues and Spanish hours when on the march are somewhat like Irish ones. They are incomprehensible to the ordinary Saxon, and so it was not until some hours more had elapsed that I found we were still three-quarters of an hour from our destination. Darkness hung about our footsteps, and a faint noise could be heard which in the distance reminded me of the crackers pulled at Christmastime. But louder and more distinct the sounds became. Our guide shook his head. "*Son tiros!*" ("They are gunshots") he ejaculated. "*Madre de Dios!* it is not over. My poor mules, whatever will become of us? Holy Virgin, Sister, Sister! Artillery, too!" It was true enough what he said, and five minutes later men with red caps and a strange fantastic garb, their heads or limbs bound up, were borne past us. "*Viva Carlos Setimo!*" they cried as we rode by – poor victims, alas! of a civil war; and louder and louder and closer the firing rang, till at last a bystander, observing our approach, asked, "How are the Señores going to enter the city? Not by the principal gate; at least, I hope not. There is no cessation to the shots in that direction. Permit me to go and I will take you in by another way where, although there is danger, the risk is not so great." I thanked him, and asked if by the road he had mentioned we could reach the Royal head-quarters, as I wished to see General Elio, the Commander-in-Chief, as soon as possible, having letters to deliver to him. General Elio lives in the Plaza. "Let the señores accompany me, I will lead them to him. Quicker!" he vociferated, "hasten your steps here, we must receive some shots"; and the words had scarcely escaped his lips when the splutter on a wall close by betokened the bullet of an adjacent rifleman. We urged our jaded beasts into a trot, and soon found ourselves in the middle of a large square and the centre of an immense armed crowd, who pressed about the horses, the more importunate repeatedly asking our business. "My business is with General Elio; I must see him directly." "The General is at dinner with His Majesty", exclaimed an officer; "but as the gentlemen wish to see him I will show them the house where he is." The officer led the way, we followed, and after entering a large portico and passing by some sentries, who presented arms as our companion strode on, I arrived on the landing of a large staircase. "Where is the General?" asked the officer. "He is dining there, before you", said a servant; "look, on the right hand of His Majesty. Why, can't you see through the half-opened door?" I turned in that direction, and saw an old man dressed in uniform at the extreme right of a long table, at the end of which sat a very prepossessing dark young man, who gave one the idea of being not more than 25 years of age. From the marked respect which was displayed by those around him, and also by a likeness to the photographs we had previously seen, I recognized the King. "It is His Majesty", added our companion. "I will send in your letters to General Elio." Five minutes later that officer came out to meet us. "You have arrived in troublous times", he observed; "but I will do everything which is in our power. An aide-de-camp has been ordered to provide accommodation for your selves, servants, and horses. Please wait one minute; I must return to attend upon His Majesty." After a short lapse of time a young man entered the room and introduced himself, saying he was the aide-de-camp and nephew of the General. "If you come with me", he said, "I will soon provide you with quarters." He had, unfortunately, difficulty in procuring them, as all the stables and hotels were full. At last a barn was discovered with room for four horses, but, alas!

there was a charger already tied up to a manger in the corner. "Take him elsewhere", shouted the officer. "Impossible", said the proprietor. "It is my order", replied the aide-de-camp, I only execute General Elio's instructions." But the horse belongs to a colonel." "Never mind; remove him and make way." In spite of the half-suppressed oaths which this somewhat brusque step gave rise to, the order was obeyed, and the charger of the Carlist colonel was placed in another stable, quite, if not more spacious than the one he had previously occupied. "Come along now," said our companion, "come and dine with the Staff in a house close by; you won't have the dinner of an English mess, but '*Que importa? en la guerra como en la guerra?*' ('Who cares? in war as in war?')." However, his prognostications proved false. The food was excellent and the wine undeniable. "The poor lady of the house is much to be pitied," said my host. "Her husband was the town Alcalde; he was killed a few days ago when fighting against us. It is too sad. How horrible for her our being quartered here, and under such circumstances." All this time the roar of artillery and small arms could be heard around as, intermixed every now and then with a strange after-report which betokened somewhat more than the ordinary rifle. "They are firing shell from the fort," said my companion; "Come and look out from the balcony. The Republicans laugh at the Geneva Convention, and they fired upon a flag of trace this afternoon. Well, it is their own look-out. They will fight it out to the death. Their blood must be on their own heads." As I write, the hands of my watch point to the third hour of the morning, the sound of rifle shots is wafted across the square, in which up to very recently a military band of music had been playing and idlers promenading. "*Que importa?*" ("What does it signify") is a Spanish familiar expression; but it is a sad sight to see a nation thus sacrificed to civil war. The Republican troops still hold out in a convent, which they have fortified but I must now take some rest. However, I shall, leave my letter open till the moment for despatching it has arrived.

19 August 7.20 a.m.
The Republicans still resist. The bombardment is going on.

FGB052
Royalist Headquarters, Allo; 19 August 1873
Burnaby to Editor – *The Times*, **27 August 1873**
We were awoke at daybreak by an incessant cannonade which shook the houses in our vicinity, and about 7 o'clock I went with some officers of the Royalist army to witness the bombardment of a fortress where the Republican garrison had retreated for shelter. When I use the term fortress, it is a misnomer, as the building in question is nothing more than the old convent of San Francisco, which has been intrenched and converted into a tolerably strong redoubt by the Government garrison. Estella is a small town which in normal times contains

some 5,700 inhabitants. It is built in a long, straggling fashion, and it is to a certain extent bisected by the River Ega, a shallow but rapid stream, which occasionally is unfordable, but at present forms no barrier of importance to impede an enemy's crossing. The River Ega is spanned by an old stone bridge in the centre of Estella. On the north-west side of the bridge stands the *Casa del Dugue*, a commanding building about 150 yards from the fort of San Francisco. Eastward is situated the convent of Santa Clara, which occupies a prominent position slightly north of the river and in the immediate neighbourhood of the Republican stronghold. There is also an eminence overhanging the *Casa del Dugue*, a little in the background, which is known by the name of the *Monte de la Cruz*. The Carlists had taken, as I stated in my yesterday's letter, the whole of the town, with the exception of San Francisco. Some of their guns were planted in the *Casa del Dugue*, others in the convent of Santa Clara, and they had contrived to mount one small piece on the summit of the *Monte de la Cruz*. The besieged had no artillery of any importance, howitzers of an old-fashioned pattern being the principal armament. However, they were well supplied with breechloaders, and a million cartridges afforded ample ammunition for the 450 Republicans inside San Francisco. On the other hand, the besiegers, with the King Don Carlos himself at their head, mustered 4,000 well-armed and excellently-officered troops. However, the artillery department was absurdly weak, and only consisted of a few pieces of 12 centimetres and two of eight. Guns of a large calibre would have speedily ousted the Federals from their stronghold, but the playthings the Royalists possess – and which, by the way, they have taken from their foes in fair fight – are of no use whatever against any average fortification. This was manifest at a first glance, and, in spite of the cannonade, no breach had been effected. But I was told by one of the King's aides-de-camp that the Republicans had no water supply, and 24 hours more must oblige them to surrender. After observing the attempt of the besiegers to force an entrance for some time, the monotony of the scene began to pall. There is a sameness in being shot at, particularly when a man is so placed that the balls cannot reach him. Such was my position in company with the King's aide-de-camp, and when he suggested breakfast, it was with feeling of anything but reluctance that I accepted the proposal. The house which the Staff inhabited is owned by a Republican proprietress, whose daughter inherits all the likes and dislikes of her mother. The arrival of these Carlists was hateful to the family, and the pretty child did her best to annoy the new comers, but their good nature was proof against every insult, I only mention this just to show that the Carlist officers are not the boars they are represented by their enemies to be; on the contrary, they studiously try to avoid giving offence, and are as gentlemanly a set of men as it has ever been my good fortune to associate with. After breakfast an aide-de-camp said His Majesty would see me, and a few minutes later I found myself in the presence of Don Carlos. The King is a fine-looking man, of commanding presence; and he towers by at least a head and shoulders over most of his suite; very dark hair, cut as short as possible, closely cropped whiskers, a rather large but aquiline nose, with eyes of great brilliancy, and a mouth which slightly deteriorates the effect produced by the other features, as both it and the chin do not correspond with the firmness depicted on the rest of the face, must complete my picture of the Sovereign. The effect is very prepossessing, but there is a sad, care-worn expression on His Majesty's countenance, and well, indeed, there may be. For a great cause is at stake, Don Carlos shares the privations which in this guerrilla warfare every one is exposed to the same as the lowest soldier in the ranks, and this added to incessant mental worry would be enough to break down most men. He exposes his life much too freely, and the Generals are continually entreating him to be more careful, but the King won't be denied, and frequently commands in person a battery when under the heaviest fire. He is in consequence idolized by the troops, who adore their leader, and the *vivas* which greet his appearance are as thrilling as a hearty British cheer. Don Carlos conversed some time with me. No one deplores the war more than the King does, but he said society was being sapped to its core by the Socialistic tendencies of the Republic, and, much as he loved peace, he would spare no effort to restore order and tranquillity to his country. His Majesty, for I suppose he maybe entitled so, as he has already been crowned by the Northern Provinces, is evidently not the priest-ridden bigot which he is declared to be by his enemies. He speaks French, German, and Italian with fluency, and is a perfect master of that sonorous, passionate Castilian oratory which so delights a Spanish audience. Half an hour after my interview with Don Carlos the King quitted the town with a force of 3,000 men, leaving a battalion behind to keep up the blockade. The reason of this step was that a column of the Republicans had marched from Mendigorria to relieve Estella, but on hearing of the Carlists' strength had advanced south to Sesma. The King has taken up a strong position near Allo, and if the Republican column, which comprises, I am told, 1,500 men and two regiments of Cavalry, with half a battery of Artillery, mean fighting, Don Carlos will not balk them of their intention. I do not know if any of my letters have reached their destination, as they have to be intrusted to peasants, who carry them to France, and as the route is frequently intercepted by the Republicans it is as difficult to communicate intelligence as it was in Paris during the siege.

FGB053
Royalist Headquarters, Allo; 20 August 1873
Burnaby to Editor – ***The Times***, **30 August 1873**
This morning the church bells began ringing at an early hour, as an order had been given out that the King would review the troops at 10 30. The excitement

can be easily imagined, as this was the Sovereign's first visit to Allo, and the people would be able to see the Monarch of whom they had heard no much. The fair sex, who are all enthusiastic admirers of Don Carlos, put on their best dresses for the occasion. Balconies assumed a gala appearance, for variegated carpets and bright-coloured shawls were fantastically wound round the pillars, and suspended from the balustrades. The soldiers were dispersed in little knots – some singing Carlist songs; others, notwithstanding the burning sun, were dancing national dances with peasant women to the strains of Basque music. A little further off were some veterans profiting by the few minutes' rest to win or lose some *sueldos* (wages) at *monte*. Officers were scattered about in all directions smoking cigarettes and eagerly discussing whether the Republicans in Estella had surrendered or not. "They do not deserve any quarter at all events", said a tall colonel dressed in a sort of Hussar uniform. "They asked for a parley the day before yesterday, and when we sent an officer with a white flag to inquire what they wanted he was fired upon. Scum of the earth, did you not hear them shout '*Muera Don Carlos! Muera la religion*'." At this moment the clang of brass instruments announced that the long wished for moment had arrived. The King was close at hand. Trumpets sounded the call to "attention". The men fell into the ranks, and on the extreme right an escort of cavalry appeared winding round a little eminence, from which point the Parade-ground commenced. Fine, well-mounted men were this body-guard of the Sovereign, but the dresses were peculiar, and characterized by their absolute dissimilarity. The officers were many of them in a sort of Hussar dress, but some with red pantaloons and Hessian boots, others in overalls, one in a busby, another in a red smoking cap. The men, for the most part, in shirts and close-fitting trousers, both of which were slashed and faced with red. The advanced guard of all, instead of carbines, were armed with gigantic trabucas, or bell-mouthed blunderbusses – obsolete weapons in these days of breechloaders, but calculated to produce great destruction when crammed with slugs and fired into bodies of men at close quarters. The infantry were well armed, principally with short Remingtons. The men were almost all as dark as Africans from exposure to the sun, but their arms were bright; and Don Carlos, who carefully inspected each man as he rode down the lines, had no occasion to be dissatisfied with his troops. The parade was soon over. The battalions returned to their quarters, and the crowd of eager bystanders, hastening from the Paseo, rushed to the church where the King was to attend High Mass. The scene was imposing. Don Carlos himself on the right of the altar, erect, with his arms crossed, a sad smile on his countenance; a little in the background Generals, Staff, and a numerous suite; behind these the crowd thronging and pushing to have a better view; but from time to time, there was a mixture of the ludicrous, as the holy fathers, losing patience with the behaviour of their congregation, reached over the heads of the officials and freely boxed the ears of the more eager and impatient of their flock. The service was at last ended, and two long lines were formed down the aisle and the King passed through; but as he issued from the church the crowd would no longer be kept back. They broke the ranks of the escort, threw themselves on the ground before their Sovereign and kissed his boots, his clothes, his horse, and an old woman, who could not get near him, the ground he had trod upon. Don Carlos took it all very good humouredly, and at last, mounting his charger – a fine bay brown of 16 hands – rode away, and the good people dispersed to their various homes delighted at the evident *bonhomie* of the King.

FGB054
Royalist Headquarters, Dicastillo; 22 August 1873
Burnaby to Editor – *The Times***, 27 August 1873**
Yesterday was a quiet day with the Royalist Army. I saw Don Carlos in the afternoon at Dicastillo, a strong position slightly to the north of Allo, and about a mile and a half distant, where the King had taken up his quarters. He appeared well pleased with the late success of his party, especially in the Basque Provinces, and told me he expected to hear very shortly of the surrender of the fort at Estella, which is now blockaded by the Carlists, as the besiegers had sunk a mine to within 12 feet of the wall. Don Carlos did not think an attack on Dicastillo at all probable. It is much too strong a position, he said, and they have not enough Artillery to shell us out.

Under these circumstances, I determined to ride over to Estella on the morrow and judge for myself what progress the Carlists were making. This morning, however, as the old church clock at Allo was striking 1, we were disturbed by the clatter of a horse's hoofs, which galloped down the street and stopped at our door. "Is the Brigadier at home?" shouted an Orderly officer, "I must see him directly." "Next house", screamed the poor old proprietress of our quarters; and in a minute or two a harried conversation could be heard. "Any news about Estella?" I inquired, putting my head out of the window. "No, No!" was the answer. "Has anything happened?" "Can't say"; and the horseman rode off. But about 6 a.m. trumpets and bugles began to sound in every direction. Presently an infantry battalion marched by, then another, followed by mules laden with luggage. A few minutes later more infantry, and finally a squadron of Hussars brought up the rear. "You had better be quick and mount", said an aide-de-camp; "the Republican column is only one hour distant. The ground on the other side of Allo is favourable for Cavalry, and they have two regiments of Horse as well as Artillery. We have only 120 Cavalry, and no guns, so General Ollo[110] means to make a stand in the olive groves, and on the heights between Allo and Dicastillo, for there we shall await the attack."

110 Nicolas Ollo (1816-1874), a Carlist general who died at the siege of Bilbao.

It is necessary for me now to go back a few days in my narrative. On the 20th of this month the Republican column had retired to Sesma. From that town they retreated to Lodosa, but yesterday, finding out from their spies that our Artillery were at Estella, they advanced to Lerin, and at nightfall commenced a march with the probable object of driving Don Carlos from his position upon Estella, and then, by means of a sally from the besieged fortress, take the Royalist troops between two fires, or if not, at all events, create a diversion and relieve the Republican garrison. I arrived on the ground between Allo and Dicastillo at 7 30 this morning, and found a battalion of Carlist Infantry lying down behind a low wall on a height which well protected the left flank of the position. About half a mile further another battalion in reserve, in *échelon* of companies in rear of an olive grove, and immediately in front of Dicastillo some more infantry prolonging the *échelon*, but with the right thrown back so as to guard against a flank attack on the King's quarters. The squadron of Carlist Cavalry was drawn up on the high road between Allo and Dicastillo. When I arrived at the last named little town, I found it full of excitement, for the King himself, accompanied by General Elio, his Minister of War, and the rest of the suite, had just mounted and ridden to a neighbouring height, which was occupied by the right of the Carlist line. I rode to the same position, and from there could command a perfect view of the whole scene. Distant about five miles, and south of me, were the hills of Sesma, and, coming down a path which leads thence to Allo, I could discern through my glass a squadron of Cavalry and then one or two guns. Presently many more Cavalry appeared, behind whom could be seen fresh Artillery and a column of Infantry. The last-mentioned troops however, were descending by another road about a mile to the east of the first division. On they came nearer and nearer, the Cavalry taking advantage of the ground to extend in skirmishing order. Soon a report told us the action had begun between these horsemen and some sharp-shooters of our side who had advanced to the exposed side of Allo. The Republican Cavalry, after a few shots, wheeled about and retired. Their guns then opened on our left battalion, which was in position behind the stone wall, and at the same time they advanced their Infantry, 1,700 strong, in two lines, the first one, which was in loose order, considerably in front of the other, and occupied Allo. The Carlist forces remained in their positions expecting an attack, but none was made, and the firing ceased, our Infantry remaining in their original positions. If the only purpose of the enemy was to take Allo, in this they have succeeded, as there was no attempt made to resist them except by a few Riflemen, who annoyed the Cavalry; but as far as relieving Estella is concerned, they are as far off as ever from the object in view, as Dicastillo commands the road to the first-named town, and they cannot pass on without turning our position. There were two killed and wounded on our side. Among the latter General Ollo, whose horse on being struck by a bullet reared and threw his rider. The poor old

General was slightly bruised on the head by his fall, but a few minutes later was again in the saddle directing the movements. The Carlist force at Dicastillo is slightly inferior in numbers to the Republican column, but the position is so strong that if General Ollo means fighting it will be very difficult for General Villarpadierna, who commands the enemy, to dislodge him here and relieve Estella. There was a great Carlist battle on almost the same ground in 1839, with 25,000 men on each side. General Elio, who is now the King's Minister of War, commanded the Carlists, and won the day. Will the battle be once more repeated on a smaller scale? To-morrow will show.

4.15 p.m.
I have just heard that the enemy's troops have withdrawn from Allo and retreated to their yesterday's position.

FGB055
Royalist Headquarters, Dicastillo; 24 August 1873
Burnaby to Editor – *The Times*, 30 August 1873
I concluded my last letter from here by stating I had been told that the Republican column had retreated from the town of Allo and retired to their previous camping ground at Sesma. I determined to verify this statement, and so rode down to our former quarters at Allo, and found that the Government troops had not only evacuated the place, but that it was re-garrisoned by Carlists. The little town had not suffered much – a few hundred bullet marks on the walls and an old lady who was complaining of the abstraction of 500 *duros* were the only signs of General Villarpadierna's hasty visit. I saw Don Carlos in the afternoon, and he said he did not expect any fresh attack, but hoped the enemy would make one as some guns had just arrived from Estella, unfortunately too late to be used in the morning's affair. The following day I obtained a guide and rode to Estella, trusting we should arrive in time to witness the explosion of a mine which the Carlists have made beneath the Convent, or now Fort, of San Francisco. General Dorregaray commands the Royalist forces in the above-mentioned town. I went to see him, and he informed me the mine was finished, and in the act of being loaded with dynamite; but that previous to blowing up the garrison a parley would be sounded, and the besieged told that if they did not surrender the charge would be fired in five minutes. From the General's I walked to the Convent of Santa Clara, which is one of the places from which San Francisco has been bombarded. The poor nuns were in a state of great excitement. First of all, the invasion of their quiet home by several hundred Carlists, was not calculated to tranquillize the minds of these celibate ladies, and then the kitchen garden had been seized, a battery established, from which an incessant fire had been maintained on the neighbouring fort; the wounded men who must be cared for, and the thousand little incidents inevitable under

the circumstances had distracted the younger sisters from an honest routine of religious duties and seriously discomposed the household. "Oh, when are you going to take the fort?" said the Lady Superior to my companion. "Is the mine laid? Horrible, horrible! Alas! the souls of the garrison; but if you are driven out, what will become of us? The Republicans will revenge themselves on our establishment because you have to fire on them from our garden. Holy Mother protect us!" And the good woman rocked herself backwards and forwards in a chair, while the other nuns handed round tumblers of sugar and water. From the convent we proceeded towards the mine, having to keep our heads well covered by the parapet, as anything moving instantly attracted attention, and drew a volley of bullets from the besieged. On arriving at the *Calle Mayor*, or principal street, which runs in an easterly direction through the town, and is at one part parallel and only 23 yards from San Francisco, my friend pointed to a large excavation which had been made. "There is the mine", he said. It commences here, passes at a depth of 12ft. beneath this house, then traverses a small garden, a demolished building, and the high road, finally terminating beneath the wall of the Fort. The garrison are making a counter mine, but they have not sunk it deep enough to reach us. We can hear them working quite plainly.

I had some conversation with the Engineer officer who was superintending the operations, and asked him when the mine would be exploded. "I am afraid we cannot blow them up to-day", he replied. "I dare not let my men go on working, as the garrison Engineer would then find out his mistake, and their line is so close to our own that before we could arrange the charge, they might spoil it all. We must wait for a moment's quiet on their part before we finish laying the charge. Probably to-morrow morning early, about 6 o'clock, but it depends upon circumstances." A little farther down the street a barricade had been erected to protect a crossing. The timber was loop-holed, and little urchins of ten and twelve years old were amusing themselves by firing rifles, lent to them by the Carlist soldiery, at the garrison. "Oh do let me see", cried a *gamin*, "if can shave a Liberal's moustache", in reply to my friend's remonstrance about the reckless waste of ammunition. "The Republicans have left off firing their howitzers at the barricade", said an officer who was stationed there, "for I hit upon a capital plan. I sent for some guns, which we loaded with shot, and kept up a continuous discharge on their embrasures. The result was we must have blinded the artillerymen, for they no longer answer our fire. The garrison is becoming discontented", he continued. "We can hear the soldiers in the fort grumbling and abusing their officers, from the roof of a house close by, when it is night and no one moving in the streets. Our best friends are the townspeople, who have been working at the mine for the last three days, and, it will greatly disappoint them if the Republicans surrender, as they look upon blowing up some Liberals as a sort of firework entertainment."

On my way back to Dicastillo I met the Bishop of Urgel,[111] who is also the ecclesiastical head of the Republic of Andorra. He had come from France to place his services at the disposal of Don Carlos. The Bishop is 70 years old, so his age will be a great drawback as far as the privations of a campaign are concerned, but he is the first Bishop who has attached himself to Headquarters, so he was treated with great distinction. An escort was sent to bring him from Estella, and a General, with two of the King's aides-de-camp, received the Bishop half-way, and rode before him to Dicastillo. It was a strange sight. First the Carlist soldiers in all their varied costumes, then the General and aides-de-camp, after them the Holy Father, followed by his Familiar, also on horseback, reading in a nasal tone prayers from a Catholic manual. Hundreds of peasants and ragged children brought up the rear, crying out, "Viva the Bishop; Viva the true religion". All the people we saw on the road knelt down in the dust and asked for the Benediction, which was gravely given by the reverend Prelate. The church bells in the villages rang in his honour, and, amid all this din and noise, we eventually arrived at our destination. I find the Bishop is lodged in he same house as myself. The honour is great, but, alas, all the best dishes which the culinary skill of our hostess can produce grace the Bishop's table, and not your Special Correspondent's.

11 30 a.m.
I have just seen the King's aide-de-camp. The mine at Estella has been fired, but with no result, save blowing up a fountain outside the fort. The mine was loaded with 800lb. of powder, besides dynamite. The Carlist Engineer officers say the mistake was owing to a defect in their instruments. They are looking everywhere for a compass.

FGB056
Royalist Headquarters, Dicastillo; 25 August 1873
Burnaby to Editor – *The Times*, **2 September 1873**
I concluded my letter of yesterday by stating that the attempt to blow up the Republican fort at Estella had failed. A few minutes after despatching it I was informed by an aide-de-camp of Don Carlos that the enemy's column at Sesma had received strong reinforcements from Saragossa; that we were sure to be attacked on the morrow, and our position was a dangerous one, as, with a besieged enemy in the line of our retreat and the numerical superiority of the assailants, we should be between two fires, and any disaster might prove a serious barrier to the success of the Carlist cause. At the same time he told me that orders had been sent to General Dorregaray, commanding the Royalist force at Estella, to commence a fresh mine with the greatest rapidity, as everything

---

111 Josep Caixal y Estradé (1803-1879).

depended on his taking the fort; for, if he could compel the Republicans to surrender before nightfall, we could be strengthened by part of the besieging garrison and have our communications free in the event of a retreat being necessary. Affairs looked gloomy indeed yesterday afternoon. Generals shook their heads, for we might find ourselves hemmed in, even as the French were at Sedan,[112] before the morrow's sun had set. Don Carlos himself was almost the only person who did not despond. He walked about cheerily on the terrace of the Cathedral, smoking a cigarette and conversing with everybody. "My men fight with a will", said the King. "We have beaten them before and we shall beat them again." But our position was not pleasant, and many pulses did not throb as placidly as His Majesty's when he retired to bed last evening. Before dawn had set in, a noise could be heard from the streets below. Louder and louder the sounds became, and *vivas* responded far and wide. What could be the matter? I was in the act of dressing when an adjutant rapped at the door and said that the Government troops in Estella had surrendered, and the bands were to play in the Plaza immediately by order of the King. All the inhabitants of Dicastillo, in spite of the early hour – 2 a.m. – were astir. Candles and lamps placed on the various balconies illumined the scene. Music struck up Carlist national airs, and any more sleep was evidently out of the question.

I was told by the King that the following were the terms accepted by the Republican garrison:– full liberty for officers and men; the former to retain their arms; all the munitions of war in the fort to be given up; and the garrison to be escorted as far as Pampeluna in order to prevent any hostile manifestation on the part of Carlist peasants by the way. It appeared that dissension had broken out among the Government troops the previous evening, and these were not allayed by the mine sprung close to them, as the besieged saw that it was only the precursor to another, which would probably prove fatal. So at 9 o'clock last evening they sounded a parley. General Dorregaray, as it may well be supposed, did not delay in offering them terms. At midnight the vanquished troops left the town in the direction of Pampeluna, and early this morning the Carlists at Dicastillo were reinforced by the battalion from Estella. The Royalist troops consist of 3,200 infantry, a handful of cavalry, and two guns. The enemy's column at Sesma were 5,000 strong, comprising six guns, two regiments of horse, besides foot soldiers. The advantage was on their side as far as numbers were concerned; but the ground leading to Dicastillo was very difficult to attack and, thickly planted with vines and olive groves, utterly impossible for cavalry evolutions. At 6 a.m. the enemy could be seen in the misty distance advancing through the defiles of the mountains in long columns,

---

112 The Battle of Sedan was fought during the Franco-Prussian War on 1 September 1870, resulting in the capture of Emperor Napoleon III and a large number of his troops. It effectively decided the war in favour of Prussia.

preceded by a thin line of cavalry, searching the country in their front. General Elio, who commanded the Carlist force, soon made his dispositions for defence. One battalion was posted in the little Plaza of the Cathedral, which commands a view for miles around, a second on some rising ground to the right front, the third in line with the second on a neighbouring hill, while our extreme right was protected by another battalion in *échelon* with the third, and placed on a position so steep that at first sight the natural defences would have appeared to the non-military eye sufficient for its protection. But no; for it was the key of our formation, as some hours more were destined to prove. Nearer and nearer the enemy came, until glasses were no longer necessary, and artillery, cavalry, and infantry could be plainly discerned traversing the plain towards us. All this time the various bands of music in the town were playing Royalist marches, and along the road from Allo to Dicastillo toiled mules and beasts of burden conveying the poor people and their chattels to Marentin, a village in the rear of the Carlist head-quarters, and out of the range of Republican projectiles. Suddenly the enemy's column appeared to detach behind a distant promontory on a new line. "They are making for Allo", said an old General, putting down his ear-trumpet, through which his aide-de-camp had been speaking. It appeared so; for dispositions were changed and the troops moved at the double to take up exactly the same ground as I described in a previous letter. But this alteration was only a feint to throw the Carlist General off his guard; and a little later a fresh change of position brought the Republican troops into their original line. Their artillery opened at an absurd range, the shells striking the ground at least a mile from the centre of our defence – a spot where Don Carlos had stationed himself with his suite. Another five minutes and a second shot fell about 200 yards from where the King was standing, and in a direct line with him. His Staff entreated their Sovereign to retire a little, as he was only exposing himself unnecessarily, but nothing would induce their leader to move until his presence was required at another point, on which the foe were advancing; for the Republican General, Santa Pau, was trying to turn our right. On his men came at the double, making every effort to gain the olive groves and rises which formed a thick network in front of the ground where our 4th Battalion stood. Ammunition was short. Many men had only 10 rounds each in their pouches and some even less. "Attack with the bayonet", was the word, and the battalion charged downhill at their Republican assailants, who were thoroughly out of breath from previous exertions. There was no collision. The enemy fled in disorder, and the two guns placed on the Carlist right played with great havoc upon the foe in his disordered flight. At the same time two companies of another battalion charged the Republicans from the centre of our position. A slight encounter ensued. The combatants were so mixed that it was hard to tell friend from foe until at last a cheer told us that the Carlists had again succeeded. The Government troops were utterly disorganised, and retiring as fast as their legs could carry them. However, the Republican cavalry then interposed, for at this point horseman could act, and, supported as they were by guns, prevented any further pursuit. But the day was over, and as I write the discomforted Government troops can be seen retiring to their original position at Sesma. If Don Carlos had as much cavalry as his opponents, would they have thus escaped? Experience teaches us otherwise, and until the Royalists are provide with guns and horsemen it will be difficult for them to convert a defeat into a rout.

FGB057
Royalist Headquarters, Estella; 26 August 1873
Burnaby to Editor – *The Times*, **1 September 1873**
I had barely finished my yesterday's letter and delivered it to the messenger who was leaving for France before the trumpets sounded, and half an hour later we were once more in the saddle, *en route* with Don Carlos to Estella. The King had taken advantage of an hour's rest to visit the wounded and say a few words of sympathy and thanks to the poor sufferers for his cause. Great was the cheering from the troops who were drawn up on both sides of the road, as the Royal *cortége* passed through and each regiment in succession fell in and marched on in rear of the escort. The church bells rang merrily in the villages as we rode by, and the welcome received by Don Carlos, and in fact everybody in his suite, was enthusiastic. Horsemen, fortunately, escaped the more demonstrative symptoms of public admiration, as mounted men could not be easily embraced and hugged by the populace, but the soldiers were freely kissed, which to my English servant who had to share in the performance was anything but agreeable. Sometime before arriving at Estella the smoke of the burning fortress could be discerned, and now and then a report as if of a shell bursting could be heard. "It is only a bomb or two which we did not find among the ammunition, and they are now exploding from the heat", said a French nobleman who has been with the Carlists since the outbreak of the war. "However, we did not do badly", he continued, "for our fellows found 1,500 rifles, 70,000 cartridges, besides engineering tools and some instruments which were greatly needed, as the want of a good compass was the cause of our failure with the mine.

The little town is full of troops, as three fresh battalions under General Lizzarraga have arrived from Guipuzcoa, and a fourth marched in last night from a village a few miles off. The day before yesterday was a critical 24 hours for the Royalists. Everything depended on taking San Francisco, the Republican stronghold. The King had only three battalions and two guns to oppose the Sesma column, which was being strongly reinforced, and his communications with the North were cut off. The personal safety of Don Carlos was at stake, as not much quarter would probably be shown him should he be taken prisoner.

However, the fall of the Fort turned the scale in his favour. An extra battalion came to the rescue. Four more were known to be on the way, and, best of all, the greatest enthusiasm prevailed among the troops on account of their comrades' success at Estella. For the same reason a proportionate feeling of despondency pervaded the Republican ranks. The Government troops had once tried to relieve the besieged garrison, and had failed. They placed no confidence in the generalship of their leaders, Villarpadierna and Santa Pau. Finally, when half an hour from Dicastillo, the news arrived that San Francisco had been surrendered to the Carlists. It was under these circumstances the column was called upon to attack a strong position held by men not much inferior to themselves in number, but vastly superior in discipline and respect to authority. It naturally failed, and will continue to do so until repeated disasters have taught the Government at Madrid – firstly, that the power of inflicting capital punishment should be vested, in time of war, with their Generals, for without this check the hot blooded southerners cannot be kept in order; secondly, that the best troops, when led by bad leaders, are uselessly sacrificed, and anything more absurd than cavalry advancing within the range of infantry sheltered by olive groves cannot be well imagined. The artillery, also, was extended over a large extent of front, and did not make itself felt, whereas if it had been concentrated there would have been more possibility of turning our right, though, from the extreme strength of the position, it would have been less than probable.

FGB058
Royalist Headquarters, Estella; 28 August 1873
Burnaby to Editor – *The Times***, 2 September 1873**
I did not give the list of Carlist casualties in my previous letters which described the engagements at Allo and Dicastillo, as from the different accounts freely promulgated I was afraid of forwarding an inaccurate return. However, it is now stated on good authority that the Royalists had two men killed and five wounded at Allo, and in the defence of Dicastillo five killed and 17 wounded. The enemy's loss is estimated to have been considerably more. This is not unlikely, as the Republicans had to advance under the fire of a well-sheltered opponent. Carlist reports assume the Government troops to have been reduced by 170 men. Of course it is impossible for me to arrive at the exact numbers, but the Royalists, I know, took 15 prisoners at Dicastillo, including a lieutenant-colonel, two sergeants, one corporal, and 11 privates.

The King's division was reinforced at Estella, as General Lizzarraga arrived from Guipuzcoa with strong battalions, and various parties had marched in from the neighbouring districts. The townspeople were much inconvenienced by the number of men billeted on them, amounting to above 7,000 infantry, 250 cavalry, and six guns. In consequence of this General Elio determined to change his quarters in 24 hours' time and to return with Don Carlos' now strengthened force to Dicastillo, in hopes that the Republican column would advance and once more try the fortune of war. Our last day at Estella was a gala one for the inhabitants. Carlist bands played national tunes in the squares until a late hour, fireworks were let off in honour of the occasion, and every available spot was occupied by hundreds of men and women slowly gyrating to provincial airs, *jotas*,[113] and other popular Basque dances. A very good-humoured crowd it was, too. Nowhere could I hear any sound of discord, and, notwithstanding the unlimited supply of wine freely lavished by the good folks of Dicastillo on the soldiery, not a symptom of drunkenness displayed itself.

The Carlist troops do not require much time to turn out in marching order. A man is considered equipped when he is provided with arms, 60 rounds of ball cartridge, his food for the day, and a spare shirt. As for marching, I have never seen their superiors, four miles an hour in six continuous hours being frequently accomplished by them, the men looking as fresh at the end of the journey as when they started. The rations are good and ample; in fact a Carlist receives a quarter of a pound more meat than the British soldier, the daily allowance for the former being – one pound of meat, two pounds of bread, and two pints of wine, which is of fair quality and far superior to average French *vin ordinaire*. In addition to this he is paid one real, or 2½d., a day. The officers, on the contrary, have but a pittance, a captain receiving but little more than a sergeant in an English cavalry regiment. However, as they are almost all persons of some position, money is not so important to them as to individuals in the higher ranks of the Republican army. There is one great drawback, speaking of the Royalist soldiery; for although they are all volunteers, who love fighting for fighting's sake, and are as brave and fine-looking a body of men as a General could wish to command, they hate the idea of drill, and very little instruction is given them, as, if much time were occupied with this particular, the Carlist troops would soon dwindle away. Their Generals are aware of this weakness, for they do not press the point too closely. The consequence is many valuable hours are consumed in idleness, and the commander of the forces cannot make an advance until he has thorough confidence in the efficiency of his troops. As far as figures are concerned, the Royalists number 22,000 well-armed men, without counting Catalonia, where Don Alfonso is said to have 11,000 more, who are fairly organised. At head-quarters regrets are occasionally whispered about that the King entered Spain so soon, and before the army was in regular working order. But the reason can be given very shortly. Don Carlos is a Spaniard, and highly sensitive. Reports were published by the Republican journals aspersing his courage, and saying that he was living a luxurious life in France while his adherents were shedding their blood in

---

113 A genre of music and the associated dance known throughout Spain.

Spain. Some of these articles were republished in French newspapers, and the King was so indignant at the term *cobarde*, "coward", unjustly attributed to him, that, contrary to the advice of his Minister of War, he crossed the frontier. Undoubtedly the Royalists are each day becoming more formidable, and, if they have rifles enough, could arm 50,000 men in a week. The latter seem plentiful enough, and each day the authorities are pestered by hundreds of volunteers, eagerly asking permission to enrol themselves. The Staff is also increasing, and the number of persons in the King's train during our march of yesterday exceeded 120 horsemen – ridiculous if our force, only some 7,000 combatants, be considered. Artillery officers arrive from day to day, and offer their services. As to Generals, there are more than 20 now in France awaiting the King's permission to join his banner. Few foreign officers have joined the Carlists, three or four Germans and the same number of Frenchman being almost the only strangers attached to the head-quarters. It is said there are some Irishmen in the Basque Division; but, as I have not seen them, I cannot vouch for the veracity of the statement – so many *canards* are continually being bandied from mouth to mouth, which, combined with the Spanish character, so prone to exaggeration and addicted to romance and invention, make the task of sifting the real from the unreal very difficult.

If I may be allowed to hazard an opinion – founded, however, merely on personal observation – I should say that any advance upon Madrid before next spring is highly improbable. Some more Castilian battalions must be raised before this can be attempted; as, if an army composed entirely of men from the Navarre and Basque Provinces were to enter Castile, so strong is the feeling of Provincial jealousy in Spain that the *Castillaños* would imagine it was an attempt of the Northerners aimed at their independence, and made with the object of conquest; but if men from Castillian villages formed part of the advanced guard all fears of this nature would vanish, and the troops be received with open arms instead of with distrust and in the light of invaders.

FGB059
Royalist Headquarters, Aras; 31 August 1873
Burnaby to Editor – *The Times***, 6 September 1873**
The principal characteristics of this guerrilla warfare now carried on by the Royalists are repeated forced marches, a perfect system of espionage, and absolute reticence on the part of the leaders as to the hour at which a change of quarters will be made. In consequence of this, if any one leaves his billet for a short walk he may find in an hour's time that not only have the troops left, but that they are not in sight and nobody can tell him where they have gone. The day before yesterday I rode over to breakfast with an officer stationed in an adjacent village, and on my return I heard that the Royal mules were packed, and saw an escort drawn up before Don Carlos's door. "Be quick", said an old colonel; "we

march directly". "Where?" "*Quien sabe?*" "Who knows?" and in a few minutes' time we had left Dicastillo. My first thought was that we were going to attack Tafalla, but no, instead of turning in an easterly direction, our advanced guard took a south-westerly course over a wretched cross country road, blocked up in places with loose stones, and extremely trying for cavalry. "We shall sleep at Los Arcos", said my companion; "but what can the reason of it be? No Republicans are there." However, after a three hours' march we halted at Los Arcos, a dirty little town, which contains under normal conditions perhaps 4,000 inhabitants. The following day two battalions were sent off long before sunrise, and the rest of our force, which comprised three battalions of infantry, 120 horse, four guns, a Bishop, and a petroleum cart, paraded at 5 a.m. Some thought we were to attack Logrono, where Espartero resides occasionally; but eventually it was whispered that our object was Viana; for 200 Republican National Guards and about 20 dismounted men of the regiment of Pavia were stationed there. They had a good supply of arms, and the plan was to capture the rifles with the view of arming a fresh battalion. On approaching Viana, some shots could be heard, for the first two battalions had already entered the town. Our own division halted, after forming in column of companies, on, some ground which stood almost as high as Viana itself, which is built on a very precipitous rise. The town, if properly defended, would have been difficult to take; but the Republicans had not made any resistance until the Carlists were already within the walls, and then the garrison retired; some went to the Convent of Santa Maria, which is in juxtaposition with a small tower called San Lorenzo, and in communication with it by means of a covered passage; the remainder established themselves in the church of San Pedro, a thick-walled building, which they loop-holed and converted into a temporary fort. General Ollo, who commanded the two Royalist battalions, had his head-quarters in the convent of San Francisco, and the guns, which had been conveyed on the backs of mules to Viana, were placed, two in houses overlooking San Pedro, the key of the Republican position, and the others in the *Calle Mayor*, ready to be used against Santa Maria, if required. The garrison evidently expected that Villarpadierna would come from Logrono with a column to their rescue, for they laughed at the idea of surrender, and – but this I am told, and cannot vouch for the fact, as I did not witness it myself – fired on the officer who proposed terms of capitulation to them. Meanwhile, Elio, the Carlist General-in-Chief, sent out some horsemen to scour the country and obtain information as to the number of Villarpadierna's force. The main body of the Carlist soldiers was scattered here and there, the men lying about in groups, drinking wine out of pig-skins. Don Carlos himself was well in the foreground, talking to the Bishop, and every now and then eagerly scanning the horizon in the direction of Logrono. "What a good picture El Rey would make now!" said an aide-de-camp, as Don Carlos put down his glasses and began to eat a large melon, without either fork or spoon. The correspondent of the *Illustrated London News* evidently thought so too, and was rapidly sketching the group. "*Mais, mon Rois, vous mangez trop vite votre melon*",[114] cried the unabashed draughtsman, as Don Carlos, taking rather a larger mouthful, slightly changed his position. The bystanders laughed, but an officer galloping up with a despatch soon gave us something else to think of. The enemy had retired, and General Elio decided that El Rey should take up his quarters at Aras, a village in the neighbourhood, with three battalions, and that the other two should continue the siege. The small cannon the Royalists possess make little impression on the walls, so in all probability the petroleum will be soon turned to account. This inflammable liquid is pumped into a fire engine worked by soldiers, and then thrown by means of a hose on to the roof of the besieged place; when the latter is thoroughly saturated fire balls are tossed into the building, and an inextinguishable conflagration is the result. The Royalists only use this measure as a last resource, and they excuse themselves on the ground of their deficiency in artillery. I must say it is a measure which savours too much of the Commune in Paris to please me. However, in war time the Carlists say everything is fair.

FGB060
Royalist Headquarters, Alsasua; 3 September 1873
Burnaby to Editor – *The Times*, 9 September 1873

A few minutes after forwarding my telegraph last Sunday announcing the surrender of the Republican garrison at Viana, I was informed that Don Carlos and his Staff were going to visit the conquered town, and that as the King's baggage was packed we should not return to our quarters at Aras. The fortifications at Viana had been almost entirely demolished, and there was nothing of interest to be seen. So after a short stay we left for Los Arcos, where I expected Don Carlos would remain at least 24 hours to rest his horses and men. But no. The following, day, at 5 a.m., he was on the march, and we soon reached Murietta. It was thought that here the Government troops might make a stand. However, they did not appear and after a night spent without any attack, save from the vermin, we paraded early to march to a destination of which all were ignorant, save the General. A redistribution was then made of the forces, the nature of which I must not mention, and we continued our route to Larion, where we made a short halt. Larion is the head-quarters of the celebrated Carlist, Cabecilla (Leader) Rosas. He is quite a character in his way, and has been of great use to the Royalist cause. Rosas knows every inch of the country, and is always on the track of the Republican columns, cutting off their communications and supplies. On one occasion when Estella was

---

114 'But my king, you eat your melon too quickly.' The artist of the *Illustrated London News* did have one of his drawings of Don Carlos published on 27 September 1873, but not this one.

held by the Government troops, he entered the town accompanied by one of his band. It was broad daylight, and two officers of the garrison were walking in the Plaza. "You must come with us whispered Rosas; or, if not, you die", at the same time pointing to a revolver, the barrel of which was concealed in his packet. The individuals thus accosted, strange to say, considering the profession to which they belonged, made no resistance, and the Cabecilla marched them off as prisoners. I relate the story as it has been frequently told me, and I believe it can be thoroughly relied upon.

After remaining, two hours at Larion, we mounted and rode through Almescuas, a narrow valley, topped on both sides by rugged mountains. Wild and romantic indeed was the scenery as Don Carlos and his followers descended the precipitous paths, where a slip to the right or left would have been fatal. Almescuas is the stronghold of the Carlists. The passes and roads are very narrow, and so exposed to a fire from the crags which overhang them that a few men can in many places bar the passage of an army, and woe betide a hostile force once entangled in the defiles. Presently we passed through Rudaire, where a factory for the repair of firearms has been established. Then San Martin lay before us, a small town, principally inhabited by old Royalist officers, who receive a daily stipend from Don Carlos on account of services rendered by them in previous wars to his family. "Look at Escala", said my companion, a German Baron, formerly an officer in the Prussian Garde Schützen,[115] but now one of General Elio's Staff, pointing to a little village on a mountain to our left, "I saw two fellows shot there last April", he continued. "One was a Carlist sergeant, the other a Republican spy. The sergeant had distinguished himself in several engagements, but, alas! he sometimes demanded more than the just number of rations in the villages where his company was stationed. This was discovered, and on the first occasion he was pardoned; but, having been detected a second time, the sergeant was sent to us escorted by two soldiers, one of whom carried an order for the immediate execution of his prisoner. The poor fellow knew what the sentence was, and did not wait till I had read the document, but saluted and said, 'Sir, I have come to be shot.' Close by Escala there are a few holes in the mountain; they are very deep, and only 3ft. or 4ft. wide at the surface. After the sergeant and spy had confessed to the priest, they were marched by a platoon of our men to one of the chasms, and placed side by side at its mouth. I was just, going to give the word 'fire' when the Carlist called out, 'I have a favour to ask.' 'What is it?' 'For that fellow', pointing to the Republican, 'to be shot elsewhere. I do not want my blood to mix with his.' The request was granted, and the spy taken further off. In the meantime the sergeant stripped himself of nearly all his clothes. 'They are new', he remarked, 'and will do for a good Royalist. *Viva Carlos Setimo!*' A volley was fired and the

---

115 Guards' rifle battalion.

body disappeared. It grieved me very much to have to execute the sentence. But what could be done? Orders must be obeyed." "Theft is severely punished", observed another officer. "The General who commands our Division in Alala has just given out that any soldier who steals an article give the value of one real – 2½d. – shall be shot."

At last we arrived at Eulata, and on being informed that some Republican officers were prisoners in Nazarachen, a village close by, I walked over to judge for myself how they were treated. We found them residing in a comfortable little house, and, on their recognizing my companion, they at once offered us *aguadiente*,[116] apologizing for the dearth of other liqueurs. I asked one of the prisoners if he was satisfied with the way the Carlists behaved to him. "Yes", was the answer, "and we have nothing to complain of except that our letters are opened and read." I was afterwards told that the prisoners had communicated Carlist military news to some Republican friends, and that this was the cause of their correspondence being examined. We left Eulata very early to-day, and marched through a district studded with magnificent timber. Fine old oak trees now and then blocked up the path with their gigantic branches as we rode towards the Barranca. One more incline, so steep that even the mules slipped as their riders, scrambling down, led them in single file, and Alsasua came in view. We are to remain here but a few hours, and then to continue our march; where, no one knows save General Elio, who is well aware that in time of war "silence is golden".

FGB061
Royalist Headquarters, Bergara; 4 September 1873
Burnaby to Editor (telegraph via Bayonne)
The Times, 5 September 1873

The garrison at Viana has surrendered. Don Carlos has granted to the prisoners of war their liberty.

FGB062
Royalist Headquarters, Bergara; 5 September 1873
Burnaby to Editor – *The Times*, 12 September 1873

The Carlists were so well received at Alsasua that it was determined to remain a night in that town, and I found myself again located in the same house as the Bishop of Urgel. The fatigues and hardships of the campaign have told upon the Prelate's health, and his Familiar thought it necessary to send for a medical man. The latter, on arriving, instantly prescribed bleeding, the invariable remedy of Spanish doctors when they do not know what is the matter with their patient. I called upon the Bishop in the afternoon and received from him a startling piece

---

116 A clear, coarse brandy.

of information – viz., that Queen Victoria is a Catholic at heart. The statement is so glaringly absurd that I only mention it to show the utter ignorance of English affairs which exists among the Spanish clergy. Our march yesterday was singularly devoid of interest, save the beautiful scenery which surrounded us, until we arrived at Zegama. Here there was a short halt, and Don Carlos, dismounting, proceeded to the church of San Martin, where is interred the body of Zumalacárregui,[117] the Royalist Commander-in-Chief during part of the Seven Years' War.[118] The Prince approached the monument and, kneeling down, prayed fervently for several minutes, while the organ poured out the grand strains of the "*Marcha Real*". He then examined, with evident interest, the altar-piece. This is not composed of the precious metals, nor of marble, but is formed of wood so exquisitely carved in the minutest details that I much regretted the short time allowed us, and which did not permit of a more careful examination. Soon after leaving Zegama we began to march down the railway, and presently entered a vast tunnel of above 2,000 metres in length. The escort dismounted, torches were carried before us, and the word "*Silencio*" was passed down the ranks. It was a strange sight, the apparently never-ending arches roofing us out completely from the exterior world. A death-like stillness reigned; unbroken save by the suppressed oaths of the troopers; as their spurred boot-heels slipped over the broken stones, or when a horse, striking his mailed hoof on the rail, created a clang which re-echoed in the distance until it faintly died away and was heard no more.

Paler and more dimly flickered the lights in the damp and fetid atmosphere. Ghastlier and more weird-like in their grim gauntness loomed out the shadows reflected on the stonework. What a chance for the Republican Generals, could they have availed themselves of the opportunity! Don Carlos and his Guards, a few hundred men, in this apparently never-ending tunnel. A few pounds of gunpowder ignited at either end would have blocked us up, perhaps, for ever, and Don Carlos might now be dead or a prisoner in the hands of his enemies.

Fortunately, however, for the Prince, the Government troops were miles away at Tolosa, not venturing to leave their quarters for fear of a surprise, and we at last emerged from what had vividly recalled to my mind parts of Dante's *Inferno*, and gladly filled our lungs with the pure mountain air. For several miles further we rode along the line, occasionally stumbling over bits of telegraph wire which encumbered the path in all directions, till at length the head of our column turned sharp to the left, and once more the high road lay stretched before us. There was one more short rest at a little town to feed the horses, and another tedious ride, when, after having placed at least 27 English miles

---

117 Tomás de Zumalacárregui y de Imaz (1788-1835) was a Carlist general.
118 Burnaby uses the phrase 'Seven Year's War' to refer to the first Carlist War of 1833-1839, rather than the better known international conflict of 1756-1763.

between ourselves and Alsasua, the clear sound of church bells ringing a merry peal announced that we were nearing our destination. Martial music then broke upon the ear, for Lizzarraga,[119] the Commander-in-Chief of Guipuzcoa had come to escort his Sovereign into Bergara.

Unluckily for the old officer, his horse reared and the rider was in the act of saluting, and the General rolled off. However, he was soon again in his saddle, and advanced before Don Carlos through long lines of Infantry composed of magnificent men, tall and broad-chested enough to form part of our own Foot Guards, to the cathedral of the town. A short mass was sung, after which Don Carlos took up his position on a balcony which commanded a good view of the square now called *La Plaza de Carlos Setimo*. The garrison of Bergara, 4,500 Infantry, then defiled by sections of fours before their Sovereign. "*Viva el Rey!*" shouted each company, headed by its officers, as they passed the saluting point. But, with the exception of these cheers, there was an absence of enthusiasm which strikingly contrasted with the heart-stirring welcome received by Don Carlos at Estella. Are the Guipuzcoans less Royalist than the people of Navarre? Carlist Generals say no, but that the character of the inhabitants is not so demonstrative here as in the Province we have left behind, though it is far truer and more sterling beneath the surface. This may be so, and, perhaps, as Bergara was only taken by General Lizzarraga on the 13th of last month, the fear of a future re-occupation by the Republican troops may in some degree have checked the popular feeling. However, the fact remains that so far the reception of Don Carlos in Guipuzcoa has not been so outwardly enthusiastic as in Navarre.

FGB063
Royalist Headquarters, Azpeitia; 8 September 1873
Burnaby to Editor – *The Times***, 15 September 1873**
When we were quartered at Bergara I had the honour of dining one evening with Don Carlos. The house which he inhabited was surrounded by an English-looking garden, and had an air of comfort about it unusual in most of the dwellings I have previously seen in Spain. It belongs to an Alfonsist Count whose children, however, were Carlists. "Their father", observed the King, "is quite right in maintaining his allegiance, for he owes everything he has to Queen Isabella, but his sons have elected for me, and are among my warmest partisans." On my expressing some surprise that we did not attack Tolosa, it was remarked that the Carlist forces were now in a state of equilibrium with the Republican troops, strong enough for defence, but not sufficiently organized for continuous aggressive steps. "However, we shall soon be able to attack the enemy in all his strongholds", observed my neighbour, "but Rome was not built

---

119 Antonio Lizzarraga y Esquiroz (1817-1877), a Carlist general.

in a day, and the Royalist movement only began 10 months ago, when 27 men crossed the frontier. At that time we were always being pursued by the columns, but now, although Sanchez Bregua knows that we are within four leagues of him and his 10,000 troops, he does not dare attack us."

Don Carlos is evidently himself the soul of his party. He has from his boyhood been impressed with the idea that he will one day be on the throne of Spain. When the Carlist insurrection failed two years ago, many of his followers lost heart. "We have no soldiers", they cried. "Men will come", said the Prince, "when I cross the border." "But there are no arms." "Never mind, we will take them from the enemy", retorted Don Carlos. "It will all come right, but we must bide our time." The Republican journals of Madrid have described the Head of the Royalist Party as being a mere tool in the hands of designing agents. This is an absurd fabrication. There are few men less easily led either in politics or military matters, for with sound common sense and a keen knowledge of character he adds a certain amount of Teutonic obstinacy and perseverance, qualities which make him either a friend to be esteemed, or a foe who cannot be trifled with. Very liberal in his opinions, and far from being a bigot in religious matters, his favourite maxim is, that with Spaniards "two and two do not make four", and he says the nation must be taught its mistake by degrees and not be pulled up too soon.

The following day we rode to Placencia and Erlar to see the manufactories of small arms. These towns can under normal conditions turn out 1,700 rifles a week, but previously to the retreat of the Republican troops they destroyed part of the machinery, and so at the present moment not more than 90 breechloaders can be supplied within the 24 hours. The firearms are all carbines on the Remington system, which is the one most in favour with the Carlists. There was little enthusiasm displayed on our arrival, and in Erlar a worker in mosaics had concealed nearly all his stock-in-trade. However, on discovering that Don Carlos and his staff paid for everything they bought in ready money, fresh boxes of goods were brought down, and I heard one shopman whisper to another, "Why, they are not the thieves the Republicans make them out, at all events." We left Bergara yesterday and marched about 14 miles to Argostea. Here everybody was Carlist to the backbone. Performers on instruments somewhat resembling the bagpipes in their harmonious strains came out to meet us, and nearly succeeded in breaking the drums of our ears with Royalist marches. Cries of *"Viva la Religion – Viva Carlos setimo"*, were intermingled from time to time with a about, *"Viva los fueros"* – the provincial privileges. For the Guipuzcoans are a canny race, like the Scotch, and with all their loyalty never forget to look after number one. The *cura*, in whose house I was quartered, had been a Colonel in the army during the former Carlist war, and he took great pleasure in showing me a passport describing his rank and services. "I am too old now", he said, shaking his silvery locks sorrowfully, "for what could my aged limbs do for the King?" We halted at the monastery of Loyola on our way here, and a religious ceremony was performed, the Bishop of Urgel administering the Communion to the King's officers and all the troops in a large church which forms the centre of the building. It was an imposing sight as battalion after battalion was marched in and the soldiers presented arms, after which they went down on their knees as one man, awaiting each his turn to receive the holy wafer. On the right of the church, which is beautifully adorned with carving and lapidary work, culminating in a magnificent dome so lofty that its rich chasing is almost lost upon the spectator, stands the monastery, once a castle belonging to the family of Loyola. Here was born the founder of the Jesuit Order, who served for some years as an officer in the cavalry, but on being wounded at Pampeluna was seized, said my informant, an old priest, with feelings of remorse, and retired to his home, afterwards converting the castle into a monastery. By the kindness of the Marquis de Valdespina and Señor Paraguirre, Don Carlos's secretary, I was permitted to visit the whole of the building. The vast refectory, once the dining room of 150 monks, was at that moment occupied by Don Carlos and his suite taking chocolate. We passed then through the library, which should contain 35,000 choice volumes and manuscripts, but, alas! is now empty, as the books are hid away and buried with the pictures and silver image of Loyola for fear of the Republican Government. The Marquis next led us through the school-room. "It was here that I finished my education", he said, and, reanimated by his boyish recollections, my companion hastened from recess to tower and from tower to dome, then down to the ruins and up again to the highest pinnacle for me to have a better view of the old convent garden and rich domains formerly belonging to the Jesuit Order.

At Azpeitia the King has been received with great acclamations. However, much time is being lost in these promenades of Don Carlos, and if another blow is not soon struck, the Republicans will quickly recover from their repulse at Dicastillo.

FGB064
Royalist Headquarters, Sequeito; 11 September 1873
Burnaby to Editor – *The Times***, 19 September 1873**
When we were at Azpeitia, it was rumoured that Don Carlos's intention was to attack General Loma, then stationed at Tolosa with a force of about 7,000 men under his command. However, on leaving our quarters, I soon saw that this was not the plan, as, instead of marching in a south-eastern direction, the Royalist troops advanced due north towards the Monastery of Loyola. Here, however, General Lizzarraga, with his division, turned off on a bypath, while the King, attended by his Staff and an escort of Lancers, took the road to Elgoular. We were then informed that the idea was to try and induce Loma to quit his

stronghold at Tolosa and pursue Don Carlos. Should the Republican General fall into the trap he would find himself between two Carlist divisions, one of 5,000 men, under General Lizzarraga, which would cut off his retreat upon Tolosa, and the Vorcasa force of 7,000 men, commanded by Velasco, which would bar Loma's progress to the front. I write thus fully as several days must intervene before this letter can be published, and the King will be miles away from Sequeito before the Republican leader could be aware of the little pitfall so carefully dug for him by General Elio.

Presently we arrived at Elgoular, a pretty little town situated in a valley, and watered by a rapid trout stream, which shone like a silver thread in the rays of the setting sun as we, gradually descending, the winding path in serpent-like column, slowly approached its banks. The news of the King's intended visit had filled the streets with eager spectators, who, anxious to see that Don Carlos of whom they had heard so much, ran before the Royal *cortége*, discharging rockets in the air by way of doing honour to the occasion. Pretty girls – and the women of Elgoular may well claim pre-eminence in eyes and lashes over those daughters of Eve we had seen in Navarre – showered bouquets of flowers from the windows, while an old woman of some 80 years, pressing eagerly up to the head of the King's charger, produced a hen, and presented the bird to Don Carlos. The poor Prince was rather at a loss to know what he could do with the fowl, the more especially as it was alive. However he accepted the offering, to the great delight of the donor, and an attendant tied the bird on to a pack mule. "*Viva Don Carlos!*" screeched the enthusiastic old lady, "but where is Doña Margherita?"[120] she added, in an inquiring tone to the King. His face lit up at the question. "She will come too, but later on", he answered in a kind tone. However, the band struck up the Royal march, the bystanders pushed and jostled to have a better view, the old woman was borne away by the throng, and pretty little Elgoular was gradually lost to view. Two hours later a succession of huge bonfires kindled on either side of the road announced that we were reaching our quarters for the night, and shortly afterwards Don Carlos with his suite rode into the market-place of Marquina. Here a rather amusing incident occurred. My companion, a German Baron, having lost his way in the narrow streets, found himself surrounded by about 15 of the fair sex, who vociferated, "*Viva Don Carlos! Viva la Religion! Abajo el Estrangero!*" (Down with the foreigner), meaning Amadeo. The German, however, took the last expression as applying to himself, so with the gravity of his nation he said, "I am a foreigner". His assailants were delighted at the avowal. The Baron was made to dismount, and accompany the whole conclave of damsels to the house of their uncle, a rich tradesman in the town. Tea was produced, and my friend was not allowed to quit his hospitable entertainers until he had promised to

---

120 His wife, Princess Margherita of Bourbon-Parma (1847-1893).

renew the visit on the morrow. However, "*l'homme propose, mais le Dieu dispose*", and the morrow we were again in the saddle, riding through mountain paths, and often having to walk on account of the precipitous nature of the road, Don Carlos himself first setting the example in dismounting. An old Italian priest who accompanies the head-quarters has brought an enormous bronze cross from Rome; in one of the arms there is a small receptacle which, he says, contains a bit of the True Cross. Occasionally, and as a great treat, the Cross is taken out of the saddlebags and handed to the bystanders, who embrace it with the greatest fervour. Yesterday it was passed into so many hands that the good priest began to be anxious about his valuable relic. However, at last it was rescued by the artist of the *Illustrated London News*, who succeeded in wrestling the cross from some devout villagers. One of them, however, on finding that she could not kiss the coveted treasure, threw her arms round its temporary possessor and embraced him instead. Gradually the hills before us appeared to be dwindling in their dimensions; this was soon clearly manifest. Lower and less steep became at each moment these barriers to our progress, until at last, on emerging from a defile, the Atlantic came in view. Before us lay the Bay of Biscay, that bugbear of bad sailors, but now smooth as a bed of glass. Another short hour, and we entered the little seaport town of Sequeito, where a salvo of artillery hailed the arrival of Don Carlos. It was very late last night before I could procure quarters for myself and horses, so I have had to rise at daybreak to write my letter and take advantage of a courier leaving for France. As I finish these lines the muleteer who conveys my luggage comes in to say the King's trumpeter is sounding the march for the Royal retinue and that the servants are saddling up.

FGB065
Royalist Headquarters, Bergara; 13 September 1873
Burnaby to Editor – *The Times*, **22 September 1873**
In my last letter, of the 11th inst., I stated that General Elio was in hopes that the Republican leader Loma might be induced to pursue Don Carlos into Vizcaya, as in that case General Lizzarraga, who had quitted the King at the Monastery of Loyola, would cut off Loma's communication with Tolosa, while Velasco, the Carlist leader in Vizcaya, attacked him in front. However, "the good thing", to use the language of the Turf, did not come off, for Santa Pau, who was at Alsasua with his division, had advanced the day before Lizzarraga left Don Carlos in the direction of Tolosa, to unite his forces with General Loma's troops. The latter, in consequence, did not leave their quarters, and Lizzarraga, finding that Santa Pau was moving on Tolosa, tried to intercept him. The Carlist leader, however, arrived too late, and did not attain his object, but he succeeded in having a brush with the enemy's rear-guard, who, I am told, entered the town in considerable disorder. Here were now concentrated

10,000 Republican troops, and in addition to this force Loma had 2,000 men stationed near San Sebastian. Lizzarraga commanded 3,500 Royalist soldiers, and, on failing in his first design, took possession of all the heights round Tolosa and completely isolated the communications, thus preventing supplies from reaching the garrison. He at the same time forwarded a despatch to Don Carlos, informing him of the enemy's position.

I must now return to Don Carlos, and explain where he was while all these events were passing at Tolosa. Don Carlos, after leaving Lizzarraga on the 9th at the Monastery of Loyola, continued his march to Marquina. He slept there that night, and the following day proceeded to Eliqueitia. We paraded early on the 11th, and General Elio had intended to march by the seashore to Ondamia, but as we were leaving Eliqueitia a large frigate was seen bearing down in our direction. It was thought that she might be a Government vessel of war, so the main body of Velasco's division were sent by a circuitous route, and Don Carlos, with his suite, rode along the coast road. However, the ship took no notice of us, and we arrived at Ondamia without any adventure, except that a little Republican gunboat fired on a soldier mounted on a mule, laden with cartridges, and who was considerably in the rear of our party. I am told the man was half asleep, and that his consternation when he suddenly awoke and found that he was being fired at while seated on a powder-magazine gave him an alacrity in hurrying his steed quite unusual among Spaniards. Don Carlos remained some hours at Ondamia to witness a regatta, and then rode on to Marquina, where, at 11 p.m., he received Lizzarraga's despatch. But it was too late; our half-day spent at Eliqueitia had just made us miss the *coup*, for five hours after the receipt of the information Santa Pau and Loma attacked Lizzarraga's positions with the whole of their force – 12,000 men. The Royalist leader kept his foe at bay with his small division of 3,500 strong for a short time, but at last, finding no reinforcement near at hand, and seeing that the enemy was turning his position, he retired to Zumarraga, and the Republican Generals succeeded in breaking out from Tolosa.

But I am anticipating, as on the morning of the 12th Don Carlos was unaware of the turn things had taken, and so he continued his march to Bergara, where we arrived yesterday morning. He then became aware that his little promenade to Eliqueitia had enabled Generals Loma and Santa Pau to escape from the net in which they had become entangled; for, if he had not gone to Eliqueitia he would have received Lizzarraga's despatch a day sooner, and could thus have arrived with Velasco's division in time to reinforce his outnumbered General. The Alava leader could also have brought 2,000 men to bear, and the enemy would thus have been held in check until General Ollo, following in the wake of Santa Pau with the Navarre brigade, had also appeared upon the scene. Fourteen thousand Carlists, occupying strong positions, would have then been opposed to 12,000 Republicans. The latter must have tried to fight their way out, on account of the scarcity of provisions. The chances would have been greatly in favour of Don Carlos, but now the opportunity has gone by. The Government forces occupy Beasain, Lezcano, and Tolosa. Their communications with Vitoria are open, and the Royalist troops will have to wait inactive until another such chance offers itself. At least, this is the opinion of General Lizzarraga, who arrived here from Zumarraga an hour ago, and from whose lips I have received the above information. The General is furious, as may be naturally imagined, at not having been reinforced. There is a proverb extant among most nations – "Never do to-morrow what can be done to-day"; it is a sad thing for the Royalists, that their leaders did not bear the saying in mind, on the present occasion.

The Republican soldiers are apparently bad marksmen, as Lizzarraga, assures me that he had only two officers wounded, and no other casualties except that six of his men were taken prisoners. He says the small loss was owing to the defensive nature of his position. The enemy is believed to have suffered considerably, but no details are known.

FGB066
Royalist Headquarters, Zumarraga; 15 September 1873
Burnaby to Editor – *The Times***, 22 September 1873**
We were informed yesterday afternoon at Bergara that Don Juan de Bourbon, the King's father, or, as he is nicknamed by the Carlists, "*El Señor con los cuartas*" (the gentleman with the half-pence), would shortly arrive at Zumarraga. Don Juan (who, it will be remembered, renounced his rights in favour of his son) has the reputation of being very rich, and, as the Royalist officers receive their pay at intervals few and far between, the rumoured approach of the rich relation was hailed with universal acclamations. On our reaching Zumarraga it was discovered that the wealthy parent was not expected till the morrow. However, there was evidently something interesting on the *tapis*, for little knots of Generals and Field Officers were standing about the Plaza eagerly discussing something important, as could be seen by the rapid gesticulations which General Dorregaray was making with his only sound arm, the other having been disabled a few weeks ago. Presently we were told that the enemy was only two leagues distant that a battle was imminent and that, of course we should win, as the Royalists could dispose of 14,000 men to their opponents 12,000. It was with visions of cannon smoke, fire and glory, coupled with the remembrance that the odds, numerically speaking, were 14 to 12 or 7 to 6 in the Royalist's favour, that most of us closed our eyes last night; some, to be the more ready for a daybreak parade, did not take off their clothes. I must say that my own experience of Spanish warfare has been such as not to place implicit credence in any announced engagement until it actually occurs, and so I slept quietly till 8 this morning, when I was disturbed by a friend, who said, "Well,

they are gone." "Of course they are", I replied angrily, "but who?" "Why the enemy, of course; they found out our strength and have retreated to Alsasua, leaving Loma with 2,000 men in the neighbourhood of San Sebastian. Loma will feel safe there, as he knows we have no artillery fit to attack a fortress. But have you heard of the outrage committed by the Carlist soldiers last night? – they have sacked the station and broken the windows of the railway carriages." Now, there are always so many *on dits* (rumours) about the barbarities performed by both Carlists and Republicans that I determined in this instance to verify the statement with my own eyes. After breakfast I walked up to the station. "What happened last night?" was my first inquiry. "Oh, early this morning, you mean", said an official who was lounging on the platform "why, five men came here; they were not armed or in uniform, but they broke open the door of the chief's office, upset the books and ink, stole a brush, and took two curtains out of a carriage." "Did they hurt anybody?" I asked, "No, but they were a little *borracho* (tipsy)." Such I found to be the real state of the case, but I can add that the Generals are furious, and if the delinquents discovered a drum-head Court Martial will be the result.

This afternoon one of Don Carlos's aides-de-camp came in to smoke a cigarette, and he informed me of the official account just received at Headquarters with reference to the affair at Balcarlos. Balcarlos contains a small fort, or sort of Spanish *douane* (border post), in the neighbourhood of the French town of St. Jean Pied de Port. There was a Spanish garrison stationed in Balcarlos, where were also 300 stand of arms and a considerable amount of ammunition. A few days ago General Argonz, with two battalions of Carlist infantry and two guns, advanced to attack the fort. Major Calderon, who commanded one of the battalions, placed his men and the artillery in the direction of French territory, but on Spanish soil. On seeing this, the Commandant of a French detachment posted close to Balcarlos advanced and spoke to Calderon with reference to International Law. A copy of the agreement between the two nations was then given to the Carlist leader, which has by him since been transmitted to head-quarters. It appears by the document that, in case an engagement should occur on the frontier, the French will not interfere unless any missiles actually cross the boundary line. Should this happen, a trumpeter is to sound a parley and a white flag must be raised. If, in a quarter of an hour's time, the violation of their territory is not discontinued the French troops are to fire on the aggressors. Now, Calderon had so stationed his men that the Republican soldiers in replying to the attack, must inevitably send their bullets into the neighbouring territory. On this ensuing a parley was sounded, and shortly afterwards the French Commander advanced across the frontier, surrounded the fort with his men, made prisoners of the garrison, and seized all the arms; he then returned into France. It is said that the Republicans have petitioned the Spanish Consul to intercede for their liberty. The Carlists, however, are furious, as, according to their line of argument, the French officer had no right to enter foreign soil, but should have confined himself to firing on the aggressors. What annoys Don Carlos's Generals the more is that the arms and munitions belonging to the Government have been seized by a neutral Power, and thus have escaped the Royalist troops.

FGB067
Lizzarraga's Division, Villa Franca; 17 September 1873
Burnaby to Editor – *The Times*, **24 September 1873**

Requisitioning is freely had recourse to by the Carlists as a means of supplying their forces with horses and mules for transport. The spectator very soon looks with indifference on the indignation of the persons whose property has been thus seized, and in a little while he begins to think that perhaps they do not mind it so much after all. Yesterday, however, I had the opportunity of experiencing in my own person what the sensation is like; for while walking in Zumarraga with my friend the German officer I was suddenly startled by a resounding "*Donnerwetter noch einmal!*"[121] which proceeded from his lips. "My horse and your horses!" he cried. "Look there! Soldiers galloping them down the road." It was true; our precious steeds were being ridden barebacked by three troopers, who were riding in a hand canter towards us. The Prussian placed himself on one side of the street and I on the other. "*Alto!*" we cried as the soldiers approached. They paid no attention, however; so springing at the heads of our horses we caught the reins and forcibly stopped the riders. "By whose orders have you taken possession of these horses?" "By command of that gentleman", they replied, pointing to a staff officer a few yards in the rear. On hearing this we walked up to him and asked by whose authority he had removed our chargers. "By orders from the General of the Alava Division." "Will you come with me to the Minister of War on the way?" "Have no time; we must be off. March!" Matters began to look rather disagreeable. I had hold of my own horse by the head, and the Prussian was playing ominously with the handle of his revolver, when, fortunately, General Valdespina came up. I instantly appealed to him, and he at once ordered our horses to be taken back to their stable. "And that one too", said the officer, pointing to a fourth which was being galloped up by a soldier. "Why, dear me", said an aide-de-camp, "that is your own horse, Valdespina!" It was the fact. The Alava General had requisitioned some horses, his troopers had entered our stable, where was also the Marques de Valdespina's charger, and, not seeing any soldier or groom in the neighbourhood, they had coolly taken possession of the animals. "Take them all back", roared Valdespina, "I shall have the matter enquired into." "We march in half an hour", he continued; the King has gone to Beasain to meet

---

121 Damn it again.

his father, but returns here and goes back to Bergara. We shall be idle probably for a few days, but Lizzarraga is going off in the direction of Tolosa. I expect there will be something going on in that neighbourhood." The thought at once struck me that I would ask permission from General Elio to accompany Lizzarraga's Division for a few days. I found the two generals together. "By all means", said Elio. "I start directly", said his companion, "but you can join me at Villa Franca this evening."

On the way we met Don Carlos and his father, a little old man, strikingly contrasting with the Herculean proportions of his son. Both were on horseback, and were accompanied by the Duque de Union de Cuba,[122] who had also come from Biarritz to place his sword at the disposal of Don Carlos. A large suite of followers and a mounted escort were also in attendance. Presently I heard my name called out, and a Frenchman, M. Laborde, who arranges for the Carlist correspondence, &c., handed me a letter. It was dated Bayonne the 5th, and had taken 11 days in transit. We are completely isolated from the world by these Carlist operations. "Ireland may have disappeared beneath the sea", observed an Irishman the other day, "and we be none the wiser." With General Lizzarraga, officers' baggage is reduced to the narrowest possible limits. No mules are allowed, and my equipment consists of one spare shirt, one pair of socks, and a pocket-handkerchief. This, combined with the weight of rations for steed and rider, is as much as a horse can carry up these mountain paths. Those English officers who complain that the 40 pounds of baggage allowed at our own Autumn Manoeuvres is insufficient would open their eyes rather wide if they could only see the slight impedimenta carried by the Carlist Cavalry.

FGB068
Lizzarraga's Division, Villa Franca; 18 September 1873
Burnaby to Editor, Reuters Telegram
The Times, 26 September 1873

The Republican General Loma, with 3,500 men, is surrounded by Lizzarraga with 9,000 men. Loma tried to escape this morning, but was repulsed and driven back by the Carlist General Laramendi. Tolosa will probably soon be taken by the Carlists.

FGB069
Lizzarraga's Division, Tolosa; 19 September 1873
Burnaby to Editor – *The Times*, 27 September 1873

I stated in a letter a few days ago that the attempt to surround the Government troops at Tolosa had failed, owing to the advance of the Royalist head-quarters to Eliqueitia, in Vizcaya. The chance given us by the enemy had been thrown

---

122 Luis Bernardo, 3rd Duke of the Union of Cuba (1844-1914).

away, and it did not seem likely that the Republican generals would again, and so soon, entangle themselves in the traps laid for them by the Carlists. However, the day before yesterday, when at Villafranca, we were informed that Santa Pau had retired with his Division in the direction of Vitoria, and that General Loma was left at Tolosa with a garrison of only 3,500 men. It also appeared that the Carlist leader Ollo had tried to intercept Santa Pau in the mountain passes, but had arrived one hour too late at the defile, having been delayed by the bad state of the roads. General Morriones,[123] another Republican leader, was said to be in Navarre with a newly-levied force of 5,000 men. The effect of all this information was to induce Lizzarraga to move on the 17th inst. to Alegria with his force, which consisted of six battalions from Guipuzcoa, three from Alava, two from Vizcaya, and two guns. At Alegria we halted for the night, to allow time to General Ollo to come up with his brigade, which consisted of four battalions from Navarre and four guns. Our division was then composed of 15 battalions of Infantry, six guns, and about 200 horse.

Yesterday morning three of the Navarre battalions were left to form a reserve at Alegria, and the remainder of the troops marched in the direction of Tolosa, to take up positions surrounding the town.

General Aizpurua was to invest the enemy on the north with three battalions; Ollo to command his own four battalions and to form the reserve – one of them, however, to be considerably advanced, to prevent any movement of Loma towards the south; Lizzarraga to march on Tolosa and establish himself with four battalions on the west of the town, and General Laramendi to station the residue of the Carlist forces on the east of the Republican garrison. Tolosa lies in a hollow, and is crested on two sides by a huge range of hills, which are covered with low brushwood. If the Carlists possessed a few good 15-pounder guns there would not be the slightest difficulty in taking the town, as it is not fortified, except by some temporary fieldworks, which, I am told, have a been recently thrown up by the orders of Loma. The high road from Vitoria to France passes through Tolosa and the valley formed at the base of the heights, above-mentioned. It was about 9 a.m. yesterday morning, and Lizzarraga had newly arrived at his position, when a lookout man posted on a neighbouring eminence called out that the Republican troops were marching out of Tolosa from the eastern side of the town. This movement caused our general to change his direction, for we turned sharp to the right and ascended a mountain path, which in places had to be repaired by pioneers to enable our cavalry to pass. Finally, after a two hours' march, we arrived on a height commanding Tolosa from the north. All this time a rapid fire could be heard east of our position. This was occasioned by Laramendi's troops, who had here intercepted Loma.

---

123 General Domingo Morriones y Murillo (1823-1881), later Marques de Oroquieta and Governor-General of the Philippines from 1877 to 1880.

Presently the steep boom of artillery, resounding and echoing through the vale, told that the action was becoming general along, the line; but Lizzarraga evidently thought Laramendi required no assistance, for he did not move towards the scene of action.

About mid-day the firing began to ring nearer, and shortly afterwards it was evident that Loma had been repulsed in his endeavours to break through the Carlists. There is, however, a hill a little to the north of Tolosa, and the Republicans, placing a battery on it, began to revenge themselves by cannonading Lizzarraga's Division, which was about 1,500 yards from them. I had just sent off my telegram announcing Loma's repulse, when the first shell burst about 300 yards short of us. "They will have our range in three more shots", drily remarked the old General. Another puff of smoke, followed by a report close at our feet, announced that the enemy's gunner had hit off the right distance. The third shrapnel exploded in the middle of our men, but, luckily, did little damage. "Take direction to the right!" was then the word, accompanied by "Don't duck your heads, my children" – an observation directed by the Carlist leader to his men, who are not yet thoroughly accustomed to the whistle of grape. At nightfall two companies were sent to take the height from which the Republicans had shelled us, and I am informed that it is now in our possession. When the sun had thoroughly disappeared, Lizzarraga, accompanied by a *cura* who forms part of his Division, made a reconnaissance in the direction of the enemy. The Priest knew every inch of the country, and explained to the general where all the cross-roads led to. *Confidentes*, or spies, were also in attendance, and now and then, after a few words whispered by the Priest in their ears, they hastened away towards Tolosa. Many of these persons were quite old men, and they are the most appreciated, as their age disarms suspicion. In one way the present war may be regarded in the light of a religious one, so deeply impressed are the Carlist soldiery that God is on their side. The priests never lose an occasion to strengthen this feeling among the peasantry, and, as every man has confessed and received absolution, he should look forward to being struck by a shot as a deliverance from this world and in the light of a removal to Paradise. This is the theory, but practice shows me that the Royalist troops are not one whit more indifferent to death than the atheistical Republicans.

I write this letter on a hill-side where Lizzarraga has posted two guns. Orders have just come to "limber up", so I must conclude.

FGB070
Lizzarraga's Division, Zumarraga; 23 September 1873
Burnaby to Editor – *The Times*, **1 October 1873**
Affairs do not look so bright now for the Royalists as they did when I despatched my last letter from the heights one mile north of Tolosa, for then the Republican leader Loma had failed in an attempt to fight his way out of

the town. He was outnumbered in the proportion of nearly three to one by the Carlists, and the key of his position, an eminence from which he had shelled our force on the previous afternoon, was in the possession of Lizzarraga. The subsequent two days were employed by the Royalist Generals in cutting off the water supply from a mill, used by the Republicans for grinding corn and in narrowing the circuit of the besieging lines. I rode one afternoon to the hill commanding Tolosa, and found there Lizzarraga, accompanied by his Staff, busily engaged in giving directions for the construction of batteries to bombard the town. The spot could not have been better chosen for aggressive operations, for it was almost precipitous on the Republican side, and about 800ft. high, being at the summit not 500 yards distant from the Cathedral in the centre of Tolosa. The batteries could have enfiladed the roads leading to Vitoria and San Sebastian, as well as to Pampeluna. It was determined to place some more guns on an adjacent height, a quarter of a mile west of the above-mentioned hill, and to establish the remainder of the artillery in a château called Iltoremeno, between the roads leading to Amezquezia and Alegria. A terribly convergent fire could thus have been maintained. The roofs of the houses are thin, and shells discharged from the Carlist positions would have created fearful havoc among the closely-packed inhabitants and soldiery. The besieged, on the contrary, could have used their own artillery with but little effect on the first two Carlist batteries, as the elevation required would have been too great, and the only means of returning the Royalist fire would have been by stationing riflemen on the roof of the Cathedral. The Republicans had not overlooked this matter, and while Lizzarraga was gazing down upon Tolosa the repeated pings (if I may be allowed the term) of bullets whistling by our ears showed that Loma did not mean to allow his opponent to continue the survey unmolested. The Navarrese under Ollo had succeeded in taking the railway station, and an animated exchange of missiles was going on between them and the garrison. It was resolved that the batteries should open fire at 5 o'clock yesterday morning, and Lizzarraga forwarded a despatch to General Ollo ordering him to have everything prepared by that hour, and to burn down a large cloth manufactory just outside the town, and on the *route* to Vitoria, should the enemy be able to avail himself of the building as an offensive post. "You can accompany my aide-de- camp to Ollo, if you like", said Lizzarraga, turning to me, "and then you will have an opportunity of seeing our works in his direction." "I have cut all the main roads round the town", continued the general, gleefully rubbing his hands; "my former comrade, Loma, is a cunning old fox, but if he does not receive reinforcements I think we shall soon have him in our power. Santa Pau and Moriones are still in Vitoria, and they cannot possibly arrive here before to-morrow night, should Moriones make up his mind to relieve Tolosa." When General Ollo was informed that he must open fire at 5 the next morning he declared that it would be almost impossible to conclude the works by that hour, and a despatch was, I believe, sent to Lizzarraga with reference to this subject.

It was quite dusk when I rode back to our headquarters at Ezquira. The track lay over mountain paths shaded with low brushwood, and below was the besieged town, silent and still. Not a hum, not a sound, met the ear. That buzzing stir of voices which is habitual to all spots where the human race is thickly congregated was absolutely unheard, and the only proof that Tolosa was not a dead city consisted in the lit-up but deserted squares and thoroughfares. Thicker and more impenetrable grew the darkness, till at last our horses refused to move as well indeed they might, for on one side was a steep ravine, ending in a precipice hundreds of feet in depth, and on the other a mountain stream dashing over huge boulders and crags, which left the existence of the riders completely at the disposal of the steeds, for the path on which they trod was in no place much more than three feet wide. The guide was sent on to procure torches, and he presently returned with long thin bundles of straw, tightly bound together by bands of the same material – such is the primitive means of illumination used by the mountaineer in these wild districts. Slowly we continued the march, our sure-footed horses feeling the ground before them with their hoofs, and never bringing all their weight to bear until they were satisfied as to the firmness of the soil. On nearing our destination an Artillery officer rode past. "There is nothing for us to do to-morrow", he said, "the batteries are not to fire, and there is a report that the enemy is advancing from Vitoria." The following morning, at half-past 4, I was awoke by an aide-de-camp with – "We break up our quarters directly." "To meet the Republican column", I inquired. "Alas, no, but to march in the direction of Vargas. The orders from General Elio are most distinct, and we are to leave this immediately. I am told that we shall join the 'King's' force at Azpeitia, but at all events make haste, as the men are on parade. Lizzarraga has desired commanding officers to take the shortest route over the mountains to Azpeitia, so we shall not march with all the troops, but independently and in various detachments. The General only takes a battalion and two companies with him." I had just time to write and despatch a telegram[124], when Lizzarraga rode by. Everybody was in a great hurry to be off, as it was thought that Loma might fall upon the rear, and for this reason our force had been divided.

Opinions were very adverse to Elio's policy, which is decidedly that of postponement for the present of all aggressive measures. The Commander-in-Chief, although a good tactician, is excessively cautious, and does not wish to risk an encounter unless the odds are three to one in his favour. "The enemy is becoming more disorganized", he says. "We must wait, arm the men better, supply ourselves with good artillery, instruct the soldiers thoroughly, and then, when we have 60,000 perfectly-equipped and well-disciplined troops, we can

---

124 This telegram has not been located.

take the initiative." This appears at first sight to be good reasoning, but there is one drawback which escapes the General – viz., that the war is confined to five Provinces – Navarre, Vizcaya, Guipuzcoa, Alava, and Catalonia. Now, the Spaniards of the North, though for the most part true Carlists, at heart, are beginning to tire of a war incessantly carried on round their homesteads. However much a man may love the Royalist cause, having soldiers billeted upon him at all hours of the day or night is not a pleasant infliction. The paralyzing of trade and commerce, which is also a result of the lingering character of this war, is ruinous in its consequences. Many people are beginning to ask themselves the question, "Is it to be another Seven Years' affair?" From the slowness of Elio's operations the fears in this respect are acquiring confirmation. Men shake their heads, and say, "Good God, how will it end?" They see the Royalist leaders leave their towns and villages, they hear the promises of Don Carlos's speedy arrival in Madrid, but a week later the troops return to be again a burden to the impoverished inhabitants, and the conclusion appears as far or further off than ever. I think I am justified in stating that a desire that the war may terminate as soon as possible, either one way or the other, is uppermost in the minds of all Guipuzcoans; and that if the Carlist Commander-in-Chief protracts his operations much longer it will not take a great deal to induce the inhabitants to act as well as to sympathize in another direction.

FGB071
Lizzarraga's Division, Zumarraga; 24 September 1873
Burnaby to Editor – *The Times***, 3 October 1873**
Considerable discontent prevails among the officers of Lizzarraga's Division with reference to General Elio's order which caused the abandonment of the siege of Tolosa. Lizzarraga himself, though he does not openly express his feelings on the subject, is evidently not at all pleased with the turn things are taking at head-quarters, for he has in the last ten days been twice foiled in his designs upon the Republican columns – the first time by the tardiness of the Vizcaya Division in arriving with reinforcements, and the second by this sudden and utterly unexpected order, which, apparently without any rhyme or reason, has prevented the taking of Tolosa.

Seldom has a town, militarily speaking, been placed in a more dangerous position – three thousand five hundred men were shut up in a confined space, so situated that they could only bring two companies at a time to return the fire of the enemy's artillery, their own guns being rendered useless by the abrupt elevation of the ground on which the Carlist batteries would have been constructed. It is true that considerable reinforcements, over 12,000 infantry, were on the way to relieve them, but Elio might have interposed with a division of 14,000 Royalist troops, and, from the nature of the road through which the Republican columns must march, he could have availed himself of numerous heights and defiles where a few hundred men, if well placed, might have barred the passage of an army. "Then what could be the reason?" is the question upon everybody's lips. Was it excessive caution, or personal feeling stimulated by the idea of another's success? It could not have been agreeable to the Navarre General, Ollo, to be commanded by the leader of the Guipuzcoans, Lizzarraga. But, when the Royalist cause is at stake, one would imagine that patriotism would obliterate the petty jealousies at being superseded. It is perfectly possible that Elio may have some deep scheme in his mind, which the Guipuzcoan officers do not fathom, and the raising of the siege of Tolosa may be followed by a Royalist success in another quarter. A general order was issued yesterday that all the men from the Provinces of Murcia, Aragon, and Valencia are to leave the Guipuzcoan, Vizcayan and Navarre Battalions in which they have been serving, and proceed to Estella. Thence they are to be forwarded to their own districts, where fresh Carlist forces will be enrolled. Several thousand stands of small arms have already been despatched to Murcia, Aragon, and Valencia. The old soldiers are to form a nucleus for the volunteers who it is said will eagerly join the banner, and as 3,000 officers and men are now precluded from remaining in the battalions belonging to the North of Spain, the initiative thus given to the new movement will be of considerable importance. At all events, something is required to outweigh the loss of prestige caused by the retreat from Tolosa, which, if not followed by a Royalist success, will more than counterbalance the advantages gained at Estella, Dicastillo, and Riana. General Ollo has returned with the Navarrese to their own Province, and Lizzarraga remains here to guard against any attempt made by the Republican columns on the rifle manufactories of Erlar and Placencia.

Despatches received last night were to the effect that the enemy was at Beasain, Villa Franca, Alegria, and Tolosa. One cannot help observing the differences that exist in the various Carlist forces, especially in relation to the religious feelings of the men. The Navarrese are not nearly so particular in the observance of the Catholic rites as the Vizcainos, and the latter are far behind the men of Guipuzcoa. The Guipuzcoans, in many respects, strongly remind me of the Scotch. Honest and frugal to the last degree, economizing every spare *cuarto* and carefully hoarding it up in the family stocking, they will go miles to perform their religious duties, and look upon any dereliction as a heinous sin. Lizzarraga's troops, in addition to attending service every morning when on the march, have the rosaries recited by the priest at the head of each battalion. No halt is made, but the officers and men bare their heads, and the chaplain, riding by the side of the commanding officer, reads out the prayers and litany. Not a word can be heard down the ranks, and there is no sound save the measured tramp of the soldiery. Impressive, indeed, is the ceremony when, as we traverse a mountain pass at nightfall, the last rays of the setting sun dimly and mystically casting a faint reflection on the wayside ridges, at the conclusion of the litany. General, officers, and men burst forth with the magnificent hymn of Ignatius Loyola as if one sole spirit animated them. The strains seem to die away in the distance until the waves of air, rebounding against some acoustic impediment of nature, re-echo back again the concluding bars of melody. The service over, general and officers laugh and talk about the ordinary topics of conversation, but for many minutes the silence down the ranks is intense. Each man seems still buried in the little world of thought which constitutes his inner being, and appears utterly indifferent to everything passing in the outer world. The devotion displayed by the lower classes in Guipuzcoa affords a striking contrast to the extreme indifference in these matters exhibited by the peasants in the South. Here the priest is a semi-Deity. There he is often a butt and a subject for ridicule.

FGB072
Royalist Headquarters, Durango; 26 September 1873
Burnaby to Editor – *The Times*, 3 October 1873
There has been nothing going on of any importance in Lizzarraga's Division since the retreat from Tolosa, and so I determined to return to the King's head-quarters. But first it was necessary to obtain my baggage, which had been left behind at Villa Franca owing to an order given that no mules were to go with the expedition to Tolosa. Now, Villa Franca is only seven miles from the above-mentioned town, and since our retreat it has been filled with Republican soldiery. However, I was told last Wednesday that the Government troops had all marched in the direction of San Sebastian, and so, mounting my horse, and accompanied by an aide-de-camp of Lizzarraga, we proceeded to recover our effects, my companion, like myself, having been compelled to abandon his valise previous to the attack upon Loma. We had not gone far when a shrill whistle announced that a locomotive was running. Don Carlos has given an order that the railway is to be repaired, and the train was full of workmen who were to repair the bridges and tunnels destroyed by the Cura de Santa Cruz.[125] Unfortunately the line is only to be used for the transport of goods and merchandise so travellers to Madrid will still have either to ride, or go by diligence. From time to time we met man and wife on horseback pillion fashion. Then came a priest in a carriage drawn by two mules as wheelers and two oxen as leaders, the vehicle itself strongly resembling a species of Noah's ark. Presently the tread of hoofs and the ringing clang of steel scabbards told us that cavalry was approaching. We leaped our horses over a crumbling wall and hid behind a low building, for it was not at all sure whether the advancing riders were friends or a reconnoitring party of the enemy. Fortunately they

125 Manuel Ignacio Santa Cruz Loidi (1842-1926), a Basque priest and guerrilla known as the Santa Cruz Curé.

proved to be a small detachment of Lizzarraga's Lancers bringing in some prisoners. Two Republican sergeants and a private marched on foot amid the horsemen, and a little in their rear, but most carefully guarded, were four peasants, with downcast mien and timid, dejected appearance. The last seemed to have lost all hope, and well, indeed, the poor wretches might despair, for they were *confidentes*, or spies, and their doom was inevitable. The soldier prisoners talked cheerfully enough with the escort. A Spaniard is indifferent to most things, provided he is fed well, not compelled to work, and allowed to sleep the postprandial *siesta*. However, for the spies there was a very different lot prepared. But of this anon. At last we reached Villa Franca, which had been evacuated that very morning by the Government troops. Notwithstanding this, quite sufficient time had elapsed for a *guerrilla partida* (guerrilla party) of Royalists to come down from mountains and locate themselves in the town. The old lady to whom my companion and myself had confided our baggage met us on the doorstep and nearly embraced my friend in her delight at seeing him again. She rapidly exclaimed, "They have gone – the negroes, the blacks" – a name applied to the Government troops. "The Virgin be praised they have left us. Their officers ate up everything I had, and not one *cuarto* did they pay. Wretches, negroes, *Ateos*! And your baggage, too, what a fright it gave me! I hid the valise in our straw loft, and there was a sword also, which a Carlist commandant had left here. I expected every moment when the negroes took some straw for their horses that they all would be discovered, and that I should be shot; but now – Maria Santisima – you have come, let me prepare a *puchero* (pot) or something nice to eat; your Excellencies must be hungry." "Why did you not take Tolosa?" was the question on everybody's lips, and before the aide-de-camp could answer they continued, "It was that General Elio, – he is so slow. We shall have another nine years' war, and again be disgraced by a foreign intervention."

There was no possibility of obtaining a mule or an ox-cart in Villa Franca, so the Alcalde gave my companion an order, and the baggage was carried to Zumarraga by two men, who were relieved at each village we came to by fresh porters. I frequently offered them money, but they would not accept it. "No", was the almost invariable answer, "we work for our religion and Carlo Setimo." The following morning I called upon Lizzarraga to take my leave. "I think you are right in going", said the general; "there is nothing doing, here. However I am preparing for another turn with old Loma." "When that happens I shall return, if you will allow me", I observed. "By all means. Nothing I like better than that foreign nations should know the truth, and what actually does occur, even if it should be unfavourable to us, instead of the garbled reports of the journals at Madrid." "What have you done with the prisoners?" I inquired. "Oh, the three soldiers; they are here, comfortable enough." "But the other four, the spies?" "Oh, the *confidentes*; I have nothing to do with them; they are always delivered over to one of the *partidas*, and are never brought before me. They have received their passport to heaven long before this." "Have you many robberies here?" I asked. "No; at present hardly ever, for I have all soldiers or civilians shot who steal an article worth more than a *real* (2¼*d*.). We had to sentence three Frenchmen and four Spaniards to capital punishment for thieving, when I first arrived, but now you may leave money or goods of any value in the street, and they will be as safe as if in your own possession. You will find the King at Durango", he continued. "Good-bye, but come back soon, as before long we shall be at work again with Loma." My Spanish servant, Lorenzo, who is from Navarre, was delighted when I told him that we should return that day to head-quarters. "*Buono*", he said, "for there Señor, I shall be able to speak. Here no one understands Castilian. Nothing but bark – yes, bark they do – when I ask for the rations; not one word do I comprehend." His joy was rather modified when it was suggested that probably we should soon return to Lizzarraga. "There is nothing but uphill and downhill with these Guipuzcoans", dolefully groaned Lorenzo. "I have worn out one pair of *alpargatas* (sandals) already; what can make his Excellency prefer remaining with Lizzarraga to being at head-quarters? Here there is little to eat, nothing to drink, marches day and night, and a good chance of being killed. But at head-quarters, if we are shot, I am sure of first having my *tripas* (stomach) filled, at all events."

I arrived at Durango very late last night, and found that Don Carlos's father had left in the morning with Saballs, the Catalonian leader. It is said that a fresh stimulus is to be given to the movement in Prince Alfonso's district. Many petty jealousies exist there between the various Carlist chiefs, and a new direction is to be given to military operations. Should nothing of any importance be likely to happen in these Northern Provinces, I shall find my way to Saballs, and then be able to form an opinion as to what is the nature of the troops under his command. There is a report to-day that the Republican General Moriones has left Tolosa and marched in the direction of Leysa, and that the Carlist leader Ollo is at Estella with the Navarre Division. If it is true, many people think that Lizzarraga will make a fresh attack upon Tolosa, but this for the moment appears to me to be very doubtful.

FGB073
Royalist Headquarters; 26 September 1873
Burnaby to Editor (telegraph via Madrid)
The Times, **6 October 1873**
The Carlist band under Merendon has been defeated and dispersed. Merendon was killed.

FGB074
Royalist Headquarters, Durango; 28 September 1873
Burnaby to Editor – *The Times*, 8 October 1873
I had a long conversation with Don Carlos yesterday afternoon. The "King" evidently thought little of the retreat from Tolosa, for he simply remarked that strategic reasons gave rise to General Elio's orders upon the subject. What those strategic reasons might have been no one seems to be aware, and the question is treated at head-quarters with that phrase which so characterizes the Spanish nation, *no importa* – it does not matter. So far as the capture of prisoners or arms is concerned, nothing has been gained by the Government, but with respect to prestige much will have been lost by the Royalists. In the meantime, it is rumoured that Moriones, the Republican General, has expressed his determination to burn Estella to the ground. Whatever the threat may have been, I hardly conceive that an attempt will be made to carry it into effect. There is no doubt that Moriones could easily take Estella, protected as it is only by the Navarre Division, some 5,000 men. But if he were to destroy the town, so strong a feeling would be created in the Province that the Navarrese would rise to a man, and the General would but have succeeded in prejudicing still more the Government. The Vizcaya Division, commanded by Velasco, is much in want of cartridges, and fresh supplies are daily expected to arrive from Bera. A disembarcation of cannon is also shortly to occur on the coast, and several artillery officers who have joined the Carlists are to take command of the batteries as soon as they are landed.

A discovery was made a few days since that a woman was serving in the Royalist ranks dressed in a soldier's uniform. She was found out in the following manner:– The priest of the village to which she belonged happening to pass through a town where the regiment was quartered, and chancing to see her, was struck by the likeness she bore to one of his parishioners. "You must be Andalicia Bravo", he remarked. "No, I am her brother", was the reply. The *cura*'s suspicions were aroused, and, at his suggestion, an inquiry was made, when it was discovered that the youthful soldier had no right to the masculine vestments she wore. Don Carlos, when he was told of the affair, desired that she should be sent as a nurse the hospital in Durango, and when he visited the establishment presented the fair Amazon with a military cross of merit. The poor girl was delighted with the decoration, but besought the "King" to allow her to return to the regiment, as she said she was more accustomed to inflicting wounds than to healing them. In fact, she so implored to be permitted to serve once more as a soldier that at last Don Carlos, to extricate himself from the difficulty, said, "No, I cannot allow you to join a regiment of men, but when I form a battalion of women, I promise upon my honour that you shall be named the colonel. "It will never happen", said the girl, and she burst into tears as the "King" left the hospital. I went over the establishment yesterday and found it the perfection of cleanliness and good management. The Spanish hospitals are, almost without an exception, admirably arranged, and the attention shown to the patients by the Sisters of Charity is of the most devoted character. I saw several wounded men as we passed through the wards. "How are you treated here?" I asked. "Our own mothers could not take more care of us than these kind nurses", was the reply. Unfortunately, the establishment is in want of funds, the Government for several months not having given anything towards the expenses of the hospital. It is consequently left entirely to the charity of some private persons in the district, and admirably do they respond to the frequent calls made upon their purses. But, in spite of this, funds are still sadly wanted, and the head sister told me they were more than 200*l*, in debt. As I was leaving the building, a nurse came forward and asked me if I would intercede in her favour. She was Andalicia Bravo, once a soldier, but now an assiduous attendant on the sick inmates. However, the confined life tries her constitution and she pines like a caged linnet for the freedom of a country life. "Do ask Don Carlos, if you see his Majesty", she eagerly exclaimed, "to allow me to return to my regiment, or at all events to quit these walls, for I am suffocated with the restraint." The poor Amazon is not likely to have her request granted, as this is the second time she has served in the ranks. On the first occasion, after an engagement with the Government troops, Andalicia, with several other soldiers, was taken prisoner. She was then banished to the Canary Islands, and to escape her fate divulged the nature of her sex. The sentence was remitted, but instead of returning to her family, as she had promised, Andalicia bought some male attire and enlisted in another Carlist battalion.

The last news we have is that the Government now permits the inhabitants of Bilbao to enter other parts of Spain. However, the blockade by the Carlists still continues. There are 3,500 Republican troops inside the fortress and about the same number of Carlist soldiers outside the walls. The outposts of both sides are said to be on the best terms, the Royalists supplying their opponents with fruit and receiving tobacco and cigars in exchange.

FGB075
Villa Real[126]**; 30 September 1873**
Burnaby to Editor – *The Times*, **8 October 1873**
Don Carlos has left Durango for Guernica, a small town three leagues northeast of Bilbao, but, as General Elio did not accompany him, it was evident that nothing interesting from a military point of view was likely to happen. I called upon the Royalist Commander-in-Chief yesterday, with the object of gathering some information as to which particular Province is now likely to be the theatre of Carlist operations. Elio said that for a short time things would

---

126 Today Urretxu.

be stationary, so far as aggressive measures on a large scale were concerned, but that I should see more with Ollo in Navarre than with the Vizcainos or Lizzarraga's division. The General attributed the retreat from Tolosa entirely to the scarcity of ammunition, the Alaveses and Guipuzcanos, according to the Commander-in-Chief, having only 12 rounds, per man, and the remainder of the force being but little better provided. "You know", he continued, "that our armament comprises, alas! almost every kind of weapon – Enfields, Miniés, and Berdans, as well as Remingtons, unfortunately, of two distinct systems. We had an ample supply of cartridges for one kind of Remington rifle, but not for the other. However, all this is remedied now, and every man will shortly receive his regulation quantity of ammunition." "With reference to Lizzarraga", Elio observed, "he is a very good General, but he has two mono-manias – Tolosa and the Republican leader Loma. If I could only have persuaded him not to attack so soon a different solution would have been the result." Such is the Commander-in-Chief's explanation of the affair. I have in previous letters stated Lizzarraga's views on the subject, and the impartial reader must now be left to draw his own conclusions.

Duels are not openly permitted in the Royalist army, but the authorities have a singular manner of arranging the difficulty. Some time ago a question arose between a French Marquis and a Spanish *Comandante*. The Spaniard finally laying his cane across the shoulders of the Frenchman, the latter went straight to headquarters and related his grievance. "You received a blow?" was the inquiry. "Yes." And you had a revolver and did not at once blow out your opponent's brains? Very well, the matter shall be inquired into." A few days afterwards, finding that nothing had apparently been done in the matter, the Marquis sent a friend – an officer formerly in the Prussian Guards – to demand satisfaction from the *Comandante*. On stating the purport of his visit the *Comandante* placed him at once under arrest. On the following afternoon the Frenchman, furious at what had happened, wrote a letter to his foe, and said in it that he should take the first opportunity which presented itself of spitting in his face. A few hours afterwards an aide-de-camp arrived and ordered the Marquis to consider himself under arrest, by order of General Elio. But this restraint did not last long, as the same evening a letter from the Commander-in-Chief was put into the Frenchman's hand. The Marquis was released from his confinement, and received a three months' leave of absence to France, to which country he was to proceed without delay, and at the same time the pay due for his previous services was given him. The other principal is, I am told, to be sent to Piña la Plata, a strong Carlist stronghold in the mountains, and here he is to remain six months. There will be time enough for both of them to moralize over their folly in appealing to head-quarters instead of at once settling the quarrel for themselves. And this is the view which Royalist officers take of the matter.

Finding that there was nothing going on in Guipuzcoa, I left Durango yesterday and made a long march to this town. At Bergara, I met a man dressed in peasant's attire and walking at a great pace. It was Simon, the chief of the Carlist spies, on his way to head-quarters. I stopped him, for a moment to inquire the news. The old man rubbed his clammy brow with a sleeve, and, recognising my face, said, "There has been a slight affair at Dicastillo; Primo de Rivera,[127] with a Republican force, attacked the Navarrese under Ollo. The enemy would all have been taken prisoners if it had not been for one of our artillery men disobeying orders and firing his gun before the time." "Any loss?" I inquired. "None on our side, and Primo de Rivera has left Navarre and led his troops in the direction of Aragon." "Where is Ollo now?" "At Estella; but I cannot wait any longer." "Go with God", I replied, and away went the old *confidente* at a good five miles-an-hour half-walk, half-run, to execute his commission. A hard life is that of a Carlist spy, and be is badly paid, for 10 *reals*, or 2*s.*, a day is not a tempting enough bait to induce most man to risk being shot at a moment's notice. We met *en route* several large parties of unarmed men coming from Navarre. They were all on their way to Vizcaya, where they will receive rifles and ammunition, and they are then to be formed into a fresh battalion. My arrangements are all upset by Simon's news, for I know Moriones is at Vitoria, having left Loma in Tolosa with about 2,000 men as a garrison, and Lizzarraga, we are informed, is again drawing a line of blockade around his old enemy. What is to be done? Go to Lizzarraga, or Ollo? Unfortunately, a correspondent cannot be ubiquitous, and Saball's division must also be visited. I think the best plan will be to proceed by the railway and through the tunnel to Alsasua, and, if I find that there is nothing likely to happen in Navarre, to make my way to the French frontier and thence to Catalonia.

FGB076
Avarzuza; 3 October 1873
Burnaby to Editor – *The Times***, 9 October 1873**
The proprietress of the house in which I was billeted at Villa Real had no sympathies with the Republicans. Party feeling, according to her account, ran high in the town, and when it was publicly announced that Don Carlos would shortly arrive great was the excitement amidst the population. My landlady assured me that her next-door neighbour was a *Negra*, and, the garrulous woman continued, "You must know, Señor, the *repugnante* slapped her elbow at me when I said that my balconies should be decorated with pieces of carpet to do honour to the King's arrival. She screamed out that Don Carlos was a *pretendiente*, and was not worth even an oil lamp by way of illumination. The

---

[127] Don Fernando Primo de Rivera y Sobremonte, 1st Marques of Estella (1831-1921), a Spanish politician and soldier.

lodgers in my house, Sir, were also Republicans, and they raged finely at me when I put three wax lights in each of their windows. They blew them out at once, but I lit them again, and finally the wretches said my house was not fit for a Liberal to be in, and that they should leave the next day. I was glad when the rooms were free, and you, dear gentlemen, were quartered here. One silver dollar did I pay, too, for the candles to welcome his Majesty's entrance into Villa Real; and the *Negros* are discontented animals, that they are."

Shortly after leaving Villa Real the day before yesterday we came upon the main road between Vitoria and Tolosa. This was the same line which the Republican General Moriones had followed in his advance to relieve Loma. But as I rode along the path no trace of the Government troops was visible. On the contrary, from time to time we were challenged by the Carlist outposts. "Halt!" they cried. "*Quien vire?*" "*España*" "*Que gente?*" ("What people?") "*Carlos Setimo.*" "Pass on." And we continued the march. During our journey, my muleteer, who hates taking any trouble whatever, even for his own animal, on finding that one pack was rather heaver than the other, instead of equalizing the weight, quietly took up a huge stone and placed it in the lighter of the two panniers. My English servant was considerably surprised at witnessing this method of balancing the saddle bags. However, the Spaniard's wonder was much greater when the Englishman, dismounting, gathered some watercresses, and tied them up in a pocket-handkerchief. "What for?" asked the muleteer, who has picked up a few sentences in English. "*Comer*", ("To eat"), replied my domestic, not wishing to be outdone in his knowledge of a foreign tongue. "What, do not you like them, Lorenzo?" I inquired. "No, most illustrious", replied the muleteer; "they may be good for clergymen and Señores like yourselves to make a salad of, but for hard workers like myself – puff!" At Alsasua, where we halted for the night, I found myself located in the town-clerk's house. Very anti-Carlist was the owner of the establishment. "It is not that I dislike the King", said our host, "he is all very well in his way; but the idea Don Carlos represents, and for him to be able to sentence me to death if he has the caprice to do so; no, I do not like that. His generals and their men behave very well, but the chiefs of the *partidas* are a perfect pest. Why, the other day one of them, a *Cabecilla*, who commands 250 men, arrested the Alcalde and his Secretary; treated them as if they were dogs; and then, threatening to shoot our magistrate, forwarded both the gentlemen to General Ollo at Estella. And all this simply because our Alcalde had not informed the *Cabecilla* that the Republican column was in the town. General Ollo released the prisoners directly, and they have returned here. However, it is not pleasant to be liable to be killed at a moment's notice by a fellow calling himself a Royalist, but who is in reality little better than a bandit."

I could not obtain much news at Alsasua of General Ollo's movements. Moriones with 12,000 Government troops, was said to have left Pampeluna and gone to Tafalla. The Carlist forces were believed to be at Estella, "but you will be sure to hear of their whereabouts on the road", was the invariable reply to my numerous inquiries. The following morning we mounted and turned our horses' heads towards Estella. Fresh information then met us at every turn. Here was a colonel laid up with fever being carried in a common country cart, with no springs, to his own home. There some wounded soldiers. "Where is Ollo?" "Near Estella, to be sure. Why, have not you heard? Moriones is advancing on the town with all his troops, and the Navarrese only muster 4,500 strong. The General forwarded a despatch four days ago to Lizzarraga asking, for reinforcements. Perhaps his men are on the way. Do you know if they are coming?" "No", I replied; "when I left Villa Real the Guipuzcoans, with their leader, were surrounding Tolosa." "Just like them", continued my informant, a wounded sergeant. "They were glad of our assistance at Tolosa, but would not now move a hand to save us all from being taken prisoners by the *Negros*. *Caramba!* If Lizzarraga does not soon arrive the Republicans will have Estella." Presently a loud booming sound made the muleteer remark "*Artilleriea*"; but, no, it was too dead a thud to have been produced by a cannon, and shortly afterwards old men, with women and children, passed us on mules laden with goods and chattels. A little later, on descending a steep ravine, our horses lost each a shoe. The position was critical. Night had thrown her dark shades around, and we were still three leagues from Estella. But Avarzuza was only five miles distant. So, under the circumstances, I thought it advisable to remain there for the night. "What is the news?" I asked of the village blacksmith at whose forge we stopped to have the horses shod. "Only that Moriones is advancing and quite enough too, is it not?" added the imperturbable farrier as he hammered on a shoe by the aid of a torchlight. "Will he be here this evening?" "*Quien sabe!*" ("Who knows?") "Where is Ollo?" "Can't say." But my horses were thoroughly knocked up, and it was very doubtful where the Navarrese leader had established his head-quarters, so I determined to take the risk and rest both steeds and riders. "The enemy is two and a half leagues off", I remarked to my servant. "Well, if they are Spanish leagues, Sir, why it don't so much matter; it is like an Irishman, his league begins in the morning and ends at night." There was some truth in the observation. A knowledge of distance is almost unknown in Spain, and with this consolation I lay down to sleep on a barn floor, the best accommodation which could be obtained under the circumstances.

We were up early yesterday morning. The enemy had not taken possession of Avarzuza during the night. However, the old women and cronies of the wine shops shook their heads, observing sadly, "The *Negros* will soon be here." But where was Ollo? No one could tell me. At last the priest remarked, "Why not go to Estella, there you will be sure to find out where the head-quarters are?" I determined to act upon his advice, and we had not long quitted the village when a patrol of Royalist troops, coming down from the mountains by a rugged track, fit only for goats or Carlists, crossed the road in front of us.

"Where is the General?" I inquired. "In one of those *pueblos* yonder", replied a sergeant, pointing to a cluster of hamlets perched like eagles' nests upon a high ridge of hills some few miles off. "But in which of them shall I find him?" "We don't know ourselves", said the officer who commanded the *partida*; "but ask at the first post and whoever is stationed there will tell you." Steeper and more impracticable became the path, and with difficulty could I induce my horse to face the loose boulders blocking up the passage. At last we emerged upon a small plot of table-land. Here in a few cottages were billeted the first battalion of Navarres. The information I sought for was readily given, and one hour later we found ourselves at head-quarters. The military aspect of affairs was anything but favourable to the Royalists. Moriones had left Pampeluna, and his own column, reinforced by the divisions of Santa Pau and Primo de Rivera, now numbered 12,000 fighting men, with 14 cannon. Seven thousand of the enemy were stationed at Oteiza, 2,000 at Laraga, and the remainder in Lerin. Moriones, it was believed, would march upon Estella, and the whole Carlist force in Grozin and the neighbourhood was only 3,500 strong, with four guns. Ollo's staff officers were in hope that Lizzarraga would bring the Guipuzcoans to their rescue; but nothing was known of the last-named General's intentions. I had barely time to swallow a cup of chocolate at the priest's house before the trumpet sounded general parade, and we were again en route. "Where are we going to?" I inquired of our leader. "To a spot that you must well remember; to Dicastillo. I mean to make a stand there, and then fight a retreating battle, as my strength is not sufficient to hold the heights." "I have just heard", he continued "that a column of the Republicans is advancing from Lorin, and if so you will soon be able to see them approaching." Shortly after our arrival I called upon the general. His windows commanded the whole of the plain that lay between Dicastillo and the mountains of Sesma. Lerin could be seen in the far off horizon, and clouds of dust slowly forming in the distance told us of the enemy's advance. Ollo's dispositions were rapidly taken. A height on our extreme right, the key of the position, was occupied by a battalion and a half. In the same direction, but slightly nearer to the town, and on a mound surmounted by an old tower, were two cannon and another battalion; four companies, two guns, and a *partida* of 250 men were stationed on a hillock about a mile to our left front, and the remainder in the *plaza* of the cathedral, the centre of our line of defence. In the meantime Ollo remained on his balcony, eagerly scrutinizing each successive wave of sand that arose in the distance, and endeavouring to ascertain the nature of the forces Primo de Rivera was bringing against him. "They are not all from Lerin", said the Carlist leader, slowly putting down his glasses. "There must be more than 3,000 men in that column, although it barely amounts to 5,000. However, the others will come later on in the day and try and turn our right. If so I must retire, or we shall be surrounded and cut off from our line of retreat."

The height which has been alluded to as being the key of our position is very strong and precipitous towards the south, but to the west it is commanded by a still loftier range of hills, and if the Republicans could have occupied these Moriones would have been able to turn our flank, and by the means of his Krupp cannon shell Dicastillo itself. The lower part of the eminence which formed the extremity to our right was covered with vines, and some thick groves of olive trees formed a network of shelter for the Carlist *partida*, should the Government troops enter Allo, a small village a mile and a half to our left front, and but 500 yards from the hillock held by the four companies. Nearer at every moment came the smoke-like clouds of sand and dust. From time to time the gleam of a bayonet flashed for a moment in the gray rays of the midday sun, and then disappeared from view in the dark shade which could each minute be more clearly defined. Presently long lines of dark spots began to emerge from the obscurity. Larger and more consistent each particle became, and, finally, we could plainly see the column debouch on the centre of Allo. A few minutes more and two batteries of artillery, taking ground to either flank, commenced shelling the right of our position, occasionally amusing themselves by throwing a shell at Dicastillo. The practice made by the Republican gunners was remarkably good, and called forth the remark, from General Ollo, that some of the old artillery officers must have returned to the corps. However, no movement was made by the enemy's infantry, which remained out of the range of fire. It was not even an artillery duel, as the Royalists did not return a shot, and the Carlist soldiers, sheltering themselves as best they could, lay at full length on the grass, smoking the eternal cigarette. Several shells burst close to the General, but no one on his staff was struck, and our casualties, I am told, were very small; this being owing not to want of skill on the part of the Republican gunners, but to the protected nature of our positions. At nightfall the Carlist troops retired to their quarters of the previous evening, and the *partidas* alone were left with orders to annoy the column in Allo by constantly firing on the outposts. At daybreak our whole force was withdrawn to this village, where we are to be reinforced by three battalions of Alaveses. Ollo will then have 7,000 men, but this is not sufficient to withstand Moriones' united columns. The latter will possibly enter Estella, as we have few troops to defend that town. In the meantime many of the inhabitants are hurriedly leaving their homes, frightened at the Republican leader's threat to burn down the city.

11 p.m.
A spy has just arrived with the information that Moriones is retiring in the direction of Lerin.

FGB077
Headquarters of General Ollo; 4 October 1873
Burnaby to Editor – *The Times*, 11 October 1873

I concluded my letter of yesterday by stating that the column of Moriones was in the act of retiring towards Lerin, but this morning, at 11 a.m., General Ollo received information that the Republican troops had continued their retrograde movement in the direction of Larraga. What can be the meaning of this apparent desire to avoid any collision with the Royalists? This is the question which everybody asks, and which, for the present at least, appears inexplicable, save by supposing one of two motives. Either Moriones is so convinced of the utter want of discipline and the demoralization of the Government soldiers that he hesitates to attack an enemy not half his own numerical strength, or else the General is influenced by some cause possibly more political than military. We have been repeatedly told by the Madrid *Official Journal* that the most energetic measures are about to be taken against the Carlists; but in what way has this announcement been carried into effect? Lizzarraga a few days since was besieging Tolosa, when Moriones, with 12,000 men and 14 pieces of artillery, advanced from Pampeluna and relieved the garrison. All the Royalist troops, with the exception of the *partidas*, or bands of *franc-tierurs*, retreated, Lizzarraga, with the Guipuzcoans, to Zumarraga, Ollo to Navarre, and Laramendi to Alava. Here was an opportunity for a vital blow. Moriones, with his own force and that of Lomas – some 16,000 men – was then only confronted by Lizzarraga, who had barely 6,000. The distance which divided him from his enemy did not exceed five leagues, a good highroad offered every facility for the transport of troops, and, Lizzarraga once defeated, Moriones could have destroyed the Carlist factories of small arms at Elbar and Placencia. The Royalist forces in Vizcaya were too far off to render Lizzarraga any assistance, and he would have been obliged either to retreat or to expose himself to fearful odds in accepting battle. But no; the Republican general, after remaining two or three days on Tolosa, retreated to Pampeluna; thence he advanced to Taffala and Lerin, finally making two attacked upon the Navarrese in Dicastillo, both of them consisting of an artillery fire, which was not returned by the Carlists. However, the numerical strength of his opponent's column was so greatly in excess of General Ollo's, that the latter did not like to risk remaining in his positions. The Navarrese retreated to Avarzuza, awaiting a reinforcement of three battalions under Laramendi; Estella was left undefended save by a few of the *partidas*; the town, I may fairly say, lay at the mercy of Moriones. However, he has not chosen to avail himself of the opportunity, and why? "*Quien sabe?*" with a shrug of the shoulders, is the general answer.

The war is carried on in a very happy-go-lucky sort of way by the leaders of both sides. Glaring blunders are frequently committed, but seldom taken advantage of; and at the rate affairs are now carried on in Spain this will not be a Seven Years' struggle, but we will see the present generation under the soil before it comes to a conclusion. Little enthusiasm was shown by the inhabitants of Estella when we entered the town to-day. The Carlist sympathizers had all fled for fear of the Republicans, and the Liberals who remained shut themselves up in their houses in high dudgeon at the unexpected turn things had taken. Nothing in the shape of meat or eggs was to be procured for love or money, as those people who had not quitted Estella, whatever their political opinions might be, preferred dining off their hens and chickens to running the risk of Republican soldiery taking them without payment. Fruit, however, was to be had in abundance, and huge melons and bunches of the most delicious grapes could be purchased for a mere song.

Some of the Carlist soldiers show a strange want of knowledge with respect to foreign countries. A friend of mine, the Baron von Wedell, formerly a lieutenant in the Prussian Uhlans,[128] is now serving with the Royalists. He was eating some grapes this morning, when a lieutenant-colonel, who shall be nameless, observed, "You have no grapes in your country." "No grapes", replied the German, indignant at his Vaterland being thus aspersed, "have you never heard of Rhine wine?" "Rhine wine! What is it, a town?" "*Donner vetter*, no!" and to the Baron's astonishment he discovered that his companion was ignorant of the existence of the world-renowned stream. Presently the Lieutenant-Colonel asked the German if it were true that in his country a man might marry four or five wives and all the children be legitimate? "Yes", replied the exasperated Prussian, "and Germany is such a fruitful country that frequently a woman has 20 and even 30 children. This will explain to you how we can afford to lose so many men in battle; a few thousand here and there make no difference whatever to us, as they are so easily replaced." "*Caramba*", said the Spaniard, and his perplexity was still greater when he was informed that Germans, Poles, and Russians possessed each a distinctive language, and were not the same nation. Such utter ignorance appeared to me unaccountable, and it was only when the Baron assured me on his word that the conversation actually occurred, and in the manner it is here described, that I ventured to write down the story.

We have no news of either Elio or Lizzarraga, but General Ollo tells me that to-morrow we shall probably advance towards Puente la Reina. Three battalions of Alaveses under Laramendi marched into Estella this afternoon, but the men cannot be compared with Ollo's troops in respect to armament or appearance. With all these drawbacks, there can be no doubt that Don Carlos is making progress: fresh arms have been landed and new battalions are being

---

128 Light cavalry armed with lances and sabres. Von Wedell later acted as a war correspondent for the *Cologne Gazette*.

organized. So, if the energetic measures which the Government announces it is going to adopt are not soon taken, the Royalists will have gained so much ground that Don Carlos's chance of eventually reaching Madrid will become each day more probable.

FGB078
Headquarters of General Ollo, Ciraqui; 6 October 1873
Burnaby to Editor (telegraph) – *The Times*, 11 October 1873
General Moriones, with 8,000 Republican troops and 16 guns, marched from Puente la Reyna this morning towards Estella. General Ollo, with 5,000 Carlists and four guns, marched to meet him.

A battle was fought at Mañeru. The Republicans at first took one of Ollo's positions, but were afterwards repulsed with considerable loss, and driven back, utterly routed, towards Puente la Reyna.

The Carlist losses are heavy. I have seen many Republican soldiers lying dead on the battle field.

FGB079
Headquarters of General Ollo, Ciraqui; 7 October 1873, 4 a.m.
Burnaby to Editor – *The Times*, 13 October 1873
The 6th of October, 1873, will long be remembered by the partisans of Don Carlos as an eventful day for the Royalist cause. My Spanish servant awoke me early. "The General has left Estella." "Has he taken any troops with him?" I asked. "No, Señor, only his aide-de-camp." Probably to make a reconnaissance I thought, or perhaps to visit the field works which were being thrown up to protect the town. But a little later a battalion followed in the same direction Ollo had taken. We hastily dressed and went to the house of General Argonz, the second in command, to inquire what the news was. "Moriones is advancing from Puente la Reyna with 8,000 men and 16 guns. Ollo is at Lorca. Heavy firing is going on in the neighbourhood of that town. We have three battalions there, and I take the rest of our forces immediately as a reinforcement." This was the state of affairs at 8 a.m. yesterday morning. The odds are long against us, I said to myself on quitting General Argonz, for the whole force Ollo could oppose to Moriones consisted of 5,000 infantry, 150 cavalry, and four guns. Our men were also short of ammunition, and the three battalions of Alaveses were badly armed. It did not take long to saddle, and ere a clock had struck the half hour, we were going over to Lorca at a good swinging trot. Quiet and peaceful looked the beautiful country which lay around Estella. It was one of those bright sunny mornings when the mere sensation of experience is a pleasure. One's lungs inhaled the pure mountain air. Life was doubly enjoyable, and so must have thought many a poor fellow who was destined never to see another sun rise. Carlist engagements have generally been the burlesque of

battles. Six or seven men killed on either side has been about the average of loss in an encounter; but what happened yesterday was an exception to the rule. Both parties at the commencement meant fighting, and the casualties were very considerable in proportion to the number of combatants. But I am anticipating. On reaching Lorca we came up with Argonz's rear guard, and on joining him were told that Radica, the colonel of the 2nd Navarrese battalion, had been in possession of the height called Santa Barbara, which commands the road between Mañeru and Puente la Reyna; that Moriones had attacked this position with the whole of his force and Radica's men, having fired away all their ammunition, had charged with the bayonet. I subsequently heard that his regiment had behaved with more bravery than prudence, and that if it had not been for two other battalions which came to the rescue not a man could have escaped being killed or taken prisoner. After this preliminary brush with the Republicans, the three Carlist battalions finding themselves so fearfully outnumbered, and having also experienced heavy losses, had retired to Artaru, a little village near Puente la Reyna. Here they were joined by the remainder of the Carlist troops, and a position was taken up on a range of heights in the form of a horse-shoe, or rather of a triangle, with the apex pointed towards Puente la Reyna, and the base a line in prolongation of Cirauqui and covering Estella. The Alaveses were given the post of honour nearest the enemy, and a deep vale divided them from the base of the position, a high ridge, almost as steep as Santa Barbara, then occupied by the Government troops.

A continuous fire was maintained by Moriones' artillery during the morning against the Alaveses; and line after line of infantry was hurled against them. Badly armed and miserably equipped are these poor sons of Alava, and little instruction has been given to them, bravely they stood their ground, repeatedly attacking with the bayonet in a manner that drew forth applause even from the self-possessed General Ollo, who is hardly ever known to become excited, no matter under what circumstances he may find himself. But the numbers were too great, and things looked black indeed, when, at 3.30 p.m., the Alaveses were forced to retire into the vale and ascend the ridge, where their comrades eagerly awaited the moment to relieve them. The enemy instantly crowned the abandoned height and advanced about a hundred yards in long lines of skirmishers. However, the Republicans had suffered great losses in taking the hill, and here lay before them the task of assaulting their foe, again established in a strong position. According to all accounts, there is not much discipline in the enemy's ranks, and it would appear so, as suddenly, and for no apparent reason, the men hesitated, faltered, and then halted. General Ollo immediately took advantage of the occasion. Two of his guns which had not been brought into action before were placed on the right of our line to enfilade those Republicans who had made their first movement towards the Royalist left front. A shell, perfectly aimed, fell in the enemy's ranks, one sergeant and two men killed being the result; a second, following an instant later, was still more destructive in its effects, and *vivas* rang from the Carlist ridge as the foe turned tail and retired behind the slope of his position. Fresh shots followed from the Royalist artillerymen, and Moriones began to withdraw his men by retiring in *échelon* of battalions from the left. The Carlist left was then ordered to attack. A deadly fire was directed at our men by the regiments formed up on the Republican right to protect their comrades' retreat; but nothing could check the hot blood of the Navarrese and Alaveses. "*Con la bayoneta*" had been the order given to them, and the bayonet is their favourite arm. Cartridges, too, were wanting, and there was nothing left but the cold steel. At a racing pace the Royalist soldiery traversed the valley; never once checking, they doubled up the hillside. Fathers might fall, struck by the deadly hail showered from above, but sons did not stop. "*Adelante!*" was the cry, and the enemy, already cowed, at last ignominiously fled. General Ollo did not spare himself; he and his son, a young aide-de-camp, were throughout in the thick of the fight, and the ordinarily calm general, for perhaps the first time in his life, became a little excited. "Let the cavalry come to the front", called out some soldiers; "*Caballeria* be ____", or something in Spanish very much to that effect, escaped the General's lips, and then, seeing me at his side, he laughingly apologized for the expression. "For what horsemen could ride over this ground", he remarked; "a little later, yes, but now it is too absurd." At this moment his servant was struck full in the chest by a shot, and, staggering back a few yards, fell heavily to the ground. A few yards further we came upon an officer shot through the throat. "Poor fellow, he is my first cousin", said Ollo; and then, the bullets began to hail around us; man after man went down; and an Artillery officer, riding up to the general, asked him where the guns should be placed. "There", was the answer, pointing to the heights of Santa Barbara, from which point some of the enemy who had rallied were devastating the Royalist files. Dead men were lying about the ground in all the varieties of grotesque and strange positions in which they had been when the Grand Destroyer laid his scythe upon them. One was behind a low mound in the act of loading his rifle; the cartridge had fallen, but the weapon was in the dead man's hand, and a stern expression still to be traced on the countenance would make the passer-by believe that if the owner of the rifle had fired his last shot it would have been aimed with a will to mete out, to another, that lot just doled out to himself.

The moon rose, and the ghastly remains of humanity were thrown still more repulsively into relief by its shadows. "Let the cavalry charge", said the general, and away went our single squadron helter skelter after the breathless Republicans. Here the ground was favourable, and if Ollo could then have disposed of two good regiments of horse, the whole of Moriones's artillery must have been captured. Presently the squadron returned. It had taken some prisoners, killed a good many of the foe, and its Lieutenant had sabred a

Republican commander. "There he lies", said the young officer to Ollo, "and here I cut him down", and the lieutenant drew a sword still reeking with his victim's gore. There is something especially repugnant when we attempt to analyze our nature and find how strong the love of destruction is prevalent with the best of us under certain circumstances. The officer in question is one of the kindest and best-hearted fellows you can well imagine, but he was positively delighted he had killed the Commandant.

But I am moralizing, which is decidedly not the province of a Correspondent, and we must return to Santa Barbara, from which height the enemy had been driven. "How pleased their artillery officers must have been to-day when they gained this height", observed my companion, "for here is the Ermita, or Chapel of Santa Barbara, the patron saint of Spanish gunners, and to lose it afterwards. Our old comrades will be sorry enough that they have thrown their swords into the same scale as the Government. It was not their fault, though", he continued, his former *esprit de corps* suddenly returning to him, "they did their best to beat us, and fired admirably, but what could the poor fellows do backed up by those *cochons*, pigs of infantry, who will not obey their officers and have no discipline whatever!" The captain of a company here came up to Ollo and asked him where he was to billet his men. "Why, I told you; there yonder", said the General, pointing, to a little village; "but since you are here, take your company to the first house in Puente la Reyna, and stay there for the night." A pleasant undertaking, considering that Moriones and his troops were in the same town but, cowed and dispirited as the Republicans were, it was not likely that much energy would be displayed by them, and the officer, saluting, went off with his men to execute the order. "Take one of your guns", said Ollo to a Lieutenant of Artillery, "and fire a shot at the very entrance of Puente la Reyna. I will let the people know that Moriones is inside like a whipped hound, and that he dares not come out."

Along the best road we marched towards Cirauqui. "Where is A?" "Poor fellow! He is dead." "And B?" "Wounded." "Glorious Victory! How pleased the King will be"; and such were the themes of conversation till we arrived at our quarters for the night. Here I found that my mule and Spanish servant had not arrived. The place was crowded, and ten officers shared my bedroom. Tired and hungry, we were too, having had nothing to eat since 8 a.m., and it was under these conditions I sent off my telegram to you and attempted to write a letter; but Nature would assert her sway, sleep overcame me in my chair. However, four hours in bed soon made me myself again, and I take the advantage of another courier going to France to despatch this letter. I forgot to mention that the Republican leader Primo de Rivera is at Logrono with 4,000 men and six guns. If he advances upon Estella, we shall have to fall back to protect that town.

FGB080
Headquarters of General Ollo, Estella; 8 October 1873, 4 a.m.
Burnaby to Editor – *The Times*, 14 October 1873

Yesterday morning Ollo was still undecided as to which course he should pursue – attack the Republicans at Puente la Reyna, or return to Estella. "The fact is", observed the General, "that I should like to strike another blow immediately, as the enemy is demoralized, but I have no cartridges, our reserves of ammunition are exhausted, and some battalions have their pouch-belts empty, while those best provided have barely 40 rounds per man." "But if we return to Estella" remarked his son, "Moriones will send a telegram to Madrid saying that he has utterly routed us, and that we have retreated." "Let him", said Ollo, coolly; "it will not be the first time that the *Official Journal* has published a falsehood. People are becoming aware of this, and but little credence will be given to the statement. Anyhow, I ought to return, for Primo de Rivera, with 4,000 men and six guns, has left Logrono, and we are told he is taking the direction of Estella. Should this movement be continued our troops must be there to meet him. However, the day after to-morrow, we shall be more than a match for Moriones' whole force, as the King is coming, with two battalions of Guipuzcoans and four of Viscayans."

At 12 a.m. we were *en route* for Estella. Ollo was not with the column, he having gone to see his wounded relation, who, it was said, could not live many hours. The general's servant had also expressed a wish to see his master. The former was lying in a villa some five miles off, and the Carlist leader, I was told, would make a point of visiting his serving man, to give him a final shake of the hand before the poor fellow died. General Argonz, the second in command, was at the head of the Division. He has the reputation of knowing every inch of Navarre, and is invaluable on account of his geographical knowledge. Carlist staff officers laugh and say, "If you wish to behold Argonz in all his glory you should see him giving directions to a *confidente*." The General will particularize each by-path, every cottage, farmyard, &c., until he at length he says, "And there, on the right or left side of the road, is a tree; it is hollow. You must get inside and count the number of battalions Moriones has when he passes." I rode for a long time with this celebrated character, being anxious to hear what opinion he had formed of the previous day's proceedings. "I do not think Moriones wished to attack us," was the reply to my question. "He wished to march his column to Pampeluna, and on leaving Puente la Reyna two of our *partidas* stationed in the neighbourhood commenced firing upon his advance guard. Moriones lost his temper, and determined to try and punish them. He advanced the Republican column in the direction of Mañeru, and there suddenly came upon the 2nd Navarre Battalion under Radica. The latter, when his men had expended all their cartridges, ordered them to charge with the bayonet. Too absurd, was it not", continued the General, gravely smiling, "800 men against 8,000? Radica is as brave as a lion, but he wishes to perform impossibilities." The next inquiry was, "How do you explain Moriones not using his artillery in the afternoon? For, with the 16 guns he is stated to possess, much damage might have been inflicted on your men when they charged up the hill." "The only solution I can find", said Argonz, "is that the Krupp artillery was too heavy to transport on mules, and so it had to be left in the plain. Or else their ammunition had run short; they have fired several hundred rounds against Dicastillo the last few days, and possibly no fresh supply of shell has been sent there. It will not be easy for the enemy to take Estella", continued the General, "for our men have thrown up field works on all the hills which surround the town; but, with the reinforcements which are to arrive to-morrow, I trust that we shall be the attackers and not the attacked."

Later on in the afternoon Ollo arrived, and I was informed by a Prussian officer who had accompanied him on his visits to the hospitals, that the wounded men were admirably looked after. He also told me that the ambulances looked clean, and the surgeons seemed to him skilful and well acquainted with their profession. The General was much affected when he saw his servant; the poor fellow had been shot through the body, and could not speak without blood pouring from the mouth. Ollo's relation was also in a dying state, and sad indeed must have been the Carlist Chief when he had to acknowledge the *vivas* of the townspeople, who cheered enthusiastically as the victorious leader rode into their town. Very true is the old saying that nothing is so saddening as defeat, and that the next degree of comparison in sorrow is perhaps a victory. For with all the joy aroused at the triumph of the Royalist arms, there are few inhabitants of Estella who have not to mourn some friend, three days ago hale and well, but now a stark corpse beneath the soil. It is difficult with Spaniards ever to obtain a true list of the killed and wounded. I inquired of General Ollo this morning, and the answer was that he had not as yet received a detailed statement from Laramendi, the leader of the Alavese. The losses, as estimated by various Royalist officers I have conversed with, should amount to 70 killed and 220 or 230 wounded. The Republicans are said to have had 1,000 men *hors de combat*, but this is probably an exaggeration, and 600 would appear to me more likely to be about the correct number. Unfortunately, in the Peninsula there is a great tendency to diminish the list of casualties even at the expense of veracity, and this renders it very difficult for a correspondent to arrive at anything like a correct return.

FGB081
Royalist Headquarters, Estella; 8 October 1873
Burnaby to Editor – *The Times*, **16 October 1873**
Don Carlos arrived here yesterday, bringing with him six fresh battalions, and, what was quite as important, a large supply of ammunition. Four million five

hundred thousand rounds of ball cartridges were landed last week in Biscay, and of these more than half are now in Navarre. Great was the enthusiasm of the good people of Estella at seeing the Prince once more, and amid the deafening peal of bells, combined with the ringing cheers of the populace, Don Carlos, dismounted and took his place in a large window looking out upon the Plaza, for here the troops were to march past, and His Majesty would then be able to inspect the weather-beaten, dare-devil soldiery of Navarre, and the equally brave, but worse armed and clad, regiments of Alava. General Ollo, with his staff, first marched by and saluted, followed by the various Navarre battalions. It was a sad sight to see how the companies had shrunk in size since the battle of Mañeru, the 2nd, Colonel Radica's, or as it is frequently called Calderon's, Battalion having lost above 100 killed and wounded in the engagement; but those left, though few in number, looked just as ready to march into the jaws of death as the other day when their leader ordered them to charge 8,000 Republicans. The regiments of Alava were also fearfully reduced, and from the small muster on parade I am inclined to think that the estimate of Carlist losses given in my yesterday's letter must have been under the mark. The infantry marched past fairly enough considering the short time the men have been enlisted; and then, came the mountain artillery, each gun being carried on a mule, its carriage on another. Much interest was awakened when the gunners approached the saluting point, for to the first three shells is attributed the sudden panic that seized the Republican ranks, and the subsequent triumph of the Royalist arms. After the review was over, General Ollo presented his various officers who had distinguished themselves in the engagement to Don Carlos. The "King" was delighted at the victory, and told me that he regretted excessively not having been able to arrive in time to take an active part in the battle. It appears that an order had been despatched to General Ollo desiring him on no account to accept an engagement until the reinforcements had arrived. However, fortunately, as it since turned out, the messenger lost his way, and the Navarrese leader did not receive the letter till the battle had been fought and won.

But now that the Royalists muster in Estella nearly 10,000 men, what will be the next step? This is the question which is on everybody's lips. The answer must necessarily depend upon the movements of Moriones. According to the latest Carlist advices, the Republican General is stated to be marching northwards in the direction of Pampeluna. Should this be the case, the road to Tafalla remains open to us. However, Primo de Rivera, with his column of 4,000 men, and it is said three regiments of horse, must then be thought of. It is believed that this leader is now at Lerin, a small town seven leagues south-west of Tafalla. Should the Carlists advance upon this last-named town, they must pass over some level ground admirably suited for the manoeuvring of cavalry. Now what would be the effect upon the Royalist newly raised infantry, if it were suddenly charged in the open by a mounted force? Don Carlos's foot soldiers have not yet had any opportunity of learning practically how weak a regiment of horse is if opposed to a battalion armed with breech-loaders, even should the infantry be simply drawn up in line. The result is, many of Elio's staff are afraid that if their men were suddenly charged home a panic might ensue. If this were to happen woe betide the Navarrese, magnificent troops, indeed, for attack, but once in retreat almost impossible to rally. Some officers think that Dicastillo would be a good position for the Carlist infantry to become habituated to Primo de Rivera's horse, for here the ground is favourable for cavalry up to a certain point, but there are many small vineyards at frequent intervals in which the foot soldiers could take refuge if broken by a charge. On the other hand, it must not be forgotten that Moriones, if at Pampeluna, is between Don Carlos and Tolosa. Lizzarraga is still blockading the garrison of the last-named town, and it would not do for the Royalists to have another failure similar to the late retreat from Tolosa. Such a combination of positions makes it appear probable that the "King" will soon return to Guipuzcoa. However, of course this can be nothing more than a surmise based upon the very indifferent knowledge that we have at present of what will be the enemy's next movements. In the meantime there are constant reports of the surrender of Valencia. According to these rumours the Royalist movement in that province has taken very wide dimensions, and I am assured that the Carlists have 10,000 armed men in the neighbourhood of the besieged city. It is said that the Royalist agents have bought a large supply of rifles from the internationalist insurgents at the price of two dollars a weapon, and with these arms the partisans of Don Carlos were first able to take the initiative. I am also told that the artillery garrison in Valencia is very anti-Republican in its sympathies, and if this should be the case, the fall of Valencia would be more than probable. Not much credence can be given to the news published in some Spanish journals, judging from the fact that I have just read in the *Español* of Seville that your Correspondent is about to organize a legion of 2,000 foreigners for the cause of Don Carlos. The statement is almost too absurd to rectify, but it shows what slight attention can be paid to information emanating from such sources.

FGB082
Royalist Headquarters, Estella; 8 October 1873
Burnaby to Editor – *The Times***, 21 October 1873**
The following is a translation of the proclamation addressed by General Ollo to the Royalist troops after the battle of Mañeru: –

To the Army of Navarre – General Order. Estella, Oct. 8, 1873.

Volunteers! – Ten months ago, faithful to the command of our august and well-beloved King (whom may God preserve), I commenced a struggle against his enemies, who are also the enemies of God and of Spain, accompanied by my inseparable companion, General Argonz, and followed by only 20 brave men. It is just that on the present occasion I should delight my heart by recalling all that you have accomplished, as a good proof that I am satisfied with you.

Scarcity of resources, want of armament, unceasing harassing by numerous armies, and the inclemency of a life in the mountains have not sufficed to prevent a handful of loyal men becoming the division of warriors whom I share the honour of commanding. Your sobriety, your valour, and your enthusiasm for the holy cause we defend have been more than sufficient to overcome every difficulty.

The arduous task of organization has been effected in the midst of the heat of battles; and at the same time, and to the magic cry of '*Viva el Rey!*' you have made the Liberals run before the points of your bayonets at Salinas, Galharra, Miravalles, Villaro, Monreal, Eraul, Ollogoyen, Udare, Allo, and Dicastillo; you have taken the forts of Irurzum, Puente, Cirauqui, Tunel, San Adrian, Campanas, Estella, Viana, Sauguesa, Lumbier, and Valcarlos; you have always conquered wherever the invariably superior number of the foe has confronted you; you have sown dismay in his ranks, and have been the means of throwing discredit on his chiefs – Catalan, Moriones, Pavia, Nouvilas, Sanchez Bregua,[129] and Santa Pau – for not one of these has been able to resist your enthusiasm and bravery, which make you invincible.

In this manner – you yourselves gaining laurels and I am proud of commanding you – we arrived at the 6th of this month; and then, on the heights of Cirauqui and Mañeru, the most important of your triumphs – obtained with the aid of our brothers the Alaveses, few in number, but always valiant and loyal – has been inaugurated.

Moriones, who easily conquers unarmed peasants – the hero of Oroquieta – came a few days ago with all the resources he could unite, resolved to destroy us and take Estella as the price of his victory. The superiority of his forces in numbers, and the destructive superiority of his artillery, have collapsed before the Alavese serenity and determination. The foe has been hurled back and cut in pieces by the *élan* of the Navarrese.

Volunteers! His Majesty the King, our august Sovereign, whose magnanimous heart is full of pleasure at so signal a victory, commands me in his Royal name to thank you, and also to thank the troops of Alava; and I have the greatest pleasure in complying with the Royal will, adding on my side that General Argonz, the chief of my Staff and my dear friend, comported himself on that day with his usual valour and skill; also, the Brigadiers Iturmendi and Mendirri. The colonels led their men with skill and bravery; the officers fought like good cavaliers; the soldiers of Alava, made a resistance not to be shaken, and to you yourselves, brave

---

129 General José Sánchez Bregua (1818-1897), later Minister of War under Castelar.

Navarrese and dear countrymen, I shall conclude by saying, as I began, that I am satisfied with you.

Your General Comandante-General, Nicholas Ollo.

FGB083
Royalist Headquarters, Estella; 11 October 1873
Burnaby to Editor – *The Times*, 17 October 1873

Nothing has been left undone to crown with pomp and ceremony the victory at Mañeru. This morning a religious ceremony was performed in the Cathedral for the souls of the Carlists killed in the late battle. Detachments from every regiment were ordered to attend, and the "King" himself, with all his suite, was present. A sombre and gloomy building at the best of times is the Church of Estella. Small windows of quaint and out-of-date pattern allow but little light to enter the edifice. Rough and hard is the architecture in the interior. Huge unsightly arches and pillars support the roof. But in the unsightliness itself there is something that stirs the imagination, more especially when the rude pile is filled with soldiery assembled to pray for the souls of their dead comrades. An altar had been erected in the centre of the nave. Tiers of candles arranged upon the shrines, pyramid fashion, threw a pale mysterious light, but dimly illuminating their immediate surrounding. Wax tapers of gigantic proportions were placed at each corner of the raised dais, and behind them stood four Royalist soldiers with ordered arms, and motionless as statues. The space between these guardians of the sanctuary and the other military devotees was filled up by rifles, arranged triangle fashion, thug giving a martial appearance to the scene, but awakening sad thoughts, as the weapons, it was said, but five days before had been in the possession of those slain at Mañeru. Long and uninteresting to many present must have been the service, sung in Latin, but a fixed attention was shown by the worshippers, and a pin could have been heard to drop, so dead was the stillness that reigned around. When the mass was over, a *cura* of Estella, Don Sebastian Urra by name, ascended the pulpit and preached a short but thrilling sermon to his soldier congregation. The rev. gentleman began:–

> Martyrs, yes, martyrs to God and the only true religion, are your departed comrades. The term is a high one, but the self-devotion manifested by our brave, alas, now dead brethren, merits the expression. They are now where God grant that you and I may one day be – enjoying the crown of martyrdom, won by sacrificing their blood for their God, for their country, and their King on the battle-field. And to what enemy is our gallant army opposed? To the enemy of the only true religion, to the enemy of the Saints, to the deadly foe of the Church, and to the supporters of an Atheistical Government, which declares illegitimate all children unless the parents have been married according to the civil law.

In similar strains the *cura* continued his discourse, the perspiration streaming down him from excitement and the violence of his gesticulations. The Bishop of Urgel was also present. Much, it is whispered, would the good Bishop like to assume temporal as well spiritual authority in the King's Council. But this Don Carlos does not allow for a moment, and if the clergy think that they will be able to make him a mere tool in the hands of the ecclesiastical party, they greatly mistake their man. Once in power, it will be seen that the Sovereign will brook no interference on the part of the priesthood. Should Don Carlos arrive at Madrid, historians will not be able to write that he was a priest-ridden Monarch and the only fault which possibly may be attributed to him can be defined in these words, that he was far too kind-hearted a man for his people.

In my last letter, I stated that Moriones was reported to have marched with all his forces to Pampeluna. However, to-day we are informed that the Republican Chief did not take any troops with him, but went there alone, remained a few hours, and then returned to Tafalla. It is also said that he has received a reinforcement of two fresh battalions; however, they are composed of newly-levied recruits, so their reported arrival does not much impress the Royalist Generals. The latter are in hopes that an advance will be made by the enemy in the direction of Estella. Should this be done and a battle be fought in the mountains, the chances will be in favour of the Carlists, flushed with triumph as their soldiers are from the recent victory, Spaniards are kept as well informed of the various actions between the Royalists and Republicans by the Generals commanding the Government forces as the French nation was of the result of the engagements at the commencement of the last campaign. It would be ridiculous, if it were not at the same time pitiful, to observe the utter disregard of truth manifested by the official organs which are inspired by the Republican Generals. For instance, I read in *La Correspondencia Navarra*, of the 8th inst., that "the invincible General Moriones, whom we have just had the pleasure of saluting, has added one more page to the glorious history of the Spanish Army." The writer continues, saying that the Government troops attacked the Navarrese and Alavese posted on the heights of Santa Barbara, near Puente, at 7 o'clock in the morning, dislodged them from the impregnable positions they occupied, and forced them to retreat to a spot two leagues distant from the field of battle; after which, at 4 in the afternoon, it was determined to execute a movement with the object of passing the night at Puente.

Such is the garbled account of the action, given, apparently, officially, as the writer states that he has "just had the pleasure of saluting the invincible General Moriones." Should this be the case the "invincible" leader of the Republican troops would appear to have forgotten to inform *La Correspondencia Navarra* that a few minutes after 4 o'clock in the afternoon in question his troops advanced to attack the united force of General Ollo, placed upon two heights in prolongation of Cirauqui; that the infantry of the "invincible" General descended the hill on which they had been stationed for about 200 yards; that then, hesitating on seeing the formidable position remaining for them to attack, they wavered and halted; that at this moment two shells were thrown into their ranks, and the Government forces hastily retired; that they were then charged with the bayonet by the Navarrese, and the retreat became a most disgraceful rout, the soldiers of the "invincible" Moriones being pursued and bayonetted up to the very entrance of Puente. It is to be regretted that a journal should present to its readers such a garbled account of the battle, while a deep slur is inevitably thrown upon that Party whose General not only loses a battle but afterwards strives wilfully to mislead the public.

FGB084
Royalist Headquarters, Estella; 13 October 1873
Burnaby to Editor – *The Times***, 20 October 1873**
We have head today that the Madrid Government, not satisfied with the conduct of Moriones, has taken away from him command of the Republican Army and given it to General Concha.[130] Judging by the results obtained by the first-named leader in his campaign against the Royalists, in which nothing has been achieved save the temporary relief of Tolosa, Señor Castela[131] would appear to have good reason for the step he is said to have taken. But if Moriones did little, will his successor do more? I had a conversation with Elio, the Carlist Commander-in-Chief, on the subject this afternoon. "Concha sleeps seldom, eats hardly anything, and only drinks enough to support existence", was the reply to my question. "If he takes the command against us we shall have plenty to do, as he is always active and on the move." I then remarked, "But it is said in Spain that Concha has been the undertaker of every Government which has employed him. Do you think he will bury the present rulers the same as their predecessors?" "That is quite a different thing", said Elio, gravely smiling. "Concha is very active, but *perhaps he will, perhaps he will.* You know", continued the General, "there was a report here yesterday of a Carlist triumph at San Sebastian, and it was rumoured that our men had captured a gun. I have just received a despatch from Lizzarraga, telling me that the Republican garrison had made a sally, but it would appear they were repulsed with loss. However, he does not mention anything about a gun, and was not personally present at the affair, so probably not much importance can be attached to it." "Any news from Catalonia or Valencia?" I enquired. "Nothing fresh", was the reply.

Little is to be gathered from the Madrid journals save the oft-repeated

---

130 Manuel Gutierrez de la Concha y Yrigoyen, Marquis del Duero (1808-1874), a respected soldier who led the Republican forces for only around a year, being killed by a stray bullet in 1874.
131 Don Emilio Castela (1832-1899), Spanish orator and statesman, who was President of the Republic in 1873.

announcement of the energetic and stringent measures about to be taken against the partisans of Don Carlos. Here, however, the lethargy which has apparently dominated the Royalist forces during the last six weeks has been thoroughly shaken off. Instruction is going on at all hours. Officers have not a moment to themselves, and the men, who have their hearts in the work, are rapidly improving in knowledge of drill and in soldierly bearing. Each failure of the Republican Generals naturally makes the Royalist officers more sanguine. But where the effect of a battle won can be best seen is in the demeanour of the soldiers themselves. At the outbreak of hostilities they feared the foe, and, as I have been told, a shell exploding in the ranks was sufficient to create a panic. But gradually the raw recruit became accustomed to his new life. A few slight successes achieved here and there in the mountains inspirited the newly-raised soldiery. After Dicastillo they considered that they were the equals of their opponents, but now, since Mañeru, they believe themselves to be far superior. Don Carlos inspected two of the Navarre battalions yesterday afternoon. The men were well handled by their commanding officers, and after having been ordered to form square repeatedly, the day's proceedings concluded with a charge in line. "I am well aware", observed one of the Colonels, "that in the first of modern armies forming square is considered an unnecessary operation, as with the breech-loading armament a line of infantry is thought sufficient to resist a cavalry attack. But we cannot afford to throw a chance away, and as our men are very young at the business it has been determined to teach them the old movement." One great drawback to rifle practice exists in the Royalist army, and this is the scarcity of cartridges. The rank and file are barely supplied with sufficient ammunition to discharge at their foe, and, in consequence, no firing ever takes place against the butts. At all events, during the last two months I have not either witnessed or heard anything like musketry instruction. The consequence is that in action half the rounds expended are literally thrown away, each man making it his principal object to discharge as many shots as possible, and paying but little attention to their direction.

    In the meantime the Engineers are busy throwing up fieldworks around Estella. This is being done with the view of leaving a small garrison in the town, and then the remainder of the forces will be able to act in the neighbourhood. Estella is looked upon as a most important point by the Carlist Generals, and any sacrifice will be made to prevent its falling into the hands of the Republicans. Strategically speaking it is of but little value. But the present idea appears to be to drive the Government troops to the other side of the Ebro, and then to make Estella the head-quarters for the winter, and this is the notion that prevails among many of the staff officers. However, all these surmises may be knocked on the head by another Carlist victory, for should Concha or the next chief of the Government troops have no better fortune than Moriones, the march upon Madrid will commence sooner than is by many anticipated.

Much attention is being paid to the organisation of fresh cavalry regiments, and we are assured that 19 mountain guns and 14 Armstrong cannon[132] have been lately disembarked. The latter, it is said, are shortly to arrive at Estella, and then I shall be able to write more fully about their calibre, &c. Several artillery officers have lately offered their services to Don Carlos, so as soon as the batteries are formed there will be no difficulty in providing them with trained commanders. More interest would seem to be taken in Spanish affairs by both Germany and Austria than formerly. Correspondents from both these nations are now at head-quarters, the Baron von Wedell forwarding his letters to the Prussian Press, and the Baron von Walterskirchen to the *Vaterland*, an Austrian journal.[133]

FGB085
Royalist Headquarters, Estella; 15 October 1873
Burnaby to Editor – *The Times*, **22 October 1873**
It is now more than nine days since the battle of Mañeru, and, notwithstanding the continual assertions of the Madrid newspapers that Moriones has achieved a great triumph, the Republican troops are further off from Estella than they were on the day of the fight. Twelve thousand Royalist soldiers are in the neighbourhood of this town. Fourteen thousand of the Government forces remain idle at Tafalla and Artajona. The enemy has also a large force of artillery and cavalry; but notwithstanding his numerical superiority, and in spite of the so-called victory of the invincible Moriones, inaction is apparently the order of the day. But this state of things cannot last long. We are informed that considerable reinforcements are being despatched from Madrid, and that when the Republican General can muster 28,000 men he will prove his invincibility by gaining a decisive victory. That he may at all events do something is the earnest wish of Don Carlos's staff officers, who are rapidly becoming weary of this town. Garrison life in the provinces is never very amusing, but where nothing can be done against a foe who will not leave his quarters, where out-door amusements in the shape of hunting or shooting cannot be resorted to, where the fair sex can be counted on the fingers, and the few who form society have not been overburdened by nature with personal attractions – where all these things are combined no one can wonder that Estella is unanimously voted an intense bore. The soldiers liked the town well enough for the first few days. Their afternoons were taken up with drill, and they could play *pelota*

---

132 More often referred to as Armstrong guns, these were breech-loading cannon with rifled barrels of a variety of calibre designed by Sir William Armstrong and manufactured in England from 1855 to the mid-1860s, when the British government made a decision to revert to muzzle-loading guns for cost reasons.
133 The *Vaterland* was a daily newspaper catering to the Austrian nobility; William, Baron von Walterskirchen, was one of its founders.

or fives against the Cathedral walls during the morning. However, now this amusement has been taken, away from them, as the people who go to pray object to projectiles in the shape of leather balls flying about their ears when they enter the church door, and a stringent order been given out prohibiting the game in the vicinity of the place of worship. It is, in consequence, now carried on in the market-place, to the great dismay of the stall-keepers, whose eggs and other fragile stock are constantly placed in jeopardy by the players. Those men who are too aged or idle to take any active exercise saunter slowly about the *plaza*, muffled up to the throat, some in mantles, and others in horse-cloths or old pieces of bright-coloured carpet. They gravely criticize the *pelota*, and never fail to remark how much better it was played in their time than at present.

With reference to Moriones himself not much is known at head-quarters, the general belief being that the Republican leader is laid up with an attack of ophthalmia at Tudela. In the meantime an impression prevails that hostilities cannot be much longer delayed. I had a long conversation with Don Carlos yesterday afternoon on the subject. He is much annoyed that his enemies will not attack him, particularly as he is remaining here now merely for the sake of public opinion, and not for military reasons. "Estella in itself, as a strategical point", observed His Majesty, "is of no advantage whatever. But if I were to leave the town the Madrid journals would instantly publish a telegram from the Republican General to the effect that he has offered battle and the Royalists have not only declined the engagement, but are no longer to be seen in the district. I have waited here seven days with only 12,000 men, and if the Republicans do not take advantage of the opportunity we shall not continue idle, awaiting our enemy's pleasure to attack, but ourselves commence the aggressive in another direction."

The idea, however, prevails that a battle must soon be fought near Estella, and if the Government really succeeds in concentrating 20,000 men at Tafalla, Don Carlos would do wisely in recalling some of his forces from Guipuzcoa, and Vizcaya. If the King chose he could easily put in the field an equally numerous force, but then the blockade of Bilbao would have to be temporarily suspended. This would in itself be no loss to the Carlists, as until they receive a supply of siege artillery all attempts on their part, unaided by treason from within, will be unavailing to take the town. Should the "King" make up his mind to remain at Estella, an engagement must be the inevitable result. The Royalists will have the advantage of ground and positions, while the enemy possesses an immense superiority in artillery, and probably also in number of combatants. Judging superficially, one would be inclined unhesitatingly to prophesy a Republican triumph. But if, on the other hand, the demoralization of the foe is considered and the extreme insubordination of his soldiery, the odds against the Carlists will, perhaps, not then appear so excessive as at first sight. If Don Carlos risks an encounter, it will probably be so far decisive that, should he be defeated, the whole of Navarre will remain at the disposal of the Government troops; but if the contrary should happen, why then, so soon as the organization of the Royalist cavalry is completed, an advance will be made upon the capital. No stones are being left unturned by the "King's" artisans to insure a victory. Agents have been sent to purchase a large supply of Gatling guns, and General Ollo has also ordered a quantity of signal lamps to be sent in for night telegraphy. Very useful they will prove in this mountainous country, where commanding heights convenient for the transmission of flashes are to be met with at frequent intervals. The only question is whether all these steps should not have been taken before this. It is somewhat late in the day to purchase arms when the foe is only 20 miles distant. That word "*mañana*", "to-morrow", which is the invariable answer to every application in Spain, is a serious drawback in military affairs. Fortunately for the Carlists, if they are slow, the Republicans are ten times slower, so the former gain by the contrast.

The system of *partidas* or *francs-tireurs*, which is most useful in the mountains, will have to be altered before any movement on the plains can be effected. These *partidas* generally consist of from 80 to 240 men, under the command of a chief chosen by themselves in the first place, and who is afterwards, should he show his efficiency in, the field, recognized officially by the Carlist Commander-in-Chief. The *partidas* are formed each, one for its own district, and many of the men have been smugglers or pedlars; in consequence they know every inch of the country, and every defile, pass, and cavern is familiar to them. Their duty is always to be on the enemy's track, by day or night no matter, to kill or make prisoners of his sentinels, capture his provisions, cut the means of communication, blow up bridges, and make themselves generally useful to the regular army, for which also they serve as *avant-postes*. Don Carlos and his troops can sleep in safety with the knowledge that these *guerrillos* are encircling the Republicans on every side. But, on the other hand, should the mountains once be left behind, the Royalist army will have to furnish its own outposts and pickets. Officers do not learn these duties so easily as civilians may imagine, and any negligence in this respect may cost the entire army its safety.

FGB086
Royalist Headquarters, Estella; 20 October 1873
Burnaby to Editor – *The Times*, 27 October 1873
No fresh engagement has occurred between the Royalist and Republican forces since Ollo's victory at Mañeru. The Carlist generals have been eagerly expecting a forward movement on the part of the enemy, but he does not seem inclined to risk an encounter. In the meantime the Government journals, till very lately so enthusiastic about the imaginary triumph at Mañeru, have lowered their tone and are beginning to ask whether the victory was so

glorious and decisive as their distinguished general had represented it to be. The *Correspondencia* observes, with some little rancour, that at the same time as the news of Moriones' brilliant success was being published in Madrid the members of the Carlist Junta in London and Paris were circulating through English and French newspapers a statement that General Ollo had utterly routed the Republican forces under the formidable Moriones. Nothing certain is known as to whether this so-called "invincible" general has been superseded, but the idea prevails that a fresh Republican general has either arrived or else is *en route* from Madrid. It was rumoured last Saturday that the foe had made an advance is our direction. However, the news was soon negatived by a *confidente* who announced that the main force of our opponents was marching towards Peralta, and Primo de Rivera with his column to Lerin, a village six miles south of Dicastillo. "We shall have a fight to-morrow", said a young artillery lieutenant, the centre of a little group of officers in the Plaza, all eagerly discussing the knotty point whether a battle would be fought or not – "We shall have a fight and then go straight to Madrid." "I wonder how the old Prado is looking", he continued, "and the Veloz (Cycling) Club and Fornos.[134] When shall we sup there again?" Several mouths watered at the last remark, for the culinary art at Estella remains very much at the same pitch as in the time of Los Reyes Catolicos. Sheep killed in the morning and cooked the same afternoon, with so-called chickens, which are in reality grandpapas among the feathered tribe, form the daily bill of fare, and many a good Carlist craves after the fleshpots of the capital. Early yesterday morning the clear bugle sounds of *Diana* the Spanish *réveillé* rang out, and it was still dusk when I noticed a few horses being led about the square. "The generals are going over to Dicastillo", was the information given by a soldier hurrying past. This turned out to be the case, and a little later I rode in the same direction. But no traces of an enemy could be seen, and the vast plain which divided us from our foe was free from those clouds of dust, the invariable heralds of an advancing column. Marks of shells on many a house and tower told the tale of Primo de Rivera's previous attempts upon Dicastillo. However, on this occasion he has been conspicuous by his absence, and warfare is a tedious business when one side is afraid to fight and the other is not strong enough to attack.

What can Moriones mean by his change of position? Is it done with the object of attempting to take possession of the Barranca, and then cut off the Royalist Division from Lizzarraga's in Guipuzcoa, or only for the purpose of comforting the Government at Madrid with a telegraphic despatch to the effect that its array has actually left Tafalla? If the first supposition is correct, Don Carlos will have to adopt one of two plans – either attack the enemy in the

---

134 The Café de Fornos, later renamed the Grand Café, was a famous Madrid restaurant, located in the Calle Alcalá.

open, regardless of his superiority in cavalry and artillery, or else march upon Tafalla, and by this means recall the Republicans to their original position. But many officers think that no aggressive measures will be taken by the generals on the opposite side, and that they will simply act upon the defensive until more confidence can be placed by them in their rank and file. Meanwhile, we are told that the latter, more and more disgusted as having been wrested from their homes and forced to serve, by a Government which climbed to power through the cry of "*Abajo las Juntas*" are each day deserting to the Carlists. I have myself seen more than 20 cavalry soldiers who are said to have come over to the Royalists only three days since. It is necessary to accept every statement in this romantic Peninsula with caution, but there can be no doubt that the Royalist army is being largely recruited from the enemy's lines.

FGB087
Royalist Headquarters, Estella; 22 October 1873
Burnaby to Editor – *The Times***, 29 October 1873**

The only military news we have received during the last two days comes from the enemy's camp, for I am assured by Don Carlos that Santa Pau has been promoted to the rank of Lieutenant-General for his Victory at Dicastillo. Wonders never cease in this land of the Cid, and since the accession to power of Castelar he has surprised us all by the vagaries of his administration.

Who, only six months ago, would have believed it possible that the champion of the liberty of the Press, the inveterate declaimer against the blood tax (forced military conscription), could have so utterly abandoned the very essence of his principles? Madrid newspapers are now forbidden, under penalty of suppression, to publish anything relating to Carlism save what is derived from official sources and printed in the *Gazette*. Can the Spaniards place any reliance on this source of information after the melancholy disregard of facts lately displayed in the journal in question? Those realms of fancy in which the President delights to roam when he inveighs from the tribune of the Cortes are now invaded by his satellites. A false despatch, and its fabricator is raised to the rank of Lieutenant-General, while the invincible leader receives the thanks of the poet Castelar. Fortune has showered her favours upon Moriones during the last eight years. Numerous revolutions in this unhappy country have not retarded his military promotion. Only a captain of Carabineers at the end of Isabella's reign, his implication in the various *pronunciamentos* and conspiracies of Prim marked him as a dangerous man, and he had to fly the country. On this occasion Moriones made the acquaintance of Simon, the chief of the Carlist spies, who guided the hunted rebel over some mountain passes into France. Thanks were the only recompense given to Simon for his service. Years, rolled by, Prim returned to Spain, Moriones with him, and very soon the latter became a Brigadier. The battle of Oroquieta – a victory achieved over a body of

Carlist labourers, many of whom were unarmed – gave him the rank of general. Twelve months more and he commanded a *Corps d'Armée* of the North. Here fate caused him once more to meet Simon, who was captured by the outposts and brought before Moriones. It appeared that the *confidente* had guided two Royalist officers into France, and was on the road back to Navarre when he was taken by the Republicans. His life was already forfeited, and nothing could have saved the prisoner if the general, who was on the point of ordering him to be shot, had not suddenly asked, "How much money did you receive from the two Carlists?" "They only gave me what you once did – *thanks*." Former recollections flashed back to the general's memory. He put some gold into the man's hand and bade him begone, but take care he was not caught again, as in that case no mercy would be shown. Quite a character in the Royalist army is the old *confidente*, and many a story is related of him. One day in Viscaya, the King was speaking to the Alcalde of a small *pueblo*. The latter, not in the least disconcerted by the presence of Royalty, did not take the pipe from his lips as he announced Don Carlos. Simon's sense of decorum was so shocked at this breach of etiquette that his feelings overcame him, and seizing the general's baton of office from the Commander-in-Chief's hand he broke the bowl of the pipe, leaving only a short piece of stem in the mouth of the astounded magistrate. The favourite *confidente* seldom leaves the head-quarters, save to convey a more than usually important despatch; however, the other day he asked for some leave of absence. "What for?" was the question. "To bury my boy"; and away trudged the heart-broken mountaineer, eight long leagues, to a cottage in the Barranca. Here lay dead his son, a lad of about 13. "Simon's notebook" he was called by the officers, for the *confidente* cannot read or write, and whenever any arms or ammunition were to be buried or hid away the father used to say, "You must remember exactly the place"; and a wonderful memory the child possessed, as months afterwards, even when snow was on the ground, which obliterated every track, he would lead a party of Carlists to the very spot where the rifles had been concealed. The old spy was not absent long; he kissed the cold forehead of his boy and returned to his former post. But the man is not what he was before, and that visit to the desolate village home has added some years to the life of poor Simon.

The report which has been freely circulated in some newspapers to the effect that a foreign legion is being formed for Don Carlos has no foundation whatever. Nothing would be so likely to prejudice the Royalist cause as the formation of such a corps. The Carlist peasantry have not yet forgotten the English Legion of the last war, and the other day, when a friend of mine inquired of an aged swineherd which he hated most, England or France, the reply was, "I would stick an Englishman for an *onza*, but I would pay an *onza* to have the chance of killing a Frenchman." While these old feelings of rancour still linger in the minds of the lower orders, it would be destruction to the hopes of the

King's party if an attempt were made to organize a force of men recruited in other countries; and as Carlos remarked with much truth at Durango, "What I require is not men, but arms."

There were some manoeuvres yesterday afternoon, a few battalions of infantry being exercised against an imaginary foe. Unfortunately for the Royalists, their generals still adhere too much to the old system of columns – possible before the new armament had been introduced, but fatal if exposed to modern tactics. A line of skirmishers was thrown out in front of three battalions. These last advanced in contiguous column at a distance not exceeding 250 yards from the skirmishers – directing them from the first line. On my remarking this to an officer, he acknowledged the justice of the criticism but observed that it was the usual method. Undoubtedly in this mountain warfare, where frequently the ground is so broken and impracticable that it is absolutely necessary for both sides to maintain a close formation, a second line or support in contiguous column of regiments may be allowed – of course premising that it is not exposed to the foe's artillery. Should the troops, however, be advanced when in this position, it is evident to the most superficial observer that they must be more than decimated by the enemy's fire. Some of the Royalist generals have studied their profession in the Seven Years' War; since that date many Spanish swords have been allowed to rust in their scabbards. What was practicable formerly is now absolute destruction, and should the system employed yesterday be adopted against the Republicans in the open, fortune, which has lately attended the Carlist arms, may prove to be a fickle goddess. When the troops had been dismissed we continued our walk to a magnificent old Benedictine monastery, now being converted into a hospital. This is sadly wanted, for the numerous wounded at Mañeru are huddled together in the scarce accommodation that can be furnished in Avarzuza. Queen Margherita de Borbon, whose interesting position does not allow her to share the vicissitudes of a campaign with her husband, Don Carlos, is doing everything she can for the wounded soldiery. Ambulances are being prepared, surgical instruments and modern appliances are on their way, while Her Majesty has herself intrusted Count Belascan with the arduous task of arranging a military hospital. The old monastery has been selected with this view, and from morn to nightfall workmen are busily at work putting in windows and repairing and thoroughly cleansing the building, which, unfortunately has, of late years, been suffered to fall into decay. More than 800 beds can be easily contained in the vast edifice, and it is calculated that in another fortnight it will be ready for use. Count Belascan was kind enough to show us all over the establishment. In one corner we came upon a heap of old books and parchments, piled up in endless disorder and confusion. "One of the workmen was to burn these works", said our companion, "and if it had not been for me they would before this have been consumed." I casually turned over the leaves of a few dog-eared tomes; they were principally treatises on religion and logic, published about the 17th century; but some of the manuscripts appeared to belong to a still remoter epoch, and Count Belascan, who greatly appreciates ancient lore, will have a long and pleasant task in wading through the volumes still left in the old monastery.

10 p.m.
I open my letter to forward you a résumé of the following despatch, just received by the Commander-in-Chief, General Elio:

> A vessel, which apparently contained supplies of war, was seen lying off Ondarrua. Her machinery was found to be out of repair, and she had been deserted by the crew. Some sailors in Ondarrua, notwithstanding an enemy's ship which steamed out of Guetaria, towed the vessel into the bay.
> The abandoned bark is 200ft. in length. She contained 5,000 rifles, system Berdan, a million cartridges, perfectly packed, with the mark 'Arsenal of Frankfort', and a great number of barrels of petroleum. An 8-pounder cannon was on deck, besides a quantity of articles which are now being disembarked and conveyed to Marquina and Durango. The vessel remains here at our disposal.
> Comandante de Armas, Nicolas Carpico, Metrico, Oct. 20.

The above despatch was first forwarded to Lizzarraga, who, in his turn, has transmitted it to Elio, accompanied by the following lines:

> I enclose your Excellency the communication which informs me of so portentous an event. I give infinite thanks to God for the immense favour which he has dispensed in guiding to a safe port a cargo for us so precious. I congratulate His Majesty the King, whom may God preserve, for the protection which Our Lord shows towards his cause.
> General Comandante-General Antonio Lizzarraga, Asteazu, Oct. 21.

The safe landing of these rifles insures Don Carlos five new battalions; for there are men in abundance, all eagerly waiting to be armed. Where the vessel came from and who she belonged to will be the next question. This I cannot answer at present, though probably some Royalist generals could easily solve the problem.

A report is being circulated this evening that Don Alfonso, the King's brother, with his wife, Doña Blanca, will arrive here very shortly from Catalonia, but I don't know this from official sources, so the rumour must be taken for what it is worth.

FGB088
Royalist Headquarters, Estella; 24 October 1873
Burnaby to Editor – *The Times*, 4 November 187

A service was held yesterday morning in the Cathedral to offer thanks to God for the safe arrival of the Carlist vessel La Ville de Bayonne. Don Carlos, with all his suite, attended the ceremony, and the church was thronged with devotees. Many religious Spaniards imagine that the Divine interposition has wrought a miracle in behalf of the Royalist cause, and the following is the account of the ship's cruise, as reported in Estella. La Villa de Bayonne is stated to have left Antwerp a few days since laden with arms for the Carlists. Fortune favoured the bark during the principal part of the voyage, but on rounding the French coast near Biarritz her boiler exploded. Great was the crew's consternation, all of whom were aware of the nature of the cargo. Petroleum in juxtaposition with a million cartridges is not the safest freight that can be carried, the more especially when smoke is seen issuing from the hold. The sailors were panic-struck, and not having faith sufficient to believe that Providence would interfere on account of the ship's cargo being intended for the slaughter of Republicans, they abandoned La Ville de Bayonne and escaped to the adjacent shore. Here the miracle commences. The fire becomes extinguished, and the vessel drifts slowly by Fuentarrabia and San Sebastian. The officers on board the Republican cruisers are blinded to the fact that a Carlist bark is passing beneath their very noses. Further and further the ship is wafted by the winds, until finally she arrives precisely at the very point where she was expected. Look-out men posted between Motrico and Ondarrua instantly inform the Commandant. Orders are at once given, and the vessel is towed into port. The captain of a Republican coaster at that moment becomes alive to the fact that war material is being disembarked. He attempts to enter the haven, but the inhabitants – all Royalists to the backbone – arm themselves with rifles taken from the Ville de Bayonne. A fire is maintained on the foe, who, enraged and baffled, returns sulkily to his former station. Such is the account of the vessel's voyage as reported in Estella. Of course, it is just possible that La Ville de Bayonne might have drifted from Biarritz to Ondarrua without being broken to pieces on the many rocks which stun that iron-bound coast. But it is excessively improbable that the Commandant, a translation of whose despatch to General Elio I forwarded to you yesterday, should not have mentioned that the country-people had fired on the Republican cruiser. So the latter part of the story can be taken at its proper value.

No fresh movement of the enemy has occurred, and the foe is more distant from this town than on the morn of Mañeru. Meanwhile, we are unofficially informed that a body of Valencians, under the command of a certain Sanchez, has entered Cuenca and carried away 25,000 *duros* (about 5,000*l.*) from the bank, besides requisitioning 75 horses, the property of private persons. As

Cuenca is not a hundred miles from the capital, should this statement prove correct Madrid will soon have to look out for its immediate environs. Many officers of known Alfonsist tendencies are serving with the Government forces. If the present Cabinet were to fall, an attempt might be made to place Queen Isabella on the throne. Should such an event ensue, the Carlists would have a much more serious foe than the one with which they are now contending.

Much attention is paid by the King's partisans to the progress which is made by the Legitimists in France, and the general opinion which prevails is that the accession of the Comte de Chambord[135] to the throne of his ancestors will not be long deferred. It may be that the wish is father to the thought, for the Royalists would probably be recognized as belligerents should Henry V. replace Marshal MacMahon in power. In the meantime, General Palacios[136] has left Estella to take command of the King's forces in Old Castille. What with the *Intransigentes* at Cartagena and the Carlists in the North, the Government has by no means an easy task to perform, and, instead of gaining ground, the Republicans appear to be further off than ever from the attainment of their end.

FGB089
Royalist Headquarters, Estella; 26 October 1873
Burnaby to Editor – *The Times*, 5 November 1873

This afternoon will long be remembered by the inhabitants of Estella, for a lady famous in the history of Carlism has entered their town. I allude to Maria de las Nieves, better known as Doña Blanca, the wife of Prince Alfonso, Don Carlos's brother. Great has been the excitement of the townsfolk during the last week as to whether the Princess would really honour them with a visit. But yesterday evening the doubts of many were set aside, as it was officially announced that the two Infantes would arrive on the morrow. Maria de las Nieves, or Mary of the Snows, is the daughter of Dom Miguel, late King of Portugal, whose other child is the sister-in-law of the present Emperor of Austria. The Princess herself, two years ago, married Don Alfonso, and during the last ten months the youthful pair – for she is only 21, and her husband 24 – have gone through all the hardships of the war in Catalonia. As a natural consequence she is idolized in Catalonia, and her presence in a battle was looked upon as a sure harbinger of victory. Doña Blanca's fame has long reached the King's followers, and his hot-blooded and passionate Navarrese were all burning with eagerness to see that lady of whom they had heard so much. I determined in consequence to ride over to a village in the neighbourhood of head-quarters, so as to meet the Royal

---

135 Henri of Artois, Duc de Bordeaux and Comte de Chambord (1820-1883) as Henry V was nominally King of France from 2 to 9 August 1830, although never officially proclaimed as such. He was the 'Legitimist' pretender to the throne of France from 1844 to 1883.
136 Romualdo Palacios Gonzalez, later (1887) Governor General of Puerto Rico.

cortége and then witness the welcome sure to be given to Don Carlos's sister-in-law. On approaching Avarzuza I found two battalions lining the principal thoroughfare, and the Marques de Valdespina,[137] at the head of a numerous suite, anxiously awaiting the expected visitors. A well-known character in the Royalist Army is this gallant General, and numerous anecdotes are related of him. He it was who confronted the notorious Cura de Santa Cruz in Lesaca. The reverend bandit was surrounded by a *partida* composed of men to whom robbery and assassination were no novelties; but Valdespina, nothing daunted, told the priest that if he did not immediately disband his force he should be treated as a rebel, and shot, the result of this energetic behaviour being the dispersion of the *cura*'s band and the flight of the holy father himself to France. Unfortunately, Valdespina is very deaf, and the only means of speaking to him is through a trumpet he carries fastened to his sash. "The Infantes will not be here for an hour", shouted the General as we rode up, "but in the meantime why not visit a hospital which is close at hand? It is a wretched place, but we have no better till the one near Estella is ready for use." Wretched in the extreme sense of the word I found the building set apart for the wounded soldiery. In many of the wards there were no windows, and light was allowed to enter only through some square holes cut in the walls; these embrasures, however, could be partly closed by means of an ill-fitting wooden shutter. A cold, damp chill was distinctly felt as we traversed one long dormitory, thickly tenanted by the victims of this civil war. Here, on some rickety pallets, and covered with a few old rugs, lay the poor sufferers. None of the many little comforts lavished by a generous public upon the Franco-Prussian ambulances were to be seen, and poverty was plainly manifest in every arrangement. Carlists were not the only tenants of the wards, as some beds were occupied by Republican soldiers. In the hospital the latter receive every attention which the scanty means at the disposition of the superintendent allow. The Royalists forget their enmity to the so-called "*Negros*", and the partisans of both sides freely talk and laugh together, while the more convalescent of the patients while away the long hours at *tresillo* and dominoes. However, the ringing of church bells announced that the Infantes were approaching, and those poor cripples who could hobble on crutches hastened downstairs, supported by the arms of their mothers and sisters, to gaze upon the far-famed Infantes. A few minutes later and General Dorregaray rode past, conversing with Don Alfonso, a slight-built young man, very like Don Carlos in face, but a pigmy compared to him in stature. A few yards in rear of her husband came Doña Blanca, the heroine of a thousand stories which are freely circulated in the Peninsular. Slight, fragile and rather under than over the usual stature, Doña Blanca sat on a coal-black Barbary charger, which once belonged to the enemy, with consummate ease and skill.

137 Juan Nepomuceno de Orbe y Mariaca (1817-1891), 4th Marques de Valdespina.

She was attired in an Hussar's dark blue pelisse jacket, embroidered round the waist, and worn over a riding habit of the same colour. Very prepossessing and decidedly pretty would have been the verdict, if a jury composed of London dowagers, and with daughters of their own to bring out, could have been asked to pass a judgement. But Mary of the Snows was eager to reach her destination, and after only a quarter of an hours' rest at Avarzuza to take some refreshment at Valdespina's house, we continued the journey, accompanied by hundreds of the inhabitants of Estella, who had purposely walked out to kiss the hand of their renowned Princess.

The escort kept slightly in rear, as there was no need of its services. The only self-constituted guardian who walked by the side of the Princess was an old *cura*, who from time to time when he saw his parishioners were too intrusive, freely boxed their ears, and cuffed them with his priest's cap. At last we reached Don Carlos's head-quarters. The streets here were literally paved with human heads, and the resounding *vivas* for Doña Blanca that rent the air as she rode into the square might have recalled a British cheer. Don Alfonso himself was almost unnoticed in the rapturous welcome given to his lady, and her reception can only be compared with that given to Don Carlos himself on his return after the victory at Dicastillo. The King was, unfortunately, not able to witness the troops' enthusiasm, as he has been confined to his room for two days with a slight attack of gastric fever. However, the last bulletin informs me that "His Majesty" will probably be able to leave his bed tomorrow, so it cannot have been a very serious illness.

FGB090
Royalist Headquarters, Estella; 28 October 1873
Burnaby to Editor – *The Times***, 5 November 1873**
Don Carlos is still too unwell to leave his bed, and the physician who attends him has pronounced the malady to be a slight attack of gastric fever. A person of much importance is now the Court Doctor – who, by the way, was formerly a Deputy in the Cortes – and during the last two days he has been the centre of all inquiries. How is the King? Has he been bled? Will he be cupped or will he be leached? And to these questions the medical gentleman, like some of his confreres in other countries, swells out his waistcoat, gravely smiles and shakes his head, looks very wise, and then, "*Vamos á ser*", which corresponds in English to "We shall see." In the meantime poor Doña Blanca is mobbed and followed by enthusiastic crowds of admirers in the shape of townspeople and soldiery whenever she leaves her house and the brave little lady has to submit to her hand being kissed at least 50 times should she walk across the Plaza to the Cathedral. M. M. Laborde, the agent in France for the Carlists, accompanied the Infantes to Estella. He knows Spain and the Spanish character better than most men, and from his promptitude and *savoir faire* is generally selected to

attend any of Don Carlos's relations who should purpose visiting head-quarters. On one occasion he arrived at Saldina, where it was found necessary to change the mules which carried the baggage. The Alcalde of the village, a man of well-known Republican tendencies, and whose duty it was to have relays of animals ready at all times, for the purposes of transport, sulkily stated that there were no mules or oxen in the place. "Indeed?" said M. M. Laborde; "then send the *Corregidor* (Municipal officer) here." When the latter came, the Royalist Agent produced an order which enjoined all Alcaldes and Corregidors to furnish the bearer with the beasts of burden he might require. On the Civil authorities still refusing to comply, M. Laborde said, "Very well; if I cannot have mules I must have *burros* (donkeys) instead"; and coolly proceeded to load the two officials, whom he compelled to carry the luggage as far as the next village. Here the effect produced on the Mayor by the spectacle of his colleagues staggering beneath the luggage was quite sufficient to induce him immediately to bring out some ox carts, and the Frenchman with his party was thus enabled eventually to reach his destination.

The Carlist officers, sadly puzzled how to break the state of *ennui* caused by their monotonous life in Estella, have at last bethought themselves of pigeon-shooting by way of a diversion. This sport is carried on here so very differently to what I have seen it in other countries, that perhaps a description of the method employed may not be uninteresting. Yesterday morning I was awoke at 5 by the nephew of General Elio, Captain Borot, who had promised to initiate me into the mysteries of *la caza de las Palonas* – the chase of the doves. My companion was attired in uniform, boots, spurs, &c., with the exception, however, of the cap, which had been replaced by a sort of wide-awake, thus giving a comical aspect to the rest of his garb. "I have only been able to get one gun", he eagerly observed, "and I do not know what we shall be able to do with it. The confounded hammer does not work; it will stick at half-cock." A wonderful piece of mechanism was the arm in question, with its single barrel at least 5ft. long; the stock, which was very short, being richly inlaid with gold and carved all over with grotesque figures representing the sport. "Very pretty to look at, but uncommonly dangerous to its owner, should he succeed in discharging his weapon" was my mental reflection; and after an hour's walk we arrived at a large wood, thickly planted with young oaks. Thousands of wood pigeons could be seen hovering about at great distances from the ground, and from time to time the report of firearms announced that we were approaching our destination. Presently the rustling of the branches in a neighbouring tree made me look up, and I saw to my astonishment a pigeon, apparently performing the evolutions of Léotard,[138] on a sort of bar which was attached to a bough, and rapidly

---

[138] Jules Léotard (1842-1870) was a French acrobatic performer who developed the art of trapeze and popularised the one-piece garment that now bears his name.

swinging backwards and forwards, the bird all the while expanding his wings and turning half somersaults in the air. "Quick!" said my companion, seizing me by the sleeve, "they are coming – run, run!" And he suddenly led us into a sort of earth-built hiding-place, a few yards from the spot where we had been standing; there I found myself in a hovel, about 7ft. high. The roof was covered with leaves and brambles, so naturally interspersed that a stranger might have passed close by and not been in the least aware of the hut's existence. The mud walls were loop-holed in every direction, and a string tied to a branch on which was fastened the acrobatic pigeon passed through one of the embrasures, the other end being in the hands of an old priest, who was franticly pulling it, thus giving rise to those strange gymnastic exercises performed by the bird outside. The attire of the *cura* himself was singularly ludicrous: a broad-brimmed, low-crowned ecclesiastical hat, very much the worse for wear, covered his closely-shaven head; for the everyday cassock was substituted a short school-boy's jacket, with sleeves very much too short for the long arms of the wearer; black trousers, protected in front from the dirt by a long, leathern apron somewhat in the style of that used by London draymen, and a pair of slippers completed his costume. Several other divines, all of them more or less funnily garbed, were seated round a heap of half-consumed embers, anxiously superintending some earthenware dishes, the contents of which emitted a most appetizing odour. Guns of every description were in the corners of the hovel, some with flint locks, others percussion, and all of them single barrels with the exception of one, the property of the *cura* with the short jacket; his was a double-barrelled muzzle-loader, and the owner was evidently immensely proud of his weapon. Our hurried entrance caused a general rise; there was no time for introductions, each man seized his weapon. My companion made another frantic attempt to make the hammer of his own piece work; and finding it was hopeless, put down the arm and came to a loophole by my side. The performances of the captive bird had caught the attention of a large flock of pigeons, which, swooping down from an immense height, settled on the neighbouring branches. They were evidently lost in astonishment at the fantastic evolutions of their feathered brother, and unconscious that several clerical gentlemen, each with his finger on the trigger, were only awaiting the word to have a family shot into the centre of their number. "*Vamos!*" suddenly shouted the *cura* with the short jacket; and at the sound of the last syllable a general explosion occurred, followed by a rush through the narrow entrance to pick up the spoil. Five birds were bagged, and everybody had shot a pigeon except the owner of the double barrel. "But I must have killed one", he said. "Why, I picked out the bird because it was only three yards, from my muzzle." "Perhaps you blew him in pieces", said his nephew, a mischievous boy, who evidently greatly enjoyed the proceedings. "No, he has gone away to die", gravely remarked the uncle; and this solution of the difficulty appeared too satisfactory for any of the other sportsmen to attempt to gainsay. At breakfast the same divine descanted for some time on the superior merits of pigeon-shooting as compared with the manner partridges are shot in Spain. The latter, I was informed, are generally killed in the breeding season, and cages with hen birds in them are placed at a distance of 12 yards from where the chasseurs are concealed; the male partridges fly up, finally settling by the females, and the moment they are quite still the sportsmen fire. "This is not sport", said the reverend gentleman; "and it is wicked to destroy the poor birds when they come, in all the innocence of their hearts, to their *amores*. It is also wrong to shoot them, as some reckless people do, on the wing, for much powder is consumed and little comes of it – mere waste of shot and no satisfaction; at least, that is the result of my experience. But pigeon-shooting, this is noble and fair; the pigeons come from curiosity and not for their natural and innocent *amores*. Curiosity was the cause of Eve's falling and she fell; curiosity, my children, should be punished." And with, these words the old man slapped his Prayer Book, which he, like the rest of his companions, had brought with him, and looked triumphantly around at his congregation, composed of the five other *curas*, the officer and myself.

FGB091
Hyde Park Barracks, 3 September [1874]
Burnaby to Delane[139]
Dear Mr. Delane, I have just received the enclosed from Lord Melgund[140] who is with the Carlists. Thinking his letter might possibly interest you I forward it for your perusal. Yours very sincerely, Fred Burnaby. P.S. If you care to make any extracts you are at liberty to do so."

FGB092
Hyde Park Barracks, 27 September 1874
Burnaby to Wright
I think the 30,000 feet of gas balloon would be too small for the journey, I propose making, as the weight of myself and friend would be 27 stone or 378 lbs., which would leave but a slight margin for ballast, of which we should require a large supply, the more particularly owing to the power the sea would have in condensing the gas. To make the journey to Germany with anything like certainty, one would require a balloon holding at least 50,000 feet of gas,

---

139 © Delane Papers (TT/ED/JTD/21/25), Times Newspapers Limited Archive, News International.
140 Gilbert John Elliot-Murray-Kynynmound, later 4th Earl of Minto (1845-1914), was a British diplomat and politician who served as Governor General of Canada. After completing his education at Eton and Trinity College, Cambridge, he was commissioned Lieutenant in the Scots Guards in 1867, but left in 1870. In 1874, in the capacity of a newspaper correspondent, he witnessed the operations of the Carlists in Spain and, in 1877, took service with the Turkish army in the war with Russia.

and the more the better. If you should know of anyone who has a balloon of that dimension, and who would hire it for the occasion alluded to, I should be much obliged by your letting me know. I hope we may meet some day, as you tell me you are a native of Bedford, where I was born.

FGB093
Hyde Park Barracks, 1 November 1874
Burnaby to Wright

Can you have the balloon ready and filled at the Crystal Palace on Tuesday morning next, the 3rd November, at 10 o'clock? Failing Tuesday, it will be necessary to postpone the ascent till next Spring, as Lord Manners will be out of town, and I also. Send answer by bearer, or if you are not in, telegraph to the Knightsbridge Barracks. You will have to communicate, in the event of compliance, with the manager of the Crystal Palace immediately – so do not waste any time. The weather will make no difference, as fine or foul we should start at 10 o'clock. Yours very truly, Fred Burnaby.

ABRM01
Suez and Souakim; 22-27 December 1874
Meyers's Journal (extract)

Dec. 22. – All at Suez last night; but preceded by Coke by two days, as he went in advance with Mohamed to see to our interests there; for not only have we to find our own supplies on board the steamer, but also a cook and kitchen utensils. Besides our own party and the two friends mentioned as going to Massawah, there are other passengers who will join our mess on board – viz., Captain Burnaby, Mr. J. Russell, and M. Marcopoli, who will land at Souakim, *en route* to Gondokoro, to join Colonel Gordon's expedition; and also the Earl of Mayo and Mr. Flower, who intend landing at Massawah on a distinctly separate shooting expedition to that of Ranfurly and Arkwright. We therefore number, with our ten servants, twenty-one in all, and we have entered into a contract with a general provision dealer here to supply us with provisions and live-stock for the voyage for 44*l*.

It is calculated that the steamer, named 'Dessouk' will arrive at Souakim, a distance of about 750 miles, in four days and Massawah, 200 miles farther, in less than six days from time of departure.

Mr. Levick, the English post-master here, has given us very useful assistance in the despatch of our goods and through him we learn that we should have been saved much trouble and expense if we had had them consigned to an agent at Suez instead of Alexandria, where the charge for landing and carriage to Suez amounted to nearly 60*l*.

Suez has not many attractions for a stranger, so we have occupied a good part of the morning in a visit to the barber, who carried out our orders to the letter according to our individual tastes, some allowing the razor to make a clean sweep of their faces, whilst others preferred the very closest application of the scissors to their heads. Thus so altered as to be hardly recognisable to one another, and more nearly resembling a party of convicts, we adjourned to the photographer, and if he does us justice it will prove a valuable and interesting group to send to our friends on our return. After luncheon we were taken on board the 'Dessouk' by a Government steam tug, as she was lying about three miles from Suez; and at 4 P.M. she got under weigh, a fresh breeze blowing at the time from the south-east, the sky overcast and the day therefore cool, Mohamed at Suez did his utmost to get into our good graces, and, fearing lest anything in his charge might be stolen, would guard our stores by night and by day.

By universal consent we have decided that a light breakfast at 8 A.M., a more substantial one at 11.30 A.M., dinner at 5 P.M., and supper at 9 P.M., will be the best way to kill time on board ship compatible with health; and our cook, Mohamed, has been appointed *chef de cuisine*.

Dec. 25. – With the thermometer standing at 84° in the shade, it is difficult to realise that this is really Christmas-day, but we have not been without the means of bearing it in mind in a social sense, thanks to a present from Mr. Grace, our Alexandrian agent, of a plum-pudding of most perfect home manufacture, and to another from the Peninsular and Oriental Company of some ice by which we were able to conceal any slight deficiencies in the quality of Cairo champagne; nor have we lacked the musical element, for Mayo has a banjo, and is accompanied by an English engineer of the steamer on the fiddle. The wind, however, is continuing to blow very freshly from the southeast, and causing the steamer to roll greatly has somewhat damped our spirits. We are, nevertheless, a very jolly party, and the 'Dessouk' is very comfortably fitted up, especially one large cabin, which was originally intended for the ladies of the Hareem.

Dec. 26. – Yesterday the Captain, an old Egyptian, told us that we should arrive at Souakim this afternoon in all probability, but in consequence of his fearing during the night that he might run the steamer on the coral reefs which abound in this part of the Red Sea, he altered the course so much to the east that we have lost ground considerably, and cannot now arrive before to-morrow. Whilst the steamer was being brought back this morning to her proper course, we had the pleasant excitement of suddenly finding that we were running right on to a coral reef; only two small points of rock appeared above the surface, but stretching along for a great distance directly in front of us the unmistakable line of breakers denoted the impassable barrier, with on one side of it a sheet of perfectly smooth water.

The excitement of the crew and the rapid bearing round again to the east, showed us pretty plainly that this obstruction had neither been expected nor observed much too soon for the general safety. At 4 P.M. we anchored in a harbour named Sheik el Baghout, where we must remain till daybreak. In the meantime we are not allowed to go on shore, owing to quarantine being in force for some parts of the coast.

M. Marcopoli has proved himself a most agreeable addition to our present circle, and it is he to whom Sir Samuel Baker refers so frequently in 'Ismailia'[141] as Marco Polo. He is a Greek, and has so thoroughly mastered Arabic that he not only speaks the language, but also reads it with perfect facility.

Burnaby is the most industrious of our party, and may frequently be seen holding a conversation with one of the crew with the assistance of an Arabic vocabulary (Sacroug), and he is making rapid progress in their language. There is a party of French Roman Catholic missionaries, including a bishop, on board, bound for Massawah, and when not occupied with their meditations they take great interest in hearing all about our future respective plans, though they perhaps would agree with the Khedive that we are putting ourselves to a very great amount of trouble merely for sport.

Dec. 27. – We arrived this morning in the harbour of Souakim, and anchored about a quarter of a mile from the town. At this distance it has a somewhat imposing appearance, as the chief buildings, with a few minarets, are collected together on a small island only separated from the rest of the town by a narrow strip of water and slightly elevated above the mainland, which extends for miles as a low flat plain, bounded in the distance by ranges of mountains that have been partially obscured from our view by a slight mist.

FGB094
Under the old tree at Aryah, Tropical Africa; 4 January 1875
Burnaby to Editor – *The Times*, 15 February 1875
It is barely eight months since an expedition was sent forth from Egypt to civilize, if possible Central Africa, and to suppress the trade in human flesh which has so long prevailed there. Although the Expedition was despatched beneath the banner of the Viceroy, it could hardly be termed an Egyptian one, as almost every State in Europe had contributed a countryman to labour in the cause, so strongly advocated by the Khedive.

An Englishman, Colonel Gordon, better known as "Chinese Gordon", was sent by England to lead the little band of pioneers, and no better person could have been found for the perilous and difficult enterprise allotted as his task. After Sir Samuel Baker's resignation the Viceroy was at a loss to find a substitute, but hearing that Colonel Gordon's services might be obtained, the same salary given to Sir Samuel Baker (£10,000 a year) was offered to him. But the modesty of spirit which characterized Gordon in China was again displayed.

---

141 Sir Samuel White Baker, *Ismailia, a narrative of the expedition to Central Africa for the suppression of the slave trade, organised by Ismail, Khedive of Egypt* (London: Macmillan and Co., 1874).

"The amount is too much", replied the open-hearted soldier, and finally, after much pressure, the man who had saved China consented to accept £2,000 a year – one-fifth of the sum given to Sir Samuel Baker as a remuneration for his labour. De Witt, a German naturalist, was only too eager to accept service under so famous a leader. Linant de Brabant,[142] a Frenchman well versed in Oriental languages and in those dialects peculiar to the savages of Central Africa, volunteered to assist as interpreter; while the New World, not to be eclipsed with such an object in view by the old one, was represented by Major Campbell, an American officer who had much distinguished himself in the War of Secession. It is scarcely nine months since all the gentlemen above mentioned, accompanied by two young Englishmen, Mr. Anson and Mr. Russell, were encamped beside the old tree beneath the shady branches of which I write. To wile away the hours of a tropical afternoon each man cut his name upon the bark; here they stand out before me – Gordon, Linant, De Witt, Russell, Campbell, and Anson; and now how many of them could answer their names at an earthly roll-call? Alas! but two, Gordon and Russell, all the others having fallen victims to the pestilential climate of the White Nile. Poor Anson did not live to see Gondokoro, but succumbed to fever some time before the Expedition had reached its destination. Linant and De Witt lie besides the remains of Mr. Higginbotham, Baker's chief engineer, at Gondokoro; and Major Campbell had the last honours a soldier can receive paid to him at Khartoum.

The place whence I write is still many miles from Gondokoro, which is the most advanced of Colonel Gordon's posts, and only 4 deg. north of the Equator. The journey to reach that spot is very nearly, in point of time equal to circumnavigating the globe. First to Suez, thence down the Red Sea for six days by the Khedive's steamers to Souakim, and on by the "ship of the desert" day and night till we reach Berba; thence to Khartoum, the former capital of the slave trade, and then up the Nile 25 days by steamer – that is to say, if we happen to find the one that Gordon has lately had constructed awaiting us in the last-named town. The excursion is not one that would be apt to tempt a Sybarite. First of all, the steamers which run from Suez to Souakim are not the most perfect of their kind. No refreshments are provided on board, each passenger has to bring his food and drink with him and the devout and odoriferous pilgrims to Mecca crowd up the steerage part of the vessel. These little addenda, combined with the want of nautical science displayed by the officers on board, are not calculated to calm the mind of a nervous passenger. For instance, one day after we left Suez the captain approached a small knot of officers in the Foot Guards, who were going shooting, and asked them to explain how he was

---

142 Burnaby has this name wrong. The person concerned was Auguste Linant de Bellefonds, one of the sons of Linant Pasha, a respected Egyptologist.

to work out his reckoning, which, by the way, had eventually to be explained by an officer in the English Heavy Cavalry, who happened to be a passenger in the same ship. The cabins, too, were infested with vermin, and this, combined with the heat, made every one sleep on deck. However, our good star was in the ascendant, and we all arrived in safety at Souakim, without having had any more exciting adventure during our voyage than narrowly missing a coral reef, and found ourselves surrounded by camel-drivers, making arrangements with them for our journey to Berba, Mr. Marcopoli, who was formerly Sir Samuel Baker's storekeeper, and who is now going to join Colonel Gordon, acting for our party; while Mr. Russell, who is returning from sick leave at Cairo, stood in the background. Our energetic companion displayed some shining Austrian coins to his gesticulatory audience. One of the minor inconveniences that the traveller has to submit to in this country is the necessity of carrying about silver Austrian dollars, as no other coin is accepted in payment, and gold is unknown; so a bag of silver somewhat similar, possibly, to that which Joseph's brethren carried down in their sacks to the land of Egypt to buy corn with, takes up a large share in the voyager's portmanteau. But at last the knotty point is settled; and after spending our first night at Souakim, with the stars for our canopy, and awaking the next morning saturated to the skin with the heavy dew that had fallen during our sleep, we found ourselves, with a cavalcade of 20 camels, slowly issuing into the open country which surrounds the quaint old town of Souakim. Wealth and poverty are there strongly contrasted, and the magnificent storehouse built by the late Governor is still more strikingly thrown into relief by the mud and pigsty-looking hovels in which the majority of the population reside. Scanty is the attire of our five Arab attendants. But whatever want of attention is displayed as to scarcity of raiment is made up by the magnificence of their head-gear. *Coiffures* that would make the first of Mr. Truefitt's[143] young men envious are possessed by each of our Arab band, and cosmetics in the shape of liquid fat bedaub and beplaster the erection of hair which is piled up some seven inches over every man's forehead. "Very beautiful!" I remarked to the Sheik of the party, who accompanied us a few miles out of the town, at the same time pointing to his hair. He was delighted at my feigned admiration, but afterwards seemed somewhat disappointed when I observed that probably he wore it so as a protection against the heat. "Can the child of the sun fear his father?" was the slightly contemptuous answer, and the man turned on his heel and strode back to Souakim, pensively scratching his head with a long silver skewer which he wore as a hairpin.

Wilder and bleaker became the country as we left the long miles behind us, and after each day's march the gazelles and sand grouse, the only living inhabitants in these arid regions, save a few Nomad Arabs and vultures,

---

143 Trueffit and Hill, 'Court Hairdressers', are still in business in Mayfair.

became more scarce. Presently our route began to be marked out by the huge white bones and skeletons of the many camels which from time to time have perished from exhaustion, while our own animals trod wearily on, every now and then crumbling into dust beneath their hoofs the cavernous skull of some unfortunate predecessor, the lazy vultures which were feasting on his carcass hardly caring to hop ten yards from their repast as we approached, so gorged were they with the carrion. The water carried in our water-skins dried up with the intense heat, and that which we found at rare intervals in the wells was so salt and brackish as to be barely drinkable. But now, after six days almost incessant travelling, we find ourselves encamped in an oasis of the wilderness which teems with vegetation, owing to an abundant supply of water. A perfect Garden of Eden it appears, if contrasted with the rugged and forbidding aspect of the country through which we have just passed. Awful must have been the convulsions of nature which at some pre-Adamite epoch have visited the regions we have left behind. Mountains of burnt pebbles, piled upon seemingly never-ending ridges of volcanic formation, barricaded on both sides the sinuous path while here and there gigantic stones of quaint and grotesque shape, almost blocked up the track itself. Not a sound could be heard, save that which arose from the faltering steps of our camels, who wearily dragged their feet over the sharp rocks. Even our guide was apparently not unimpressed by the wildness of the scene. A geologist would find endless scope for research in this almost unexplored, district, where the ranges of hills ascend 3,000ft. above the level of the sea, and in some places quantities of primeval fossil remains would doubtless reward his labours. But the sun is setting like a great ball of fire beneath the loftiest of these huge piles of charred stones and the foliage of the old tree throws a darker shade over my writing-paper. "When shall we reach Berba with our tired camels?" asks Russell of the chief camel-driver. "*Inshallah* in ten days more", is the answer. "Then *inshallah*, you shall have 50 blows with the koorbatch when you reach Berba", mutters the indignant Marcopoli, who, coming up suddenly, overhears the last remark.

FGB095
Berba, Tropical Africa; 13 January 1875
Burnaby to Editor – *The Times*, **2 March 1875**

It was singular to meet with the telegraph in the heart of the desert between Aryah and Berba[144] – not the telegraph put up and in working order as we see

---

144 Berba (18°N 34°E), now usually spelled Berber, is a town in the Nile state of northern Sudan, 50 km north of Atbara, near the junction of the Atbara River and the Nile. This town was the starting-point of the old caravan route across the Nubian Desert to the Red Sea at Souakim (or Suakim), now usually spelled Suakin. Berbera (10° N 45°E) is a seaport, now in Somaliland, with the only sheltered harbour on the south side of the Gulf of Aden. It would have been impossible for Burnaby to travel from Soubat to Berbera in two days, so the last letter cannot be his.

it in Europe, but all the appurtenances of that instrument of civilization carried on the backs of hundreds of camels, which, laden with coils of wire and hollow iron posts, trod their toilsome path through the burning sand. Every now and then we met one of these poor beasts which, over-weighted and broken down by the weight of his load, had fallen on the ground and been abandoned a victim to the vultures. All this telegraphic gear was marked "Siemens Brothers, London", and was *en route* to Khartoum, from which town it will be forwarded on to span the desert between Kordofan and Darfour. A good many lives will probably be sacrificed before the line can be considered open, as the Arabs, who eagerly steal every piece of iron they can meet with for their spear points, have to be severely punished before they leave off cutting down the poles. However, this difficulty once got over, the telegraph will be as easily worked as the one between Khartoum and Cairo, which, when it was first laid down, was continually being interrupted.

Onwards we march through the desert, and find that we are near the spot where a few years ago a whole battalion of Infantry perished through its Colonel not following the guide's advice and not halting at the proper watering-places. The result was the men found themselves tortured with the pangs of thirst, and without anything to drink in their water-skins. The scene that followed was fearful. The soldiers left their ranks, disobeying the commands of their officers, and ran here and there over the desert, attracted by the mirage, which, giving the appearance of lakes and crystal streams to the burnt ground immediately before the poor follows, enticed them still further on towards destruction. Only five or six eventually escaped and arrived at their destination with the Colonel of the battalion, through whose obstinacy this fearful tragedy had occurred. He was tried by Court-Martial and sentenced to be banished to the Blue Nile – a very light sentence, considering the hundreds of lives sacrificed to his folly.

Our guide, who, as a rule, was not at all inclined to make any long marches, here hurried us on; for there were no wells, he said, to be met with for 48 hours and the water our camels carried was being evaporated by the heat. He also proposed that we should continue our march throughout the night, so as to reach Berba the more quickly.

The sun had long set when Mr. Marcopoli and Mr. Russell, who were riding some distance ahead of the party, heard the sounds of an approaching caravan. "Very strange", said the former, "What can it have left Berba so late for? Arabs, as a rule, do not like travelling by night when there is no moon." Presently a few dark outlines of camels loomed in sight through the dusky atmosphere, and we came face to face with some well-dressed Arab merchants, behind whom marched, in little bands of four and five, a number of boys and girls, whose ages averaged from about 10 to 16 years. Then some more camels some of them carrying two and three young girls; and further in the rear men with *koorbatches*, or long whips, and swarthy Nubians, armed with spears, closed the cavalcade.

"*Salam a leïkom*" ("Peace be with you"), said my companion to the chief of the caravan. "Where are you going?" "We are all pilgrims and are on our way to Mecca, *viâ* Souakim", was the answer given in an undertone to Mr. Marcopoli's interrogation. The latter continued his path, for two or three minutes, apparently buried in deep thought. Suddenly he exclaimed, "They are not pilgrims. Boys and girls do not go to Mecca. It is a slave caravan. Now, what is to be done? We are only ten hours from Berba. Shall we hasten on and inform the Governor that, in spite of the stringent orders given by the Khedive and the endeavours of Colonel Gordon in the interior, the slave-traders are laughing at his beard within 25 miles of Berba? Or shall we return and take the slave-traders ourselves? "The last-mentioned course of action was thought to be the best one; and, hastily loading our revolvers, we turned our jaded beasts and trotted back towards the caravan. After some time we came up with it, and Mr. Marcopoli, accosting the chief merchant, told him that his statement about the boys and girls being pilgrims was a false one, for they were slaves, and that in the name of His Highness the Khedive he (Mr. Marcopoli) arrested him. "But how can I know that you have any authority to detain me?" was the reply of the man addressed, who now seemed thoroughly frightened. "How can we tell that you are officers of the Government?" said a trader, riding up to the side of the leader of the caravan. "If they are officers they must have soldiers with them", called out a third. "Where are your soldiers?" "I believe they are robbers", shouted another. "Our soldiers are close by", said Mr. Marcopoli. (Fortunately, it happened that there were two with the main body of our party.) "Well", said the chief merchant, after muttering something in an undertone to one of his subordinates, "in that case I will accompany you, and if you really have soldiers, why, then you can return for the remainder of our party." "Will the rest of the slave-dealers not escape with the slaves if we leave them", I inquired. "No", said Mr. Marcopoli; and at all events, we have the chief merchant as a hostage." We soon fell in with our caravan, and desired the soldiers to arrest the merchant. It appeared, however, that they were old acquaintances; for, after saluting each other, they commenced consulting in a dialect not known even by our polyglot Italian friend. "Go and bring the rest of this man's caravan here", was the order next given, "and take him with you, but do not let the fellow escape on any account; upon your heads be it." However, in about ten minutes' time the soldiers came and said that the merchant had escaped, favoured by the darkness. "He has bribed you to let him go, you scoundrels", was our answer, and we all of us hastily dispersed over the desert in search of the slave-dealer and his party. But the night was very dark, and after about an hours' fruitless search we had to give up the attempt. "Never mind", said Mr. Marcopoli, "the man will never be able to efface the tracks of himself and party, and an Arab guide can distinguish the prints of his own camel from a hundred others. We will make a forced march tomorrow to Berba, and ask the Governor to send some soldiers mounted on dromedaries in pursuit. They will overtake the caravan before it arrives at the next wells; and, if the soldiers are not to be bought over by a bribe as our fellows have been, we shall see the whole party brought back to Berba before we leave for Khartoum."

The Governor, who received us very hospitably, could at first hardly be induced to believe Mr. Marcopoli's affirmation that we had passed a slave caravan. "Quite impossible", he said; "such a thing could not happen within the limits of my authority." "But it has happened", vociferated his informant, "and they have already 24 hours' start. Send out some soldiers on dromedaries immediately, and tell the officer, if he does not bring the caravan back, that you know the reason why he has not done so – namely, that he has accepted a bribe from the merchants. It is too bad when not only Europeans but hundreds of your own countrymen under Colonel Gordon are sacrificing their lives to put down the slave trade on the White Nile, that the dealers should, in spite of the Viceroy's rigorous orders, carry on their trade almost under your nose." This last remark apparently quite convinced the Governor, who said soldiers should instantly be despatched; and yesterday, to our great satisfaction, we were informed the slaves had all been brought to Berba. We went to see them in the afternoon, and if any one who disbelieves in the cruelties of the slave trade had been there to judge for himself, he would have been speedily undeceived. Twenty boys, with 18 women and girls, some of the tenderest age, many marked with the lash of that fearful instrument the *koorbatch*, which had been relentlessly applied by the merchants when the poor worn-out victims flagged in their endeavours to toil over the heavy sand – were living witnesses of the brutalities which had been enacted. Some had their cheeks scarred with the knife to brand them as the property of a particular owner. We were informed by the officer in charge that when the wretched captives found that they were free and their masters prisoners in the hands of the soldiers, some of them, showing their torn feet and flayed sides to the captured rascals, cursed them for all the cruelties they had perpetrated, and could with difficulty be restrained by the guard from retaliating on their former persecutors. "The retaliation will come soon enough, for all the slave-dealers shot", said an old Arab Captain, in reply to my inquiry as to what punishment awaited them. "The Viceroy's orders are very strict in this particular."

I hope that in the instance just mentioned they will not be allowed to remain a dead letter, and the merchants be permitted, after a few weeks' imprisonment, to return to their old location with more experience how to evade detection, for it is only by stern repressive measures that this disgrace to humanity can ever be effaced in Egypt. The slaves, it appears, were originally seized near the Bahr Gazelle River and brought to Khartoum. Here they were detained some time, for a few of them could speak Arabic, and had only recently been bought by the merchants we were fortunate enough to fall in with in exchange for wares brought from Souakim. The slaves would afterwards have been re-shipped to Jedda and Suez, where the lowest price any could have fetched would be about $50 and some, especially the better looking of the girls, a great deal more, so the absolute loss to the trader is above £1,000. He and his companions made some resistance to the soldiers on being arrested, but a few shots fired over their heads soon cowed them and they surrendered. The chief merchant then offered a large sum to the officer in command if he would allow them to escape, but fortunately the official proved himself capable of resisting the temptation. Whether the slaves will finally be much benefited is another question, for the women will be given as wives to the Egyptian soldiers and the boys enlisted in the army, such being the fate that invariably awaits all persons taken from traders in human flesh.

FGB096
Soubat, Central Africa; 5 February 1875
Burnaby to Editor – The Times, 30 March 1875

On arriving at Khartoum, after a five days' journey on the Nile from Berba, through a most beautiful country, well irrigated by huge waterwheels, and rich in doura and cotton plants, we found Mr. Jesse,[145] Colonel Gordon's agent, at Peshoda, a small town in Ismail Pasha's district and that there was no boat available to take us up the White Nile. Khartoum itself is on the Blue Nile, about two miles from its junction with the first-mentioned stream, and is a clean-looking town of, perhaps, 20,000 inhabitants. It formerly was the head-quarters of the principal merchants in the Soudan, who found the spot a most convenient one for despatching slave expeditions into the interior, and for forwarding their human prey to the various other towns where slave agencies were established. Khartoum was a few years since in the most flourishing condition on account of the activity and energy displayed by these speculators, but since the Viceroy made up his mind to suppress the slave trade, the inhabitants have assumed that appearance of apathy and listlessness so peculiar to the inhabitants of almost all Egyptian towns. A few of the leading people are Greeks and Germans; these last are very indignant at the change which has been made in their pecuniary gains since Gordon was appointed Governor of Central Africa. They complain that the town was once rich and prosperous, and declare that business is now paralyzed. They say that, where they cleared £2,000 a year they can now barely pay their expenses, and inveigh deeply against the active British Officer who is incessantly engaged in blocking every means of communication that the slave merchants had with the interior. It must not be supposed that the Europeans alluded to engaged directly in the expeditions themselves. No; they would not expose their precious lives to

---

145 Again Burnaby has the name wrong, this was the Italian mercenary, Romulo Gessi (1831-1881).

the many dangers and deprivations which every slaver must undergo. So they remained quietly at Khartoum, and lent out money at 300 and 400 per cent. to those men who were about to organize a band of desperadoes for a raid upon the natives in the interior. If the expedition was successful, as it would be nine times out of ten, the European speculators quadrupled their investments, and in the course of a few ventures accumulated large fortunes; but now all this has come to an end, and they find themselves without any so lucrative an employment for their capital, and all their former business at a dead-lock. The European merchants at Khartoum exacted far higher interest from the slave traders than the Arab money-lenders; but as the latter had not the necessary funds at their disposal, the slavers were obliged to have recourse to the Germans and Greeks alluded to in my letter.

There was nothing for us to do at Khartoum but to have patience and resignation, and await Mr. Jesse's arrival, which occurred a few days later on. He instantly placed his vessel, the *Embaria*, at our disposal, and said that he would accompany us up the White Nile, till we met a boat on its way down, which he would send back to Gordon with the mails and ourselves, and that we should reach the Colonel in about 14 days. *L'homme propose, mais Dieu dispose*, and we found this out to our cost. The first steamer we fell in with had damaged her cylinder, and could not return against the stream. Then we ran aground, and our crew, stripped to the skin, worked several hours up to their waists in water and mud to get us off. Poor fellows! they were indeed to be pitied. Many of them were half prostrate from fever, and others suffering from fearful sores on their legs, the result of the sharp cutting grass which grows in the river and the poisonous character of the water. The pilot himself was unable to stand up, so exhausted was he from repeated attacks of fever; and as his voice was too weak to be heard by the steersman, a sailor was stationed beside him to shout out the various directions. The country, however, which we passed through was magnificent in the extreme – splendid timber on each side, and fine lofty trees which would have ennobled an English park were studded here and there in all directions. Every now and then we came to long avenues or vistas of trees; beneath whose shade we could discern quantities of gazelles, tebals, and oriel deer; along the banks swarmed hippopotami and crocodiles, while in the rich grass that grows luxuriant from the river to the edges of the wood ran thousands of guinea fowl, so tame that they utterly ignored the presence of our steamer. The country between Khartoum and Peshoda is a veritable sportsman's paradise; every species of deer abounds, while elephants, giraffes and buffaloes, as well as lions and leopards, are to be met with at two hours' distance from the banks. Monkeys chatter at us from the top-most branches of the huge trees as we glide along the stream, and birds of every variety of plumage fly around our boat, apparently unconscious of man's presence in their locality. We are more than 2,000 miles from the mouth of the mighty river and several hundred beyond that point where Herodotus describes it as being unknown and impassable, and from shore to shore the distance is far greater than that of the Thames at London-bridge – a broad, rapid, shallow stream, of a whitish gray colour, whence it derives its name El-Bahr-Abyad, or the White Sea. Presently we meet another of Gordon's seven steamers, bringing mails and sick soldiers to Khartoum; but she has also had an accident and broken her paddles against a sandbank. So it is impossible to continue our journey in her, and Mr. Jesse determines to take us on in his own boat to Soubat, the first of Gordon's stations in Central Africa. Almost every 30 hours we have to stop for wood, which replaces coal in Gordon's steamers; sometimes we found it already cut, but, if not, two or three days would be employed by our worn-out crew in providing a sufficient supply or our onward journey. At last we pass Peshoda, the last town in Ismail Pasha's Government, and on emerging into the territory where Gordon's authority commences we find that we have left behind even those traces of civilization which were the appurtenances of our first parents. For here the male savage has not even a fig-leaf to cover himself with, and disdains the cloth worn by the inhabitants of the Soudan. But yet there is some little attention paid to personal decoration, and this is displayed by both sexes tinging their hair with a fine red or golden ointment, and magnificent natural chignons are worn by the men which might make even a Bond-street hairdresser envious. At length we arrive at point where the Soubat river runs into the White Nile, having left behind us Taufynia, or Baker's Settlement, which is now abandoned, and a wilderness, a few blades of doura corn growing in the distance being all that marks this former station; and, leaving the Bahr-Abyad, we steam a few hundred yards up the Soubat and find ourselves beside a clean little square of straw-thatched huts, surrounded by a defence made of heaped-up thorns and brambles. Quantities of naked natives are bringing down piece of wood to the river side, for here is the principal fuel depot for Gordon's vessels which ply between Khartoum and Ragaff, the farthest point where the Nile is navigable, and about 120 miles below the falls. The Governor of Soubat, a black officer, came down to the steamer. He had been in Mexico during Napoleon's Expedition, and was very proud of the few words of Spanish he had mastered during his stay there. He informed us that he had been sent here three months ago with 17 men, and that he had already lost four through fever, and that three of the ten donkeys sent down from Khartoum for the Expedition had already succumbed to the climate. The natives, however, who were carrying wood to our vessel did not bear in their faces any signs of the unhealthy nature of the soil. Splendid fellows many of them were, some being considerably over 6ft. in height. The women were also much above the average female stature, and Frederick of Russia could have found in Soubat wives worthy of the tallest of his Body Guard. The news received here was very welcome, for Gordon, we were told, was himself on his way to this station, where he is expected to-morrow. From here he may, perhaps, make an exploring expedition up the Soubat, as nothing whatever is known of the river within two or three days from this settlement; and later on, the indefatigable Colonel is going to Fatico, which Baker terms the paradise of Africa, and which is at a considerable elevation above the sea.

Gordon has certainly done wonders since his stay in this country. When he arrived, only 10 months ago, he found 700 soldiers in Gondoroko, who did not dare to go 100 yards from that place, except when armed and in small bands, on account of the Baris, who were exasperated at the way Baker had treated them. With these 700 men Gordon has garrisoned eight stations – viz., at Soubat, at Ratichambé, Bor, Lardo, Raggoff, Fatico, Duffe, and Makraka, the frontier of the Nam Jam country. Baker's Expedition cost the Egyptian Government £1,170,247, while Gordon has already sent up sufficient money to Cairo to pay for all the expenses of his Expedition, including not only the sums required for last year, but the amount estimated for the actual one as well. It is Gordon's aim and ambition to make his district more than pay for itself, and from the absolute trust the savages about Lardo and Gondokoro are said to have in him, there is every reason to believe that Egyptian commerce with the interior will be greatly developed during the next few years.

FGB097
Soubat, Central Africa; 7 February 1875
Burnaby to Editor – *The Times*, **27 March 1875**
Soubat, which is the first of Colonel Gordon's stations that is reached after leaving the Soudan and the Provinces under Ismail Pasha's rule, does not strike the observer as being at all a formidable post, or one easy to be defended, if the natives, of whom there are hundreds in the neighbourhood were to attempt any hostile measures. The soldiers' huts are built of mud and straw, and the only defence in the shape of a fortification is a circular, thick, piled-up hedge made of thorns and brambles; in fact, the whole place is so combustible that a few red-hot arrows would suffice to set the station in a blaze, if the Shillouks or inhabitants of the country ever thought seriously of attempting to drive out the Egyptian invader. But there is now no reason to fear any surprise on the part of the Shillouks. They appear to have accepted the new ruler and their changed circumstances with the usual apathy of an Oriental or African race, and do their best to assist the garrison by cutting wood for the steamers which stop at Soubat for fuel when *en route* to and from Khartoum. A few years ago affairs were very different; the Shillouks were then a united and powerful race, perpetually at war with the Egyptians, who could not leave their most advanced station at Pashoda, save in large armed parties, and the garrison there had several narrow escapes of being surprised and put to the sword. In those days the Shillouks had grievances enough, in the shape of the constant

inroads made on their villages and hamlets by slave-traders, to stir the most peacefully-disposed people to retributive measures, and the suppression of the slave trade by the Viceroy has done more to tranquillize the country than his most formidable fortifications or armed stations. Very contented and happy appear the natives who have established themselves within a stone's-throw of Soubat, and the huts in which they dwell are clean and weatherproof. In point of cleanliness the comparison would not be in favour of the houses inhabited by some of the lower orders in London, if contrasted with the beehive-like cottages of the Shillouks. Two attributes of civilization, money and religion, are equally unknown, and the natives do not trouble their heads with any endeavour to fathom the great secret of the future, while instead of money they use Doura corn, two handfuls of which are considered ample payment for a day's wood-cutting and the conveyance of it to the station. A man who has sufficient Doura to last himself and family for a week is looked upon as a sort of Croesus by his less fortunate brethren. When no corn is to be had the people live upon fish, which are to be found in abundance in the marshes all round the river, and are not particular even as to eating crocodiles, for one that was shot by an officer in the expedition and left on the banks for the vultures was wrested from these voracious birds by the natives, who, cutting up the huge reptile with their spears, carried the pieces away for themselves. They are not troubled by those attacks of fever which undermine the strongest European constitution, and are just as much at home in their reed-made barks or up to their necks in the muddy river as any South Sea Islander in the surf and in his fragile canoe. Great delight was evinced by the natives when they heard that the "Pasha Kabeer", or "Great Pasha", was daily expected to visit the settlement; for Gordon is very popular with the people in this district as he listens to and remedies any real grievances they may have, and severely punishes the soldiers if they ill-treat them. His principle in China, as here, has always been that you can get more out of a man by kindness than by any other method, and the confidence which is placed in him by the Shillouks and Baris has done much to obliterate the traces of the stern rule of his predecessor.

About 12 at noon yesterday a watchman, who was perched upon a tree commanding a good look-out on the White Nile, rushed to the station with the glad tidings that the steamer Khedive (one put together by the late Mr. Higginbotham for Baker at Gondokoro) was in sight. Immediately the settlement was in a state of commotion. The bugle sounded "Turn out", and the garrison, consisting of 17 soldiers, under a black captain, who is also the Governor, hastily donning their smartest uniforms, hurried down to the bank beside which the steamer was expected to anchor. Some aged natives were actually so moved as to put down their huge pipes, out of which they were slowly inhaling the stupefying fumes of pure charcoal, and join the different little knots and bands of their excited wives and children who lined the riverside. Nearer and nearer came the steamer, and, gracefully rounding the sharp curve where the White Nile is joined by its still whiter-looking Soubat tributary, anchored within a few feet of the shore. The one bugler nearly burst his lungs in ringing out the clear strains of a general's salute, the black captain lowered his sword, and the 17 men composing the garrison brought their arms to the "present", as a short, thick-set man, who appeared to be the picture of health, and was attired in the undress uniform of a Colonel of Engineers, hastened down the side and, approaching the officer and his small force, rapidly, inspected the men and their accoutrements. He was accompanied by Mr. Watson, an officer in the Engineers, whose services had been lent by the British Government to the Viceroy, but who is now going back to England, owing to his health having become affected by the trying climate of the White Nile. A few soldiers, who formerly were in Baker's Guard, which was termed by him the Forty Thieves, and who now act as orderlies to Gordon, brought up the rear of the procession. Fine-looking fellows they are, too, not a man of them under some 6 feet in height, with magnificently formed chests and shoulders. They looked remarkably clean and smart in their scarlet tunics, with black faced sleeves and collars; and there was a resolute and sort of devil-may-care expression in their faces, which betokened that the late chief had not been unwise in estimating his bodyguard as equal to cope with a hundredfold their number of hostile savages.

The inspection was over in a minute, and, after a few words to the Governor, Gordon returned on board, and there, beneath an awning on deck, began the business of the day. The number of things he had to settle and arrange would have been enough to turn the head of any ordinary mortal, but the Colonel went steadily ahead, giving out one order after another, administering justice to the natives, censuring or praising the officials, ordering punishment here and reward there; all this through an Egyptian interpreter, who gravely rendered every word of Gordon's French, into Arabic. Some of the news brought by the last mail was enough in itself to disconcert most men. Two English engineers had arrived at Khartoum, to put up a steamer which had been sent out in pieces. The engineers were there, and so were the pieces, but there was no plan of the vessel in the storehouse at Khartoum, and there was no list of the different pieces, to show where and in what boxes they were separately packed. The keel of the ship must be laid before the approaching rainy season or be deferred till next year, and all this time the engineers would be doing nothing and drawing the Viceroy's pay, which was the most aggravating of all to Gordon, as he is far more careful of the Khedive's money than of his own, which he throws away right and left in backsheesh and presents. If he were to leave the Expedition tomorrow he would be personally poorer, it is said, than when he first assumed the command. The next letter opened informed him that Raouf Pasha was *en route* to Khartoum and Lardo, with 500 soldiers and a band of music. Now, the captains of all the steamers belonging to the Expedition had received orders to remain at Khartoum to bring up the horses bought for the Expedition, and here were 500 men who would require transport before the rains had commenced, or else half of them would die on their way to Lardo. In addition to this a supply of Doura corn must be provided to last them for the next seven months. Then came the Governor with a report that 12 slaves who had been taken from the traders had stolen some guns and rifles from a station further up the Soubat and come to him, saying that they had been ill-treated by Nazar, Gordon's agent there. The Governor had given them food and lodging preparatory to an inquiry being made as to their grievances, but they had broken out of his station at night and had fired upon the soldiers who were sent in pursuit of them. On investigation it appeared that their grounds of complaint against Nazar were groundless; so they were sentenced to receive each a hundred lashes with a knotted cord, and then to be sent to Fashoda, which is the receptacle of all Egyptian convicts or exiles – a sort of fiery Siberia, in fact, but far more unhealthy, as fever and dysentery decimate the population, which is only kept up by the constant addition it receives in the shape of embezzling Pashas, cut-throats, and thieves.

At last everything was settled to everybody's satisfaction, save to the 12 runaways, who were each receiving their hundred lashes in the background, and were lamenting their fate – calling upon Allah, their fathers, mothers, and all their departed relations to intercede for them and not let the blows be quite so hard, but just a little, little softer Bismillah, in the name of Allah and his blessed prophet – and Gordon had some minutes to himself take a few mouthfuls of refreshment and drink several cups of strong coffee, which is believed here to be a capital specific against fever. After luncheon he told us what had been done by the Expedition during the past year and of his plans for the next few months. On arrival in the Provinces intrusted to his care he found that there were only three stations – viz., Fatico, Foweira, and Gondokoro; but that at this last-named post the garrison did not dare go more than a few hundred yards from their intrenchments for fear of the Baris, who were always on the alert to pick off any stragglers. The new Pasha's first object was to conciliate the Baris, and after that to establish the following detached armed settlements; all of which were formed from the few hundred men he found at Gondokoro. First, he established one station, two days up the Soubat River, called Nazar's Station, from the name of the agent there, who, by the way, was formerly a slave trader, but who, like many others of his class, has been taken into Gordon's service. Then was formed this post at the junction of the Soubat and the White Nile – a most important point strategically considered, as it effectually debars the slave traders from ascending or descending either stream. Next comes the Ratichambé Settlement, 250 miles up the river, which has now been abolished on account of its extreme unhealthiness and removed six days' march to the west, for the purpose of opening up an ivory trade with the natives. Ninety miles from Ratichambé, and on the river, is the Bor Station. The appearance of the country here improves a little and has a more wooded aspect than that between Soubat and Ratichambé, which is dismal in the extreme. There we find nothing but dreary miles of swamp and morass on either bank; here and there a solitary tree, adding by its very loneliness to the bleak appearance of the waste – naught save floating islands and decaying vegetation – a hot-bed of malaria and fever – the water bubbling incessantly from the gas which arises from the vegetable matter undergoing decomposition beneath the surface. Not a human being to be seen, and, save for the animals which infest the marshes, the traveller might almost fancy himself floating down the Styx. South-west of Bor and far inland, a settlement has been made at Makraka, which is now being visited by Major Long, an American officer serving under Gordon, and a Mr. Marno, an Austrian explorer, whose expenses are defrayed, I believe, by the Geographical Society at Vienna.[146] Long is the officer who a few months since, when on his road back, after having visited King Mtesa, was attacked by Camárragga's people, on the Victoria Nile, near Foweira. The Major was in a canoe, and accompanied by only two Egyptian soldiers. However, the three managed to keep up such a hot fire on the natives, who were shooting at them with arrows from the banks, that the savages were eventually driven off, having suffered, as was afterwards ascertained, a loss of over 60 killed and wounded. On leaving Bor, and continuing the journey up the river, we arrived, after about 90 miles steaming, at Lardo, which is the most important station that Gordon has hitherto established. It is 10 miles only from Gondokoro, that post of which so much is said in Sir Samuel Baker's last book, and which has replaced Gondokoro as the head-quarters of the Province, everything having been moved from the old station, which is now entirely deserted. The distance from Khartoum to Lardo, as ascertained by Lieutenants Watson and Chippendale,[147] is as nearly as possible 1,000 miles, and these two young Engineer officers who were at Ragaff, the next station, some 12 miles further up the stream, succeeded in making some important observations during the transit of Venus, which are to be transmitted to the Royal Geographical Society. Ten miles above Ragaff the Nile becomes un-navigable, and it has been proposed to connect the station with Duflé, the next settlement, which is 12 days' march distant, by either a canal or a railway, but this, of course, is a work for future consideration. At the present moment Gordon is using every effort to get a small steamer put together on the Nile at Duflé. The more portable parts of this vessel were taken there overland from Ragaff, a few months back by Mr. Kemp, a civil engineer

---

146 Ernst Marno (1844-1883) was an Austrian explorer and author. He travelled widely through the Blue Nile area and along the Sudan-Ethiopia border, as well as in Kordofan and southern Sudan.
147 Actually Lieutenant William Harold Chippindall, RE.

then in Gordon's service, but now invalided, and when the Colonel returns from visiting the station up the Soubat he is going to forward the heavier parts of the boat in carts, drawn by men, from Ragaff. This will be a work of great difficulty on account of the nature of the country. Duflé is on the left bank of the Nile and opposite Ibrahimia, which is mentioned by Baker. Lieutenant Chippendale is now on his way to Duflé. He has received orders to march with 180 soldiers and 500 carriers from Ragaff through a post called Laboré, and, as best he can, across the Ashua river to Ibrahimia. This river is navigable in the dry season, but an almost unsurmountable torrent when the rains commence. Chippendale is to leave the greater part of his men at Ibrahimia, and to continue the march with only those soldiers he deems absolutely indispensable for his enterprise, striking inland for the Albert Nyanza Lake. He is there to obtain a canoe at any cost, either by purchase or force, and return, if possible, from the Albert Nyanza down the Nile to Duflé, thus establishing the fact whether the great river is navigable between those two points. The task confided to this young officer is extremely arduous, and he will merit the highest praise should he succeed in the dangerous undertaking. If the result of his investigations is that the Nile is un-navigable, there will be nothing for it but to carry the steamer in pieces overland to the Albert Nyanza and launch the vessel on the lake, a labour the duration of which it is impossible to forecast. After Duflé, Gordon's next settlement is at Tatico, an important ivory station, south-east of the former post and inland, whence we finally arrive at Toweera, the most advanced point where there are Egyptian soldiers. It is on the Victoria Nile, near the Albert Lake. Major Long passed through Toweera a few months ago on his road to Urondagani, the last navigable point on the Victoria Nyanza, in Mtesa's territory. It was on his way back that he discovered the lake of which so much has been said lately, but as unfortunately, he had no instruments with him, he was unable to take any observations so as to define its exact position and boundaries. He was also very unwell at the time, and is not at all clear as to its dimensions, so it is as yet uncertain whether the new discovery may not turn out to be simply an overflow of the Victoria river.

Camárragga, who was Baker's foe, and whose people lately attacked Long, has just sent down to Lardo Sir Samuel's uniform, that of a deputy lieutenant – which was taken from him, it is believed, at Masindi, probably during the retreat from that part.

As so much has been written about Abou Saood, who is Sir Samuel's *bête noir* in his publication "Ismailia", it may not be uninteresting to state the reasons why Gordon took Abou into the Khedive's employ, and the causes which led to his ultimate dismissal. When Baker's successor arrived in Central Africa, he found the Dongolouese (really inhabitants of Dongola, but now a name given to the men who engaged themselves to serve under the slave traders), established in three stations – viz., at the Bahr Giraffe, Bor, and Ratichambé.

These people had great influence with the natives and were still powerful in those districts, so Gordon – when their bread and butter so to speak, was taken away by the suppression of the slave trade and by the ivory commerce in which they had also been engaging having become exclusively a Government monopoly – determined, if possible, to conciliate the men; and at the same time to make use of them by enlisting all who chose to serve beneath the banner of the Viceroy. Abou Saood had great influence with the Dongolouese, he had headed them successfully on numerous expeditious, and directly he accepted service under Gordon they all followed his example. From Abou Saood and the Dongolouese, the Colonel was able to obtain a vast quantity of useful information and gradually, as the old slave traders became better acquainted with Gordon, who came among them a stranger utterly ignorant of their language and customs, the new Governor's influence rose and Abou Saood's fell. In the meantime Gordon had learnt all he required, and when a few months later Abou became somewhat impertinent, and tried to get more ivory than was due to him from the Government, he suddenly received his dismissal. "May I still remain here?" asked the surprised intriguer. "Certainly", said Gordon; "stop here or go to Khartoum as you please." Abou stayed on, but all his prestige with his old followers subsided, and this sudden disgrace produced no reaction whatever, Gordon now having thoroughly established his own authority. Abou remained but a few days, and seeing that there was no chance of his being reinstated, returned to Khartoum. He frequently writes to the Colonel in the most humble terms entreating re-employment. This, however, he is not likely to obtain, as Abou Saood, in Gordon's opinion, cannot be trusted. No more use can be made of him, and, for these reasons, he is discharged from the Expedition. The energetic Governor of the Provinces in Central Africa will next year be further removed than ever from civilization, as he is about to make over all the country between Soubat and Lardo to Raouf Pasha. His own district will begin at Ragaff, from which point he will establish military posts a day's journey apart, and by this means form a connecting link with his more remote stations, at the same still time pushing still further into the interior. All speculators in ivory would do well to lay in large stocks of that precious commodity, and that soon, as it is now in these regions a Government monopoly. The supply which is yearly forwarded to Egypt is not the result of 12 months' chase, but taken from the stores which are the accumulations of native Chiefs and Kings for many years past. These people exchange their valuable treasure with the officers in charge of Gordon's stations, requiring 2½ piastres' worth of beads for the *oke* (2¾ pounds avoirdupois) of ivory. In the course of a few years the supply will diminish, and consequently the value in Europe will become enormously enhanced. At present the Egyptian Government, in addition to paying all the expenses of the Expedition, realizes several thousands a year by the tusks, which are forwarded to Cairo from Central Africa, the cost price of the ivory being barely £1 a cwt., and its value in Egypt being about £40 for the same quantity. Of course there may be many teeth stored up in unknown regions south of the lakes, this is as yet uncertain. It may seem somewhat strange that no attempt was ever made to open up any commerce with the natives, save that of ivory and slaves, but as slave trading gave quicker and larger returns than any other kind of speculation, and also required less capital, no merchant cared to attempt a different business. However, the country is rich in every sort of skin; gum trees abound in some localities; sugar and tobacco might be cultivated at a large profit between Khartoum and Soubat; while the oil of the hippopotami in the Bahr Giraffe[148] would alone yield any speculator a handsome yearly income. One of the principal reasons that these sources of wealth were left unworked was the existence of the slave trade which absorbed all the energies of the leading merchants at Khartoum, while the perpetual wars and disturbances which it occasioned so depopulated the country that there were no arms left to till the ground should anybody have desired to promote agriculture. But now that the great curse to Central Africa has been removed, there is no reason why the capitalists at Khartoum should not speedily recoup their temporary losses in a manner honourable to themselves and beneficial to their countrymen, by opening up fresh branches of industry in the interior.

As the evening wore on the sounds of a native drum announced that the Shillouks in the neighbourhood were assembling in the station for the purpose of having a fantasia or dancing entertainment in honour of the Pasha's arrival. Very picturesque was the scene an hour or two later when the moon rose, and threw its pale silvery rays on the animated picture. For here, round a high post on which was slung an instrument now undergoing a frantic beating from the hands of a drummer, ran the nude savages of all ages from the veteran of perhaps 70 summers to the urchin who had barely completed his first decade, making rapid gesticulations with hands and body, combining movements with panther-like bounds into the air. Their women, who were looking on, sang a guttural ditty, and, clapping hands to the frequent cadences in the drum, incited the performers to still more strenuous feats of agility. Presently a gigantic native bounded within the living circle and brandishing his spear, placed himself in the attitude of an attacking warrior, then changing his gesture he assumed the position of a cringing supplicant at the mercy of a victorious foe, the other dancers going through all their motions with their weapons as if they were actually engaged in battle. To the spectator unaccustomed to such scenes, the performers seemed so thoroughly raised to frenzy, that he could easily imagine the mimic fight at any moment turning into stern reality. Far away in the

---

148 Also known as the Bahr el Zeraf and by other variations, it is an arm of the White Nile in the Sudd region of South Sudan.

background a magnificent spectacle presented itself. Miles upon miles of the prairie were on fire, and the roaring flames leaping up into the air as they embraced tree after tree within the pitiless element, reflected coruscating flashes from the glassy surface of the Nile and its tributary, frightening away the crocodile, geese, and hippopotami, which infest the shores, the latter with their deep bass grunting forming an accompaniment to the discordant music and wild yells of the Shillouks. Mountains of white smoke fanned into a thousand grotesque forms and shapes by the soft breeze were slowly sailing away towards the distant horizon, and an eruption of Vesuvius could not have surpassed in either grandeur or brilliancy the glowing mass of devouring flame which pursued its headlong course across the tinder-like grass and forest. Myriads of fire-flies sparkling over the heads of the dusky savages, and then disappearing like meteors in space, completed the picture, and it was one well worth a journey even to Central Africa.

CMW01
[Shepheard's Hotel,] Cairo; 2 April 1875
Watson to sister
Having been of late a regular beast in the matter of writing to you, I must try to atone to some small extent for my remissness in this matter, and the rather as your excellent letter of the 24th has this morning reached me and given me exceeding pleasure. If you can forgive me for my wickedness, pray do so, and attribute the fault to the disadvantageous circumstances under which I have been lately placed.

And now, to become egotistical, let me say that I have had really a most pleasant journey this time, and that I now feel all right, and would be quite able to go up again and have another shot at the old Lake, if that were to the mind of Gordon; but as it wasn't, we need not discuss the matter. Historically, here is my voyage down in brief:

January 25. Preparing to start for South; got note from G[ordon] to say 'don't'.
6. Started in nuggar for Lado.
27. Arrived at Lado. Gordon gone to Sobat.
30. Started for Sobat in steamer.
31. Caught up Gordon at Bor.
February 7. Arrived at Sobat. Found Captain Burnaby of Horse Guards, who had come up to see the country.
9. Started with Burnaby for Khartoum in steamer.
17. Arrived at Khartoum.
22. Started for Berber by camel.
25. Shendi.
March 1. Arrived at Berber.

2. Started for Abu-Hamed by camel.
6. Arrived Abu-Hamed.
9. Started across desert to Korosko.
15. Arrived at Korosko.
17. On this day we got an open boat and made the best of our way to Aswan, or rather to the top of the first Cataract, which we reached at sunset on the 19th. The Temple of Philae is just at this point, and I must say I have never seen anything more beautiful than the view on approaching it. I saw the scene under perhaps more advantageous circumstances than 999 persons out of a 1,000, seeing that I was coming down the river without having come up it first, which, as you can understand, made the greatest possible difference. Probably, too, not having expected anything, I was more struck with the general aspect. The sun was setting on one side with a most beautiful after-glow, and the full moon rising on the other.

On arrival we immediately visited the temple, which certainly impressed me more than Thebes or Karnak or any of the others which we saw afterwards. The following morning we found that some friends of Burnaby's, Lord F. Cecil and wife, were alongside in a large dahabiah, being engaged in wedding touring. They asked us to breakfast and to shoot the rapids with them, which we did, sending the baggage to Aswan by camel. Going down the rapids is amusing, and the excitement of the Arab sailors immense; but I could not decide how much was real and how much put on for the benefit of the onlookers. It felt comfortable sitting down again to a table with a table-cloth on it, and to know that our travels were practically at an end and we had again reached civilization.

Aswan attained, I immediately got a small dahabiah from the Mudir, and we started without delay down the Nile.

22. Reached Essné.
23. Reached Luxor at 9 a.m. There we stopped, of course, but as we could not afford more time than until sunset (as Burnaby's leave was rapidly drawing to a close), rapidity was essential. In Murray's Guide-Book it is stated that, if travellers are very quick, they may get through in three days; so we thought that seven hours ought to be enough, and, seizing donkeys, galloped off to Karnak (which is certainly a very big place), returned to the boat, had something to eat, crossed the river, took more donkeys, went to the Tombs of the Kings, Kurna, saw all the temples, the Colossi, etc., etc., were back at the boat by 5.50, and immediately started on our voyage. Thebes is certainly a wonderful place and well worth seeing, even though Cook's tourists do go there. By the way, we just missed meeting a steamer-load of them.

24. Reached Kiné.
27. Reached Girgeh.
29. Reached Siout (Asyut), and made fast alongside the railway.
30. Went to the railway, and found that the train for Cairo started, or

rather was supposed to do so, at 7.30 a.m. After many delays, we got off at 8.15, proceeding until the engine burst a cylinder, which delayed us an hour fixing another. We then proceeded until the second engine also broke down, and eventually got to Cairo four hours late, and were soon established in Shepheard's Hotel, which presented a very different aspect to what it did when I was here last, as now it is nearly full, while then we were almost the only inhabitants.

CGG01
Lado, Sudan; 25 June 1875
Gordon to Watson (extract)
My dear Watson ... Marcopoli is angry, and with reason, at being written about by Burnaby in *Times*, for it does him harm. If you see or hear from Burnaby, tell him that it is on the understood ground that he ceases this sort of correspondence and limits it to descriptions of country and *dead objects*, etc., and that he will not write again after he leaves, that I accept his presence. I am going to refuse Stanley leave to stay in Province. I object to being daily logged. No one can like it ...

FGB098
Demout's Hotel, St. Petersburg; December 1875
Burnaby to General Milutin
Sir,– I trust that you will pardon the liberty I am taking in writing to you without having the honour of your personal acquaintance.

I wish to have the permission to go to India via Khiva, Merve and Cabul. But as I had read in some English papers, previous to my departure from London, that the Russian Government had issued an order forbidding Englishmen to travel in Russian Asia, I thought that I ought to address myself to Count Schuvalov, the Russian Ambassador in London. He said to me, "I cannot personally answer your question, but when you arrive in St. Petersburg, the authorities there will give you every information." Before I quitted London I received a letter from Count Schuvalov, informing me that he had written officially to the Minister of Foreign Affairs at St. Petersburg with reference to my journey, while the Count enclosed me a letter of introduction to his brother, and concluded by wishing me a happy journey. Now, sir, I should much like to know if I can have this permission. If it cannot be granted me, will you do me the honour of writing two lines and tell me frankly, Yes or No. If the answer is No, I shall leave St. Petersburg immediately, because my leave of absence will soon be over, and I do not wish to remain here longer than it is necessary to receive your answer.

I have the honour to be, etc.'[149]

GWFC01[150]
War Office, [April 1876]
Duke of Cambridge to Gathorne Hardy
My dear Hardy, I saw Captain Burnaby yesterday & a more interesting conversation I never remember holding with anybody. He is a remarkable fellow – singular looking, but of great perseverance and determination. He has gone through a great deal & the only surprise is how he got through it. I think you ought decidedly to see him & and I think he had better also be interviewed by the Foreign and Indian Offices after you have heard what he has to say. He has been in Khiva where no Englishman has ever been but for Abbott & Shakespear years ago.[151] He will tell you very remarkable things, which is quite sufficient I think to cause us much anxiety & great alarm & he says if we don't act now it will be decidedly too late & the Russian will easily reach Merve and Kabul & then the empire of India, which the officer says clearly is the great object they have in view & towards which they have made such tremendous strides, particularly of late. I've arranged that he should be with Horsford about 12.30 when if at the office you might like to see him or you could fix your own place for doing so. But pray see him, for it is very important that you should do so. I remain yours most sincerely George.

FGB099
Cavalry Barracks, Windsor; 13 April 1876
Burnaby to Editor – *The Standard***, 14 April 1876**
Sir, – Having seen my name mentioned in a Reuter's telegram from St. Petersburg, published in your issue of this morning, where it states that I was expelled from Khiva for having evaded the requisite presentation of a passport and other papers testifying to my identity, and in consequence of complaints raised by the Khan of Khiva, permit me to remark that there is no truth whatever in that statement, and that the reasons for my leaving Khiva are better known to General Milutin, the Russian Minister of War, than the St. Petersburg correspondent of the *North German Gazette*. – I have the honour to remain, Sir, your obedient servant, Fred Burnaby, Captain Royal Horse Guards.

---

149 This letter is reproduced by Burnaby in his *Ride to Khiva*, but is probably an approximate recollection, rather than a draft.
150 Courtesy of Ipswich Record Office: The Earl of Cranbrook Family Archive; correspondence with the Duke of Cambridge (HA43/T501/264). NB This undated letter is filed out of sequence at the beginning of December 1875.
151 Lieutenants James Abbott and Richmond Shakespear, both of the Bengal Royal Artillery, were at Khiva in early 1840 and succeeded in arranging for the Khan of Khiva to release a large number of Russian slaves in his possession.

[Reuter's Telegram. St. Petersburg, April 12. Several newspapers discuss the article published by the *Army and Navy Gazette* regarding the expulsion of the British Captain Burnaby from Khiva, and refer to the St. Petersburg letter of the *North German Gazette* of the 9th inst., according to which the captain, who had evaded the requisite presentation of a passport and other papers testifying to his identity, was expelled in consequence of complaints raised by the Khan of Khiva.]

FGB100
Regent's Park Barracks; 30 May 1876
Burnaby to Houghton
Captain Burnaby has much pleasure in accepting Lord Houghton's invitation for the 8th of June.

FGB101
Cavalry Barracks, Windsor; 2 August 1876
Burnaby to unknown[152]
Dear Sir, Thank you for yr letter. It has amused me very much. Yrs vy truly, Fred Burnaby

FGB102
Regent's Park Barracks; 16 September 1876
Burnaby to Wright
In the event of your having a balloon ascent from the Crystal Palace on Tuesday next, I should like to take your place in the balloon and go alone with my friend. Of course no one would be told of this, and it would have to be a private matter between you and myself. I suppose that in the event of our making some sort of an arrangement like this, I should not have to pay for the gas, as this would be found by the company for your ascent. I should like your largest balloon, so as to make a long ascent, and would pay for any damage done to it, as well as a certain sum to you for the hire. What time would the balloon be likely to go up, as the earlier the better, and what would be your terms for the hire? Send me an answer by telegraph, as tomorrow is Sunday and there is no post.

FGB103[153]
Marlborough Club; 31 October 1876
Burnaby to Beaconsfield
Dear Lord Beaconsfield, I hope you will do me the honour of accepting this

---

152 Courtesy of University of Reading, Special Collections, Longman Archive II 71/1/29.
153 Courtesy of the Bodleian Libraries, University of Oxford, Special Collections: Hughenden papers BXXI/142-1402 (ff. 133/4).

book minus the maps which are not yet engraved, but which shall be sent to you as soon as they are completed. Believe me, Yrs very truly, Fred Burnaby.

FGB104[154]
Marlborough Club; 2 November 1876
Burnaby to Beaconsfield
Dear Lord Beaconsfield, Many thanks for your kind wishes as to my success in Montenegro, but I have just received the enclosed communication from the Horse Guards telling my me that my services will not be required. Yrs very truly, Fred Burnaby.

FGB105
Regent's Park Barracks; 15 November 1876
Burnaby to Wolseley[155]
Dear Sir Garnet – I am going to ask you a great favour. In the event of there being a war, will you take me on your staff or in any other capacity how humble it might be – as nothing I should like better to serve under you. I know Russian thoroughly, and leave this evening for Turkey to study the Turkish language. I have got 5 months leave and mean to travel in Asia Minor in the direction of the Caucasus. I hope you will pardon the liberty I am taking in writing to you on the subject and pray believe me Yours very sincerely, Fred Burnaby.

FGB106
Grand Hotel de Luxembourg, Rue de Pera, Constantinople;
30 November 1876
Burnaby to his mother[156]
I arrived here last Saturday, a tolerably fair passage lasting 7 days from Marseille. I leave this on Tuesday next for a 1000 miles ride to Erzeroum and to Kars. It will be a road that few Europeans have travelled and of which little is known. Erzeroum is very highly situated being very nearly the highest tableland in the world. Close to Erzeroum is Mount Ararat where the old Ark settled. Shall I bring you back a bit of the wood of which it was made? It will be a very cold journey, but I have made my preparations against the enemy. I have been ten hours in the saddle today, going over the ground which is to be the English position in the event of Constantinople being attached by the Russians. The position is very strong and almost impregnable.

154 Courtesy of the Bodleian Libraries, University of Oxford, Special Collections: Hughenden papers BXXI/142-1403 (ff. 135/6).
155 Courtesy of Brighton and Hove City Council, Hove Central Library, Wolseley Collection, GB 0510/1.
156 Courtesy of the University Librarian and Director of the John Rylands Library, The University of Manchester.

FGB107
Grand Hotel de Luxembourg, Rue de Pera, Constantinople; 4 December 1876
Burnaby to Lady Molesworth[157]

Dear Lady Molesworth[158] – I had a pleasant journey here from London, to as far as Paris I travelled with the celebrated Cocotte Mrs. Phoenix the Authoress of *La Americaine á St. Petersburg*.[159] She had been turned out of Paris for writing her a book against the Czar, but since then permission has been given to her to return. – She was all for free love if accompanied with by a full purse and advised me "that trade was very dull in London and that the Ladies in her line of business in our capital were all grumbling – In summer it is well enough she said but in Winter the men only care for riding after the stinking foxes, and you will scarcely believe it, but I have hardly seen 2 men in a week since the middle of October." Travelling from Paris to Marseille I fell in with Mr. Ballantyne [sic][160], he was going to Toulon to see a Mrs. Peter Robinson about a divorce case. Happened that her husband Mr. Peter had lately come into £350,000, and since the acquisition of this fortune he had begun to look upon Mrs. Robinson as an encumbrance. He is prepared to pay anything to get rid of her and Ballantyne's fee for going to Toulon was 500 and all expenses. How lawyers, like Ballantyne, must like the divorce court and that incongruity of disposition which makes husband & wife quarrel. I only stayed a few hours at Marseille and in the afternoon embarked on board a steamer belonging to the Messageries Maritimes. We had a fair passage as far as Smyrna. There Here our cargo complement of passengers was increased by a Pasha with 4 wives – a black eunuch and 150 Turkish recruits all going to the seat of war in tight hoses, and 2 pointer dogs in hampers made up the list of new arrivals. The Pasha was accommodated in a first class cabin, his 4 wives were accommodated on deck – a very pleasant place on a fine summer night – but a most disagreeable berth in wet weather – However the Pasha evidently went in for economy – at least as far as his female appendages were concerned, and the only attempt made to shelter them was made by the Captain of the vessel. – This polite Gaul ordered one of his sailors to erect a tarpaulin as a sort of shelter above the heads of the Seraglio. One of the wives was not bad looking – they all wore the thinnest of

---

157 © Somerset Archive and Record Service: DD\SH/59/274 N.D. WW56/1-16. Emphasis and corrections as in original letter.
158 Née Andalusia Grant Carstairs (1803-1888), widow of Sir William Molesworth, 8th Bt. (1810-1855) of Pencarrow, Cornwall, mathematician, philosopher and one-time Secretary of State for the Colonies. "Lady Molesworth became the leader of all that was best in society of her day, the friend of kings and queens, and holding political salons of importance." (*Further Indiscretions by a Woman of No Importance* by Mrs. Stuart Menzies, London: E.P. Dutton & Co., 1918, p. 302.)
159 A cocotte was a fashionable prostitute; 'Mrs. Phoenix' was perhaps better known as Fanny Lear.
160 Probably Serjeant William Ballantine (1812-1887), who had acted for the plaintiff, Mr. Hooker, in the assault case in which Burnaby was the defendant, *Hooker vs. Burnaby*, in 1864.

gauze veils so their ~~faces~~ features could be easily discerned – the other three ladies were ugly and very fat, the ugliest of the party obese to a degree quite unknown in a London ball-room, and the Duchess of Westminster, Mrs. Hennike or Hannah Rothschild would have been fairies in comparison – It was a light and glorious night as I walked along the deck and gazed on the recumbent beauties, the 150 recruits were all engaged in singing songs about the number of Serbians they would slay and about the number of houris that awaited each true believer in the world to come. – The melody was occasionally varied by sounds from the other side of the deck. These emanated from the dogs which disturbed in their slumbers vented their annoyance by howling at frequent intervals. The 4 wives were all fast asleep beneath the awning, the sable eunuch ~~lying~~ lay at their feet, his ebon face contrasting strongly with the white dresses his mistresses wore. It was a picturesque scene. However things were not destined to go on so quietly. In the early morn the winds rose the waves tossed our bark to and fro – No longer the bellicose warriors sang songs relating to war and houris, a change had come over the spirit of the dream. Sounds suggestive of anything but martial enthusiasm broke upon the ears of the listeners. The first to succumb was the fattest of the Pasha's wives. Her head held tightly between the arms of the black eunuch (it was too big for him to encircle with his hands) was as Artemus Ward[161] would have said a caution to the snakes. The vessel backed – a heavier wave than usual had struck her, the sable attendant lost his balance and was precipitated on the hampers containing the dogs. They raised an angry growl. If they could have used their teeth they would have done so to some effect. As it was their fierce tones made the ebon mass of humanity rear itself up like a flash of greased lightning, but at that moment, there was another roll. His mistress ~~called~~ screamed to him, she ~~was~~ frantically called for assistance – the basin had fallen from her side – duty called the black gentleman but nature called too, the eunuch first rushed to the side of the vessel and ~~then in~~ a few seconds later he returned to ~~the side of~~ his mistress. Their faces were green. He held her head & she held the basin. I need say no more. Constantinople was at last reached, the winds had fallen, the sun shone bright in the heavens and on ~~one of the~~ a lovely morn we anchored in the world renowned Bosphorus. Here we first found how little difficulty is experienced with the officials whose duty it is to examine the passports. One of his hands was held out for <u>Baksheesh</u> the other for the document. A few extra coppers were given to this Official and the papers were returned to us unlooked at. The same free and easy system awaited us with our luggage and I soon found myself ensconced within the hospitable walls of this hotel. In the evening I

---

161 The *nom de plume* of Charles Farrar Browne (1834-1867), an American humour writer.

dined with Sir Henry Elliot,[162] – Admiral Drummond[163] who commands the fleet is staying with him. As far as I could make out their idea was that Russia is only blustering and that there will be no war. – There is not much love lost between the Russian and the English Embassies and Ignatieff[164] was represented as an Ananias of the first class.[165] In fact if all the stories told of this Russian gentleman are true, Ananias would be out of the hunt altogether. Everybody was very anxious to have the feeling in England about Russia and Constantinople and Mr. Gallenga[166] the Correspondent of the *Times* here, and Mr. Gahan [sic][167] the Correspondent of the *Daily News* – the 2 journals which, to a certain extent have sided with Russia were inveigled at very strongly. – In the morning I called upon Gallenga this *bête noir* of the British Embassy, he was very good natured and civil and has been of great use to me in giving me letters of introduction to various officials. Mrs. Gallenga soon who is with him, soon let the cat out of the bag as to the feud between her husband and the Embassy. It appeared that Gallenga not being able to obtain any information from the British Embassy procured it from the Russian Ambassador and certain people connected with the British Embassy were so foolish as to say that Gallenga was in the Russian pay. – Hence These remarks came to Mrs. Gallenga's ears and hence the row began. – I went a few days ago to the line of defence which it has been proposed to occupy with British troops in the event of a war and of a Russian advance upon Constantinople. The line extends from the Sea of Marmara to the Black Sea the position is immensely strong by nature, and almost impregnable save in the rear of the right flank about 2 miles from the Black Sea. Here the nature of the ground is not so favourable for defence. The position to be defended is not quite 20 miles in extent, and it would require 60,000 men for to defend hold this line, which as the crow flies is about 25 miles from Constantinople. The Turks are making great preparations for war and men are continually being sent on to the Balkans. Nothing however has been done as yet about throwing up works to defend the above mentioned important line of defence which is being carefully surveyed by some of our Engineer Officers. One thing is absolutely necessary – should it ever be determined to occupy the position – and that is the construction of a railway, for about nine miles, as a branch from the actual line of rails which runs from Constantinople along the shores of the Sea of Marmara. As the roads are now,

---

162 Sir Henry George Elliot (1817-1907) was a British diplomat, noted for his period as ambassador at Constantinople.
163 Admiral Edmund Charles Drummond (1841-1911) was a Royal Navy officer who went on to be Commander-in-Chief, East Indies Station.
164 Count Nikolay Pavlovich Ignatieff (1832-1908) was a Russian statesman and diplomat.
165 Ananias was the disciple of Jesus sent to restore the sight of Saul (Paul) and convert him to Christianity.
166 Antonio Carlo Napoleone Gallenga (1810-1895) was an Italian author and patriot.
167 Januarius Aloysius MacGahan (1844-1878) was an American journalist and war correspondent.

it would be impossible to get up stores without a railway, to the position to be defended and a short line such as should be made, would not cost more than 20,000. The railroad we constructed in the Crimea cost 200,000, but it would have been cheap at half a million if it had been made a month earlier. Lord Salisbury is expected here tomorrow and he is to be escorted into the Bosphorus by two steamers of our Ironclads. I breakfasted this morning with Schuyla [sic] the American Consul General and the Author of *Turkistan*[168]. We were a queer party. An American surgeon just arrived from Alescinato, Gallenga, Mr. White our Consul at I believe Bucharest, and George Sala the Correspondent of the *Daily Telegraph*, who had just arrived from Odessa via St. Petersburg & Moscow. He assured us that the Russians were are making immense preparations in the South of Russia and said that the Railway Stations were filled with troops and that everyone he spoke to with was full of martial ardour. – He thinks that there will be war and so does Schuyla, the latter on my asking him his reasons replied, "Why every one of the cusses at the Conference wants something which the other cusses won't allow and a tarnation fight will be the end of it", – Gallenga does not believe in war & no more do I for the matter of that – Wolf has been cried too loudly – and the little fire which has been kindled comes from damp wood it gives out a great deal of smoke, but I doubt whether it will this time immediately burst into flame. Our idiot of an Ambassador at St. Petersburg that wretched imbecile Lord Augustus Loftus[169] is – I am told – for England extending the right hand of friendship to Russia and joining her in the proposed dismemberment of Turkey. It will be a fatal day for England should such a step ever be taken by our rulers. For my own part though I am of the opinion that war will not break out immediately. I feel concerned that sooner or later we shall have to fight the ambitious Muscovites, and the sooner the better for we are not likely to have our army increased, and shall be no better prepared 5 years hence for the struggle than we are at present, whilst our foe is each day putting his forces into a greater state of efficiency. – Russia is on the verge of bankruptcy it is true, but no nation was ever prevented from going to war through lack of money, and money is not everything as the French found out in the Franco-German war. – I leave this on Friday for a long ride of more than 2000 miles through Asia Minor & all the way must be done on horseback. I mean later on to go to Erzeroum and Kars, so if you are not bored by the perusal of this long letter, write to me Poste Restante Erzuroum Turkey in Asia. I have bought five horses and am going with my English servant a Blue, and a Circassian whom I have engaged. The latter can only speak Turkish so I hope to make good progress in that language. – It will be a bitterly cold ride

---

168 Eugene Schuyler (1840-1890) was an American scholar, writer, explorer and diplomat.
169 Lord Augustus William Frederick Spencer Loftus GCB, PC (1817-1904) was a British diplomat and colonial administrator.

and for the greater part of the way the ground will be covered with snow. I mean to spend some time amongst the Kurds and to try and learn something about their customs and way of living. – I am also going to have a good look at the roads which lead from the Caucasus through Asia Minor to Soutane, very little is known of the country through which I shall travel so perhaps I may pick up a little information for our Military Authorities which in all probability will be pigeon holed as soon as it reaches London and will never reach the Duke. Good bye dear Lady Molesworth.

I have written you the prosiest of letters. Give my best love to Lord T, and to Hayward – Ask the latter if he would like a Circassian young lady – I am told that one can be bought for a few sheep. I am taking out some tins of Australian mutton with me which I mean to offer in exchange for a young lady Circassian belle and Believe me always, Yrs very sincerely, Fred Burnaby.

FGB108
Constantinople; 8 December 1876
Burnaby to unknown (extract) – *Mayfair*, **20 February 1877**
I am just about to start upon a journey overland – the whole way from Scutari to Erzeroum and Kars. I have bought five horses and engaged a Circassian servant; but he can speak nothing but Turkish, so I shall have to learn that language, *nolens volens*.[170] My party will consist of my English servant, the Circassian and myself. By the time I have finished my ride, I shall have got over more than 2000 miles, as the route is very circuitous. From Kars I shall probably turn south to Van, and afterwards see what the Kirghiz are doing. It will be a very rough journey and very cold, as the thermometer in January in Erzeroum is often 30° below zero. I expect to get over 30 miles a day, that is if the horses will stand the work; but they are not half as strong as the Kirghiz horses.

FGB109
Erzingan, Turkey; 2 February 1877
Burnaby to unknown (extract) – *Mayfair*, **6 March 1877**

Paradise Regained

We have been favoured by permission to publish the following extracts from a private letter from Captain Burnaby, addressed to a friend in London. It is dated 'Erzingan, Turkey in Asia, February 2nd, 1877', and reached London on Thursday night. It shows that the gallant captain is well advanced in his long and perilous ride through the unfrequented paths by the banks of the

170 Willy-nilly.

Euphrates:

All the way along the road I have met numbers of soldiers *en route* for Erzeroum and Kars – soldiers I mean only in name, as they have none of them received but two months' drill, and have no uniform or rifles. They are, however, to receive arms and clothes at Erzeroum. They are all in high spirits, and do not seem at all faint-hearted at leaving their homes; and the priests (Mullahs) who go with them sing out at intervals 'There is but one God, and he is great – the only God, and Mahomet is the prophet of God.' The recruits take up the strain, and keep on repeating it till the peasants in the neighbouring village hear the sounds, and re-echo them back over the mountains.

The people are everywhere very civil, but it has been a roughish ride over above 1,100 miles of chiefly snow-covered mountains, down slippery passes with precipices, and every sort of bedevilment. And now I am reaching Erzeroum, the supposed abode of our first parents, and I ride each day along the banks of the Euphrates, forward bound to Kars.

The people here are all convinced that the Conference will end in smoke, and that there will be war.[171] In fact, they are sanguine about victory, and say God is on their side. Poor deluded creatures! They forget Napoleon's saying that '*Le Dieu des victoires c'est le Dieu des Grandes bataillons*'.[172] Kars, Erzeroum, and Van will fall an easy prey to the Russian invader should he determine to cross the frontier, for the Turks have no officers, and, though the men are as brave as possible, brains are wanting to lead them to victory.

In the meantime all the stories about cruelty, torture, &c., on the part of the Turkish authorities to the Christians in Asia Minor are pure lies, and the government, though venal to the last degree, is not a cruel one. I am informed that the Russian consul at Erzeroum, who has *carte blanche* from his government, is intriguing amongst the Armenians in the event of a Russian advance in this direction.

I had a narrow escape of being suffocated the other evening in a village. The room in which I slept caught fire. The next apartment was inhabited by my host, and his two wives. I woke up in the middle of the night half suffocated by smoke, and called for assistance. No one came. It was a question of going into the harem, and arousing my host, or letting himself and his house be burnt down. I determined to make another endeavour to arouse the sleepers, so taking

---

171 The Constantinople Conference was held from 23 December 1876 to 20 January 1877, at which the Great Powers handed to Turkey a plan agreed among themselves for political reforms in Bosnia and those Ottoman territories with a majority Bulgarian population. The plan was formally rejected by the Ottoman Empire on 18 January, leading to the dissolution of the Conference. Failure to accept the proposed reforms led to the failure of the other Great Powers to support Turkey when war was declared on her by Russia later that year.
172 The God of victories is the God of the big battalions.

my revolver out, I fired two shots in the air. It was a comical sight. I did not go into the harem, but the harem came to me. Soon half the village arrived, and the flames were speedily extinguished.

The Armenian women are veiled just as closely as the Turkish females, and no man is hardly ever permitted to see their faces. 'I keep my wife for myself, and not for my friends', was the reply made by an Armenian who was interrogated as to why he did not introduce his wife.

It is bitterly cold, and my English servant is quite knocked up. Instead of looking after me I have to look after him.

FGB110
Erzeroum, Turkey; 8 February 1877
Burnaby to unknown (extract) – *The World*, February 1877

This place is close to the Garden of Eden. The thermometer is near to zero. If the weather was like this at the creation, Adam and Eve must have found it uncommon cold in fig leaves.

FGB111
Erzeroum, Turkey; 9 February 1877
Burnaby to unknown (extract) – *The Times*, 27 February 1877
(sent by Special Correspondent)

I have a letter from Captain Burnaby, dated Erzeroum, February 9th. Captain Burnaby arrived at Erzeroum on the 7th, after a long and very hard march through deep snow and over very high mountains, his route being made by Ismid, Angora, Yuzgat, Tokat, and Sivas, from which latter place he made a detour by Arabkir and Egin to Erzingan, and hence to Erzeroum. He describes the roads or rather tracks, for roads do not exist, as being in a fearful state, the spots where no snow was being quagmires with the mud 2ft. to 3ft. deep. The journey, however, has been an interesting one. The captain tells us he has visited Circassian, Tartar, Kurd, Turkoman, Armenian, and Greek villages, besides the Turkish, and he has had a fair opportunity of learning the actual state of affairs in that out-of-the-way part of the world. He found that the Armenians get on tolerably well with the Turkish authorities in all towns he went through, with the exception of Direcke; but, he adds, they are certainly bullied by the Turkish lower orders, who are in their turn bullied by the Circassians. Captain Burnaby attributes this to the prostrate and cowed disposition of the Armenians, who are not as ready with the cold steel as the Circassians. He seems to have no very high opinion of the Armenians, whom he describes as Christians only in name, and superstitious to the last degree. The fact, however, that their women are kept in similar bondage to the Mussulman women, and are usually shut up in the harem, admits of an easy explanation, for, wherever Armenian women are safe, as here in Constantinople or at Smyrna, and other large towns, the yasmak has been laid aside, and harem seclusion has ceased. Captain Burnaby has visited some of the prisons, and has taken care to come upon them unannounced, giving the authorities no time to prepare for his visit. He found very few Armenians among the prisoners, and witnessed no instances of torture or of cruel treatment of the inmates. He says that things at Erzeroum look very warlike, and everyone believes war imminent. He purposed, when he wrote, to leave Erzeroum on the following week, and proceed to Van, a twelve days' march over the mountains. From Van he intended to make his way through Bayazid, Kars and Ardahan to Batoum. His English servant was knocked up, and he had to get a fresh Turkish one, having been robbed by the Turkish attendant he had hired at Constantinople. Of his various adventures he will have not a little to tell when he gets back "all right", as is always the case with him, to his friends.

FGB112
Erzeroum, Turkey (The Garden of Eden); 11 February 1877
Burnaby to his mother (extract)

It has been a hard journey. Over 1800 miles, and all on horseback, through deep mud at first, and in some places up to the horses' girths. I stayed at Angora three days. Then on the track again; over mountains and crags, passing over ground that abounds with mineral wealth, and alas! left idly in the earth, till I reached Yusgat.

"Why do you not introduce your family to me?" I enquired one day of my host (an Armenian gentleman). "I keep my wife and daughter for myself, and not for my guests", was the reply. All through this part of the world the same custom exists. Poor Armenian women. They are indeed to be pitied. They receive no education whatever. What they do not know themselves, it is impossible to teach their children; the result is that the whole population, Christian as well as Mussulman, is steeped in the deepest slough of ignorance.

FGB113
Hoy, Persia; 2 March 1877
Burnaby to unknown (extract) – *Mayfair*, 17 April 1877

We have again been favoured by permission to publish extracts from a private letter received in London from Captain Burnaby, author of the 'Ride to Khiva'. It is dated 'Hoy, Persia, 26th February'. Its political significance is discussed in another column. The accompanying map will enable the reader to trace Captain Burnaby's route, which is marked by lines running thus:

> The Persians are very disappointed at the state of affairs. They were in hopes of war. They meant to join Russia and their idea was to get back Kotoor and all the territory which Turkey took from them forty years ago.

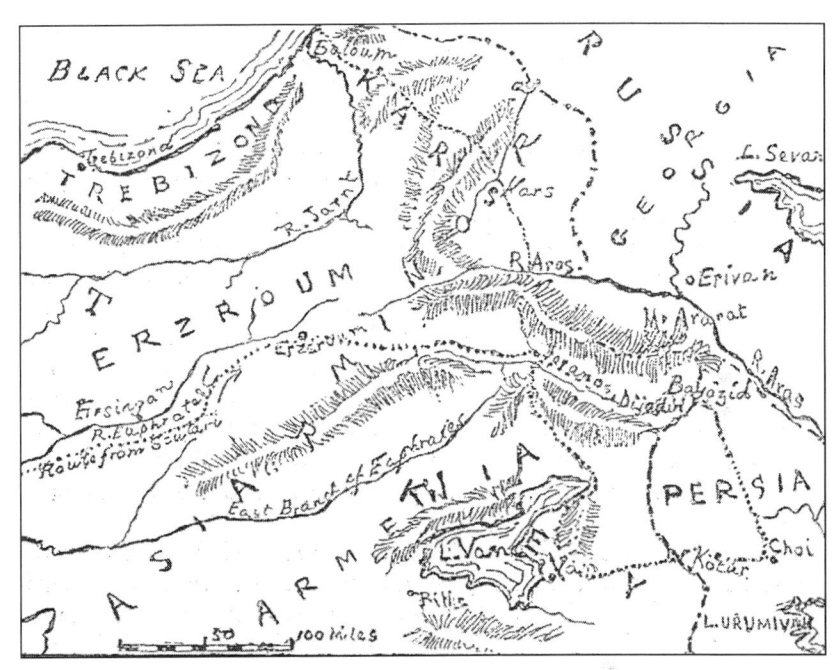

The region around Lake Van, 1876/7

They would, in all probability, have been disappointed, as Russia would have made use of them only as a cat's paw, and would have marched their troops through their territory to Van, when, in my opinion, all that part of Turkey, from Van through to Erzeroum, and thence east to Kars, would have fallen into the hands of the Russians. The Turks have no troops in Anatolia to stop them, and they could have done what they liked had the war begun. Fortunately, however, he has no money, and is afraid of Austria and ourselves.

It would be a serious thing for England if Russia were once to take Van, as then she would have another arm around Persia, and that Power would eventually fall, whilst Russia would extend herself to the Persian Gulf.

I have been living with the Yeseeds, or Devil-worshippers, a funny race of people divided into two sects; the one thinks that the Devil is the Almighty's grand vizier, the other his adviser. The priests of these people when they arrive in a village send for the prettiest girl; she is brought, and is considered highly honoured by the attention of the priest.

The Kurds, ancient Assyrians, are a fine race of men, and their chiefs live much as the Highlander did of old, by robbery and pillage. I stayed for a few days with one of those chiefs, and found him a very good sort of fellow, though rather savage at times.

Another Kurdish chief in the neighbourhood of Van has promised the Turkish

Government 20,000 men in the event of war, and has offered to arm them all at his own expense. Should war take place, and his offer be accepted, there will, I fancy, be a great deal of Bashi-Bazoukery.

The Armenians in Anatolia are a poor lot, more degraded than the Jews in Syria, and utterly given up to money-making. No wonder that the Turks despise the Christians after the specimens that they see around them.

Good-bye; I am going from here to Van, and thence to Kars, across the mountains, and so on to Batoum. I shall hope to see you in town about the end of April. By the time I arrive at Batoum I shall have ridden 2,000 miles, and brought my four horses, Inshallah (please God), all the way from Scutari.

SHN01[173]
House of Commons; 5 March 1877
Northcote to Ponsonby
Sir Stafford Northcote presents his humble duty to the Queen.

The chief business of the House of Commons this evening has been the introduction of the Army Estimate. Mr. Hardy's speech has been very well received, and there do not appear to be any difficulties.

A question was raised by Mr. Grant Duff, before the House went into Committee, with regard to Capt[ain] Burnaby's having been recalled by a telegram from HRH the Duke of Cambridge when he was on his celebrated "Ride to Khiva" in the winter of 1875. Mr. Grant Duff asked whether it was true that such a telegram had been sent, and whether it was sent at the request of the Russian Government. Mr. Hardy replied that it had been sent, not at the request of the Russian Government, but at the wish of the Foreign Office, it being thought at the time that there were reasons which rendered it undesirable that an English officer should travel in Central Asia, and should arouse jealousy. Mr. Goschen made some sarcastic remarks on this answer, observing that if a Liberal Government had taken such a step they would have been charged with truckling to Russia.

It seems not impossible that the question, which is one entirely belonging to the Foreign Office, may be brought forward again.

HFP01[174]
Windsor Castle; 6 March 1877
Ponsonby to Northcote
General Ponsonby in humbly returning Sir Stafford Northcote's letter cannot understand the difficulty about Captain Burnaby.

He had not leave to travel in Khiva and therefore disobeyed orders in going

---

173 RA/VIC/MAIN/B/28/20.
174 RA/VIC/MAIN/B/28/21.

there.

This is sufficient reason for recalling him.

But the anxiety to get him back certainly requires a little explanation. The Foreign Office objected to his going there, and Colonel Wellesley[175] was indignant at him slipping past as he did.

FGB114
Regent's Park Barracks; 21 April 1877
Burnaby to Houghton
Dear Lord Houghton. With great pleasure. Yrs vy sincerely, Fred Burnaby

FGB115
Regent's Park Barracks; 27 April 1877
Burnaby to Stafford House Committee
In the course of my recent travels through Asia Minor, I visited several Turkish military hospitals, and conversed with the surgeons in charge. They often complained to me of the great scarcity of drugs, and said the authorities at Constantinople found it impracticable to supply many of the necessary specific medicines and surgical instruments, all of which have to be obtained in Europe.

If people in this country could only realize to themselves the sufferings which the wounded will undergo when being operated upon without chloroform and with worn-out surgical instruments, I think they would willingly subscribe to the Stafford House Fund.

The soldiers from the southern part of Anatolia suffer very much from the change of climate, and are utterly unsupplied with warm underclothing. Many a time I have met battalions of Redifs on the march, the men with bare feet and wading through deep snow while the thermometer stood at zero. Many were frost-bitten on the march to Erzeroum and Kars. A supply of warm stockings and flannel shirts and blankets would save thousands of lives.

FGB116[176]
St. John's Wood Barracks; 17 May 1877
Burnaby to Corry
Dear Corry.[177] Do you think that you could procure for me any of the reports of our Consuls at Angora & Scutari during the last 6 or 7 years. I want some

---

175 Lieut.-Colonel the Hon. Frederick Arthur Wellesley (1844-1931), of the Coldstream Guards, who was Military Attaché to the British Embassy at St. Petersburg.
176 Courtesy of the Bodleian Libraries, University of Oxford, Special Collections: Hughenden papers BXXI/142-1404 (ff. 137/8).
177 Montagu William Lowry-Corry, 1st Baron Rowton (1838-1903), was a British philanthropist and public servant, best known for serving as Lord Beaconsfield's (Benjamin Disraeli's) private secretary from 1866 until the latter's death in 1881. He was highly regarded by Queen Victoria.

padding for my book – if there are any reports from our Consuls relating to Russian misrule in the Caucasus they w^d be very useful.

I think Lord Derby's[178] answer to the R[ussian] Declaration of War is capital. I only hope we shall not find it all smoke but that there will be a little fire from that sleeping animal the British lion before long. Yours very truly, Fred Burnaby.

TGB01
London; 11 June 1877
Bowles to the Prince of Wales (extract)
It is impossible I can avoid seeing that this is not an isolated case, but one of many beginning four years ago, by which your Royal Highness has shown a feeling of personal animosity towards me for which I am at a loss to account. And I cannot refrain from recalling here the conversations which in previous years your Royal Highness has had with Captain Burnaby in which you have intimated to him your opinion that he would do well to cease to be what for many years he has been, my intimate friend.[179]

FGB117[180]
St. John's Wood Barracks; 5 October 1877
Burnaby to Beaconsfield
Dear Lord Beaconsfield, I have taken the liberty to forward you a copy of my last book which I hope you will accept, from yrs very sincerely, Fred Burnaby.

BD01
~~10 Downing Street~~ **Brighton; 15 October 1877**
Beaconsfield to Burnaby
Dear Captain Burnaby, I am reading your book with much interest, & I think everybody will do the same. The subject is … [Fragment only survives.]

DWF01
London; [30] October 1877
Freshfield to Editor – *The Times*, **31 October 1877**
The circulation which, from their merit as spirited narratives, Captain Burnaby's

---

178 Edward Henry Stanley, 15th Earl of Derby (1826-1893) was a British statesman who served as Secretary of State for Foreign Affairs twice, from 1866 to 1868 and from 1874 to 1878. After the Declaration of War by Russia on Turkey on 24 April 1877, he warned the Russian Government that any attempt by Russia to blockade the Suez Canal, launch an attack on Egypt, occupy Constantinople, or alter the existing arrangements for the navigation of the Bosphorus or the Dardanelles might compel England to abandon her neutrality.
179 Quoted in Leonard E. Naylor, *The irrepressible Victorian, the story of Thomas Gibson Bowles* (London: Macdonald, 1965), pp. 50-1.
180 Courtesy of the Bodleian Libraries, University of Oxford, Special Collections: Hughenden papers BXXI/142-1405 (ff. 139/40).

books deservedly obtain, and the importance attributed to them as political evidence by a portion of the public Press, render the nature of the statements put forward in them [a] matter of public importance.

I trust, therefore, that you will allow me the use of your columns to respond to a challenge conveyed by Captain Burnaby through one of his Caucasian informants in his recent work 'On Horseback through Asia Minor' (vol. I., p. 250): – "Tell your countrymen to travel through our country – that is, if the Russians will let them – to go to our villages and talk to the country-people, but not in the presence of Russians ... then let them form an opinion about the merits of the case." I went to the Caucasus in 1868, two years only after the last revolt with strong anti-Russian prepossessions. I travelled through the mountains, in districts where no Russian was met for weeks, and though I did not penetrate far among the Black Sea tribes, I had for companion a competent Mingrelian interpreter,[181] who had himself previously lived in and travelled through Abkasia with an English Consul and was always ready to recount his adventures. I have since supplemented my personal experience by communication with other travellers, German and English, and by the study of every book on the Caucasus I could lay hands on, especially the writings of such Circassian sympathisers as Mr. Gifford Palgrave[182] and Mr. Bell. From the knowledge thus acquired I am convinced that since in 1838 the stern choice between submission and abandonment of their ancestral practices of making border forays and kidnapping human beings and removal to the banks of the Kouban or into Turkey was first offered to the mountaineers, there has been no want of efforts on the part of Russia to make them accept the former alternative, and that her policy – in the words of an English Ambassador at St. Petersburg – 'though unrelenting, has not been deliberately sanguinary'. It is only just to add, what in more than one passage Captain Burnaby would seem to have forgotten, that so far from showing any fear "lest Englishman should travel through the Caucasus and discover their method of dealing with the Circassians", the Russian authorities have from 1868 up to the present year afforded travellers all the facilities in their power for visiting the most remote corners of the Circassian Provinces.

The greater part of the hearsay stories about Russians or Armenians repeated by Captain Burnaby are probably not intended for, and are certainly quite unworthy of, serious notice. But he brings forward with some show of evidence and much emphasis of type two grave charges against the Russians which call for close investigation.

---

181 Mingrelians are a sub-ethnic group of Georgians, who mostly live in the Samegrelo region of Georgia.
182 William Gifford Palgrave (1826-1888) was, at various times, a soldier, traveller, Roman Catholic priest and Arabic scholar.

The first is a statement founded on a despatch sent from Soukhoum Kalé on the 17th of March, 1864 by Consul Dickson, and received in London the 17th of May, announcing that at a village on the Soubash river men, children and women with child had been, after surrender, killed by a Russian detachment belonging to Count Yevdokimov's army, and predicting, in consequence, a desperate resistance of the tribes. Consul Dickson was living about a hundred miles from the spot where the slaughter is supposed to have occurred, and gives no clue to the manner in which the details came to his knowledge. There is however further evidence in the case.

Captain Burnaby can hardly have failed to notice that the same batch of Parliamentary papers from which be extracted Consul Dickson's report contains a detailed account of the movements of each detachment of Count Yevdokimoff's troops taken from the *Journal de St. Petersburg* of the 19th of May. From this account it would seem that no Russian column even approached the Soubash until the 31st of March (new style), and that the elders of the principal tribes in their submission to the Grand Duke a fortnight later. From the dates it is impossible that this account could have been framed with any reference to the Consul's charge. A Consul is, as everyone who has been in the East knows, much at the mercy of bazaar gossip for distant news; a military report is seldom falsified without purpose. It is for Captain Burnaby to explain why he has ignored the latter document, which deserved at least, I think, the respect of refutation.

The second charge is contained in the following passage, which has been copied in newspapers and widely circulated throughout England: – "Among other ways of compelling the Circassians to submit to their conquerors was one so fiendish that if proof were not at hand to confirm the statement I should hesitate to place it before the reader. In order to frighten the mountaineers and civilize them *a la Russe*, the Czar's soldiers cut off the heads and scooped out the eyes of several men, women, and children; then nailing the eyeless heads on trees, they placed placards underneath them, saying, 'Go now and complain to the Kralli of the English and ask her to send you an oculist.'"

An Englishman, Mr. Stewart Rolland of Dibden, Hants, has travelled in Circassia. He can authenticate my statement. One of these blood-stained placards is in his possession. He will show it to anyone who wishes to see for himself a proof of Russian civilisation.

Of this reference I have availed myself, and I think it is only right the public who are now reading Captain Burnaby's book should know with what result. I must, however, in the first, offer my sincere thanks to Mr. Stewart Rolland for the very prompt, frank, and full manner in which he has responded to my enquiries.

It appears that in 1862 two Circassian chiefs came to England to seek assistance against Russia. At the Foreign Office they found no encouragement, but in other quarters they were warmly received. Mr. Rolland accompanied them in a provincial tour, and spoke in their favour at public meetings, enlarging at once on the wickedness of Russia and the "high treason" of Lord Palmerston, who be considered ought to have been replaced by the late Mr. Urquhart. A committee, presided over by Mr. Edmond Beales, was formed to assist the Circassians, but failed to turn sympathy into subscriptions. Mr. Holland, however, subsequently went back with the Circassian delegates to their own country, and following in the steps of Mr. Urquhart and Mr. Spencer, concerted with them a plan of revolt in furtherance of which on his return to England he despatched a vessel laden with arms and ammunition to the Circassians, which reached its destination in safety. We now come to the point of the story.

In the Spring of 1863 after his return to England Mr. Rolland received from Constantinople, through a certain Sefir Bey, three pieces of rough paper, bearing inscriptions in bad Turkish to the effect given above. Two have been lent and lost, but one he still possesses. The narrative of the circumstances under which they were found came through the same Sefir Bey. This individual was a Circassian noble who after an education in the Russian Fort of Anapa, and a youth spent in military service in Egypt, returned to his native land to marry, and having been subsequently (about 1830) commissioned by the Circassian chiefs to proceed to Constantinople to look after their interests, preferred to reside on the shores of the Bosphorus, drawing heavy contribution from his countrymen, while his wife and children were left in a state of penury at home. His character is thus described by Mr. Oliphant in 1856, "Sefir Pasha is a Circassian by birth, but he has been in Turkish employ long enough to have acquired a taste for political intrigue, and the art of replenishing his purse and satisfying his private schemes of ambition at the expense of those he thinks he has a right to subject to such treatment. The Circassians as yet are too unsophisticated to have discovered this," &c.

No date has been given to me for the commission of the fiendish acts more precise than the spring of 1863, and the massacre is vaguely described as having been committed at two villages "in the Abasek country not far from Ghelendjik" a port in reality far distant from the nearest spot in the Abasek country. Nor is any light thrown on how the placards travelled from the Caucasus to Constantinople, if they ever did so travel. Such is the proof of the correctness of Captain Burnaby's statement placed before me by the gentlemen to whom the Captain's readers are referred for confirmation of it.

It must be added that although the Circassian Committee already mentioned was in full activity, and had a most energetic head in Mr. Edmond Beales, as well as an organ ready to welcome any stories telling against Russia in the *Free Press*, this tale seems never to have been put before the public until after a lapse of 14 years it was thought worthy of notice by Captain Burnaby.

That the simple enthusiasm of Mr. Rolland should have led him, like the "unsophisticated Circassian", to put implicit faith in Sefir Bey we can easily understand. But Captain Burnaby has a keen sense of the worthlessness of hearsay evidence in the East, as he shows elsewhere in his book in a case where Moslems were the aggressors (vol. II. p.17). An Armenian relates an insult offered to the symbol of Christianity. "This is very horrible" I remarked, "did you see it yourself?" "No, but I heard of it." "Who told you?" "A man in Arabkir." "Had he seen it?" "No, he had not been in Malattia, but he had been told the story." "We are in the East," I observed to my host, "and it appears to me that you Christians are very much given to exaggeration."

Captain Burnaby must surely be in a position to supply the missing link and to trace the placards beyond Constantinople and Sefir Bey. Otherwise he would never have thought of passing on to his readers as an incontestable fact a story which as it stands is, to say the least of dubious origin. He has made this story a text for frequent allusions throughout his book, to the political portion of which it forms, as it were, the keystone and he will, no doubt, welcome an opportunity to remedy his oversight and complete his evidence.

I make these enquiries not from any love of Russia, but in the interest of historical truth. I shall be glad, for Captain Burnaby's sake, if he can prove that he has not in some of his fiercest and most positive accusations been blinded and led away by political passion. It is far from my wish or intention at any time to attempt a general justification of Russia's dealings with subject or neighbouring races. She has probably done many harsh and some cruel acts elsewhere than in Poland. But even a criminal has a right to a fair trial. For the sake of English common sense, not to say of English honour and honesty, let the charges against her be investigated as impartially as those brought against Turkey have been. Let us have witnesses; who show candour, accuracy of statement and some little critical insight, and above suspicion of being influenced by petty personal spites. Finally, when we have given atrocities on both sides their due weight, let us remember there are broader grounds on which Governments must eventually be judged; that, although to restrain its agents and subjects from needless bloodshed in times of war and revolt is part of the duty of a civilized State, it is very far from its whole duty. If every Government which occasionally fails in this respect is to be condemned as uncivilized, what country will be found to deserve the title? Let Turkey have all the advantages she may gain by this admission; and then let her system of government and that of Russia be dispassionately judged by their fruits during the last century. To do this may require some little mental effort, but those who will not so far exert themselves have no right to the opinion, which society loves to express in the easy common-place "*Arcades ambo*", "barbarians both".

FGB118
Marlborough Club; 31 October 1877
Burnaby to Editor – *The Times*, 1 November 1877

Sir, You have allowed Mr. Freshfield to comment in a column of your valuable space upon some Russian atrocities mentioned in "On Horseback through Asia Minor". Will you permit me to reply in a few lines to his criticism? Referring to vol. I., page 250, of the work in question, my would-be critic quotes the following remarks made by a Circassian:–

"Tell your countrymen to travel through our country – that is, if the Russians will let them – to go tour villages and talk to the country people, but not in the presence of Russians ... then let them form an opinion about the merits of the case."

Mr. Freshfield, in the above quotation, purposely omits these words, "as the poor sufferers would be afraid to speak, knowing well the fate which would await them when their questioners had departed." My critic remarks that in 1868 he went to the Caucasus accompanied by an interpreter, and is convinced that since 1838 the policy of Russia though unrelenting, has not been deliberately sanguinary. Mr. Freshfield states that his companion was a Mongrelian. Now some Mingrelians hold official positions in Russia, and it is not likely that the country people in the Caucasus would dare to speak about their sufferings to a man who might be a paid spy.

My critic next complains that in giving *in extenso* Consul Dickson's report to Earl Russell about the massacre of two Circassian women in an advanced state of pregnancy and of five small children by the Russian troops, I have not added an extract from the *Journal de St. Petersburg* in which it is affirmed that there was no Russian column at the place where Consul Dickson reports the massacre to have been committed. Mr. Freshfield may be a believer in Russian journalists and prefer their statements to an official report from a British Consul. I must say that, for my part, I prefer the simple word of an English gentleman. Here Mr. Freshfield and I may differ in opinion.

The next thing my critic finds fault with are some remarks in which Mr. Rolland's name is mentioned. I shall leave it to Mr. Rolland to reply to him about this matter.

Mr. Freshfield appears to believe that since the year 1838 the Russians have changed their skins. Let me ask him, then, to entreat Mr. Gladstone to accept the challenge conveyed to the author of the pamphlet entitled the "Bulgarian Horrors", in page 286 of the second volume of my book. The question whether the Russian officers and soldiers have become less brutal since the year 1838, which Mr. Freshfield seems to think the turning point of Russian barbarism, will then be definitely settled. In conclusion, let me suggest to Mr. Freshfield that the next time he travel in a foreign country with the object of obtaining information it might be as well if he were to learn the language and dispense with an interpreter.

I have the honour to remain, Sir, your most obedient servant, Fred Burnaby.

EB01
London; 1 November 1877
Beales to Editor – *The Times*, 2 November 1877
Sir,–Mr. Freshfield, in his communication published in *The Times* of yesterday, refers to me as presiding over the Circassian Committee formed in 1862 for the purpose of enlisting public sympathy in favour of the Circassians, then struggling for their independence against Russia, and I think it right to make the following statement in support of the reason he gives for questioning the truth of one of the grave charges brought by Captain Burnaby, in his recent work "On Horseback through Asia Minor", against the Russians in their dealings with the Circassians.

I was in frequent communication with the Circassian Chiefs who came as delegates to this country in 1862. They had much to tell of the ill-treatment of their countrymen by the Russians, but nothing of the nature of the horrible tale published by Captain Burnaby. In the course of 1863 the committee endeavoured to obtain from all other reliable sources the best information on the subject of the Russo-Circassian struggle and most assuredly if they had received any hint even of such a frightful atrocity as that imputed to the Russians by Captain Burnaby, they would have availed themselves of so powerful a means of exciting a warm and indignant interest in favour of the cause they espoused.

I have no recollection of any notice of such a tale before I read Mr. Freshfield's letter.

I am, Sir, your obedient servant, Edmond Beales.

SER01
Erskine Lodge; [2] November 1877
Rolland to Editor – *The Times*, 3 November 1877
Sir,–As my name has been dragged into your columns by Mr. Freshfield, and as I am called on by Captain Burnaby to answer, I very unwillingly trouble you with a few remarks, requesting the favour of your inserting them.

When Captain Burnaby's book appeared, one paragraph in it, inserted by him with my permission, caused me to receive many letters of inquiry. To all these I replied as well as I was able, and among others to Mr. Freshfield. I sent that gentleman some matter previously published, which he was naturally at liberty to use. It comprised documents relating to Circassia, and also a sentence of a speech I delivered at Macclesfield, substantially the same as Captain Burnaby's paragraph. But I never gave permission to Mr. Freshfield to publish or quote from my private letters, which, as usual among gentlemen, I considered confidential.

Mr. Freshfield has not only done this, but he has garbled and falsified the sense of what I did write. I never told him that I put implicit faith in Sefir Bey, nor did I tell him that the narrative came from Sefir Bey.[183] I never said that I laid before Mr. Freshfield "a proof" of the correctness of Captain Burnaby's statement, as he says I did. I said to him that I do believe in the authenticity of the placards. This belief is shared by some of the best living Orientalists from certain internal evidence. I invited Mr. Freshfield to come here and see for himself, and I told him I would not take the trouble of walking across my room to convince anyone who doubted. Possibly this is what he calls "my simple enthusiasm". If it were worthwhile, the placards, even now, after the lapse of 14 years, could with some trouble be distinctly authenticated. I am not disposed to undertake this task to please or convince a man whose conduct in commenting on the contents of private and unpublished letters does not command my respect. In my last reply to him I gave him the grounds why, when asked formerly to exhibit them about the country, I had refused to do so. I held then, as I do now, that the recital of an act of cruelty may be used to illustrate a political subject; but that the public exhibition of blood-stained placards would be an unworthy way of supporting a cause which I consider sacred, as it is that of a handful of brave men defending their country's independence to the last.

I am, Sir, your obedient servant, Stewart Erskine Rolland, Dibden-lodge, Hants.

FGB119
St. John's Wood Barracks; 2 November 1877
Burnaby to Editor – *The Times*, 3 November 1877

Sir, –Mr. Edmond Beales, in a letter published by you this morning, remarks that he presided over the Circassian Committee formed in 1862, and that he has no recollection of the Russian act of brutality to which Mr. Freshfield refers. Mr. Beales does not say whether he has at any time travelled in the Caucasus. Mr. Stewart Rolland, my authority for the statement to which your correspondents allude, has, I know, spent several months with the Circassians. He is a gentleman of high social position and education and not a simple enthusiast, as Mr. Freshfield would seem to believe. Mr. Edmond Beales declares that he has "no recollection of any notice of such a tale". Mr. Stewart Rolland, who gave me the information, and who read the proof-sheets relating

---

183 Sefir (or Sefer) Bey Zan (?-1859), a Shapsugh by origin, was the chief intermediary between the British Embassy in Constantinople and the Circassians during the latter part of the Russo-Circassian War of 1817-1864. He later became an important leader of the Circassian military forces. See Kadir I. Natho *The Russo-Turkish War* http://www.circassianworld.com/russo_circassian_war.html [accessed 12 April 1884].

to this Russian atrocity before my book, "On Horseback through Asia Minor", went to press, remembers it perfectly. I pin my faith upon Mr. Stewart Rolland's memory, and not upon Mr. Edmond Beales's failure to recollect.

I have the honour to remain, Sir, your obedient servant, Fred Burnaby.

DWF02
London; [4] November 1877
Freshfield to Editor – *The Times*, 5 November 1877

Sir, –I shall reply very briefly to Captain Burnaby's personal remarks, and only in so far as they misrepresent facts. I do not know whether the author of "On Horseback through Asia Minor" has, any more than Mr. Beales, been in the Caucasus; he has apparently read very little about it. If he ever reads or travels more about this region, he will probably discover that something besides open ears is needed in the East to obtain information worth retailing, and he will certainly find that in the recesses of "the mountain of languages" even a linguist like himself could hardly travel at all without an interpreter, and would certainly learn very little if he did. He may further ascertain, whenever he has time, what my interpreter's antecedents were; that, he came to me full of anti-Russian ideas from the household of one of the ablest men in the English service, then resident in Turkey, Mr. Gifford Palgrave, and that, as a fact, the Caucasians frequently discussed with us Russian rule and opened their grievances without the least reserve.

I did not, and I will not – for I believe the accusation would be unfair – accuse Captain Burnaby of any purpose in omitting the, as it happens, all important words, "on the Soobash river" in quoting in his text the report of Consul Dickson, given verbatim in the appendix. He would have consulted discretion as well as courtesy by imitating my reserve. To an unimpassioned reader it can hardly be necessary to explain that I left out the words he has supplied because, as my interviews with Caucasians occurred many miles from any Russian, they were not at all to the point.

It is now time for me to bring this matter to a practical conclusion by making of Captain Burnaby the demand which his book and letter justify.

With respect to the first of the two charges to which you have allowed me to call attention, Captain Burnaby admits that the choice lies between believing a British Consul to have been misinformed as to events at a distance, or believing the official Russian report of the plan of the campaign to have been palpably and purposelessly falsified in all its details and dates. Of course Captain Burnaby is at liberty to prefer the latter belief; but he has no longer any right to suppress all mention of any difficulty in taking this view. In support of the second charge Captain Burnaby has not a word to say; he throws the whole weight of defence on Mr. Rolland. That gentleman has, as I believe, frankly told me all he knows, and he has stated that it is his firm belief in the wickedness of

Russia that makes him believe in this "atrocity", and that he would not "walk across the room" to convince those who do not share his prepossessions. All that Mr. Rolland now adds is that living Orientalists believe in the authenticity of the placards. No one disputes that they are authentically Oriental.

In this matter Captain Burnaby does not yet seem to have realized his responsibility. He has lent the weight of his name and position as a writer and an officer to a terrible charge which he declines, when challenged, to substantiate. Such a position is not to be escaped from by a few empty sarcasms covering a total evasion of the main issue. As a matter of honesty and fair dealing, I call upon Captain Burnaby, in any future edition of his book, to withdraw or qualify the language he has used in commenting on these "atrocities", and to tell the whole truth as to the evidence concerning them.

I am, Sir, yours obediently, Douglas W. Freshfield

DWF03
6 Stanhope Gardens; [6] November 1877
Freshfield to Editor – *The Times*, 7 November 1877

Sir, –A personal charge of breach of confidence, as well as that of garbling and falsifying the information given me, has been made against me by Mr. Rolland. I must therefore ask of you the favour of inserting the following statement:– In reply to a question of Mr. Rolland's as to the object of my inquiries, told him that I meant to make use of his information for the purpose of commenting on Captain Burnaby's book. I posted this letter more than a week before I wrote to you, and Mr. Rolland raised no objection in the interval. I call upon Mr. Rolland, if he proposes to make any further comment on my conduct, to produce the whole correspondence which has passed between us, including his letter of the 1st of November. As to Mr. Rolland's second accusation, I have to say that I have done my best to reconcile the various statements placed before me and to tell the story as Mr. Rolland believes it. If, as is possible, I have failed in any respect, or if, as is also possible, Mr. Rolland now wishes to correct the facts as given me (he stated the year of the massacre differently on October 10 and 14) let him come forward and tell his own story. My only wish is that the whole truth should be told. I much regret if any expression of mine has given pain to Mr. Rolland or induced him to withhold that information which I asked as a member of the public, and which, by the use he has allowed Captain Burnaby to make of his name Mr. Rolland has pledged himself to give.

I am, Sir, yours obediently, Douglas W. Freshfield.

FGB120
St. John's Wood Barracks; [6] November 1877
Burnaby to Editor – *The Times*, 7 November 1877

Sir, –Mr. Freshfield again writes to you in reference to some paragraphs in 'On

Horseback through Asia Minor'. After what has passed between the aforesaid gentleman and Mr. Stewart Rolland – an account of which appeared in *The Times* of last Saturday – it is unnecessary for me to take any more notice of Mr. Freshfield or trespass any longer on your valuable space.

RMM01
[Fryston Hall]; November 1877
Lord Houghton to Henry Bright (extract)
Sumner speaks of me amiably, which is more than I do of him. I like Burnaby very much, but think his book over-praised. The truth is people are amazed at anything but the merest commonplace coming from a soldier, especially a Lifeguardsman!

FGB121
Sofia; 2 December 1877
Burnaby to Editor – *Morning Post***, 3 December 1877**
On Wednesday and Thursday some hard fighting ensued on the Russians attacking Mehemet Ali. He, however, succeeded in driving them back from the positions they had gained, threatening the line of redoubts on the Camarli Pass and Camarli Heights.

FGB122
Sofia; [3] December 1877
Burnaby to Stafford House Committee –
*The Times***, 27 December 1877**
The following communication has been received from Colonel Burnaby:

> Gentlemen,– I have the honour to report to you that I arrived at Adrianople last week and visited the hospital which is under the supervision of the Stafford-house surgeons now stationed in that town. The hospital forms part of what was formerly a very large cavalry barrack. This has been vacated by the troops. Part of the building has been given to the Stafford-house surgeons, and the remainder is used by the Turkish authorities as a hospital under the direction of their own medical men. There were 1,400 patients in all, of whom 260 were attended to by three surgeons, and by one assistant-surgeon, all sent out by the Stafford-house Committee.
> You will be glad to hear that every attention is being paid to the wounded. The wards are clean, lofty, and well-ventilated. The food supplied is of good quality, and there was an expression of pleasure which passed over the poor sufferers' countenances as the English surgeons walked around the wards and inquired after each man's ailment. I conversed with several of the patients, and they expressed their hearty gratitude to the subscribers to the Stafford-house Fund – the 'Inglis',

as the wounded men termed them – who had sent out such skilful and kind practitioners. I inquired of the medical men if any difficulty was placed in their way with reference to surgical operations, &c., by the Turkish authorities. I was assured that this was not the case. In no instance had any opposition been made to the performance of an operation, provided that the wounded man himself (the most interested individual) was a consenting party. In several instances the Turkish surgeons had called on the Stafford-house medical men to amputate in that part of the building which is set aside for the Turkish hospital – thus freely acknowledging that the Englishmen were more skilful operators than the Turks themselves.

Dr. Sandwith, one of the English surgeons, had recently visited the district between Tirnova and Karabunar. He had there attended to several Turkish and Jewish women and children who bad been wounded during this war. One Jewess had been ravished by 16 Cossacks. I was informed, that there were 2,600 women and children – the former the widows of massacred Turks – in the Kezanlik district. Many of these poor creatures are destitute of any means of sustenance.

From Adrianople I proceeded to Philippopolis. In that town I met Captain Fife[-Cookson], Her Majesty's Military Attaché in this part of Turkey. Our conversation turned upon the events which have recently happened in Eski Saghra. He informed me that he had questioned a missionary who was in that place as to what had occurred there. The reverend gentleman replied to a question as to whether the Russians had committed any atrocities in the town – 'No; but the Bulgarians were let loose, and they did so.' Captain Fife had also visited Kechi Dere, near Kezanlik. Here some Turkish women had been seized by the Cossacks. The trousers of the ladies had been taken from them, and the victims were then told that their nether clothing would not be restored until such time as they consented to be baptized and embraced Christianity. Now, if there is one part of her body which a Turkish woman dislikes to be exposed more than her face, it is her legs, and, frightened at the outrages perpetrated upon them, several of the females consented to become Christians. Their trousers were then restored, and the ladies were marched in rear of a military band to a Bulgarian church, and there publicly baptized by the priest. In the meantime the mosque in the village had been burnt to the ground.

I next arrived at Philippopolis. Here there is only one Stafford-house surgeon, as Dr. Eccles, the other doctor, has been lately invalided to Constantinople. There are a great many wounded men in this town; 75 of them are looked after by the Stafford-house surgeon to whom I have referred. He has more work to do than he can properly perform, and the sooner he has some more assistance the better. The hospital was not so well ventilated as could be desired, and a very disagreeable smell could be perceived in some parts of the building. This was owing to the bad construction of the edifice, the water-closets being next to the principal ward. Many of the patients were suffering from typhoid fever. You can understand the rest. I was informed by the surgeon that this defect in the building arrangements was about to be remedied.

I arrived in this town, Sofia, yesterday, and today visited the Stafford-house wards. The wounded men have every attention paid to them; they are as well looked after and cared for as they would be in any London hospital. There are altogether 150 patients, who are attended to by the Stafford-house medical gentlemen. Wounded men, however, are passing in every day, and if there were three times as many surgeons there would be more work than they could do. I append to this letter a communication from Mr. Master, who is special agent for Lady Burdett Coutt's Fund. Her subscription list, like your own, has every right to invite the sympathy of the British public. In conclusion, I may mention that when at Philippopolis I made the acquaintance of Dr. Smith, of the Red Crescent. He was in Plevna a few weeks ago. Now, it has been publicly stated that Osman Pasha had behaved in a barbarous manner towards his wounded countrymen. I have Dr. Smith's authority for saying that it was impossible for Osman Pasha, taking into consideration the circumstances under which he found himself, to have treated the matter from merely a medical point of view, and that the General to the best of his ability alleviated the distress of the sick and invalid soldiers. It appears there was some little misunderstanding between the Turkish commander and one of his visitors. The latter thought that Osman Pasha had not shown him proper courtesy, as he had not been offered coffee. The real fact was, that Osman Pasha had very little, if any coffee for himself, much less for all his self-invited guests.

There is a great deal of excitement in Sofia at present, as the Russians are said to be in force about 24 miles from here, before Kamarli. This town is not fortified in any way, and should the enemy succeed in forcing Mehemet Ali Pasha's lines at Kamarli, there will be nothing between the Russians and Adrianople. The result of all this is an exodus of many of the inhabitants. The banker has announced that after to-day he can cash no more checks, as all his gold is to be sent to Constantinople. He is afraid lest the Russians might requisition some of his safes. Several hundred Circassian families from the neighbourhood of Orkhranie are migrating further south. Many of these people have literally nothing with which to feed their wives and little ones. The consequence of this has been that some robberies of food and wearing apparel have taken place, unaccompanied, however, by any violence to the owners. It is a piteous sight to see the women and children wading through the deep mud which is on the road between this and Tatar Bazardjik. I have had an opportunity of speaking to some of the men. They bitterly curse the invaders who have produced all this misery. 'They are not satisfied with driving us out of our own country and murdering our women', observed one of my informants, 'but they follow us even here, where we have been offered shelter by the Turks.' I think if the gentlemen who has been styled the Divine Figure of the North could only see all the horrors he has caused, his conscience might suffer some few pangs of remorse. It may naturally be supposed, this town being so close to the Russian outposts, spies abound here. Five were hanged this morning, compromising documents having been found on their persons. Indeed, I am assured that the culprits did not attempt to deny their guilt. Should the Turkish lines be forced, and Mehemet Ali's army have to retreat, the Turkish population in Sofia will have everything to fear from the Christian inhabitants of the town; indeed, the latter do not hesitate to say that they will pay off the Turks on the first opportunity for hanging the five spies in question. Judging from the fearful reprisals that have already taken place in the Kezanlik district, this is not at all impossible. I have the honour to remain, yours obediently, Fred. Burnaby.

FGB123
Camarli; [4] December 1877
Burnaby to Editor – *Morning Post*, 5 December 1877

There is fighting every day. The Russians attach vigorously, but are repulsed on each occasion.

FGB124
Pera; 5 December 1877, 1.20 a.m.
Burnaby to Editor – *Morning Post*, 6 December 1877

Suleiman Pasha has gained Elena and taken six guns. Hopes to take Tirnova tomorrow. Mehemet Ali has repulsed the Russians at Orkhranie.

FGB125
Pera; 3 January 1878, 7.00 a.m.
Burnaby to Editor – *Morning Post*, 5 January 1878

Chakir Pasha and Baker Pasha having, by a most brilliant victory, cut through a large Russian force which barred their way, are marching to Tatar Bazardjik. Major Fawcett is to join Baker Pasha.

FGB126
Chakir Pasha's Headquarters; 9 January 1878
Burnaby to unknown – *Mayfair*, January 1878

Mayfair has permission to publish the following extracts from a private letter addressed by Captain Burnaby to a friend in London. The despatch is dated from Chakir Pasha's head-quarters, January 9th, 1878:

> For the last three weeks we have been constantly on the move, and it has been a very exciting time, not only for the Turkish troops, but also for non-combatants like myself. When the news reached us that Plevna had fallen it became clear that 120,000 Russians and Roumanians would be free to march against the

corps under Chakir Pasha, stationed at the southern extremity of the Kamarli defile, and amounting to about 20,000 men. These figures, however, were rapidly diminishing, on an average 200 men going into hospital every day, owing to frostbites, dysentery, ague, &c., without counting those who were continually being put *hors de combat* by the Russian artillery. Under these circumstances it was manifest that a speedy retreat on the part of our troops would be the best policy, and a concentration of the Ottoman forces at Adrianople, or the Busuk Chekmagee lines. However, orders came from Constantinople for Chakir Pasha to hold his position at Kamarli as long as possible. This he did, in spite of several attacks made by the Russians; but at last, on the 27th of December, they succeeded in marching a force of 30,000 men by a mountain pass across the Balkans, and were thus enabled to attack it in its flank as well as in front, with the evident ultimate intention of cutting our line of retreat upon Tatar Bazardjik, our communications with Sofia being already closed. Baker Pasha, with a small brigade of 2,800 men, was sent to the village of Tashkessan to hold the newly arrived Russian force in check, whilst Chakir Pasha determined to retreat with the remainder of our troops in the direction of Slatiza. I accompanied Baker, and on the last day of the year 1877 saw the best-contested battle against overwhelming numbers that it has ever been my good fortune to witness. The Russians, as I have said before, had 30,000 men, we only 2,800. The odds were great against us. Things looked very black for Valentine Baker and his little force. From our position at Tashkessan we could see lines upon lines of the foe coming forward to attack. The battle raged from day-break to sundown, and if I had only time or a table I would describe it in full; but my desk is a barn-floor, and you must wait till we meet again for an account of the many incidents which occurred during the fight, and of Baker's conspicuous courage, good generalship and *sang froid*. Briefly, the battle was a desperate one, and Chakir Pasha's reply to Baker's repeated requests for reinforcements was that he had none to give, and that we must at all cost hold the position; as if it were carried by the foe, the whole of his (Chakir Pasha's) army, which was retreating, would be taken in flank and annihilated. The Turks fought splendidly. They struggled for every inch of ground with extraordinary tenacity. Each minute of daylight seemed a year, and Baker kept looking at his watch, the Turks meanwhile gazing at the sun, old Nature's timepiece – as until nightfall it would be impossible for us to abandon the position. The hours rolled on, and our men died in their places. The Turkish ranks became each moment more thinned by the bullets of the foe, and the plucky survivors of the little brigade stood up on the mountain ridge with their forms standing out in bold relief against the sky-line, and returned volley for volley to the slowly but steadily, advancing enemy. Just before sunset the Russians collected themselves for a supreme effort and charged home at the Turks. Our men burst forth with their battle-cry, an invocation of the one true God, and the '*Ya Allah!*' '*Ya Allah!*' re-echoed over the mountains. The Russians cheered in response, but their hurrahs were of no avail. The Mussulmans dashed at their foe. Shoulder to shoulder, there was no flinching on either side and the steel was driven home. Baker ordered his bugler to sound the '*Ya Allah!*' and the Ottoman soldiers again took up the strain. They seemed possessed of superhuman energy. Each man looked as if he possessed the strength of ten. Another charge, and the Russians were driven back a few hundred yards. It was now too late for the enemy to make another effort. In the dark we marched to the plain below. Here Baker, assisted by Colonel Allix, his A.D.C., who had behaved with great gallantry during the battle, mustered his little force. Out of 2,800 men more than 600 of the brave fellows had bitten the dust, nearly 400 being killed outright. There was little quarter given on either side. You can understand the disproportion between the lists of the killed and wounded at the roll-call. The Muscovites must have suffered very severely, owing to their generals persisting in attacking us in column, the more particularly towards the end of the day. I am informed that Gourko commanded the Russian forces, but can hardly think so after the way his praises have been sung in some of the English newspapers. Baker managed his retreat across the mountains very well, and in consequence of the battle at Tashkessan has been named by the Sultan a general of division. Allix is also to have a medal, which, by the way, he well deserves. Two days ago, Baker made a reconnaissance towards the village of Meska, about five miles from this; he discovered that a Russian brigade was stationed there. A sharp engagement took place, and when the reconnaissance was over he returned to our previous quarters. This morning, before daybreak, when on the march to Tatar Bazardjik, Chakir Pasha was met by a messenger from Suleiman Pasha. We were informed that an armistice had been proclaimed. This is not at all pleasing to many of the troops, though possibly it is not so unsatisfactory to the Porte. It is to be hoped that Russia will not be able to obtain the right of passing the Dardanelles as one of the terms of peace. It will be bad enough if she is allowed to take Batoum and keep Kars; but once turn the Black Sea into a Russian lake, and England, as far as her naval estimates are concerned, will have to spend half as much money again as before. What will Mr. Gladstone say to this? When he was Chancellor of the Exchequer he was not one of those who wished to swell the national expenditure. I am sick to death of all the nonsense that has been written about the oppressed Bulgarians. I have been in a number of their villages and find the people very much better off than many of our English peasantry. Why does not Mr. Gladstone spend a few of his leisure hours in making a tour through Bulgaria? He would then be able to see for himself, and a walk through the Balkan passes would afford him quite as much exercise as chopping down trees at home. If the news of the armistice be confirmed, I shall turn my horse's head towards Constantinople. It is about a three hundred mile march; however, Radford and my steed are in capital condition. The former says he 'don't think much of them Bulgarians'.

FMS01
Constantinople; 2 February 1878
Drs. Sandwith and Hume to Stafford House Committee (extract) –
Morning Post, 18 February 1878

On January 15, a battle in the plain furnished Dr. Hume and myself with some patients, who, after being dressed, were sent to the Stafford House Hospital. We proceeded to the railway station on the afternoon, and placed ourselves under the orders of Safret Pasha. At midnight we started with the Pasha and troops for Stanimana, when the enemy, who had advanced within a distance of 300 yards, opened a very brief musketry fire as we left the station. Our servants and arabajis on this occasion showed the greatest fortitude, and exhibited no anxiety to leave their posts, in spite of the confusion and flight of the Turkish cavalry around us.

Reaching Stanimana the next morning at six o'clock, we rested there until the night of the 17th. During our stay, we attended the wounded who had accompanied us from Philippopolis, and those who resulted from the fighting then going on immediately without the town. We now learned from Captain Burnaby that it would be impossible to take wheeled vehicles further, and accordingly procured pack-saddles, onto which we transferred as many of our stores as it was possible to carry on horses. Carriages, stretchers, and some stores were of necessity abandoned.

Starting with the staff of Baker Pasha at 2 a.m. on the 18th, we proceeded, with the exception of four hours' halt, until 8.30 p.m. After five hours sleep in the snow we proceeded once more, and at daybreak commenced the ascent of the Rhodope mountains. The hill-side, covered with deep snow, except where its many zigzag paths had their surface beated into glassy ice, seemed an almost insuperable problem to tired men and horses. On every side, upon the ice and in the snow, struggling and falling horses, soldiers and wounded mixed in frightful confusion, with women and children fleeing from their burnt houses, all toiling wearily upwards. During the ascent, the explosion of an ammunition box, which had fallen from a mule, added not a little to the general confusion.

In the plain below could be seen the Cossacks advancing to the foot of the hill, and as, from there, they fired on the struggling masses, soldiers with pack-horses on all sides cut loose their baggage and so hurried to escape. Our servants exerted themselves so well, they made their ascent with the loss of only one box, a somewhat heavy case of provisions. After the climb of three hours, we halted on the hill-top, and cautiously advanced through the district, where roads from Hakeni offered an opportunity to the enemy to cut off our retreat. We went on through the hills, the bitter cold gradually relenting from day to day as we travelled southwards, until after spending a night at the small town of Kirikh-Ali, on the banks of the Arda, halting at various hamlets, and traversing the almost pathless mountain gorges, we reached Gumurd-jina on the morning of January 23. Here we were very hospitably entertained by the Greek bishop and other inhabitants of the town, who afforded us most welcome food and rest.

On the afternoon of the 24th we proceeded four hours to Bumbaya, and on the following day, by fording two arms of the sea, reached Porto Lagos (Karagatch). On the 26th and 27th we were occupied in dressing the wounded, of whom we had succeeded in bringing some through the hills. During these two days our patients were gradually embarked and placed on board the steamship *Sultanié*, where we joined them on the evening of the 27th, having been specially requested by Suleiman Pasha to accompany them to Constantinople.

The decks being covered with between 3000 and 4000 troops, the wounded and sick, the former numbering 380, the latter 120, were crowded together in a state saloon and the after-cabins of the vessel. The authorities were unable to provide them with anything but biscuit, and it was with great difficulty that we succeeded in obtaining a very inadequate supply of water for them. By the kindness of Mr. Young, chief commissioner of the National Aid Society, who arrived in the steamship *Osmanié* on the morning of the 28th, we were enabled to supply them with soup, bread, and under-clothing. To the same source we are indebted for several hundred bandages, of which our stock was by this time nearly exhausted. They were assisted on board by a willing staff of Turkish dressers. Eight men succumbed during the voyage, but we had the satisfaction of relieving to a great extent the sufferings of the wounded, and of curing a large proportion of the sick.

At Gallipoli we were enable to procure oranges and tobacco, for which our patients were deeply grateful. We arrived at Constantinople on the eve of February 2, and on the following day the wounded were removed to various hospitals. This report cannot be closed without acknowledging the unfailing kindness of General Baker and Captain Burnaby.

Anon03
Constantinople; 8 February 1878
The Times, 15 February 1878 (possibly written by Francis Francis)

The Retreat from Tatar Bazardjik

To give in a letter any detail of the incidents with which this eventful march was replete would be impossible. There are many, though, who will be glad to know that Captain Burnaby was taking copious notes of all that passed, and it is, I believe, his intention to write a book on the winter campaign in the Balkans.

The sufferings of the troops during the march were terrible. The road lay almost entirely across mountains where food and fuel were often scarce; men died by the wayside in great numbers from pure exhaustion; others were frozen to death, the cold being intense, and the clothing of the men, in many instances, very poor and scanty. Both the General and Captain Burnaby lost all their baggage early in the march, and for 14 days had to live without changing their clothes, and without the luxury of blankets or wrappers to protect them from the cold while bivouacking at night. The numbers who died by the wayside testified to the severity of the privations that had to be endured. General Baker, however, soon succeeded in getting his own division into something like order; the troops and men were kept together; he himself was constantly with them talking to them at their camp fires, cheering them on their march, and, by the way in which he bore hardship and rough living, setting them an example that had the most excellent effect. Had it not been for the masterly way in which he covered the retreat, it is, extremely doubtful whether the remainder of the Turkish forces would have succeeded in escaping, for the enemy were hanging about the rear of the army the whole time and only waiting for a good opportunity to attack in earnest. The General, however, left them no such chance; by dint of constant watchfulness and energy he at length passed the mountains and arrived in sight of the sea without being forced into any serious engagement. At Gumurd-jina the troops were quartered for one night. General Baker, with Captain Burnaby and Shakir Bey, lodged in the Archbishop's house, and on the following morning breakfasted with that dignitary, being waited on during the meal by several priests. Immediately afterwards they left for Karagatch, and after an hour's ride on the road all three were taken violently ill. Fortunately, Dr. Gill, of Tashkessan (as he is familiarly called), who was so highly complimented for his conduct at Kamarli by Mehemet Ali, was present, and on discovering strongly-marked symptoms of their having been poisoned, administered very powerful antidotes. With the greatest difficulty they were able to reach Karagatch; the whole party suffering from intense pains in the loins and back, accompanied, by constant vomiting. According, to the doctors, if antidotes had not been promptly administered, fatal consequences would probably have ensued. It is, of course, possible that the poisoning might have been occasioned by the uncleanliness of one of the vessels used in cooking, but it is, nevertheless, a remarkable fact that Colonel Studdy, of the Gendarmerie, who breakfasted at the same time, did not experience the slightest indisposition afterwards. The only way in which this could be accounted for was by the fact that neither that gentleman nor the Archbishop drank any of the wine that was on the table, while those who were ill had not only done so, but had, moreover, remarked its peculiar taste. It is only fair to state that neither the General, Captain Burnaby, nor Shakir Bey attached the slightest suspicion to the Greek Archbishop. They seemed to think that they suffered from the fanaticism of one of the attendant priests.

FGB127
Turkey; 17 February 1878
Burnaby to his mother (extract)
Things here look very unsettled. I hope that the Russians will not be allowed to enter the city. However, as the enemy is slowly creeping on, and the Turks are doing nothing to stop them, the Muscovite will probably be here before long. And so England does not mean to fight for Constantinople after all. What a wretched lot of shopkeepers we are! The country would seem to have lost all its backbone.

HEC01
Constantinople; 13 March 1878
Crook to Editor (extract) – *Bristol Mercury*, 27 March 1878
I omitted to mention in my last letter to you anything about the so-called poisoning of Baker Pasha. He, with Captain Burnaby, Chekir Bey, the chief of our staff, and Colonel Studdy, lodged at the palace of the Greek Archbishop, at Gumurd-jina, for two days. We left there for the coast, which was about six hours distant. After riding about two hours, Chekir Bey was taken very ill and vomited violently. A few minutes afterwards Captain Burnaby was likewise affected, and then Baker Pasha. Several doctors were present, and we all agreed that a good draft of salt and water would be beneficial, and this was administered. Very copious vomiting was produced, and then the party, all feeling better, rode on to the coast. Colonel Studdy was not in the least affected; he had not taken any wine at the dinner. So it was generally reported that the wine was poisoned intentionally. Copper saucepans are generally used in Turkey for cooking purposes, and I fancy that a new pan must have been used to cook their last meal, and so caused the alleged poisoning.

FGB128
St. John's Wood Barracks; 25 March 1878
Burnaby to Toole
Dear Mr. Toole, I have great pleasure in accepting yr invitation. Yrs vy truly, Fred Burnaby.

FGB129
Cavalry Barracks, Windsor; 10 June 1878
Burnaby to 'Dolly'
Dear Dolly. Some time ago I left instructions at Cox's to sell out my Dunaburg & Vitebsk shares on their reaching a certain price. I now wish to cancel these instructions & to let the Dunaburg & Vitebsk shares stand.[184]

---

184 The Dunaburg & Witepsk Railway Company was formed in 1863 to carry out a concession from

Please acknowledge this letter. Yrs vy sincerely, Fred Burnaby

FGB130
Marlborough Club, Pall Mall; 18 July 1878
Burnaby to Wolseley[185]
Dear Sir Garnet,–Dr. John Gill who was with Valentine Baker during the retreat across the Balkans, and who is really a very determined & energetic man besides being a good Doctor, has been to see me. He wishes to know if there is any opening for him at Cyprus. Now if you should ever want a really first class man – & I would not say he was if he was not – you could not have a finer specimen of a Doctor as well as a man than Gill. I enclose his card in case you might wish to make use of him, and apologise for troubling you, pray believe me Dear Sir Garnet, Yours very sincerely, Fred Burnaby.

---

the Russian government; first registered on the London Stock Exchange on 2 June 1863; and its name changed in 1893 to the Dvinsk and Vitebsk Railway Company Limited. It went into voluntary liquidation on 21 May 1894 after acquisition by the Russian government – shareholders received cash or Russian government bonds.

185 Courtesy of Brighton and Hove City Council, Hove Central Library, Wolseley Collection, GB 0510/2.

Part 3

Speeches (1878)

Introduction

This section comprises almost entirely speeches given by Burnaby, as reported in newspapers (by date of speech). A full list of all speeches contained in this section together with an explanatory key is provided in the Appendix in Volume 2. There are some meetings that Burnaby is known to have addressed where no record has thus far been located of his speech and there are doubtless other recorded speeches that have yet to be found. Two speeches given by Joseph Chamberlain are also included here, since in both he refers directly and at length to Burnaby. Burnaby's own speeches fall naturally into two categories, with one exception.

The first category comprises political speeches given between 5 March 1878, shortly after Burnaby's return from the Russo-Turkish War, and 1 April 1880, the day following his defeat at Birmingham in the General Election of that year. The vast majority of these speeches were given at various venues in Birmingham and more than half of them were given in the three weeks before that election. The only important exception in this category is that given at the Savage Club on 21 March 1878, in which he described Baker Pasha's outstanding generalship at the battle of Tashkessan. This speech is generally regarded as an important step in Baker's rehabilitation and led directly to his re-election to the Army and Navy Club.

The second category comprises political speeches given between 12 May 1881 and 14 November 1884, of which the majority were given from May 1882 onwards. For almost the whole of this period Burnaby and Lord Randolph Churchill believed they would be fighting jointly the three Birmingham seats held by the Liberal triumvirate of Chamberlain, Bright and Muntz, although by the time the 1885 General Election was held there had been a redistribution of the seats in Birmingham. During this period Burnaby was an active speaker not just in Birmingham, but around the country on behalf of his fellow Conservative aspirants and he also addressed gatherings such as the first annual dinner of the Primrose League. Two speeches given on successive evenings (15 and 16 April 1884), although given for political purposes, were important as they contained Burnaby's descriptions of the two battles of El Teb and what led up to them.

FGB001S
Burnaby at Exeter Hall; 5 March 1878
The Star, 9 March 1878

Captain Burnaby, who just entered the Hall, then came forward, and on his name being made known to the meeting he was loudly cheered. He said— When I came here this evening, I had not the slightest intention of making a speech, as you appear to wish me to do. ("Hear, hear".) Under the circumstances, then, if I do not make a good one you must remember that it is not a prepared speech, and I must ask your indulgence (cheers). The meeting is held, as I understand it, to support our Government against Russia (cheers), against the designs of a Government which, in my opinion, and in the opinion, I believe, of every Englishman who has studied the Eastern question, has for its object the destruction of our Indian Empire. I have the greatest pleasure in saying what my own opinions are about the matter. Russia has been as we know systematically pushing Eastward for years and years. She has had recourse to every conceivable means of advancement. She has intrigued; she has not hesitated to use means which in England we should describe in terms which would not be strictly parliamentary, and I, as an officer in her Majesty's army on full pay, am not entitled to use. Under these circumstances, if I do not apply expressions that I should like to use, all I can say is that I feel them (laughter and cheers). I know from official despatches written by Colonel Mansfield, now at Bucharest, but who was Consul General at Warsaw, how Russian officials have permitted women and children to be flogged simply because they would not change their religion (groans). Well, I object to the particular form of Christianity which Russia is pleased to call the right one (cheers). I also, as an Englishman, uphold every form of Constitutional Government which exists, but I read in a despatch from Mr. Layard to her Majesty's government that a high Russian official speaking to him, said that Russia could not submit to an established Constitution in Turkey, because it would be considered as an insult to Russia. (Laughter and hear, hear). I have to thank you very much for the kind manner in which you have listened to the very few words I have had to say (go on), and I only regret that I cannot make my expressions towards Russia stronger because my position in her Majesty's service prevents me from do doing so (loud cheers).

FGB002S
Burnaby at the Savage Club; 11 March 1878
The Star, 21 March 1878

Captain Burnaby, speaking at the Savage Club on Wednesday week, described the conduct of General Baker in command of 2,400 against 30,000 men of the Russian Guard in the following words, which we take from a verbatim report in *Mayfair*.

It was a cold grey morning, on the last day of 1877, when that distinguished officer found himself in command of a small force of 2,400 men protecting the retreat of the army of Chakir Pasha. Against him were thirty thousand men of the Russian Guard, the choicest soldiers of the Czar. The sun was just rising; when a soldier on outpost duty came galloping in with the news that the enemy were advancing to attack. General Baker had asked for reinforcements on the previous day, and they had been refused. The answer was that it was impossible to give them. He had again written for them. The only answer was, "You must hold out", and the last information we had from the officer commanding was that thirty thousand Russians were advancing to attack us. I need hardly tell you what were the feelings of individuals there who like myself bore no part in the proceedings, but were simply spectators. It seemed to me as if the odds were not merely a guinea to a shilling, but a shilling to thousands of pounds. The only man there who was perfectly cool and calm, perfectly cool and self-possessed, was the man who had made up his mind from the night before to hold out until every soldier there, including General Baker, was dead. We saw them coming on, their long lines extending from right to left, advancing along the road, and covering the snow capped ground. They came closer; they brought seventeen guns against our position, where we had but seven, and those small ones. They came on, and when they were within about four or five hundred yards, the whole of the Russian Guard broke out with one unanimous cheer of "Hurrah!". We heard their cheer as they closed around our position, overlapping us to the right and left, advancing against our centre. We feared that we should be forced to retreat, when General Baker turned at that moment to his trumpeter, and said, "Sound the Turkish cry—the cry to God." Then, as if from one throat, there re-echoed through the mountains the shout of the 2,400, "*Allah-il-Allah!*" It was a grand feeling at that moment, a sensation worth living for, to hear those men, poor raw levies at the time, cheering back in defiance of those thirty thousand warriors, the choicest troops of the Czar. General Baker had sent again to ask if it were possible to give him reinforcements, and the answer again came back, "You must hold on. The whole safety of the army depends on you." At that moment we saw our left retiring, driven back to the crest of another hill, it was absolutely necessary that General Baker should retire his right from the vicinity of the rapidly-advancing enemy. This was an exceedingly difficult military operation, yet it was performed with the greatest accuracy and care of the men. Between eleven and twelve, just as the sun was at its height, the Russians rested for an hour. General Baker sent his aide-de-camp to inquire if he could not have reinforcements, or, at least, two or three guns. The message that came back was "General, all is lost. Chakir Pasha has retired, and has deserted you. You must fall back." Now came the self-possession and the generalship of a true commander. Ninety-nine men out of a hundred would have thought all was lost; but our General said, "No; my orders have been to hold the position, and until every man is killed, I will remain here." The day wore on, and the Russians again gathered to the attack. General Baker stood there, looking at his watch. Would that day ever finish, or would the sun ever go down? While we looked at our watches, the Turks looked at the great clock of nature hung high in the distant horizon. Again the Russians came on in dense columns to assail our last line, but still General Baker remained at the head of his troops, exposed to the hail of bullets, standing in the most dangerous position, encouraging his men. He had confidence in his men, and I must say the Turks had confidence in their general. It was five o'clock, and the sun was going down, when the Russians again attacked is. It was a critical moment. We could see the infantry and the guns of Chakir Pasha hurrying along in retreat, and if the Russians had succeeded in breaking our thin line, the whole of the force must have been lost. The Russians could see them also, and they advanced cheering—not now thirty thousand men, for they had lost more than two thousand men in the fighting. Again their cheers were met by the Turkish cry. General Baker's trumpeter was shot by his side, another was brought up, and he continued to sound the cry. The Russians came up the hill, broke at the continuous fire, and then the Turks, as they retired, charged down and drove them into the village below. All was over, the day was won, and slowly the general retired down the plain. There he reviewed his small force, now smaller than ever, for more than one-third had bit the dust. But the rest cheered as pluckily as ever, and were only disgusted that they had to leave their position. General Baker addressed a few words to the men, telling them how bravely they had fought for Turkey and the Sultan; but they replied with one voice, "It is not we who have fought well, it is you our general. It is not our bravery that has carried us through, but your skilful generalship."

Only ephemeral passion can obscure so great a feat—a feat which will eventually rank among deeds as familiar to military men as our household "Balaclava Charge" is to every Englishman. The "Balaclava Charge" was indeed "*magnifique, mais ce n'était pas la guerre*" but this deed of two thousand four hundred under General Baker against thirty thousand "*c'était magnifique, et c'était la guerre*". The moral we draw from it is very simple, perhaps too simple for Chambers of Commerce, certain loanmongers now busily at work in certain quarters, and certain officials, the safety of whose character is abundantly consistent with hiding the truth from their own country in the interest of any country. The moral we draw is that, with trifling help from Great Britain, the Turks, under such officers as General Baker, if the Turks only saw that we are in earnest, are abundantly capable of disposing of Russian aggression for any time material to consider. And a further consequence is that, if we abandon the Turk, it can only be because my Lord Derby is secretly playing the game of the Chief of the Police of the Great Despotism of the North. We deliberately challenge the alternative from all comers. The "Greek" notwithstanding. Do people remember that the Queen of Greece is a Russian?[1]

1 The Grand Duchess Olga Constantinova (1851-1926), daughter of Grand Duke Constantine Nikolaievitch and Princess Alexandra of Saxe-Altenburg.

Part 4

Other Writings by Fred Burnaby (1875-1878)

1 *Annual Report of Proceedings of the Aeronautical Society of Great Britain* (1875), pp. 28-30.

2 'The practical instruction of staff officers in foreign armies' in *Journal of the Royal United Services Institute* vol. 16, no. 68 (January 1872), pp. 633-44. Reprinted with the same title as a pamphlet (London: W. Mitchell & Co., 1876).

3 'In Memoriam' from *On horseback through Asia Minor* (London: Sampson Low, 7th edition 1878), pp. xxxii-xl.

Introduction

Burnaby's two books of travel writings, *A ride to Khiva* and *On horseback through Asia Minor* remained in print throughout his life and for some years thereafter, going through numerous editions. In recent years several new editions of these two books have appeared, although they have usually lacked the fine maps contained with the first editions and often do not include the original appendices in full. Both books remain readily available, including those published by the Oxford University Press with introductions by Peter Hopkirk (author of *The Great Game*).

'The practical instruction of staff officers in foreign armies' was originally a lecture given at the prestigious Royal United Services Institute in 1871, almost certainly based on direct observations made during his visit to Russia in the winter of 1870/71. As was customary the lecture was printed in the *Journal* of the RUSI and reprinted as a pamphlet in 1876, by which time there was beginning to be a demand for anything written by the hero of Khiva.

The reviews of Fred's second book, *On horseback through Asia Minor*, had not all been entirely positive. At least one reviewer went as far as suggesting that the real hero was not Burnaby, but his servant, Radford. For the seventh edition of *On horseback*, published in 1878, Burnaby wrote a short additional chapter that he entitled 'In memoriam'. Ostensibly a memorial to Radford, who had died on his return to England after their participation in the Russo-Turkish war, it also contained a description of the battle of Tashkessan and of some other incidents that they had shared. Since this edition is not always easy to find, the 'In memoriam' has been included here.

A ride across the Channel and other adventures in the air came in for even more criticism on its publication than had *On horseback*. Burnaby had thrown it together within only a few days of completing the journey and, even with a considerable amount of padding, it only amounted to some 18,000 words.

'The possibilities of ballooning', which Fred wrote for his friend T.H.S. Escott, editor of the *Fortnightly Review*, to some extent covered ground well-trodden in *A ride across the Channel and other adventures in the air*, but with a certain amount of additional material.

Although not strictly written by him, a report of a ballooning experiment carried out by Burnaby and reported in the 1875 *Proceedings* of the Aeronautical Society of Great Britain is also included here.

The common denominator of these five items is that they have not been readily available to the general reader since their original publication, which, taken together with their relative brevity, is the justification for including them here.

1 *Annual Report of Proceedings of the Aeronautical Society of Great Britain*, **1875, pp. 28-30.**

Captain Burnaby gave some notes of experiments at the Crystal Palace. These, he said, had reference to an instrument he had invented some time previously for the purpose of ascertaining the direction the balloon was going when floating in space above the clouds, and more particularly at night. As many gentlemen present knew, he had made ascents at night when it was almost impossible to get a line. The compass indicated East, West, North, and South, but the earth was hid from their view, the clouds were going the same way as they were, and for anything they knew, they might be going towards France or Germany. He had, therefore, thought of employing two small parachutes to indicate the direction in which the balloon was travelling. The parachutes could be made of silk. They would have magnesium wire in their cars, and must be attached the one to the other by a long silken thread.[1] This, in turn, is fastened to a reel in the car of the balloon. On dropping one parachute it would at first fall on the

---

1   Although it is nowhere commented upon, magnesium wire is inflammable, burning with a bright white light, and must have been used so that the position of the parachutes could have been seen even in the dark.

motion of the balloon, but the attraction of the earth would gradually make the parachute descend. In a few seconds he would let fall a second parachute. This would act in a similar manner; and then by drawing an imaginary line in the mind's eye from the first to the second parachute, the aeronaut could discover the direction in which he was travelling. This, he believed, was most important with respect to warfare, and particularly in respect of postal balloons sent out of a fortress at night; otherwise they would not know whether they were going into the country of the enemy or that of friends. By this invention they would be able to ascertain the course of the balloon, and to know whether they should descend or continue their course. This was a subject which he believed had never been worked, and he had thought it of sufficient importance to bring it before the Society.

Mr. Wenham asked whether the parachutes could be drawn up again.

Captain Burnaby: Yes; that is the advantage, because you have a silk cord connecting the two parachutes and connected with the car by a reel, so that you cannot lose the parachutes.

The Chairman said whenever he had been above the clouds and lost sight of the earth he could always determine the direction of motion by means of the hanging grapnel rope. If the balloon was standing still the grapnel was vertical, if moving at all it was out of the vertical, and by looking at the compass he always knew in which direction he was moving. That was by daylight; but in night ascents he had still seen the rope. Captain Burnaby, who had been with him, must have remarked that the rope could be seen at night.

Captain Burnaby said they might be able to see it, but he had known cases where he could not see his hand before him. It had been so dark that he could see nothing. He had had the opportunity of talking on this subject with several of the men who went up from Paris during the siege.[2]

The Chairman: They were sailors and inexperienced men, with the exception of M. de Fonvielle and two or three others.

Captain Burnaby thought this did not meet the case. The balloon ascents were mostly made by day because there were no means of knowing the direction at night.

Mr. Wenham said he could not exactly see on what principle an anchor, suspended from a balloon, should deviate from the perpendicular. Captain Burnaby's parachutes, if left at rest, would, after a time, partake of the motion of the car; but while the parachute was being quickly raised or lowered it would have a tendency to fall perpendicularly, and the balloon at the time traversing in a direction away from the line of gravitation taken by the parachute, a sensible inclination of the suspending cord would indicate the direction in which the balloon was travelling.

---

2   The siege of Paris took place during the Franco-Prussian War in 1870/71.

The Chairman remarked that the grapnel always followed the balloon.
Captain Burnaby: At times you cannot see the anchor at all.
The Chairman: I have been in the car of a balloon when we could not see the balloon itself.
Captain Burnaby: That is what I make a great point of. That is the time when it is impossible for the aeronaut to know the direction in which he is going, but this invention of mine will enable him to do so.
The Chairman observed that Captain Burnaby spoke from practical knowledge, and that the Meeting was much obliged to him for giving the result of his experience.
A vote of thanks was given to Captain Burnaby.

2 'The Practical Instruction of Staff Officers in Foreign Armies' in *Journal of the Royal United Services Institute* vol. 16, no. 68 (January 1872), pp. 633- 44. Reprinted with the same title as a pamphlet (London: W. Mitchell & Co., 1876).

"The art of war" has greatly changed during the last fifty years, and railways and telegraphs have given it quite a different aspect to that which it originally possessed. Topography was formerly but little known; maps were few and far between, not many Officers had the aptitude to read them, and Generals used to trust much more to their guides than to the frequently inaccurate maps then published. Armies are much larger now than they have ever been during the annals of modern warfare, it was formerly so difficult to feed a large army, and railroads did not exist; roads were few and often impassable, supplies were cut short, discontent was the consequence; the army became demoralised, and defeat was inevitable. But if armies are much larger now than they have been during the annals of modern warfare, it must not be forgotten that in the earlier pages of the world's history, enormous forces took the field. Herodotus tells us that Xerxes invaded Greece with an army which exceeded five millions of men, with its combatant and non-combatant strength. But war in those days was not conducted on the same civilised and, comparatively speaking, humane principles as at present. The conquered had to supply the conquerors with every means of subsistence that lay in their country; and those wretched sufferers who were not killed or sold as slaves, had no alternative left but to die of hunger.

But notwithstanding the exacting manner in which warfare was carried on in those early days, every now and then we read of special instances of large expeditions having their ends entirely frustrated owing to a deficiency in the Commissariat. For instance, Darius, King of Persia, crossed the Bosphorus 513 B.C. on a floating bridge, and led his army of 700,000 men into the country which lies between the Lower Danube and the Don – a country, by the way, which it is interesting to study now, as it may again be the theatre of military events, perhaps sooner than we think. The Scythian retired and carefully avoided battle; Darius pursued; but in those wild steppes there were no means of feeding his army, and eventually be had to beat a retreat. Some historians say that many thousands of his men died of hunger. Again, Alexander of Macedon, on his homeward return from India, divided his forces into three columns. The southern column he sent by ships; the centre one along the coast; and the northern one he led himself through the desert plains of Gedrozin. Here there were no means of feeding his troops, and 80,000 men, or two-thirds of his army, perished, principally from hunger. Again, in later years, General Dumouriez's expedition, at the latter end of the last century, was a failure principally on account of the deficiency of his Commissariat arrangements; and, finally, we have but to look back to the year 1812, and to perhaps the most distinguished General that ever lived, and who had planned his campaign in Russia with the greatest care and forethought. But how disastrously it ended, owing to his army being cut off from its supplies when in an enemy's country.

I think I have given you instances enough to prove that in all times and in all ages, one of the greatest difficulties that a General has had to contend against, has been to feed his troops when he has been in an enemy's country.

I now propose to tell you what is done by the Prussian, Russian, and Austrian military authorities to ensure having in their Commissariat, or, as they call it, "Intendance" Department, Officers thoroughly acquainted, both practically and theoretically, with every part of that branch of the profession.

In Prussia, every Officer who wishes to enter the "Intendance" Department has to pass an examination. He has to know all the various divisions of the Prussian Army, and the relation of the separate military commands to the higher civil and military authorities; also the rights and duties of the military administrative depots with reference to the separate military commands. He has to possess a qualified knowledge of finance, and a thorough knowledge of military economy in times of peace and war. In addition to this, he has to know all statistics relating to the clothing and feeding of an army. No Officer is admitted as a candidate to this examination unless he has served six years with distinction in the regular Army. In some few cases, junior Officers of the Intendance are admitted as candidates; but then they must have shown special aptitude for their profession, and have served previously in the Line or in the Reserve.

In Russia, the Staff Officers of the "Intendance" have not only to know all the resources of their own country, but they have to know all the resources of every country with which Russia may at any time have to go to war. It is not sufficient for them to know that the country in question is rich, but they must know in what that richness consists, whether in corn or in pasturage, whether in commerce or in manufactures. They must know the network of railways of the country in question, and in what way they are connected with the Russian railways. They must be able to speak French and German, and be able to state how many Russian troops could be fed in that country in the event of war, by means of "requisition". We read in a very interesting article in the *"Voennye Shornik"*, or *"Russian Military Magazine"*, a magazine, by the way, in which the articles are written almost entirely by Officers of the Staff, and which is edited by Major-General Menkoff of the Russian Staff, that Bohemia, which is one of the richest countries in Austria, and which has a population of 5,000 people to the square mile (German mile), would not long be able to support a foreign army, as the richness of Bohemia consists principally in its manufactures, but that in Hungary, Wallachia, or Banat, a foreign army would be able to subsist for a very long time, provided only it had sufficient mills to grind the corn, which is the principal produce of those countries.

The "mill" question is an important one as connected with the Commissariat. The Russians have not forgotten that shortly before the outbreak of hostilities in the Crimea, they had 140,000 quarters of wheat lying in the ports of the sea of Azov ready for shipment to Europe; but this corn was almost all lost to them, owing to their having but very few mills to grind it. We know that Napoleon, previous to his expedition to Moscow, ordered 5,000 hand-mills to be sent with the troops. The order was fulfilled too late, and the mills did not arrive till he was on his retreat from Moscow, and when they arrived, there was nothing for them to grind. Now, if you will follow me through a small calculation, you will see how important the "mill" question is. For instance, let us suppose that Silesia has 2,000 people to the square mile, and that there are mills enough there to grind corn for 3,000. Now, let us presume that an army of 360,000 men is brought to bear upon that country. To grind corn for such a force, it would require that all the mills extending over an area of 120 square miles should be kept going day and night. You can see clearly what a difficulty that would be in the event of war.

The Austrians became so thoroughly aware of their shortcoming in the "Intendance" after the battle of Königgratz,[3] that they determined to start a special military school for all men who wished to acquaint themselves practically with the Commissariat department. And in addition to this they instituted a two years' course of military instruction at the Academy for all Officers who wished to enter the "Intendance". The course of instruction and the system of examination is very similar to what takes place in Prussia. I need not, therefore, detain your attention any more on this subject.

There is yet another element in modern warfare to which great importance is attached on the continent. I allude to railways and to the military carriages for all arms which foreign countries now possess, and, in addition to this, to

---

3   Also known as the Battle of Sadowa, taking place in 1866 it was the decisive battle of the Austro-Prussian War, in which the Kingdom of Prussia defeated the Austrian Empire

the military railway commands; and how Officers and men are both practically and theoretically taught everything connected with the railway department. Railways in modern warfare occupy such a very important position as a means of rapidly mobilising and feeding troops, that it is not to be wondered at, that in Russia—which is a country where the want of railways was so signally felt during the time of the Crimean war—great attention bas been paid to this matter. In June, 1869, a special committee of Staff Officers was ordered to sit at St. Petersburg and to report upon the nature and number of military railway carriages for all arms that every railway company in Russia should be compelled to keep. The result of their deliberations and recommendations was forwarded to the Emperor and signed by him. At present in Russia all the railway companies have to provide a certain number of carriages for wounded, fitted up with litters, and well ventilated; also a number of trucks, specially fitted up with every appliance for the transport of heavy artillery in the event of war; and, in addition to this, a large number of horse-boxes or horse-trucks; and there seems to be a very useful device in connection with them, for they are so contrived that the sides of the trucks can be let down and formed into a bridge, so that the cavalry can be got out at any point on the line without waiting for their arrival at a station. The railway companies have also to provide a large quantity of carriages fitted up with racks and every sort of contrivance for hanging up soldiers' knapsacks and arms. At present in Russia they have enough of these carriages to transport 54,000 infantry, 1,500 cavalry, a proportionate quantity of artillery, 1,464 slightly wounded, and 732 severely wounded men; and the railway companies are still constructing more of these carriages.

In imitation of the Prussian military "railway commands", which proved of such signal use during the Austro-Prussian war, the Russians determined to institute a force of their own, founded on the same model. For this purpose they dispatched 432 men and 8 Officers to all the different railways in Russia. This was three years ago. The men had to learn both practically and theoretically everything connected with the management of the line, and the Officers were ordered specially to study the duties of station-masters. In June last year it was thought by the military authorities at St. Petersburg that it would be a very useful thing to ascertain in some manner the exact amount of knowledge which every Officer and man had attained in his new calling. For this purpose it appeared that the best possible means would be to construct a railway during the manoeuvres. This was determined upon, and it was resolved to unite the Peterhof and Warsaw lines, and make a branch from the Ligovo station to the ninth verst of the Warsaw line. This line, if left standing, would be very useful as a means of connecting Peterhof with Tsarskoe and Krasnoe Selo; and if prolonged as far as Kolpino, on the Nicolaev line, it would facilitate communication with Oranienbaum, where it bad been proposed to construct a port. This Nicolaev has nothing to do with the Nicolaev near Odessa, but the railway is called Nicolaev because the Emperor Nicholas was the person who ordered its construction, and it was the first line laid down in Russia. Major-General Annenkoff, of the head-quarters' staff, was requested to take command and to make all the necessary arrangements. The men and Officers who had been sent to the different lines were telegraphed for to come to St. Petersburg, and on their arrival they were formed into two companies of 216 men and 4 Officers in each company. In the companies there were engineers, engine-drivers, stokers, guards, constructors of trains, points-men, signal-men. The 22nd infantry division and one reserve engineer battalion were ordered to assist in the work. The whole length of the line, I should have told you before, was eight versts, or seven miles. The work was commenced on the 28th of July, and it was finished on the 4th of August. There were two stations constructed, one at each end of the line, and ten bridges, one over the Ligors Canal, which is there more than 50 yards broad. The Emperor was so pleased with the celerity with which the work had been performed that he was determined it should be left as a permanency. The entire expense of it to the country was 150,000 roubles, or a little more than £21,000, and it is said that the Government will not be a loser by the transaction, for the exploiting of the line will thoroughly pay for its cost. Russia is more dependent upon these military railway commands than perhaps any other nation, because almost all the men who are working on the line from Vilna to St. Petersburg are either Poles or Germans, and in the event of war, it would be necessary to replace them with Russians. For this reason Russia has more reason to be particular about these matters than either Prussia or Austria.

There is, however, yet another military element, which I am now going to speak to you about. This element in warfare is perhaps the most important one of all; for no matter how well a campaign may be planned, no matter how skilful the General who plans it, if his subordinates during the time of war do not properly execute their independent trusts, signal disaster is sure to take place. I allude to "strategy". For let us imagine that a country has an army, that that army has its railway commands in the highest possible degree of efficiency, and that its Commissariat is perfect; let us further suppose that that army is well clothed, well armed, and well disciplined. Still, the nation which possesses such a force cannot even then be assured that it has a trusty defence in the moment of danger; for it is necessary to give all armies in time of peace a thoroughly warlike education. Sad will be the fate of those forces whose leaders think that the moment of commencing hostilities is the moment for commencing, and not for terminating, their military education. Bravery and superhuman exertions will not compensate for the want of strategy in modern battles. The "Kriegs Spiel", or war game, is an admirable means of theoretically studying the art of war in time of peace. It may be made most useful as a method of studying tactics and learning the ground over which double manoeuvres, or what we call "autumn manoeuvres", are to take place. But where Prussian and Russian Officers find the "Kriegs Spiel" of such advantage is, that they are enabled by it to play the game over a foreign country, where they have no opportunity of manoeuvring their troops until actual warfare commences.

In England the "Kriegs Spiel" has to be played with the 6-inch map; for the Ordnance survey 1-inch map is too small; and while I am on the subject of maps, and as maps play such an important part in modern warfare, perhaps I may be allowed to make a few remarks with reference to our own Ordnance survey. The English Ordnance survey map, as far as its trigonometrical lines go, is perhaps the most accurate one that has ever been published; in fact it is so accurate that I remember last year Captain Moncrieff, the inventor of the celebrated gun carriage that bears his name, saying that he believed it would be possible in the event of war and of a foreign foe being on our shores, to place a battery of guns behind a hill, and then to send out an Officer to mark down the exact point where the enemy were, and if they were not more than a mile off, he would be able, without seeing the enemy, to shell them from their position, and by means of the map, direct his guns and make the shells fall into a piece of ground not larger than 100 yards square. But if the English Ordnance survey map is so wonderfully accurate as far as its trigonometrical lines go, it must not be forgotten that it is a very old survey, and does not represent the present actual condition of the country. A country changes very much. Roads are turned, roads are altered, fresh roads are made. What was marsh is now cultivated ground; what were woods may be arable country; and what were arable grounds may now be woods. If we take the Ordnance survey map of England and draw a line from Essex to Glamorgan, and again from Cornwall to Kent, we find that the intermediate country was surveyed in 1816. Since then the railways have been inserted; but the roads remain in exactly the same state on the Ordnance survey map as they did in that year. Again, if I turn to sheet 8, counties of Surrey and Hampshire, I see that this map was published also in 1816. Since then the railroads have been put in, and the camp at Aldershot; but the roads five miles from the camp remain exactly in the same state on that map as they did fifty-six years ago. It is true we have the 2.5-inch parochial scale map, but this is a partial map, and not the Ordnance survey. I cannot help thinking if the "Kriegs Spiel" could be played on a raised or modelled map, showing the height of the hills and the ridges, it would be a great advantage, especially to artillery Officers.

Double manoeuvres, or what we call "autumn manoeuvres", are undoubtedly the best means in the world, short of actual warfare, for teaching Generals strategy, provided that the number of men employed on both sides is sufficiently great to make their handling as intricate a matter to the Officers concerned, as it would be in actual warfare. But manoeuvres are costly things. Again, in

England they can only take place once a year, on account of our climate and our agricultural conditions; and in some counties they cannot take place at all without great opposition being made to them by the game and landed proprietors. Now, in the event of war, and of Mr. Vernon Harcourt's theory proving incorrect, we cannot expect our enemy to ask our opinion as to which should be the best route for him to move upon London. It is, therefore, advisable that the closer and confined counties should be as well known to our Staff Officers, as the more open expanses of country, which are in England, alas! becoming each year more scarce. Again, double manoeuvres, though admirable practice for Generals, are not so beneficial to Colonels, particularly to junior Colonels, who only command their own battalions; because these Officers have exactly the same command in the "autumn manoeuvres" as they would have in their own barrack field. In addition to this, on returning to camp each evening, they have their time so thoroughly occupied with the care and management of their horses and men, that they have but very few moments left to consider what have been the tactical problems of the day. Now the very men who are now Colonels commanding regiments, in all probability in the course of a few years—or, if war should take place, much more quickly—may be Generals, and then we might see the strange anomaly in the nineteenth century, of Officers placed in positions of high responsibility, who had not been sufficiently prepared for them in time of peace.

The Russian military authorities have long had their attention drawn to this question. They saw plainly that their autumn manoeuvres would only be a source of useful instruction to the senior Colonels and Generals; it was therefore determined to institute some means of practically teaching their junior Colonels and other Field Officers the higher commands in warfare. For this purpose they resolved to send out parties of Staff and Field Officers from every military district into which Russia is divided, to divide each party into two sides, and to let them manoeuvre against each other exactly in the same way as they would during the grand manoeuvres, but with this difference, that the armies, divisions, and brigades should be skeleton ones, and that two or more infantry men should represent an infantry regiment, two or more cavalry men a cavalry regiment, and a gunner a gun or a battery, as the case might be. Two similar expeditions were sent out from the head-quarter Staff of St. Petersburg in the spring of last year, and three others were sent out from Moscow, Kiev, and the Warsaw districts in the autumn. My present object is to tell you what was done by the party of Officers who were sent out in the Moscow district.

Before I commence, however, I must tell you that the subject of manoeuvres is naturally a dry one, and full of details; but I will endeavour to make them as clear and interesting as possible by means of this large military sketch. It is taken from a Russian military map which was drawn out by a Colonel of the Russian Staff. This rough military sketch shows all the fortresses in Russia,

Other Writings by Fred Burnaby (1875-1878) 353

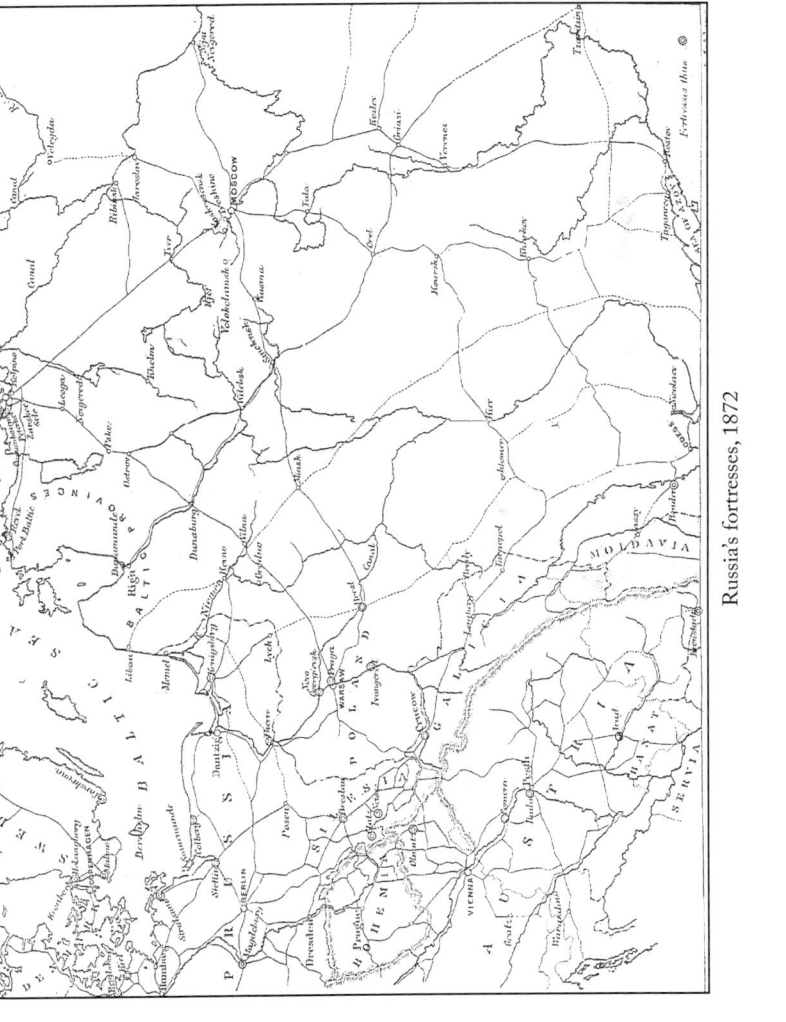

Russia's fortresses, 1872

and it also shows the railroads, and their connection with the Austrian and Prussian railroads. I know that many people in England look upon a war between Prussia and Austria against Russia as a great improbability, but I can assure you that Prussian and Austrian Staff Officers do not think so. I have often heard people in England say, "Ah, but remember the friendly relations that exist between the two countries; and look how well Prince Frederick of Prussia and General Moltke were received at St. Petersburg last year." Did family connection preserve his throne to the poor King of Hanover? and was the reception given by the Emperor Napoleon to the King of Prussia a few years ago one whit less hospitable than that shown by the Russians to the Prussian Prince and to General Moltke. There is a great deal of difference between saying what you think, and thinking what you say. Do you think Napoleon said what he thought to the King of Prussia, when he paraded his Imperial Guard before him in Paris? And was not King William himself, perhaps, an example, a living example of the old adage or saying attributed to the celebrated French philosopher, that "words were given to man to disguise his thoughts".

I remember hearing an admirable speech made two years ago in the House of Commons. The orator, after alluding to the causes which led to the Franco-Prussian war, said, no man in Europe who has carefully followed the course of political events during the last few years, could have failed to observe that after the battle of Sadowa, there was a train of gunpowder laid from Berlin to Paris, which only required the spark to set Europe in a state of conflagration. It is the opinion of many people in Prussia and Russia, amongst whom are Officers and persons whose opinion is well worth having, that after the battle of Sedan there was a train of gunpowder laid from Berlin to St. Petersburg, which only requires the death of one aged monarch to kindle not only Europe, but also part of Asia in one general bonfire. I know some people in England think that we have reason to apprehend Russia in India. This is a question which, though now like a cloud no bigger than a man's hand, will as certainly loom up in the far-off future, as that the Southern States of America will at some distant period again try to cast off the hated yoke of the Northerners.

But you may ask me why should Austria be dragged into this war? If Prussia and Russia go to war, nominally on account of the Baltic provinces, but in reality and as is the case in most wars for the sake of statesmen's ambition, and for the desire inherent among nations as amongst men, to determine which is to be the master, it would be far more disadvantageous for Austria to remain neutral than to throw her sword into the same balance as an ally with her late foe. Poor Austria! the Kaiser who rules her heterogeneous empire has a difficult task to perform in endeavouring to govern a variety of nationalities, who all want to govern themselves; and in the event of victory or in the event of defeat, Austria's lot will be equally an unenviable one. Her eight million Germans, and sixteen million Slavs and their territory are as tempting a morsel in the eyes of

Prussia and Russia as Naboth's vineyard was to the Jewish King.

But I must return to the manoeuvres, and I will now tell you what was done by the party of Officers which went out in the Moscow district. It consisted of 2 Generals, 16 Staff Officers, 29 Field Officers, 2 Officers of the Intendance, and 3 medical men; 75 infantry soldiers, 60 cavalry soldiers, and 28 artillerymen, were ordered to join the expedition to act as markers; and 120 horses were attached to it for the use of the Officers during their exercise in the field. The following was the plan of the manoeuvres:—A western army, evidently a Prussian one, has crossed the River Niemen between Kovno and Grodno. I should here tell you that the Russians intend to build a fortress at Kovno. They have all the plans drawn out for it, but the works are not yet commenced. Well, this army has crossed the River Niemen, between Kovno and Grodno, has invested Dunaburg, and occupied Pskov, and from Looga it marches on St. Petersburg. A southern army, probably an Austrian army, in alliance with the western one, has occupied Jitomir, and from Jitomir marches on Kiev. A detached force of the western army, after the occupation of Pskov, receives orders to march forward and clear the line of operations for the main body, and then to march on through Rjeff to Volokolamsk, and thence to Moscow, if possible to occupy Moscow, and to prevent the formation of reserves for the eastern army, which was defeated at a battle supposed to have taken place when the western army crossed the River Niemen between Kovno and Grodno.

The Officers having been divided into two sides, one side was assumed to represent the party marching from Pskov on to Moscow, and the other was supposed to be a detached force of the eastern army stationed at Voskresensk, with the view of impeding the attempt of the western army to take Moscow. This was the plan of campaign. The assumed strength of each of these detached forces was three divisions of infantry, eight regiments of cavalry, and a proportionate quantity of artillery, one engineer battalion, one pontoon half battalion, and a railway command. The colonel of an infantry regiment was to command one side, and the colonel of a cavalry regiment the other. Previous to commencing their operations, the Officers on both sides had to go through a preliminary course of instruction. The Officers of the western army had to study the military topographical description of the road between Pskov and Moscow, and had to give a detailed account of the railroads, roads, and other means of communication. They had to ascertain the numerical strength of every division in their assumed army with reference to existing statistics, and to state the best manner of forwarding troops through Pskov and Ostrov to Volokolamsk. They had also to send in reports upon the best means of covering their front during their march, and of keeping up their line of communications, and to state where it would be most advisable to leave depots, and the quantity of men that it would be necessary to leave at each depot for its defence. The Officers of the "Intendance" had to study the nature of the country through which the expedition would have to pass, and to report in what districts they would be able to provide the troops with provisions by means of requisition, and in what districts they would be compelled to use transport. The Officers of the artillery had to give a detailed account of the exact amount of ammunition assumed to be with the Force and in store, and also of the best means of forwarding stores. The Officers of the medical department had to inform themselves as to the formation and construction of military hospitals, and the furnishing them with every requisite. The Officers of the eastern army had to study the military topographical description of the Moscow, Kiev, and Smolensk districts, and in addition to this, they had to draw up a plan for the fortification of Moscow. By this plan it was proposed to fortify Moscow on the western side, to throw up thirteen earthworks, and to place in an efficient state of defence the cemetery and large buildings outside the town. It was calculated by this plan that 10,000 men would be required to defend the fortifications, and that those fortifications would be able to shelter an army of 100,000 men. The Officers of the "Intendance" had to report upon the best means of providing Moscow with provisions for the space of ten months, and also upon the best method of despatching supplies to the troops when they were engaged in the field. The Officers of the railway command had to report upon the time required and best means of forwarding an infantry division from Nijni Novgorod to Moscow, and a cavalry brigade from St. Petersburg to Moscow.

As the conclusion of these preliminary tasks, the commanding Officers on both sides gave their Officers instructions that, during the operations in the field, they would have to make reconnaissances, to prepare routes for marches, to select the best place for camps, bivouacs, &c., to arrange expeditions for foraging, and also from time to time to draw up their men in battle order, and to report upon the best means of fortifying the positions taken up by them by the means of field works, and to give a detailed account of the number of men, and the time that would be employed in throwing up each field work.

With the solution of each tactical problem the Officer would have to furnish a map of the locality, and also a written statement showing the disposition of his troops; and, previous to an assumed assault, a survey would have to be made of all approaches to the position. The Commander-in-Chief of the Moscow district was to be the head umpire. He was to have charge of both sides, and to be assisted by eight senior Officers, who were to aid him in verifying the tasks performed by the Officers in the field. The military medical inspector at Moscow had to verify the work done by the medical men attached to the expedition. A day was allowed for the solution of each more complicated problem; and all the Officers had to keep diaries in which everything they had done in a military sense during the day had to be noted down, and a printed journal was kept on both sides stating the progress of the day's marches, and the course of the manoeuvres.

Every morning at 12 o'clock the head umpire sent to the Commander-in-Chief on each side, information as to the enemy, and according to this information they had to make their arrangements and all dispositions, and forward the same in writing to the head umpire, at the same time telling him what had been the tasks performed by the Officers under their command the day before. The head umpire on receiving this information sent back word when, and where, and by whom the tasks would be verified. If the two sides approached so closely that a collision appeared inevitable, the head umpire desired the Commanders-in-Chief on both sides to make all arrangements exactly the same as they would during actual warfare, and that they were to mark out the ground chosen by them by means of the men with flags. During the course of the engagement, the different umpires rode about, and informed the various division leaders and brigade leaders of what was being done by the division leaders and brigade leaders on the opposite side, and according to this information, the division leaders and the Brigadiers had to act. If they changed their position they had to make a rough sketch of the place, and to state how they had disposed of their men. If an infantry regiment had to attack, the commander of the infantry regiment had to design a map, and state exactly the nature of the ground, and how he would have led his men to the assault without exposing them too much to the enemy's fire; or, in case of resisting an assault, how he would have availed himself of the nature of the ground in the locality. Every order during the manoeuvres was sent in writing; for it had been found during the autumn manoeuvres at St. Petersburg, that very often mistakes had arisen. In time of war we know what disastrous consequences may ensue through any error in a message. During these "skeleton manoeuvres" every order was sent in writing, and these orders were to be kept for the inspection of the umpire at the end of the day, so, that should any mistake arise, the umpire might be able to see whose fault it was, and whether the fault lay with the Officer who sent the order, and who had not worded it properly, or whether the fault lay with the receiver of the message, who had shown a dearth of comprehension. A certain quantity of young Officers were also attached to the expedition to act as "gallopers", to convey messages. They from time to time received written orders for the different division or brigade leaders, with the exact time marked upon the envelope. When they had received them, they then had to ride perhaps six or seven miles, and find their way by means of a map to the person to whom the order was addressed. When he received it, he marked down the exact hour; and the following day the head umpire compared the two times, when it was clearly ascertained whether the Officer had carried the message with due and proper celerity. In addition to this, the Officer who carried the message had to make a rough sketch of the ground over which he had galloped, and to give an account of the nature of the country. The day after a battle, the head umpire rode over the battle ground with all the Officers' maps and plans, and compared one with the other, and pointed out the mistakes which ought not to have been made, or approved, if he thought it right to do so.

Twenty-one days in all were allotted to these manoeuvres; seven days were devoted to preliminary instruction, seven days were allotted to work in the field, and seven days to verifying the problems and tasks performed by the Officers. The following were the tasks that were performed by Officers in the field:—The Officers of the western army fought a battle at Voskresensk, then from that place they made a flank march on the Smolensk high road, and fought three retreating battles as far as Viazma. The Officers of the eastern army fought a battle at Voskresensk, then they made a retreat march to Tooshino and Kinsk, and thence an advance, with three battles, along the Smolensk high road.

At the conclusion of the manoeuvres, the Officers of artillery sent in reports to the military authorities, how they would have supplied the forces under their command with ammunition after the battle at Voskresensk. The Officers of "Intendance" reported upon the means they would have employed to remove their baggage when they made their retreat. The medical men also sent in reports as to how they would have supplied their hospitals with every requisite, and how they would have forwarded the wounded to Moscow and Viazma. The other Officers sent in a report of the survey they had made of the River Moskva, and the River Istra. At the conclusion of the manoeuvres in the three districts, the chief umpire on each side sent in a detailed report to St. Petersburg, and these reports were submitted to the inspection of a board composed of the senior Generals in the Russian army. These Officers, after carefully reading the various remarks, came to the conclusion that these manoeuvres are most useful. In the first place, they cost the country very little; secondly, in an enclosed and confined district you can manoeuvre with freedom, and without doing any damage to the crops; and, thirdly, you give the opportunity to Colonels and other Field Officers who do not command brigades, during the autumn manoeuvres, to command brigades and divisions, and learn the higher commands in warfare. It was resolved that these "skeleton manoeuvres" should take place in every military district in Russia, certainly once, if not twice, a year; but that first of all the direction of the manoeuvres should be specially confined to the western frontier.

From the various subjects I have brought before you to-day, it would be very easy to make deductions, and possibly to draw comparisons. But if I were to do so it might be misconstrued into an attempt at criticism, so I shall leave it for Officers who are older and far wiser than myself to consider whether any of the systems I have mentioned this afternoon might be beneficial if adopted into our own service.

3 'In Memoriam' *On horseback through Asia Minor* (London: Sampson Low, 7th edition, 1878), pp. xxxii-xl.

It may seem strange to the general public thus introducing into a book a dedicatory chapter after five thousand copies of the work are in circulation, and it has gone through six editions. The author's excuse must be that since these pages were written he has lost his fellow-traveller and faithful friend. Wishing to leave some lasting tribute to his memory, this chapter has been written.

George Radford, the object of these remarks, commenced life as a sailor-boy. He grew rapidly and was soon six feet in height. One day he came to London. His smart appearance attracted the attention of a recruiting corporal. A short time afterwards George Radford found himself a trooper in the Royal Horse Guards. He gained the good-will of his comrades and officers. Whenever there was any extra work to be done, he was one of the first to volunteer assistance and, strong himself, he was always ready to protect the weak against the strong.

Years rolled by. George Radford would have been promoted to the rank of non-commissioned officer, but, in soldier's language he was no scholar. The old spirit of adventure which had prompted him when a lad to go to sea, had not died away. I wanted a servant. He knew that I liked travel. He applied for the situation. I took him.

I will pass over the numerous journeys in, so to speak, civilized countries, where he accompanied me. It is now about five years ago since General Kaufmann commenced his march upon Khiva. I wished, if possible, to be with the Khivans at the time of the attack. When on the road, I caught a typhoid fever at Naples, and for four long months was nursed by my faithful servant. That same autumn the Carlist war broke out. The editor of the *Times* wanted a military correspondent, and asked me if I would go to Don Carlos's head-quarters. I consented. At first I tried to dissuade Radford from accompanying me by pointing out that he had a wife and children – that he might be shot. These arguments had no effect, "Must die someday, sir," was his reply; "may be run over by an omnibus at home! I nursed you through your fever. You will let me go, won't you?"

Many a risk the poor fellow ran in that campaign. He was under fire at the battles of Allo, Dicastillo, Viana, and Mañeru, besides being present during the siege of Tolosa and the capture of Estella. Always cheery, he was equally at home in the trenches before Tolosa, or cooking a beefsteak for Don Carlos's staff in the redoubt at Dicastillo.

On our way back to France, and when crossing the mountains near Bera, Radford had a very narrow escape for his life. There were two paths winding round a rock. They overhung a mountain stream. The lower path was some fifty feet from the water. The rivulet dashed over the pebbles below. It was in no place more than a foot deep. The side nearest the precipice was broken away.

To my surprise the guide who accompanied us chose the topmost track. He was followed by Baron von Wedell, the correspondent of the *Cologne Gazette*, then came Mr. O'Shea, on the staff of the *Standard*. As I reached the upper path, thinking that the lower one was the safer of the two, I called out to Radford, who was about fifty yards behind me, "You had better take the undermost track." He did so. A minute or two later, a sound as of some falling rocks reached our ears. I looked in the direction of the noise, and saw Radford on his back; his foot was fast in the stirrup, the horse with only his forefeet on the path – the animal's body half over the precipice, and the ground crumbling away beneath his exertions to free himself. I jumped off my own animal and drew my hunting knife to cut Radford's stirrup-leather and free his foot; but, before I could reach him, by a frantic effort he had managed to extricate himself. Almost as he did so, the struggling horse disappeared over the edge of the precipice. A dull thud reached our ears as the poor brute's body struck against the rocks below.

"Had better go down and get my cloak – it is strapped to the saddle – had I not, sir?" inquired Radford, a little exhausted by his struggle to release himself, but with his usual air of composure. "Yes", I replied. Baron von Wedell and Mr. O'Shea remained on the path, looking at the horse, which lay on its back on the rocks below us, perfectly motionless. My servant commenced unstrapping his waterproof from the saddle – the animal began giving some signs of life.

"*Donnerwetter*, he is not killed!" remarked my German companion. The baron was right. The horse, after a few minutes, appeared to recover from his stupor, and endeavoured to rise; presently he did so. Later on I brought him back to London – Radford ever afterwards taking the keenest interest in the animal's welfare – a horse which, according to him, had fallen the height of Knightsbridge barracks, and had been none the worse for the tumble.

Sleeping out in the open during the Carlist campaign had somewhat impaired my servant's health. I did not let him accompany me during my next two journeys to Central Africa and Khiva. However, just before I started for the travels related in these volumes, he so entreated to be allowed to accompany me that I consented. In November, 1877, and when the Russo-Turkish war was at its height, he again went with me to the East – this time not to Asia Minor, but to European Turkey and the Balkans – never grumbling no matter how great were the hardships and privations which he had to undergo. The only thing which could make him lose his temper was the idleness of a Turkish servant called Osman, and who was just as lazy as the individual of the same name mentioned in these volumes.

Radford was present during the memorable battle of Tashkessan, when General Baker, with 2400 Turks, proved more them a match for thirty battalions of the Russian Guard, the choicest troops of the Czar, and hard my servant worked throughout that life-long day carrying water to the wounded, and aiding the doctors in their work of humanity.

The battle of Tashkessan was certainly the most brilliant action during the campaign. As on this occasion the Turks were led by an Englishman, it may perhaps be considered a sufficient excuse for my relating very briefly what occurred during the memorable fight.

It was the last day of the year 1877, General Baker, who commanded a small Turkish division, had received orders to cover the retreat of Shakir Pasha's army from Kamarli. This retrograde movement had become necessary owing to General Gourko having crossed the Balkans and reached Curiae, thus virtually turning Shakir Pasha's left flank; and threatening his communications with Sofia. The village of Tashkessan lies on the main road between Sofia and Kamarli. It is about six miles from the last-named village. Two mountains in the shape of saddles slope down towards the Tashkessan road, which runs through a sort of gorge for a few hundred yards, and then debauches on to the plain of Kamarli. Shakir Pasha's left flank was threatened by 30,000 Russians under the command of Gourko. At the same time, he had opposite to him, and entrenched before Kamarli, a hostile force estimated at about 22,000 men.

Shakir Pasha's *corps d'armée* itself originally – that is, on the first of November, 1877, consisted of about 20,000 Turks. Owing to the intense cold and want of medical stores, this force was continually diminishing – some days as many as 350 men being rendered unfit for service, owing to disease, frostbite, and other causes. At the time of which I write, Shakir Pasha's troops did not amount to 14,000 men.[4] Two thousand four hundred of these soldiers with seven guns, and about two squadrons of cavalry, had been detached under General Baker. This officer was to hold the Russians in check at Tashkessan, whilst Shakir Pasha with, it must be remembered, a hostile force considerably superior to his own, and immediately in front of him, was to effect his retreat across the Kamarli plain towards Petric and Tatar Bazardjik. I had ridden on with General Baker the previous evening to Tashkessan.

The first faint gleam of the sun was just beginning to appear when a mounted soldier rode into our head-quarters at a gallop with the announcement that the enemy was advancing to attack. General Baker had asked for reinforcements on the previous day; Shakir Pasha had refused to give them. "Not a man can be spared", was his reply. "You must hold on and till the death, for the safety of the whole army depends upon you." We could see the enemy advancing. Their long lines of infantry extended from right to left across the plain. Their cavalry along the Sofia-Tashkessan road, looking in the distance, and through

---

4 'I received the information as to these figures from one of Shakir Pasha's staff officers; I believe it to be accurate. General Baker is writing a book about the recent campaign in the Balkans. He had every means of knowing the number of Shakir Pasha's force. I must refer the public to General Baker's more detailed account of the engagement.' [FGB]

the telescope, like interminable black dots speckling the snow-covered ground. The dots came nearer and nearer. They were no longer dots: they were long lines of horsemen. They came closer. The Russians brought seventeen guns against General Baker's position, where he had but seven, and these small ones. The firing became hot and fast, and when at about 500 yards distance, the whole of the Russian Guard broke out into one unanimous cheer of "Hurrah!".

As the cheer died away we appeared to be surrounded. The enemy overlapped us on our right and left, whilst he was steadily nearing our centre. Things looked very black at that moment. It seemed as if General Baker would be forced to retire for a few hundred yards, and take up another position, when that officer, suddenly turning to his trumpeter, remarked, "Sound the Turkish cry – the appeal to God!" Then, as if with one voice, there burst from the lips of the 2400 the shout, "*Allah il Allah!*".

It was a sensation worth feeling; it was a moment worth ten of the best years of a man's life; and a thrill passed through my heart at the time – that curious sort of a thrill – it can only be described as a thrill – the sensation which you experience when you read of something noble and heroic, or see a gallant action performed. It was grand to hear these 2400 Mahometans, many of them raw levies at the time, cheering back in defiance of those thirty picked battalions, the choicest troops of the Czar.

"By Jove, there is a devil of a lot of them!" The voice came from a bystander who was standing in the direction of the Russian left. General Baker, whose attention had been called by the remark, and who was scanning the enemy's movements through his field-glasses, without removing the latter from his eye, quietly observed, "I think we shall be able to account for them yet."

Presently his aide-de-camp rode up to him with the announcement, "All is lost! Shakir Pasha has retired; he has abandoned you. We shall be taken prisoners." It was a critical moment, but now came out the genius of a first-class British general, and the sturdy pluck of a true British soldier, "It is not so hopeless as you think", replied General Baker, "Anyhow, we will die in our places ere we surrender to the enemy. Here! Colonel Allix!" – this to an English officer, formerly in the Guards, and now on General Baker's staff – "there is a good position a little to the left of the road; take a couple of guns there, and annoy those masses of infantry which are advancing in that direction." This was done. The artillery fire, ably directed by the colonel, did enormous execution in the enemy's ranks, and checked for a time his advance. In the meantime, Captain Thackeray, who had arrived at Tashkessan a few days before, volunteered to lead two squadrons of horse down the hill in the direction of some Russian cavalry which were gradually advancing towards our right. The movement was skilfully executed, and the gallant manner in which this officer led his men against a force ten times their number elicited hearty cheers from the Turkish infantry.

But the enemy, though held in check for a moment, was not baffled. On he came in never-ending streams of skirmishers, which, as they reached our position, formed into seas of desperate soldiery. An exclamation from General Baker, who was eagerly scanning the left of our position with his field-glasses, called my attention in that direction. We could see our men retiring, but in good order. They had been forced back by sheer weight of numbers. It now became necessary to withdraw our right and centre from the vicinity of the rapidly advancing foe, and to take up a fresh defensive line on the second saddle or height, which was about half a mile in rear of the first position. Four guns were playing with considerable effect from the road below us on the advancing foe. The Russians had concentrated a very heavy cross-fire on this point. The Turkish gunners became unsteady. They limbered up one piece, and commenced retiring. If the other had followed, the day would probably have been lost. General Baker saw this at a glance, and, sticking his spurs into his horse, he galloped down the slippery height – his animal now up to the haunches in the snow, then sliding down the steepest of declivities – the loose stones and pebbles flying like hail in the faces of those who attempted to follow him. He rode up to the retreating artillerymen, made them return with the cannon to the original position, and remained there for more than an hour, in the most exposed part of the field – his presence so encouraging the gunners that they redoubled their exertions, and fired so fast and accurately that for a time they completely paralyzed the Russians' movements.

It was between eleven and twelve o'clock; the great orb of day was at its height, nature above us looked calm and peaceful; below us wounded men and corpses, and horses without riders galloping to and fro. Shakir Pasha's troops could be seen in the distance, in full retreat across the plain; and if the Russians had succeeded in breaking through Baker's line, every man of this force must have been lost.

The Russians probably saw their foe, as it were, escaping from their grasp.[5] The Russian officers again cheered on their men to that attack – not now thirty battalions, for ere this more than 2000 Muscovites had bit the dust. The afternoon wore on. General Baker sat on his grey horse, gazing at his watch. Would that day ever finish? Would that sun ever go down? As we sat looking at our watches, the Turks gazed at the great dial of nature gradually descending

---

5 'I was at this time with Mr. Francis Francis, the *Times* correspondent. As we were ascending the height leading to the second position, my breast plate broke, the saddle turned, I found myself in the snow. I had sprained my ankle a few days previous; the pain was very great, and I could not put my foot to the ground. The Russians were not more than a quarter of a mile from us. It is not every man who will dismount from his horse on such an occasion to help a friend, and the more particularly when the bullets are flying about in close proximity to his person. Mr. Francis, however, did not hesitate for a moment. Springing from his horse, he coolly took off his coat and waistcoat, unwound a long sash from his waist, mended with it the breast plate, then helped me on my horse, and I was able to reach the position.' [FGB]

towards the western horizon. All this time a life and death struggle was going on between the two forces. It was the last position that the Turks could hold. Every moment gained was so much time lost to the enemy. The Russian general knew this: he collected his men for a final effort. The Czar's officers gallantly advanced to the attack: their cheers were met by counter-cheers.

General Baker was in the foremost and most exposed place, standing in a hail of rifle bullets and shell fire. He was encouraging his men. He had confidence in his men, and the men had confidence in their general. The Russians came up the hill at the double, but broke with the Turkish fire; and the Turks, as their foes retreated, charged home with the cold steel, and drove them into the valley below. When our force was mustered that evening, it was found that more than 800 of the 2400 Turkish heroes had given their lives for Turkey.[6]

Radford saw this memorable engagement, and was with me on the occasion of the retreat to Petric. He was of great use to Doctors Gill and Heath, helping them to dress the wounded during the battle of Meska.

It was in this engagement that Colonel Allix performed an act of bravery which in our own army would have won him the Victoria Cross. General Baker had received instructions from Shakir Pasha to make a reconnaissance in force and destroy Meska. The Russian troops had been driven out of this village, the Turks were almost in possession of it, when a panic seized the Mahometans. It was afterwards said that some lieutenant had cried out that the Muscovites had made a flanking movement, and were about to take the Turks in rear. Anyhow, all the Sultan's troops ran away as fast as possible, leaving General Baker and Colonel Allix about 300 yards from the village. This was filled with Bulgarians; the latter were amusing themselves by butchering the Turkish wounded as they lay helpless on the ground. "We must burn that village", remarked General Baker, and Allix, without saying a word, galloped into it, accompanied only by one orderly. Once inside, and when in the midst of the Bulgarians, and with the Russians advancing towards him from the other end of the hamlet, he set fire to some straw stacks, which speedily ignited the houses. Many shots were fired at him by the Bulgarians and Russians; however, the gallant officer escaped, and returned afterwards to Constantinople to receive the order of the Osmanli, a decoration which he had so nobly won.

From Othlukoi to Tatar Bazardjik, and during the disastrous retreat of Suleiman Pasha's army across the mountains to the sea at Kara Atch, Radford accompanied me, never complaining, never murmuring, in spite of the

---

6 'For the account of the muster and the loss incurred, I am indebted to Dr. Gill. This gentleman, with Dr. Heath, had been in the thick of the fight throughout the day, performing the duties of a good Samaritan, regardless of the Russian fire. Dr. Gill, whose gallantry under fire and devotion to the cause he served had repeatedly won the applause of Mehemet Ali, Rejib Pasha, Shakir Pasha, besides General Baker, was subsequently decorated at Stamboul by Raouf Pasha, the Minister for War.' [FGB]

incessant privations, amounting sometimes almost to starvation, to which he was exposed. On one occasion, having had no sleep for more than forty hours – being nearly all that time on the march – and after having to wade through deep snow, the poor fellow fell asleep on his horse seven times, each time losing his balance, and coming on the ground. In the last tumble he put his thumb out of joint. Dr. Gill coming up after Radford had mounted, the latter put out his hand and had his thumb pulled into joint without even dismounting for the operation.

Many a time my servant would bring a piece of biscuit, his own ration for the day, and try and persuade me that he had already partaken himself, whilst food had not perhaps passed his lips for twenty-four hours. At last we reached Constantinople, and shortly afterwards left for London. A typhus fever, contracted during the retreat of Suleiman Pasha's army, showed its first symptoms in Radford in Vienna; indeed, as were leaving for England. When we arrived at Dover he was almost unconscious. Everything that human skill could devise was brought to bear, the best medical attendance was secured, but it was too late.

Radford's constitution, already enfeebled by the hardships of the recent campaign, was not proof against the fatal malady. Forty eight hours after reaching England's shores, one of the noblest souls that ever tenanted a human frame soared away towards that unknown bourn from which no one can ever return.

George Radford lies in Dover cemetery. Can more be said about him than is contained in the lines engraven on his tomb, "He was a brave soldier, a faithful servant, and as true as steel"? Yes, there might have been added, "In him I have lost a sincere friend." There are not many men who would give their lives for their friends. Radford would have readily given his life for his master.

Part 5

Sketches, Obituaries and Extracts from Selected Memoirs

1 William Henry Lucy 'Portraits in Oil. XCII: The Latest Lion', in *The World* (26 April 1876).

2 Thomas Gibson Bowles 'Men of the Day. No. CXLIII: Captain Frederick G. Burnaby', in *Vanity Fair* (2 December 1876).

3 Anonymous 'Men and Women of the Day. No. LXXXVIII: Capt. Frederick Gustavus Burnaby' in *The Hornet* (24 October 1877).

4 William Henry Lucy 'Radford in Asia' in *Mayfair* (20 November 1877).

5 Anonymous 'Pictures in Little, – N° 12. "His name the Synonym of Daring"' in *The Owl* (20 May 1882).

6 Edmund Hodgson Yates 'Colonel Fred Burnaby at Home' in *The World* (17 July 1882).

7 John Augustus O'Shea (1) 'Explorers I have met' in *Tinsley's Magazine* vol. 33 (August 1883); (2) extract from *Roundabout Recollections* (London: Ward and Downey, 1892), p. 58-9 & 337-8.

8 Eugene Schuyler, 'Colonel Fred Burnaby: recollections of his career' in *New York Tribune* (22 January 1885).

9 Anonymous, 'Colonel Burnaby as a journalist' in *Northern Echo* (27 January 1885).

10 Henry Tracey Coxwell, 'Colonel Burnaby's ballooning' in *Pall Mall Gazette* (27 January 1885).

11 Edward Marston, 'Colonel Fred Burnaby' in *Publishers' Circular* (1 February 1885). Reprinted in *After work: fragments from the workshop of an old publisher* (London: W. Heinemann, 1904), pp. 168-72.

12 Thomas Gibson Bowles, 'Colonel Frederick Gustavus Burnaby' in *Vanity Fair* (February 1885).

13 Martin Farquhar Tupper, 'Colonel Fred Burnaby' in *The Brooklyn Magazine*, vols. 2-3 (1885), pp. 89-90. Reprinted in *My life as an author* (London: Sampson Low, Marston, Searle & Rivington, 1886), pp. 328-30.

14 Henry William Lucy, 'Fred Burnaby' in *Faces and Places* (London: Henry & Co., 1892), pp. 1-22.

15 Evelyn Burnaby, extract from *A Ride from Land's End to John O' Groat's* (London: Sampson Low, Marston & Co., 1893), pp. ix-xxii

16 Archibald Forbes, extract from *Czar and Sultan: the adventures of a British lad in the Russo-Turkish war of 1877-78* (Bristol: J.W. Arrowsmith, 1894), pp. 316-8.

17 William Henry Lucy, extract from 'Ups and Downs in My Life' in *Strand Magazine*, vol. 31 (January 1906), pp. 33-40. [A reprint of the article 'A balloon journey with Captain Burnaby' in *Mayfair* (3 July 1877).]

18 Julian Hawthorne, 'Fred Burnaby, the hero that was' in *New York Tribune* (26 April 1908).

19 Amy Charlotte Stuart Menzies (née Bewicke), extract from *Memories Discreet and Indiscreet by a Woman of No Importance* (London: Herbert Jenkins, 1917), pp. 52-60.

Introduction

Quite how Burnaby first came to be involved with the literary community is unclear, but by the 1860s he was on very close terms with Thomas Gibson Bowles and it may have been through him that he met Algernon Borthwick (later Lord Glenesk), who had taken over as editor of the *Morning Post* on the death of his father. Bowles had started his writing career with the *Morning Post* and it would therefore have been quite natural for Burnaby to send in letters to the *Post* in parallel to those he wrote to *Vanity Fair* after its foundation in 1868. In 1873 Burnaby persuaded John Thadeus Delane, editor of *The Times*, to employ him as a 'special correspondent' with the Carlist forces in Spain. Although Burnaby's was not a household name by 1873, he was increasingly well connected and had almost certainly met Delane before he approached him for this commission. Once in Spain he not only met several others acting there as reporters, but became a member of the wider, but close-knit community of special correspondents and war artists. After his return from Central Asia in 1876 and the publication of *A ride to Khiva*, Burnaby became eminently newsworthy in his own right. Many of those called upon to write sketches about him therefore knew him personally and there were very few occasions when he received anything other than a good press (a point noted by Lord Wolseley). With the possible exception of Bowles, most of these contacts would have been made after the mid-1860s and it is therefore not surprising that none of them mentioned in detail the journeys he made before his trips to Spain in 1868 to 1870. Slightly more surprising is their failure to mention the trip (or trips) he made to Russia other than that in the winter of 1870/71.

The sketches given here are typical examples of those written while he was alive, to which is added a sketch of Radford, who also became a minor celebrity after the publication of *On horseback through Asia Minor*. The author of the sketch in *The Hornet* has not been identified.

Edmund Hodgson Yates (1831-1894) had wide journalistic experience before founding *The World* in 1874, one of the objectives of which was to feature a regular gossip column (which he wrote himself, using the alias 'Atlas') and features on celebrities. Although not at the top of the social ladder Burnaby was a larger than life character well known around the clubs and featured in the gossip column from time to time, almost invariably being mentioned favourably. Yates and Burnaby evidently became close, with sketches of Burnaby being included in two of his long-running series ('Portraits in Oil', written by William Henry Lucy (1842-1924), and 'At Home', probably written by Yates himself).

Burnaby and Lucy, later to be knighted and become one of the most respected parliamentary sketch writers of his time, had met in September 1874, shortly after Lucy had joined the staff of the *Daily News*. They made a balloon ascent together from Crystal Palace and thereafter became close friends. Lucy wrote an account of the ascent in the *Daily News* of 15 September 1874 ('A balloon journey with the French aeronauts: from Sydenham to Highwood') and expanded this in an article in *Mayfair* of 3 July 1877, followed by another *Mayfair* article, this time about Radford, of 20 November 1877. Lucy was the co-founder of the short-lived *Mayfair* in 1876, but resigned as its editor in 1879, not long before it ceased publication. Meanwhile, he had written the

'Portraits in Oil' sketch for *The World* of 26 April 1876. Large sections of this sketch in *The World* (omitted therefore in the extract given here) were reprinted in the chapter on Burnaby in Lucy's memoirs, *Faces and Places*, which is also reproduced here. The memoir is important since it provides the closest we have to a chronology of Burnaby's early travels, albeit with some obvious errors. The *Mayfair* description of the balloon ascent was reprinted almost verbatim in the *Strand Magazine* many years later, but with new illustrations. Burnaby hosted a dinner for Lucy before his departure on a trip to the United States and Japan in 1883.

As described in his own sketch, John Augustus O'Shea (1839-1905) and Burnaby became friends while both were covering the Carlist War in 1873 and remained on good terms thereafter. Burnaby chaired the farewell lunch for O'Shea prior to his departure for the United States in 1884. Before his work in Spain O'Shea had become known for his despatches from the siege of Paris, where he would have been reporting alongside Tommy Bowles. Later he covered the Bengal famine and worked on *Tinsley's Magazine*, to which he contributed the article on explorers that included Burnaby. O'Shea also wrote two memoirs: *Leaves from the Life of a Special Correspondent* (1885) and *Roundabout Recollections* (1892). Burnaby was mentioned again briefly in the latter.

Tommy Bowles was probably Burnaby's closest friend and their relationship has been described already in some detail. The sketch accompanying the caricature of Fred in *Vanity Fair* is one of several to stress Fred's independence of spirit and firmness of friendship. Bowles's sad, angry obituary is one of the shortest included here, but nonetheless neatly encapsulates Fred's life and character.

When news of Fred Burnaby's death reached London, the popular press devoted not just columns, but pages to his obituaries. Many of these were little more than recapitulations of his life by journalists who did not know him well, but others were by journalists and others who had actually known him, in some cases intimately. The obituaries and memoirs contained here are all in the latter category.

The anonymous obituary may have been written by Fred's personal secretary, James Percival Hughes, or someone with access to him.

Henry Tracey Coxwell (1819-1900) trained originally as a dentist, but by the late 1840s had become a professional aeronaut with a balloon factory in Sussex. He made literally hundreds of ascents, many with the equally well-known balloonist James Glaisher (1819-1903). Like Burnaby he was a member of the Aeronautical Society of London and they knew each other well.

Archibald Forbes (1838-1900) was a British war correspondent. Entering the Royal Dragoons as a private, he gained considerable practical experience of military life and affairs. Being invalided from his regiment, he settled in

London and became a journalist, working mainly for the *Daily News*. Among the campaigns he covered were the Franco-Prussian War, the Carlist War and the Russo-Turkish War. He also covered the Bengal famine of 1873/4 and accompanied the Prince of Wales on his tour to India of 1875/6.

Julian Hawthorne (1846-1934) was an American writer and journalist, the son of novelist Nathaniel Hawthorne (of *Tanglewood Tales*) and Sophia Peabody (a writer and painter). He wrote numerous poems, novels, short stories, mystery/detective fiction, essays, travel books, biographies and histories. He travelled widely, reporting on the Bengal famine for *Cosmopolitan* magazine, and the Spanish-American War, for the *New York Journal*, and met Burnaby on several occasions. The alternative description of how Burnaby met his end probably needs to be taken with a pinch of salt.

Edward Marston (1825-1914) was a publisher who joined the firm that had originally been founded in London by Sampson Low. In addition to Burnaby, Marston published many of the best selling authors of the day, including Jules Verne, Harriet Beecher Stowe, Wilkie Collins, Thomas Carlyle, Sir Henry M. Stanley, Charles Dickens and Sir Edward Bulwer Lytton.

Eugene Schuyler (1840-1890) was an American scholar, writer, translator, explorer and diplomat. Like Burnaby he was fluent in Russian and had travelled widely in Central Asia. Whether he and Fred were actually friends is unclear, but he dined with Fred and Valentine Baker at the Marlborough Club during a visit to London in 1878, commenting: 'Baker is sad and quiet. Burnaby is full of spirits.'[1]

Martin Farquhar Tupper (1810-1889) was an English writer and poet, the author of *Proverbial Philosophy*. Although his books sold well, when he fell upon hard times Fred was one of those who provided financial support to him.

Mrs. Stuart Menzies (née Amy Charlotte Bewicke-Bewicke, 1846-1933) was the wife of an army officer, Captain Stuart Alexander Menzies of the Gordon Highlanders, who had been a contemporary of Burnaby, and whom she divorced in 1887. In the early years of the twentieth centuries she wrote a number of colourful memoirs (one of which led to her being sued successfully for libel by Brigadier-General F.P. Crozier), including sketches of both Fred and Evelyn Burnaby.

---

1   Eugene Schuyler, *Selected Essays, with a memoir by Evelyn Schuyler Schaeffer* (New York: Charles Scribner's Sons, 1901), p. 112.

1 'Portraits in Oil. XCII. The Latest Lion' in *The World*, 26 April 1876.

One evening in the autumn of the year 1874, two strangers might have been observed slowly sauntering on the outskirts of a concourse of citizens gathered in the grounds of the Crystal Palace at Sydenham. The elder was of dark and somewhat sallow complexion, and there was something in his appearance which indicated that, though at present clad in the narrow trousers and tightly-fitting coat of the Frank, he was not unfamiliar with the more loosely-designed costume of the Turk. The younger man was unmistakably English, and held his umbrella with a firm yet light grasp which to the keen observer showed an intimate acquaintance with the climate of London. His figure was one that would have attracted attention in any company, for he measured six feet four in his stockings. As he towered head and shoulders above the crowd, a cloud brooded over his handsome face, with its quick-glancing resolute eyes, and the kindly merry smile that ever played about his moustached lips. In the centre of the crowd a vast balloon was being filled with gaseous matter, and as the gusts of wind, born of the autumnal evening, caught the broad expanse of silk, it swayed hither and thither, making lanes through the crowd and disclosing to the two strangers the roomy car attached. The cloud deepened on the brow of the younger stranger, and striding forward he watched more closely the preparations for the departure of the balloon. It was known that there had been great competition on the part of an adventurous public for seats in the car. But the adventurers had counted on a pleasant trip, and evidently did not care about the journey on this gusty evening, when experienced aeronauts prophesied calamity, and held back. Deeper still grew the cloud on the face of the stranger, and he drew nearer yet to the balloon. The wind moaned through the trees overhead; the balloon rolled about like a thing possessed; the car had already received its full complement of passengers; the ropes that held it to the ground were being loosened; in another second it would be sailing through space. Then suddenly the cloud fell from the face of the younger stranger, and with a quick '*Au revoir!*' to his Excellency, his companion, he jumped into the car and tumbling down amongst its occupants sailed away with them out of sight.[2]

The younger stranger was 'Fred' Burnaby of the Royal Horse Guards, just now returned from Central Asia in time for the season in London; and it is pardonable to dwell on the incident with some elaboration, because it illustrates vividly the character of the soldier who has since modestly performed a feat unprecedented in the history of civilised man. When a year and a half ago

---

[2] It may be inferred from this that Burnaby's companion was the Turkish Ambassador to the Court of St. James, Constantine Musurus Pasha (1807-1891), who had come to London in 1851.

Captain Burnaby strolled down to the Crystal Palace to see the Duruofs off in the balloon, he had no more intention of forming one of the party than he had of walking across the glass-roof of the central transept. He had, in fact, a little dinner-party *chez lui*, and it was the recollection of this circumstance that troubled him when he saw the unexpected opportunity of joining an expedition from which others had retreated because it was too highly spiced with danger. That was the one spice found irresistible by his appetite; and so, stubbornly closing his eyes upon the prospect of the perplexity and despair that would gradually open around a company of guests invited to a feast the founder of which had two hours before dinner gone off to the clouds, he tumbled into the car and began to enjoy himself.

[The following paragraphs, describing his early life and ride to Khiva, are duplicated in Lucy's memoir (see later) and omitted here.]

It is whispered in the mess-rooms, where all these things are talked of, that Fred Burnaby has made a report to the Horse Guards on the military situation in Central Asia which justifies the perils of the journey, and since the Victoria Cross is out of the question, ought to be worth a majority to the gallant captain. But even if no substantial benefit were derivable from the dashing ride, it is one upon the story of which Englishmen may dwell with grim satisfaction, and the British soldier may linger around with pride. We have heard a good deal lately in the necessity of keeping up British prestige in the continent of Asia, and have even, in our anxiety to checkmate Russia, agreed to call our Queen 'Empress'. But we may be sure the sight of this gigantic sheepskin-clad Guardsman galloping into Khiva, having crossed over from Windsor in the depth of winter *pour passer le temps*, will have an effect upon the Russians scarcely less desirable than that which will follow upon the proclamation of the Queen as Empress of India; while the story of the dauntless horseman, slowly passing, as it will pass, from mouth to mouth along the Asian frontier, will be worth a pitched battle fought and won for India.

2 'Men of the Day – No. CXLIII: Captain Frederick G. Burnaby' in *Vanity Fair*, 2 December 1876.

The son of a Leicestershire parson of good family and possessions, Fred Burnaby was sent to Harrow, and thence into the Blues, for which he seemed to be particularly suited, by reason of his great stature and strength. The first years of his discretion he devoted to feats of activity and endurance, and that with so much success that he soon became reputed the strongest man in the British Army, as well as a more daring and agile gymnast than had ever yet been seen in an amateur of his size. The back-lifts and hock-swings he threw and the weights he lifted are matters of club-history, and his boxing earned for him the name of "Heenan".

But he soon developed other aims than these. The perseverance and untiring application which are his distinctive qualities being sated with physical pursuits, which brought him through much exertion into sickness, he cast about for other laurels; and, after a career of ballooning, in which he made himself sufficiently expert to conduct his ascents without other captaincy than his own, he devoted himself to the study of languages. By dint of incredible labour he mastered Russian more perfectly than perhaps any other Englishman of our time; by continual sojourns in Seville he learnt to speak Spanish almost like a Castilian; and he has recently acquired a respectable knowledge of Arabic, besides that current smattering of French and German to which all Society lays claim. Thus fortified he essayed literature, and, coincidentally with a visit which he paid to the Carlist camp, the *Times* was enriched with some excellent letters, with the hot breath of battle in them, which some to this day would attribute to the Infant Blue, who was known to be a spectator in the front of the fighting. As his experiences grew, so grew the wish to extend them, and he has been several times at St. Petersburg, once to Central Africa, and last to Khiva, by way of spending to some better purpose the leave which the Household Cavalry commonly give to shooting in England or to amusement on the Continent.

One of the special characteristics by which "Fred" is marked out from among the order of young men with whom he might hastily be classed, is that he has never sought to be popular in the Society sense, and that he is no great respecter of persons. With ladies, indeed, he takes an inordinately deferential and mincing tone, yet he is by no means a ladies' man; with men he is blunt, outspoken, and on the defensive always, yet those of them who know him know that to his friend he is staunch and true as steel, and to all incapable of any mean or ungenerous action. He is simple and *naïf* in his ways of speech, yet not easily duped, and like most big men modest and retiring unless there be some exacting physical business on hand. Although he courts the Muses, he is above consulting the Graces, and perhaps there is no man in the Service who off parade looks less like a British Cavalry officer than he. He has had every kind of illness and tried every kind of remedy, from exclusive milk-diet for a fortnight to exclusive bacon for a month. Nevertheless his temper is agreeable and gentle, his industry and application prodigious, and having in him no tinge of conceit, he may be said to possess all those qualities which in an idle and self-sufficient age go to the making of its best kind of men.

Jehu Junior[3]

---

3   Jehu Junior (in allusion to a biblical prophet who effected the downfall of his enemies) was a pen-name of Thomas Gibson Bowles, a great friend of Burnaby and from whom he had obtained £200 to found *Vanity Fair* and the name of which he had suggested. Spy's caricature shows Fred in evening dress, with his chin powdered to make it less blue, his usual habit after shaving. It was said that only in evening dress and uniform did Fred ever look remotely respectable. That he did not like the caricature is shown in a letter quoted by Alexander: "I do not like it, it makes me as ugly as nature has. The artist reminds me of a Chinaman who sketched old K. The admiral complained that the likeness was not flattering. The old Chinaman replied: 'How can I handsome face make when handsome face no have got.' I am like K. I wish for a little more flattery."

3 'Men and Women of the Day. No. LXXXVIII: Capt. Frederick Gustavus Burnaby' in *The Hornet*, 24 October 1877.

"Is there danger, and how much of it?" is a question a large class of Englishmen are now in the habit of asking themselves. The Grand Tour, as it was understood by our ancestors, is ignored. What suited Horace Walpole, or Sterne, or Dr. Tobias Smollett is only an outing with the new generation. To ask a man pretending to the character of a traveller if he has crossed from Harwich to Rotterdam, and made a tour of the dead cities of the Zuider Zee, would be to affront him. The Rhine and the Black Forest are for your tailor; Venice and the cities of Italy are common-place; Syria and the Holy Land are for humdrum tourists who peregrinate the Levant under the guardianship of Cook or Gaze. To be an excursionist in our day is to have risked life on the summit of some unknown Alp, to have fought a passage through Indians on a trackless prairie in America, to have crossed equatorial Africa, or explored the inhospitable steppes of Central Asia. Of this class of adventurers, Captain Burnaby is, perhaps, the most illustrious type. He must not be classed with the foolish Alpine tourist who ascends a mountain for the purpose of doing what nobody has done. Like his two compeers – and the twain are more than his compeers – Captain Burton and Mr. Stanley, Burnaby has had an object in his exploits. At the moment when the Eastern Question, as it is called, once more was presented to Europe, Captain Burnaby determined to contribute to the solution. He resolved to throw light on that mysterious region which, according to those who despair of the future of England, is the legacy of Russia. He had no encouragement at home. But he made an adventurous incursion into Central Asia, which ought to dissipate all alarm as to the progress of Russian Arms in the direction of our Indian Empire. Towards the end of November, in 1875, Captain Burnaby started from London with the intention of entering Khiva. It would be presumptuous in us to enumerate the dangers and difficulties he experienced, inasmuch as everybody who reads is acquainted with the record of the adventurous and perilous journey he accomplished. His 'Ride to Khiva' has taken its place among the most fascinating books of travel we possess.

In 1873 the Russian emissary to England assured Lord Granville that not only was it "far from the intention of the Emperor to take Khiva, but positive orders had been given to prevent it". In face of this declaration – every act of Russia has been made against such a declaration – Khiva has been taken and, according to captain Burnaby, Russian officers talk as coolly of going to India as English officers do of going to Aldershot.

"In my opinion", says Capt. Burnaby, "Russia, from the present position, has not the power of even threatening British India. However, she has the power of threatening points which, should she be permitted to annex them, would form a splendid basis of operations against Hindostan. Merve, Balkh, and Kashgar would make magnificent *étapes*.[4] Russia ought to be clearly given to understand that any advance in the direction of Kashgar, Balkh, or Merve will be looked on by England as a *casus belli*. If this is done, we shall no longer hear from the authorities at St. Petersburg that they are unable to restrain their generals in Turkestan. At the present moment Great Britain, without any European ally, can drive Russia out of Central Asia. If we allow her to keep on advancing, the same arms which we might now employ will one day be turned against ourselves."

Captain Burnaby's book is one of the best specifics against any fear that may be entertained on this head.

As for Captain Burnaby himself, it is enough to say that he is 36 years of age, was educated at Harrow, and subsequently at a German university; that he joined the Royal Horse Guards Blue as cornet in 1859; that he has visited almost every country in the world, and that he is one of the greatest favourites of society.

---

4 In this context *étapes* are military supply bases.

4   "Radford in Asia Minor" in *The World*, 20 November 1877.

"Well, you see, sir, the Capting rides sixteen or seventeen stun, and it's o' no use him getting across a horse what has no bone and sinew, though when we was in Asia the Capting had a very little horse, and it was wonderful to see how it carried him through, day after day, too, with very little to eat, and a great deal to put on, as you may say, the Capting being, as I said, between sixteen and seventeen stun."

The speaker was a tall, straight, well-made young fellow, who, though he was now comfortably attired in civilian dress, bore about him unmistakable marks of the soldier. He might be about forty years of age, though he looked younger, having the advantage of a fresh, frank face, eyes that looked you straight in the face, and a smile of humour always ready to gather about his lips. On this point of age there was, indeed, forthcoming later authentic and detailed information.

"I was forty-two on the 28th of February, and the Capting was thirty-five on the 3rd of March" he said, apparently mentally discovering in this close neighbourhood of dates a distinction not common between distinguished officers and privates in the Royal Horse Guards. Not to make a mystery of the matter, the speaker was Radford, known all over the world as the faithful servant and companion of Captain Burnaby in his ride on horseback through Asia Minor, and, next to Osman, perhaps the most living and distinctive character recently added to English literature. I had always felt a great desire to converse with Radford, the sententious, faithful, courageous, and thoroughly English groom whom circumstances and a habit of obeying his superiors suddenly landed in the midst of the unknown territory washed by the Black Sea and bisected by the Euphrates. A friend of mine had a horse to sell, and was in treaty with Captain Burnaby for its purchase. Radford was to be sent to inspect the animal, and here was the desired opportunity of getting a new view of Asia Minor. What did Radford think of it all? What view did he take of the respective qualities of Turk and Christian, and of the difference between travelling by 'bus from the Bank to the Marble Arch and riding on horseback from Scutari to Batoum?

Radford had been carefully passing his hand down the forelegs of the horse, when he made his observation about the Captain's weight. But the passing reference to Asia brought him bolt upright, and with eyes fixed on the towers of Windsor Castle, which could be seen from the stable-yard, he was evidently thinking of the mosque at Erzeroum. Radford is not prone to be communicative touching adventures which have passed the experience of an average trooper. In truth he is at the outset inclined to dole out his views on foreign affairs as if they were horse pills. But as the subject grows upon him he is not failing in words to describe his impressions. He has been in the Royal Horse Guards for twenty years, during the last half of which period he has fulfilled towards Captain Burnaby the functions performed for "my Uncle Toby" by Corporal Trim.[5] His experience of foreign parts began some four or five years ago, when he was sent for from Rome to attend his master, then lying sick almost unto death, with a fever which had stricken him down whilst on his way to some impossible place in Central Africa. He afterwards accompanied Captain Burnaby through an adventurous residence in Spain during the Carlist War, and was on speaking terms with Don Carlos, whose kingly heart he had moved by the superior succulence of a steak he cooked for him by the camp-fire. Radford smelt a good deal of gunpowder in Spain, his master having an irresistible tendency to get in the neighbourhood of the whistling of rifle balls or the boom of cannon. Once master and man found themselves shut up in a beleaguered town, with a storming party at the walls, and within hasty preparations for mitigating the horrors of a sack.

As for his journey through Asia Minor, Radford regards it much as he would have looked upon an extra parade, "Living hard, working hard, and lying hard". There was of course some privation, crystallised in Radford's mind by the mathematical fact that he "lost three stun two pounds before he got home". But, for the rest, it was not so bad, and "if the Capting was agoing again tomorrow" Radford would cheerfully pack his saddle-bags for the journey. Mrs. Radford, the mother of six children, regards the expeditions with the same unswerving eye to duty. Radford is a soldier, and goes where honour and duty call; Mrs. Radford stops at home and minds the children.

Of the Turks as a nation, Radford, regarding them from quite another point of view, is scarcely less favourable than his master. They are, he says, a kind people, and will share with you anything they have got; "though", as he adds, his mind travelling back to the miserable huts and scanty fare of his entertainers, "it isn't much". Meat is a matter of no moment to them, at least it forms a very small proportion of their daily fare. "Sweets" are, according to Radford, what they generally live upon – sweets and bread, this latter being "not bad stuff", though of course not to be mentioned on the same day with the honest British quartern loaf. Once, somewhere in Armenia, Radford forgets the precise name of the place, he saw a lot of women making bread after "the curiousest fashion". He called Mamut (as he names Mahomet) and, by signs, invited him to accompany him on a visit to the household thus engaged. There were an old lady and three daughters, young girls, one twenty-seven years of age, "and very pretty", Radford says, with an emphasis in which Mrs. Radford might find some significance. Also, there was an "old gentleman" of about seventy. The three daughters were engaged in making bread, which they did with flour and water. When it was made and rolled out thin they, as Radford

---

5   A reference to characters in *The Life and Opinions of Tristram Shandy, Gentleman*, a novel by Laurence Sterne.

says, "dabbed a sort of pillow on it, and carried what stuck to the pillow to an earthenware pan" under which fire was burning. The dough stuck to the heated pan, and left "the pillow" free. When the bread is all baked the pan and the fire-place are, "in Asia", put to other uses. The family, and such neighbours as are privileged to join the family circle, sit round the fireplace, with their feet as close to it as may be convenient, and a cloth spread over their knees to keep the heat in. Thus they sit and converse or work, and as, the fire goes down, and the bread-pan becomes cooler, they put their feet into that, and so make the most of the available heat.

"Were they friendly, or did they regard the call of the stranger as an intrusion?"

"Oh yes, they are friendly – particularly", adds Radford, in his sententious manner, "if they know they are to get anything out of you".

What they looked for at the hands of Radford was a pinch of tea, and for this, according to his account, men and women in, this part of the world will do anything. The old lady, the head of this household, absolutely fawned upon the stranger whose reputation as a purveyor of tea had spread for miles round. Also the old gentleman sitting in the corner did his best to conciliate the powerful stranger. He was "reading away at the bible", Radford says, "and he began reading it to me, though he might just as well have read to the bread-pan". But it was his way of "going for the tea", and doubtless having heard that in the land from which the tea-dowered stranger came there were such things as divergences of opinion among Christians, he attempted further to endear himself to the Englishman by explaining that he was "a Protestant Christian". This was, of course, lost upon Radford, and it was when Mamut reported the conversation to Captain Burnaby, that the Captain translated it for the edification of his servant.

Of this passion for tea Radford was once witness of a remarkable testimony. After having finished the evening meal, he emptied the spent leaves out of the pot into a zinc basin, full of garbage and greasy water. He had been eagerly watched all this time by a young lad of sixteen years of age, who, when, he saw the precious leaves dropped into the basin, swooped down upon it, and, as Radford puts it, "sucked all the water up", and then devoured the leaves. The aged Armenian ladies drawn by the remarkable passion of tea followed Radford about everywhere. It was the most potential bribe, and on one occasion, when the travellers were snowed up for two days, Radford, for a single cup of tea dispensed to an elderly Armenian, got the whole of his master's and his own stockings darned. His process of concluding this bargain was eloquent, though inarticulate. Taking out a pinch of tea from the canister, he held it up in one hand, whilst with the other he displayed a stocking, much in need of darning. Then he made signs of darning the hole, having first held the stocking and then the tea out to the old lady. "She smelt it in a moment", Radford says complacently, evidently regarding this triumph over Asiatic ignorance with feelings of pride. "She clutched at them stockings and some other things I gave her and was off like a shot. She came back in an uncommonly short time with them all darned, and neatly darned too. Then she had her cup of tea, and lor! it were a sight to see her sipping it down and trying to get her head into the cup when it was all gone to finish the last drop. I made her a present of the spent tea-leaves, and she went away as delighted as if I had given her a handful of sovereigns." What they drink in Asia (Radford always refers to "Asia", in an offhand familiar way as if the place were about the size of Windsor, and you went down in the Parliamentary train) is coffee. There is no such thing as beer there. But once at Erzeroum Radford managed to get a bottle of rum, "leastways they called it rum, and it was not so bad for Asia". That rum, Radford believes, or at least such portion of it as he was privileged to drink, saved his life. He had kept it somewhat openly in his quarters at Erzeroum, being under the impression that "them Turks never drunk". But he was cruelly undeceived. Going to bed about half-past ten he took out his bottle of rum, thinking he would have a glass. It felt very light, and he proceeded to make further inquiries by the assistance of a lamp – "a thing with a wick in it which sucks up oil, and smells very bad when it goes out" – which stood on a box. He saw that half of the rum had been abstracted; and his suspicions fell upon "a humbashee". To this functionary Radford attempted by signs to convey his conviction that he was not as honest as was reasonably to be expected on the part of a representative of the law. But though his eyes had a rather fixed look, the man shook his head, and certainly knew nothing about the rum. Radford then called Mamut, to whom he communicated his suspicions. Mamut, who lived under the protection of "the great English Pasha" immediately "went for" the otherwise dreaded omnabashee, and attempted to extract the truth by the physical process of shaking it out of him. But the officer persisted in asserting his innocence, till Mamut dexterously got in a position to smell his breath, "when", as Radford says, "it was all hup with him". He confessed everything, and begged of them not to tell the Pasha (Captain Burnaby) to whom, on the following morning, the unblushing fellow went to prefer a petition for influence in securing his promotion. Radford speaks of his earliest companion, Osman, with the forbearance of a generous nature. Osman was a thorough scamp: shifting, thieving, lying, and grasping. And yet Radford was half sorry when matters came to a crisis, and the scoundrel was finally dismissed under the affecting circumstances related by Captain Burnaby. "We had got to understand each other", Radford says, "and he would not have been half so bad only for his praying. He was always on his knees, specially if there was any work to do. As soon as he got up in the morning he was at it. I used to ask him to do the horses first, but he wouldn't. At first he used to pull off his shoes and stockings, put his feet in water, and then daub his wet hand over his face before he said his prayers. But this took such a time I wouldn't stand it. And, specially after his only pair of stockings wore out, Osman used to keep his boots on, and when he found any water, he put his hand in it and drew it over the outside of his boots. He crowed a good deal about saving time in this way, but I generally had to clean the horses." Mamut Radford found a much better fellow, less given to prayer and more to doing his duty. On the whole, Radford looks back with tenderness upon his fellow servants in his memorable journey, and if by chance Osman's steps were to wander in the direction of Windsor he would be sure of a welcome at Radford's humble home, with liberal provision of every convenience for conducting his frequent religious ceremonial. Only Radford thinks that if Osman were on a visit to England, and there was no work to do "he wouldn't be so particklar about his prayers".

Burnaby at Birmingham
(*The Owl*, 20 May 1882)

5   'Pictures in Little, – Nº 12. "His name the Synonym of Daring"' in *The Owl*, 20 May 1882.

When Australians beat us on the cricket field and a Canadian on the river, when Zulus and Boers worst us in fight, and a British officers leads a skurry at sight of danger we may well ask whether our old supremacy is leaving us, and whether the race capable of going anywhere and doing anything is deteriorating. At such a time it is pleasant to turn to the Colonel, whose name is associated with "pluck" that might be called reckless. It is a pity that such a man cannot find sufficient employment off the platform of political spouters, where his appearance seldom brings him credit. War is a bad game, but it is only in that game that he would be seen at his best, and when England has need of him as a soldier he will do her good service and himself much credit. Meanwhile, though he is a big success as an advertising agent, as a traveller on Conservative nostrums he is a failure; whether from want of demand for old-fashioned remedies or from his unadaptability for the work, it is not easy to say. Perhaps if he tried some other town he might do better.

6 'Colonel Fred Burnaby at Home' in *The World*, July 1882.

Like the ancient travellers who made Jerusalem the centre of their world, or the Bostonians who consider their court-house the "hub" or axle-box of the universe, Colonel Fred Burnaby has established a centre for himself in Mayfair. His topographical skill has decided that it is about equidistant from the Cavalry barracks, in which his regiment, the Blues, is stationed when in London.[6] The gigantic soldier radiates, as it were, from No. 18, Charles-street, since Mrs. Burnaby's delicate health compels her to live abroad. Whether there is regimental duty to be done, or the important functions of Silver Stick to be performed, a *pied-à-terre* in Mayfair is always convenient, No. 18, Charles-street is just this and nothing more. There is a little boudoir crowded with superb Dresden and Sèvres, and in every corner are presents from friends, many of them made on the occasion of Colonel Burnaby's wedding. There are tokens of regard from Mr. Labouchere as from Mr. Yates, handsome souvenirs of the friendship of the Royal Princes, and a beautifully inlaid and mounted revolver from Don Carlos. Essentially the dwelling of a travelled man, the writing room upstairs shows signs unmistakeable of a literary workshop. Apart from the official table, cumbered with the reports and printed forms incidental to the command of a regiment, is another, with heaps of manuscript in the strange scrawl with which the writer thinks it well to tax the intelligence of compositors, and which he likes to see in type before attempting to put the final touches to his novel; for he will not be satisfied any longer with rides to Khiva or Channel voyages in a balloon. Nothing will serve his purpose but the authorship of a novel dealing with political questions and personages. This is the *magnum opus* on which the colonel of the Blues gets to work early in the morning, before his regimental duties take him away to barracks. His manuscript, like his acts and deeds generally, is on a large scale. There are certain men who require elbow-room, and whose height makes ordinary furniture appear absurd. At an ordinary table Colonel Burnaby would find writing crippling work. So he employs a writing-board – like a drawing-board – made out of the side of an old portmanteau. Resting this on one knee, he describes, with great rapidity, the calligraphic puzzles he intends for the printer, sometimes in blue ink, sometimes with a xylographic pen, often with a lead pencil. The rider to Khiva is a living contradiction to the assumption that large and ponderous people are necessarily slow and dull, for the huge form of the descendant – as the genealogists make out – of Edward Longshanks has ever been an obedient and untiring engine, driven hither and thither by an unrestful brain and courage beyond proof. It is not quite certain whether Colonel Burnaby believes in the Longshanks story, but he has at least an unflinching

---

6 The two barracks concerned were at Knightsbridge and Regent's Park.

faith in his own power to pull through in almost any situation. And he has an undeniable knack of succeeding. His last balloon excursion of the many he has made is a case in point. Poor Mr. Powell had just lost his life, and another gentleman had completely failed in a Channel balloon voyage; but Colonel Burnaby succeeded perfectly. It cannot be all luck; but everything he has attempted, except winning a seat at Birmingham, has, in Newmarket parlance "come off". One is constantly hearing it explained that such and such a one has succeeded in such a feat because of his peculiar construction. This was said of "attenuated Wilton",[7] and other eminent horsemen; but the man who rode to Khiva, and through the wildest and roughest part of Asia Minor, is six feet four in his stockings, and massively built into the bargain. He is, therefore, not specially constructed by Nature for ballooning or riding; but, as Americana say "he gets there". The fact is that he is gifted with great tenacity of purpose and with immense physical power. Educated at Harrow and in Germany, he found himself at seventeen, not a "cornet in the Coldstreams" as Mr. Anthony Trollope wrote the other day of one of his heroes, but in the Blues, and soon became distinguished for his extraordinary athletic feats in fencing, boxing, dumb-bell exercise, carrying a pair of ponies under his arms, and so forth. Athleticism, however, played some pranks with young Fred Burnaby's health, and, being a capital linguist, he turned his thoughts to travel. It followed, as a matter of course, that he chose strange routes by earth and air. Like some other eminent persons, Fred Burnaby soon discovered that travelling, unless the traveller writes a book, is a vain thing. It was hard luck for him that MacGahan got first to Khiva, for it was only a sudden attack of typhoid at Naples that prevented him from accompanying, or attempting to accompany, General Kauffman on his memorable expedition to that celebrated oasis. Not being able to go to Khiva, Captain Burnaby went to Spain, and foregathering with the Carlist faction, wrote a series of letters to the *Times*. Accompanied by his faithful servant Radford – now no more – he assisted at Allo, Dicastillo, Vera, and Mañeru, as well as at the capture of Estella and the siege of Tolosa. When the Carlist rebellion collapsed, Captain Burnaby made for Africa, in quest of Chinese Gordon, whom he finally encountered on the Sobat River. In his writing-room now hangs an interesting memorial of this African expedition – a photograph of a group of travellers, including Gessi Pasha,[8] Major Campbell, and several others, every one of whom has since joined the majority, excepting Mr. Russell, Consul at Mosul, son of Dr. William Howard Russell. On his return from the White Nile, Captain Burnaby determined to renew his long-deferred endeavour to ride to Khiva. This expedition commenced on the last

---

7   Thomas Egerton, 2nd Earl of Wilton (1799-1882), a leading sportsman and politician.
8   Romolo Gessi (1831-1881) was an Italian soldier and an explorer of north-east Africa, especially Sudan and the Nile River.

day of November, 1875, and continued through the depth of winter until Khiva was reached, and an amusing and spirited book of travel was written. Next came the famous ride on horseback through Asia Minor, an excursion of two thousand miles through a rough and difficult country, and then the varied experience of the Russo-Turkish war gained with General Baker, but in the purely civil capacity of agent of the Stafford House Committee. How exactly Fred Burnaby kept within the limit of his civil functions will be accurately guessed by anybody who knows him. As on the Khivan expedition, some frightfully cold weather was endured. Poor Radford fell off his horse seven times, overcome by the severity of the frost. The faithful follower only survived this terrible exposure to die subsequently at Vienna of typhus fever, contracted during the retreat of Suleiman Pasha's army. Since the war Colonel Burnaby has taken an active part in politics. A Jingo of the deepest dye, and of tried courage and confidence, he was put forward by the Tories to contest Birmingham in the Conservative interest. It was thought that a popular man, of good presence and dashing style, was the only one to break up the celebrated "cocked-hat constituency", the Radical trilateral fortress *par-excellence*. Colonel Burnaby was evidently the man for Birmingham – if any Tory were possible – and he was encouraged to make the attempt. When "speaking his piece", Colonel Burnaby has the great advantage of a good voice and immense height; and, so far as speechifying went, did very well. His tall figure, striking olive-hued features, and coat thrown well back, after the manner of Lord Rosslyn, are very effective with a mixed audience. It is true that he waves his body about after the manner of Lord Rosslyn and other reeds shaken by the wind; but he propounds the right Jingo stuff – red-hot abuse of Mr. Gladstone, and scornful observations on the degeneracy of the age, the effeminacy of a once warlike race, and so forth. Colonel Burnaby is, as becomes a soldier, a strong advocate for a soldierly way of looking at things, holding strong views concerning flogging in the army, the Eastern Question, and the government of Ireland. If his ideas seem a little old-fashioned, his friends put this down as a peculiarity of a survivor of the Anakim;[9] but, whether they agree with him or not, contrive to separate the man from his opinions. Whether the latter be sound or not, the former has a host of friends not particular to a shade or two of Jingoism, but glad to recognise in the stalwart Horse Guardsman that (according to the late Mr. Carlyle) rare specimen of humanity, a genuine man with a distinct character of his own, full of strong convictions and strong antipathies, a sturdy friend and a "good hater". At his marriage in 1879 with the beautiful heiress, Miss Elizabeth E.F. Hawkins-Whitshed, he was overwhelmed with good wishes by his numerous friends – royal, military, literary, aeronautic. Unfortunately, all the

---

9   Biblically, the Anakim (literally 'long-necked') were the offspring of Anak, a Rephaite (Deuteronomy 2:11).

hopes then formed have not been realised, for Mrs. Burnaby is compelled to live abroad during a great part of the year on account of her delicate health. But no one can expect to be completely happy in health, wealth, success, and reputation. In his present position Colonel Burnaby, yet in the flower of his age, has three avenues open to ambition – politics, war, and literature. It is not often that an Englishman has so many safety-valves for that "last infirmity of noble minds".

7 'Explorers I have met' by John Augustus O'Shea in *Tinsley's Magazine*, vol. 33 (August 1883); and extracts from *Roundabout Recollections* (London: Ward and Downey, 1892).

Explorers I have met

It was in the public room of a hotel off the principal square of Estella, in Navarre, at that time the head-quarters of his perambulatory Majesty uncrowned, King Charles VII, I first saw one explorer. That is some nine years ago, and he was an explorer then, but not celebrated. A tall fellow, with crisp black hair and moustache, swarthy Spanish complexion, and dancing eyes. He was dining heartily on campaigning fare, in company with a stout young officer in Carlist uniform. They were speaking the most guttural of German. That did not surprise me much, for we had fellows of many nationalities in our army – French, Americans, Italians, and, of course, Irishmen. The following morning I met the Carlist officer at breakfast and we foregathered. He told me he had been a Lieutenant of Uhlans, was a cousin of the War Minister, at Berlin, and had come to share in a little guerrilla fighting in the Pyrenees, to add to the stock of military experience acquired in a more regular service in the Franco-German war. Naturally he was a Baron – the Baron von Kamecke. Later in the day I saw the German chatting to his companion of the table of the previous evening under the colonnade outside the inn. What a very tall man the stranger was. I had not noticed his great height when he was sitting. He wore a cork helmet, a cutaway coat, cord breeches, and high boots. The German approached me and said in his characteristic French:

"M'sieu, c'est un gompatriote à fous, un gapitane dans les Gardes de la Reine d'Angleterre", and he presented me to my "gompatriote".

"How d'ye do?" said the giant, in an off-hand fashion, and in accents that savoured more of the West End than Whitechapel.

"How d'ye do?" said I, bowing as stiffly as he had; "pardon me, I didn't quite catch your name."

"Burnaby", he condescended to inform me.

"Delighted, I'm sure. I took you for a groom."

"Haw, haw!" laughed the giant, "you're a rum customer."

"You're a rummer", I said; "but I suppose you didn't know who I was at dinner last night, or you would have exchanged a few words in the vernacular with me in this strange land."

"Wrong", he quickly added; "I did know, but I had a prejudice against you. Now I know it to have been un-just."

"How did the prejudice arise?"

"I was told you opened a letter of mine at Bayonne, and telegraphed the contents to London as your own. I have since learned it was the Junta did the dirty trick."

I was mortified beyond measure, and coloured at the suspicion that I could have been guilty of the dishonourable act.

"Hum! As a rule of life, I believe only half what I see, and nothing that I hear", and I was turning on my heel; but Capt. Burnaby smilingly extended his hand, saying: "I think we shall be friends." I grasped his hand. May I flatter myself with the hope that we are friends. A few weeks roughing it; together among soldiers, when fighting is going on begets more trust and liking, if the sympathies are there, than years of automatic London acquaintanceship. We rode knee to knee for weeks after that, slept under the same roof and sometimes on the same boards, and exhausted all our anecdotes in the endeavour to carry out the provisions of a joint-stock guild we had formed for the Reciprocal Recreation of Animal Spirits and Combined Curtailment of the King's Highway. Some of the haps and mishaps we met it is my present intent briefly to set down.

Spain is the land of romance; it is the only country I know of in this hemisphere where fans and flowers speak the language of love, where the very mendicant is dignified and the courtesan devout, where honour is punctilious and coin is base, where gentlemen in jail are free to take lessons in forgery, and gentlemen at large have the enterprise to say "stand and deliver" to a railway train – the most ignorant, backward, bigoted, greedy, lovable, simple, delightful and chivalrous of all countries. I treasure Spain, and am tempted to say much about it and Spanish adventures; but that the portion of the disturbed realm we were in was the patriotic barrier of the north, which is to the true Spain what Piedmont is to the true Italy. Besides, the six-feet-five of explorer I have in hand and I were sufficiently independent and original to make our own adventures.

Captain Burnaby (he is now Colonel, but I call him by his then title) I discovered was an athlete, and overdid the thing as ambitious athletes are wont; was an accomplished linguist, being qualified to slang a cab-driver in six tongues; was well up in the science, technicalities and practice of his profession; was anxious for fame and had a predilection for balloon ascents. He had called on Colonel Gordon in the Soudan before I had seen him, and since then he has ridden to Khiva, and made a horse-back tour in Asia Minor. His faithful henchman, Radford, who died after one of his master's trips and is buried in Dover, was with him in Navarre. The Captain was summoned back to his regiment before he anticipated, a complaint having been made from Madrid, as I understand, that the Carlists were sedulously propagating a rumour that the English sympathised with them, and that one of Queen Victoria's "Blue Guards" was giving military counsel to the King. When we returned towards the French frontier von Kamecke accompanied us. We were treated with extreme consideration, by the peasant-farmers, because we were taken to be good Carlists and true hidalgoes. All of the party, except myself, were very tall men. As we entered, one by one, the common room in a house at St. Esteban, after a day's ride, the country folk respectfully stared, and remarked admiringly of what noble stature Englishmen must be, if these cavaliers were specimens of them.

"Pretty fair", said Burnaby, "though as my grandfather, who is coming in, will tell you, we were much more finely built in the last century."

I was on the threshold, and overheard the words.

"Your grandfather; but he is as short as we are, Excellency, and he looks young."

"True, he looks young, but he is not. Will you kindly inform our good friends how old you are, august sir?"

"Why ask me, boy? Do you not know as well as myself? I am one hundred and eighty-four."

There was a chorus of astonished exclamations at this announcement, and I was ushered into a chair almost as venerable as myself.

"In England", continued the humourist, "it is not as it is here. Up to a certain age, the prime of life, one hundred and fifty or so, we grow – grow; then we shrink – shrink. My grandfather there was taller than I am, much taller thirty years ago."

"Wonderful", said the village schoolmaster, "but easy of understanding to the enlightened mind. It is the effect of fog."

This anecdote is introduced for the purpose of showing that Captain Burnaby is possessed of that cheery temperament and power of story-telling which are indispensable to the traveller. Those people of St. Esteban are unsophisticated. To amuse them I borrowed some of their loose coins, and performed sundry silly conjuring tricks with them. They refused to take the money, back, vowing that it was bewitched and would, bring them ill-luck.

It was the next day, I think; that Radford had a close shave for his life. We were traversing a mountain-pass by a bridle-path on a tree-covered slope, overhanging a gorge with a brawling rivulet in its depth. Radford took a short cut by a track underneath; when suddenly his mare stumbled. In trying to recover herself she displaced the soil, which was slippery, and, despite all the gallant fellow's efforts, we saw she must, topple over.

"Let her go", shouted Burnaby, "save yourself."

Radford lifted his off-leg free, threw himself towards a bush on the hill-side, which he caught with both hands and held tightly as the mare snorted and plunged; his near foot was caught in the stirrup. It was an appalling position even to look at. The man, pale and silent, grimly clinging to his frail support, and desperately wrenching at the stirrup, the terror-stricken horse frantically struggling. At last the animal reeled over, and by some chance Radford's foot came loose.

"There goes eighty pounds", said Burnaby; "but, thank God, Radford is safe!" as the mare threw a series of somersaults, like a bounding ball of the arena, in her rapid descent-of the steep slope. At the edge of it there was a sheer fall of quite thirty feet; over she went and rolled on to her back, in the stony bottom of the rivulet. Radford clambered towards his master, but Burnaby did not upbraid him.

"Are you hurt?'"

"No, sir; more frightened than hurt."

"Beware of short cuts in future. Take a pull at the *bota*.[10] Now try and get down to strip the beast; you'll have to tramp it for the rest of the journey."

Radford did succeed in getting to the bottom of the ravine, and here comes the most marvellous part of the adventure. When he stooped to undo the bridle, the mare began to struggle, and by his help she was enabled to regain her feet. She trembled in every limb; the saddle tree was snapped across, but, except for an abrasion on the forehead and a patch of bared hide on one of the hind quarters, she was unhurt – bore no traces of her terrific act of horsemanship. Next day, of course, she was stiff, but *Caoutchouc*[11] lived to be patted by the Prince of Wales, shrugged at by sceptical Blues, and ultimately sold, I believe, for a respectable figure at Tattersall's.

As we travelled along at a walking-pace to keep time with our pack-mules, Burnaby started a philosophical discussion. At this writing, I am convinced neither of us is a don at philosophy. He maintained that nobody did any service to another in this world without an object. Selfishness was the hinge on which humanity turned. I held that his theory was heterodox. With what object does a mother kiss her babe? Pure selfishness, to be repaid with a smile! It is needless to pursue the argument, which nearly led to the break-up of our guild, for although it curtailed the king's highway, it did not recreate animal spirits.

But I had a plot in my mind that was better than any of the processes in Aldrich or Mill. At Elizondo next morning the Captain executed the "boot and saddle"[12] on a trumpet improvised from paper outside my bed-room door. I groaned wearily; he burst in.

"What's the matter, old man?"

"Fear I can't travel to-day; you must go without me."

"Seedy? Let me feel your pulse; it is irregular."

The amateur was unaware that I had knocked my elbow violently against the wall some moments previously.

"Seedy!" I echoed dismally, "I should think so. I have a volcano in my head

---

10 A *bota* was a leather wine bottle with a wooden top used by travellers, still occasionally seen at bullfights and fiestas.
11 *Caoutchouc* is the French word for native or Indian rubber.
12 Reveille.

and an earthquake in my stomach."

"Here", cried the generous soldier, flinging back the casement, "Radford, have those mules unpacked, and send me up the landlord: I want a doctor."

"Surely you are going on! Your leave has been stopped, and the Duke – "

"Surely I'm not, until I see you better, or trenched. What do you take me for?"

"An excessively clumsy logician", said I, jumping out of bed. "What object had you in stopping for me?"

For an instant he was non-plussed, but only for an instant. Nonchalantly he replied: "Pure selfishness! I expect you would do the same for me under similar circumstances."

We were comparatively silent as we rode along that day; philosophy was at a discount, but I could notice an occasional shrewd glance, half mirth, half reproach, of those dancing eyes directed at me.

Our last adventure in Spain was at Bera, on the border, where we had a difficulty about securing pack-mules. The *alcalde* – dog in office that he was – was impudent, and almost threatening. Burnaby was, cool and resolute as when he stood in the front of the battle at Dicastillo a few weeks before.

"If you don't procure me mules, as my order empowers me to demand, I shall saddle yourself and compel you to carry my luggage like a beast of burden."

This to a functionary whose station in the district was like to that of a Lord Mayor of London; and this, too, in the presence of his fellow-townsmen! The *alcalde* was galvanised with rage. As soon as he could find voice he spluttered:

"I – I am the *alcalde*!" and half lifted his clenched fist.

"You dare not", said Burnaby, quietly.

"Dare not, dare not! Why?"

"*Io tengo mas caballerosidad*[13] *que usted.*"[14]

This is the most straightforward insult you can offer to any Spaniard. It was so straightforward that it completely stunned the *alcalde*. He was speechless, and stuttered when he came to his speech. While the row, which occurred in a stable crowded with loafers, was being waged, I heard an ominous click. It was von Kamecke, surreptitiously looking to his revolver. We felt that a tough fight was imminent, I had my fingers on my own in my pocket, and was calculating would it be wise to discharge it through the lining, in the approved Colorado style. Radford, who did not understand the words that were spoken, but guessed that they were angry, looked mischievous.

"Tell me, sir", he whispered to me, "when it's time to go in, and I'll land that cove one on the conk!"

Providentially, hostilities were not proclaimed. We got the mules, but the

---

13 O'Shea added that '*Caballerosidad* was not precisely the word, but Spaniards will know what it was.' He probably had in mind the word '*cojones*'.

14 Literally, 'I have more chivalry than you'.

gay muleteer refused point-blank to cross the imaginary boundary line on the mountains, and deliberately landed our impedimenta on the heather and disappeared. We were in a sorry strait, in the midst of a drenching shower in the bleak Pyrenees. But Burnaby laughed, and set the example of strapping a portion of the luggage to his own charger. He is not the man to despair in an emergency. Readiness of resource is the first faculty in an explorer, and he possesses it in abundance. I have seen him do farrier's work on his horse when it had cast a shoe. The rain was lucky, after all, for there was a nice Scotch mist out, and under its screen, and by my local knowledge, we succeeded in insinuating our cattle right through the cordon of customs' guards without permit.

When next I saw the Captain, he was in the car of a balloon in the Crystal Palace, with Duruof and de Fonvielle. Dining with him a few evenings after, Radford, who was handing me a plate of soup, was so startled when he recognised me that he nearly let the liquid slop over and brocade my nether habiliments. That would have been a grievous catastrophe, indeed, for they were not the leather galligaskins I wore in Spain, but the fancy dress trousers reserved for state occasions, and funerals in Westminster Abbey. To sum up, Colonel Burnaby is a thoroughly good fellow and will oblige me and the world much if he give to the light his maiden volume, that on his experiences with the Carlists, which is wasting in manuscript, and stowed away somewhere. If he does I wish him every success in his designs on Birmingham. Should he get into Parliament for that constituency, with his present political programme – well, I think it may be admitted he has achieved a bigger task than riding to Khiva.

Roundabout Recollections

[At the Battle of Mañerú, 6 October 1873.] Burnaby, conspicuous and self-possessed, was present at this encounter, taking notes in a somewhat exposed position, his man Radford beside him. A shell exploded in perilous proximity. Radford was startled and almost meditated shifting his ground, until his master's eye caught him. "He's more afraid of me than the enemy", was Burnaby's comment. Burnaby was much attached to Frank,[15] and Frank in return almost worshipped him. At leaving, the kindly guardsman bequeathed him his functions as *Times* correspondent, but Frank, though excellent as an artist, had not in him the timber of a contemporaneous war-chronicler. (vol. 1, pp. 58-9.)

---

15 Frank Vizitelly (1830-1883), war artist for several papers including the *Illustrated London News*, who covered the American Civil War and the Third Carlist War. He was with Hicks Pasha's force in the Sudan when it was annihilated in 1883.

[In reference to his Spanish colleagues.] Knee to knee with Burnaby of the Blues I rode through the sierras of Navarre, and cultivated an attachment which only closed with his life. The manner of his death there is no need to describe; he was killed in action at Abu Klea. I have written of him elsewhere, and here I only present an anecdote which has not before been given in print. We were chatting about danger, and he declared he feared nothing particularly, but that he could not help feeling a latent nervousness about his neck. We both laughed, I taking it as he had probably intended it, as one of those jokes which are cracked to shorten a tedious road. I understood that he meant playfully to indicate that he would be hanged. It is remarkable that he should have succumbed to a wound in his neck – a spear-thrust in the jugular. (vol. 2, pp. 337-8.)

8   Eugene Schuyler 'Colonel Fred Burnaby: recollections of his career' in *New York Daily Tribune*, 22 January 1885.

Poor Fred Burnaby! Dead, thrust through the throat by some unknown Arab in the Soudan, where he had gallantly volunteered to go to the relief of Gordon. He might have had a better death, perhaps a worse one, for with his disposition he never could be tranquil. Thirsting for adventure, he was condemned to home service, and he lost no opportunity during his leaves of absence of seeking what might be least accessible. As [an] officer in the Blues, one of the crack regiments in the Guards, he was a favourite in society. With a large income he had never found the opportunity of spending it, for his habits were simple and he was ever in search of the impossible.

I first knew him in St. Petersburg, whither he had come again to improve himself somewhat in the Russian language. A tall, heavy man, who should have been and had been in a way, an athlete, with black hair and a drooping black moustache. We frequently dined together at the Hôtel de France, where he told me of his adventures in Spain, in South America and Central Africa, and of his attempts in ballooning. He had made then nineteen or twenty attempts, and was afterwards one of the first to cross from England to France. He was one of the best story-tellers that I have ever known, and his stories had that great charm that, though concerned exclusively with his personal adventures, he allowed himself to sink out of sight and concentrated the interest on the other characters. He never put himself forward or magnified himself, except as the hero of some most absurd mishap. He had great facility in learning languages; knew Spanish and all its dialects more thoroughly than anyone I have ever met; could tell a Spanish folk tale in the dialect of the province with an accent which would deceive even a Spaniard; and had already been up the Nile farther than Khartoum, and had a current knowledge of Arabic, to say nothing of the ordinary European languages, with which he was quite familiar. He would drink nothing but weak whiskey and water, for he professed to be suffering from a liver complaint, though he admitted that it was in great part owing to a strain received in carrying a young calf to his rooms at the top of the barracks as a bet.

After meeting him often in London in the spring of 1874 I saw him again in St. Petersburg in 1875. This time he had come for an excursion to Central Asia. He wished to go to Khiva, but was uncertain as to the best way of getting there. He knew that the Russian authorities would object to his journey, as he had resolved if possible to penetrate to Afghanistan. I was able to give him some details about the routes and to recommend him to the persons who might facilitate his journey. After two or three days he started off. He had asked official permission, but owing to the ill-will of the military attaché of the British Embassy this had been delayed, and he went without it. It really was of no consequence except so far as it called attention to his movements, and therefore it did him more harm than good. From Orenburg he rode to Fort No. 1, then straight through the steppes on the track of MacGahan arrived easily at the Russian outposts and notwithstanding the hard journey across the desert, and then succeeded in outwitting the Russian commanders and found his way to Khiva and the headquarters of the Khan. He had no sooner arrived there than an enquiry was telegraphed back from the Russian general in command as to his movements. The English Embassy professed to have no knowledge of him, and the result was that as he was simply on leave and without military orders the Duke of Cambridge ordered him to return at once. This command was sent through the Russians and reached him at Khiva. He obeyed, reluctantly it is true, but not before he had seen the whole country and had secured the materials to write his extremely interesting book, "A Ride to Khiva".

After meeting Burnaby frequently in London when he was busy writing his story, we came together again at Constantinople in the autumn of 1876. His book had been a success. He himself was a success except in his strictly professional career, where the Duke of Cambridge, manager-in-chief of the English army, thought it right for no one to depart from the strict lines of his duty. Thirsting for some opportunity to display himself, he had come to offer his services to the Turks in case of war with Russia, and to assist our common friend Valentine Baker, who, after having served a term of imprisonment for a fault in which he was more sinned against than sinning, had become a Pasha and a General in the Turkish service. The war did not begin as soon as was expected, and, after the abortive results of the Conference, Burnaby made up his mind to take a trip to the Armenian frontier. After a short preparation he started out on horseback, and the results of his excursion are summed up in his "On Horseback through Asia Minor". This book, even his friends must admit, is far inferior to his first, the whole interest lying in the talk and adventures of a soldier servant, who unfortunately died soon afterwards from a fever and could not therefore give the subject for a new book.

A year later Burnaby came again to Constantinople, this time with the intention of joining Baker Pasha, the besieged at Plevna. One of my pleasant recollections is a little dinner at which Baker and Burnaby were the chief guests, and at which both were gradually induced to relate their adventures. I recall now but one story. Burnaby had made mention in his Khiva book of Cockle's pills, and the paragraph was quoted and used largely as an advertisement by the proprietor. "Burnaby's Ride to Khiva." "Try Cockle's Pills." "Burnaby says, etc." stared at you for months in constant alternation over whole sides of the London papers. On returning from Armenia Burnaby found, he said, a letter which looked so suggestive of a bill that he put it aside till the last. When he opened it he found to his astonishment a letter from Mr. Cockle offering him a gross of pills and a check for £200 as his share of the profits gained from the advertisement. "I of course accepted the money", he said, "but replied to Cockle that I should apply it in his name to some benevolent object. I was at a loss how to get even with him, but as I had noticed that he chiefly advertised in the Liberal papers I concluded that he sympathized with the Russians, and therefore subscribed in his name to the Turkish Relief Fund."

Both Baker and Burnaby left on the following morning, but arrived too late to relieve Plevna. Baker himself went with many misgivings. It was a plan which he had proposed two months before, and which only the delays of a Turkish administration had prevented from being executed immediately. On this expedition Burnaby came very near being captured. He had, or it was said that he had, made a bet that he would enter Plevna. General Skobeleff heard of this and within a short time, according to my informant, the American attaché with the Russian armies, had an exact description of Burnaby's personal appearance and a knowledge of his history up to three days before. Strict orders were given to all the scouts and outposts to arrest any such individual and shoot him on sight. Knowing Skobeleff as well as I did, I should have been very sorry had this happened, although I cannot but admit the justice of the order, for Burnaby was a simple volunteer with the Turkish army, and under such circumstances might rightly have been considered a spy. Fortunately for himself he did not make the attempt, and after the disastrous defeat of Suleiman Pasha, where all the merit must be ascribed to Baker and all the faults to the Turks. Burnaby returned to Constantinople in as good spirits and in as good humour as ever. Again we had a little dinner, and fortunately all were able to forget the misfortunes of the numerous defeats and of the happy retreat. Burnaby was as good in recounting the little adventures of war as was Skobeleff afterward, when with Tserebeleff, MacGahan and Green he dined at the same table.

A year passed. I had then been sent as Consul to Birmingham. This was a great Radical stronghold, with a caucus in the Birmingham sense and a strict party organisation under the control of a German named Schnadhorst. There were rumours of a new general election. Under these circumstances Burnaby, as then one of the most popular men among the Conservatives – for Lord Randolph Churchill had scarcely yet appeared on the political scene – undertook to run as a Conservative candidate for Parliament from Birmingham. It was rather dangerous. There were three members, all Liberals – Mr. Bright. Mr. Chamberlain, now, but not then, in the Cabinet, and Mr. Muntz. According to the English law the electors could vote for only two persons. At first, when the Liberals and radicals had a vast majority, this would have been easy, but now that it had become more divided Mr. Schnadhorst, as secretary of the Liberal Club, had to make a careful calculation and tell each elector for which two candidates he should vote in order that all three might get in. It was plain, therefore, that if a defect in the calculation should occur the Conservatives would elect not one but two. I laughingly told Burnaby one morning as we went on the train down to London after a very strong and amusing speech he had made the night before, that if he would give me notice of the election I should undertake to put Schnadhorst in such a condition that he would make a mistake in his calculations. Within a month I had left Birmingham and gone to Rome. Imagine my surprise on the eve of the general election of 1880, when found that, American official as I was then, I was inserted on the election lists of Birmingham as a Conservative, and that tickets for Burnaby and Calthorpe were sent to me to vote.

About that time I met Burnaby frequently in London. We dined at the Marlborough Club, where among others I had the pleasure of seeing at the same table Sir Allen Young, who recently on the 'Pandora' had made an excursion to the Arctic regions in an attempt to discover the last relics of Sir John Franklin's expedition. Burnaby had then obtained his promotion and had become lieutenant-colonel of the Blues, one of the crack regiments of the Guards. I dined with him at the mess, where the sole talk was of India, Central Asia and Russia, intermingled with light gossip about theatres and the actresses of the day. It was about this time that Burnaby married a young Irish lady, a ward in Chancery, for her fortune placed her under the special safeguard of the Lord Chancellor, and I remember well that the last time I saw him was in Hyde Park, where he and his bride reigned up their horses to the railings to greet us and beg us to stay for a few weeks longer in England to come to their wedding.

I never saw him again. We exchanged, as always, occasional letters giving the news, and especially the gossip of the day. Just a year ago I happened to go to Cairo for ten days. It was at the time when the English were advancing from Suakin. Shepheard's Hotel was full of English, among whom I fortunately found many friends, and Cairo was full of anti-English – French, Italians, Russians, Germans, and others, among whom I found as many; but all had a sad moment when the telegram reached us one Friday that Burnaby had been wounded. All who had met him personally, no matter of what nation, could not but be charmed by him, and all, therefore, felt a personal interest in a man who, after having braved so much, had finally, while Colonel of one of the best of English regiments, gone as a simple volunteer to the Soudan and had been wounded by an Arab spear or by one of those fearful knives which the savages used.

Now in nearly the same place, a year later, at Abu Klea, on January 17, 1885, he has gained a far higher cross, the brave death on the battlefield, which is the worthiest reward of the true soldier.

9   Anonymous 'Colonel Burnaby as a journalist' in *Northern Echo*, 27 January 1885.

There will be found among Colonel Burnaby's papers the completed manuscript of a novel. He began it about five years ago, laid it on one side when half through, took it up again in 1883 and finished it off. It is what is called a novel of society, and would create some sensation if it were published. It also dealt with political personages, in a manner that left little to be desired in the way of means for identification. From the portion I was privileged, to see, I do not think the novel would rival in popularity the "Ride to Khiva". The humour was rather given to horseplay, and the novelist treated his political adversaries in chance conversation much after the fashion in which the candidate for Birmingham discussed them at meetings of enthusiastic Conservatives. I remember one scene depicts the breaking out of a fire in Downing-street during a Cabinet meeting. The affrighted Ministers rush on to the balcony, where they betray a ludicrous timidity. Overtures were made by two publishers to secure the novel, but Burnaby was in no hurry to publish, and locked the MS up in his desk.

Indirectly, Burnaby had a powerful influence upon English journalism. But for him the Society journals, which form a prominent feature in modern journalism, would not have existed.

The pioneer of "Society journals" was a friend of Burnaby's. He had long brooded over the project of his ideal journal. He had everything save one necessary for its birth. He could write himself, knew others that could wield a facile pen, and was in society. But he had no money. In this dilemma he went to Burnaby and asked him for a loan of £500. In those days relays of £500 were not come-at-able by the young captain in the Guards. But Burnaby's friendship was not of the kind that too narrowly weighs sacrifices. He would do anything for a friend, so he lent the £500 "And I got it back again", he said, with a pleased smile, as if that was the only remarkable part of the story. He had a strong hankering after journalism, and has himself done some good work in the field. He wrote some graphic letters for the *Times* during the last Carlist War. Of late years his special attachment has been to the *Morning Post*. Here again one of the leading impulses of his life—the desire to help a friend—came into action. Sir Algernon Borthwick was a friend of his, and accordingly Burnaby, both during the Russo-Turkish War and the operations in Egypt sent valuable contributions to the *Post*. He was a man who liked his dinner and an interminable succession of cigars after it. But in order to do a service to a friend he scorned delights, and lived the laborious days of a special correspondent. Pay was pressed upon him, but he would take nothing but the satisfaction of having served a friend.

10 Henry Tracey Coxwell 'Colonel Burnaby's ballooning' in *Pall Mall Gazette*, 27 January 1885.

Among the military aeronauts who ascended with me more than twenty years since was the lamented and distinguished Englishman who has met with a soldier's death, but who never, I believe, suffered any personal injury during his numerous aerial travels. Long before his famous ride to Khiva we journeyed together with the balloon I made for the experiments in behalf of the British Association. It was in the year 1864 that a party of the Royal Horse Guards engaged every available seat in one of my trips from the Crystal Palace grounds. We were nearly, if not quite, twelve, all told, and the most prominent figure seated on the hoop, with a bugle or cornet in his right hand, was "Burnaby of the Blues", as that officer was familiarly styled on being introduced. No sooner had we started than this majestic companion struck up a lively tune, and his conversation afterwards, by no means ostentatious, afforded evidence of minute and extensive observation, impressing me with the idea that his first, or perhaps second, experience in mid-air was undertaken *con amore*. After crossing the Thames and bearing away over the Essex marshes, I was reminded of having, albeit reluctantly, consented to attach a certain hamper outside the car, which appeared to me a very ponderous addition to the weighty occupants who allowed me to conduct them to cloud-land. I now retain a vivid recollection of the amiable and jocular manner with which Captain Burnaby at that time received my protest. It was excused, and, indeed, withdrawn, when Mr. Boswell whispered that a messman had brought down the hamper expressly from the Albany Barracks, and that it was charged with all sorts of creature comforts, including pies, pasties, chicken, and various other tempting morsels, admirably calculated to shake the most stoical objection, so that it was at last attacked. The diverting incident of a luncheon aloft having passed off with not a single fault-finding as to the chef's proficiency in the culinary art, some meteorological records were made, but they were in all truth extremely limited, as the hygrometric state of the atmosphere was no sooner pronounced dry than the hamper, rather than the attached thermometer, was again consulted. This time the solids were permitted to rest, but a flighty cork, as it careered downwards, watched with attention, and in justice to the moderation of our thirst it should, in fairness, be recorded that a full half of the champagne, which was of course well up, escaped ere the glasses were forthcoming. I can vouch for it that an infinitesimal portion of the contents of that basket was all that we consumed, and that the remainder rejoiced sundry good fellows at the descent who had been alarmed at our sudden appearance, as a brisk breeze had sprung up before we landed, and the grapnel tore down the branch of an elm tree and trailed over a meadow, much to the consternation of the country folk, but considerably to the diversion of Captain Burnaby and his brother officers. The journey was pronounced—if I remember rightly by Lieutenant Westcar—a most enjoyable one. There is, however, more than one melancholy association connected with the three names I have mentioned. Those who bore them have all gone over to the majority. Burnaby, Boswell, and Westcar all stood quite six feet four, and were noble, handsome men. If the fittest survive, they are not always the finest.

Just a decade after this event Captain (then Major) [sic] Burnaby made another ascent in one of my balloons. It was on a remarkable occasion, a French balloonist and his wife having ascended from Calais when the wind blew towards the sea. They were carried away northwards, and thereby increased the dangers of their venture. A descent was made, but it was on the wild waves in the line of the Dogger Bank, and there they struggled until a Grimsby smack rescued them. M. Duruof and his faithful partner met with a warm reception in England. He was invited to appear at Sydenham, but his balloon was damaged, and I was enabled to offer some attention to this young Frenchman, who had the honour of being the first aeronaut who passed out of Paris during the siege. Major Burnaby, hearing probably of the fact that I had given M. Duruof the free use of my balloon, together with the proceeds of the car, determined to patronise them. It was a great day at the Crystal Palace, and the muster roll of celebrities was unusually large. Major Burnaby seated himself near M. Duruof and the enterprising M. de Fonville, several paying passengers being in by their side. There was nothing worth chronicling in this ascent beyond the circumstance of its being a fraternal proof of goodwill and sympathy between English and French air travellers, not forgetting the respective nationalities represented. In reference to Colonel Burnaby's Channel voyage I cannot lay claim to having provided a balloon for this daring feat, but I hold a correspondence in which a similar suggestion was made as to my loaning my largest balloon to promote a voyage to Belgium. My conditions proved scarcely acceptable. I could only consent to the pilot being myself, and I incurred, possibly, some slight odium by not resigning the proposed seat of honour and providing a balloon. Not the slightest degree of resentment, however, followed, although it has been my lot to meet with this sort of feeling; but I have point-blank declined to gratify amateurs and meteorologists whenever our views were not in unison. I may here allude most opportunely to a recent proof of this. In an article by Colonel Burnaby, which appeared in the *Fortnightly Review* of May Day last, on "The Possibilities of Ballooning", my own experiences were alluded to in the kindest and most complimentary terms. Again, in his narrative of the Channel voyage was this friendly notice expressed. As to the application of balloons in Egypt and the Soudan, we were clearly of one way of thinking. When I heard that the Colonel had embarked for the Nile, I was hoping that, as he was to be working with the Intelligence Department, balloons might be utilized (or at any rate, miniature despatch balloonets, either composed of skin or thin gutta percha) for signalling with. Major Jones proposed cipher messages, or as I have long advocated in my own way. In the *Times* and *Standard* of February, 1884, I sent forth, and not before it was wanted, a timely war balloon cry. The purport of my letter was literally in the following words, "Be ready with your war balloons", and had this been heeded I have no hesitation in saying General Gordon would have been materially helped; and if Sir Herbert Stewart in his desert march had been provided even with a huge paper fire balloon, such as men have gone up in, and capable of being inflated on an emergency with a bundle of sticks, who can say but what our brave opponents might have been descried the other side of the hills, or in force on them, and that the British square at Abu Klea might have been in consequence better able to bear the shock of ten thousand Arabs, and Colonel Burnaby preserved to us, besides many others who can ill be spared at this momentous period of our national history, when at least the resources of science should be brought into requisition, and the opinions based on long practice treated with proper and polite respect?

There are one or two aspects in which General Gordon and others have been recently placed which makes the blood of an aeronaut almost boil to think what balloons might have achieved in the Soudan. It is true that an aerial fleet has gone to South Africa; but is that a spot more in need of aerial observatories than Khartoum and the surrounding country? On January 2, we read that at sunrise the General "daily mounts to the roof and makes a survey of the whole country with his telescope". Only suppose that he was in command of a balloon, and how much more might he overlook! "But where", ask many supposed far-seeing people, "would the General get his gas from?" Well, he might do without gas. How did Pilatre de Rosier mount a hundred years ago? Secondly, it appears that Colonel Barrow's Hussars took the old Bayuda track, while Major Kitchener's scouts followed the road to the east and got seven miles to the westward. Now, signalling by balloon, even on a small scale, might have kept them from such an extreme divergence. Thirdly, General Earle's column might have received *en route* a message per balloon, or the 1,000 warriors near Metammeh might, if they only possessed toy balloons, make known their state at this critical moment.

11 Edward Marston 'Colonel Fred Burnaby: a publisher's reminiscence' in *Publishers' Circular*, 1 February 1885. Reprinted in *After work: fragments from the workshop of an old publisher* (London: W. Heinemann, 1904), pp. 168-72.

The death of Colonel Fred Burnaby will be felt by a larger number of people and by a greater variety of classes that perhaps that of almost any soldier, or, indeed, of few men, of the present day. He made friends and could not help being popular, wherever he went, and in whatever grade of society. Other papers have done full justice to him in his career as soldier, journalist, explorer and politician. We who came into personal contact with him in his literary career may be pardoned if we say a few words about him from this standpoint. How well do we remember his splendid and gigantic figure as he used to stroll into our office when he had some grand literary project in view – his hearty grip of the hand, his twinkling eye – and loud ringing laugh! There was a sort of magnetism about him which made us all jolly in his presence. Notwithstanding his joviality, however, he had a keen eye to business, he was a splendid hand at striking a bargain, and by no means under-estimated the value of his literary work. He seemed to take more pride in overcoming a *publisher* than in winning a battle! However unpromising his project may, at first sight, appear, he managed to cast over it such a rose-coloured glamour that he soon made it assume a more attractive aspect, and in this way he carried his point; it must be admitted that in the result he was generally not very far wrong, for he made his influence to be felt for the good of his new book wherever he went, and it should be added that in the case of failure he was always as generous in the end as he was exacting in the beginning. He was somewhat fidgety about his proof-sheets; if none came for a short interval he would write: "Two days! And I have received nothing: this makes me swear – puts my liver out of order and does away with the effect of the waters." One on occasion when a slight inelegance of style was pointed out to him he wrote: "You are probably right about the repetition ... I write as I talk, and do not pretend to have any style. You are not the only person who has remarked about the repetition of the word. I have let two or three people look at the proofs. They are not connected with the press, but are average mortals – I call them my *Foolometers. They* like the book. I think they represent the majority of the reading public! ... You will make a success!" Hardly a compliment, perhaps, to the "reading public".)

Never would he admit the possibility of failure in any literary venture he undertook, and therefore insisted upon being himself well paid beforehand. Writing about a certain cartoon he says 'I do not like it. It makes me as ugly as nature has. The artist reminds me of a Chinaman who sketched old K____. The admiral complained that the likeness was not flattering. The Chinaman replied, "How can handsome face make, when handsome face no have got!" I am like K____, I wish for a little more flattery. At the time when he was lying dangerously ill with congested lungs, he sent for the present writer, who found him lying on a small bed in a room furnished with Wellington-like simplicity. "Ah, my friend", he said, "I'm glad to see you, how are you?" And on sorrow being expressed at his painful illness, "Yes", he said, "I am ill; but I *mean* to get over it; I have done it before, and I shall do so now; my doctor shakes his head, but I shall be all right soon"; and then after a terrible fit of coughing he added, "Go to that cupboard; you will find a box of splendid cigars, and come sit down here and have a smoke." Feeling that the smoke of even so good a cigar could hardly be congenial to that fearful cough or in accordance with the doctor's wishes, the kind request was not complied with; and after a long chat, interrupted by much coughing, the writer left him – with a sad foreboding that, notwithstanding the gallant colonel's confident determination to get well, there was little chance of ever seeing him about again.

The last letter from him is dated June 6, 1884, and contains the following characteristic remark: 'I am still suffering from my left lung, which is congested, and *later on mean to make one more big travel through Morocco to Timbuctoo*! When I will write you a book, such a book – "Khiva" nothing to it – that will make your fortune." Alas! how gladly would we have sacrificed the chance of "making a fortune" to have seen his fine handsome face and have heard his cheery genial laugh once again! That journey to Timbuctoo was not a pleasant joke; it was, we believe, a serious project of his, as he had often spoken about it; and it would in all probability have been undertaken, had not this accursed war in the Soudan broken out; the scent of battle was too strong for him, and he abandoned his projected and possibly, to his somewhat shattered constitution, equally perilous travel into Central; Africa, to meet the fate most honourable to a soldier, which awaited him in the north of that "Dark Continent".

12 Thomas Gibson Bowles 'Colonel Frederick Gustavus Burnaby' in *Vanity Fair*, February 1885.

Fred Burnaby has left a name that will never die; but it will also be cited as one who was treated with quite a remarkable neglect, not to say contempt and disfavour, by his Sovereign, or rather by those who dispense the honours supposed to be awarded by the Sovereign. In spite of exploits as brilliant as those of any paladin of old, he never once received so much as a word, a ribbon, or a medal, or even the C.B. that is thrown to a Board of Trade clerk when he signs some ridiculous convention. After his Ride to Khiva, and again after his journey through Asia Minor, he made most full and valuable reports to the Horse Guards; they were received and used and no notice was taken of their author. After the Russo-Turkish war, when he accompanied and assisted Baker Pasha in his masterly retreat across the Rhodope Mountains, and in the various hard-fought battles incidental thereto, he again made the most valuable reports to the Horse Guards; but no notice was taken of their author. In last year's operations in the Sudan he was severely wounded, was specially thanked in general orders read out before the troops by the General-in-Chief for his services, and was named in despatches; and again no notice was taken, though on the breasts of those engaged at Tel El Kebir crosses were growing like mustard and cress. For the manner in which he commanded the Blues, and the remarkably high state of efficiency and soldier-like smartness to which he brought what had hitherto been regarded as a regiment of loungers, he was repeatedly commended in the highest terms; but from first to last no mark whatever of the Sovereign's favour, not the very least mark, was ever conferred upon him. It is but too true that, like so many more of England's best and bravest sons, Fred Burnaby remained to the day of his death a splendid example of England's ingratitude.

13 Martin Farquhar Tupper 'Colonel Fred. Burnaby' in *The Brooklyn Magazine*, vols. 2-3 (1885), pp. 89-90. Reprinted in *My life as an Author* (London: Sampson Low, Marston, Searle & Rivington, 1886), pp. 328-30.

I am asked to give a short note of personal reminiscence about my lately departed friend, Colonel Fred. Burnaby, with whom I was intimate for three years before his death. Everyone has read of his popular life, and heard of his many exploits; how alone in mid-air he navigated a balloon across the Channel; how he accomplished, in spite of State telegrams to the contrary, his adventurous and patriotic ride to Khiva in dead winter and defying perils of all sorts; how he stood six feet four in his stockings (with another foot to be added to that magnificent specimen of manhood when in jack-boots and in his plumed helmet); how he was strong enough to bend a kitchen poker round his neck, to crack cobnuts in his fingers, and to carry a pair of Shetland ponies upstairs under his arms, how also the genial giant, quite the Arac of Tennyson's Princess, was the gentlest and kindest and least dangerous of knights-errant (unless, indeed, his just wrath was aroused by anything mean or insolent, when doubtless he could be terrible), and how he was the idolised of men, especially his own brother giants of the Royal Regiment of Blues, and naturally was also the adored of women wherever he showed himself. This Admirable Crichton had every social accomplishment, but as he was also gifted with a knowledge of many tongues, even to Turkish and Arabic, beyond the more familiar French, German, Italian, and Spanish, of course he must dare all sorts of perilous travel, if only to prove that he was no carpet-knight, no mere 'gold stick' [sic] at court, or silver-casqued statue at the Horse Guards. So he fearlessly risked his life in all ways on every possible occasion which the War Office routine gave him on holiday.

Khiva and Kars, and of late at last the fatal Mahdi war, had fascinations for him of danger which his thirst for active service (too much refused to him as obliged officially to be a stay-at-home) had not power to resist; and we all know how gallantly, if indeed too rashly, he fought and fell on what his Viking blood loved best as a deathbed, the field of battle. For he came of an old Teutonic family, and on his mother's side was also a direct descendant, as he told me himself, of our heroic and gigantic King Edward III, whom he is said greatly to have resembled, as the portrait at Windsor Castle proves. We were talking about ancestry and the anecdote came out naturally enough.

In politics a strong Conservative, he, with characteristic antagonism, chose radical Birmingham for his coveted seat in Parliament, but alas! he has not lived to hazard the election. He was a neat, fluent, and epigrammatic speaker, as potent with his tongue as with his sword; and as for the pen (albeit his handwriting must have puzzled compositors), the myriads of readers who have enjoyed his stirring books in print, can testify how brilliant and eloquent he was for the matter of authorship. He told me of a new novel – of the satirico-political sort – which he had written for the press, but as yet we hear nothing definite of its publication.

My own personal acquaintance with the familiar Fred. Burnaby was confined to several hospitable dinner-parties at the house of his relative, Lady W----, my near neighbour and friend at Norwood, about which I might anecdotise to any extent; but I never allow myself to record private conversation nor to reveal domesticities. All such are sacred in my memory, and on principle I despise the modern mischief-maker whose reminiscences are practically 'reminuisances'. On a certain public occasion, however, Burnaby stood by me, to my great pleasure and advantage, and let me record his kindness thus. When I gave my lecture on Flying at the Royal Aquarium, he most appropriately took the chair, and made some excellent remarks. Altogether, let my testimony, however brief, however inadequate, to the merits of Fred. Burnaby be this: I lost in his too sudden death a friend, as I had hoped, for many years to come, and my regrets are for him as one of the noblest of mankind. Let me add a word further, as the worthy witnessing of one, quite a kindred spirit, whose acquaintance I made some long time back, and look for great things from his energy and enterprise, and multifarious talents, Charles Marvin, then the famous Eastern Pioneer, who in his book on Asia, says: "Yes, our Burnabys, our Bakers, our MacGregors, our Gordons – these are the real pillars of the Empire. These are the men who confer provinces upon England, who risk their lives to guard them. When the world is a little older, and the working man's vote is worth more than the statesman's opinion, then the splendid achievements of such men will be more generously appreciated: and the warm English feeling expended to-day on torpid, stupid, unpatriotic party politicians will be directed towards heroes whose steady undaunted patriotism, in face of public indifference and bureaucratic disdain, conveys a moral as grand as their careers."

14 Henry William Lucy 'Fred Burnaby' in *Faces and Places* (London: Henry and Co., 1892), pp. 1-22.

I made the acquaintance of Colonel Fred Burnaby in a balloon. In such strange quarters, at an altitude of over a thousand feet, commenced a friendship that for years was one of the pleasantest parts of my life, and remains one of its most cherished memories. It was on the 14th of September, 1874. A few weeks earlier two French aeronauts, a Monsieur and Madame Duruof, making an ascent from Calais, had been carried out to sea, and dropping into the Channel, had passed through enough perils to make them a nine days' wonder. Arrangements had been completed for them to make a fresh ascent from the grounds of the Crystal Palace, and half London seemed to have gone down to Sydenham to see them off. I was young and eager then, and having but lately joined the staff of the *Daily News* as special correspondent, was burning for an opportunity to distinguish myself. So I went off to the Crystal Palace resolved to go up in the balloon.

"No", said Mr. Coxwell, when I asked him if there were a seat to spare in the car. "No; I am sorry to say that you are too late. I have had at least thirty applications for seats, and as the car will hold only six persons, and as practically there are but two seats for outsiders, you will see that it is impossible."

This was disappointing, the more so as I had brought with me a large military cloak and a pair of seal-skin gloves, under a general but well-defined impression that the thing to do up in a balloon was to keep yourself warm. Mr. Coxwell's account of the position of affairs so completely shut out the prospect of a passage in the car that I reluctantly resigned the charge of the military cloak and gloves, and strolled down to the enclosure where the process of inflating the balloon was going on. Here was congregated a vast crowd, which increased in density as four o'clock rang out, and the great mass of brown silk into which the gas was being assiduously pumped began to assume a pear-like shape, and sway to and fro in the light air of the autumn afternoon.

About this time the heroes of the hour, Monsieur and Madame Duruof walked into the enclosure, accompanied by Mr. Coxwell and Mr. Glaisher. A little work was being extensively sold in the Palace bearing on the title-page, over the name "M. Duruof", a murderous-looking face, the letter-press purporting to be a record of the life and adventures of the French aeronauts. Happily M. Duruof bore but the slightest resemblance to this portrait, being a young man of pleasing appearance, with a good, firm, frank-looking face.

By a quarter to five o'clock the monster balloon was almost fully charged, and was swaying to and fro in a wild, fitful manner, that could not have been beheld without trepidation by any of the thirty gentlemen who had so judiciously booked seats in advance. The wickerwork car now secured to the balloon was half filled with ballast and crowded with men, whilst others hung on to the ropes and to each other in the effort to steady it.

But they could not do much more than keep it from mounting into mid-air. Hither and thither it swung, parting in swift haste the curious throng that encompassed it, and dragging the men about as if they were ounce weights. The wind seemed to be rising and the faces of the experienced aeronauts grew graver and graver, answers to the constantly repeated question, "Where is it likely to come down?" becoming increasingly vague. At last Mr. Glaisher, looking up at the sky and round at the neighbouring trees bending under the growing blast, put his veto upon Madame Duruof's forming one of the party of voyagers.

"We are not in France", he said. "The people will not insist upon a woman going up when there is any danger. The descent is sure to be rough, will possibly be perilous, so Madame Duruof had better stay where she is."

Madame Duruof was ready to go, but was at least equally willing to stay behind, and so it was settled that she should not leave the palace grounds by the balloon. I cast a lingering thought on the military cloak and the seal-skin gloves, in safe keeping in a remote part of the building. If Madame was not going there might be room for a substitute. But again Mr. Coxwell would not listen to the proposal. There were at least thirty prior applicants; some had even paid their money, and they must have the preference.

At five o'clock all was ready for the start. M. Wilfrid de Fonvielle, a French aeronaut and journalist, took off his hat, and in full gaze of a sympathising and deeply interested crowd deliberately attired himself in a Glengarry cap, a thick overcoat, and a muffler. M. Duruof put on his overcoat, and Mr. Barker, Mr. Coxwell's assistant, seated on the ring above the car, began to take in light cargo in the shape of aneroids, barometers, bottles of brandy and water, and other useful articles. M. Duruof scrambled into the car, one of the men who had been weighing it down getting out to make room for him. Then M. de Fonvielle, amid murmurs of admiration from the crowd, nimbly boarded the little ship, and immediately began taking observations. There was a pause, and Mr. Coxwell, who stood by the car, prepared for the rush of the Thirty. But nobody volunteered. Names were called aloud; only the wind, sighing amongst the trees made answer.

"Il faut partir", said M. Duruof, somewhat impatiently. Then a middle-aged gentleman, who, I afterwards learned, had come all the way from Cambridge to make the journey, and who had only just arrived breathless on the ground, was half-lifted, half-tumbled in, amid agonised entreaties from Barker to "mind them bottles". The Thirty had unquestionably had a fair chance, and Mr. Coxwell made no objection as I passed him and got into the car, followed by one other gentleman, who brought the number up to the stipulated half-dozen. We were all ready to start, but it was thought desirable that Madame Duruof should show herself in the car. So she was lifted in, and the balloon allowed to mount some twenty feet, frantically held by ropes by the crowd below. It descended again, Madame Duruof got out, and in her place came tumbling in a splendid fellow, some six feet four high, broad-chested to boot, who instantly made supererogatory the presence of half a dozen of the bags of ballast that lay in the bottom of the car.

It was an anxious moment, with the excited multitude spread round far as the eye could reach, the car leaping under the swaying balloon, and the anxious, hurried men straining at the ropes. But I remember quite well sitting at the bottom of the car and wondering when the new-comer would finish getting in. I dare say he was nimble enough, but his full arrival seemed like the paying out of a ship's cable.

This was Fred Burnaby, only Captain then, unknown to fame, with Khiva unapproached, and the wilds of Asia Minor untrodden by his horse's hoofs. His presence on the grounds was accidental, and his undertaking of the journey characteristic. He had invited some friends to dine with him that night at his rooms, then in St. James's Street. Hearing of the proposed balloon ascent, he felt drawn to see the voyagers off, purposing to be home in time to dress for dinner. The defection of the Thirty appearing to leave an opening for an extra passenger, Burnaby could not resist the temptation. So with a hasty *Au revoir!* to his companion, the Turkish Minister, he pushed his way through the crowd and dropped into the car.

I always forgot to ask him how his guests fared. As it turned out, he had no chance of communicating with his servant before the dinner hour. The arrival of Burnaby exceeded by one the stipulated number of passengers, and Coxwell was anxious for us to start before any more got in. For a minute or two we still cling to the earth, the centre of an excited throng that shout, and tug at ropes, and run to and fro, and laugh, and cry, and scream "Good-bye" in a manner that makes our proposed journey seem dreadful in prospect. The circle of faces look fixedly into ours; we hear the voices of the crowd, see the women laughing and crying by turns, and then, with a motion that is absolutely imperceptible, they all pass away, and we are in mid-air where the echo of a cheer alone breaks the solemn calm.

I had an idea that we should go up with a rush, and be instantly in the cold current of air in view of which the preparation of extra raiment, the nature of which has been already indicated, had been made. But here we were a thousand feet above the level of the Palace gardens, sailing calmly along in bright warm sunlight, and no more motion perceptible than if we were sitting on chairs in the gardens, and had been so sitting whilst the balloon mounted. It was a quarter past five when we left the earth, and in less than five minutes the Crystal Palace grounds, with its sea of upturned faces, had faded from our sight. Contrary to prognostication, there was only the slightest breeze, and this setting north-east, carried us towards the river in the direction of Greenwich.

We seemed to skirt the eastern fringe of London, St. Paul's standing out in bold relief through the light wreath of mist that enveloped the city. The balloon slowly rose till the aneroid marked a height of fifteen hundred feet. Here it found a current which drove it slightly to the south, till it hovered for some moments directly over Greenwich Hospital, the training ship beneath looking like a cockle boat with walking sticks for masts and yards. Driving eastward for some moments, we slowly turned by Woolwich and crossed the river thereafter steadily pursuing a north-easterly direction.

Looking back from the Essex side of the river the sight presented to view was a magnificent one. London had vanished, even to the dome of St. Paul's, but we knew where the great city lay by the mist that shrouded it and shone white in the rays of the sun. Save for this patch of mist, that seemed to drift after us far away below the car, there was nothing to obscure the range of vision. I am afraid to say how many miles it was computed lay within the framework of the glowing panorama. But I know that we could follow the windings of the river that curled like a dragon among the green fields, its shining scales all aglow in the sunlight, and could see where it finally broadened out and trended northward. And there, as M. Duruof observed with a significant smile, was "the open sea".

There was no feeling of dizziness in looking down from the immense height at which we now floated – two thousand feet was the record as we cleared the river. By an unfortunate oversight we had no map of the country, and were, except in respect of such landmarks as Greenwich, unable with certainty to distinguish the places over which we passed.

"That", said Burnaby from his perch up in the netting over the car, where he had clambered as being the most dangerous place immediately accessible, "is one of the great drawbacks to the use of balloons in warfare. Unless a man has natural aptitude, and is specially trained for the work, his observations from a balloon are of no use, a bird's-eye view of a country giving impressions so different from the actual position of places."

This dictum was illustrated by the scene spread out beneath us. Seen from a balloon the streets of a rambling town resolve themselves into beautifully defined curves, straight lines, and various other highly respectable geometrical shapes. We could not at any time make out forms of people. The white highways that ran like threads among the fields, and the tiny openings in the towns and villages which we guessed were streets, seemed to belong to a dead world, for nowhere was there trace of a living person. The strange stillness that brooded over the earth was made more uncanny still by cries that occasionally seemed to float in the air around us, behind, before, to the right, to the left, but never exactly beneath the car. We could hear people calling, and had a vague idea they were running after us and cheering; but we could distinguish no moving thing. Yes; once the gentleman from Cambridge exclaimed that there were some pheasants running across a field below; but upon close investigation they turned out to be a troop of horses capering about in wild dismay. A flock of sheep in another field, huddled close together, looked like a heap of limestone chippings. As for the fields stretched out in wide expanse, far as the eye could reach, they seemed to form a gigantic carpet, with patterns chiefly diamond shape, in colour shaded from bright emerald to russet brown.

At six o'clock the sun began to drop behind a broad belt of black cloud that had settled over London. The mist following us ever since we crossed the river had overtaken us, even passed us, and was strewed out over the earth, the sky above our heads being yet a beautiful pale blue. We were passing with increased rapidity over the rich level land that stretches from the river bank to Chelmsford, and there was time to look round at each other. Burnaby had come down from the netting and disposed his vast person amongst us and the bags of ballast. He was driven down by the smell of gas, which threatened to suffocate us all when we started. M. Wilfrid de Fonvielle, kneeling down by the side of the car, was perpetually "taking observations", and persistently asking for "the readings", which the gentleman from Cambridge occasionally protested his inability to supply, owing either to Burnaby having his foot upon the aneroid, or to the Captain so jamming him up against the side of the car that the accurate reading of a scientific instrument was not only inconvenient but impossible.

When we began to chat and exchange confidences, the fascination which balloon voyaging has for some people was testified to in a striking manner. The gentleman from Cambridge had a mildness of manner about him that made it difficult to conceive him engaged in any perilous enterprise. Yet he had been in half a dozen balloon ascents, and had posted up from his native town on hearing that a balloon was going up from the Crystal Palace. As for Burnaby, it was borne in upon me, even at this casual meeting, that it did not matter to him what enterprise he embarked upon, so that it were spiced with danger and promised adventure. He had some slight preference for ballooning, this being his sixteenth ascent, including the time when the balloon burst, and the occupants of the car came rattling down from a height of three thousand feet, and were saved only by the fortuitous draping of the half emptied balloon, which prevented all the gas from escaping.

At half-past six we were still passing over the Turkey carpet, apparently of the same interminable pattern. Some miles ahead the level stretch was broken by clumps of trees, which presently developed into woods of considerable extent. It was growing dusk, and no town or railway station was near. Burnaby, assured of being too late for his dinner party, wanted to prolong the journey. But the farther the balloon went the longer would be the distance over which it would have to be brought back and Mr. Coxwell's assistant was commendably careful of his employer's purse. On approaching Highwood the balloon passed over a dense wood, in which there was some idea of descending. But finally the open ground was preferred, and, the wood being left behind, a ploughed field was selected as the place to drop, and the gas was allowed to escape by wholesale. The balloon swooped downward at a somewhat alarming pace, and if Barker had had all his wits about him he would have thrown out half a bag of ballast and lightened the fall. But after giving instructions for all to stoop down in the bottom of the car and hold onto the ropes, he himself promptly illustrated the action, and down we went like a hawk towards the ground.

As it will appear even to those who have never been in a balloon, no advice could have been worse than that of stooping down in the bottom of the car, which was presently to come with a great shock to the earth, and would inevitably have seriously injured any who shared its contact. Fortunately Burnaby, who was as cool as if he were riding in his brougham, shouted out to all to lift their feet from contact with the bottom of the car, and to hang on to the ropes. This was done, and when the car struck the earth it merely shook us, and no one had even a bruise.

Before we began to descend at full speed the grappling iron had been pitched over, and, fortunately, got a firm hold in a ridge of the ploughed land. Thus, when the balloon, after striking the ground, leapt up again into the air and showed a disposition to wander off and tear itself to pieces against the hedges and trees, it was checked by the anchor rope and came down again with another bump on the ground. This time the shock was not serious, and after a few more flutterings it finally stood at ease.

The highest altitude reached by the balloon was three thousand feet, and this was registered about a couple of miles before we struck Highwood. For some distance before completing this descent we had been skimming along at about a thousand feet above the level of the fields, and the intention to drop being evident, a great crowd of rustics gallantly kept pace with the balloon for the last half-mile. By the time we were fairly settled down, half a hundred men, women, and children had converged upon the field from all directions, and were swarming in through the hedge.

Actually the first in at the death was an old lady attired chiefly in a brilliant orange-coloured shawl, who came along over the ridges with a splendid stride. But she did not fully enjoy the privilege she had so gallantly earned. She was making straight for the balloon, when Burnaby mischievously warned her to look out, for it might "go off". Thereupon the old lady, without uttering a word in reply, turned round and, with strides slightly increased in length, made for the hedge, through which she disappeared, and the orange-coloured shawl was seen no more.

All the rustics appeared to be in a state more or less dazed. What with having been running some distance, and what with surprise at discovering seven gentlemen dropped out of the sky into the middle of a ploughed field, they could find relief only in standing at a safe distance with their mouths wide open. In vain Barker talked to them in good broad English, and begged them to come and hold the car whilst we got out. No one answered a word, and none stirred a step, except when the balloon gave a lurch, and then they got ready for a start towards the protecting hedges. At last Burnaby volunteered to drop out. This he did, deftly holding on to the car, and by degrees the intelligent bystanders approached and cautiously lent a hand. Finding that the balloon neither bit nor burned them, they swung on with hearty goodwill, and so we all got out, and Barker commenced the operation of packing up, in which task the natives, incited by the promise of a "good drink", lent hearty assistance.

We had not the remotest idea where we were, and night was fast closing in. Where was the nearest railway station? Perhaps if we had arrived in the neighbourhood in a brake or an omnibus, we might have succeeded in getting an answer to this question. As it was, we could get none. One intelligent party said, after profound cogitation, that it was "over there", but as "over there" presented nothing but a vista of fields – some ploughed and all divided by high hedges – this was scarcely satisfactory. In despair we asked where the high-road was, and this being indicated, but still vaguely and after a considerable amount of thought, Burnaby and I made for it, and presently succeeded in striking it.

The next thing was to get to a railway station, wherever it might be, and as the last train for town might leave early, the quicker we arrived the better. Looking down the road, Burnaby espied a tumble-down cart standing close into the hedge, and strode down to requisition it. The cart was full of hampers and boxes, and sitting upon the shaft was an elderly gentleman in corduroys intently gazing over the hedge at the rapidly collapsing balloon, which still fitfully swayed about like a drunken man awaking out of sleep.

"Will you drive us to the nearest railway station, old gentleman?" said Burnaby cheerily.

The old gentleman withdrew his gaze from the balloon and surveyed us, a feeble, indecisive smile playing about his wooden features; but he made no other answer.

"Will you drive us to the nearest railway station?" repeated Burnaby. "We'll pay you well."

Still no answer came from the old gentleman, who smiled more feebly than ever, now including me in his intelligent purview. After other and diverse attempts to draw him into conversation, including the pulling of the horse and cart into the middle of the road, and the making of a feint to start it off at full gallop, it became painfully clear that the old gentleman had, at sight of the balloon, gone clean out of such senses as he had ever possessed, and as there was a prospect of losing the train if we waited till he came round again, nothing remained but to help ourselves to the conveyance. So Burnaby got up and disposed of as much of himself as was possible in a hamper on the top of the cart. I sat on the shaft, and taking the reins out of the old gentleman's resistless hand, drove off down the road at quite a respectable pace.

After we had gone about a mile the old gentleman, who had been employing his unwonted leisure in staring at us all over, broke into a chuckle. We gently encouraged him by laughing in chorus, and after a brief space he said, "*I seed ye coming.*"

As I had a good deal to do to keep the pony up and going, Burnaby undertook to follow up this glimmering of returning sense on the part of the old gentleman, and with much patience and tact he succeeded in getting him so far round that we ascertained we were driving in the direction of "Blackmore". Further than this we could not get, any pressure in the direction of learning whether there was a railway station at the town or village, or whatever it might be, being followed by alarming symptoms of relapse on the part of the old gentleman. However, to get to Blackmore was something, and after half an hour's dexterous driving we arrived at the village, of which the inn standing back under the shade of three immemorial oak trees appeared to be a fair moiety.

We paid the old gentleman and parted company with him, though not without a saddening fear that the shock of the balloon coming down under his horse's nose, as it were, had permanently affected his brain. At Blackmore we found a well-horsed trap, and through woods and long country lanes drove to Ingatestone, and as fast as the train could travel got back to civilisation.

This was the beginning of a close and intimate friendship, that ended only with Burnaby's departure for the Soudan. He often talked to me of himself and of his still young life. Educated at Harrow, he thence proceeded to Germany, where, under private tuition, he acquired an unusually perfect acquaintance with the French, Italian, and German languages, and incidentally imbibed a taste for gymnastics. At sixteen he, the youngest of one hundred and fifty candidates, passed his examination for admission to the army, and at the mature age of seventeen found himself a cornet in the Royal Horse Guards. At this time his breast seems to have been fired by the noble ambition to become the strongest man in the world. How far he succeeded is told in well-authenticated traditions that linger round various spots in Windsor and London. He threw himself into the pursuit of muscle with all the ardour since shown in other directions, and the cup of his joy must have been full when a precise examination led to the demonstration of the fact that his arm measured round the biceps exactly seventeen inches. He could put 'Nathalie' (then starring it at the Alhambra) to shame with her puny 56-lb. weight in each hand, and could 'turn the arm' of her athletic father as if it had been nothing more than a hinge-rusted nut-cracker. His plaything at Aldershot was a dumb-bell weighing 170 lbs., which he lifted straight out with one hand, and there was a standing bet of £10 that no other man in the Camp could perform the same feat. At the rooms of the London

Fencing Club there is to this day a dumb-bell weighing 120 lbs., with record of how Fred Burnaby was the only member who could lift it above his head.

There is a story told of early barrack days which he assured me was quite true. A horse-dealer arrived at Windsor with a pair of beautiful little ponies he had been commanded to show the Queen. Before exhibiting them to her Majesty he took them to the Cavalry Barracks for display to the officers of the Guards. Some of these, by way of a pleasant surprise, led the ponies upstairs into Burnaby's room, where they were much admired. But when the time came to take leave an alarming difficulty presented itself. The ponies, though they had walked upstairs, could by no means be induced to walk down again. The officers were in a fix; the horse-dealer was in despair; when young Burnaby settled the matter by taking up the ponies, one under each arm and, walking downstairs, deposited them in the barrack-yard. The Queen heard the story when she saw the ponies, and doubtless felt an increased sense of security at Windsor, having this astounding testimony to the prowess of her Household Troops.

Cornet Burnaby was as skilful as he was strong. He was one of the best amateur boxers of the day, as Tom Paddock, Nat Langham, and Bob Travers could testify of their well-earned personal experience. Moreover, he fenced as well as he boxed, and the turn of his wrist, which never failed to disarm a swordsman, was known in more than one of the capitals of Europe. Ten years before he started for Khiva, there was much talk at the Rag of the wonderful feat of the young Guardsman, who undertook for a small wager to hop a quarter of a mile, run a quarter of a mile, ride a quarter of a mile, row a quarter of a mile, and walk a quarter of a mile in a quarter of an hour, and who covered the mile and a quarter of distance in ten minutes and twenty seconds.

Fred Burnaby had, whilst barely out of his teens, realised his boyish dream, and become the strongest man in the world. But he had also begun to pay the penalty of success in the coin of wasted tissues and failing health. When a man finds, after anxious and varied experiments, that a water-ice is the only form of nourishment his stomach will retain, he is driven to the conviction that there is something wrong, and that he had better see the doctor. The result of the young athlete's visit to the doctor was that he mournfully laid down the dumb-bells and the foil, eschewed gymnastics, and took to travel.

An average man advised to travel for his health's sake would probably have gone to Switzerland or the South of France, according to the sort of climate held to be desirable. Burnaby went to Spain, that being at the time the most troubled country in Europe, not without promise of an outbreak of war. Here he added Spanish to his already respectable stock of languages, and found the benefit of the acquisition in his next journey, which was to South America, where he spent four months shooting unaccustomed game and recovering from the effects of his devotion to gymnastics. Returning to do duty with his regiment, he began to learn Russian and Arabic, going at them steadily and vigorously, as if they were long stretches of ploughed land to be ridden over. A second visit to Spain provided him with the rare gratification of being shut up in Barcelona during the siege, and sharing all the privations and dangers of the garrison. Whilst in Seville during a subsequent journey he received a telegram saying that his father was seriously ill. France was at the time in the throes of civil war, with the Communists holding Paris against the army of Versailles. To reach England any other way than via Paris involved a delay of many days, and Burnaby determined to dare all that was to be done by the Communists. So, carrying a Queen's Messenger's bag full of cigars in packets that looked more or less like Government despatches, he passed through Paris and safely reached Calais.

A year later he set forth intending to journey to Khiva, but on reaching Naples was stricken with fever, spent four months of his leave in bed, and was obliged to postpone the trip. In 1874 [sic] he once more went to Spain, this time acting as the special correspondent of *The Times* with the Carlists, and his letters form not the least interesting chapter in the long story of the miserable war. In the early spring of 1875 he made a dash at Central Africa, hoping to find "Chinese Gordon" and his expedition. He met that gallant officer on the Sobat river, a stream which not ten Englishmen have seen, and having stayed in the camp for a few days, set out homeward, riding on a camel through the Berber desert to Korosko, a distance of five hundred miles. After an absence of exactly four months he turned up for duty at the Cavalry Barracks, Windsor, with as much nonchalance as if he had been for a trip to the United States in a Cunard steamer.

It was whilst on this flight through Central Africa that the notion of the journey to Khiva came back with irresistible force. It had been done by MacGahan, but that plucky journalist had judiciously started in the spring. Burnaby resolved to accomplish the enterprise in winter; and accordingly, on November 30th, 1875, he started by way of St. Petersburg, treating himself, as a foretaste of the joys that awaited him on the steppes, to the long lonely ride through Russia in midwinter. At Sizeran he left civilisation and railways behind him, and rode on a sleigh to Orenburg, a distance of four hundred and eighty miles. At Orenburg he engaged a Tartar servant, and another stretch of eight hundred miles on a sleigh brought him to Fort No. 1, the outpost of the Russian army facing the desert of Central Asia. After this even the luxury of sleigh-riding was perforce foregone, and Burnaby set out on horseback, with one servant, one guide, and a thermometer that registered between 70° and 80° below freezing point, to find Khiva across five hundred miles of pathless, trackless, silent snow.

Two Cossacks riding along this route with despatches had just before been frozen to death. The Russians, inured to the climate, had never been able to take Khiva in the winter months. They had tried once, and had lost six hundred camels and two-thirds of their men before they saw the enemy. But Fred Burnaby gaily went forth, clothed-on with sheepskins. After several days' hard riding and some nights' sleep on the snow, he arrived in Khiva, chatted with the Khan, fraternised with the Russian officers, kept his eyes wide open, and finally was invited to return by a telegram from the Commander-in-Chief, who had been brought to understand how this strange visitor from the Cavalry Barracks at Windsor had fluttered the military authorities at St. Petersburg.

This adventure might have sufficed an ordinary man for a lifetime. But in the very next year, whilst his *Ride to Khiva* remained the most popular book in the libraries, he paid a second visit to the Turkomans, seeking them now, not on the bleak steppes round Khiva, but in the more fertile, though by Europeans untrodden, plains of Asia Minor. He had one other cherished project of which he often spoke to me. It was to visit Timbuctoo. But whilst brooding over this new journey he fell in love, married, settled down to domestic life in Cromwell Gardens, and took to politics. It was characteristic of him that, looking about for a seat to fight, he fixed upon John Bright's at Birmingham, that being at the time the Gibraltar of political fortresses.

The last time I saw Fred Burnaby was in September 1884. He was standing on his doorstep at Somerby Hall, Leicestershire, speeding his parting guests. By his side, holding on with all the might of a chubby hand to an extended forefinger, was his little son, a child some five years old, whose chief delight it was thus to hang on to his gigantic father and toddle about the grounds. We had been staying a week with Burnaby in his father's old home, and it had been settled, on the invitation of his old friend Henry Doetsch, that we should meet again later in the year, and set out for Spain to spend a month at Huelva. A few weeks later the trumpet sounded from the Soudan, and like an old war-horse that joyously scents the battle from afar, Burnaby gave up all his engagements, and fared forth for the Nile.

At first he was engaged in superintending the moving of the troops between Tanjour and Magrakeh. This was hard work admirably done. But Burnaby was always pining to get to the front. In a private letter dated Christmas Eve, 1884, he writes: "I do not expect the last boat will pass this cataract before the middle of next month, and then I hope to be sent for to the front. It is a responsible post Lord Wolseley has given me here, with forty miles of the most difficult part of the river, and I am very grateful to him for letting me have it. But I must say I shall be better pleased if he sends for me when the troops advance upon Khartoum."

The order came in due course, and Burnaby was riding on to the relief of Gordon when his journey was stopped at Abu Klea. He was attached to the staff of General Stewart, whose little force of six-thousand-odd men was suddenly surrounded by a body of fanatical Arabs, nine thousand strong. The British troops formed square, inside which the mounted officers sat directing the desperate defence, that again and again beat back the angry torrent. After some hours' fighting, a soldier in the excitement of the moment got outside the line of the square, and was engaged in a hand-to-hand conflict with a cluster of Arabs. Burnaby, seeing his peril, dashed out to the rescue – "with a smile on his face", as one who saw him tells me – and was making irresistible way against the odds when an Arab thrust a spear in his throat, and he fell off his horse dead. He sleeps now, as he always yearned to rest, in a soldier's grave, dug for him by chance on the continent whose innermost recesses he had planned someday to explore.

The date of his death was January 17th, 1885. His grave is nameless, and its place in the lonely Desert no man knoweth.

Brave Burnaby down! Wheresoever 'tis spoken

The news leaves the lips with a wistful regret
We picture that square in the desert, shocked, broken,
Yet packed with stout hearts, and impregnable yet
And there fell, at last, in close *mêlée*, the fighter
Who Death had so often affronted before;
One deemed he'd no dart for his valorous slighter
Who such a gay heart to the battle-front bore.
But alas! for the spear thrust that ended a story
Romantic as Roland's, as Lion-Heart's brief
Yet crowded with incident, gilded with glory
And crowned by a laurel that's verdant of leaf.
A latter-day Paladin, prone to adventure,
With little enough of the spirit that sways
The man of the market, the shop, the indenture!
Yet grief-drops will glitter on Burnaby's bays.
Fast friend as keen fighter, the strife glow preferring,
Yet cheery all round with his friends and his foes;
Content through a life-story short, yet soul-stirring
And happy, as doubtless he'd deem, in its close.

Thus *Punch*, as it often does, voiced the sentiments of the nation on learning the death of its hero.

15 Evelyn Burnaby *A Ride from Land's End to John O'Groat's* (London: Sampson Low, Marston & Co., 1893), pp. ix-xxii [Introduction]

My brother's ride to Khiva suggested the idea of a ride from Land's End to John O'Groats.

It has often been suggested to me, Why not write a book and publish some anecdotes of your reminiscences? My brother's ride to Khiva, and his experiences in the Khan's dominions, I suppose, had led people to believe that I too was gifted with innate literary talent. I am afraid I cannot hope to emulate his effort. The subject of his adventures on horseback from Russia in midwinter across the frigid Steppes was a fascinating one. The objections offered by the Russian Government, the strange tactics of General Milutin, minister of war, who was always inconveniently "out" when my brother called to obtain the necessary permission for his journey, helped to intensify the interest of the public in the book. Novelty always has its charms, no matter whether it is a fresh religion, or a new dress. The "Ride to Khiva", from a political point of view, as regards the position of our Eastern Empire, possessed intrinsic value. I remember my brother telling me that on a railway journey from Petersburg to Orenburg, the conversation of three Russians in their native tongue was most instructive. Being well acquainted with the language, he was able to learn much of the feeling of Russia towards England, and he found out that Mr. Gladstone at the head of affairs was regarded by the Russians as a powerful factor to assist their hopes of aggression in regard to our Indian Empire. A remark, however, made by my brother to them in their own language when he had learnt all he wished to know, brought the political conversation to an abrupt termination. Fred's fame as an athlete and his prodigious weight to say nothing of his dumb-bells, and his favourite hobby of breaking the pokers of our domestic hearth, had secured for him a signal reputation. His pugilistic encounters with Heenan had gained for him the sobriquet of that champion with the gloves. His perils again by land, and his journeys in the air, with his exploits in Spain as a volunteer, in the army of Don Carlos, had also made his name famous.

However I bethought myself, that though I could not expect to rival his literary productions, still, perhaps, a ride through England and Scotland might be interesting, and that a sketch of one's experiences on horseback from Land's End to John O'Groats would help to fill up a few leisure moments for those who have visited the many lovely spots in which our island abounds. It is true the tour has often been made before, and the bicycle has made it a matter of every-day occurrence; still there is always something original to be learnt, and a general election being imminent, it struck me I might be able to pick up a few wrinkles from the conversation in the various hotels *en route* and also from the rustics by the wayside. Why is it that Englishmen are so reticent? The ordinary traveller, as a rule, does not care to unbosom himself, and a journey from Edinburgh to King's Cross will often provoke no further remark than some forced expression in reference to the weather, or it may be a request that the carriage window may be raised or let down.

I believe much of Fred's success was derived from the fact that he associated with all sorts and conditions of men. Before commencing an account of my adventures in the saddle, it has struck me that a few characteristic anecdotes connected with my brother's life, and which have never appeared in print, might interest my readers. Since his death a book has been written purporting to be a record of his romantic career; but inasmuch as the author could not have had the information at hand necessary to make the work perfect, the result was rather meagre and incomplete. "Lor', master Freddy, you have got a contradictorious spirit", was the oft repeated remark of the faithful old nurse who watched over our infancy days. This same spirit which induced him to contemplate his ride to Khiva, I fancy had shown signs of existence in his early life; at the old rectory-house of St. Peter's, on the Green at Bedford, now rendered famous by the statue erected to the memory of Bunyan. There Fred gave evidences of pugilistic tendencies, when still of tender years, by proving himself the better boy in a stand-up fight with another lad who was a fellow-student at the famous grammar school and ancient seminary of learning, founded by the bounty of the late Sir William Harpur and Dame Alice, his wife. Little did this benefactor imagine when he bequeathed a few houses in Holborn which returned a small rental, to found a school on the banks of the Ouse, that the property would so increase in value as to produce an income little short of 20,000*l. per annum*, whereby Bedford Grammar School has become one of the foremost institutions in the country. Sunday after Sunday, Sir William Harpur and his spouse are remembered in the bidding-prayer. In reference to this curious custom, before an assize sermon preached at Saint Mary's at Oxford, the countenance of an eminent judge, who has lately retired from the bench and who is famed for his knowledge of criminal jurisprudence, was an interesting study; especially when the sheriff's chaplain alluded to the bounty of some of Henry the VIIth's wives, "Benefactresses of this ancient university." Fred was barely ten years of age when he was sent to the academy of that excellent divine, the Rev. Chas. Arnold of Tinwell, near Stamford, whose father's contribution to classical literature will never fade from the memory of students of that era.

The wall that Balbus was building, and never built, — the bloodthirsty encounters between that gentleman and Mr. Caius, which never proved fatal, as they seemed to go on for ever — what reflections their memories suggest to those whose early life was spent under a strict discipline, administered with the free use of the cane. Mr. Arnold was a firm believer in this instrument of torture.

It was whilst at Tinwell, where my brother had as a companion the late Duke of Marlborough, then Lord Blandford, that he met with a serious accident. He was trying to poise himself on the cross-bar of a gymnastic apparatus, and finding he had lost his balance, he exclaimed, "Look out, fellows, I am coming", and jumping from the perilous position he occupied, fully twenty feet from the ground, the result was a broken leg which laid him on his back for several months.

From Tinwell to Harrow was the next move in the course of events. Here the reports of his monthly progress were eminently satisfactory, inasmuch as though the place in the shell[16] or form was not very high, my brother's aptitude for foreign languages was always honourably mentioned. After leaving Harrow, and whilst a pupil of the late Rev. Stephen Donne of Oswestry, my brother made himself famous in more ways than one. His prodigious appetite, whilst on a walking tour through North Wales, will never be forgotten in the principality. My brother, soon after leaving Oswestry, passed ninth in order of merit into the army, and it was after he had joined the Blues, and during his subsequent extraordinary career that his name was brought prominently before the public.

His great weight was not, I imagine, conducive to health, and he often used to complain to me that the vulture of Prometheus had fastened on his liver, and seldom ceased to devour its prey.

It was during his early career in the Blues that he made a wager that he would reduce himself four stone in weight in as many months. Frequent visits to the Turkish Baths in Jermyn Street and a very large drain on the firm of Cockle, accomplished the result.

As soon as the period of training for the wager was won he dined with my father at the old University Club in Suffolk Street, and on taking his weight after a sumptuous dinner, the scales revealed a spasmodic increase of seven pounds. Later on in his life, there was a speedy loss of nine stone — but here the cause was an attack of malignant typhoid contracted at Naples, and in one of his many letters to me, he alludes to his sylph-like waist, and taper form. He was a firm believer in the climate of Spain as a tonic to his constitution, and in looking over pages of his correspondence, I find numerous anecdotes which tend to prove how powerful was his sense of humour and appreciation of the ridiculous. He was spending one winter at Seville and on returning to his hotel late one night from the theatre, he became aware that he was followed by three men, whom he describes as Spaniards of the worst type. The streets through which he had to pass were very dark and narrow, and as my brother smoking a huge cigar slowly sauntered along, he felt that his would-be assailants were rapidly gaining on him. The position was critical, and it became necessary to

---

16 In this context a shell, at a public school, is a preparatory year before that in which public examinations are usually taken.

display promptitude. Fred therefore began to soliloquize audibly as he walked, in the native tongue, at the same time letting the rays of the moon flash along the barrel of a small revolver which he always carried. His soliloquy took the form of a rule of three sum; though expressed in the Spanish language, the desperate trio became aware that they were not going to have it all their own way. "How many men could I kill", inquired my brother, "with six bullets which are at the present moment in my pocket; if I accept as a fact that two bullets would effectually polish off one man — answer three. Right." The effect of the soliloquy was very remarkable. Muttering some rather violent imprecations, the Spaniards at once decamped, and Fred returned to his hotel master of the situation.

On another visit to Spain, when staying at Seville, he got the best of an avaricious station porter, who having carried his luggage, shrugged his shoulders when he was offered as a gratuity twice the amount to which he was entitled. "Ah, quite so", said Fred; "I find I have made a trifling mistake; give me back the coin", and he promptly paid him the exact amount, and handed the surplus to a beggar who was standing close by.

A large crowd was immediately attracted to the entrance of the hotel, and Fred proceeded to deliver a political address to his audience, who at that time were inflamed by a spirit of revolution. "Anarchy is caused", he remarked, "by a desire of equal rights and privileges. Now you, a porter, have no right to complain. The beggar has an equal right to a gratuity, especially when you demanded more than your lawful dues." There was a sally of laughter when the oration had been delivered, and the mendicant tribe were very importunate for some days to come.

Many are the anecdotes which might be recorded during the many years he served in the Blues, from 1859 till his death on 17th January, 1885. One of his many exploits may be interesting to the public.

The regiment was quartered at Windsor, and he laid a wager that he would run, row, ride, hop and walk five successive quarters of a mile within one quarter of an hour. A boat and a horse were in readiness on the Banks of the Thames, and the feat was accomplished in a little over twelve minutes.

It was from Windsor that Fred started one summer afternoon on one of his first balloon excursions, in company with the late Captain Westcar. The car was at the mercy of the wind, and sailing over the playing fields of Eton, after many divers courses in their transit over the adjoining counties, fate brought the balloon over the little town of Bedford. It was a lovely June evening, when we sighted the balloon, as it peaceably sailed over our garden, and my father, the moment he sighted it, expressed his belief that Fred might be one of the passengers — and sure enough he was, for shortly after midnight, the slumbers of our peaceful household were rudely disturbed by my brother's voice, who awoke us with, "Hulloa, Governor, here we are; we came down in the balloon eight miles from Bedford."

An *al fresco* supper was prepared, and the fatted calf was killed in his honour. I happened to be in London, a few years before his death, when he started for his perilous voyage across the channel. A bottle of Apollinaris and a tin of biscuits were the rations provided, when he left Folkestone for his journey in the air.

I had been much perplexed as to the reason for his repeated inquiries in regard to the gas supply at that popular sea-side resort; and at last I was induced to believe that he was interested in the lighting of the town, from being a large investor in gas shares; but, no, I was on the wrong track, and the announcement in the morning papers, that he was about to start on a trip across the channel apprised me as to the cause of his interest in the Folkestone gas works.

It was announced that in the event of his safe return to London, he would deliver a lecture at the Aquarium the same evening to the Balloon Society; but no news of his safe arrival in France being received during the day, I was invited to attend the meeting, and so enthusiastic was the reception I met with, that I was at once enrolled a member of that august society. I had no intention, however, of being more than an honorary member, as flights in the air, I felt convinced, would have no charms for me. After the meeting was over and towards midnight much anxiety was expressed; as no tidings had been received of my brother or the balloon. I spent some of the early hours of the morning at the offices of many of the leading newspapers in the Strand, thinking that the first tidings of his safe arrival would be received there; but after a long and weary waiting I went home to bed, and the next morning, in driving down St. James's Street, I caught sight of the immense form of my lost brother, enveloped in an overcoat of about twenty-eight pounds in weight, as he was on his way to breakfast at his club. He seemed much amused at the excitement which his non-appearance had caused, and he confessed to me that at one time during his journey there seemed to be a prospect of dissolution for himself and the balloon. By good luck, however, a change of wind brought the car to anchor on the coast of France, and after accepting the hospitality at a neighbouring farm-house he returned to England, thinking very little of the perils of his journey.

My brother has himself recorded the history of his adventures. A fire balloon started from Cremorne Gardens many years ago. M. Goudat [sic], the French aeronaut, on this occasion, refused to take him as a passenger, owing to his bulky form, but Fred was not to be beaten, and as the balloon commenced to rise gracefully from the ground, amid the plaudits of thousands, interspersed with strains of martial music, my brother, with much dexterity, seizing the ropes, vaulted into the car.

The effect was magical, and the descent of the balloon to the ground was the work of a moment. The aeronaut's language was far from polite. In broken

French he ejaculated, "Weel, sare! you spoil de effect. De band play, de people shout, we rise, we mount! Magnifique! and then you – why, you put your ugly carcase into my balloon, and we go down, plomp; dare, dat is vot you do." However, my brother gained his ends, and as the balloon made its second ascent, he was found to be amongst the enterprising party.

It was during one of his visits on leave to Bedford that in discharging a pistol it burst, and his hand was seriously lacerated in the part adjoining the thumb. Naturally the consequences could have been serious, and lockjaw might have supervened; but without saying a word Fred walked quietly down the street, found our medical adviser at home, sat patiently whilst stitches were inserted into the inflamed wound, and returned little disconcerted by the result of the accident. When over eighteen stone in weight my brother determined to make himself proficient in the art of riding a bicycle. Most of his practice was carried on in a secluded path in the Crystal Palace grounds, as he was anxious to conceal from all his friends the scene of his labours. However, by hook or by crook, I found it out, and on arriving at the Palace I inquired of a visitor whether he had seen a gentleman on a bicycle. "Well, sir", he replied, "I can't exactly say that, but there is a big gentleman a falling and a tumbling about in the direction of yonder path", and sure enough there he was, gyrating with an enormous machine, and rather put out by my unexpected appearance. However, he went on with the practice until he became proficient, and the remarkable agility with which he vaulted on to his machine was astounding, when one remembered the extraordinary weight he drew in the scales.

He was throughout his life a martyr to indigestion, and I believe constant field days at Wormwood Scrubs, which did not find favour with dancing subalterns, were the result of his firm conviction that early hours and active exercise were the best stimulants for a sluggish liver. He had no taste for race meetings, and during the latter part of his life the only race-course he was in the habit of attending was at Ascot on the cup day. His horses received extraordinary names: Obadiah, Ahasuerus, and Beelzebub, were his principal chargers, and on his offering to mount a timid friend on the latter, I was appealed to as to whether the name was not suggestive of tricks and vice.

Amongst my brother's characteristics, one stood out prominently. He was ever in the habit of making light of his many feats. He considered that the world was too highly prized by most men, and that life was intended to be seen and studied from every point of view. His firm friendship with the late Baker Pasha was evidenced in the fact that in the event of his widow's death he had appointed him the guardian of his little son. He was in company with that gallant cavalry officer when he was wounded in the East. The bullet which was extracted from Col. Baker's cheek came into my brother's possession, and at his request I had it mounted on a letter-weight and forwarded to one of our most gallant cavalry officers as a token of my brother's regard. Utter recklessness of danger seemed to predominate over Fred's short-lived career, and the exemplary patience which he displayed during his long illness of typhoid in Southern Italy in 1873, was only equalled by his courage in the Soudan, when having started to the relief of his old friend Gordon, he coolly met his death at the hands of an Arab, whose spear-wound from behind caused mortal injury to the jugular vein.

His appreciation of services rendered to him by others was very marked, and the record on poor Radford's (his servant's) tomb, in the little cemetery on the hill above Dover, "True as steel. This stone is erected by the man he served so well", is a proof that he valued in others that sterling kind-heartedness which was a prominent trait in his character. The English public have shown that they recognized the good service he rendered to his country, and that they regret the premature loss of a life of no ordinary value. The monuments to his memory in the chapel of Harrow School, in the church of Holy Trinity, Windsor, the Memorial Window in St. Peter's Church, Bedford, and at Somerby in Leicestershire, besides the large obelisk placed in St. Saviour's Churchyard at Birmingham as the result of humble contributions of those to whom he had endeared himself when he was a candidate to represent that town in 1880, are an evidence that true British pluck will ever be appreciated by British people.

16 Archibald Forbes *Czar and Sultan: the adventures of a British lad in the Russo-Turkish war of 1877-78* (Bristol: J.W. Arrowsmith, 1894), pp. 316-8.

On the evening before our departure from Plevna my father had sent me down from Tutchenitza a *Daily News* of December 5th, which contained a telegram from Sophia stating that several English officers, Colonels Allix, Baker, and Maitland, Captains Fife and James, and other English officers were now with Mehemet Ali's army in the Kamarli position; that Valentine Baker Pasha and Captain Fred Burnaby of Khiva renown had recently arrived, and that the former had taken command of Mehemet Ali's left wing on either side of the Baba Konak Pass. It had occurred to me as I read this telegram that it would be a pleasant thing for me, although circumstances had placed me on the side where there were no fellow-countrymen in arms, to see British officers well out to the front as they were sure to be. Millett was an American, and could not be expected to feel as I did in this matter.

But he was a fellow who was always ready for an adventure; and he said in his humorous way that he was specially anxious to see Burnaby because when the war was over he had an idea of going into the showman business, and would be glad to ascertain whether the biggest man in the British army would suit him as his "boss" giant....

... I asked Count Schuvalov whether any English officers had been recognised on the Turkish side. "Yes, indeed", he exclaimed — "quite a number of them! You can see them for yourself if you care to go up yonder. Two of them are old friends of mine, and I should like nothing better than to ask them to come over and dine with me. You are too young to have been in the Aldershot autumn manoeuvres in 1871, else you might remember the officer of the Russian Guards who rode with the Prince of Wales and Valentine Baker at the head of the 10th Hussars. I was that officer; and poor Baker was the finest light-cavalry officer I ever saw. Had he belonged to us, do you think we should have lost him to the service he adorned because of a piece of wretched private folly? Pshaw! what a square-toed prudish folk you English are! If Valentine Baker would only forsake those tatterdemalion Turks and come over the trenches to us, I'll engage the Czar would make him a full general within a month! Burnaby! yes, you may see that huge droll fellow as like as not, if you care to go up into the entrenchments. He is quite mad of course — always was, and he hates us. But he was my guest at the mess of the Garde du Corps when he was last in St. Petersburg, and our crack giant, old Protassoff-Bakmetieff, was not in it with Burnaby either in stature or in strength." "By George!", exclaimed Schuvalov, "I'll give you a flag of truce, and if you can persuade Baker and Burnaby to come back with you and dine with us, I shall be delighted beyond measure!" Just then there broke out the rattle of a sharp musketry-fire. "Oh, that is nothing!" exclaimed Schuvalov; but Millett and I ran up the steep ascent, passed through the quiescent batteries, and scudded out into the advanced entrenchment. Schuvalov's orderly officer came with us, and pointed out how easily the Russians could work down into the valley below without using the Baba-Konak pass at all. There were not 150 paces between the Russian and Turkish entrenchments. The firing was pretty sharp, and we were not at all ashamed to accept the cover the breastwork afforded. "Look!" exclaimed Schuvalov's orderly — "You see these two men on the top of the Turkish parapet? The big man standing up and showing us his full front is Burnaby; the other one in the fez, sitting down with his legs dangling over the entrenchment is Baker!" Yes, there they were, calm and unconcerned in the Russian fire! My heart swelled, and the water came into my eyes. The Russians are brave men; but in all the Russian host I had seen but one man so daring — that was Skobeleff, and he only when urgent occasion demanded. And there were my two countrymen, quietly and undramatically exposing themselves as a matter of course, to hearten their wretched "Mustafiz" — I knew by the uniform that their men were not "Nizams".

17 Henry William Lucy, extract from 'Ups and Downs in My Life' *Strand Magazine*, vol. 31 (January 1906), pp. 33-40.

Scene, Crystal Palace; locality, a bit of meadow inside the Palace grounds, consecrated to the departure of many balloons; epoch, the sixteenth Handel Festival; time, high noon; weather cloudy, with a strong wind blowing southwest. There are not many people about, the tens of thousands who throng the Crystal Palace being happily unconscious that a renowned traveller is about to make another journey. Up on a knoll near the gate leading into the field are two nursemaids in charge of four children, the latter amusing themselves by dragging each other through a hedge, whilst the maids are profoundly occupied — the one reading a letter, the other listening.

In the centre of the sward a balloon is swaying about ineffectually, held down by innumerable bags of sand hooked on to the netting. A gentleman in semi-police attire is diligently pumping gas into the balloon. Another gentleman, in his shirt-sleeves, is superintending operations. Others, also in shirt-sleeves, are holding on to ropes, sniffing at the gas, or performing other functions understood to be essential to a successful balloon ascent.

Captain Fred Burnaby (of the Blues) stands smilingly looking on, his colossal figure draped in a thick, far-reaching overcoat, his head crowned by a comical little tweed cap, guaranteed not to blow off unless the balloon goes within a mile of Saturn. Near him is another gallant captain, of the Grenadiers, who has not thought the occasion worth special preparation in the way of dress. He has turned out in an ordinary shooting-coat, and "billycock" hat warranted to blow off on the slightest provocation. There is no particular reason why the Grenadier should go up in a balloon, except that there is a strong spice of danger about the enterprise; for whomsoever else may join the expedition, it is stipulated that there shall be no professional aeronaut. Burnaby, however, has a purpose. Back from his ride to Khiva, he has now been in this effete land several weeks, and its commonplaces begin to pall upon him. Life is scarcely worth living in a country where a man regularly goes to bed under cover; where he dines at stated hours, has his morning and evening newspapers, goes to dinner-parties and balls, and from Sunday to Saturday comes no nearer danger than that which may lurk under the probability of a mob suddenly breaking in upon the Horse Guards, when he might at the head of his troops defend it to the last drop of his blood.

Growing discontented with the horrible regularity of life in London, the thought occurred to him that he would have a balloon all to himself, where, freed from the counsels or the fears of an aeronaut, he might go whither the wind should drive him. As some men, finding themselves in low spirits, not sound in the liver, take a pill, so the captain decided to take a balloon. Thus it comes to pass that, whilst the wind is bending the mighty trees, swaying the balloon to and fro as if it were a feather, he looks on with contented smile, the colour already coming back to his cheeks, the light returning to his eyes.

"Now, sir", said Wright, the envied owner of a real balloon, "the sooner you are ready, the better I shall be pleased."

"Have you given us plenty of gas?" asked the captain.

"Yes, sir; you will go up like a shot."

"Give us some more gas", said Burnaby, firmly.

The gentleman in the semi-police uniform shook up the hose, and the balloon, trembling and snorting like a maddened horse, threatened to break away.

Crawling in under the netting, skilfully evading the swaying cords that threatened to strangle him, the Grenadier boarded the car. Sitting down at the bottom, with his head thrust through the netting, after the fashion of an ambitious bird on the way to market in a twine bound basket curiously regards the surrounding scenery, he had a bad five minutes. The balloon was tossed about with increased frenzy. Every time it pitched over, right or left, the netting swept across, threatening to create a flow of promotion in a crack regiment.

Burnaby, scorning to dodge in among the netting, strode fiercely over it towards the car, his illimitable legs dangerously entwined at every step. He

On the ground, Crystal Palace, 14 September 1874
(*Mayfair*, 3 July 1877)

In the air, Crystal Palace, 14 September 1874
(*Mayfair*, 3 July 1877)

got over safely, just escaping being ripped up by the anchor as the balloon lurched over, and the Grenadier's head, still safe on his shoulders, disappeared on the other side. The captain has every qualification for an aeronaut except moderate size. No one except those who have made an aerial journey with him can imagine the curiously complete way in which his legs pervade the car. It is a case of Eclipse first and the rest nowhere. If he did not find a fresh charm in the danger of sitting on the edge of the car whilst it careers through space, it would be absolutely impossible to dispose of him in any aerial contrivance built on a smaller scale than the dome of St. Paul's Cathedral.

Now the car is loaded the balloon grows madder and madder, dashing off towards the side on the edge of which the captain sits, holding on to the netting. Then it lurches back, the Grenadier, now master of the situation, deftly dodging the netting as it sweeps across with murderous intent to strangle him.

"Let go!" cried the captain, and the men begin unhooking the bags of sand.

The balloon is positively going out of what passes with it for a mind, surging and swaying in a manner that threatens to pitch the occupants out of the car.

"Let us have another bag of ballast."

"You have got plenty", Wright expostulates.

"Another bag of ballast", says the captain, in the same uncompromising manner with which he had ordered and obtained more gas. The bag was

(*Strand Magazine*, January 1906)

pitched in.

The sand-bags that anchor the balloon to earth are unhooked one by one. The men in charge grow more and more excited. The two nursemaids on the far-off knoll stop reading their letter to watch the balloon. Of the four children one has been finally overcome, and, lying prone on its face, its back affords a convenient coign of vantage whence an elder brother may observe the proceedings. The last link with earth is loosed. The mad surging of the balloon ceases. To the throbbing and jumping there succeeds a condition of absolute steadiness, whilst the world and all that therein is seem suddenly to sink beneath the occupants of the car.

The prospect swiftly widens, and, without feeling that we have stirred an inch, lo! we are motionless many feet above the topmost pinnacle of the Crystal Palace. All around, for miles and miles, lies the verdurous country with a cloud of smoke towards the north, through which chimneys and spires appear, indicating that there lies London.

Driven by the south-west wind the balloon was carried swiftly on at the rate of forty miles an hour. So steady and motionless was the progress that the only way of ascertaining that one moved was to fix the eye on some landmark. Being well loaded with ballast, the balloon was kept at a pretty low level for some

(*Strand Magazine*, January 1906)

miles, thus affording a view of the country stretched below, the fields showing in varied pattern like a drawing-room carpet, the towns and villages, with all their streets singularly straight, dotted about like neatly-made toys. Clear away to the north-west London loomed large, the principal object in the congeries of buildings being St. Paul's Cathedral.

The balloon made straight for the river, crossing it just below Greenwich. Harking back, it trended farther east, crossing again at Woolwich. Whilst sailing in this direction the captain's heart was light. Balloon ascents are a comparative nothingness to him, for, having long ago made his twentieth, he has given up counting how many times he has been up. In the present instance there was the special spice of delight in the fact that he was untrammelled by the presence of an aeronaut, and that consequently something might happen. What he wanted, and chiefly hoped for, was to get to the sea.

"It is a curious thing in this country", he said, looking moodily at his compass, "that one never or rarely gets a good stiff north breeze that would carry a balloon over the Channel. This westerly gust, if it lasted, would take us out into the German Ocean. But we shall have it changing again, and will be off on the usual journey across Essex."

There fell dead silence. The balloon sped steadily eastward till Woolwich was

(*Strand Magazine*, January 1906)

passed. Looking far out the eye beheld, under a gleam of sunshine, something that shone like molten silver.

"The sea!" cried the captain.

A voice, which sounded strangely — as voices do in the unearthly stillness of this upper air—slowly spoke:—

> Then felt I like some watcher of the skies
> When a new planet swims into his ken;
> Or like stout Cortez when with eagle eyes
> He stared at the Pacific, and all his men
> Look'd on each other with a wild surmise
> Silent upon a peak in Darien.

Burnaby's prognostication proved true. After catching a glimpse of what seemed to be the sea, though it was probably only the broad mouth of the river at Gravesend, the balloon, spinning round, began to re-cross the river, and swiftly made its way over the low-lying land of Essex.

"Shall we go higher?" said the Grenadier.

"Yes", said the captain.

A bag of ballast was emptied, the earth seemed to sink farther, and the top of the balloon suddenly came upon a cloud. Like everything else, the cloud soon dropped below the car. The balloon went sailing on. Above, a cloudless sky of blue; below, no earth, nor sight nor sound of human life.

Only a broad sea of fleecy cloud, on which was pictured the shadow of the balloon, with the heads of the occupants as clearly traced as if it were a colossal photograph. It was worth a much more perilous journey to see this picture, and to feel all that was made possible by the sight. Overhead, the bewitchingly blue sky, tempering with softened light the blazing ball of the setting sun; beneath, the fleecy clouds with the shadowy companion balloon; afar off, beyond the ravelled edges of the cloud, glimpses of glade and trees and sunlit fields.

"It is confoundedly hot", said the Grenadier.

"Yes", said the captain, taking off his gigantic coat and hanging it on to the anchor, as if he were in a mess-room.

"One comfort in being above the clouds is that a man can sit in public in his shirt-sleeves."

The balloon sped on and presently cleared the cloud. All the nether world lay spread below, with the Thames glittering far away behind, suggesting the idea that the sea-serpent had got himself electro-plated and was leisurely crawling up towards London, intent upon seeing the great city. After sailing for an hour and a half, the wind still keeping southerly, the sea again became visible to the east. A glance at the map showed that this must be the Blackwater River, and that, with the wind as it now was, the balloon would, in course of time, arrive at Norwich. Some distance ahead was a wood — not Epping Forest, as the Grenadier surmised, for Epping lay away to the left.

"We had better get down before we reach the wood", said the captain; "so here goes."

And he gave the gas-pipe a turn. The earth, contrary to its usual practice, now began to ascend. Suddenly the fields assumed larger dimensions; trees grew up as if by magic; animals, which looked like hares as they capered about the meadows, turned out to be horses; cattle, which one thought were mice, disclosed themselves in their true dimensions. With the sound of the wind rushing in the ears, and a vague sense that if the earth did not cease behaving itself in this ludicrous manner there would shortly be a collision, things continued to grow larger and larger.

"Out with the anchor!" shouted the captain. The anchor was dropped, the earth thereupon suddenly taking a dive, leaving the balloon some hundred feet higher than when freighted with the iron load. You may throw an anchor out on a field, but you cannot make it bite. This particular anchor amused itself by dancing about on the hard earth, diligently grubbing up the grass, passing through hedges, and skilfully avoiding anything that offered a firm clutch.

The earth, having thus insisted upon coming up to the balloon, brought the wind with it. The captain was now in improved spirits. The pertinacious conduct of the anchor was quite an unlooked-for treat.

Fullness of joy was promised by approaching the wood, which was rushing on the balloon with far more velocity than Dunsinane approached Macbeth.

"We shall be into the wood in half a minute", said the captain, cheerfully.

"At the charge!" responded the Grenadier. Amid the rushing of the wind might be heard an inspiriting whistle sounding the charge.

"Here is the wood!"

Into it went the balloon, crashing against a tree and tearing a large strip out of the silk, spreading abroad a perfume as if the main pipe of the gasworks had suddenly burst. If the anchor would only catch the ground now all would be well.

But there never was, since the days of the Ark, an anchor like this. To observe the way it carefully eluded trees, which grew about as plentifully as gooseberry bushes, was exceedingly interesting. It would go half a yard out of its course to avoid an eligible tree, whilst it fiercely grubbed up any weeds that raised aloft their feeble stalks. From tree to tree the wind hurried the balloon, making fresh gashes in the canvas, threatening to leave not a rag behind. Also the balloon now began to droop heavily, and it was evident that the end could not long be delayed.

Midway in the wood the anchor carefully selected an exceedingly rotten elm, on a branch of which the car calmly reposed, the anchor taking this opportunity — when it was absolutely of no use — to fasten itself in the root of a giant oak. There was nothing for it but to drop on to the ground, and this was done without other harm than a few scratches. There remained the balloon to release, and this the Grenadier volunteered to do. Climbing up the tree like a cat, he, though half suffocated with gas, loosened the folds of the balloon, and lowered the car into the arms of the captain.

"How do you feel now?" asked the Grenadier, when, at midnight, he met his companion of voyage at the Queen's ball at Buckingham Palace.

"Better", said Burnaby, emphatically. "That was a capital anchor. I am going to buy it from Wright, and will keep it for future balloon journeys."

18 Julian Hawthorne 'Fred Burnaby, the hero that was' in *New York Tribune*, 26 April 1908.

It was at a Lord Mayor's dinner in the Mansion House, London that I first met the man. I did not know who he was. He sat low in his chair at my right hand; but his face, with its dark complexion, large, soft, black eyes, dark wavy hair, and charming play of expression, was the handsomest I ever had beheld. His conversation was fascinating, and covered a great variety of subjects, and the intonations of his mellow voice were a delight to the ear. He was as simple and unaffected as a boy. He looked to be hardly beyond his first youth, and I took him to be some yet unrenowned scion of a good family, who had exceptionally improved the opportunities afforded him by the conventional grand tour. But some remark that he presently made indicated connection with the army and he admitted that he belonged to one of the British cavalry regiments. I then noticed, and commented on, the exceptional breadth of his shoulders.

"Yes, the fellows used to consider me pretty strong", he replied, with his light laugh, "A couple of years after I joined, we were in barracks at Aldershot, and our mess room was, for some reason, at the top of the building, up three flights of stairs. Our Colonel, a bit of a martinet, owned a couple of Shetland ponies, which his wife drove to a little basket carriage. They were cunning little fellows, and might weigh twenty-two or three stone apiece [about three hundred pounds]. The Colonel was very proud of them; and he once said, when scolding us for some blunder on parade, that his Shetlands had more brains than any of us. 'They can't talk', he said, 'but I'd about as lief have them at the mess table as some of you young gentlemen who fancy you know all about cavalry manoeuvres. It was only his fun, of course; but it stuck in my crop; perhaps because I imagined, with good reason, no doubt, that he had been pointing particularly at me. Next evening I was late for mess; and passing by the stables an idea struck me, and I went in and got the groom to let me have the two ponies. I led them along to the barracks, and then got one under each arm, and lugged them up stairs, kicking and squealing; till I fairly landed them in the mess room on the third floor. I walked up with them to the Colonel, who was carving a leg of mutton, and put them down beside him. I was a bit winded, for the little beggars got to be pretty heavy at the last; but I managed to say, "I thought you might be in need of a little rational society, Colonel", and then went to my seat. "But my word!" added my unknown friend, laughing, "I never heard such an uproar in my life!"

At this juncture, the functionary behind the Lord Mayor's chair hammered for silence, and called out, "The Lord Mayor drinks to the health of Captain Fred Burnaby!" Whereupon, to my amazement, up rose my companion, unfolding himself to greater and greater heights, till he stood at his full stature of six feet six of magnificent manhood, and gracefully acknowledged the cheers that greeted him. For he was at that time one of the most famous men in England; the hero of the 'Ride to Khiva', the pride of the army, the darling of society, the author of several popular books, and, without doubt, the strongest man then wearing the British uniform. So I had been entertaining an angel—or, rather, he had been entertaining me—unawares.

How He Met His End

Fifteen years later, in 1893, I happened to be at the World Trade Fair in Chicago, and found myself in the viewing of the British building, down near the lake. I knew that my friend Villiers[17], the war correspondent, was stopping there; but as I put my hand on the gate of the front yard, the sentinel on guard stopped me, saying that the house was closed to visitors for the day.

He was a tall, bony, soldierly fellow, with the stripes of a sergeant on his arm; and the number of the regiment on his cap prompted me to ask him I whether he had been in the recent campaign in Egypt, where the British were attacked by the "Fuzzy-wuzzies".

The man's eyes glowed. "Indeed, then, I was", he replied. "I was in the front of the line that day."

"Why, in that case", said I, you must have seen Burnaby."

He straightened up instantly, as if on parade, and stared at me with a sort of fierceness. "Did you know him?" he said, and went on immediately, "I saw him, sir—and I saw him when he died."

We went into executive session forthwith, and the sergeant told me his story. Burnaby had joined the expedition, having been assigned no command, but for the sake of adventure and for the sport of the thing. He soon became the favourite of the officers, and the idol of the rank and file. His experience in campaigning in wild countries, his quick perceptions, sound judgment, and dare-devil courage made him a valuable stimulating companion.

On the day of the battle, he assisted in choosing the position for the British force, and in forming the square. When the Fuzzy-wuzzies charged, and in spite of the fire of the infantry, engaged in hand to hand fighting with parts of the British line, Burnaby stepped to the point where the attack was fiercest, and with his drawn sabre fenced with the native spearmen. "He didn't try to kill none of 'em, sir", said the sergeant, "being there unofficial as I might say, though he had chance enough, as I could see, being only about fifteen paces to his right; but he just stood there and played with 'em, as a man plays with boys, parrying the thrusts, and sometimes taking on two or three of 'em at once, and he was laughing, in a quiet way he had all the time. It was just pastime for him,

---

17 Frederic Villiers (1851-1922), British war artist and correspondent. Along with William Simpson and Melton Prior, Villiers was one of the most notable 'special' artists of the later nineteenth century.

Burnaby at Abu Klea
(*New York Daily Tribune*, 26 April 1908)

you could see that. By and by, my mate, that was standing next me, got prodded through the stomach by one of those devils; and it made me that mad that, in place of giving the fellow the bayonet, I clubbed my rifle and bashed his head open. I'd stepped a bit forward to do it; and as I stepped back, I looked round toward Burnaby. A big blackamoor, pretty near as tall as he was, had made a thrust at his face, and Burnaby's sword had sent the spear up in the air. Just then, as his arm was raised, a fellow who'd been crouching down close to him gave a jab upward with his weapon and sent the point right through Burnaby's heart. He was dead before he fell—and so was the fellow that killed him, for Phil Bowman, a private in the ranks, gave him a kick that broke his jaw, and then pinned him through the neck with his bayonet. But Burnaby was dead, and if we'd killed every Fuzzy-wuzzy in Egypt it wouldn't have made up for him."

This account of the young hero's death, though differing slightly from some of the stories, has the credit due to an eye witness at close quarters. It seems a life thrown away; and yet the example of such a man helps to inspire the spirit in British troops that has made their "far thin battle line" victorious all round the world.

19 Amy Charlotte Stuart Menzies (née Bewicke), *Memories Discreet and Indiscreet by a Woman of No Importance* (London: Herbert Jenkins, 1917), pp. 52-60.

I am now about to take a very big jump from King Alexander and Queen Draga, with the Tweedales thrown in, to Colonel Burnaby, who had a most romantic career, though passed in a prosaic era! A restless wonderful man, never happy unless passing through some fiery ordeal of adventure, crossing the Channel in a balloon, riding to Khiva, and such-like little enterprises. I have never been in a balloon, but there does not appear to be much room in them for such big men as Colonel Burnaby, who stood six feet four inches in his socks, and had a chest measurement of forty-six inches, or Captain Templer, who was, I believe, in the 60th Rifles before he became a Government aeronaut; he was a big man, tall and broad. How cramped they must get!

When I first knew Colonel Burnaby he was in the Royal Horse Guards, just before he gained his majority. He was the son of one of the good old sporting parsons.

From all I hear, he and my grandfather were much of the same calibre, both of a proud and dignified bearing, inspiring respect and awe, living in some state, hunting, attending race-meetings, with well-turned-out carriages, horses and servants. The sporting parson was generally greatly esteemed by his flock. I was boasting one day to Colonel Burnaby of a feat of my husband's in his early youth, when he started from our landing-stage on the Derwent, which runs through the Park of our Yorkshire home, in a small canoe with only a paddle and an umbrella to use as a sail. He travelled down the river to its mouth, then round to Hull and back again without mishap. My little boast was quite thrown into the shade by an account Colonel Burnaby gave me of a jaunt of his own when at Harrow. He started alone at the age of thirteen on a journey of some hundreds of miles in a boat, returning in three weeks, having been on the move all the time.

I used to hear Colonel Burnaby spoken of as the strongest man in the English army, as, indeed, I think he may well have been, for I have seen him do prodigious things. I remember my husband bringing him in one night from the club, with a few other old friends, when we were staying at the Langham Hotel in London. My partner was somewhat of an athlete, and had won various medals and prizes for running and walking. Soon they began to do tricks, which went on into the early dawn, amusing me so much I felt I could not go to bed, but must stay and watch. They began, that is to say, Burnaby and my husband began, with a hopping match over the chairs placed in a row equal distances apart. This was a dead heat, but was an expensive game, as Burnaby was no light-weight, and we were informed next morning that the concussion had brought down a chandelier in the room below. Rather doubtful whether the extent of the mischief was as bad as it had been painted, we went to see what damage was done, and there truly enough lay more or less wrecked one of those enormities, which consisted of endless hanging glass icicles, much valued and very fashionable at one time. Of course the one in question was valuable according to the hotel manager.

But more gymnastic feats were performed before morning arrived and we were confronted by the results. After the hopping match Burnaby vaulted over a largish round table in the middle of the room, using his left hand, and without the least apparent effort. My husband then followed suit, not so successfully; he certainly eventually arrived at the other side, and that is all I can say. A cousin of mine in the Black Watch who was in the room at the time said, "You can't lift the 'Old Man'" (this was a name given to my husband by his chosen and familiar friends in consequence of his hair being white at the age of twenty-five) "with one hand." The 'Old Man' looked anxious, as six feet four inches advanced towards him, and seized him by the back of his collar and coat, popping him down at the other side of the table much as a dog would a rat. Although slight my husband was above the average height.

Colonel Burnaby nearly always called his horses by Biblical names. I can remember a Moses, Boaz and a Nimshi. Although a good horseman, I never thought he looked well on a horse, too untidy and all abroad as they say in the south. On State occasions when he rode before the Queen as Silver Stick and Colonel of the Blues, he managed to brace himself up and look smart.

He was rather a trial to his valet, as in the first place he would wear cheap boots, and what is almost worse, if it were possible he would manage to fasten up his waistcoat wrongly, leaving a button somewhere not doing its duty, its proper button-hole being engaged elsewhere. Yet his servants were much attached to him. Most people have heard of his devoted soldier servant Radstock [sic], and of his master's tender nursing of him during his last illness.

A weakness for puns was a little failing of Burnaby's, and at the time when he was piqued with Colonel Owen Williams and there seemed every likelihood of a flare up, he told me his views on the matter and his opinions of his one-time friend, winding up with, "Never mind, I am owing Williams one!" The fact that he did not get on very well with his superior officers, and at times with his brother-officers, did not trouble him a little bit; he used to laugh about it and went on his way rejoicing. One of the chief causes of offence to his superiors was that, when he asked for leave and it was not granted, he usually managed to circumvent the authorities and turn up wherever he wished to be. Daringly independent he cared nothing for a wigging.

One of the reasons why he did not always "hit it off" with some of his brother officers, Burnaby declared, was because he did not wear stays, paint his face, wax his moustache and dye his hair.

There is, however, no denying that he was untidy, although he would never admit it. A certain lock or two of hair, which should have been swept back off his brow, had a way of almost invariably hanging down over it. This helped to give him an untidy appearance.

When he crossed the Channel by balloon in 1882 he left England without permission, so on his return the Duke of Cambridge was turned on to him, but the Duke spoke very nicely, for I happen to know he was much interested in the enterprise, and admired Burnaby's pluck, and said he would like to go up in a balloon himself with Burnaby, only he feared "there would be such a hullabaloo".

The aircraft of to-day fascinate me, but I decline to go up in a balloon, too much has to be left to chance and luck to please me. Not many women have taken up ballooning, but Mrs. May Harbord loves it.

There have been various conflicting accounts of how Colonel Burnaby met his death at Abu Klea, and it is curious that out of the accounts given to me by friends present at the battle, no two are alike. Lord Binning's of the Blues was the most graphic, but too long to quote verbatim. From it I gathered that when the square was broken by the camels being wounded and unable to advance with the troops, the enemy quickly saw the weak spot and rushed it. Lord Binning saw Burnaby riding backwards and forwards on Moses trying to get the men to fall back quickly and then lost sight of him in the *mêlée*.

When the battle was won and there was time to think and breathe again, a general cry arose of "Where's Burnaby?" Lord Binning went in search of him, and a little way from the square found him on the ground dying, with his head lying in the lap of a young private in the Bays. The lad was crying bitterly, and said, "Oh, Sir, here's the bravest man in England dying, and no one to help him." Colonel Burnaby tried to speak, and seemed to recognise his friend, but was dying fast from loss of blood from three mortal wounds: a spear wound in the throat, a bullet wound in the forehead, and part of his head cut away. Lord Binning remarked that it was wonderful that he had lived as long as he did with three such ghastly wounds. Poor Moses was lying near his master covered with spear wounds.

On the other hand, Mr. Melton Prior told me that when Colonel Burnaby met his death he was outside the square fighting six Arabs single-handed, and that when he heard an order shouted to retire he turned his head to see who gave it; this gave his opponents their opportunity and they at once speared him in the throat.

Another friend writing to me almost directly after the battle describes it thus: "Burnaby was on the back of Moses when the poor beast was killed. Burnaby continued to fight on foot with his four-barrelled Lancaster pistol, but fell from loss of blood from three wounds, each one serious enough to have killed him."

Yet another account tells me: "It was Burnaby's own fault he was killed, he asked for it; went out of the square as if he wished to fight the lot single-handed, and by so doing jeopardised the square, and if we had lost the battle it would have been Burnaby's fault and his alone."

A letter written quite recently by one of the Blues who took part in the engagement says:

> Burnaby arrived the day before Abu Klea, and we were told he had been sent up to take command in case anything happened to Herbert Stewart, who was in command as second senior officer. Sir Charles Wilson, though a clever man and excellent political officer, had never commanded a regiment in his life. Eroll was not there, but when the Arabs from without and the camels from within broke the square formation in which we were fighting, Burnaby went out of the square near to our (the Blues') face.
>
> Binning, seeing him wounded and in difficulties, went and spoke to him, but he was mortally wounded in several places, and notably by a shot in the forehead at the roots of the hair. Burnaby went out [from England] on his own hook, I believe, and Sir Garnet Wolseley wanting a man employed him at once and pushed him up to our column.
>
> Binning did tell me he was killed while the fighting was still going on, as I was busy trying to shut the face of the square and get the ammunition and camels back inside it. Stewart being mortally wounded two days afterwards at Abu Kru and Burnaby being killed, we found ourselves under Sir Charles Wilson surrounded by the Arabs. Luckily Charlie Beresford was there, Star Boscawen (Falmouth), and Mildmay Wilson, or we should be there still under ground.

I have been told by a friend who was at the side of Colonel Burnaby when he died that his face alone of all the dead and dying that lay around him bore a smile, the smile we all knew so well; and I have always hoped perhaps he heard the cheers of victory before the end came.

All who have ever spoken to me of this time said Colonel Burnaby's death caused a feeling of consternation. This hero of so many fights, so many narrow escapes, dead; and not one but many of the men cried over his dead body.

In England, at the very time he was dying, the authorities were talking about court-martialling him on his return for having gone out to the Soudan without leave; they were saved the trouble.

As I look back over the years I knew Burnaby I think what I noticed more markedly than almost anything else was his intolerance of conventions; his very attitudes and way of sitting down were protests against convention.

I have lately been turning over some old letters refreshing my memory of these old times, and have come across some notes of Colonel Burnaby's: his writing was like that of a child having its hand held and taking great pains. One of these notes refers to a promise he had made me of introducing to me

Garibaldi, whom I had told him I should much like to meet. Colonel Burnaby's promises were not made of the proverbial pie-crust, and although I had quite forgotten he had said he thought he could arrange a meeting between the lovable old revolutionist and myself, his note told me that Garibaldi was expected in England very shortly, and when would I be ready to receive the Red Shirt?

I was staying at the Alexandra Hotel, Knightsbridge, at the time, and the meeting was to take place there. My husband fled when he heard he would have to speak in French, so I received my guests alone; they presented a remarkable contrast as they entered the room. Colonel Burnaby, looking a Hercules with his broad shoulders and abnormally long legs, smiling as was his wont all across his face, with his untidy rebellious lock of hair falling as usual across his forehead. Beside him the poor old man suffering much from rheumatism, the son of a poor Nice fisherman, with the manners of a courtier and a soft almost pleading voice for which alone I shall always remember him.

I had been warned by Burnaby that I should have to talk Italian or French. He was a born linguist, I am not, and my Italian being of the order of the school-room Miss, taught just enough to be able to sing Italian songs without giving herself away, I decided to try French, although I must confess I am not as expert even in that as I should be, considering my many opportunities. But never did an hour pass more pleasantly for me, never did I feel less ignorant, thanks to the charming manners and understanding of General Garibaldi, who seemed to anticipate and understand what I wished to say almost before I spoke.

We all paid each other charming compliments. The General spoke with affection of Colonel Burnaby, while he in return told me of the General's individual influence and power that had worked so powerfully in Italy.

He drew the old man into talking of some of his astonishing enterprises. I ventured to suggest that Count Cavour and Mazzini[18] had thrown all the weight of their rebellious spirit on to his, Garibaldi's, shoulders, letting him do all the work and reap all the punishments that should have been theirs if punishment were deserved. He smiled his sad, sad smile, and said he had been a very willing tool, that those who had the fire burning in them and who had nothing to lose were the proper people to do the work, and it had been a work of love for his country. I asked him if his life could be lived over again, would he pursue the same policy. He replied, "Yes, given the same conditions." I wondered why, if he was so content with his life, he had such a sad look in his eyes, whether it was the outcome of thwarted desires, ambitions, and hopes. Not that he had any ambitions for himself, they were all for Italy he had

---

18 Camillo Paolo Filippo Giulio Benso, Count of Cavour (1810-1861) and Giuseppe Mazzini (1805-1872), also leading figures in the Italian unification movement.

refused riches, preferring to remain poor.

I asked him to tell me of the Countess della Torre,[19] who acted as his Joan of Arc, riding at the head of his Who's Who Legion, wearing the same Red Shirt as all his army. A sparkle came into his eyes; he said she was splendid, she was superb, she was brave, and sang as she rode along, inspiring all his plucky rabble, and she was a mother to them all.

Every now and then I became entangled with my flow of French, then Colonel Burnaby came to the rescue and carried on for me. Garibaldi spoke with gratitude of the way the English people had treated him, of the way they had received him when he visited this country in 1864, and expressed his great pleasure at the way the English people had responded to his call for help, of the many of all sorts and sizes who had joined his army.

At the end of this delightful visit Garibaldi stooped down and kissed my hand, saying he hoped we should meet again, but he was growing an old man.

He lived just three years after this. His handwriting was fine and pointed like the running hand of the ladies in the early sixties. The Italian language and characters rather lends itself to this.

I have not forgotten that it was to Colonel Burnaby I owe the pleasure of meeting the pathetic old Revolutionist.

---

19 Little is known of the Countess Maria della Tore, who spent some time with Florence Nightingale in the Crimea and met Garibaldi in London, before following him to Italy and becoming one of his mistresses.

Part 6

Poems and Songs (1879-1885)

Even while he was alive Burnaby became a subject in the weekly journals for songs and poems. The earliest, relating to his political aspirations, were not always entirely complimentary.

> 'The Captain's Song' by unknown author (*The Owl*, 30 January 1879)[1]

Captain	I am a Captain in the Caval–ry
Chorus of	And a budding Politician too,
Conservatives	For no one else I could
	Have consented to have stood,
	But I knew I could represent you.
	Though my knowledge is not great
	Of the nation or the State,
	I firmly swear by Reciproci–ty;
	And I never, never quail,
	At the *Post* or *Daily Mail*,
	And I never feel the shafts of great J.C.[2]
Chorus	What never?
Captain	No, never!
Chorus	What, never???
Captain	Well – hardly ever.
Chorus	He never quails before the sharp J.C.
	Then give three cheers, and one cheer more,
	Call it a demonstration, as we did before.
	So give three cheers, and one cheer more
	For the Bobadil of the Tory Corps.
Captain	I do my best to satisfy you all,

---

1 Adapted from the Captain's Song in Gilbert and Sullivan's *H.M.S. Pinafore*.
2 Joseph Chamberlain.

Chorus	With your efforts we are forced to be content.
Captain	'Tis for you I spout and write,
	And I think it is only right
	You should send me to parliament;
	That's if you have the power,
	Which I doubt more every hour
	The more of your Birmingham I see,
	Though on my chance I may
	Occasionally lay,
	I never think you'll carry an M.P.
Chorus	What never?
Captain	No, never!
Chorus	What, never???
Captain	Well – hardly ever.
Chorus	He never thinks we'll carry an M.P.
(Diminuendo)	Then give three cheers, and one cheer more,
	And the Caucus it shall tremble 'fore our mighty roar;
	Then give three cheers, and one cheer more
	For the Captain of this beaten corps.

'The Tory Two' by unknown author (*The Owl*, 18 March 1880)

The Tories their men have proclaimed,
And chosen a wonderful pair;
A fire-eating swash-buckler one,
Defineless the other, I swear.
The first "ne'er set squadron in field,"
Though his prowess he loudly can boast;
On his shrill penny trumpet he blows
A blast that might serve for a host.

"To Khiva I've ridden, you know,
On a horse that was rapid and strong;
And the pills, named of Cockle, I've strewn
The colic-torn natives among.
For a war with the Russ I have prayed,
Though others the fighting should do;
'Tis pleasant in safety to shout;
And a Jingo I am through and through."

"To commerce my mind I have turned,
Reciprocity still is my cry;
What matter though beef should be dear,
And the price of your bread should be high;
What is plenty with glory compared,
And gladly your taxes you'll pay,
While the trumpet the onset resounds,
And your brothers are slain in the fray."

With loud shouting the Tories reply,
To his cry of fee, fo, and fum,
But his resonant notes are as flat,
And hollow as t'hollowest drum.
This he raves, and he pleads, and implores,
But the only return he will get,
Is a ticket for London again,
But not to the Commons, I'll bet.

Who is this that so ghost-like appears –
The speechless, the silent, the dumb?
A school-boy could better repeat
His political rule of the thumb.
He has riches in money and land,
And springs from the blue-blooded kind,
But Nature, in giving him wealth,
Omitted to give him a mind.

What then? Your Tories ne'er trouble for that;
They prefer what is stupid and dull,
And measure their favours to all,
By what's out, not what's inside the skull.
They seek not a Statesman, but one
With the Lord of the Jingos to vote;
And in Calthorpe they've found just the man
Who has learned his short lesson by wrote.

But vain are their tricks and their craft;
They cannot throw dust in our eyes,
We know when the true metal rings,
And the false we still shall despise.
No Burnaby-Calthorpe for us;
We and they could never agree;

Such a pair we for ever reject,
And shall vote for the Liberal Three.

Acrostic 'Burnaby' by unknown author (*The Owl*, 25 March 1880)

Few men have dared to take, with flippant tongue,
Rude liberties with Gladstone's work, or flung
Embittered scorn upon his spotless name,
Deriding his great life and lofty fame;

But you – a household, unfledged soldierling –
Unknowing any wise or gracious thing,
Rush in with rash and renegade delight,
Not heeding e'en where angels fear to tread,
And pour with deep, envenomed party spite,
Base Tory calumnies upon that head
You cannot harm – whose righteous wrath you dread.

'A True and Authentic Copy of "Major Burnaby's" Lament' by unknown author (*The Owl*, 25 March 1880)

These Liberal lads they puzzle me quite,
I wish I never had come here;
When I call for "Dizzy" they shout for "Bright,"
There isn't a Tory Brum here.

Oh, Liberal here! and Liberal there!
And the Tory cause is undone!
But I'll smoke my pipe and devil may care,
For I'll go back to London.

My folded arms and tragedy air
These Liberal lads all laugh at;
For the cream of my jokes they've a vacant stare
That I've laboured a year and a half at.

Chorus

Muntz's seat is as sure as the base of the hills, –
That's plain as a steeple to read here, –
I must take a good dose of my favourite pills
And pack up my trunks with all speed here.

Chorus

A waspish lot has buzzed in my ear,
That Chamberlain I could molest here,
When I call him "tyrant," they laugh out "no fear!"
And I find him as safe as the rest here.

Chorus

It was powerful mean of Stone and Lowe,
To lead me this beast of a dance here;
For a fellow with half an eye might know
There wasn't a ghost of a chance here.

Chorus

'Epitaph' by 'a Burnabyite' (*The Owl*, 25 March 1880)

Here lies poor Fred,
Who was alive and is dead,
Had it been another,
I'd rather 'twere his brother,
But since it's only Fred,
Who was alive and is dead,
There's nothing more to be said.

More songs and poems followed Burnaby's death at the Battle of Abu Klea, some written within hours of the news reaching London. The following are a selection. They include some that dealt principally with the deaths of fellow officers or even associated events, but Burnaby's death was considered sufficiently important to be mentioned alongside them.

'*In Memoriam*. "Colonel Burnaby and his comrades"' by unknown author (*Western Mail*, 21 January 1885)

Britannia, twine another wreath around thy saddened brow,
But mingle with its conqu'ring bays some leaves of cypress now;
And swell thy song of victory, but mingle in the strain
A wail for that one dauntless heart who ne'er shall fight again.
His race is run; his broken sword lies on the bloody sand,
And cold and chill around its hilt the hero's mighty hand;
No more his gallant form shall tower above the charging line,

Where vict'ry's beams, mid steel and sleet, high o'er the colours shine.
He sleeps, but not alone, for their the wild siroc shall rave
O'er many another's humbler rest in some forgotten grave.
They fought as Englishmen will fight; they died as soldiers must,
With ne'er a thought of home or aught but England's sacred trust;
Whilst that same light of valour blazed in each determined eye
As when their serried squadrons rode into the gorge to die.
O England! stricken England! wouldst this last sacrifice
Of blood that thou canst hardly spare but pay the fearful price
Of dastard counsels, wav'ring will, and all the shameful tale
That bids the orphan's piteous cry with anguish load the gale!
But no; for coming fields of blood stern vengeance plumes her wings;
And death will march in her red track with fiercer, deeper sting
When comrades, burning for revenge, sweep on the savage foe
To find, when steel meets steel, the joy revenge can only know.
Another battle-roll will loom ere many suns have set,
And hearts now full of pluck and pride must drain their life-blood yet;
But O, Britannia! 'tis for thee the soldier courts his death,
And thy proud name is murmured with his last expiring breath.
No storied fame, no sculptured stone shall tell his need of praise –
No drooping willow bend above to shield the desert rays;
The bowling wind, the jackal's cry, alone will seek his rest,
But in a nation's tears his deeds will live and last the best.
Then turn thee to that far off plain, and, mid thy sobbing, say
No braver life 'mong all the brave than his was quenched that day.

'Colonel Burnaby, Royal Horse Guards' by Sphinx (*The Sporting Times*, 24 January 1885)

By the wells of Abu Klea,
On Afric's arid plain,
A battle has raised and ended,
And a hero has been slain.
There is grief in the hour of triumph,
In the hour of victory – gloom;
And all hearts mourn the soldier
Who has met a soldier's doom.

A giant in strength and stature,
A giant in heart and arm;
A grand ideal of a warrior,
With all a warrior's charm,

Of gentleness born of courage,
Of mildness born of might,
Whom naught could turn from duty,
Nor hinder from the Right.

He fell in the thick of battle,
His knell the cannon's roar;
'Twas the death he would have chosen
And oft had faced before.
And there's grief in the hour of triumph,
In the hour of victory – gloom,
For a nation weeps in silence
O'er a gallant soldier's tomb.

Untitled poem by Fred Albert (*The Era*, 24 January 1885)

Hail, victory, once more, for the telegraph tells
How Stewart struck hard near Aboo Klea Wells,
And the pluck of old England was shown once again
In the Desert where Burnaby fought and was slain.

'Colonel Fred Burnaby' by unknown author (*Fun*, 28 January 1885)

Oh, dauntless heart! And gallant mien!
In worthier cause could life be spent?
To fall for country and for Queen,
On 'leaguered comrade's rescue bent
With sword in hand and face to foe,
'Mid clash of steel and battle cry,
The comrades round who loved him so;
'Twas sure the death he'd wished to die!

'Colonel Burnaby' by unknown author (*Moonshine*, 31 January 1885)

["But Colonel Burnaby was full of the spirit of other times." – *Daily News*.]

And where was this reflex of other times? –
In honour unsullied, beyond gainsay;
In courage undaunted; in heart so true;
In will that was through and felt no stay?

Or was it the spirit of deeds – not words?
His love of old England, no thought behind;
His giving a life that had won a realm
Away in the days when men knew their mind?

So much the prouder those "other times" –
Those times had a purpose, a country's gain.
Yes, he reflected them, last of the knights;
Staunch to the death, though to die in vain.

'Colonel F.G Burnaby' by unknown author (*Punch*, 31 January 1885)

Brave Burnaby down! Wheresoever 'tis spoken
The news leaves the lips with a wistful regret.
We picture that square in the desert, shocked, broken,
Yet packed with stout hearts, and impregnable yet.
And there fell, at last, in close *mêlée*, the fighter,
Who Death had so often affronted before;

One deemed he'd no dart for his valorous slighter
Who such a gay heart to the battle-front bore.
But alas! for the spear-thrust that ended a story
Romantic as Roland's, as Lion-Heart's brief!

Yet crowded with incident, gilded with glory,
And crowned by a laurel that's verdant of leaf.
A latter-day Paladin, prone to adventure,
With little enough of the spirit that sways

The man of the market, the shop, the indenture!
Yet grief-drops will glitter on Burnaby's bays.
Fast friend as keen fighter, the strife-glow preferring,
Yet cheery all round with his friends and his foes;
Content through a life-story short, yet soul-stirring
And happy, as doubtless he'd deem, in its close.

'Colonel Burnaby' by Andrew Lang (*Punch*, 31 January 1885)

Thou that in every field of earth and sky
Didst hunt for Death, who seemed to flee and fear,
How great and greatly fallen dost thou lie,
Slain in the desert by a nameless spear!

'Not here, alas!' may England say, 'not here,
In such a quarrel was it meet to die;
But in that dreadful battle drawing nigh,
To shake the Afghan mountains lone and sere!'
Like Aias[3] by the ships, shouldst thou have stood,
And in some pass have stayed the stream of fight,
The bulwark of thy people and their shield,
Till Helmund or till Lora ran with blood,[4]
And back, towards the Northlands and the Night,
The stricken Eagles scattered from the field!

'In the ranks' by unknown author (*The Owl*, 6 February 1885)

[Slightly altered from a poem in *Harper's Monthly* for February.]

His death-blow struck him, there in the ranks –
There in the ranks, with his face to the foe:
Did Burnaby's lips utter curses or thanks?
    No one will ever know.

Still he'd marched on with the rest –
Still he'd marched on with his face to the foe
To Khartoum's bitter business sternly addrest:
    Dead – did they know?

Laurels or roses, all one to him now –
What to brave Burnaby's glory or glow?
Rose wreaths for love, or a crown on his brow?
    Dead – does he know?

Yet there they all saw him march on with the rest –
None than Fred Burnaby a goodlier show –
In the thick of the savages, jostled and prest:
    Speared – would you know?

---

3 Ajax.
4 Helmund and Lora are both provinces of Afghanistan.

'Pens of the War' by unknown author (*Punch*, 7 February 1885)

[*In Memoriam* for John Alexander Cameron, war correspondent of the *Standard* and St. Leger Algernon Herbert, war correspondent of the *Morning Post*, killed at the Battle of Gubat, 19 January 1885.]

Not only in the battle's rangéd ranks,
Not only under soldier's cloth and casque,
May manhood earn what Bayard's[5] self would ask,
A Hero's ending and a country's thanks.
Cameron, Herbert! These are names to mate
With Burnaby's and Stewart's on the roll
Of militant honour, men of kindred soul,
Equal in hearty and matched in glorious fate.
Pen *versus* sword? But now the hasty phrase
Loses its glib significance since the two
Co-operate are in a splendid risk; and who
Will weigh their service or divide their praise?
In steadfast valour, danger-scorning toil,
Penmen like these are plumeless knights indeed,
Ready to face war's death-rain, and at need
To stain with life-blood free a foreign soil.
What may a soldier more? No more they claim,
Gallant sword-wielders, than to these brave men,
Comrades in duty, Paladins of the Pen,
They gladly yield of glory and of fame.
And England, watchful of all high deeds done
By all her children dutiful and brave,
Lays tear-stained laurel on the desert-grave
Of gallant Herbert and stout Cameron.

Untitled poem by Walton Hook (*The Sporting Times*, 21 February 1885)

[*In Memoriam* for Captain J.W.W. Darley and Lieutenant C.W.A. Law, 4th Dragoon Guards, killed at the Battle of Abu Klea, 17 January 1885.]

Afar, where Stewart led his gallant band,
Their blood has slaked some patch of thirsty sand:

---

5   Pierre Terrail, seigneur de Bayard (1473-1524) was a French soldier, generally known as the Chevalier de Bayard.

At home, the starting tear, and half-drawn sigh
Pay wistful homage to their memory.
Blithe sons of Erin! Summer saw them face
Less deadly aim, wielding the willow-mace
In many a well-fought game, where skill and pluck
Singled them both from out the common ruck
Foremost in manly sport; and foremost they
Were picked among their comrades for the fray.
Foremost on that arena – who can doubt? –
At Abu Klea's hand to hand death-bout,
Even of those who knew them but in part,
Not one but, hearing, felt the blow at heart.
And when the middle months come round again,
And Cricket, lithe-limbed queen, resumes her reign,
Many shall be the tributary thought
To those returnless absent ones who fought
And died on Afric's waste; while reverie
Contrasts the arid desert where they lie
With England's meadows, fresh, and trim, and green;
Contrasts the desolation of that scene,
In all its lonesome, dreary solitude,
With nature's gifts, life's pleasures, here renewed!
Yet, so we die with honour, unforgot
By friends, what matter where our bodies rot?
Remembered kindly, have we not a grave
Beneath some of stone of memory's hallowed cave?
DARLEY and LAW, farewell! Nor could a friend
Wish you aught better than a soldier's end,
Would you had died, indeed, in some wild charge
Where havoc death set hero-souls at large,
'Mid tramp and blare of nation's battle roar!
And yet, in passing to that further shore,
What braver comrade-spirit to defy
The shadows of Death's vale than Burnaby?
'Tis solace that a hero fell with you –
Too little, and too lately known, adieu!

'The opening speech of the G.O.M.' by 'R.M.' (*The Dart*, 27 February 1885)

[The 'G.O.M.', or 'Grand Old Man' was Gladstone.]

I, Mr Speaker, the prince of red-tapers,
Beg permission to lay on the table some papers,
These papers, I hardly need say, are Egyptian,
The contents of a non-controversial description.
The members most readily will understand
That the telegrams, which, day by day, come to hand,
If they suit us, we publish, if not we retain –
They don't suit us at all, I confess, in the main;
But if you've no objection, the news by the cable
I'll lay, if I may be allowed, on the table,
A course, I believe, sir, by no means unusual,
So I think to my motion there'll be no refusal.
Some come from Lord Wolseley, and tell us of Gordon,
He's dead (perhaps buried,) we'll treat him accordin',
And not allude to him, he's bothered us sadly,
He's disobeyed orders, and treated us badly,
Defending the garrisons, as per instruction,
To his own, and may be to the party's destruction.
A decision was come to. To leave the Soudan,
Which we should have done but for this pig-headed man,
And to give to the Mahdi, and his Soudanese,
The country to rule, as it might them so please.
Gordon craved for assistance, I own we were tardy,
We trusted he'd give up the place to the Mahdi –
A man of intelligence, knowing and subtle,
But Gordon was stupid, refusing to scuttle,
And fought him without us, alone, single-handed,
And it finds us in this sad predicament landed –
That Gordon is killed, and the Mahdi, I fear,
Tickling up our contemptible force in the rear,
A most awkward dilemma, and all I am able
To do, is to place all the facts on the table.
Now as to the action pursued by our forces,
I beg to submit to your notice three courses –
To collar the Mahdi, and hither embark him,
To smash Osman Digna by taking Suakim,
Or lay through the desert, a railroad to Berber,

To get off troops quickly, and quash a disturber;
Of all these three courses, one course must be taken
If England's to save, at this crisis, her bacon.
'Twas the vote for the purpose that was our objection,
When there seemed to be looming a general election,
So we've put off the matter, till now, for that reason,
And our generals say it's too late in the season.
Poor Burnaby, Stewart, and Earls are no more,
And the murder of Gordon is placed at our door,
The army's retreating, it's awkward for Buller,
The despatches of bad news get fuller and fuller,
The river's so low, it don't help us a bit,
An example of *"nihil* (Nile) *ex nihilo fit."*[6]
To decide on a policy being unable,
Permit me, these papers, to lay on the table.

'The Battle Of Abu Klea' by Sir William Topaz McGonagall

Ye sons of Mars, come join with me,
And sing in praise of Sir Herbert Stewart's little army,
That made ten thousand Arabs flee
At the charge of the bayonet at Abu Klea.

General Stewart's force was about fifteen hundred all told,
A brave little band, but, like lions bold,
They fought under their brave and heroic commander,
As gallant and as skilful as the great Alexander.

And the nation has every reason to be proud,
And in praise of his little band we cannot speak too loud,
Because that gallant fifteen hundred soon put to flight
Ten thousand Arabs, which was a most beautiful sight.

The enemy kept up a harmless fire all night,
And threw up works on General Stewart's right;
Therefore he tried to draw the enemy on to attack,
But they hesitated, and through fear drew back.

But General Stewart ordered his men forward in square,
All of them on foot, ready to die and to dare;

---

6   Nothing comes of nothing.

And he forced the enemy to engage in the fray,
But in a short time they were glad to run away.

But not before they penetrated through the British square,
Which was a critical moment to the British, I declare,
Owing to the great number of the Arabs,
Who rushed against their bayonets and received fearful stabs.

Then all was quiet again until after breakfast,
And when the brave little band had finished their repast,
Then the firing began from the heights on the right,
From the breastworks they had constructed during the night.

By eight o'clock the enemy was of considerable strength,
With their banners waving beautifully and of great length,
And creeping steadily up the grassy road direct to the wells,
But the British soon checked their advance by shot and shells.

At ten o'clock brave General Stewart made a counter-attack,
Resolved to turn the enemy on a different track;
And he ordered his men to form a hollow square,
Placing the Guards in the front, and telling them to prepare.

And on the left was the Mounted Infantry,
Which truly was a magnificent sight to see;
Then the Sussex Regiment was on the right,
And the Heavy Cavalry and Naval Brigade all ready to fight.

Then General Stewart took up a good position on a slope,
Where he guessed the enemy could not with him cope,
Where he knew the rebels must advance,
All up hill and upon open ground, which was his only chance.

Then Captain Norton's battery planted shells amongst the
         densest mass,
Determined with shot and shell the enemy to harass;
Then came the shock of the rebels against the British square,
While the fiendish shouts of the Arabs did rend the air.

But the steadiness of the Guards, Marines, and Infantry prevailed,
And for the loss of their brother officers they sadly bewailed,
Who fell mortally wounded in the bloody fray,

Which they will remember for many a long day.

For ten minutes a desperate struggle raged from left to rear
While Gunner Smith saved Lieutenant Guthrie's life without
    dread or fear;
When all the other gunners had been borne back,
He took up a handspike, and the Arabs he did whack.

The noble hero hard blows did strike,
As he swung round his head the handspike;
He seemed like a destroying angel in the midst of the fight
The way he scattered the Arabs left and right.

Oh! it was an exciting and terrible sight,
To see Colonel Burnaby engaged in the fight:
With sword in hand, fighting with might and main,
Until killed by a spear-thrust in the jugular vein.

A braver soldier ne'er fought on a battle-field,
Death or glory was his motto, rather than yield;
A man of noble stature and manly to behold,
And an honour to his country be it told.

It was not long before every Arab in the square was killed.
And with a dense smoke and dust the air was filled;
General Stewart's horse was shot, and he fell to the ground.
In the midst of shot and shell on every side around.

And when the victory was won they gave three British cheers.
While adown their cheeks flowed many tears
For their fallen comrades that lay weltering in their gore;
Then the square was re-formed, and the battle was o'er.

'Abu Klea' by R. Menn (*The Dart and Midland Figaro*, 30 January 1885)

With British blood the desert sand is red,
Hovers above the fell expectant kite,
More noble souls are numbered with the dead,
God knows what else is happening whilst I write.

Poor Burnaby! He seemed, for long, to seek
To quench the vital fire which in him lay
By strange adventurous whim, and dangerous freak,
To hasten on the end we all delay.

Once cannot curse the dark fanatic bands
Who bravely fought and for their country fell;
We but retrieve the fault of nerveless hands,
What else we strive for it were hard to tell.

For Gordon's rescue? Well a blunder first,
A senile scheme, quixotic and inane,
And, much I fear, we have not seen the worst
Of grim disaster following in its train.

Brave English sons, ghastly with blood and sweat,
Fall in yon arid wilderness to rot,
Though, truly, I am not determined yet
Whether our course is justified or not.

Those dusky Arabs, conscious of the right,
Oblivious of all thought of fear and death,
Swoop in a horde of overwhelming might,
Shouting aloud their Moslem shibboleth.

They turn, they falter, and the battle's won,
The desert rings with our victorious cry,
But on the sand lies many a British son,
And none less brave than gallant Burnaby.

'Vitai Lampada'[7] by Sir Henry Newbolt (1892)

There's a breathless hush in the Close to-night –
Ten to make and the match to win –
A bumping pitch and a blinding light,
An hour to play and the last man in.
And it's not for the sake of a ribboned coat,
Or the selfish hope of a season's fame,
But his Captain's hand on his shoulder smote
'Play up! play up! and play the game!'

7 'Torch of life', a quotation from Lucretius.

The sand of the desert is sodden red, –
Red with the wreck of a square that broke; –
The Gatling's jammed and the colonel dead,
And the regiment blind with dust and smoke.
The river of death has brimmed his banks,
And England's far, and Honour a name,
But the voice of schoolboy rallies the ranks,
'Play up! play up! and play the game!'

This is the word that year by year
While in her place the School is set
Every one of her sons must hear,
And none that hears it dare forget.
This they all with a joyful mind
Bear through life like a torch in flame,
And falling fling to the host behind –
'Play up! play up! and play the game!

Unknown song by unknown author

Come listen to my story boys,
There's news from overseas,
The Camel Corps has held their own
And gained a victory.

Weep not my boys for those who fell,
They did not flinch nor fear,
They stood their ground like Englishmen,
And died at Abu Klea.

No more our colonel's form we'll see,
His foes have struck him down.
His life on earth alas is o'er
But not his great renown.

No more his merry voice we'll hear,
Nor words of stern command,
He died as he had often wished,
His sabre in his hand.

Chorus

Now Horse Guards Blue both old and young, Each man from front to rear,
Remember Colonel Burnaby at sandy Abu Klea.
And when Old England calls her blues to battle soon or late,
We shan't forget how soldierly the Colonel met his fate.

Chorus

'Brave Burnaby' by H. Burrows Smith

He lies in silence with the dead,
So strong, so brave;
In rustling folds above his head
A flag doth wave;
Scenes that his wand'ring fancy weaves
Crowd on his mind,
And disappear like autumn leaves
Before the wind.
He lies upon the blood-red plain,
So strong, so fair;
Dew mingling with the drops that stain
His dark-brown hair.

'A Lion Hearted Soldier was Colonel Burnaby' by John Read

Let the drums be muffled! Play the march in "Saul"!
For a brave and gallant soldier, has in battle chanced to fall
While fighting for Old England, his country and his Queen;
His name was Colonel Burnaby, You all know who I mean:

He was a soldier, no man bolder, The foremost in the fight, To lead his men to victory
Always daring, never caring, A lion-hearted soldier, was Colonel Burnaby.

As a linguist few were better; at politics "A1"
Perfect to the letter, A true born Briton's son.
His manly form and figure were look'd upon with pride
And with the daring Nubians he bravely fought and died:

Chorus

It's known in every action, he always proved "true blue",
Giving satisfaction. What more could mortal do?
A credit, to the nation; an honour, to the Corps
He caused a great sensation, Although he is no more:

Chorus

And just by way of moral, I think 'tis only right
That those that make the quarrel, Should be the men to fight
But Burnaby the Colonel, he was eager for the fray
His sole delight it was to fight, And all that I can say:

Chorus

Appearing beneath a chromolithograph of the Battle of Abu Klea, probably published shortly after Burnaby's death

Removed from succour, through a desert land
Our gallant Stewart led his little band,
Prepared to fight – more eager still to save,
His cry was "Gordon! Victory or the grave."
No feat in martial history excels
His bold and brilliant struggle for the Wells,
Whence, sorely wounded he was borne away
To die and leave a hero's name for aye.
With him was Burnaby, whose matchless sword
Spread wide destruction through the dusky horde,
Till on that fatal day near Abu Klea
He fell, – but in the arms of victory.
Why for such warriors should Britain weep?
They've done their duty, and in peace they sleep.
Their praises shall resound from shore to shore
Till Doom has struck and Time shall be no more!

Mourn Britons, mourn; Weep, Britons, weep!
Brave Burnaby, thy boldest son, has fallen asleep;
No more his stalwart arm, thy sword will wield,
He's dead! He's dead! slain in the battle field.
Heroic Burnaby thy name will live in story
Escutcheoned 'mongst the boldest deeds of glory;
As long as pen can write, or tongue can tell,
How Britons fought at famed Aboo Klea well,

Ay! fought and conquered, dear bought victory –
'Twas purchased with thy life, brave, bold Fred Burnaby.

They marched from Korti thro' the drifting sand,
Their hearts were beating high with hope, each thought of native land;
'Neath burning sun o'er Egypt's Plain they strode and onward bent,
One mind, one purpose, one desire, one firm yet bold intent,
Gordon the watchword, Gordon's relief; for he beleaguered lay
In Khartoum, where he nobly holds the Mahdi's force at bay.
On, on they stride another day, Gakdul is reached and past,
No sign of foe, they onward press, they sight the well at last;
The bold Hussars go forward then – they are full of dash and dare –
But soon return with bated breath, "The foe! the foe! are there."

Then goes the signal round, then sound alarms
And columns formed, our standard moves mid cries "To arms, to arms."
Those few brave men were firm and true, though tired and parched
    with thirst,
Respond at once, at danger's call, each striving to be first.
The Guards and Lancers, Infantry, Dragoons and bold Scots Grey,
Are on their camels instantly, and hastening to the fray.
But night draws on too soon, its thickening gloom and shade,
Too dark, too dark for battle, so now the halt is made;
And in the camp that night, the comrades watch in sorrow,
And hand in hand, with brave resolve, look forward to the morrow.

The morrow came at length, and with first dawn of day
The enemy are advancing seen in all dread war's array,
With wavering flags, with shield and spear, and noise of beating drum
Ten times our number all full told, mid cries of "Allah!" come.
Our square is formed, each man on foot. On, on the foe advance,
'Gainst withering fire; 'Gainst shot and shell, and well directed lance,
O'er dying comrades, see they leap. On, on, still on, they rush;
Our Heavies staggered, yet they stand against that fearful crush.
Oh! how they fought; Oh! how they stood, 'twill live in future story,
How Guards and Lancers fighting fell, for Britain, home, and glory.

See, still they stand, they form again, each well directed blow
Makes fearful havoc, hand to hand, among the murderous foe.
Our Stewart falls; he's up again, only his horse is slain,
He shouts "All, right; keep up my lads," implores his men again.
"The battle's ours! we win," he shouts. "Hold on brave Guards and Lancers,"

With thudding blow, with compressed lip, and lighted eye, they answer;
And Arabs falling, heap on heap, around that fated square,
Dying and dead, yet fighting still, mid shrieks that rend the air.
Then all is o'er, the day is ours, but Death's destroying blast
Had stricken down, amongst those braves, bold Burnaby at last.

Oh! what a wail of grief was there – 'twas echoed 'cross the sand'
And borne to every home and hearth in this his native land.
He's dead! he's dead! brave Burnaby, hero of Khiva, El Teb, Merve;[8]
The man of dauntless courage, heroic God-like nerve.
Fanatic hand had sped the shaft that laid our hero low,
He met his fate, a soldier's death, fell striking down the foe.
From every town and hamlet, from every hall and tower,
From club, from field, from forest, from every maiden's bower,
Shall rise that wail of anguish, when men the story tell
How Burnaby fought and bled, and died, at famed Aboo Klea well.

Mourn, Britons, mourn; weep, Britons, weep, for those who fighting fell –
For Burnaby, for Atherton, for Gough, and Carmichael;
For Captains Darley, Law and Wolfe, for Piggot and de Lisle,
And all those braves who fought and died for this our native Isle.
A greater battle ne'er was fought, nor lesser victory won.
For in the fight so many fell of these thy bravest sons.
Old men shall mourn, and maidens weep, as long as tongues can tell
How Burnaby, the Guardsman, fell at famed Aboo Klea well.

'Burnaby the Brave' by J.S. Haydon, composed by Harry Braham (1885)

Across the plains of Egypt, and
The desert of Soudan,
Amid old England's sons of war
Rode one brave Englishman;
A better soldier ne'er drew sword
Upon the tented field,
Prepared to prove this motto true:–
"We die but never yield."

A British hero, staunch and true,
Has found a soldier's grave;

---

8 Burnaby never did manage to reach Merve (or Merv).

He died as British heroes do,
This dear old land to save.

He e'er was foremost in the van,
He ne'er knew taint of fear;
He fought as Britons only can,
He heard the British cheer!
But ere the shout of Victory
Rose o'er the savage yell,
His blood had stained the dessert sand,
Our fighting hero fell.

Chorus

Still onward pressed our little band,
The foemen strove in vain;
For Britain's sons with dauntless hearts,
Avenge their comrade slain.
On that rude field at Abu Klea
They made a soldier's grave,
And in that grave our hero lies:–
Fred Burnaby the brave.

Chorus

'Homage to Colonel Burnaby, "We talk of deeds of glory"' by Charles Tracy, composed by T. Kent, sung by Charles Godfrey (1885)

England is wrapt in mourning,
She mourns for one great son,
Whose greatest enemy in life,
Could only say "Well done!"
I speak of Colonel Burnaby,
A Britain Bold and true,
A good six feet of British pluck,
Who always proved true blue.

We talk of deeds of glory,
We talk of tales of old,
Repeat the good old story,
But was ever man more bold;

That Burnaby the Valiant,
Who made a right good stand,
And died a British warrior,
With his good sword in his hand.

'Tis not till we have lost them,
How terribly we feel,
The loss of one great valiant life,
Whose heart was true as steel.
'Tis not till we have lost them,
And pondered o'er their grave,
How great the man has been in life,
How generous, how brave.

Chorus

England weeps in anguish
And yet with pride will tell,
How Burnaby rushed to the front,
And like a lion fell;
England glories in his pluck,
And sheds a silent tear,
To think his manly silent face,
Will never more appear.

Chorus

'Our men at Abu Klea' by J.C. Lynch, composed by C.E. Damian (1885)

Throughout the vast dominions
Where Britain's Queen holds sway,
All hearts with joy and deep emotion
In unison beat today
All hearts with joy and deep emotion
In unison beat today.

With pride we view our gallant men
Who stoutly kept at bay,
The wild fanatic savage host
Near the wells of Abu Klea
Near the wells of Abu Klea.

All honour, all honour, all honour to our soldiers,
Who bravely won the day
'Gainst fearful odds like heroes fought
Near the wells of Abu Klea
'Gainst fearful odds like heroes fought
Near the wells of Abu Klea.

Forth from their more congenial home,
With ready step they go,
Nor Sparta worthier children had
In the days of long ago
Nor Sparta worthier children had
In the days of long ago.

Over the torrent's wave they push'd,
Und' Afric's burning ray
The boundless stretch of sand they cross'd
To the wells of Abu Klea
To the wells of Abu Klea.

Chorus

Upon our squares like demons,
With frantic yells they rush
Unflinchingly the shock we meet,
Then on the en'my rush,
Then on the en'my rush.

Rain'd shot and shell, rain'd shot and shell, still on we press
The Arabs flee but round there lay
Too many a soldier's grave
Had found at Abu Klea
Too many a soldier's grave
Had found at Abu Klea.

Chorus

Frederick Gustavus Burnaby by John Payne, *c*.1908

He was of those with heart and hand who reared
Our England in high imperial place
And her therein maintained, despite the base
Curst crew that fain upon the rocks had steered, –
Her constant son who none and nothing feared
Nor at life's hand asked any greater grace
Than leave to look far danger in the face
And pluck rebated peril by the beard.

And first, so last, the Fates to him were kind,
Vouchsafing him the true man's most desire,
Occasion for the land he loved so well,
Fighting, to fall and on the dessert wind
Pass, borne of Battle's chariots of fire,
To where, death-shrined, the high-souled heroes dwell.

In March 1885 it was reported that Mr. William Davies of Bangor Cathedral had composed a song on the late Colonel Burnaby that was due to be sung at a forthcoming concert and was likely to become popular. In fact it was performed by him at the Penrhyn Hall on 24 April, entitled '*In Memoriam – Colonel Burnaby.* "By the walls of Abu Klea."', but this has not been traced.[9] Within a few months there was also an Abu Klea waltz (by Samuel Holloway) and an Abu Klea quick march (by René Franck).

---

9 *North Wales Chronicle*, 14 March and 25 April 1885.

Related titles published by Helion & Company

The Thinking Man's Soldier. The Life and Career of General Sir Henry Brackenbury 1837-1914
Christopher Brice
ISBN 978-1-907677-69-4

The If Man. Dr Leander Starr Jameson, the Inspiration for Kipling's Masterpiece
Chris Ash
ISBN 978-1-907677-74-8

Ice, Steel and Fire. British Explorers in Peace and War 1921-45
Linda Parker
ISBN 978-1-908916-49-5

Man of Steel and Honour: General Stanislaw Maczek. Soldier of Poland, Commander of the 1st Polish Armoured Division in North-West Europe 1944-45
Evan McGilvray
ISBN 978-1-908916-53-2

HELION & COMPANY
26 Willow Road, Solihull, West Midlands B91 1UE, England
Telephone 0121 705 3393 Fax 0121 711 4075
Website: http://www.helion.co.uk